GET IT RIGHT!

*A Cyclopedia
of Correct English Usage*

GET IT RIGHT!

A CYCLOPEDIA
OF CORRECT ENGLISH USAGE

By
JOHN BAKER OPDYCKE, M.A., D. Litt.

Author of DON'T SAY IT,
TAKE A LETTER PLEASE,
SAY WHAT YOU MEAN,
THE OPDYCKE LEXICON

REVISED EDITION

FUNK & WAGNALLS COMPANY, INC.

NEW YORK

To

T. H.

THIS BOOK

—so vulnerably titled *Get It Right*—is meant primarily to serve as a sort of first-aid kit in expressional emergencies. It is an omnibus of usage to be consulted whenever and wherever decisions have to be made between what is exact and precise in speech and writing and what is merely passable or downright wrong. An exhaustive index makes such consultation easy and immediate. The contents of the book are alphabetically arranged. Major treatment is accorded grammar, punctuation, spelling, and word study, for the reason that most errors and the most serious violations of good usage occur in these departments of the language. While doubtless "more could be said" about any one of the subjects treated in the book, all are adequately and amply dealt with for the purposes it is calculated to meet. It cannot, for instance, be called "the complete and perfect letter writer," but letter writing is nevertheless comprehensively explained and illustrated. It does not attempt to define and illustrate all literary terms known to man, but more than one hundred of those most helpful to the understanding and enjoyment of literature are treated. It is certainly not a "universal cyclopedia" in the principles and practises of journalism and publicity, but its abridged treatment of these subjects will be useful and instructive to laymen who are required to do occasional or even frequent work in them. Nothing so ambitious has, in other words, been undertaken as was indicated by that naive medieval historian who called his comparatively brief manuscript *The Complete History of the Heavens and the Earth*. The aim has been, rather, comprehensiveness without presumption or preciosity.

There are many excellent handbooks and manuals and dictionaries of usage. This, it is hoped, will prove to be something more than just another one. Like most other books of its kind, this is for business and industrial office desks, for secretaries and managers and executives.   But it will be found of imperative service also in the professional and literary study, in schools and colleges of every grade, and in individual homes where correct conversation and intelligible writing are still considered a part of good manners. It is therefore not only for the office and the library and the school but for the bed-table likewise.   It is to be studied as well as merely consulted.   It is a book for leisure hours as well as for working hours.   It should, indeed, have the unmodified approval of that automobile executive who a little while since at an educational convention said: "What our office forces need more than any- thing else is a book that will yield lubrication for straightaway driving and at the same time start the engine when it stalls in crucial traffic places."

This is not an ultra-conservative book.   It is not a book for those who would still persist in spelling *honor* with a *u*.   It is not an extreme or radical book.   It is decidedly not for those who would weakly and lazily succumb to the momentum of illiteracy abroad today and sanction such usages as:

It is me	He is different than John
Try and do it	I don't know if I can
Can I go now	Who are you looking for
Loan me a pencil	The reason is because it is raining

It is a strictly no-compromise book as far as such expressions as these are concerned.   Modifications in English usage—and espe- cially modifications downward—are not enforced by edict.   Learned (?) authorities (?) in formidable conference assembled do not debase the Mother Tongue by ukase.   Certainly no mere book could authorize the parts of speech to sow their wild oats and expect to have such authorization taken seriously.   The growth or change of language comes by the slowest possible evolution, never by revolution and scare headlines.

There are moot points in our language, to be sure.   They are, indeed, wholesome signs that language is alive.   There are no moot points in a dead language, or none that can matter now.   But the moot points of English, as of every other living language, do matter. They offer challenge and stimulus at the same time that they make writers and speakers cautious. They demand respectful analysis; they defy arbitrariness and dogmatism. In any book of this kind they must be treated in such a way as to establish expressional confidence in those who are sincere in their efforts to improve and perfect their use of English. If they to some extent invalidate such a title as *Get It Right*—make it an approximation only—they nevertheless spur to research and ratiocination.

And there are many who still do care about correct speech and writing, indications to the contrary notwithstanding. Many, both young and old, still do honestly care to make and to keep their expression indisputably correct; still do strive to avoid the spoken or written word that will merely pass, to find the word that consummately expresses their meaning. How much of a trial their striving may be made by the general laxity in English usage was to a degree realized by the author recently when in a brief afternoon he suffered the following experiences: He read in a popular column of a leading newspaper "among we literary people"; he read in a novel advertised as a best-seller "some of whom what has become I do not know"; he heard a well-known university professor in a radio talk belabor the word *describe* when *explain* was the word he should have used; he heard a fashionably dressed lady say to a sales-person: "I want a hat what nobody aint got one like"; he heard an educator (*sic*) say to three thousand pupils in a school assembly: "Youse young people has the uppertoonity of your lifes"; he found on a single page of a widely used high-school textbook ten positive solecisms and three misstatements of fact. He hastens happily to add that this particular afternoon is not typical of his experience. But he knows that such looseness of expression as these instances point, cannot be said to be uncommon even in so-called educated and literary circles.

The depression in American speech and writing antedated the economic depression by many years, and the upturn in some of the most important quarters would seem yet to be a long way off. But hope is not to be abandoned entirely. It is heartening to find this editorial exhortation in a leading literary weekly: "The thirties have been prolific of shoddy books got out while the news was fresh, and of dull, clumsy, badly written books, claiming attention because their subjects were new, and of extravagant, egoistic books that read like the shouts of drunken college boys, and of cheap, cynical, smutty books whose philosophy of life, when any, was so shallow as to disgust an honest humorist. It seems time to call off the hunt for the new and the sensational, stop the praise for the bright young men who make bad novels out of the rich materials of economics or psychology, and go back on the trail to find out where good writing lost its way and went off somewhere into the night.

"Ideas fascinate us as they seem to fascinate every one nowadays. But, if books are to be made, ideas are not enough. A novel should do what narrative was meant to do. A biography should be a Life. A history should be historical. A poem should communicate as well as be. And all should share in that heritage of hard thinking and intense imagination, competently applied, and of craftsmanship adequate to bridge the gap between writer and reader, which is the core of literary tradition, and its real excuse for being. New books are well enough, but let them be good." *

Even among those who should especially pride themselves upon the habitual use of good English—professional writers and speakers, and teachers of the Mother Tongue in particular—there is very often today a kind of high disdain for precise grammar and nice diction. As result of the deterioration in teacher training during the past decade, young teachers of English have been known to make it a boast that they "know no grammar," and to greet its champions with a condescending shrug. This attitude has become a prepossessing pose with them, or, at least, so they apparently hope and think. Their disillusionment comes, if at all, when they are confronted with some problem of expression that is of vital interest to their own personal welfare and that they

* *The Saturday Review of Literature.* May 4, 1935 Used by permission.

are unable to solve advantageously. Disagreements and disputes and failures in whatever walk of life, more frequently now than ever before, have their source in bad English. Its correction and clarification by one who knows the underlying principles of grammar and who is called in to "render grammatical services" save the day. Many a legal case or public question is settled by getting grammar right. True, a negative consolation—a sort of saving grace—has been salvaged from the frenzied phraseology that besets on every hand, namely: "If those who so ardently champion dubious causes were as enthusiastic about the language they use in advocating them as they are about the causes themselves, society would have more to fear. Most agitators render their preachments negligible and harmless by 'virtue' of ambiguities, redundancies, solecisms, and malapropisms." But this is beggarly comfort indeed.

If logic is the science or doctrine of correct thinking, then grammatical expression is logic made audible and visible. Incorrect and inaccurate speech and writing reflect loose and irrational processes of thought. People who habitually make errors in their expression—diction, grammar, spelling, punctuation—get themselves not only misunderstood but disregarded. What is worse, they get themselves accused of bad manners, and rightly, for in these days of public education that is not only free but actually aggressive and intrusive, bad English is the worst of bad manners. Muddled and erratic thinking, with its assured concomitant, muddled and erratic expression, has defeated many an ambitious and otherwise worthy person. Precise and tasteful expression has nine times out of ten been the greatest contributory factor in personal success. He who has little to say but is able to say that little well, is of infinitely greater value to himself *and to society* than he who has little or much to say and says it vaguely and bunglingly and otherwise badly. To know really is to be able to express correctly. Expression is at once a part and a manifestation of knowledge.

It is, moreover, much easier to be consistently correct in speech and writing than it is to be consistently incorrect. And no small part of all bad expression is the illogic of its seeming defiance of rule in one place and its seeming observance of rule in another —the catch-as-catch-canniness of communication. It is both more enjoyable and more advantageous to play a game strictly according to rule than otherwise. One violation of rule may undo the whole game, spoil it not only for the violator but for all others. Never this side of sheer genius is there—can there be—any trick or knack or sleight-of-hand that will enable a person regularly to do anything offhand and do it consistently well and satisfactorily to himself and others. Language has its rules to be mastered and followed. Try to follow them at some times and not at others, observe one standard of usage for your immediate family and another for your employers or coworkers, and you are doomed to die the death of your own diction.

There are those, it is said, who contend that a knowledge of the fundamentals of grammar, that is, of logic, is by no means essential to precise and correct expression; that such expression is, rather, to be gathered through reading it and hearing it and assimilating it from that "elusive something" that educators so glibly and so vaguely discuss as *background*. This is bad doctrine and worse logic. And language has its revenge upon all those who so flippantly or otherwise abuse and defy and ignore its principles —it commits them to saying so much that they do not mean, to revealing so brazenly what they do not know.

––––––––

Few if any claims to originality can be made by the author of a book of this kind. No adequate acknowledgment of indebtedness is therefore possible. There is much indirect or unconscious plagiarism, for the book represents cumulative reading and study and observation over a long period of years. The content is largely dictionary and encyclopedia content, and to the leading dictionaries and encyclopedias of the world first acknowledgments are undoubtedly due. Closely thereafter—if not, indeed, in parallel— come such important and dependable publications as *The World Almanac; The Brooklyn Eagle Almanac; The Chicago Daily News Almanac; Almanach de Gotha;* Burke's *Peerage, Baronetage,*

Knightage; Whitaker's *Almanac;* Whitaker's *Peerage, Baronetage, Knightage, and Companionage;* Kelly's *Handbook to Titled, Landed, and Official Classes;* Black's *Titles and Forms of Address —a Guide to their Correct Use,* and the year-book, the who's who, the index, the directory, the blue book, the social register, the digest, the guide, and other issues of their kind in various countries and in various fields of human activity.

Such reliable reference authorities as the following have likewise been consulted for verification and substantiation and variety of points of view. They must form a first line of defense—a two-and a-half-foot bookshelf—for any one who is concerned with correct usage: *The Style Manual of the (United States) Government Printing Office; A Manual of Style of the University of Chicago Press;* C. O. Sylvester Mawson's *A Style-Book for Writers and Editors* (Thomas Y. Crowell Company); George B. Ives' *Text, Type, and Style—a Compendium of Atlantic Usage* (The Atlantic Monthly Press); Taintor and Monro's *The Secretary's Handbook* (The Macmillan Company); Frank D. Halsey's *A Handbook of Style* (Princeton University Press); Horace Hart's *Rules for Compositors and Readers at the University Press* (Oxford University Press); Frank H. Vizetelly's *Twenty-five Thousand Words Frequently Mispronounced* (Funk & Wagnalls Company); James C. Fernald's *English Synonyms and Antonyms, with Notes on the Correct Use of Prepositions* (Funk & Wagnalls Company); George Crabb's *English Synonyms* (Harper and Brothers); Peter Mark Roget's *Thesaurus of English Words and Phrases* (Thomas Y. Crowell Company); Henry Watson Fowler's *A Dictionary of Modern Usage* and *The King's English* (The Clarendon Press, Oxford); Maurice H. Weseen's *Crowell's Dictionary of English Grammar* and *Words Confused and Misused* (Thomas Y. Crowell Company); William Livingston Klein's *Why We Punctuate; or, Reason versus Rule in the Use of Marks* (The Lancet Publishing Company, Minneapolis, Minnesota); George Summey's *Modern Punctuation* (Oxford University Press); Reginald Skelton's *Modern Punctuation* (Pitman Publishing Corporation); Benjamin Sherbow's *Making Type Work* (The Century Company); Edmund

G. Gress' *The Art and Practice of Typography* and *Fashion in American Typography* (Harper and Brothers); Theodore L. DeVinne's *Book Composition* (United Typothetae of America), *The Practice of Typography* (Oswald Publishing Company), *Manual of Printing Office Practice* (Press of Ars Typographica); Goold Brown's *The Institutes of English Grammar* (S. S. and William Wood and Company); Alfred S. West's *Elements of English Grammar* (The Macmillan Company); and the style-books (or sheets) of the leading newspapers, periodicals, and commercial and industrial houses of the English-speaking world, especially those of *The New York Times, New York Herald Tribune, The (New York) Sun, New York World-Telegram, Chicago Daily Tribune, Springfield Daily Republican, The Atlanta Constitution, St. Louis Post-Dispatch, The Kansas City Star, The (London) Times, The (London) Daily Telegraph, The (London) Morning Post, The Manchester Guardian,* and of the National City Bank and the Guaranty Trust Company of New York City.

The following books are recommended for collateral reading and study, the titles themselves serving as sufficient identification with chapters in *Get It Right* with which they correlate. Many other excellent books in the same fields might, of course, be named. These, however, happen to be works with which the author is best acquainted. They constitute an excellent consulting library for all those who are interested in using the Mother Tongue accurately and impressively in a wide variety of subject-matter: W. Davenport Adams' *Dictionary of English Literature* (Cassel and Company, Ltd.); Ray Palmer Baker's *The Preparation of Reports, Engineering, Scientific, Administrative* (Ronald Press Company); Francis K. Ball's *Constructive English, a Handbook of Speaking and Writing* (Ginn and Company); H. I. Barrett's *Modern Methods in the Office* (Harper and Brothers); R. F. Brewer's *The Art of Versification and the Technicalities of Poetry* (John Grant, Edinburgh); Marie F. Cahill's *Junior Office Practice* (The Macmillan Company); Lee Calloway's *Office Management, its Principles and Practice* (Ronald Press Company); Paul T. Cherington's *Advertising as a Business Force* (Doubleday, Doran, and

Company); Arthur F. Church's *The Training of a Secretary* (J. B. Lippincott and Company); Paul D. Converse's *Marketing Methods and Policies* (Prentice-Hall, Inc.); Mary Owen Crowther's *The Book of Letters* (Doubleday, Doran, and Company); W. J. and Coningsby Dawson's *The Great English Letter Writers* (Harper and Brothers); G. Binney Dibblee's *The Newspaper* (Henry Holt and Company); Edward William Dolch's *Business Letter Writing* (Ronald Press Company); Gayley and Scott's *Methods and Materials of Literary Criticism* (Ginn and Company); John L. Given's *Making a Newspaper* (Henry Holt and Company); Roland S. Hall's *Writing an Advertisement* (Houghton Mifflin Company); Max J. Herzberg's *New Style Book of Business English* (Pitman Publishing Corporation); George Burton Hotchkiss' *Advertising Copy* (Harper and Brothers); Hotchkiss and Kilduff's *Advanced Business Correspondence* (Harper and Brothers); E. R. Hudders' *Indexing and Filing: a Manual of Standard Practice* (Ronald Press Company); George Philip Krapp's *A Comprehensive Guide to Good English* (Rand, McNally, and Company) and *The Knowledge of English* (Henry Holt and Company); James Melvin Lee's *Language for Men of Affairs* (Ronald Press Company); E. W. Lord's *The Fundamentals of Business Ethics* (Ronald Press Company); E. V. Lucas' *The Gentlest Art* and *The Second Post* (The Macmillan Company); William C. Marshall's *Graphical Methods* (McGraw-Hill Book Company, Inc.); Edward L. McNamara's *Secretarial Training* (Ronald Press Company); H. L. Mencken's *The American Language* (Alfred A. Knopf); Elizabeth Meyers' *The Social Letter* (Brentano); Frank Arthur Mumby's *Letters of Literary Men* and *Letters of Literary Men: Sir Thomas More to Robert Burns* (George Routledge and Sons, Ltd.); J. C. Nesfield's *Modern English Grammar* (The Macmillan Company); John B. Opdycke's *Advertising and Selling Practice* (A. W. Shaw Company), *The English of Commerce* (Charles Scribner's Sons), *The Literature of Letters* (Lyons and Carnahan), *Business Letter Practice* and *The Language of Advertising* (Pitman Publishing Corporation); Emily Post's *Etiquette* (Funk & Wagnalls Company); Robert E. Ramsay's *Effective Direct Advertising* and *Effective House Organs*

(D. Appleton and Company); Byron Johnson Rees' *Nineteenth Century Letters* (Charles Scribner's Sons); Charles G. Ross' *The Writing of News* (Henry Holt and Company); George Saintsbury's *A Letter Book* (George Bell and Sons); Walter Dill Scott's *Psychology of Advertising* (Small, Maynard, and Company); G. H. Sheldon's *Advertising, Elements and Principles* (Harcourt, Brace, and Company); Walter K. Smart's *Handbook of Effective Writing* (Harper and Brothers); Sorelle and Gregg's *Secretarial Studies* (The Gregg Publishing Company); Daniel Starch's, *Principles of Advertising* (A. W. Shaw Company); Sloan and Mooney's *Advertising the Technical Product* (McGraw-Hill Book Company, Inc.); Sarah Augusta Taintor's *Training for Secretarial Practice* (McGraw-Hill Book Company, Inc.); Taintor's and Monro's *The Book of Modern Letters* (The Macmillan Company); Eugenia Wallace's *Filing Methods* (Ronald Press Company); Maurice Weseen's *Write Better Letters* (Thomas Y. Crowell Company); William Dwight Whitney's *The Life and Growth of Language* (D. Appleton and Company); Edwin C. Woolley's *The Mechanics of Writing* (D. C. Heath and Company); John L. Young's *Books from the Manuscript to the Bookseller* (Pitman Publishing Corporation).

The author is specifically indebted to the following publishers, business organizations, educational institutions, and individuals for the courteous extension of privilege to use copyrighted materials, acknowledgment being also made in the text itself: Harper and Brothers, New York City; The Macmillan Company, New York City; Charles Scribner's Sons, New York City; Henry Holt and Company, New York City; Funk & Wagnalls Company, New York City; Little, Brown, and Company, Boston, Mass.; Elbert Hubbard II, East Aurora, New York; Isaac Pitman and Sons, Bath, England; Oxford University Press, London, England; The Chicago University Press, Chicago, Illinois; the United States Government Printing Office, Washington, D. C.; The American Specification Institute, Chicago, Illinois; the American Library Association, Chicago, Illinois; the United Typothetae of America, Washington, D. C.; American Institute of Filing, Buffalo, New

York; the Spelling Reform Association, Lake Placid, New York; Gaylord Brothers, Syracuse, New York; Doubleday, Doran, and Company, New York City; Frederick A. Stokes and Company, New York City; the New York State Board of Regents; New York University Bureau of Publications; *Chicago Daily Tribune;* General Electric Company, Cleveland, Ohio; Pencil Supply Company of New Jersey; Thomas M. Gregory, Advertising Service, Akron, Ohio; Achison, Topeka, and Santa Fe Railway System; St. Louis (Missouri) Sticker Company; Oak Rubber Company, Ravenna, Ohio; Mr. E. P. Archibald, Advertising Counsel, Boston, Mass.; Jimm Daugherty, Inc., Advertising Agency, St. Louis, Missouri; the Western Union Telegraph Company; the Postal Telegraph Company; the New York Telephone Company; the New York City Police Department; the New York City Hall of Records; Trade Ways, Inc., New York City; Carnegie Hero Fund Commission, Pittsburgh, Penna.; the Beck Engraving Company, Philadelphia, Penna.; *The Atlantic Monthly; The New York Times; New York Herald Tribune; The (New York) Sun; New York World-Telegram; The New Yorker; The Saturday Review of Literature;* The Vocational Survey Commission, New York City; Miss Charlotte Tyler of the Institute of Pacific Relations, personal representative in America of Professor C. K. Ogden, Cambridge, England; Professor George Burton Hotchkiss, New York University, New York City; Mr. Charles E. Vautrain, Holyoke, Mass. To Mr. Edwin L. Shuman, of the Funk & Wagnalls Company, the author acknowledges indebtedness for many valuable suggestions and for painstaking work on proofs.

J. B. O.

CONTENTS

CONTENTS

GET IT RIGHT!

*A Cyclopedia
of Correct English Usage*

GET IT RIGHT!

CHAPTER ONE

ABBREVIATIONS

Abbreviations should not be used in "straight copy," that is, in formal composition written for solid straightaway reading in connected sentence and paragraph form. They are permissible and justifiable in informal copy only when and because haste and lack of space make them desirable. They are freely and properly used in billheads, receipts, tabular matter, statements, and other similar content pertaining to commerce and industry. They are likewise allowable in all kinds of footnote, cross-referencing, and other such addenda materials.

I As to names and titles

    A Such commonly used terms of respect as *Mr., Mrs., Messrs., jr., Sr.* are exceptions to the first statement above. Used with proper names these are altogether proper in straight copy as elsewhere. The first three are always capitalized; the last two may or may not be.

    B Such abbreviations as *Gen., Gov., Hon., Prof., Rev*, are properly used before full names but not before surnames only. In the latter usage they should be written out.

Gen. U. S. Grant	General Grant
Prof. Jay C. Cole	Professor Cole
Gov. Alfred E. Smith	Governor Smith
Honorable Watson	*not* Prof. Hartman
Reverend James	Gen. Blanford

But in the most formal matter such abbreviations should be written out even when preceding full names. The abbreviation *Dr.* is excepted from the above rule because of its common usage, but the tendency is to conform to the rule in its use also.

    Dr. James Pedersen   Doctor Pedersen
        Dr. Pedersen (allowable)

2 GET IT RIGHT!

C Christian names should be abbreviated only in emergencies of time and space. In abbreviating them care should be exercised to use the real abbreviations.

Benj. is an abbreviation   *Ben* is probably not
Danl. is an abbreviation   *Dan* is probably not

Similarly:

Edw.	and	*Ed*
Jas.	and	*Jim*
Saml.	and	*Sam*
Thos.	and	*Tom*
Wm.	and	*Will* or *Bill*

D Titles and degrees following proper names are properly designated by capitalized abbreviations. But titles used before a name and after it should not repeat each other.

     Dr. Thomas Atkinson, Thomas Atkinson, M.D.
not Dr. Thomas Atkinson, M. D.

But these are correct since two *different* title meanings are conveyed:

     Dr. Thomas Atkinson, Chairman
     Prof. Harold Briggs, D.D.S.

E When title designations are used without a name they should never be abbreviated.

     I hope, Doctor, that he is recovering
     The professor came in late

F The form of signatures should be respected. This rule is important for the letter writer. Both individuals and firms have their own particular usage very often, and it is an evidence of courtesy on the part of any one who addresses them to comply with their preferences. Such preferences cannot always be ascertained, of course, but signatures and letterheads constitute documentary evidence that a certain form has been adopted by the person or the firm using them. It is sometimes said that the misspelling of a proper name and the mistitling of its holder are the most forgivable of errors. But let it also be remembered that every individual has a right to be meticulous—"fussy" if you please—about both of these apparent details.

One Mr. Chapman may prefer his name written out—his signature after the complimentary closing indicates this.

You will therefore please address him *Mr. John Robert Chapman.* His brother may prefer plain *Tom Chapman.* To you, therefore, he must be *Mr. Tom Chapman.* Still another brother may sign off as *J. Bernard Chapman,* and that, then, is your cue. Observe the signature variations below. Used in addresses these should, of course, be preceded by *Mr.* Everybody is entitled to the courtesy of *Mr* or *Esq* or *Miss* or *Mrs,* but nobody should affix such title in signing his own name. The forms *sr, jr, II,* and so forth, however, are appropriately used by the signer. Abbreviations following proper names are usually preceded by a comma, but there is increasing variation in this usage.

Harold Romano, Sr.	Archibald Robinson, Third
Harold Romano jr.	Archibald Robinson, II
Elsie Eno Foote, Second	A. Gregory Robinson, President

The abbreviation *Esq. (Esquire)* after a man's proper name is a British form. It is used occasionally in the United States in addressing lawyers, architects, and retired gentlemen of wealth and distinction. It derives from usage in connection with the name of the landed country gentleman who, in former times, was the legal authority of his community. The esquire in England is the English rank of gentry next below a knight. When knighthood was in flower the esquire was attendant upon a knight and was by this token himself a candidate for knighthood. *Mr.* should never be used before a name when *Esq.* is used after it.

G Letterheads, advertising copy, and other company forms should be the guide in regard to correct spelling, correct punctuation, correct capitalization, and correct abbreviation of firm names and addresses. There is wide variation among business houses in all these respects, as witness:

> Lord & Taylor
> R. H. Macy & Co.
> The Wentworth Brothers, Inc.
> Walters & Mahon, Ltd.
> American Title and Mortgage Company
> The Excelsior Stone & Mortar Works
> Brand Bros. and Company
>
> Pitman Publishing Corporation
> Two West Forty-fifth Street
>
> Philip Morris & Co., Ltd., Inc.

The ampersand (&) is preferably never used between individual names either in business titles or in collaborations other than business. But this rule is frequently violated in firm names, as the foregoing list indicates. In other cases it is seldom violated.

> Beaumont and Fletcher
> Gilbert and Sullivan

When, as result of the decease of the individual members of a firm, their names are still carried as the firm name, the ampersand may be used with somewhat more justification. Used in straight copy and in formal composition of any kind it savors a little of the discourteous and the uncomplimentary.

The word *The,* used as part of a name or title, should be clearly differentiated from the use of *the* as a definite article before a name or title.

> *The New York Times*
> the *Los Angeles Times*
> *The Five Gables* (name of an estate)
> the *Five Gables*

Examples two and four are really abbreviated titles—*The* is omitted as a part of the title. In writing these titles the difference should be respected.

> I read it in *The New York Times*
> I read it in the *Los Angeles Times*
> We visited at *The Five Gables*
> We visited at the *Five Gables*

H   Never abbreviate any title in the salutation of a letter except *Mr., Mrs., Messrs.,* and *Dr.* (?) and the French *M., MM., Mme., Mmes., Mlle.,* and *Mlles.*

> Dear Major Rollins   Dear Mrs. Jones
> Dear Professor Smith   Dear Lieutenant Fry
> Dear Governor Cross   Dear M. Le Fevre
> Dear Mr. Underwood   Dear Commissioner Waters
> Dear Dr. Burnley   but also (preferably)   Dear Doctor Burnley

*J   Never abbreviate any word in the complimentary closing of a letter.

> Yours very respectfully   *not*   Yrs. very resp'y

K   Never abbreviate the first name or names of a well-known author.

* See page 435.

| William Shakespeare | *not* | W. Shakespeare |
| Percy Bysshe Shelley | *not* | P. B. Shelley |

This rule applies to the treatment of names in present-day usage. Do not use the single initial before a surname. *A. Barnes* is bad. *A. C. Barnes* is somewhat better, perhaps. But *Alfred C. Barnes* or *Alfred Coe Barnes* is preferred usage, for it indicates gender, and the person who addresses can tell whether to use *Mr.* or *Mrs.* or *Miss* before the name. It is not in the best of taste ever to write a name with a single initial. Short-cuts never are.

L Titles of writings should not be abbreviated, with the possible exception of *v.* or *vs.* for *versus.*

> *Government Ownership versus Private Enterprise*
> *not*
> *Gov'nm't Ownership vs. Private Ent'rprise*

II As to dates and places

A Names of the days of the week, of the months of the year, and likewise of states and cities are preferably never abbreviated. The longer state names, however, are more or less commonly written in abbreviated form in addresses. Authorities are fairly well agreed that these names should always be written out: *Alaska, Canal Zone, Guam, Hawaii, Idaho, Iowa, Maine, Ohio, Utah, Virgin Islands,* and *March, April, May, June, July.*

This rule is given in various other ways: Short words should never be abbreviated. Geographical names must never be abbreviated, because they are used, as a rule, in connections where accuracy is important and abbreviations easily get themselves misunderstood. Monosyllabics and dissyllabics should never be abbreviated (but this form of the rule is inapplicable because some words of three syllables may be comparatively short and some of one syllable comparatively long). Still another rule says that names of insular possessions and of foreign countries should never be abbreviated. To be on the safe side it may be concluded that it is preferable not to abbreviate important place and time names.

B The words *fort, mount, point,* and *port* used as part of proper place names should never be abbreviated.

C It is sometimes ruled that the word *saint* must never be abbreviated when used in connection with the name of a religious character or place, but that in other uses it may quite properly be abbreviated.

St. Louis (Missouri)	Saint Louis
St. Paul (Minnesota)	Saint Paul
St. Helena	Saint Ann's Church

D The letters *U.S.* and *U.S.A.* may be used for *United States* and *United States of America* respectively. The former may also be used before the names of divisions and departments of the Government. But neither set of initials should be used in straight copy. In connection with Government sea and air ships it has become acceptable to use U.S. before the proper name or U.S.A. beneath it. The word *ship* is commonly abbreviated to S. in such usage.

X—4	US57
U.S.A.	U.S. Army Plane *Dare*
U.S. Cruiser *Cavanagh*	U.S.S. *Brooklyn*

E The words *avenue, boulevard, place, street* should not be abbreviated in formal letter copy, tho there is much violation of this rule even in printed letterheads and much inconsistent usage. Some people consider the abbreviation of these words in headings and addresses as brusque and discourteous.

F The forms *d, nd, rd, st, th* should *not* be used after date and place numbers in letters or other straight copy. (As a matter of fact *nd* and *rd* are themselves incorrect forms of *d* in such usage.) Our forefathers always used these after dates—*June 20th, 1864*—but we rarely do so today. The *th* and the others have passed in this connection. They are passing too—and wholesomely—from place numbers, tho evolution here as elsewhere works slowly. It is not only unnecessary but it is even bungling to write *114 West 23rd Street*. Even in run-in date references these forms are quite superfluous and should not be used; *I met him on the 20 of April* is better than *I met him on the 20th of April*. The best form, of course, is *I met him on the twentieth of April*. All such expressions are primarily to be *seen* rather than to be *heard*. If they are to be read aloud it is perfectly easy for the reader to pronounce the ordinal form. Moreover *20th* and *23rd* are hybrid or impure forms. Any letter-carrier will testify to the fact that *31* is more easily and more quickly read than *31st*. The latter form frequently delays reading, especially on the part of the near-sighted, for at a glance it may be mistaken for a number of four digits.

G In inner house notes it may be permitted to break all the "forbiddens" and enjoy an orgy of abbreviating. This is happening constantly—*Jones ph'n'd Dr. C. 4 p.m. Tues. 2/9/35*—and speed, space, and occasion may all justify it in strictly informal communications. It is well to remember that the short form for day, month, and year—*2/9/35*—means in America February 9, 1935, but that in England and other European countries it means September 2, 1935.

H The points of the compass are abbreviated by capitals sometimes with and sometimes without the period.

N.	S.	E.	W.	NW.	SE.	NNE.	WSW.
NW. by N.		SE. by S.		SW. by S.		SE. by NW.	

J The word *o'clock* should not be used with meridian abbreviations to indicate the time of day.

12 m (noon)   10 a.m.   2.30 p.m.   12 p.m. (midnight)

III Capitalization, punctuation, and so forth

A Abbreviations are capitalized in accordance with the words they stand for (see list below). They are sometimes capitalized also for the sake of emphasis; thus, A.M. in order to emphasize that ten o'clock in the morning is meant rather than ten o'clock at night.

B Abbreviations and, as a rule, their parts are followed by periods. The forms *d, nd, rd, st, th* are not abbreviations really, and do not require the period. The numerals I, II, III, IV, V, and so forth, may or may not be followed by periods when they are used for partitioning copy or for tabulations. Usage is increasingly omitting the period when numerals are used in this way. The same is true of Arabic numerals and of letters. Roman numerals pronounced as ordinals after names—*George V*—are preferably not to be followed by the period. Usually each element in an abbreviated form is followed by a period, but not always (see points of the compass above and note variations to this rule in the list below).

C Hyphenated abbreviations follow the hyphenation of the words they stand for.

ft.-lb.   foot-pound   hf.-bd.   half-bound

D Care must be exercised not to confuse certain short words that have been introduced from foreign tongues (chiefly Latin) with abbreviations. The Latin word *via*, for instance, tho used for abbreviating or short-cutting expression, is nevertheless not an abbreviation and should not therefore be followed by a period. Some others are *ad, circa, et, ex, finis, in, in re, par, per, per cent, pro, re, versus.*

It should be noted here that many firms and institutions today omit the period after *Dr, St, Mr, Mrs,* and *Messrs,* a usage that, it is hoped, will be increasingly adopted by large and influential organizations. The letter-names of radio stations are written without periods or spaces—*WOR, WEAF.* So, too, are TNT (trinitrotoluol), TB (tuberculosis), US40 (United States Highway Number 40), SOS (suspend other service—wireless distress signal), and all the metric abbreviations.

E These last are written in lower-case and the initial letters of the component parts of the word are used as abbreviations. They may or may not be followed by periods.

WEIGHT		LAND AREA		CAPACITY OF CONTAINERS		LENGTH	
kg	kilogram	ha	hectare	kl	kiloliter	km	kilometer
hg	hectogram	a	are	hl	hectoliter	hm	hectometer
dkg	dekagram	ca	centare	dkl	dekaliter	dkm	dekameter
g	gram			l	liter	m	meter
dg	decigram			dl	deciliter	dm	decimeter
cg	centigram			cl	centiliter	cm	centimeter
mg	milligram			ml	milliliter	mm	millimeter
						μ	micron (0.001 mm)
						mμ	millimicron

AREA		VOLUME	
km^2	square kilometer	km^3	cubic kilometer
hm^2	square hectometer	hm^3	cubic hectometer
dkm^2	square dekameter	dkm^3	cubic dekameter
m^2	square meter	m^3	cubic meter
dm^2	square decimeter	dm^3	cubic decimeter
cm^2	square centimeter	cm^3	cubic centimeter
mm^2	square millimeter	mm^3	cubic millimeter
μ^2	square micron	μ^3	cubic micron

PREFIXES AND THEIR MEANING

m milli = one thousandth (0.001)
c centi = one hundredth (0.01)
d deci = one tenth (0.1)
   [The unit equals 1]
dk deka = ten (10)
h hecto = one hundred (100)
k kilo = one thousand (1,000)

METRIC UNITS

m meter (for length)
g gram (for weight or mass)
l liter (for capacity)

F Weights and measures—British and American—are abbreviated as follows. Usage varies as to their pluralization, but it is preferable to make the one form serve for both singular and plural:

LENGTH	AREA and VOLUME
in., inch	sq. in.
ft., foot	cu. in.
yd., yard	sq. mile(s)
mile(s), rarely abbreviated	cu. ft.

WEIGHT	CAPACITY
grain(s), rarely abbreviated	gill(s), rarely abbreviated
dr., dram	pt., pint
oz., ounce	qt., quart
lb., pound	gal., gallon
cwt., hundredweight	pk., peck
ton(s), rarely abbreviated	bu., bushel
	bbl., barrel

G It is better to use abbreviations with periods after them than it is to use their corresponding contractions with apostrophes. In other words, *dept.* is preferable to *dep't, sec.* to *sec'y.* Never should both styles of shortening—abbreviations and contractions—be used in the same unit of work. Both the period and the apostrophe should never be used with the shortened form. The form *s'g't.* is wrong. In cases where the abbreviation with a period after it would constitute a complete word and thus tend to confuse the context, the apostrophe may be justifiably used instead of the period. Thus, *for'd* or *fwd.* is preferable to *ford.* But many first syllables of words used for abbreviations constitute independent words—*art., ill., log., mar., mat., max.*— and it would be difficult to adopt others for such of these as have been long in use.

H Abbreviations are sometimes pluralized by adding *s* to the singular form and sometimes by doubling the initial letter used as the singular number abbreviation: *bl.* (bale), *bls.*

(bales); *p.* (page), *pp.* (pages). The latter is more unusual than the former. Note the following abbreviations used in footnotes, marginal notes, tables, and so forth, in connection with literary work, principally the compilation of bibliographies:

art., arts. (article, articles)	p., pp. (page, pages)
bk., bks. (book, books)	par., pars. (paragraph, paragraphs)
ch., chs. (chapter, chapters)	pl., pls. (plate, plates)
fig., figs. (figure, figures)	pt., pts. (part, parts)
l., ll. (line, lines)	sec., secs. (section, sections)
no., nos. (number, numbers)	vol., vols. (volume, volumes)

In using such words as *article, figure, section* in listings and enumerations, it is preferable to write them out and capitalize them in the first instance and to abbreviate them thereafter.

Section	A	Article	1
sec.	B	art.	2
sec.	C	arts.	3, 4, 5

J. The words *north, south, east, west* are not abbreviated when used in connection with proper names unless the proper names themselves are abbreviated. Thus, *No. Amer.* is correct for *North America,* but *No. America* is wrong.

IV   A list of commercial and general abbreviations in common use

Abbreviations and contractions, in the main, just happen. Haste in writing, labeling, and classifying, or lack of space, or both, compel a more or less haphazard and unorganized formation of even the most logical of abbreviated words and expressions. Sometimes the first letter and the last letter of a word suffice for its abbreviation, as *ht.* for *height;* sometimes the first letter, the last letter, and a letter or letters from between them, as *mdse.* for *merchandise;* sometimes the first two or three letters are used, as *art.* for *article,* or the first two letters and the last, as *amt.* for *amount.* In the abbreviation of expressions of more than one word, the initial letters only may be used, as *c.o.d.* for *cash on delivery;* the initial letters of the two most important words may be written in fractional form, as *b/s* for *bill of sale;* the first letter of the first word and two or more of the second may be used, as *b. rec.* for *bills receivable.* Again, the abbreviation may be so condensed in form as to be a sign only, as @ for *at,* or % for *per cent,* or $, the monogram of the United States, for *dollar.*

According to the old story, a Yankee porter once wrote on a delivery note "orl krekt." This he adopted for all satisfactory deliveries. To save himself work he began to sign them OK. This has come down to us as he wrote it, OK. It has come down as O.K. It has come down as O K and as o.k. This single example illustrates the variation of practise that exists in the writing of abbreviations. The periods and the omission of periods in the following list should be noted carefully, as should also the spacing and the use of the diagonal. In certain mathematical fields exponents are used—N° (numero)—for *number*. The French likewise sometimes use the exponent letter, as in Cie (compagnie) for *company*. Certain metrical abbreviations are similarly written with exponents, as are the terms indicative of book sizes (see page 445).

Many establishments adopt their own system of abbreviations for special operations or products, and these come to constitute a sort of shorthand known for most part by employees only. In making up such individual abbreviations those upon whom the task devolves would help the cause of simplified English usage if they were to observe such fundamental rules and preferences as have been indicated in the foregoing pages.

The dictionary is the last resort for a comprehensive list of abbreviations. The unabridged dictionary gives thousands of them. The list below cannot, of course, pretend to exhaustiveness; but even an abridged list may prove helpful in puzzling cases.

a. at, acre, adjective
aar against all risks
A.B. Bachelor of Arts
abb. or **abbr.** abbreviation
acc., acct., a/c account
A.D. (*Anno Domini*) in the year of our Lord
ad inf. (*ad infinitum*) without end
ad int. (*ad interim*) in the meantime
adj. adjective
ad lib. (*ad libitum*) at pleasure
admr. administrator
admrx. administratrix
ad val. (*ad valorem*) according to value
adv. adverb, advertise, advocate
advg. advertising
advt. advertisement

ae., aet. (*aetatis*) aged, of age
A.E.F. American Expeditionary Forces
A.F. of L. American Federation of Labor
agt. agent
A 1 first class
Ala. Alabama
A.L.A. American Library Association
a.m. (*ante meridiem*) before noon
A.M. Master of Arts, (*anno mundi*) in the year of the world
amt. amount
anal. analysis, analogous
A.N.C. American Nurse Corps
anon. anonymous
annot. annotation, annotator

ans. answer
ant. antonym
a/o account of
a/or and or
a.p. additional premium
app. appendix, apprentice
appt. appointed, appointee, appointment
Apr. April
apt. apartment
A.R.A. Associate of the Royal Academy of Arts
A.R.I.B.A. Associate of the Royal Institute of British Architects
Ariz. Arizona
Ark. Arkansas
arr. arrangement, arrival, arrived
art. article
A.R.V. American Revised Version (of Bible)
A.S. Anglo-Saxon
a/s account sales
A.S.C.E. American Society of Civil Engineers
A.S.M.E. American Society of Mechanical Engineers
assg. assigned, assignment
asst. assistant, assistance
asstd. assorted
att. attention
atty. attorney
at.wt. atomic weight
Aug. August
aux. auxiliary
av. average
A.V. Authorized Version
ave. avenue
avoir., avdp. avoirdupois

b. book, born
B.A. Bachelor of Arts
bal. balance
Bapt. Baptist
B. Arch. Bachelor of Architecture
batt. battalion, battery
b.b. ball bearing, bank book, bill book
bbl. barrel
B.C. Before Christ
B.C.E. Bachelor of Civil Engineering
B.C.L. Bachelor of Civil Law
B.D. Bachelor of Divinity
bdl., bdle. bundle

bds. beds, boards, bonds, bound in boards
b.e., b/e bill of exchange
bg. bag
bib. bibliographer, bibliography
Bib. Bible
biog. biographer, biography
bk. bank, bark, book
bkg. banking, bookkeeping
bkt. basket
bl. bale
b.l., b/l bill of lading
B.L. Bachelor of Law
bldg. building
B.L.E. Brotherhood of Locomotive Engineers
B. Litt. Bachelor of Literature or Letters
blk. black, bulk
b.m. board measure
B.Mus. Bachelor of Music
b.o. branch office, buyer's option
bosn. boatswain
b.pay. bills payable
B.P.O.E. Benevolent and Protective Order of Elks
b.rec. bills receivable
br. brand, brief
brev. brevet
bros. brothers
B.S. Bachelor of Science
bu., bull. bulletin
bu., b/s bushel
bus. business
bx. box

c. cent, chairman
c., cir. (*circa*) about
C. (*centum*) one hundred
C. Catholic, Centigrade
c.a. chartered accountant, chief accountant, commercial agent, controller of accounts
C.A.C. Coast Artillery Corps
c.a.f. cost and freight
Calif. California
cap. (*caput*) capital, head
capt. captain
car., k. carat
carp. carpenter
cash. cashier
c.b. cash book
C.C. Construction Corps
C.Cls. Court of Claims
cd. command

C.D. Chief of Division, Colonial Dames
C.E. Church of England, Civil Engineer
C.E.C. Civilian Engineering Corps
cent. (*centum*) one hundred
Cent. Centigrade
cert., certif. certificate, certify
cf., cp., conf. compare, consult
c.f.i. cost, freight, insurance
ch., chap., cap. (*caput*) chapter
Ch.C. Chaplain Corps
c.h. courthouse, custom house
ch.clk. chief clerk
chem. chemist, chemistry
chf. chief
chgd. charged
chr. chairman
Chron. I Chronicles I
Chron. II Chronicles II
cir. circulation
c.i.f. cost, insurance, freight
C.J. Chief Justice
ck. cask, check
cl. class
cld. called, cleared
clk. clerk
cm. centimeter
cml. commercial
co. company
c/o care of
c.o.d. cash on delivery
col. colonel, column
Col. Colossians
coll. collection, collector
colloq. colloquial
Colo. Colorado
com. commission, committee, common
comdr. commander
comm. commentary, commerce, commonwealth
con. (*contra*) against
con., cont. continued
Cong. Congregational
conj. conjunction
Conn. Connecticut
cons. consolidated, consolidation, constitution
cont. contents, continental, continued, contract, contractor, contrary
constr. construction, constructor
contr. contraction, contrary
conv. convention

Cor. I Corinthians I
Cor. II Corinthians II
corp. corporal, corporation
corr. corrupted
cor.sec. corresponding secretary
C.P.A. Certified Public Accountant
C.P.R. Canadian Pacific Railroad
cr. crate, credit, creditor
c.r. company's risk
cr., crim. criminal
crit. critic, criticism
cr.8vo crown octavo book size
cs. case
C.S. Christian Science, Civil Service
C.S.C. Conspicuous Service Cross
CST Central Standard Time
c.t. commercial traveler
ctge. cartage
cts. cents
cur., curt. current, current month
c.w.o. cash with order
cwt. hundredweight

d. day, died, dime, dose, pence (*denarius*)
D five hundred
D. Democrat
Danl. Daniel
D.A.R. Daughters of the American Revolution
dbk. drawback
D.C. Dental Corps, District of Columbia
D.C.L. Doctor of Civil Law
d.d. day's date, days after date
D.D. Doctor of Divinity
D.D.S. Doctor of Dental Surgery
d.&w.tf. daily and weekly till forbidden
deb. debenture
dec. deceased, declaration, decoration, decrease
Dec. December
def. defendant, definite, definition
del. (*delineavit*) drew or drawn
Del. Delaware
Dem. Democrat
dent. dental, dentistry
dep. deposit
dept., dpt. department
deriv. derivation, derivative, derived
Deut. Deuteronomy
dft. draft

D.G. (*Dei Gratia*) by the grace of God
dial. dialectic
dict. dictation, dictionary
diff. difference
dim. diminutive
disc. discovered
dis., disc., disct. discount, district
dist. distance, distinguished, district
distr. distribution
div. dividend
D.L.O. Dead Letter Office
D.Litt. Doctor of Literature or Letters
dm. decimeter
D.Mus. Doctor of Music
do. ditto, the same
d/o delivery order
dolls. dollars
doz. dozen
dr. debit, debtor, doctor, drawn, drawing
D.R. Daughters of the Revolution
ds. days
d.s. days after sight
D.Sc. Doctor of Science
D.S.C. Distinguished Service Cross
D.S.M. Distinguished Service Medal
D.S.O. Distinguished Service Order (British)
D.V. (*Deo Volente*) God Willing
dwt. pennyweight

e. earl, earth, east, engineer, English
ea. each
Eccles. Ecclesiastes
ed., edit. edition, editor
e.e. errors excepted
E.E. Electrical Engineer
e.g. (*exempli gratia*) for example
8vo octavo
ejusd. (*ejusdem*) the same
e.&.o.e. errors and omissions excepted
elec. electric, electrician
enc., encl. enclosed
e.n.e., ENE east northeast
Eng., E. English
engr. engineer, engraved, engraver
ens. ensign
entd. entered
e.o.m. end of month
Eph. Ephesians

E.R.V. English Revised Version (of Bible)
e.s.e., ESE east southeast
esp. especially
esq., esqr. esquire
EST Eastern Standard Time
et al. (*et alii, aliae*) and others, and so forth
etc., &c. (*et cetera*) and others, and the rest
et seq. (*et sequentes, sequentia*) and following, what follows
etym. etymology, etymological
et ux. (*et uxor*) and wife
E.V. English Version
ex. examiner, example, exceptional, executive
exc. except, excuse
exch., ex. exchange, exchangeable, exchanged
excl. exclusive
ex cp. without coupon
ex div., xd. without dividend
exec. executive
Exod., Ex. Exodus
exp. expense, export, express
exr. executor
exrx. executrix
ext. extra, extract
Ezek. Ezekiel

f. fabric, farthing, fathom, feminine, folio, following, foot, fort, franc
F. Fahrenheit, French
f.a.a. free of all average
Fahr. Fahrenheit
f.a.q. fair average quality
f.a.s. free alongside ship
F.& A.M. Free and Accepted Masons
F.B.A. Fellow of the British Academy
fcp. foolscap
f.d. free dock
Feb. February
fec. (*fecit*) he or she did it
ff. following
F.G. Foot Guards (British)
f.g.a. free of general average
fgt. freight
f.i.c. freight, insurance, carriage
fig. figure, figurative
fin.sec. financial secretary
fir. firkin

fl. florin, flour
Fla. Florida
f.o.b. free on board
f.o.c. free of charge
fol. folio, following
f.o.r. free on road, free on rail
for'd, fwd. forward
f.o.s. free on steamer
f.o.t. free on truck
4to quarto
f.p. fire plug
fr. fragment, franc, frequent, from
F.R.A.S. Fellow of the Royal Astronomical Society
F.R.C.P. Fellow of the Royal College of Physicians
F.R.C.S. Fellow of the Royal College of Surgeons
F.R.G.S. Fellow of the Royal Geographical Society
Fri. Friday
F.R.I.B.A. Fellow of the Royal Institute of British Architects
F.R.S. Fellow of the Royal Society
frt. freight
F.S.A. Fellow of the Society of Antiquaries
ft. feet, flat, foot, fort
ft.-lb. foot-pound
fth. fathom
fur. furlong

g. general, good, goods, gram, guinea
g.a. general average
Ga. Georgia
gal. gallon
Gal. Galatians
gas. gasoline
G.A.R. Grand Army of the Republic
G.C.B. Grand Cross of the Bath (British)
G.C.I.E. Grand Cross of the Indian Empire (British)
G.C.L.H. Grand Cross of the Legion of Honor (French)
G.C.M.G. Grand Cross of the Order of St. Michael and St. George (British)
G.C.S.I. Grand Cross of the Star of India (British)
G.C.V.O. Grand Cross of the Victorian Order (British)

gen. general
Gen. Genesis
gent. gentleman
G.H.Q. General Headquarters
gi. gill
gm. gram
g.m.q. good marketable quality
gov. government, governor
G.P.O. General Post Office
gr. grain, gram, great, gross
G.R. (*Georgius Rex*) King George
gram. grammar, grammatical
G.S.C. General Staff Corps
guar. guarantee, guaranty
gun. gunner

h. harbor, height, high, hour, house, hundred
Hab. Habakkuk
Hag. Haggai
h.c. held covered
H.B.M. His or Her Britannic Majesty
hdkf. handkerchief
h.e. (*hoc est*) this or that is
H.E. His Excellency
Heb. Hebrews
hf. half
hf.-bd. half-bound
H.G. Horse Guards (British)
hhd. hogshead
H.I.H. His or Her Imperial Highness
H.I.M. His or Her Imperial Majesty
H.M. His or Her Majesty
H.M.S. His or Her Majesty's Ship or Service
ho. house
hon. honorable
Hon.Sec. Honorable Secretary
Hos. Hosea
h.p. half pay, horse power
h.p.n. horse power nominal
hr. hour
h.r. house record, house of representatives
H.R.H. His or Her Royal Highness
ht. height
hun., hund. hundred
h.w.m. high water mark

i. island
i.a. incorporated accountant
i.b. invoice book

ib., ibid. (*ibidem*) the same, in the same place, from the same source
id. (*idem*) the same
i.e. (*id est*) that is
I.E. Indian Empire
Ill. Illinois
ills. illustrated, illustration
imp. imperative, imperial, imported, improved
in. inch
inc. incorporated, increase
incl. inclusive
incog. incognito, unknown
ind. independent, index, indigo
in f. in fine, final, at the end
inf. (*infra*) below or back
init. (*initio*) in the beginning
in lim. (*in limine*) at the outset
in loc. (*in loco*) in its place
in pr. in principle
in re in regard to, pertaining to
in s. (*in situ*) in its original position
ins. inspector, insurance
inst. (*instant*) in the present month, instant, institute, institution
int. interest, interim
inv. invention, inventor, invoice
i.o. in order
I.O.F. Independent Order of Foresters
I.O.O.F. Independent Order of Odd Fellows
I.O.U. I owe you—acknowledgment of money lent
i.q. (*idem quid*) the same as
I.Q. intelligence quotient
I.R.O. internal revenue officer
irr. irregular
Isa. Isaiah
ital. italics
I.W.W. Industrial Workers of the World

j. judge, justice
Jan. January
j/a joint account
Jas. James
Jer. Jeremiah
Jon. Jonah
Josh. Joshua
jour. journal
J.P. Justice of the Peace

jr., Jr., jun. junior
Judg. Judges

k. karat, keg, king, knight
Kans. Kansas
K.B. King's Bench, Knight of the Bath (British)
K.C. King's Counsel (British)
K.C.B. Knight Commander of the Bath (British)
K.C.I.E. Knight Commander of the Indian Empire (British)
K.C.M.G. Knight Commander of the Order of St. Michael and St. George (British)
K.C.S.I. Knight Commander of the Star of India (British)
K.C.V.O. Knight Commander of the Victorian Order (British)
kg. keg, kilogram
K.G. Knight of the Garter (British)
K.L.H. Knight of the Legion of Honor (French)
km. kilometer
K. of C. Knights of Columbus
K.P. Knights of Pythias
kt. knight
K.T. Knight Templar, Knight of the Thistle (British)
kw.-hr. kilowatt-hour
Ky. Kentucky

l. law, league, left, length, line, lira, liter, long, (*libra*) pound
L fifty
L. Latin
L., l., £ pound sterling
La. Louisiana
l.a. law agent
lab. laboratory
Lam. Lamentations
lat. latitude
Lat. Latin
lb. pound
l.c. (*loco citato*) in the place quoted or cited, lower case or small letter, label clause (insurance term)
l/c letter of credit
leg. legal, legislation, legislature
Lev. Leviticus
L.C.J. Lord Chief Justice (British)
l.f. ledger folio

ABBREVIATIONS 17

lib. (*liber*) book, liberty
lieut. or lt. lieutenant
lieut. or lt. col. lieutenant colonel
lieut. or lt. comdr. lieutenant commander
lieut. or lt. gen. lieutenant general
liq. liquid, liquor
lit. liter, literally, literary
Litt.B. Bachelor of Literature
Litt.D. Doctor of Literature
LL.B. Bachelor of Laws
LL.D. Doctor of Laws
loc. cit. (same as l.c. above)
log. logarithm
lon., long. longitude
loq. (*loquitur*) he or she speaks
L.S. (*Locus Sigilli*) place of the seal
l.s.d. pounds, shillings, pence
l.t. long ton
ltd. limited

m. noon (*meridies*), mark, married, masculine, meter, mile, minute, month, moon
M., M Monsieur
M one thousand
M.A. Master of Arts
mach. machine, machinery, machinist
mag. magazine, magnitude
maj. major, majority
Mal. Malachi
man. manager, manual
Man. Manhattan
Mar. March
marg. margin
Mass. Massachusetts
math. mathematics
Math. C. Mathematics Corps
Matt. Matthew
max. maximum
M.C. medical corps, member of Congress, Military Cross (British)
Md. Maryland
M.D. medical doctor
mdse. merchandise
Me. Maine
M.E. mechanical engineer, Methodist Episcopal, mining engineer
meas. measure
mem. member
memo., mem. memorandum
Messrs., Messrs Gentlemen

mfd. manufactured
mfg. manufacturing
mfr., manuf. manufacturer
mgr. manager
Mic. Micah
Mich. Michigan
mid. middle, midshipman
M.I.M.E. Member of the Institute of Mining Engineers
min. minimum, minority, minute
Minn. Minnesota
misc. miscellaneous
Miss. Mississippi
M.L.A. Modern Language Association
Mlle., Mlle Mademoiselle
mm. millimeter
MM., MM Messieurs
Mme., Mme Madame
mo. month
Mo. Missouri
m.o. money order
m.o.m. middle of month
Mon. Monday
Mont. Montana
M.P. member of Parliament, municipal police, marine police
m.p.h. miles per hour
Mr., Mr mister or master
Mrs., Mrs mistress
ms. manuscript
m/s months after sight
m.s.l. mean sea level
MST Middle Standard Time
mt. mount, mountain
mtg. mortgage
mus. museum, music, musical
Mus.B. Bachelor of Music
myth. mythology

n. news, north, noon, note, noun, number
N Navy, North
n/a no account
N.A.D. National Academy of Design
Nah. Nahum
nat., natl. national
nav. naval, navigation
n.b. (*nota bene*) note well, take notice, important
N.C. North Carolina
n.d. no date
N.Dak. North Dakota
n.e., NE northeast

N.E.A. National Educational Association
Nebr. Nebraska
Neh. Nehemiah
nem. con. (*nemine contradicente*) unanimous, no one contradicting
n.e.s. not elsewhere specified
Nev. Nevada
n.g. no good
N.G. National Guard
N.H. New Hampshire
N.J. New Jersey
n.l., n.lat. north latitude
N.M. New Mexico
n.n.e., NNE north northeast
n.n.w., NNW north northwest
no. north, (*numero*) number
nol. pros. (*nolle prosequi*) to be unwilling to prosecute
non. seq. (*non sequitur*) it does not follow
n.o.p. not otherwise provided for
Nov. November
N.P. notary public
n.r. no risk
n.s., n/s not specified, not sufficient, new series, new style
n.u. name unknown
Num. Numbers
N.Y. New York
N.Y.C. New York City

o. old, order, oxygen
O. Ohio, Ontario
ob. (*obiit*) died
ob. (*obiter*) by the way
Obad. Obadiah
obj. object, objection
obs. observation, obsolete
obt., obdt. obedient
oct. octavo size
Oct. October
o/d on demand
o.e. omissions excepted
o.k. correct, satisfactory
Okla. Oklahoma
O.M. Order of Merit (British)
on a/c on account
op., opp. opposite
o.p. out of print
op. cit. (*opere citato*) in the work cited or mentioned
opt. optician

o.r. owner's risk
O.R.C. Officers' Reserve Corps
ord. ordinary, ordnance
Ore., Oreg. Oregon
org. organ, organic, organization
orig. origin, originally
o.s. ordinary seaman, old style (calendar)
o/s out of stock
o/s or return on sale or return; that is, retailer may return goods if they cannot be sold
O.T.C. Officers' Training Corps
oz. ounce

p. page, parallel, part, participle, party, pay, penny, period, person, piano, pint, pipe, pole, population, post, profession
p.a. private account, particular average
Pa. Pennsylvania
par. paragraph, parallel
pass. tr. passenger train
p.clk. pay clerk
payt. payment
pc. piece
p.c. per cent, postcard
pd. paid
Pd.B. Bachelor of Pedagogy
Pd.D. Doctor of Pedagogy
P.E. Protestant Episcopal
Penna. Pennsylvania
peo. people
per. period, person
per, par by, at, thru
per ann. (*per annum*) by the yea1 annually
per cent, per ct. (*per centum*) by the hundred
per m. by the thousand
per pro., p.p., p.pro. (*per procurationem*) on behalf of
pert. pertaining
Pet. I Peter I
Pet. II Peter II
pfd. preferred
pharm. pharmacist, pharmacy
Ph.B. Bachelor of Philosophy
Ph.D. Doctor of Philosophy
Ph.G. Graduate in Pharmacy
Phil. Philemon, Philippians
phr. phrase, phraseology

P.I. Philippine Islands
pk. pack, peck
pkg., pkge. package
pl. place, plate, plural
p.l. partial loss
p. & l. profit and loss
plf., plff., pltf. plaintiff
plur. plural, plurality
pm. premium
p.m. (*post meridiem*) afternoon, postmaster
P.M.G. Postmaster General
p.n. promissory note
p.o. post office, postal order
p.o.d. pay on delivery
poet. poetical, poetry
pol. political, politics
p.o.o. post office order
pop. populace, popular, population
pos., poss. possession, possessive
pp. pages
p.p. parcel post, past participle
p.p.c. (*pour prendre congé*) to take leave
pph. pamphlet
p.p.i. policy proof of interest
p.p.m. parts per million
pr. pair, printed, printer
P.R. Puerto Rico
pref. preface, preferred
prem. premise, premium
prep. preparation, preposition
prin. principal
pro tem. (*pro tempore*) for the time
prob. probably
proc. proceedings, proctor
prof. profession, professor
pron. pronominal, pronounced
prop. proposition
prov. province, provincial
Provs. Proverbs
prox. (*proximo*) next month
prs. pairs, personality
p.s. (*post scriptum*) postscript
pseud. pseudonym
pss. postscripts
Pss. Psalms
PST Pacific Standard Time
pt. pint, point
p.t. post town
p.t.o. please turn over
pvt., pte. private
pwt. pennyweight
p.x. please exchange
pxt., pnxt., pinx. (*pinxit*) painted

q. quart, quasi, queen, query, question, quire
Q.C. Queen's Counsel (British)
q.d. (*quasi dicat*) as if he should say
q.e. (*quod est*) which is
q.e.d. (*quod erat demonstrandum*) which was to be proved
q.e.f. (*quod erat faciendum*) which was to be done
q.e.i. (*quod erat inveniendum*) which was to be found out
q.l. (*quantum libet*) as much as you please
Q.M.C. Quartermasters Corps
qr. quarter, quire
q.s. (*quantum sufficit*) enough
qt. quart
qu. question
quad. quadrangle
quar., quart., qu. quarterly
ques. question
q.v. (*quod vide*) which see
qy. query

r railroad, rare, received, recipe, rector, regina, residence, resides, retired, right, river, rise, road, rod
R. (*rex*) King, (*regina*) Queen
R.A. regular army, Royal Academy, royal artist
R.Adm. Recovery Administration
R.A.F. Royal Air Force (British)
R.A.M. Royal Academy of Music (British)
rc., rcpt., rect. receipt
R.C. Roman Catholic
re regarding
rec. record, receipt
recd. received
ref. referee, reference, reformed
reg. regular, regulate
rep. reporter, representative, republican
retd. returned
R. et I. (*Rex et Imperator*) King and Emperor
(*Regina et Imperatrix*) Queen and Empress
rev. reverence, reverend
Rev. Revelation
R.F.D., RFD rural free delivery
R.G.S. Royal Geographical Society (British)
R.I. Rhode Island
rm. ream, room

r.n., R.N. registered nurse, Royal Navy (British)
R.N.R. Royal Navy Reserve (British)
Rom., rom. Roman, roman (type)
Rom. Romans
R.O.T.C. Reserve Officers' Training Corps
r.p.m. revolutions per minute
R.P.O. railroad post office
rpt. report
R.R., RR railroad
r.s. right side
R.S.V.P. (*Répondez s'il vous plaît*) respond if you please, please answer
r.s.w.c. right side up with care
R.V. Revised Version (of Bible)
ry. railway

s. second, see, series, shilling, sign, south
S. Sabbath, Saint, Saxon, Signor
s.a. subject to approval
Sam. I Samuel I
Sam. II Samuel II
S.A.R. Sons of the American Revolution
Sat. Saturday
S.A.T.C. Students' Army Training Corps
s.b. sales book
sc., scil. (*scilicet*) to wit, namely
sc., sculp. (*sculpsit*) he or she engraved it
s.c., sm.caps. small capitals
S.C. South Carolina
sch. school, schooner
scr. scruple
s.d. (*sine die*) without naming a date
S.Dak. South Dakota
s.e., SE southeast
sec. second, secretary
sect. sectional
sel. selected, selection
sen., sr., Sr. senior
Sept. September
seq., seqq. (*sequentia*) next, following
ser. series, sermon, service
sergt., serg., sgt. sergeant
sh., s. shilling
ship., shipt. shipment
s.i. short interest

sic so, thus (sometimes inserted after a quotation to indicate that the quoted matter is literal and surprizing)
s.j. (*sub judice*) under consideration
S.J. Society of Jesus
s.l. salvage loss, south latitude
sld. sailed, sold
so. south
s.o. seller's option, sub-office
soc. society
s.o.d. seller's option to double
Song of Sol. Song of Solomon
SOS suspend other service (wireless distress call at sea), "save our ship"
sp. special, spelling
S.P.C.A. Society for the Prevention of Cruelty to Animals
S.P.C.C. Society for the Prevention of Cruelty to Children
spec. special, specialty
S.P.E. Society for Pure English
sp.gr. special grant, specific gravity
s.p.q.r. small profits and quick returns
spt. seaport
sq. square, 'squire
sr., Sr. senior
S.S., SS steamship (before name)
s.s.e., SSE south southeast
s.s.w., SSW south southwest
st. saint, stand, strait, street
s.t. short ton (2000 pounds)
stat. (*statim*) immediately
S.T.B. Bachelor of Sacred Theology
stbt. steamboat
sten. stencil, stenographer
stet (*sto*) restore, let it remain (as of some writing that has been wrongly crossed out)
stg., ster. sterling
stge., stor. storage
stk. stock
str. steamer
Sun. Sunday
sund. sundries
sup. (*supra*) above, superficial, su perfine, superior, supervisor supplement, supreme
sup. ct. supreme court
super. superfine

ABBREVIATIONS   21

supp. supplement
supt. superintendent
surg. surgeon
s.v. (*sub verbo*) under word or title
s.w., SW southwest
syn. synonymous

t. temperature, time, ton, township, transitive
t.b. trial balance
t/c till countermanded
tcs. tierces
Tenn. Tennessee
Tex. Texas
t.f. till forbidden
t.g.b. tongued and grooved and beaded
t. & g. tongued and grooved
Thess. I Thessalonians I
Thess. II Thessalonians II
Thurs. Thursday
t.l. total loss
t.l.o. total loss only
t.m.o. telegraph money order
t.o. telegraph office, turn over, turnover
ton. tonnage
tr. tare, train, transfer, translation, translator, transpose, trustee
treas. treasurer, treasury
t.t. telegraph transfer
t.u. trade union
t.u.c. trade union congress
Tues. Tuesday
12mo duodecimo

u. uncle, union, upper
u.c. upper case
ult., ulto. (*ultimo*) last month
univ. universal, university
u.s. (*ut supra*) as above
U.S. United States
U.S.A. United States of America
U.S.M. United States Mail
U.S.M.C. United States Marine Corps
U.S.N. United States Navy

v. valve, verb, verse, version, versus, very, vicar, village, violin, volume, vocative, von
V five
Va. Virginia
V.C. Veterinary Corps, Victoria Cross (British), Vice Chancellor

ven. venerable
ves. vessel, vestry
v.g. (*verbi gratia*) for example
v.i. verb intransitive
via by way of
vid., vide (*vide*) see
viz. (*videlicet*) namely, to wit
V.O. Victoria Order (British)
vol. volume
v.pres. vice-president
vs., v. (*versus*) against, opposed
v.t. verb transitive
Vt. Vermont

w. week, west, wide, wife, with, work
Wash. Washington
w/b waybill
W.C.T.U. Women's Christian Temperance Union
Wed. Wednesday
w.f. wrong font (wrong type face)
whf. wharf
wk. week
w.n.w., WNW west northwest
w.s.w., WSW west southwest
wt. weight
W.Va. West Virginia
Wyo. Wyoming

X ten
x.d., x.div. ex-dividend
Xmas., Xms. Christmas
Xtian., Xn. Christian

y. yard, year
yd. yard
Yᵉ the
yr. year
Y.M.C.A. Young Men's Christian Association
Y.M.H.A. Young Men's Hebrew Association
Y.P.S.C.E. Young People's Society of Christian Endeavor
Y.W.C.A. Young Women's Christian Association
Y.W.H.A. Young Women's Hebrew Association

z. zinc, zephyr
Zech. Zechariah
Zeph. Zepaniah
z.g. zoological garden
zool. zoology

V   Abbreviations as national slogans

Abbreviations have been used for centuries as "war-winning" or "cause-winning" slogans, and by voice as well as by pen. The United States Government has always to some extent designated certain departments by initial letters rather than by full and labored titles. The practise popularizes at the same time that it "short-cuts" time and space in making reference to them. It became almost a vogue early in 1933 when Franklin Roosevelt took office as President. He organized government machinery to fight economic depression. The new departments set up came to be known popularly by initials, and there were so many of them that they constituted a sort of legislative shorthand. The chief of these are listed below. Some have ceased to function, but their records are intact and usable. Some have been organized as result of World War II. Note that most are designated by three letters only (without periods) and that very few of them spell an actual word or a syllable that suggests a word. The original NIRA,* for instance, constituted an easily pronounceable word, dangerously suggestive of the obnoxious NAZI. When this is the case people tend to remember the unified letters *as a word* and to forget the individual letters and what they stand for. In a few instances a governmental title is so complex and extended that initials are not attempted for popular use, as, for example, Director of Production in the Motion Picture Division of the Office for Coordination of Commercial and Cultural Relations Between the American Republics under the Council of National Defense. The asterisks in the following list mean that these particular forms and the departments they represent existed before Mr. Roosevelt took office.

THE WASHINGTON ALPHABET: NEW DEAL AGENCIES

AAA   Agricultural Adjustment Administration (Department of Agriculture)

ACA   Advisory Committee on Allotments

ALB   Automobile Labor Board

AVA*   Administration of Veterans' Affairs

BAC   Business Advisory Council

BCD   Bituminous Coal Division (Department of the Interior)

BLS   Bureau of Labor Statistics (Department of Labor)

BOB*   Bureau of Budget

BPI   Bureau of Plant Industry (Department of Agriculture)

CAA   Civil Aeronautics Administration (Department of Commerce)

CAB   Civil Aeronautics Board (Department of Commerce)

CAB   Consumers' Advisory Board

CCC   Civilian Conservation Corps (Federal Security Agency)

CCC   Commodity Credit Corporation (Department of Agriculture)

* National Industrial Recovery Act. The *i* was soon dropped and the organization was popularly known as *NRA*. It was authorized June 16, 1933, and discontinued by decision of the Supreme Court May 27, 1935.

ABBREVIATIONS 23

CEA Commodity Exchange Administration (Department of Agriculture)
CES Committee on Economic Security
CSB Central Statistical Board
CSC* Civil Service Commission (1883)
CWA Civil Works Administration
DAI Division of Applications and Information
DCADA District of Columbia Alley Dwelling Authority
DCB Defense Communications Board (National Defense)
DLB Deposit Liquidation Board
DLC Disaster Loan Corporation (Federal Loan Agency)
ECW Emergency Conservation Work (Civilian Conservation Corps)
EHC Emergency Housing Corporation
EHFA Electric Home and Farm Authority (Federal Loan Agency)
EIB Export-Import Bank of Washington (Federal Loan Agency)
EZAACMO Eastern Zone Army Air Corps Mail Operations
FAC Federal Aviation Commission; Federal Advisory Council
FACA Federal Alcohol Control Administration
FBI Federal Bureau of Investigation (Department of Justice)
FCA Farm Credit Administration (Department of Agriculture)
FCC Federal Communications Commission
FCIC Federal Crop Insurance Corporation (Department of Agriculture)
FCT Federal Coordinator of Transportation
FCUS Federal Credit Union System
FDA Food and Drug Administration (Federal Security Agency)
FDIC Federal Deposit Insurance Corporation
FEHC Federal Emergency Housing Corporation

FERA Federal Emergency Relief Administration
FESO Federal Employment Stabilization Office
FHA Federal Housing Administration (Federal Loan Agency)
FHLBB Federal Home Loan Bank Board (Federal Loan Agency)
FICB Federal Intermediate Credit Banks
FLA Federal Loan Agency
FMC Farm Mortgage Corporation
FPC* Federal Power Commission
FPI Federal Prison Industries
FRB* Federal Reserve Board
FS Fiscal Service (Department of the Treasury)
FSA Farm Security Administration (Department of Agriculture)
FSA Federal Security Agency
FSEC Federal Securities and Exchange Commission
FSHC Federal Subsistence Homestead Corporation
FSLIC Federal Savings and Loan Insurance Corporation
FSRC Federal Surplus Relief Corporation
FTC* Federal Trade Commission
FTZB Foreign Trade Zones Board
FWA Federal Works Agency
GFA* Grain Futures Administration
HLB (Federal) Home Loan Bank (Board)
HOLC Home Owners Loan Corporation
IAB Industrial Advisory Board
ICC* Interstate Commerce Commission (1887)
IEC Industrial Emergency Council
JEB Joint Economy Board
LAB Labor Advisory Board
MLB Maritime Labor Board
NACA National Advisory Committee for Aeronautics
NCB National Compliance Board
NDAC National Defense Advisory Commission (National Defense)
NDMB National Defense Mediation Board (National Defense)
NEC National Emergency Council
NIRB National Industrial Recovery Board

NL(R)B National Labor (Relations) Board
NMB National Mediation Board
NPB National Planning Board
NPPC National Power Policy Committee
NRB National Resources Board
NRPB National Resources Planning Board (Executive Office of the President)
NRRB National Recovery Review Board
NRS National Reemployment Service
NYA National Youth Administration (Federal Security Agency)
OCD Office for Civilian Defense
OEM Office for Emergency Management (Executive Office of the President)
OPACS Office of Price Administration and Civilian Supply
OPM Office of Production Management (National Defense)
PA Petroleum Administration
PAB Petroleum Administrative Board
PBA Public Buildings Administration (Federal Works Agency)
PJBD Permanent Joint Board on Defense (National Defense)
PLPB Petroleum Labor Policy Board
PRA President's Reemployment Agreement
PRA Public Roads Administration (Federal Works Agency)
PRRA Puerto Rico Reconstruction Administration (Department of the Interior)
PSAC (Non-member) Preferred Stock Advisory Committee
PWA Public Works Administration (Federal Works Agency)
PWAP Public Works of Art Projects
PWEHC Public Works Emergency Housing Corporation
RA Resettlement Administration
RACC Regional Agricultural Credit Corporation
REA Rural Electrification Administration (Department of Agriculture)
RFC* Reconstruction Finance Corporation (Federal Loan Agency)

RRB Railroad Retirement Board
SAB Science Advisory Board
SAPFT Special Adviser to the President on Foreign Trade
SBPW Special Board for Public Works
SCS Soil Conservation Service (Department of Agriculture)
SEC Securities and Exchange Commission
SES Soil Erosion Service
SHD Subsistence Homesteads Division
SLIC (Federal) Savings and Loan Insurance Corporation
SLRB (National) Steel Labor Relations Board
SMA Surplus Marketing Administration (Department of Agriculture)
SSB Social Security Board (Federal Security Agency)
SSS Selective Service System (National Defense)
TEC The (President's) Executive Council
TFI Textile Foundation, Inc.
TLRB Textile Labor Relations Board
TVA Tennessee Valley Authority
TVAC Tennessee Valley Associated Cooperatives
TWAB Textile Work Assignment Boards
USCS United States Conciliation Service (Department of Labor)
USES United States Employment Service
USHA United States Housing Authority (Federal Works Agency)
USIS United States Information Service
USMC United States Maritime Commission
USO United Service Organization (for National Defense)
USTC* United States Tariff Commission (1916)
VA* Veterans Administration
WAB Work Allotment Board
WHD Wage and Hour Division (Department of Labor)
WPA Work Projects Administration (Federal Works Agency)
WPD Works Progress Division

CHAPTER TWO

ALPHABETIZING—FILING—INDEXING

A All items to be alphabetized should be arranged strictly in the sequence of the alphabet. All letters in the first word of a given item should follow this sequence to the last letter of the word. If the first alphabetized names (surnames) in a series are the same, then the second or given names in the list must key the alphabetization.

Bakar, Inc.	Bakeri, Anderson
Baker, (Dr.)	Bakerim, Samuel
Baker, (Mrs.)	Bakerite Company
Baker, A.	Bakerivitz, Serge
Baker, A. C.	Bakerson and Brothers
Baker, Alfred	Bakerworth Nurseries
Baker, Horace	Bakerzoned Cook Stoves
Baker, Horace G.	Bakerzoned Cooking Utensilry

Note closely the order of the foregoing listing. The alphabetical listing develops from the surname alone to the surname with title, with single initial, with Christian name, with Christian and other given names. Following is the regulation itemization as observed by listing companies, including the telephone companies thruout the country.

1 Surname (or proper name) followed by comma
2 First given name or initial (or equivalent of either)
3 Second given name or initial (and other given name, if any)
4 Title, if any
5 Designation, if any
6 Street name (or equivalent)
7 Building number

B Such prefixes to names as *D', Da, De, Della, Di, Du, El, Filz, L', La, Le, M', Mac, Mc, O', St., Van, Vom, Von* key the alphabetization, that is, the first letter in these prefixes decides the placement in the alphabetical or filing list. Note that this is true when the prefix stands for *the* in a firm name.

D'Artagnan, Alphonse	Della Robbia, Antonio
Da Bretagne, Gaston	Di Rouggi, Carminita
De Laverelle, Marie	Du Vois, André

El Via Garage
Fitz Maurice, Jonathan
L'Aller, Lorenz
La Fondre, Jacques
Le Grégoire, Georges
Le Perrault Compagnie
M'Gillicuddy, Andrew

Mac Andrew, Michael
Mc Cann, Jacqueline
O'Leary, Patrick
St. John, Horace G.
Van Waveren, Martin and Sons
Vom Bauer, Franklin & Company
Von Bernuth, Lawrence

As indicated above, abbreviations (*St.* for *Saint*) are alphabetized as if spelled out. This is true of *Mt.* for *Mount, Gt.* for *Great, N.* for *New,* abbreviated points of the compass, and other directive and definitive modifiers of names.

The same ruling applies to names preceded by numbers—these are alphabetized as they would be were the numbers spelled out, thus:

1st National Bank	*under F*	First National Bank
2nd Church of Christ	*under S*	Second Church of Christ
10th Avenue Bazaar	*under T*	Tenth Avenue Bazaar

C Cross referencing is imperative in connection with all names about which confusion is likely to occur.

1 Hyphenated names:

Cholmondeley-Jones, Alfred Thomas
Jones, Alfred Thomas Cholmondeley
    (*see* Cholmondeley-Jones, Alfred Thomas)
Bradley-Mahoney Coal Corporation
Mahoney Coal Corporation (*see* Bradley-Mahoney
    Coal Corporation)

2 A surname spelled in more than one way:

Donnelley	*see also*	Donnelly
Donaly	*see also*	Donelly
Trevor	*see also*	Trevour

3 Institutions—schools, churches, foundations:

Woodrow Wilson Hotel	*see*	Wilson
Wilson, Woodrow, Hotel		
Cathedral of Mount Olive	*see*	Mount Olive
Mount Olive Cathedral	*see*	Olive, Mount
Olive, Mount, Cathedral		
Thomas Jefferson High School	*see*	Jefferson
Jefferson, Thomas, High School	*see*	Schools, High
Schools, High, Thomas Jefferson		

4 Company names:

Atlantic Seaboard Airline
Seaboard Airline, Atlantic
Airline, Atlantic Seaboard

British-American Investment Company
American-British Investment Company

Corporation Counselors' Bureau
Counselors, Corporation, Bureau
Bureau, Corporation Counselors'

Granger, Jones, and Company
      Selig, Robert, Superintendent

Selig, Robert, Superintendent
      Granger, Jones, and Company

The last listing is for dealings directly and personally with
Mr. Selig. The one above it is for dealings with Granger,
Jones, and Company thru Mr. Selig. Note the importance
of the commas in these names. The names are not Granger
Jones and Selig Robert, but the commas are necessary to
make this clear.

Bros., Co., Sons, Inc., Ltd. key the alphabetization when
they follow company surnames that are alike. The connectives *&, of, for,* and *and* are not considered in alpha-
betizing.

Johnson, Aaron
Johnson Bros.
Johnson and Brother
Johnson Brothers and Company
Johnson Brothers, Inc.
Johnson Brothers, Ltd.
Johnson Brothers of Mavondale
Johnson Brothers' Patent Leather Plant
Johnson Company
Johnson-Daniel Company
Johnson & Daniel Corporation
Johnson Patent Leather Plant
Johnson's Patent Leather Plant

5 Subordinate descriptive terms:

Columbia University, Board of Trustees
Guaranty Trust Company, Directorate

These are the preferred listings in general directories. In
private files, however, these two entries would be cross-
references:

Trustees, Board of, Columbia University
Directorate, Guaranty Trust Company

The subordinate descriptive term *estate* is usually cross-referenced in both general and house directories:

> Estate of Robert C. Coe
> Coe, Robert C., Estate of

6 City, county, and state listings:

> Chicago, City of
> New York, City of (departments of are cross-referenced)
> Cook County
> Illinois, Counties of,
>   Accounts, Commissioner of ⎫
>   Education, Board of   ⎬ cross-referenced
>   Hospitals, Department of   ⎭

> Denver Insurance Company
> Denver Steam Fitting Corporation
> Denver Warehouse Company
> Denver, Warren P.
> Denver, Young, and Co.
> Denver-Zircon Corporation

D The following illustrations* are self-explanatory of the degrees of alphabetical splitting. The mere twenty-six divisions afforded by the letters of the alphabet are seldom sufficient for accommodating the filing demands of the average business house. Different colors are sometimes used in an alphabetic set (beginning with vowels if five only are enough) for the purpose of affording quick discernment to the eye.

25 divisions		40 divisions		60 divisions		
A	Si	A	M	A	H	Pe
B	T–V	B	Mc	Am	He	Pi
Bi	W	Bi	Me	B	Ho	Q
C	Wi	Br	Mo	Be	Hu	R
Co	X–Y–Z	C	N	Bi	I	Ri
D		Ch	O	Br	J	Ro
E		Co	P	Bu	K	S
F		D	Pi	C	Ki	Sch
G		Do	Q	Ch	L	Se
H		E	R	Co	Le	Si
Ho		F	Ro	Cr	Li	St
I–J		G	S	D	M	Su
K		Gr	Se	De	Mar	T
L		H	Si	Do	Mc	To
M		He	St	E	Me	U
Me		Ho	T	F	Mo	V
N–O		I–J	U–V	Fl	Mu	W
P–Q		K	W	G	N	We
R		L	Wi	Gi	O	Wi
S		Li	X–Y–Z	Gr	P	X–Y–Z

* Used by permission of the American Institute of Filing, Buffalo, New York.

THREE METHODS OF CORRESPONDENCE FILING

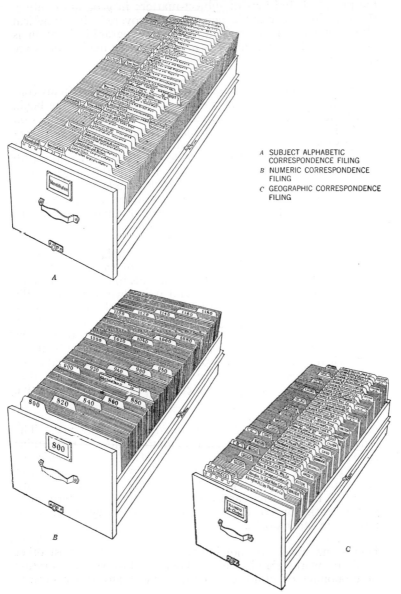

A SUBJECT ALPHABETIC
   CORRESPONDENCE FILING
B NUMERIC CORRESPONDENCE
   FILING
C GEOGRAPHIC CORRESPONDENCE
   FILING

A

B

C

In subject filing the main headings, it will be noted, follow
the principal divisions of subject-matter; in geographic filing,
the principal geographic points to be covered; in numerical
filing, an individual or a subject or a geographic location is
given a number, and thru this number as key file locations are
easily traced.

E   An index is a detailed alphabetic list of the subject items contained in a book.   It is always placed at the end of the book.
After each item listed is the number of the page or pages on
which its treatment is to be found.   An item may be exhaustively subdivided, the subheads all being followed with exact
page numbers.   In order to enable the reader to find easily
and quickly any item that he wants to find, the index should
be complete and subdivision should be made wherever possible.   Cross-referencing should likewise be made wherever
subject-matter obligates, that is, wherever separate treatment
of a subject on more than one page occurs.

The index is not to be confused with the table of contents of
a book.   The latter is a general outline of the contents of a
book sequentially arranged from the beginning to the end.
It is the author's working plan, and it is always placed at the
beginning of the book.   The topics listed in the table of contents are of course included in the index, but they are very few
indeed in comparison with the large number of items that
must be alphabetized in the index if it is to be valuable at all.
It is clear, then, that the page references in the table of
contents are regular from page one to the last page, but that
the page references in the index cannot possibly be consecutive
or sequential.

And the index must not be confused with a glossary.   The
latter is sometimes called an explanatory index.   It pertains
always to a special work, as of *The Merchant of Venice* or
L'Allegro, and its principal function is, not to tell the exact
page upon which a term is to be found (tho it does this
usually), but to define and explain and discuss the term both
in the work concerned and comparatively, very often, as it
appears in other works.

Poems and novels are not indexed as a rule.   But most other
kinds of works should be.   A book on history or literature
or economics or philosophy or on almost any other subject,

that is not indexed, cannot be said to be a complete book. An index is especially valuable in any sort of book that one expects to "live with"—to take up and put down, to consult frequently. Not so very long ago a book with an index cost more than a book without one, and this was as it should be, for good exact indexing is a most laborious task. Strictly speaking, the author himself is the best person to index the book he writes. He is the one person who knows what he has treated of and where. But there are many authors who leave the indexing of their works to special indexers, many of whom have made a particular study of indexing and can thus turn out a good job.

As an author writes a book he sometimes jots down items to be indexed. More often he does not do so until he receives galley proofs—long sheets of paper upon which the first printing set-up of his book appears. Most often, perhaps, he does not begin indexing until he receives page proofs. Here he has not only the items to be indexed but the page numbers as well, and he can jot down item and corresponding page at once on the card—preferably a library card with a hole at the bottom. If he makes his item index from copy or from galley proofs, he is unable to write in page numbers, for his copy pages do not correspond to the printed pages and the galleys do not carry page numbers.

Pages must be scrutinized for subject items. These should be written on individual cards. It is wise not to try to be economical with the cards. Let an item to a card be the rule. Then when all the pages have been searched, the cards should be arranged alphabetically in accordance with the rules above illustrated. It will be found at this stage of the process that item after item will be repeated on different cards, each with a different number after it. This means that the different page numbers must be accumulated in sequence on the item card having the lowest page number. It will be found also that many cards bear items that should be listed under more general card items. Thus, subentries have to be made on the general card, and sometimes there are so many that they run to two or more cards. When this is true the alphabetization will keep the cards in order, but the cards may be numbered and the words *Continued on card 2*, and so forth, may be written at the bottom of the card bearing subentries. The waste cards, after the accumulation is made, may be thrown

away.   The others may be kept together without danger of
pieing by running a string thru the holes, and may be sent to
the printer in this form.

Books are sometimes written in numbered sections.   It is
necessary in indexing them to include two sets of numbers,
one to refer to sections and one to refer to pages.   This is
usually done by printing one kind of notation in bold or heavy
face and the other in body face.   But such double reference
is not recommended, for it invariably causes some confusion.

The rules for alphabetization, for capitalization, for punctuation, and for italicization pertain strictly to indexing, as will
be noted in the following unit illustrations of good indexing.
Note that sometimes the items of an index are run in after
the first extended item; that sometimes they are listed by
division and subdivision in columns; that sometimes subordinate topics are preceded in each case by a dash.   Note also
that inclusive item groups are separated by semicolons and
that page numbers pertaining to the same item are separated
by commas.   Items in columnar indexing are not followed
by periods.   The period is not used at the end of a run-in
group of index items.   In other words, the period is not used
in indexing except for abbreviations.   Strict alphabetization
of subject-matter must be observed, and strict sequence of
page numbering after each entry.

The run-in method of indexing (the first illustration below)
is the one in most common use.   In some publishing houses
there is an established style for indexing that is followed in
all departments of publication.   In most, however, the style
of indexing used is left entirely to the author or to his particular indexer.

1	2
Typography, 141-167; alphabet, 141-143; capitals, 150; character, 147, 149; color in, 161-164; con-densed, 145-148; devices, 159-161; expanded, 145-148; faces, 151-156; headlines, 164; impor-tance of, 143-144, 166-167; lines of, 156-159; monograms, 149-150; optical center letters, 144-145; paragraphing, 164; punctuation, 166; serialization, 165-166	Grammatical Expression, studies in, 78-149 adjectives better, 116 either, both, 90 elder, 100 foot, 93 good, 107 less, fewer, 88 many, much, 129 real, 85

ALPHABETIZING—FILING—INDEXING 33

CHAPTER THREE

CAPITALIZATION

I As to persons

A Always capitalize the personal pronoun I.

B Always capitalize the names and initials of names of individuals.

Woodrow Wilson   Susan B. Anthony
J.B.O.   Kate M. Monro

C Capitalize nicknames and epithets applied to individuals.

William the Conqueror   Catherine the Great
Reddy Anderson   Happy-Go-Lucky Carver

D Capitalize *father* and *mother* in direct address.

Please, Father, let me go

The words *father* and *mother* are not capitalized when preceded by a possessive pronoun.

I shall tell my mother what you say

E Capitalize *sister, brother, uncle, aunt* when they precede the proper name of the relative indicated, but not otherwise.

While Sister Jane and I were out we saw Uncle William and Aunt Sara

F The particles *d', da, de, della, di, l', la, le, van, von* are usually not capitalized when preceded by a given name or by a title of any kind. Inasmuch as American usage is not strictly established in this connection it is advisable to seek individual family preference, as far as it is ascertainable, whenever and wherever the writing of such names is important. American usage tends to merge the particle with the name.

34

Mary d'Ascolo
Leonardo da Vinci
Guy de Maupassant
Leonora della Monica
M. de Galaup
Captain di Cesnola

Marie l'Ario
Mlle. la Monte
Harry le Fevre
Marion Lefevre
Eben van Dyke
Count von Zeppelin

Harold Vandewater is visiting us
They like our Di Lauro cousins
He spoke of the De Forest service
The Lafarge family lives there
We have four Von Gogh paintings

G Capitalize all degrees and all titles of honor, profession, rank, and respect used in connection with individual names. Even where the individual name is not given, the principal word or words in a title should be capitalized when an individual is unmistakably referred to.

Mr. Albert Seabury
Mrs. Blaine McKinley
Miss Allison Rogers
Dr. Samuel Barnes
Professor Coe
Dean Jacob Masterson
President Trainor
Captain K. L. Messer
Alderman Elias Jacobs
Father Brown
Rabbi Goldman
Governor Horner
Justice Weatherbee

Commissioner Baldwin
Speaker C. V. Webber
Monsignor Applegate
George Thompson, A.B.
Sylvia Fox, A.M.
James Weldon, A.B., A.M., Ph.D.
Thomas Brown, Esq.
the Director-General
the First Vice-President
the Acting Secretary
His Honor the Mayor
Wynne Aldon, C.E., Chief of Division
Harrison Wiggin, LL.D., D.C.L., Litt.D.

Patrick Gillan, Jr.
Patrick Gillan jr.

John Gillan, Sr.
John Gillan, sr.

The abbreviations *jr.* and *sr.* may or may not be capitalized. Usage is about evenly divided.

The words *reverend* and *honorable* are not really titles but complimentary adjectives, and they should always be followed by the first name, the initials, or the appropriate title. When preceded by *the* they should not be abbreviated.

Hon. Elihu Root
The Honorable Elihu Root
Rev. Ogden Richards Conrad
The Reverend Doctor Thomas Blaine
The Very Reverend Monsignor Stephen Joseph Donahue

It is not the best practise to use more than one title or degree with the name of a given individual, but more than one or both are sometimes used for the purpose of making a record complete (and imposing?). The multiplication of titles and degrees with a given name is not objectionable when each one represents a different kind of status from the others:

> The Reverend President Adam Halliburton, D.D., LL.D.
> The Reverend Professor Archibald Bedford, B.D., D.D., D.C.L.

Two or more degrees after a name should be arranged chronologically. This usually means in order of increasing value and importance:

> Horace M. Constable, A.B., A.M., Ph.D., LL.D.

There is much disputed usage in regard to the capitalization of written-out titles when they follow the name. Such titles as *under-secretary, foreign attaché, vice-consul, cabinet officer, assistant editor* are consistently capitalized by some organs and consistently lower-cased by others. The following represent the best usage in run-in matter:

> Hamilton Holt, president of Rollins College
> Lewis J. Smith, professor of English
> Harrison Wentworth, director of art
> Benjamin Holworth, chief of division

But when such names and titles are set up for listings, as in catalogs, all important words are capitalized, for each complete item constitutes a title.

> Harold Wainwright, Ph.D., Associate Professor of English

The Style Manual of the United States Government Printing Office lists the following "certain specified instances regarding the title following the noun *which is most often regarded as a common noun*":

> Franklin D. Roosevelt, President of the United States
> the President   the President-elect
> the Executive   the Chief Magistrate
>   the Commander-in-Chief

> *Similarly*

> the Vice-President
> Albert C. Ritchie, Governor of Maryland
> the Governor of Maryland
> the Lieutenant
> Cordell Hull, Secretary of State

> the Secretary
> the Under-Secretary
> the Acting Secretary
> the Assistant Secretary
> Hugh S. Gibson, Ambassador Extraordinary and Minister Plenipotentiary
> the Envoy Extraordinary
> the Chargé d'Affaires

But

> Charles F. Hughes, rear admiral, United States Navy
> John Smith, chairman of the committee

The words *defendant, plaintiff, appellant, respondent* are not capitalized in titles of legal cases.

> Jay Bronson, plaintiff, *vs.* James Brown, defendant

H The foregoing rule with its modifications means, conversely, that such words as *commissioner, governor, president, professor, rabbi, speaker* are not capitalized when they are generic in reference. This distinction applies also to place names (see page 42). As a general working principle, *words are capitalized according to the company they keep.*

> I saw the priest enter the cathedral
> I saw Father Stommel enter Saint Patrick's
> The Commissioner of Education will speak tonight
> The educational commissioner is the most important official
>   in any country

The word *governor* is capitalized when closely linked to the name of a state:

> The Governor of Connecticut will be here tonight

As indicated under G, the word *president* is capitalized when used to refer to the presidency of the United States, as are also any other special terms referring to him. This rule applies also to any titles given specifically to his wife:

> His Excellency   the First Lady of the Land

The adjective form—*presidential*—is capitalized when referring unmistakably to the President of the United States, tho many newspapers do not observe this usage and there is, therefore, widely divergent practise:

> the presidential train   the presidential party
> the Presidential camp   the Presidential yacht
> the Vice-Presidential box   the vice-presidential car

The same variation is to be observed regarding "President-elect" and "President-Elect" (see G above). *But* "ex-President Roosevelt" and "ex-Governor Cross" are generally accepted. The following is nevertheless worth noting. When *ex* is prefixed to *president,* the word *president* is capitalized in case the president is living; it is lower-cased in case he is dead. This rule, however, is by no means universally observed.

> The ex-president's widow receives a pension
> The ex-President attended the ceremony

J Capitalize *cabinet* when it refers unmistakably to the members of the Cabinet of the President of the United States. Capitalize *court* if it is a part of the name of a national or international court, a United States court, a district court, or a state court, and thus connotes judicial personality; it is lower-cased if part of the name of a city or county court. And the general rule under H applies:

> the President's Cabinet
> the British Cabinet
> the United States Supreme Court
> Court of Appeals of the State of Wisconsin
> Circuit Court of the United States for the Southern
>   District of New York
> International Court of Arbitration
> Covenant of the League of Nations
> Court of Customs and Patent Appeals
>
> They took him to the police court
> They took him to the magistrate's court

K Titles of direct address should be capitalized, but ordinary terms of respect, used within sentences, such as *madam, sir, ladies and gentlemen,* should not be.

> Your Honor, Your Excellency, Your Majesty
> Madam Chairman, please observe this
> Mr. Secretary, may I ask a question, please?
> May I inquire, Senator, what you intend to do?
> I reply, sir, that I shall do nothing whatever
> This, madam, is the fabric I mean
> And now, ladies and gentlemen, I am done

L Capitalize all names of deities and specific references thereto:

Almighty	Holy Spirit	Providence
Brahma	Jehovah	Redeemer
First Cause	Jupiter	Savior
God	King of the Jews	Son of God
Godship	Krishna	Supreme Being
Holy Ghost	Messiah	Zeus

The words *fatherhood, goddess, messiahship, sonship* are not capitalized unless they are used in some special and directly personal connection.

> The Fatherhood of God is basic to the faith
> The goddesses gathered unto her

But capitalize *Virgin Mary* and *Virgin* and *Blessed Virgin, Madonna, Our Lady, Holy Mother, Mother of God* in biblical and religious allusion.

Capitalize also *Pontiff, Supreme Pontiff, Holy Father, Pope, Popes, Apostolic Delegate, Archbishop, Cardinal,* and other church titular names, both before and after individual names themselves and elsewhere in direct personal reference.

M Capitalize personified words and terms. This rule was formerly regarded with precision. Present-day writers, however, are increasingly inclined to ignore it. Longfellow wrote

> All are architects of Fate

But were he living now he would probably write

> All are architects of fate

The figure is just as apparent and just as good without the capital as with it.

Under this rule the words *devil, evil one, evil eye, adversary, his satanic majesty,* and other such allusions may or may not be capitalized.

> The Prince of Demons is Beelzebub
> The prince of demons is Beelzebub
> And Satan finds some mischief still for idle hands to do

N Pronouns used in reference to deities and to personified things are preferably not capitalized. There is, however, much contradictory usage in this respect. The increasing tendency is to lower-case all such pronominal references.

> And Jesus entered into Jerusalem . . . and when he had looked round about. . . . *Mark xi:11*

> And that inverted Bowl we call the Sky,
> Whereunder crawling coop't we live and die,
> Lift not thy hand to It for help—for It
> Rolls impotently on as Thou and I.
> *The Rubaiyát*

O Capitalize words that identify people with different countries or with different sections of a country.

Westerner	Easterner	Britisher	New Zealander
Southerner	Northerner	Canadian	Papal Statesman

II As to places

A Capitalize the names of city and state legislative bodies when they are accompanied by the particular name of city and state; capitalize the names of all national legislative bodies.

the United States Congress	the Sixty-eighth Congress
the French Chamber of Deputies	the Ohio State Legislature
the British Parliament	the Colorado Senate
the German Reichstag	the New York City Board
	of Aldermen

The word *nation* should be capitalized only when it is strictly synonymous with the United States or when it is preceded by the proper name of a specific country. The word *national* is frequently a part of a title and thus used it should, of course, be capitalized; used otherwise it should not be capitalized.

the National Capital	the National Association
the national policies	of Boy Scouts

The words *state* and *city* should be capitalized when used with corresponding proper names and when, standing alone, they stand clearly for certain commonwealths and municipalities respectively.

New York City	the State election
the City of New York	the City prison
the State of Iowa	the State representative
the City Board of Control	the State House of Correction
city life vs. country life	

B It follows as a corollary to the foregoing rule with its modifications, that names of places in general—churches, cemeteries, statues, towers—should be capitalized.

Arlington Cemetery	Grant's Tomb
Empire State Building	Hilliard Boulevard
Eiffel Tower	Lenox Avenue
Fifteenth Street	Saint Patrick's Cathedral
Frick Gallery	Washington Monument
the Goshen Home	the World's Fair

Usage varies greatly in application of this rule. Many organs lower-case the generic term when it follows the proper name and most do so when the generic or descriptive name precedes the proper name (see next page).

the river Nile	the valley of the Wye
the tower of Babel	the tomb of Napoleon

But *Tenth street* and *Sixth avenue* are not recommended

C   When the generic noun in place names is preceded by two or more proper nouns the preferred usage is to write it with small letter (this in spite of the fact that *The Style Manual of the United States Government Printing Office* rules oppositely). Pluralization tends to make nouns common.

Prospect and Central parks	Union and Madison squares
Yale and Harvard universities	Baker and Dexter fields

There is much confusion of authority regarding the rule. In the main, individual house practise must be the ultimate guide, as it must be in many other cases. The manual above referred to lists the following words to be capitalized "if part of proper name; capitalized, standing alone, only if well-known short form of specific name; lower-cased in general sense":

> aqueduct, archipelago, basin, bayou, beach, bend, bight, boro, branch, breakwater, butte, camp, canal, canyon, cape, channel, chute, cove, crater, creek, dam, desert, dock, ditch, dike, dome, draw, dry dock, dune, falls, ferry, flats, forest, fork, fort, gap, glacier, gulch, gulf, harbor, head, highway, hill, hollow, hook, inlet, island, isle, islet, jetty, lake, landing, levee, light, lighthouse, light station, lock, mesa, mole, mount, mountain, narrows, oasis, ocean, park, pass, passage, peak, peninsula, pier, plateau, point, pond, port, range, reef, reservoir, ridge, river, roads, rock, run, sea, shoal, ship, sound, spring, strait, tunnel, valley, volcano, weir, wharf, woods

The list is given for purposes of comparison with the common usage as observed in daily, weekly, and monthly organs, which represent majority practise, and not at all because it should be learned by rote for application of the rule.

D   Capitalize all geographical names that pertain to countries and states and cities and regions thereof, and to topographical parts and sections, such as, bays, coves, islands, isthmuses, mountains, oceans, peaks, peninsulas, points, rivers. This rule also applies to fanciful appellations.

Boston Common	Indian Ocean	the Orient
the Channel Islands	Isthmus of Panama	Old World
City Island	Murray Hill	South Dakota
East Drive	the Nickel Plate Road	Strait of Magellan
East Side	the Nutmeg State	Warwick Township
the Hub	the Occident	West End

E   Capitalize the names of the points of the compass when they are used to indicate geographical areas.

> The South voted solidly for him
> The great Northwest was developed by Hill

They toured the West
We are visiting in the East
The Orient is settled and content
The Occident is under continuous agitation

Used for descriptive or explanatory or merely directional purposes the words *north, south, east,* and *west,* and their various forms of combination, should not be capitalized.

He hails from western Tennessee and therefore likes southern cooking and southern hospitality in general

She is well acquainted with both oriental and continental customs, for she has lived in Eastern Siberia as well as in Northern and Central Europe

F Capitalize the names of political sections of a city, state, and country:

the Vatican State	the Fifteenth Precinct
the Dominion of South Africa	the Upper West Side
the Commonwealth of Colorado	the Twelfth Ward

Here again the usage of special organs and houses should be observed, inasmuch as there is much variation in the application of this rule.

G Capitalize the words *academy, cathedral, chantry, chapel, college, high school, institute, school, seminary, synagog, university,* and other generic references to educational and religious buildings and organizations when they are connected with proper names and when, standing alone, they refer unmistakably to individual buildings and organizations:

Ardmore Academy	the Methodist Episcopal Church
Beth Sholaum Synagog	the People's Temple
Blair Institute	the Roman Church
Blaine High School	St. Paul's Cathedral
the Church of England	the Spence School
Columbia Chapel	Salvator School
Grace Chantry	Ursula Park Retreat
the Liberal Congregation	Warrensville Business School

but

the chantry ceremony	the cathedrals of England
the chapel dedication	the synagog attendance
the church influence	the churches of Canada

H Capitalize the names of stars and constellations and of heavenly bodies generally, but do not capitalize *earth, moon, sun, star, planet* unless they are used with proper names or are personified.

Mars	Saturn	the Milky Way	the Big Dipper
Venus	Orion	the Great Bear	Ursa Major

Capitalize *hades, heaven, hereafter, paradise, purgatory,* and their synonyms when they are used figuratively to refer to a special place or condition. The word *hell* is rarely capitalized in present-day usage.

III   As to composition proper

A   Capitalize the first word of every sentence and of every word, phrase, and clause standing alone as an independent unit of expression:

> The way of the transgressor is hard
> A horse! A horse! My kingdom for a horse

In quotations from poetry that do not adhere to line-by-line arrangement, capitals are retained exactly as in source, regardless of incongruity thus caused in punctuation and capitalization:

> Longfellow's lines: "Life is real, life is earnest, And the grave is not its goal" were never in greater need of emphatic revival than they are today

B   Capitalize the first word of every line of conventional poetry. In free verse the first word of the first line of a stanza or a thought is frequently the only initial capitalization observed.

> Thus let me live, unseen, unknown,
>   Thus unlamented let me die;
> Steal from the world, and not a stone
>   Tell where I lie.
>
> ALEXANDER POPE
>
> My only fear
> is of growing careless
> in a universe that is perfection's model
>
> God always finishes off his handiwork:
> the roundness of the spheres,
> the rhythm of the tides,
> the coming and the going of the sun,
> the melodious recurrence of the seasons,
> the harmony of birth's cancelation of death,
> the perfect bias-cut of mountain ranges,
> and the organized cavalcade of the Milky Way
>
> And Betelgeuse,
> I'm sure,
> would cap God's very climax

C Capitalize *O* always. Capitalize *oh* only where it opens a sentence or stands alone as an independent expression. Capitalize all letters of the alphabet used to mark off certain main divisions in outlining and paragraphing. Small letters are used in outlining to indicate minor divisions (see page 435). Main divisions or partitions of outlines and compositions are likewise indicated by capital roman numerals.

And, oh, the difference to me!   I   II
                                                        A   A
He said: "O what's the use?"   B   B

D Capitalize the first word and the last word of the salutation of a letter and the first word of the complimentary closing. The word *dear* used as the second word in the salutation is preferably lower-cased.

Dear Sir	Dear Friend	Dear Mr. Jones
My dear Sir	Dear Lady Alice	Yours very truly

E Capitalize all principal words in titles. This means the first and usually the last word of titles and all nouns, principal verbs, and important pronouns, adjectives, and adverbs. This rule applies also to displayed slogans and special headings and captions.

The Very Good Young Man
The Happiest Day of My Life
The Last Days of Pompeii
The Hague
The Last Supper
The Moonlight Sonata
Gershwin's Rhapsody in Blue
The Man Who Was Laughed at
Ask the Man Who Owns One
The Report of the Committee of Fifteen
A Report on the Opium Traffic in Great Britain
The New York Times
New York Herald Tribune
Chicago Tribune
Boston Evening Transcript

It is important always to observe whether the article is or is not used in titles and in company names. The usage in company publications and in company letterheads must be observed and followed, tho these are sometimes inconsistent. The letterheads of a company may, for instance, carry *The;* its reports or minutes may not. Note that *The* is a part of the title of *The New York Times* but not of the last three newspaper titles above named.   See capitalization (page 44) and letterheads (pages 235 and 236).

It is somewhat better to capitalize none but noun parts of hyphenated titles and terms, tho the adjective and verb hyphenates may in some cases be too important to set in lower case.

> Twentieth-Century Progress
> Well-known Authors
> The Fifty-first Street Case
> The Economy of High-Speed Pumps
> World-Union of British-born Patriots

F Do not capitalize abbreviations of common nouns and minor parts of speech unless it is desirable to do so in rare instances for the sake of emphasis (see page 7).

a.m.	i.e.
e.g.	lb.
etc.	p.m.
ft.	pt.

This rule applies likewise to abbreviations in cross-referencing in reports and in literary matter, as *art.* for *article, sec.* for *section, par.* or ¶ for *paragraph, div.* for *division, pp.* for *pages.* The words themselves are lower-cased in minor references.   They are capitalized, however, in major headings, especially when subordinate matter is placed beneath them, as *Vol. X. bk. i.* or *Volume X, book i; Chap. III, sec. xii,* or *Chapter III, section xii.*   Note that nouns followed by capital roman numerals are capitalized; nouns followed by lower-case numerals are not.

G Capitalize adjectives and other derivatives (see page 155) formed from proper nouns when they are used with their original special meaning.   Do not capitalize those that thru common usage are no longer especially identified with the words from which they were derived.

> American, British, Canadian, Caucasian, Chesterfieldian, Darwinian, Elizabethan, English, French, Georgian, Gregorian, Homeric, Indian, Johannean, Johnsonian, Kentuckian, Latin, Mexican, Napoleonic, Olympian, Papal, Pan-American, Roman, Rooseveltian, Russian, Semitic, Sistine, Swiss, Venetian, Victorian, Virginian, Wilsonian, Welsh, Wordsworthian, Yankee, etc.

But note

> anglicize, artesian well, babbitt metal, boycott, bristol board, britannia ware, brussels sprouts, burley tobacco, canada balsam,

cashmere shawl, china clay, chinaware, chinese blue, colossal,
delftware, derby hat, dutch windmill, fedora hat, fullers' earth,
georgette crepe, german silver, gothic architecture, gothic type,
harveyized steel, india ink, india rubber, italics, japanese varnish,
kafir corn, kraft paper, leghorn hat, levantine silks, levant
(leather), lima beans, london purple, lynch law, lyonnaise potatoes, macadamized roads, manila paper, mansard roof, mercerized
fabrics, mercurial, merino sheep, messianic, morocco (leather),
navy blue, navy cloth, newmarket coat, osnaburg cloth, pagan,
palm-beach suit, panama hat, pasteurized milk, parian ware, paris
green, plaster of paris, portland cement, prussian blue, raglan
coats, roentgen rays, roman numerals, roman type, russia
(leather), scotch plaid, surah silk, tantalize, timothy grass, titanic,
turkey red, ulster coat, utopia, venetian blinds, vulcanize, wedg-
wood ware

Do not capitalize the verbs *americanize, anglicize, boycott,
fletcherize, germanize, pasteurize.* When used as nouns,
however, these words are preferably capitalized.

Americanism	Anglicization	Fletcherization
Americanization	Boycott	Germanization
Anglicism	Fletcherism	Pasteurization

The prefixes *anti, ex, pro, un* prefixed to proper nouns and
adjectives are not capitalized.

anti-Romanist	un-American
pro-British	ex-President

H Capitalize the word following a colon when it is the first
word of a complete and elaborating sentence. Do not
capitalize the word following a colon (or an exclamation
point or an interrogation point) when the words, phrases,
clauses, or sentence following are merely supplementary,
repeating or making fuller and clearer what has gone before.

Wars are not made: they grow
What, not started yet? not even ready?
You ask for help from me! from me whom you hate!

The completely organized sale should follow these steps: attention, interest, desire, conviction, action

The five steps of the well-organized sale are: Arouse attention,
beget interest, create desire, establish conviction, induce action

In case, however, words, phrases, clauses, sentences following
a colon are listed on separate lines beginning below the line
on which the colon stands, the first letter of each is preferably capitalized.

    I The five sales steps:
        A Attention
        B Interest
        C Desire
        D Conviction
        E Action

Some authorities insist that the words listed after the colon in a run-on statement (as in the second illustration above) should be capitalized inasmuch as they constitute topics in an outline to be developed. There is wide variation of usage in regard to this point. They may or may not be capitalized. The important thing for the writer is to be consistent in all such cases. Usually, major topics in either a run-on or a tabular outline are capitalized and minor ones are not. All may be capitalized or all may be lower-cased (see page 435).

J Capitalize the first word of every complete direct quotation. Conversely this means that the first word of a fragmentary or part quotation is not capitalized unless, of course, it is itself capitalized in the text from which it is taken. It also means that the first word of the second part of a broken or interrupted quotation is not capitalized unless, again, such word is one that would otherwise be capitalized under some rule of this section.

> The speaker said: "The first commandment of every religion should be: Thou shalt work"

> "The first commandment of every religion," said the speaker, "should be: Thou shalt work"

> "The first commandment of every religion should be," said the speaker, "Thou shalt work"

> He took exception to the "disorder, the general attitude toward the work, and the downright lack of respect evidenced"

Do not capitalize the first word of an indirect quotation, declarative or interrogative.

> He asked whether we believe in the ten-hour day
> He said that work is the one solution of all our problems

For purposes of clarity and emphasis the first word of a direct question that is not quoted is capitalized. This form is followed also by some authors and some houses in direct but unquoted declarative expressions. Serial questions and exclamations should be capitalized.

He asked the class: Is that contention supportable? Does it appear to be logical? Upon what premise is it based?

And so he thought to himself: The girl is competent to do the work but she probably won't do it

What's that? Why, what do you mean! Well, I never!

Typographical variation is being increasingly used to take the place of quotation marks (see page 437) and hence to settle some of the problems of divided usage in capitalization. The small capitals and italics below illustrate. In copy, underlining would, of course, be used to indicate italics.

He said PLEASE HAND ME THE LEDGER

He asked WHAT IS THE CAPITAL? WHERE IS IT LOCATED? WHAT IS ITS POPULATION? WHAT IS ITS PRINCIPAL INDUSTRY?

The first commandment of every religion should be *thou shalt work*

Typographical display is increasingly depended upon for quoted matter used as title or chapter heading or as any other outstanding part of composition. The first word of a part quotation so used should not be capitalized unless the first word is itself a proper noun, and such part quotation need not be placed in quotation marks. Leaders should be used to indicate omitted parts of such quotation (see pages 447 and 524).

........advertising of the first quality is business electricity

Advertising........is business electricity

Do not capitalize the first word of a parenthetical expression when such expression is functionally a grammatical part of the content in which it appears (see also 524).

I suspected that he had lost his job (since he had returned so much earlier than usual) and, sure enough, after some embarrassment, he confessed that he had

I suspected that he had lost his job. (He had returned much earlier than usual.) Sure enough, after some embarrassment, he confessed that he had

K Capitalize *Resolved* and *Whereas, Be it resolved* and *Whereas furthermore* when used in resolutions, propositions, petitions, and other formal writings. The word following such expressions should also be capitalized.

Resolved: That happiness is the perpetual possession of being well deceived

Whereas, The stamp tax is a form of taxation that makes everybody tax-conscious........

Be it therefore resolved: That stamp taxes be levied on all objects of purchase costing ten cents or
more

L Capitalize such trade names as *Pebeco, Nabisco, Astring-o-
sol, Packard Twelve, Quaker Oats.* But note that derivations sometimes "wear so long" and so well that the original
connection is lost sight of and lower-case thus tends to be
substituted for capital. While *Kodak* is today properly
capitalized, it is frequently written without the capital *K*
and every sort of handy camera has come to be known as a
kodak. The same is true to a degree of *Sapolio* and *Multigraph.* The ultimate of publicity achievement is to make a
trade name so well known that it is wrongly changed from
capitals to lower-case. Trade names are correctly capitalized.

M The capitalization of words used in a piece of composition
to refer to specific parts or sections is recommended by some
authorities, but the practise is highly questionable. It is
unwise to use the capital letter too freely for purposes of
emphasis. There is already considerable confusion in the
use of capitals. Excess of capitalization for the two purposes above indicated simply tends to make confusion more
confused. It is better to write

The foreword of the book is too argumentative
See the table of contents

than

The Foreword of the book is too argumentative
See the Table of Contents

Foreword and *Table of Contents* are not proper nouns.
Those who advocate their capitalization in such connections
as those above, would probably not write

The Last Chapter is very exciting
See the Index to the last volume

There are so many mechanical devices other than capitalization that may be used for emphasis—principally typographical variations of one kind and another—that it
would seem best to confine capitals to their specific and
already abundant purposes.

IV As to things and events

A Capitalize titles of religious literature—bibles, books or divisions of bibles, creeds, confessions of faith, religious legislative documents, and the like.

Bible
New Testament
Old Testament
Lord's Prayer
the Sermon on the Mount
the Four Gospels
the Ten Commandments
the Gospel according to St. Mark
the Twenty-third Psalm
the Book of Proverbs
the Revised Version
the Authorized Version
the Nicene Creed
the Apostles' Creed
the Pentateuch
Deuteronomy

the Koran
the Talmud
the Apocrypha
the Breeches Bible
the Holy Scriptures
the Book of Mormon
Science and Health
the Septuagint
the Lord's Supper
the Thirty-nine Articles
the Westminster Confession of Faith
the Douai Bible
the Book of Esther
the Beatitudes
Vedanta
Zoroastrianism

But note that adjectives derived from or related to these terms are usually not capitalized.

apocryphal
apostolic
biblical

koranic
gospel
pentateuchal

proverbial
scriptural
talmudic

B Capitalize names of religious denominations, of holidays, and of holy days and events.

Adventist
Bahai
Baptist
Congregational
Disciples of Christ
Episcopal
Jewish
Latter-Day Saints
Lutheran
Mennonite
Methodist
Moravian
Presbyterian
Quaker
Reformed
Roman Catholic
Salvation Army
Society of Friends
Spiritualist
Unitarian
United Brethren
Universalist

All Saints
Ash Wednesday
Christmas
Columbus Day
Easter
Feast of Tabernacles
Fourth of July
Good Friday
Holy Thursday
Labor Day
Lincoln's Birthday
Memorial Day
Michaelmas
New Year's Day
Passover
Feast of Purim
Rosh Hashana
Sabbath
Thanksgiving
Washington's Birthday
Whitsuntide
Yom Kippur

C Capitalize the names of the days of the week, and of the months of the year, but do not capitalize the names of the four seasons except when they are used figuratively or are identified in history with some special event or date.

> The fateful Winter of 1917
> Now Summer blinks on flowery braes

D Capitalize period and scientific names—era, epoch, age, genus, event—when they are closely identified with specific proper nouns and adjectives and are thus made to stand for recognized particular happenings or things.

The name of a species is not capitalized, but the name of the class or order or family usually is.

the Civil War	the Dark Ages
the World War	the Battle of Chattanooga
Armistice Day	the Neolithic Age
the Renaissance	the Elizabethan Period
the Exodus	the Oncidium orchid
the Alaska Purchase	the Wassermann test
the Wars of the Roses	Dakin's solution
the Crusades	Canis familiaris
Lower Silurian	Spathyema fœtida

E Capitalize the names of particular organizations—clubs, companies, dynasties, families, institutions, mercantile establishments, orders, parties—when they are closely identified with specific proper names, and when, standing alone, they refer unmistakably to special units.

American Legion	Rockefeller Foundation
American Merchants' Association	Socialists
	Soviets
Chi Phi Fraternity	Tammany Hall
Democrats	University Club of Chicago
Drys	Wanamaker and Brown
Fascisti	Yamanaka Company
House of Hapsburg	Young Men's Christian Association
Knights of Columbus	
Masonic Order	Young Men's Hebrew Association
Order of Odd Fellows	

Usage is disputed in regard to the capitalization of *party* under this rule. Some organs write Republican Party; others, Republican party.

The tendency is, when such words as *club, company, order* form the third or fourth (or more remote) word in a title combination, to write them with small letters, thus:

the Alfred M. Hitchcock Industrial College association
the University of Texas Social Problems club

F   Capitalize *constitution* and names of other official documents
of great importance.

the Constitution of the United States
the Constitution of the Union of Soviet Socialist Republics
the Declaration of Independence
the Emancipation Proclamation
the Bill of Rights
the Treaty of Versailles
Magna Carta

G   The words *administration, bureau, committee, commission,
commonwealth, confederation, department, government,
office, powers, service, station, union,* and so forth, are capitalized when used with or as proper names or as proper
adjectives in definite reference to the United States Government or to divisions of the Federal Government or to any
other specific government or divisions thereof.

The new Administration has achieved wonders
the National Reconstruction Administration
the Civil Works Administration
the Farm-Credit Bureau
the Reconstruction Finance Corporation
the Patent Office
the Treasury Department
the Norfolk Naval Station
the Federal Board of Health
the Federal Government
the National Government
the British Government
the Imperial Government
the South African Union
the Cherokee Nation
the Allied Powers
the Air Service, Ltd.
the Swiss Confederation
the Commonwealth of Ohio

When capitalized the word *government* refers, according to
most general usage, to national rather than to state government.

Every state government must pay back the loans made to it by
the Federal (National) Government

The words *commission* and *committee* should be capitalized
always when they refer to bodies appointed by Congress.

Interstate Commerce Commission
United States Tariff Commission

the Senate Finance Committee
the Ways and Means Committee
the Democratic National Committee

H Capitalize the names of steamships, special trains, airplanes, and zeppelins.

The Majestic	The Twentieth-Century Limited
The Leviathan	The Orange-Blossom Special
The X-4	The Spirit of St. Louis

J Usage pertaining to the capitalization of terms referring to the army and navy is vastly fluctuating and contradictory. Newspapers and periodicals disagree in their practise regarding their capitalization. *The Style Manual of the United States Government Printing Office* authorizes the following:

Adjutant General	Inspector General
Air Corps	Judge Advocate General
the Air Service	the Marine Corps
the Army	Medical Museum
the Army Band	the Navy
the Army Establishment	Navy (Naval) Establishment
Army officer	naval officer
army shoe	naval station
British Army	Navy officer
the brigade	navy yard
Brooklyn Navy Yard	navy-yard hand
the Cavalry	Nurse Corps
Coast Artillery	Pay Corps
the corps	Paymaster General
Coldstream Guards	the regiment
Confederate Corps Area	the Regulars
Eighty-first Regiment	Regular officer
Engineer Corps	the Regular Army
First Brigade	Reserve officer
First Corps	Revolutionary Army
Field Artillery	Robinson's brigade
French Army	Royal Air Squadron
French Navy	Royal Navy
General Headquarters (GHQ)	Scouting Force
General Staff	Special Service Squadron
General Staff College	the Staff
General Staff Corps	Surgeon General
Grant's army	United States Army
Headquarters	United States Navy
the Headquarters	the Volunteers
Hospital Corps	volunteer officer
the Infantry	War College
infantryman	

CHAPTER FOUR

DIRECT-MAIL COPY

Advertising thru the mails is called direct-mail advertising for the reason that the copy goes *directly* to the individual prospect. It may be changed frequently and easily, and it is thus versatile and elastic. It may be sent to lists of people representing many different kinds of interests, and it is therefore selective and adapt-able. And it may be used for many different purposes—to sell primarily, but also to follow up, to supplement other kinds of advertising, to cope with changing conditions of one kind and another, to precede and accompany and follow prospects' visits or inquiries or salesmen's approach, to go out into places unreachable to the ordinary operations of salesmanship, to make buying and selling and *delivery* easy and automatic, and so on.

Everything depends upon good lists in direct-mail selling. If you were to make lists of people in a neighborhood or even in a school according to the different interests they represent, you would have a fair concrete idea of the importance of differentiated mailing lists to a large mail-order establishment. Those having one par-ticular occupation or interest would be appealed to in one circular; those having a different occupation or interest, in another, and so forth. In a class of forty pupils and in a community of forty families, there will be an average of ten distinct occupational and recreational special interests to appeal to. Multiply these simple cases by the population of a state or section or country, and you will have some idea of the tremendous task of setting up differ-entiated lists for use by mail-order salesmanship.

Lists are derived from directories of all kinds, from assorted newspaper files, from social and business club memberships, from government (town, county, state, federal) records—tax, license, building, marriage, election, and the like. They must be "shuffled" almost constantly to be kept alive and up-to-date. It is a most complicated service that the listing department of a large mail-order house and the independent listing companies

54

render. It is comparable, again, to the subject listings of students in a large high school or college who are doing their work under broad and varied elective privileges.

Any circular made up for wide distribution thru the mails with the purpose to advertise and sell a commodity, a service, or an idea, may be classed loosely as direct-mail advertising or as direct advertising. Letters (printed or so generally processed that they cease to be personal communications), catalogs, house organs, almanacs, booklets, leaflets, broadsides, portfolios are sometimes called the conventional direct-mail pieces. This name is given them because they are more or less standardized in size and shape and form and are usually sent out independently—"on their own." Enclosures of all kinds—cards, blotters, small calendars, coupons, envelop stuffers, package inserts, and the like, are the unconventional pieces. They are more frequently "surprize" pieces, that is, they are made up in unconventional and unstandardized form, and as a rule accompany other matter.

It is not possible to define or describe exactly any one of the above-named pieces. Those in both groups are subject to the taste and judgment of the one who devises them, and to the circumstances under which they are composed. The names are loosely used. A booklet may be anything from a small envelop-contained piece to a publication of more than one hundred pages. And the names are not important. The strategy and beauty and impressiveness of make-up are the things that count. One of the best rules for guidance in the building of a piece of direct-mail copy is the tripartite one of *use-attraction-interest*, that is, the piece should be made useful so that it will be kept, attractive so that it will hold attention immediately, interesting so that it will impress and thus carry conviction. Color, line and space, illustration, headline, typography, quality of paper, and English must be depended upon to realize these ends.

I Color

Use backgrounds that are less intense in color than the objects shown upon them. The larger the surface the less intense the background has to be, and vice versa.

Contrast warm colors against cold ones; contrast tints against shades. When two different shades are used for expository purposes, emphasize the parts by means of tints or lighter colors.

Keep the tone of display lines in harmony with that of border and typography. Do not allow the one to neutralize the other. Usually, the larger the type face or the heavier the design, the lighter should be the color tones. In two-color printing—and for the vast bulk of direct advertising work two colors are all that are ever necessary—the reading matter should be in the heavier tone and the decorative matter in the lighter.

Make the type face stronger as a rule than anything else, in case it is the message that you wish to impress upon the reader. This means that reading matter is to be placed upon color, not color placed upon reading matter. The rule applies to the border, to the decorative lettering, to head pieces and tail pieces. Do not allow these to steal the glory of the tout ensemble and thus negative the real message.

Use color for distinctiveness and attention-arrest, with good taste and great discretion. Otherwise nothing may be left in the mind of the prospect but a big splash of red or green or some other color. Red is the color most commonly and most successfully used for attention value. It makes spaces appear larger than any other color does; it seems nearer than blue or green or yellow at the same distance away. It creates greater depth and perspective than any other color for general uses.

Make color, first of all, tell the story of actuality. It may be used to convey texture, grain, pattern, outline, quality, atmosphere. This is the primary reason for using color. To sell rugs by direct mail and not to reproduce their colors, is like trying to sell china eggs and paper roses for the real articles. Moreover, color protects against fraud in enabling the purchaser to picture the article exactly as it looks and is.

Aim to make the color you use—and pay for (remember that color work costs five or six times as much as simple black and white, but that it has five or six times the attention-getting and sales value)—give real distinction to your copy. This means that color may be so used as to lengthen the life of a piece cf copy, to give it better class appeal, to convey a decorative note to a room when the direct-mail piece on which it appears is left on a table or a chair.

The following color chart is worthy your study. It has proved very valuable to many copy men and women who have had to make nice color adaptations in their direct-mail pieces.

CORRELATION CHART OF COLOR INTERPRETATION *

1 Light Values   2 Medium Values   3 Dark Values

HUES	SYMBOLISM	CHARACTERISTIC	MOOD	Influence	Temperature
Redpurple	2 Battle 3 Heroic Virtues 2 Valor 3 Prowess	2 Stateliness 2 Impressiveness 2 Haughtiness	3 Cold 3 Chilly 2 Tragic		
Purple	3 Loyalty 2 Patience 2 Fidelity 3 Allegiance	3 Dignity 3 Royalty 3 Seriousness 3 Imperialness	3 Dark 3 Ceremonious 3 Cold Grave 3 Austere 3 Pompous	SUBDUING COLORS	COOL COLORS
Purpleblue	3 Solemness 3 Majesty 2 Reverence 2 Sublimity	3 Apathy 3 Harshness	3 Stern 3 Unyielding 3 Cold		
Blue	3 Truth 3 Consistency 3 Justice 2 Sincerity	2 Tranquillity 2 Calmness 1 Expansiveness	2 Passive 3 Cold 3 Deep		
Bluegreen	2 Peacefulness 2 Serenity 3 Placidity	2 Retiredness 3 Unexpressiveness	2 Sedate 3 Sober 3 Cold	TRANQUILIZING COLORS	
Green	2 Fruitfulness 2 Hope 2 Immortality 2 Prolification	2 Youth 2 Vigor 2 Life 2 Appeal	2 Cool-Passive 1 Refreshing 2 Restful 3 Quiet-Retiring		
Greenyellow	2 Encouragement 1 Happiness 2 Success 1 Prosperity	1 Cheerfulness 1 Refreshingness 1 Vivacity 1 Alacrity	2 Springlike 1 Gentle 2 Stimulating 2 Flush or Warm		WARM COLORS
Yellow	1 Supreme Wisdom 1 Goodness 1 Inspiration 1 Prudence	1 Joyfulness 1 Gaiety 1 Merriment 3 Sickness	1 Warm 1 Light 1 Joyous 1 Active 1 Stimulating	EXCITING COLORS	
Yellowred	1 Knowledge 2 Benevolence 2 Home 1 Light 2 Benignity	1 Liveliness 1 Warmth 2 Gravity 3 Somberness 3 Strength	1 Mellow 1 Warm 2 Rich 2 Luscious		
Red	2 Love 2 Valor 2 Passion 2 Truth	2 Danger 2 Sanguinity 2 Fire 2 Anger	2 Intense 2 Fierce 2 Hot 2 Vital 2 Active 2 Exciting		
White Silver	Chastity Innocence Purity	Peace Modesty Reservedness	Dignified Clean Chaste		
Gray	Tribulation Humility Distress	Quietness Subduedness Repressiveness	Calm Serene Mild		
Black	Death Mortality	Gloom Darkness	Mournful Sad		
Gold	Richness Glamour Enchantment	Money Gold Glory	Glorious Powerful Distinctive		

* Used by permission of the author, Charles E. Vautrain, Holyoke, Mass.

II   Line and space

Use vertical lines to give height, horizontal lines to give breadth. A vertical line appears longer than a horizontal for the reason that we look from side to side more easily than we look up and down. Verticals may be broken for relief, as may horizontals. The breakage foreshortens. Closely paralleled horizontals give accented breadth.

Do not use zigzag or otherwise broken lines except for the purpose of showing actually how something looks. They invariably confuse the picture and dissipate the reader's attention. This is especially likely to be the case when typography is required to follow in and out to accommodate itself to irregular borders and figures.

Keep purely decorative lines harmonious in shape and alinement. This is a corollary of the foregoing rule. Triangles and circles may be combined, as may parallelograms and ovals, but if the combination is bizarre or grotesque, attention will be detracted from the actual message of the advertisement. Ornament is subjective—it asserts itself. Decoration is objective—it subordinates itself. Ornament perverts attention value. Decoration helps to focus attention value upon the copy it accompanies. As pointed out on page 72, poor paper stock may be disguised by profuse ornament, but this is the only excuse for its use in direct-mail copy —if indeed this be an excuse.

Make shapes and sizes consistent and agreeable. One space should never be made three or four times as large as another that accompanies it in a piece of copy. One area twenty times the size of another with which it is used gives a restless and inharmonious effect. Areas and distances should not be more than one half or two thirds larger than each other in copy units. Space and distance ratios should be about as five to seven to eleven. Bottom marginings should be eleven; top, seven; side, five. On pages that are wider than long the bottom margin should remain eleven, but the top should be five and the sides seven, for the sake of picturing consistent balance and symmetry. The double square upright is called the vertical golden proportion; the double square side by side, the horizontal golden proportion. These or their approximates are the two predominant shapes. The vertical oval golden proportion, and the horizontal oval golden proportion are likewise more or less common shapes, but they require line drawings for reproduction, whereas square forms can be set up easily by means of the printer's rules.

Play up important words or lines or illustrations at the optical center of the page. This is always a little above the real or mathematical center—that point on either of the golden proportion areas to which the eye first naturally goes.

Aim to balance copy so that no tendency to tilt will be conveyed by it. One side heavier than another may throw your whole message out of key, and the prospect will not be able to concentrate upon word, sentence, and paragraph. Bisymmetrical balance means perfect evenness of numerical allotment on both sides. One large vase in the middle of a table and one small one at each end, both equidistant from the central vase, and both of the same size, give bisymmetrical balance. Occult or compensatory balance means the balance of unequal parts thru some device. If the large vase is placed nearer to one side of the table than the other, then the vase nearer it should be smaller than the one farther from it. If the large vase is placed three-quarter distance toward the right of the table, then the small vase at the right edge should be only half as large as the vase at the left edge:

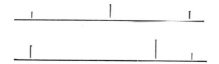

Remember that the principle of movement is the opposite of the principle of balance, but that it is equally important. Balance makes for rest and repose; movement for alertness and action. Movement may be directed by sign or token or "lean" in copy. The old Spencerian style of writing led the reader forward by its forward lean. Eyes tend to follow the meeting point of two or more lines. Arrows and pointers direct the eye. The point of a pencil and the tip of a shoe should focus into copy, not out of it. These are all structural devices for movement. There are numerous others to be discovered in almost any good piece of direct copy. But in content itself rhythm and euphony make for movement, as do also good-looking type and fine quality of paper. It may be said that anything that makes for agreeableness makes for movement.

Increase the attention-value in copy in proportion to the decrease in space size. A space four by five should have twice the attention-value of a space eight by ten. Color intensity, line display, marginal or other in-pointing lines, unusual out-pressing lines such as a circle pushing against the four sides of a square, two columns that are related and continuous in make-up with different matter between them, concentration of color and line and word focus upon a central point (as the members of the chorus are trained to look at the star)—any device that protrudes to *you*—all of these make for creating an illusion of larger space than is really occupied by the copy. A large space is usually more impressive and has greater cumulative momentum than a small space. Its very magnitude tends to negative competition and to convey stability and reliability. But by the exercise of skill and care the writer and designer of small direct-mail pieces may do much to build mere size into their copy.

Make line and other styles of borders sustain and unify copy. They may at the same time express ideas in keeping with the message they enclose. Inappropriate decorative designs—borders, tail-pieces, head-pieces, intermediate pieces—may entirely nullify otherwise excellent copy. But appropriate decoration may be made to strengthen, to convey the impression of permanence and compactness, to emphasize taste and delicacy and refinement without at all radiating weakness. Repetition of the same figure in borders with variety by way of periodic breaks is the commonest style of enclosure for copy (the well-known egg-and-dart border illustrates). But the border should, whenever possible, be made to grow out of the picture of the commodity advertised or in some way have bearing upon it.

Keep borders strictly subordinate to copy proper. They may express ideas, they may individualize copy, but this does not mean that they should dominate it. Borders must be regarded as decorative, not as ornamental. Sometimes copy is held together and unified centrifugally rather than centripetally, that is, lines radiate from the center and seem to gather in everything that is contained in the copy (see page 62). Broken borders and broken lines, however, like irregular spaces and sizes, may be used effectively to surprize and therefore renew attention. The danger in resorting to such devices is that shock may be conveyed rather than surprize, and thus the intended emphasis may be destroyed. Tricks unsell quite as often as they sell.

A FEW STOCK BORDERS

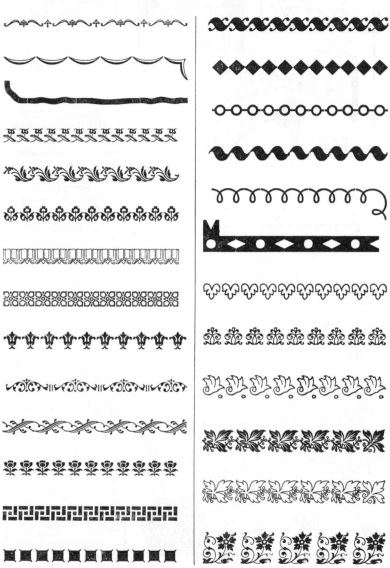

STRIKING USES OF LINE AND SPACE

62

III Illustration (including pictures, photographs, line drawings, reproductions, and so forth)

Keep illustration simple. If you attempt too many details you will destroy both the unity and the coherence of the theme you attempt to convey. Inasmuch as copy aims to say as much as possible in as few words as possible, advertising designs should tell as much as possible with as few strokes as possible.

Keep illustration appropriate. Let the bearing of illustration be apparent at sight. If the reader is required to make an effort to catch the derived application, the force of the illustration may be lost. Even in illustration that is merely atmospheric, in which form and action and story play little part, appropriateness may be definitely suggested and built in.

Keep illustration beautiful. Beauty will oftentimes compensate for any inappropriateness in an illustration. Mere abstract beauty arrests, tho it may not always hold the attention. Vacuous beauty begets only passing notice. Meaningful beauty clinches attention with interest and memory. Let the illustration, therefore, convey quality of refinement and tone.

Keep illustration true. This means that nothing insincere or inconsistent should be permitted to weaken by rendering suspicious any advertising illustration. If your picture is expository or descriptive, let the exposition or the description be exact. Genuine photographic reproduction suggests honesty and reality. There is some insincerity and inconsistency, surely, in using the same illustration with a dozen different write-ups in as many different mediums. If singleness of thought dominates the whole copy make-up, then a certain illustration peculiarly belongs to a certain piece of copy. Do not allow the illustration and the copy to falsify to each other or both to falsify to the prospect.

Keep illustration agreeable. Ugliness of any sort repels. Serpents, disasters, robberies, holdups, storms, fires, cesspools, and the like, are distinctly disagreeable to most people. Made permanent, by way of line and color design, they become tableaux that may be permanently carried in the imagination, and thus possess more than mere passing negation and repulsion of association. And good positive constructive illustration is so easily possible in insurance copy or firearms copy or welfare copy, by showing results rather than causes, that it is a pity ever to resort to any other kind, as these classes of copy so frequently do.

Keep illustration emphatic. This may be done in many ways but a few of which can be touched upon here. Youth is, as a rule, more emphatic than old age, for it is fresh and vigorous and forward-looking. Illustrations of good-looking, "strong-charactered" men and women are emphatic. Positive color is emphatic. Action about to commence or just concluded, that is, initial action or final action, is emphatic. But action in suspense, that is, incomplete and suspended action, is indecisive and therefore weak. You may find both interest and amusement in connection with this principle in the reproduction of illustrations of athletic contests in the Sunday supplements. Suspended action is usually a bit blurred by the camera. It in the same way blurs mental conception of it. But strong character and sharp, positive, decisive action make for clarity and emphasis of impression.

Keep illustration suggestive. Do not attempt to say all that may be said in the copy illustration. If you do you will have ignored one of the most salable of human attitudes, namely, suspense. Let the illustration create certain unsatisfied fancies in the mind of the prospect, certain suggestions for thought long after it ceases to be seen merely by the eyes. The most suggestive illustration is the one that gets itself impressed clearly upon the imagination, and that is consequently "carried around" in the prospect's mind, and applied by him to everyday situations.

Keep illustration atmospheric. Every copy illustration should leave an impression of strength, or delicacy, or daintiness, or dignity. And this atmosphere should likewise have the qualities of permanence and persistence. If the illustration is weak or gross or loose in make-up, its atmosphere and its impressiveness are consequently nullified. If the illustration can be made to say something to the prospect that he has himself felt many times previously, but that he has been at a loss to visualize or put into words, it probably has atmosphere—"that elusive inexpressible quality that is felt rather than heard or seen." Illustrations are justifiable for the creation and maintenance of atmosphere alone.

Keep illustration harmonious with copy. If there is a deep gulf of disagreement between your illustration and your copy, you may be accused of trying to sell needles under the name of sewing machines. It is a good policy to have illustrations not merely bear upon or suggest or grow out of copy, but to follow the style of copy used in the theme they present. If your copy is narrative, let your illustration suggest narrative. Conversely, if your illus-

tration is dramatic, let your copy be dramatic. If your illustration is expository, let expository copy grow out of it. If your illustration is merely a scene, let your copy be descriptive. If you write character, picture character. If you picture a climax in action, write the climax, and so forth.

Keep illustration conventional. The world runs true to form in a very large measure. Any attempt to do the unusual in advertising art is certainly a risk, and probably a losing one. Remember that painting and sculpture and architecture are very highly conventionalized arts. Cubism and futurism are interesting schools of departure, but they *are* departures. The tenets of conventionalized art say that curves are more attractive than straight lines, ovals than circles; that uprights and oblongs are more attractive than squares; that the vertical oblong and the vertical oval are more practicable as well as more striking than horizontal oblongs and ovals. The double square, or golden proportion, is probably the most practicable, as it is the most advantageous shape for illustration. You will be interested in observing the prevalence of this form in the things that you come into daily contact with.

IV   Headlines

Make your headlines and sub-headlines advertise your copy. Remember that the newspaper headline (see page 397) takes the content out of the copy, that the advertising headline takes the reader into the copy.

Express headline content by means of active present-tense verbs, and by nouns, adjectives, and adverbs. These parts of speech are listed in order of importance as far as their use in headlines is concerned.

Use no punctuation in headlines if you can possibly avoid doing so. A straightaway sweep of reading in your headline is the most impressive composition.

Get emphasis on the first word and on the last word.   In *FIRE CONSUMES YOUR DIVIDENDS* note that the first word and the last word of the headline are important words and are strategically placed. Note also two other valuable characteristics of this headline: It is strictly rhythmic and it is short enough to be grasped at a glance, that is, it is of "eye-gulp" length. These are two characteristics that make for quick and easy memorization.

Make declarative and imperative headlines periodic in construction whenever possible. *LET US PAINT YOUR HOUSE* is better than *LET US PAINT THAT HOUSE OF YOURS.*

Break your headline by sense in case it has to be run over from one line to another. This means that the first line should not be suspended by a syllable of a divided word or by an unimportant word such as a preposition or an article or a pronoun. These are bad:

FIRE CONSUMES YOUR
DIVIDENDS

TRY THIS INTER-
ESTING METHOD

TAKE ME HOME TO
OLD VIRGINNY

DRESS UP FOR
SPRING

These are better:

FIRE CONSUMES
YOUR DIVIDENDS

TAKE ME HOME
TO OLD VIRGINNY

TRY THIS
INTERESTING METHOD

DRESS UP
FOR SPRING

Do not use words that look alike at a glance in close proximity to each other. *Study* is often taken for *sturdy,* or vice versa; *tabasco* for *tobacco, Armenian* for *American.*

Do not use blind headlines, that is, headlines that are generic and consist of a single word or of two generic words at most (see page 399). The words *INSURE, SATISFACTION, DESTINY,* and the like, require interpretation before they can be understood in their connection. One of the chief purposes of the headline is immediacy. The blind headline is never immediate.

Make your headline connect copy with illustration, or at least show definite relation between them. The headline of an illustration or picture is called the caption or the legend. It has for many decades been placed beneath the picture, but there is now a growing tendency to place the caption at the top of the illustration. This is as it should be, for it is desirable to know what we are going to see before we see it. So placed the caption is sometimes called the overline (see page 416).

Place and devise headlines so that they will dominate the copy or that part of it to which they strictly belong. To this end a head-

line may be broken and distributed in parts thru the copy; it may
be divided into principal and intermediate headlines; it may be
extended beyond the normal margin; it may be boxed, that is,
placed in rules and set thus to one side or elsewhere; it may be
isolated in white space or protruded into it in such a way as to
arrest attention; it may be written in appropriate character type;
it may paraphrase a familiar saying or apply a figure of speech
subtly.

Use plain, simple, direct declarations for headlines, until such time
as tests may prove other forms better. The command or imperative headline, the question or interrogative headline, the negative
headline, the predicament headline, the Pollyanna headline have
all been put to the test in connection with certain commodities and
services. The declarative in the majority of uses makes the best
showing, with the command a close second. The latter is sometimes called the autosuggestion headline, for the reason that
people instinctively obey commands. *Shut the door, open the
window, take this paper,* and the like, induce spontaneous reactions.

Here are a few good advertising headlines:

FOR ALL THE FAMILY

One Step does not make a Dance

BUILD YOUR OWN HOME

SAY SOMETHING!

WRITE FOR THIS PORTFOLIO!

THE MOON IS FULL TONIGHT

E-a-s-y, THERE!

Are letter-writers born?

Mail Men Don't Wait on Benches

NATURE'S WAY WITH COLORS

Bachelor Girls

Keep in Mind The Fact

AT LAST...

what you have been looking for

OBSOLETE AGONIES   *The Tale of an Elephant*

PICK THE RIGHT ONE!

ECONOMY

for Letter Users

V   Typography

See to it that the typography of your direct-mail piece is clear, legible, and inviting. The last word means that typography must be agreeable to the eye, not forbidding, not even arresting unless it is at the same time intriguing.

Use character type only when it is certain to enhance the value of your copy. By character type is meant type that carries with it the idea of the thing it stands for. It is to typography what onomatopœia or echoism (see page 107) is to literature.

Make type emphasize but not overemphasize your copy. Mechanical typographical devices for emphasis are capitals, italics, underlining, spacing, certain punctuation marks such as dashes and hyphens and exclamation points, signs such as ¶ and #, tabulations, initialing, acrostics, and type arrangements of all other kinds. But more than one mechanical device should not be used at any one place. To italicize and capitalize both, to underline and also to separate letters by hyphens would be to emphasize by mechanics unnecessarily. Two or more devices for emphasis may, indeed, weaken rather than strengthen emphasis.

Permit no freakishness of type for the sake of emphasis or attention. It, again, may defeat the end desired. Do not allow excessive use of condensed type or of expanded type. This is condensed: **Twelve** and this is expanded: TWELVE. Each may sometimes have character value, but used to excess either one will become a monotone and lose all point or significance. Too many type faces in a single piece of copy will confuse the reader. Aim to secure uniformity of type face without making it seem monotonous. Aim at some variety of type face for the sake of emphasis without making it appear incoherent and confused.

Adjust type size to line length, that is, increase the size of type as the line increases in length. This will make for easier reading. The small type of the newspaper is adjusted to the short line— about two inches in length. But in reading longer lines of small type a person may unconsciously skip a line when he reaches the right-hand margin, or start reading the same line again. Larger type face will prevent this to a large extent. The longer the lines the wider the spacing that should be made between them. This is true of handwriting and typewriting as well as of printing. Long lines tend to wave or swing. But spaces left between them absorb the wave spread and it does not therefore run over into the line above or the line below.

Do not permit space trickles or gutters to follow thru on a page of print (or of typewriting). You may have seen little rivers of white space here and there on a printed page, thus:

> ALBANY, Nov. 20.—The Con-
> servation Department ordered
> State foresters, rangers and
> game protectors today to patrol
> closely all forested areas to
> prevent theft of Christmas trees.
> The illegal removal of such
> trees from State land, the de-
> partment said, may cost the
> offender $10. a tree. Similar
> theft from privately owned land
> is a misdemeanor, punishable by
> a fine of not more than $100.

The printer can always obviate this by resetting a little, as here:

> ALBANY, Nov. 20.—The Conser-
> vation Department ordered State
> foresters, rangers and game pro-
> tectors today to patrol closely all
> forested areas to prevent theft of
> Christmas trees. The illegal re-
> moval of such trees from State
> land, the department said, may
> cost the offender $10. a tree. Sim-
> ilar theft from privately owned
> land is a misdemeanor, punishable
> by a fine of not more than $100.

See to it that all reading in your folder or leaflet or broadside or other form runs in the same direction. Do not require the reader to turn the mail-piece around or upside down to continue any part of your message from one page or part to another. This rule is especially important when connected reading is required. Matter on a multi-page piece should, of course, be so arranged that each page or smaller part constitutes a unit of reading in itself. But this is by no means always possibie.

VI Paper

Use a "personality paper," that is, a paper that shows body and quality immediately it is seen and felt.

Test paper for opaqueness by holding it up to the light. Test also for agreeableness of surface and edging. Highly glossed papers are not durable. Sharp-edged papers are likewise to be avoided —they may cut the prospect's fingers! Plain surface and deckle edge are preferable in papers calculated for wide general use.

Be sure your paper is durable and fadeless. Tear a sheet in half and put one half away in the dark for a few days. Then compare it with the half that has been left in the light.

Put your tongue to the paper. If the moisture comes thru to the other side, the stock does not have proper body or sizing for first copies. If the moisture remains on the surface, the sizing may be regarded as satisfactory.

Bend or break your paper, or rub it firmly. Then hold it up to the light and look thru it. If there is a rough corrugated edge where the break was made or a fuzz where the rubbing was done, the surface of the paper is not well "fixed," that is, it is not firm; it will not stand hard usage.

Cut and tear paper with the grain. This will make the separated pieces less likely to fray. To discover which way the grain runs cut two strips from a sheet—one across, one lengthwise. See then as you hold the two pieces which will support the other. The strip cut or torn with the grain will show itself to be the stronger.

Use tinted papers rather than those with heavier color or shade, if you prefer variation from pure white. Printing on shades is more difficult to read than printing on tints and plain white. If you vary your tints by departments, be sure to use the more cheerful colors for collections, the pure white for formal and official use, buffs and yellows and blues and grays for general use and for sales.

Remember that dull finish is more artistic than highly glossed or enameled papers, and is at the same time easier on the eyes. If you use the cheaper papers, cover them well with print so that their quality will not be so easily noticed. And adapt the typography to the quality. India paper, for instance, is best suited for very fine print (cf. the Bible); the coarse-grained papers used for book jackets demand stronger and bolder type. All too seldom is this adaptation of print to paper considered by direct advertisers.

VII English

As elsewhere in business composition, simple words and simple sentences should be used in direct-mail copy. Specific concrete nouns, pictorial adjectives and adverbs, panoramic verbs should be the primary tools of expression. The appeals—human-interest and reason-why—mentioned on page 341, should be used wisely, as should also the sales regimentation—attention, interest, belief, resolution, action—mentioned on page 346. Such generic words as *good, beautiful, useful* are of little value. Their specific equivalents should be applied. And such general statements as *The best made, The last word, It leads them all* are coinages of such common mintage as to be practically useless. Here, again, the expression must needs be close-up and definite.

One idea and one idea only should be presented in a single circular. No direct piece should be constructed to sell more than one thing at a time. Concentration upon one commodity or service, adaptation of it to the prospect's tastes and needs, treatment of it in such a manner as to make purchase easy and automatic—these should be the aim of the copy writer. Color, typography, and so forth, may be made of inestimable value in accomplishing this. But suppose you are required to depend upon your use of English alone. You will then have to choose your words with such precision and construct your sentences with such directness and simplicity that they will do the work of all other devices combined. The good mail catalog description that is unillustrated is in most cases an excellent example to be followed. Unless it is clear, concise, correct, and honest in regard to every detail it presents, transactions are bungled and the claim and adjustment department finds more work on its hands than it can do.

VIII House organs

The so-called house organ is a company publication issued for the purpose of knitting together all departments into a sort of family, keeping employees informed of company happenings, advertising and promoting the interests of the company internally, and so forth. In some concerns there are more than one house organ —each department may, indeed, have its own organ. There may be an organ for salesmen, one for dealers, one for prospects, one for users or consumers, one for executives. The general internal organ, however, in which all of these are covered, is the most common, and the one that is likely to be conducted most successfully.

The contents of such publications vary to some degree, naturally, according to the character of the house of issue. But in the main all house organs aim to include material that appeals to the interests of those connected with the house, and in order to do this they solicit contributions from all departments either for the same issue or for rotation issues. In particular, the editor of a house organ sees to it that functions in which the entire personnel of his concern is interested, are given prominent placement. He should be a person capable of adapting materials from all sources in the company to the columns of his organ.

The general rules above set forth in connection with direct-mail copy apply to this kind of publication. Indeed, the organs of many establishments are frequently used for distribution thru the direct-by-mail lists. It sometimes happens that a house organ graduates out of its immediate aim and environment and becomes a regular trade publication on its own. But this ultimate is not and should not be made the aim of the well-managed house organ. As a rule the company issuing the house organ sets aside a fund from the general advertising appropriation for its maintenance. The little publication is therefore distributed free of charge to employees of the firm.

The titles of the house organs of some of the leading business houses are almost as well known as those of the leading magazines. *Business* of the Burroughs Adding Machine Company, Detroit, Michigan; *Gas Logic* of the Consolidated Gas Company, New York City; *Knott Knotes* of the Knott Hotel Chain, New York City; *N C R News* of the National Cash Register Company, Dayton, Ohio; *Number Eight* of the National City Bank, New York City; *The Lamp* of the Standard Oil Company of New Jersey; *What Next?* of the Dennison Manufacturing Company, Framingham, Massachusetts; *The Y and E Idea* of the Yawman and Erbe Manufacturing Company, Rochester, New York; *Shopmark* of the Berkey and Gay Furniture Company, Grand Rapids, Michigan, are a few of the best-known house organ titles.

In more respects than one the average school or college paper is a house organ for its group. It is made up of contributions both voluntary and assigned; it contains exchanges and general announcements of interest to the student body; it occasionally contains contributions from the outside; it publishes inspirational editorials, humorous paragraphs, and personal notes; it publishes pictures, drawings, cartoons, and so forth; *and*—its aim always is or should be to "sell" the institution just as the aim of the house organ is to "sell" the house. It is edited and managed in very much the same manner as the house organ, with editor-in-chief, circulation manager, business manager, and their respective assistants. The house organ does not, however, except in rare cases, carry advertising matter. School publications have been known to improve as their officers have increasingly become conscious of the fact that their papers are really house organs.

The completed layout of arrangement of content for any publication such as a house organ is called the dummy (see page 470). This, page by page and column by column, is a rough picture of what is to be included and where and how it is to be arranged. When the galleys (see page 467) come back from the printer for first reading, they are pasted in the dummy according to the proposed arrangement, with continued parts correctly linked and with headings and illustrations and all other special matter definitely fixed as they should be. The dummy is now "dressed" and sent back to the printer, who follows it in dividing the galleys into type pages. The page proofs then go to the editors for final corrections, and the booklet is printed and made ready for distribution.

The following editorial is taken from the house organ of a large industrial company. It was written at a time when the depression was felt most keenly in all departments of the enterprise, and the organ thus initiated a campaign toward fighting it successfully. In the parlance of the street, this is a good "boost" editorial:

WE WANT YOU TO KNOW

It's time—high time—that the buying public were made aware of two particular facts regarding Maximo Products Company. One is a fact of appreciation. One is a fact of obligation. The former means that the company is deeply appreciative of the growing customer enthusiasm for Maximo Products—an enthusiasm that is now well-nigh country-wide. The latter means that Maximo Products customers the country over are deeply obligated to three groups of workers who ARE the company and who are responsible for its phenomenal growth and development

NAMELY AND TO WIT

The factory hands whose sturdy workmanship, unwavering loyalty, and indefatigable industry have evolved a product second to none and first to most of its kind. Concentration upon their job for the sake of the job

LAYOUT FOR AN ILLUSTRATED PAGE
OF A MODERN MAGAZINE

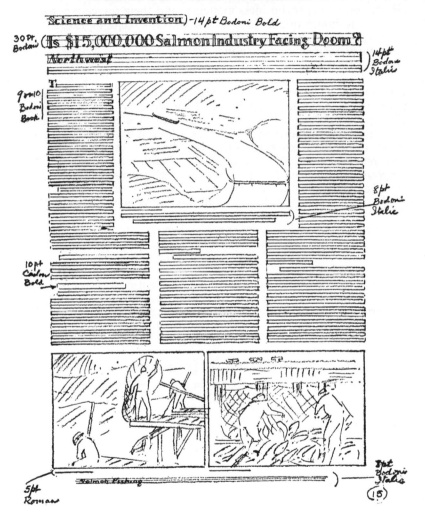

itself has brought them, almost without their knowing it, such preeminently deserved rewards as the five-day week with the six-day wage, housing and educational facilities that are the pride of the home town, job insurance and pension rights, PLUS a share in semi-annual profits from all sources

AND THEN

The white-collar workers — the sales, advertising, managerial, auditing, clerical, shipping, and still other members of the personnel, who by their skill and accuracy and reliability, and devotion to a trust, have built for themselves all those outstanding cooperative privileges above listed. They serve between the factory and YOU. They personally convey the product to the people. The office records show that they do this thing surpassingly well. And letters from just about everybody everywhere attest extravagantly in their behalf

AND OF COURSE

The dealers—the middle men—the keystone men—the over-the counter men—whose dependability in keeping Maximo Products within your every momentary call has made them the distinguished service experts in your community. Organized as they now are on the LIGGETT PLAN and backed by Maximo in every promise and in every transaction they make, these dealers—almost ten thousand of them!—are, too, actual members of the company as well as mercantile missionaries to your homes

[Here a row of illustrations in color of certain standard products]

AND SO—PRESENT CUSTOMERS and FUTURE CUSTOMERS—know that the Maximo Products House is in great order, that down to the last kiddie born to the latest employee there is a unity of spirit and enterprise focusing always in YOUR service and welfare. Join the happy and wholesome family if you have not already done so, for to be identified with such a goodly company is really to be a policy-holder in merchandising insurance. *The Monthly Maximo* will come to you regularly if you don't mind. On page twenty of this issue you will find initial ordering made easy. Please look it up?

CHAPTER FIVE

FIGURES OF SPEECH AND RELATED TERMS

Figures of speech have been called the romance of composition. They are derived from feeding thought with imagination. They exist, not at all because some one first devised and defined them and then set about speaking and writing in accordance with his device and his definition, but because somebody was at a loss to express himself in a new experience. The best he could do in the emergency was to strike up a resemblance, and primitive man did it very well (as children do), as witness fire-water for whisky, happy hunting-ground for heaven, iron-horse for steam engine. These are romantic expressions yet, even tho they are now somewhat hackneyed.

Figures of speech are devices, both comparative and mechanical, used for the purpose of beautifying, clarifying, vivifying, energizing, and picturizing language. They lift language out of the merely literal or ordinary ways of expression into striking and arresting and memorable phraseology. In strictly literal, man-of-the-street English Macbeth would have said "I am no longer young" or "My youth is passing." But Macbeth was a personality of tragic and intriguing interest, and it was fitting that he should express himself in this way (Act V, Scene iii):

My way of life
Is fallen into the sear, the yellow leaf;

and thus build into the expression a connotation that evokes pity, fear, reminiscence, tragic consequence, and still more. The expression, in other words, has "overflow" or "radiation"; it means more than meets the ear.

The language of romance is aided by figures of feeling and content; the language of realism, by figures of form and workmanship. The figures of romance have to do with resemblances and comparisons; the figures of realism with mechanics and arrangement. Loosely grouped or classified, the former include simile, metaphor, personification, apostrophe, vision, prolepsis, allegory,

78

metonymy, synecdoche, exclamation, interrogation; the latter include antithesis, parallelism, climax, anticlimax, litotes, inversion, repetition, hendiadys, alliteration, onomatopœia, euphemism, epigram, epithet, hyperbole, irony, paradox, oxymoron.

But as realism and romanticism are themselves inextricably mixed in literature, so these figurative vehicles of expression are impossible of rigid classification. A simile may be worked out with such thorogoing nicety as to make it quite as much a figure of form as of resemblance (see page 121). The figures of exclamation and interrogation, while usually the most emotional and spontaneous of all, are nevertheless sometimes wrought and placed with mechanical precision.

Strictly speaking, a different kind of word used to convert the literal into the pictorial is called a *trope;* a different arrangement of words, a *figure of speech* proper. Those in the first classification above are tropes, and those in the second, figures. But the term *figure* is used generally in reference to all, and this is as it should be, for the reason that the different kind and the different arrangement are so frequently used together to enforce and vivify and beautify both prose and poetry. *The king lay dead* is a most literal, not to say pedestrian, statement. Change in both kind (trope) and arrangement (figure) to *So like a shattered column lay the king,* and it has literary distinction.

The figures of sound—alliteration, hendiadys, euphemism, onomatopœia—are necessarily very often steeped in feeling, and like most other figures are as important for emotional emphasis as for intellectual emphasis. The pictorial quality of a good simile constitutes emphasis of content, but its very arrangement also yields structural emphasis. The arrangement of the parts of a sentence so that one balances or offsets another constitutes structural emphasis primarily, but such construction as a rule makes a strong appeal to the feelings. This latter is, however, not to be confused with mechanical emphasis—italics, capitalization, and other typographical variations (see page 70), tho all three methods for emphasis—contentual, structural, mechanical—are frequently to be found used together in figurative language in order to make the emphasis inescapable.

The list below includes the principal figures of speech as well as many other literary terms that pertain to figures and that belong to literary style in general. It is a brief style lexicon. The illustrative excerpts are taken chiefly from poetry, tho many are from prose. Figures of speech are used in both prose and poetry, but in the latter more abundantly.

Acrostic is a verse or prose writing in which certain letters (usually the first or last of each line), read up and down, form a word, name, phrase, motto, or sentence. There are numerous arrangements of acrostic; usually the first letters, read vertically, yield the secret. When the end letters do it, the acrostic is called a *telestich*. In the following sonnet by Edgar Allan Poe the acrostic begins with the first letter and is then continued with the second letter of the second verse, the third letter of the third verse, the fourth letter of the fourth verse, and so on, the name *Sarah Anna Lewis* having fourteen letters in it, and the last letter of the name being the fourteenth letter in the fourteenth verse:

AN ENIGMA

"Seldom we find," says Solomon Don Dunce,
"Half an idea in the profoundest sonnet.
Through all the flimsy things we see at once
As easily as through a Naples bonnet—
Trash of all trash!—how can a lady don it?
Yet heavier far than your Petrarchan stuff—
Owl-downy nonsense that the faintest puff
Twirls into trunk-paper the while you con it."
And veritably, Sol is right enough.
The general tuckermanities are arrant
Bubbles—ephemeral and so transparent—
But this is, now—you may depend upon it—
Stable, opaque, immortal—all by dint
Of the dear names that lie concealed within't

Allegory in the strictly figurative sense means the continuance of a figure of speech thru many verses or thru a whole work, either prose or poetry. The thought or symbolism of allegory is expressed thru simile, metaphor, personification, and still other figures. "Allegory," said Samuel Taylor Coleridge, "is the employment of a set of agents and images (figures) to convey in disguise a moral meaning—those agents and images being so combined as to form a homogeneous whole."

Shelley's *The Cloud* is one continuous personification, and in toto is, therefore, a poetical allegory.

I bring fresh showers for the thirsting flowers,
From the seas and the streams;
I bear light shade for the leaves when laid
In their noonday dreams.

From my wings are shaken the dews that waken
  The sweet birds every one,
When rocked to rest on their mother's breast,
  As she dances about the sun.
I wield the flail of the lashing hail,
  And whiten the green plains under;
And then again I dissolve it in rain,
  And laugh as I pass in thunder.

I sift the snow on the mountains below,
  And their great pines groan aghast;
And all the night 't is my pillow white,
  While I sleep in the arms of the blast.
Sublime on the towers of my skyey bowers,
  Lightning, my pilot, sits;
In a cavern under is fettered the thunder,
  It struggles and howls by fits;
Over earth and ocean, with gentle motion,
  This pilot is guiding me,
Lured by the love of the genii that move
  In the depths of the purple sea;
Over the rills, and the crags, and the hills,
  Over the lakes and the plains,
Wherever he dream, under mountain or stream,
  The spirit he loves remains;
And I all the while bask in heaven's blue smile,
  Whilst he is dissolving in rains.

The sanguine sunrise, with his meteor eyes,
  And his burning plumes outspread,
Leaps on the back of my sailing rack
  When the morning star shines dead;
As on the jag of a mountain crag,
  Which an earthquake rocks and swings,
An eagle alit one moment may sit
  In the light of its golden wings.
And when sunset may breathe, from the lit sea beneath,
  Its ardors of rest and of love,
And the crimson pall of eve may fall
  From the depth of heaven above,
With wings folded I rest on my airy nest,
  As still as a brooding dove.

That orbèd maiden, with white fire laden,
  Whom mortals call the moon,
Glides glimmering o'er my fleece-like floor,
  By the midnight breezes strewn;
And wherever the beat of her unseen feet,
  Which only the angels hear,
May have broken the woof of my tent's thin roof,
  The stars peep behind her and peer;
And I laugh to see them whirl and flee,
  Like a swarm of golden bees,
When I widen the rent in my wind-built tent,
  Till the calm river, lakes, and seas,

Like strips of the sky fallen through me on high,
Are each paved with the moon and these.

I bind the sun's throne with a burning zone,
And the moon's with a girdle of pearl;
The volcanoes are dim, and the stars reel and swim,
When the whirlwinds my banner unfurl
                    PERCY BYSSHE SHELLEY, *The Cloud*

The continuance of the personification in the following excerpt
from *The Vision of Sir Launfal* constitutes allegory in the strictly
artistic and literary sense; the moral quality usually so insistently
present in such full-length allegories as Edmund Spenser's *The
Faërie Queene* and John Bunyan's *The Pilgrim's Progress*, of
course, is not present.

Down swept the chill wind from the mountain peak,
    From the snow five thousand summers old;
On open wold and hill-top bleak
    It had gathered all the cold,
And whirled it like sleet on the wanderer's cheek;
It carried a shiver everywhere
From the unleafed boughs and pastures bare;
The little brook heard it and built a roof
'Neath which he could house him, winter-proof;
All night by the white stars' frosty gleams
He groined his arches and matched his beams;
Slender and clear were his crystal spars
As the lashes of light that trim the stars;
He sculptured every summer delight
In his halls and chambers out of sight;
Sometimes his tinkling waters slipt
Down through a frost-leaved forest-crypt,
Long, sparkling aisles of steel-stemmed trees
Bending to counterfeit a breeze;
Sometimes the roof no fretwork knew
But silvery mosses that downward grew;
Sometimes it was carved in sharp relief
With quaint arabesques of ice-fern leaf;
Sometimes it was simply smooth and clear
For the gladness of heaven to shine through, and here
He had caught the nodding bulrush-tops
And hung them thickly with diamond-drops,
That crystalled the beams of moon and sun,
And made a star of every one:
No mortal builder's most rare device
Could match this winter-palace of ice;
'T was as if every image that mirrored lay
In his depths serene through the summer day,
Each fleeting shadow of earth and sky,
    Lest the happy model should be lost,
Had been mimicked in fairy masonry
    By the elfin builders of the frost
        JAMES RUSSELL LOWELL, *The Vision of Sir Launfal*

Alliteration is the repetition of the same sound in consecutive or almost consecutive words. Usually the repetition is at the beginning of words or *initial alliteration,* but it may also be at the end —*final alliteration*—or in the middle—*medial alliteration.* The alliteration is *merged* when it occurs in more than one place in a given line, as

> The *s*ulfurou*s* ri*fts* of pa*ss*ion and woe
> JAMES RUSSELL LOWELL

In general, however, alliteration refers to repetition of initial letters in successive words, as

> The *f*urrow *f*ollowed *f*ree
> SAMUEL TAYLOR COLERIDGE

Alliteration is common to epigram (see page 94), hendiadys (see page 98), epithet (see page 95), onomatopœia (see page 107), and still other figures, and it is very often due to the alliteration in household proverbs that they are so easily remembered and thus become proverbs. Used with restraint alliteration adds beauty and memorableness to both prose and poetry. Used to excess, it begets a kind of claptrap that is downright damaging to expression. In early English poetry alliteration was a major device, but it is today a subordinate one, only so much of it being employed as makes for euphony (see page 97). It is considered somewhat better art to use alliterative sounds, not in successive words, but in occasional or alternate ones. It is thus made insinuating rather than aggressive, accidental rather than designed and tricky. Alfred Tennyson's "misty moonshine" and "his heavy shotted hammock-shroud," Percy Bysshe Shelley's "though frosts may blight the freshness of its bloom," and James Young's

> When fortitude has lost its fire
> And freezes into fear

are excellent illustrations of the artistic use of alliteration. It is obvious that many of the catchy advertising slogans depend for their catchiness and their lastingness, for that matter, upon alliteration. And such expressions as these have become current for the same reason, the sound doing more to perpetuate them in most cases than any logic of meaning:

> blind as a bat, brown as a berry, cool as a cucumber, dead as a doornail, fit as a fiddle, flat as a flounder, good as gold, part and parcel, rough and ready, safe and sound, spick and span, through thick and thin, tip to toe (see also pages 96 and 127)

Allusion in the literary sense is a reference to contemporary or past events or personages. Classical allusion means that the reference is made to something belonging to the classical—Greek and Latin—periods of history and literature. John Milton's poetry has been called classical poetry partly because it abounds with allusion, as

> But come, thou goddess fair and free,
> In Heaven yclept Euphrosyne

and

> Hence, loathèd Melancholy,
> Of Cerberus and Blackest Midnight born

Allusion must be quite sure of itself; that is, it must be both accurate and applicable. To pay compliment to Bacchus, the ancient god of wine, at a prohibition dinner or in a temperance poem would not be "in keeping." Do not attempt to call the ancient gods and goddesses and muses into your speaking and writing unless you know what they stand for and are quite sure that your reference to them is appropriate.

Ambiguity is not a figure of speech (see page 172), but it may easily result from the use or the misuse of figures of speech. In ordinary composition ambiguity arises when ideas are so loosely put together that either one of two meanings may be taken from an expression. It is sometimes colloquially used to refer to expression that conveys more than two meanings. In *John told Bill that his work was done* the reference of *his* may be *John* and it may be *Bill*. The sentence is therefore ambiguous. John Ruskin wrote in *Munera Pulveris:*

> We don't want to produce more fuel just now, but much less, and to use what we get for cooking and warming ourselves, instead of for running from place to place

His omission of *for* before *warming* makes *ourselves* the object of both *cooking* and *warming*. In the following use of inversion (see page 103) Thomas Gray got himself wrongly accused of solecism:

> The boast of heraldry, the pomp of power,
> And all that beauty, all that wealth e'er gave,
> Awaits alike th' inevitable hour—
> The paths of glory lead but to the grave

Hour is the subject of *awaits*, not *boast* and *pomp* and *all* as more than one editor has erroneously supposed. There is, however, apparent ambiguity caused by this inversion. While the mixed metaphor (see page 91) is not completely ambiguous, it nevertheless has the elements of ambiguity in it.

Amplification is a kind of repetition, made for the purpose of insuring the understanding of a point. As in music the musician takes a chord and builds upon it and expands it—*amplifies* it— until he has a complete musical composition, so in speaking and writing the author may take a saying and amplify it into a theme. You amplify a composition subject. Amplification is especially important in oratory, for the ear has but fleeting memory and much may be lost in an orator's efforts unless he takes pains to amplify his points for the sake of impressing them. In printed matter it is the privilege of the reader to turn back if need be in order to gather points here and there. Still, even in writing, the practise of amplifying without becoming repetitious and monotonous is to be recommended. If you touch your important points too lightly you may fail to fix any in your reader's mind. The refrain in the old ballad was a form of continuous amplification for the sake of "aural contagion." It must not be overdone, however, or mere wordiness will result.

But amplification at its probable worst is illustrated in this poem, written by Francis Quarles in amplification of Psalm xxxi: 11—*My life is spent with grief, and my years with sighing.* It runs to forty-eight verses, the following being the first ten. A critic has said that Quarles took pains to gild the lily in dull finish.

> What sullen star ruled my untimely birth,
> That would not lend my days one hour of mirth?
> How oft have these bare knees been bent to gain
> These slender alms of one poor smile in vain?
> How often, tired with the fastidious light,
> Have my faint lips implored the shades of night?
> How often have my nightly torments prayed
> For ling'ring twilight, glutted with the shade?
> Day worse than night, night worse than day appears;
> In fears I spend my nights, my days in tears. . . .

Anacoluthon is an incoherent or grammatically inconsistent expression. Grammatically it may be run-on construction; it may be confusion of tense or person; it may be illogical or inharmonious arrangement of parts. The following is a common type of grammatical anacoluthon, especially in the conclusion of letters:

> We shall be pleased, therefore, if you will kindly look into the matter, and awaiting a reply we assure you, sir, of our very best wishes at all times

Obviously, the first sentence should be ended after the word *matter*. Note the following example from John Milton:

> Both turned, and under open sky adored
> The God that made both sky, earth, air, and heaven,
> And starry pole. Thou also madest the night,
> Maker Omnipotent, and Thou the day

Here *both* refers to five rather than to two, and the third person of the first two verses is changed to second in the last two. This pàrticular form of solecism (see page 610) may, however, be used rhetorically for humor or energy or dramatic effect, and thus become a figure similar to *aposiopesis* (see page 89), that is, the deliberate breaking off of an expression and the immediate continuance with a new one that is unrelated and irreconcilable to it. Grammatical anacoluthon usually happens thru carelessness; rhetorical anacoluthon is designed.

Analogy is a resemblance drawn between two things in which the resemblance is itself analyzed to some extent. It is specifically a resemblance of relations, and is a more deliberate comparison than is indicated by the simile (see page 119). It has been aptly called applied example. The following taken from Abraham Lincoln's address at Cooper Institute, February 27, 1860, illustrates:

> But you will not abide the election of a Republican president! In that supposed event, you say, you will destroy the Union; and then, you say, the great crime of having destroyed it will be upon us! That is cool. A highwayman holds a pistol to my ear, and mutters through his teeth, "Stand and deliver, or I will kill you, and then you will be a murderer!" Same in principle

Anticlimax is the opposite of climax (see page 92). It is used to bemean or to make little or laughable or inferior. It is achieved by devices exactly the opposite of those employed for building climax, that is, by arranging successive words, phrases, clauses, sentences, and paragraphs in less interesting and important order. Impressions are weakened by anticlimax as expression continues. The most striking trick in the construction of anticlimax is that of permitting thought to build toward what promises to be climax, and then suddenly letting it down to a weak or ridiculous ending. Intentionally used, anticlimax makes as a rule for comic or ironic effects; unintentionally used, it is, of course, a rhetorical blunder. The dash is frequently used for structural emphasis before the final step of an anticlimactic sequence. Following are examples of literary anticlimax:

Not louder shrieks to pitying heaven are cast
When husbands or when lapdogs breathe their last
ALEXANDER POPE

What female heart can gold despise?
What cat's averse to fish?
THOMAS GRAY

The Chief-Justice was rich, quiet, and—infamous
THOMAS BABINGTON MACAULAY

Is it not monstrous that this player here,
But in a fiction, in a dream of passion,
Could force his soul so to his own conceit,
That from her working all his visage wann'd,
Tears in his eyes, distraction in's aspect,
A broken voice, and his whole function suiting
With forms to his conceit? And all for nothing!
WILLIAM SHAKESPEARE

Antithesis is the forceful expression of contrast. It is constructed usually by the paralleling of adversative clauses, one showing the applicable side of the thought and the other the inapplicable side. Wit, brilliance, cleverness are usually expressed antithetically, but such expression may easily be overdone, thus resulting in mere pyrotechnics rather than in steady illumination. Alexander Pope, who was a master of this style, nevertheless reproved a contemporary who followed it, in these words:

His wit all see-saw, between that and this,
Now high, now low, now master up, now miss,
And he himself one vile antithesis

The balanced sentence is most commonly used for throwing one expression into strong relief by another, as

Contempt is the proper punishment of affectation, and detestation is the just consequence of hypocrisy
SAMUEL JOHNSON

They never taste who always drink:
They always talk who never think
MATTHEW PRIOR

Epigram (page 94) and paradox (page 110) and antithesis frequently occur together.

Stone walls do not a prison make,
Nor iron bars a cage
RICHARD LOVELACE

In this antithesis there is chiasmus (see page 92):

His back was turned, but not his brightness hid
JOHN MILTON

Antonomasia is the appropriate use of a proper name or descriptive epithet for some one rather than his own name. The Czar was called *Little Father;* a wise man is sometimes called a *Solomon;* Napoleon was dubbed *The Little Corporal.* Charles Dickens made use of antonomasia in calling Mme. DeFarge *The Vengeance* in *A Tale of Two Cities.*

Apheresis is the dropping of an unaccented letter or syllable from the beginning of a word, as *squire* for *esquire, neath* for *beneath, mend* for *amend, dobe* for *adobe.* When the first letter only is dropt, and when such shortening is gradual and unintentional, the process is sometimes called *aphesis.* In the early stages of such shortening the apostrophe is used—'*dobe,* '*mend*—but this is gradually dropt also and the short form stands as a complete word. By extension apheresis may mean the dropping of the whole first part of a word or phrase or sentence or longer expression, as *bus* for *omnibus, cello* for *violoncello, phone* for *telephone.* It may thus be any conversational shortcut, such as *Coming?* for *Are you coming? See?* for *Do you see? And then?* for *What happened then?* The term *prosiopesis* is sometimes used for apheresis in the latter extended forms.

Aphorism or *apothem,* according to John Morley, is "the compression of a mass of thought and observation into a single saying . . . It conveys some portion of a truth with such point as to set us thinking on what remains." It is somewhat similar, therefore, to epigram (see page 94). Unlike the axiom, the aphorism states a truth without the enforcement of teaching. Aphorism is good in proportion as it is the outgrowth of its author's experience; hence, the aphorisms of Poor Richard (Benjamin Franklin) are among the best to be found. Essayists and poets have for centuries kept notebooks in which they jotted down experiential aphorisms later to be developed into essays or poems. Bacon, Overbury, Pope, Walton, Emerson, Thoreau, are a few of the great aphorists in the field of English literature. One of the most pointed aphorisms on record is that of Henry Wotton, who suffered for saying that an ambassador is an honest man sent to lie abroad for his country. And Jonathan Swift's equally pointed one, for which he also suffered, is this: "Happiness is the perpetual possession of being well deceived."

Apolog is a kind of fable or moral tale, one that is derived for the most part from oriental environment and character, and in which the emphasis is placed upon the instruction contained rather than upon the method of narration. It therefore contains most of the qualities of the parable, but it is usually told thru the medium of animals or inanimate objects of nature. The following apolog of Jotham (Judges ix:6) is one of the best in all literature:

> And all the men of Shechem assembled themselves together, and all the house of Millo, and went and made Abimelech king, by the oak of the pillar that was in Shechem. And when they told it to Jotham, he went and stood in the top of Mount Gerizim, and lifted up his voice, and cried, and said unto them, Hearken unto me, ye men of Shechem, that God may hearken unto you. The trees went forth on a time to anoint a king over them; and they said unto the olive tree, Reign thou over us. But the olive tree said unto them, Should I leave my fatness, wherewith by me they honor God and man, and go to wave to and fro over the trees? And the trees said to the fig tree, Come thou and reign over us. But the fig tree said unto them, Should I leave my sweetness, and my good fruit, and go to wave to and fro over the trees? And the trees said unto the vine, Come thou and reign over us. And the vine said unto them, Should I leave my new wine, which cheereth God and man, and go to wave to and fro over the trees? Then said all the trees unto the bramble, Come thou and reign over us. And the bramble said unto the trees, If in truth ye anoint me king over you, then come and take refuge in my shade: and if not, let fire come out of the bramble and devour the cedars of Lebanon. Now therefore, if ye have dealt truly and uprightly, in that ye have made Abimelech king, and if ye have dealt well with Jerubbaal and his house, and have done unto him according to the deserving of his hands (for my father fought for you, and adventured his life, and delivered you out of the hand of Midian, and you are risen up against my father's house this day, and have slain his sons, threescore and ten persons, upon one stone, and have made Abimelech, the son of his maid-servant, king over the men of Shechem, because he is your brother); if ye then have dealt truly and uprightly with Jerubbaal and with his house this day, then rejoice ye in Abimelech and let him also rejoice in you: But if not, let fire come out from Abimelech, and devour the men of Shechem and the house of Millo; and let fire come out from the men of Shechem, and from the house of Millo, and devour Abimelech. And Jotham ran away, and fled, and went to Beer, and dwelt there for fear of Abimelech his brother

Aposiopesis is an abrupt curtailment or stoppage of a word or phrase or sentence or longer form of expression, as the long-since adopted *chapel* for *chapelle* and *program* for *programme*. It is one of the principal sources of shortcuts and slang—*photo* for *photograph, spec* for *speculation, exam* for *examination, L* for *elevated road;* it is also a common form in conversational English —"Stop it or I'll" . . . "Give me my hat or you'll" . . . , and so forth. In literary usage, especially in oratory, it means the sudden and deliberate break in a train of thought for the sake of dramatic effect (see *anacoluthon,* page 85). This, while it commonly causes what the rhetoricians have called a "grammatical earthquake," is nevertheless a justifiable violation of the principle of coherence for the sake of the ends to be achieved. It is customarily signaled by the dash, as the following examples indicate:

> I never had shade or shadow of a doubt of my petrified and indestructible honesty until now—and now, under the very first big and real temptation, I—Edward, it is my belief that this town's honesty is as rotten as mine is; as rotten as yours
>
> MARK TWAIN

> Ay me, I fondly dream!
> Had ye been there—for what could that have done?
>
> JOHN MILTON

> Be still a symbol of immensity;
> A firmament reflected in a sea;
> An element filling the space between;
> An unknown—but no more: we humbly screen
> With uplift hands our foreheads. . . .
>
> JOHN KEATS

Apostrophe is addressing some one or something absent as if present, the dead or inanimate as if capable of response. It is second-personal, whereas personification (see page 114) is third-personal. The orator commonly appeals to the absent, invokes some dead patriot, apostrophizes a historical memory, in order to emotionalize his effects. Observe these samples of apostrophe:

> Frailty, thy name is woman
>
> WILLIAM SHAKESPEARE

> Milton! thou shouldst be living at this hour
>
> WILLIAM WORDSWORTH

> These were thy charms, sweet village! sports like these,
> With sweet succession taught e'en toil to please
>
> OLIVER GOLDSMITH

> Hold, hold, my heart:
> And you, my sinews, grow not instant old,
> But bear me stiffly up
>
> WILLIAM SHAKESPEARE

Asyndeton (not linked or connected) is the omission of connectives for the sake of directness and energy. The most famous example, perhaps, is Julius Cæsar's *Veni, vidi, vici*—I came, I saw, I conquered. The abruptness caused by the omission of conjunctions gives a sense of speed and precision and decisiveness. Insert the connectives—*I came and I saw and I conquered*—and you slacken the pace, make the idea leisurely instead of swift. The opposite of asyndeton is *polysyndeton* (much linked or connected). Biblical style sometimes illustrates this excessive use of connectives—*And he spoke and said*. Rhetorically the complete connection or overconnection of expressional units gives them ease and poise and simplicity, retards the pace for deliberation or meditation. Note in the following that anaphora (page 117) is achieved thru polysyndeton:

> And there the King will know me and my love,
> And there the Queen herself will pity me,
> And all the gentle court will welcome me,
> And after my long voyage I shall rest!
>
> ALFRED TENNYSON

Bathos is a sudden fall from worthy and dignified expression to unworthy and undignified expression. It occurs not infrequently in conversational description. Continued anticlimax (see page 86) is likely to descend to the level of bathos. The young woman who said that she thought Niagara Falls *"majestic* and just too *cute* for anything"* descended from the sublime to the ridiculous in her description. The following couplet by Alexander Pope, of which a war steed is the subject, illustrates further:

> His eye-balls burn, he wounds the smoking plain,
> And knots of scarlet ribbon deck his mane

Bombast is hyperbole (page 101) or climax (page 92) that "misses fire." It is inflated and extravagant expression "full of sound and fury signifying nothing." It results usually from insincere attempts to impress and from excessive or misapplied figures of speech. In the following couplet on bull-baiting the language is far too pretentious, too "big," too bombastic, therefore, for the thought contained; it is rant or grandiloquence:

> Up to the stars the sprawling mastiffs fly,
> And add new monsters to the frighted sky
>
> RICHARD BLACKMORE

Shakespeare applied the term to circumstance in *Othello* (Act I, Scene i) and thereby defined it.

> A bombast circumstance
> Horribly stuffed with epithets of war

Catachresis is a mixed metaphor (page 85), and, loosely used, any mixed figure. Do not mix either metaphors or similes. If you confuse your figures, or intermingle them too closely with literal language, you will convey absurd and laughable meanings. In "The Blankley branch office at York is once again tossed upon

the waves, a sheep without a shepherd," the meaning is evidently
that the branch manager has left or has been discharged, and that
this situation has existed frequently before. But to refer to the
branch office first as a ship, and then as a sheep, is quite incoherent. The illustration shows, however, that a mixed figure may
have value for purely humorous purposes. Note the absurd
mixture of literal with figurative language in this excerpt: "You
are now, my son, entering upon your life work, manufacturing.
Before you the doors of opportunity open wide, and like a colt
escaping from his tether, you launch forth to navigate the seas
of industry upon your own wings." There is also the classic
example of Addison's mixed figure, and Johnson's criticism of it.
Addison had written in his *A Letter from Italy:*

> Fired with that name, which I so oft have found
> The distant climes and different tongues resound,
> I bridle in my struggling Muse with pain,
> That longs to launch into a bolder strain
>
> JOSEPH ADDISON

This was Doctor Johnson's critical analysis of Addison's poetic
flight: "To *bridle a goddess* is no very delicate idea; but why
must she be *bridled?* because she *longs to launch;* an act which
was never hindered by *a bridle;* and whither will she *launch:*
into a *nobler strain.* She is in the first line a *horse,* in the second
a *boat;* and the care of the poet is to keep his *horse* or his *boat*
from *singing.*"

> SAMUEL JOHNSON, *Lives of the Poets.*

Chiasmus is throwing parallel expressions somewhat out of balance. Instead of expressing them *a b a b*, the writer expresses
them *a b b a* or otherwise, as John Milton's *Love without end,
and without mercy grace* and Henry Thoreau's *The waves generously rise and dash angrily,* instead of, respectively, *Love
without end, and grace without mercy* and *The waves generously
rise and angrily dash.* Chiasmus carries with it the emphasis of
variety and surprize. It must not be permitted, however, to
shock or confuse. The following, while a correct form of
chiasmus, is nevertheless strongly objected to by some editors.
He is a good worker not only, but as well a thorogoing student.
Inasmuch as *not only* and the correlative *as well* pertain each to
an entire clause, their placement is unimportant so long as each
is permitted to remain in the clause to which it belongs.

Climax is the arrangement of words and phrases and clauses in
a sentence, or of sentences in a paragraph, or of paragraphs in

an entire theme, so that each in turn rises in strength or interest or suspense or general importance of content above the other. In the shorter units of composition the periodicity of structure constitutes climax; in the longer, the deliberate delay of the most striking thoughts for presentation at or toward the end builds climax. The following arrangement for climax from Cicero's oration against Verres still remains the master example of this important figure. The verbs, it will be noted, build the climax:

> It is an outrage to bind a Roman citizen; to scourge him is an atrocious crime; to put him to death is almost parricide; but to crucify him—what shall I call it?

In the following poetical example climax is built by the accumulation of details in which nearly all parts of speech are involved:

> When, fast as shaft can fly,
> Bloodshot his eyes, his nostrils spread,
> The loose rein dangling from his head,
> Housing and saddle bloody red—
> Lord Marmion's steed rushed by
>
> WALTER SCOTT

The last speech of Othello (*Othello,* Act V, Scene ii) is one of the best examples of dramatic climax in our literature.

> Soft you; a word or two before you go.
> I have done the state some service, and they know't;—
> No more of that.—I pray you, in your letters,
> When you shall these unlucky deeds relate,
> Speak of me as I am; nothing extenuate,
> Nor set down aught in malice; then must you speak
> Of one that lov'd not wisely, but too well;
> Of one not easily jealous, but, being wrought,
> Perplex'd in the extreme; of one whose hand,
> Like the base Judean, threw a pearl away
> Richer than all his tribe; of one whose subdu'd eyes,
> Albeit unused to the melting mood,
> Drop tears as fast as the Arabian trees
> Their medicinal gum. Set you down this;
> And say, besides,—that in Aleppo once
> Where a malignant and a turban'd Turk
> Beat a Venetian and traduc'd the state,
> I took by the throat the circumcised dog,
> And smote him—thus
>
> WILLIAM SHAKESPEARE

The strictly correct use of climax presupposes that the sound and thought combine in the same word or phrase or longer expression. But in Edmund Burke's famous reversal of this rule consideration of sound alone was the guide (see page 187). In his *high crimes and misdemeanors* the least important but more high-sounding term is deliberately placed second, the more important but less high-sounding term first. Crimes are much more serious than misdemeanors—except to the ear. The reverberating echoism of *misdemeanors* leaves accusation in the very air. The colored preacher who dwelt tearfully but persistently upon *for the glory of God and Mesopotamia* just before the collection, attributed the bountiful contributions of his congregation to his placement of *Mesopotamia* after *God* rather than before.

Elision or *apocope* means the omission of letters from a word principally for the purpose of accommodating rhythm. When a word ends with a vowel, for instance, and the next word begins with one, the two may be merged by eliding the final vowel of the first, as in *L'Oiseau Bleu* rather than *Le Oiseau Bleu, t'afford* for *to afford,* th'*end* for *the end* (see also *aposiopesis,* page 89, *haplology* and *syncope,* page 122).

Ellipsis means the omission of words for the sake of economy, but without risking the conveyance of complete sense to an expression. In conversation words are commonly omitted. The subject of the second verb in a compound predicate is frequently elliptical. The *to* is elliptical in the infinitive after *please, bid, dare, let,* and other verbs (see page 174). We speak of the Atlantic for *The Atlantic Monthly* or the Atlantic Ocean. In poetry the demands of meter and rhythm make it desirable sometimes to omit words. Alexander Pope's

> Man never is, but always to be, blest

is rhythmically spoiled if *blest* is used also after *is.* Ellipsis is wrong in case the word to be supplied has not been used elsewhere and in the same form (see pages 174 and 209).

Epigram is a brief witty expression, finished, precise, cleverly turned. It is usually rhythmic, sometimes rimed, always complete in itself as far as meaning and construction are concerned. Close synonyms for epigram are adage, aphorism, axiom, dictum, maxim, motto, precept, proverb, saw, truism. The Greek original of the word meant inscription, as for a monument or tombstone, but the word *epitaph* is now used in this connection and *epigram* is applied to apt sayings, quotations, slogans—any short pointed expression that "sticks" in the mind. A couplet or quatrain or other brief form of versification is, by extension of definition, also called an epigram. An epitaph on a tombstone may be both epigrammatic and epithetical (see next page), as

Beneath this stone there lies interred
In cruel death's rigidity,
A man who always broke his word
With exquisite stupidity

The following have the pith and smack and finality of the true epigram:

An apple a day keeps the doctor away

A little learning is a dangerous thing

Let us be of good cheer, however, remembering that the misfortunes hardest to bear are those which never come

JAMES RUSSELL LOWELL

The three following resultant parallelisms (see page 111) are all epigrammatic:

How far that little candle throws its beam—
So shines a good deed in a naughty world!

WILLIAM SHAKESPEARE

Know then thyself, presume not God to scan—
The proper study of mankind is man

ALEXANDER POPE

Ward has no heart, they say; but I deny it:
He has a heart, and gets his speeches by it

SAMUEL ROGERS

Epithet is a term or short expression so happily composed and applied that it comes to have immediate association with the subject with which it is used. The adjective and the noun are usually wed in forming the lasting epithet, and alliteration (page 83), hendiadys (page 98), epigram (page 94), periphrasis (page 114), and still other turns of expression are frequently called upon to add piquancy and aptness. Sometimes the epithet is merely decorative, as in Alfred Tennyson's "misty moonshine" and George Eliot's "slanting sunbeams." Sometimes its value lies in its sheer descriptive compactness, in its potent "capsule quality," as in George Chapman's "solid flames" for precious stones, John Keats' "the green and juicy hay" for grass, Homer's "swift-footed Achilles." Many popular advertising slogans depend upon epithet quality for their permanence, and our everyday conversation abounds in epithetical phrases. Following is a list of some of the most outworn epithets, combining various other figures in their make-up. Whether he wills or not, many of these "creep and intrude and climb" into the average individual's speaking and writing every day:

advice and counsel
aid and comfort
alive and kicking
all in all
better or worse
body and soul
bread and butter
by and large
cats and dogs
do or die
down and out
each and every
fame and fortune
fast and loose
fine and dandy
fire and water
flesh and blood
forgive and forget
free and easy
gall and wormwood
gay and lively
give and take
good and all
goods and chattels
grand and glorious
hale and hearty
hammer and tongs

hand and foot
hand and glove
hand to mouth
hard and fast
head and shoulders
heart and soul
heaven and earth
here and there
hide and seek
hit or miss
hook or crook
house and home
hue and cry
joy and solace
length and breadth
letter and spirit
long and short
man and message
milk and honey
now or never
null and void
one and all
one and same
over and above
over and done with
peace and plenty
pillar to post

quit and quittance
rain or shine
rank and file
rime and reason
root and branch
safe and sane
short and sweet
shoulder to shoulder
sink or swim
sixes and sevens
take or leave
time and tide
tooth and nail
top and bottom
touch and go
up and doing
up and down
warp and woof
ways and means
wear and tear
well and good
whim and fancy
wild and woolly
wish and will
yea and nay
you and yours
young and foolish

bell, book, and candle
cribbed, cabined, and confined
eat, drink, and be merry
first, last, and always
health, wealth, and beauty
healthy, wealthy, and wise
here, there, and everywhere
hop, skip, and jump

life, liberty, and the pursuit of
   happiness
lock, stock, and barrel
love, honor, and obey
stop, look, and listen
time, place, and the girl
way, shape, and form
wine, woman, and song

Euphemism is an unoffending term used for an unpleasant or disagreeable thing, or the use of mild terms for strong ones in the effort to spare the feelings of others. In primitive times euphemism (as well as euphemistic behavior) supposedly warded off the wrath of evil spirits. The supposed bad gods were given pretty names, as well as presents, in order that they might thus be placated. The term *passed on* is euphemistic for *died,* as are *mistake* for *crime, error* for *lie, plain* for *ugly, appropriated* for *stolen, under the weather* for *drunk, inexpensive* for *cheap.* It is sometimes used very much as litotes. During the World War, for instance, that part of the sea thickly laid with mines was said to be "not too healthy for vessels." Note also these examples:

After life's fitful fever, he sleeps well
WILLIAM SHAKESPEARE

..........and, as you say,
There was a'gaming; there *o'ertook* in's rouse
WILLIAM SHAKESPEARE
How sleep the brave who sink to rest
By all their country's wishes blest!
WILLIAM COLLINS

Euphony refers to sound. Literally it means "well sounding." In all writing and speaking the aim should be to make composition sound well, unless of course deliberate pains are taken to accumulate discordance (see page 107) for special effects. Euphony is not a figure of speech, but it is part and parcel of most figurative language. The harsher sounding letters of the alphabet are *g, h, j, k, s, t, x, z;* the smoother sounding ones are *b, f, l, m, n, r, v, w.* Lullabies are written with the latter predominant; invectives, with the former. This is not to say that a speaker or a writer deliberately sets about securing euphonious letters in a theme, tho he may do so; but it does mean that "polishing" a work after the actual composition is completed should include the deletion of uneuphonious terms and the substitution of euphonious ones. And this is especially true of poetry and oratory, both of which are highly concerned with sound values. The following stanza on Italian from Byron's *Beppo* is interesting in connection with the subject of euphony:

I love the language, that soft bastard Latin,
    Which melts like kisses from a female mouth,
And sounds as if it should be writ on satin,
    With syllables which breathe of the sweet south,
And gentle liquids gliding all so pat in,
    That not a single accent seems uncouth,
Like our harsh northern whistling, grunting, guttural,
Which we're obliged to hiss and spit and sputter all
GEORGE GORDON NOEL BYRON

Euphuism is a style of writing that became the vogue in Elizabethan England as result of John Lyly's *Euphues and his England.* Its influence was felt by Shakespeare himself, one of his most notable euphuistic passages being in Act I, Scene ii of *The Merchant of Venice.* Antithesis, alliteration, simile, allusion, and numerous illustrations and resemblances based upon the natural sciences—botany, zoology, mineralogy—as these were known at the time, characterize this highly artificial style. The following illustrates:

The *s*un *s*hineth upon the *d*unghill and is *n*ot *c*orrupted; the *d*iamond lieth in the fire and is *n*ot *c*onsumed; the *c*rystal *t*oucheth *t*he *t*oad and is not poisoned

Any highly balanced or otherwise artificial style is now referred to as euphuistic. Walter Scott burlesqued this false fashion in Sir Pierce Shafton's talk in *The Monastery*. The monotonous artificiality of euphuism prevented its ever becoming more than a merely temporary fashion. It nevertheless had an extraordinary contemporary vogue and its influence is still felt to some small extent.

Exclamation, as a figure of speech, means the turning of an assertion or a denial or a question into the exclamatory form in order to accentuate its importance. Used in this way for rhetorical and emotional effects it is called *rhetorical exclamation.* A question may be followed by the exclamation mark, and thus become the figure of exclamation. So also may a declarative sentence, and an imperative sentence. Everything depends upon the mood of expression. Exclamation is used figuratively in impassioned prose, oratory, and highly wrought poetry. The following excerpt from Daniel Webster's *First Bunker Hill Oration* illustrates the figurative use of exclamation:

> But—ah!—Him! the first great Martyr in this great cause! Him! the premature victim of his own self-devoting heart! Him! the head of our civil councils, and the destined leader of our military bands; whom nothing brought hither, but the unquenchable fire of his own spirit; Him! cut off by Providence, in the hour of overwhelming anxiety and thick gloom; falling ere he saw the star of his country rise; pouring out his generous blood like water, before he knew whether it would fertilize a land of freedom or of bondage! how shall I struggle with the emotions that stifle the utterance of thy name!—Our poor work may perish; but thine shall endure! This monument may moulder away; the solid ground it rests upon may sink down to a level with the sea; but thy memory shall not fail! Wheresoever among men a heart shall be found that beats to the transports of patriotism and liberty, its aspirations shall be to claim kindred with thy spirit!

Hendiadys is the use of two (or more) words, usually nouns, connected by *and,* one of which repeats the other adjectively. This is an oratorical figure, the sound and rhythm value of the "teamed" words having a moving effect and leaving a rounded-out impression. The fact that the two (or more) words mean the same thing is ignored as result of the aptness of pairing and the agreeableness of impression upon the ear. Edmund Burke's *waste and desolate;* Patrick Henry's *entreaty and supplication;* Abraham Lincoln's *conclusive and final;* Daniel Webster's *one and inseparable;* Woodrow Wilson's *the square and right thing,* and the everyday expressions *might and main, touch and go, by and large* are illustrative. The double or triple phrase is usually reducible to a single term of a word or two. John Milton's *with joy and tidings fraught* means *fraught with joyful tidings.* Daniel Webster's *one cause, one country, one heart,* means *unanimous patriotism.* William Shakespeare's *flint and hardness* means *flinty hardness* or *hard as flint.*

Hiatus means an opening, a gap, a failure to keep close together. In poetry it is the opposite of elision. *The infernal* requires for clear pronunciation a definite pause after *the* in order to catch the *i* in *infernal.* This poised stop or gap makes hiatus. Elision requires *th'infernal,* thus making the first syllable *th'in.*

Humor, according to George Eliot, is "thinking in jest while feeling in earnest." Humor is more sustained than wit (see page 123), more basic, more lasting, and therefore more general in its appeal. Wit sparkles; humor shines. It is, indeed, universal, whereas wit is special and fleeting. Humor is warm and tender, and has none of the "bite" in it that characterizes wit and sarcasm and irony (see pages 104, 118). Joseph Addison said that Wit married Mirth and that Humor was their child. Wit usually requires you to open your mouth to smile or to laugh aloud. Humor may do the same, but it is more likely to "tease your insides," to make your eyes sparkle, to cause you to pause in contemplation, even to make you weep gently, for humor may be pathetic as well as lively. Humor is always tolerant and sympathetic—it may make you pity some weak and helpless person without in the least wishing him different. Oliver Goldsmith considered that the height of the humorous was manifested by the fastidiousness of a noseless man in selecting his own snuff-box. An entire book may be continuously humorous, and humorous in event, in situation, in characterization, as, for instance, Mark Twain's *Tom Sawyer,* Miguel de Cervantes' *Don Quixote.* But an entire volume of "sustained" wit is as unthinkable as it would be undesirable.

Following is an excellent example of sustained humor, not without its element of pathos. A young upstart of a viscount is being humorously taken to task for poking fun—wit—at Cyrano de Bergerac's nose.* This is Cyrano's cue for enlarging upon the viscount's thrusts and going him one better. By the very extension of this speech Cyrano reveals his sensitiveness and at the same time plays to it with satisfaction.

* Reprinted from Charles Renauld's translation of *Cyrano de Bergerac* by permission of the publishers, Frederick A. Stokes Company. Copyright by Charles Renauld, 1898.

You might have said at least a hundred things
By varying the tone, . . . like this, suppose, . . .
Aggressive: "Sir, if I had such a nose
I'd amputate it!"　*Friendly:* "When you sup
It must annoy you, dipping in your cup;
You need a drinking-bowl of special shape!"
Descriptive: " 'Tis a rock! . . . a peak! . . . a cape!
—A cape, forsooth! 'Tis a peninsular!"
Curious: "How serves that oblong capsular?
For scissor-sheath? or pot to hold your ink?"
Gracious: "You love the little birds, I think?
I see you've managed with a fond research
To find their tiny claws a roomy perch!"
Truculent: "When you smoke your pipe . . . suppose
That the tobacco-smoke spouts from your nose—
Do not the neighbors, as the fumes rise higher,
Cry, terror-struck: 'The chimney is afire?' "
Considerate: "Take care, . . . your head bowed low
By such a weight . . . lest head o'er heels you go!"
Tender: "Pray get a small umbrella made,
Lest its bright color in the sun should fade!"
Pedantic: "That beast, Aristophanes,
Named Hippocamelelephantoles,
Must have possessed just such a solid lump
Of flesh and bone beneath his forehead's bump!"
Cavalier: "The last fashion, friend, that hook?
To hang your hat on? 'Tis a useful crook!"
Emphatic: "No wind, O majestic nose,
Can give *thee* cold!—save when the mistral blows!"
Dramatic: "When it bleeds, what a Red Sea!"
Admiring: "Sign for a perfumery!"
Lyric: "Is this a conch? . . . a Triton you?"
Simple: "When is the monument on view?"
Rustic: "That thing a nose? Marry-come-up!
'Tis a dwarf pumpkin, or a prize turnip!"
Military: "Point against cavalry!"
Practical: "Put it in a lottery!
Assuredly 'twould be the biggest prize!"
Or . . . parodying Pyramus' sighs . . .
"Behold the nose that mars the harmony
Of its master's phiz! Blushing its treachery!"
—Such, my dear sir, is what you might have said,
Had you of wit or letters the least jot;
But, O most lamentable man!—of wit
You never had an atom, and of letters
You have three letters only!—they spell Ass!
And, had you had the necessary wit,
To serve me all the pleasantries I quote
Before this noble audience, . . . e'en so,
You would not have been let to utter one—
Nay, not the half or quarter of such jest!
I take them from myself all in good part,
But not from any other man that breathes!
　　　　　　　EDMOND ROSTAND, *Cyrano de Bergerac*

Hypallage is the transference of epithet, that is, the transference of an adjective from the noun to which it belongs. The purpose of its use, if any, appears to be to give the reader or hearer pause—to make him dwell upon an expression—in order that he may fix the expression in his mind by making the proper adjustments. In Alfred Tennyson's oft-quoted line from *The Princess,*

> Robed in the long night of her deep hair,

it is obvious that *long* properly modifies *hair* and *deep* modifies *night*. Some one has called this a disjunctive oxymoron (see page 108), that is, an oxymoron in which the contradictory elements are separated. Similarly, Tennyson's "Melissa shook her doubtful curls" means literally "Doubtful Melissa shook her curls," and Goldsmith's "seated over a pensive dish of tea" means "pensively seated over a dish of tea." Again, Macaulay's "shouting streets," Wordsworth's "lowing meadows," Shelley's "wrinkled legends" all illustrate the transference of the adjective to a noun that it really does not modify, from the one (understood or elsewhere expressed) that it does. Note that the transference carries with it sometimes personification (see page 114), sometimes metonymy (see page 106), sometimes metaphor (see page 105), and still other figures.

Hyperbole is exaggeration for the sake of emphasis. As a matter of fact all figures of speech are hyperbolic. Hyperbole is overstatement made not for the purpose of deceiving but for the purpose, rather, of impressing. It is "apparent on its face." It may easily fall into mere emotional rant, and thus defeat its own end. The use of exaggerated adjectives and adverbs—*awfully lovely, excruciatingly hungry, staggeringly beautiful, outlandishly insulting*—is probably the commonest form of hyperbole. When you say "I have a thousand errands to do" you use hyperbole in the form of synecdoche (see page 123). When you say "He eats like a bear" you use hyperbole in form of simile (see page 119). When you say "This is a pretty kettle of fish" you use hyperbole in forms of irony (page 104) and metonymy (page 106), and so on. Hyperbole is frequently used for the sake of evoking prompt or unusual reactions, as when the small boy tells his mother that he is "hungry as a bear." When Ralph Waldo Emerson wrote

> Here once the embattled farmers stood,
> And fired the shot heard round the world

he deliberately overstated in order to stir pride and patriotism in the hearts of his countrymen. Note that the basis of his hyper-

bole is synecdoche. Any figure of speech may be used in the
sense of hyperbole. Note also the following:

Our tears shall seem the Irish seas,
We, floating islands, living Hebrides

JOHN MILTON

Shall blow the horrid deed in every eye
That tears shall drown the wind

WILLIAM SHAKESPEARE

Will all great Neptune's ocean wash this blood
Clean from my hand?

WILLIAM SHAKESPEARE

Falstaff sweats to death,
And lards the lean earth as he walks along

WILLIAM SHAKESPEARE

Hypobole is akin to paralipsis and euphemism (see pages 112 and
96) and is the opposite of hyperbole. It is deliberate understatement—sometimes misrepresentation—used for the purpose of
making people believe that you agree with them when the opposite is really the truth. Portia used the trick of hypobole—and
it is a rhetorical trick—when she pretended to go along with
Shylock in his demands for a pound of Antonio's flesh. He was
delighted with her attitude—until she discontinued her hypobole
and said "Tarry a little; there is something else." Then came her
confounding arguments that not one drop of blood was mentioned
in the bond, and that exactly one pound must be cut. Most
famous of all examples of hypobole in literature is Marc Antony's
opening of his funeral oration (*Julius Cæsar,* Act III, Scene ii),
in which he seems to concede everything.

I come to bury Cæsar, not to praise him.
The evil that men do lives after them;
The good is oft interrèd with their bones;
So let it be with Cæsar. The noble Brutus
Hath told you Cæsar was ambitious:
If it were so, it was a grievous fault,
And grievously hath Cæsar answer'd it

WILLIAM SHAKESPEARE

Hypocorisma is a kind of apostrophe or personification in which
pet names are accorded to inanimate things, as, *nightie* for night-
gown, *goody* or *goodie* for sweets, *drinkie* for drinking-cup,
bathies for bathing togs, *undies* for underwear. The pet name
quality is evidenced by the diminutive *ie* ending.

Innuendo is a hint or a suggestion instead of a complete statement. Well made, innuendo flatters the reader or hearer into the

mental act of supplying the complete statement and thus makes
him a party to the theme. In "Mr. Balaman has been playing
the races—and looks so!" there is an invitation to fill in the picture. Either Mr. Balaman has won, and looks prosperous, or he
has lost and looks the opposite. Similarly,

> A word to the wise is sufficient
> He accepted the job I offered him—and thus did me a very bad turn

Portia makes use of innuendo when she has the song about fancy
sung at Bassanio's choosing the caskets. She hints that the eyes
are not to be dazzled and deceived by the fanciful appeals of gold
and silver. He takes the cue by beginning "So (therefore) may
the outward shows be least themselves; the world is still deceived
with ornament." Gold and silver are the materials from which
outward shows and ornaments are made; hence, he chooses the
dull leaden casket which makes no appeal to the eyes at all.

Interrogation, as a figure of speech, means the turning of an assertion or a denial into question form in order to accentuate its
importance. It is sometimes called *rhetorical question*—a question
to which no answer is required or desired. It is a challenge, and
usually an ironic challenge, made with feeling. An answer to
a rhetorical question indeed would be superfluous, for the one
who makes interrogation in the figurative sense has already in
reserve in his own mind the answer that he wants to convey.
The figure of interrogation is an everyday conversational form.
What do you mean by doing such a thing? Do you mean to tell
me that you are not going? and the like, constitute figurative
interrogation. It is a favorite method in all kinds of literature,
especially in oratory and poetry. Note these few examples:
Marcus Brutus' "Who is here so base that would be a bondman?"
John Milton's "Who would not sing for Lycidas?" And Thomas
Jefferson's

> Sometimes it is said that man cannot be trusted with the government
> of himself. Can he then be trusted with the government of others?
> Or have we found angels in the form of kings to govern him? Let
> history answer this question

Inversion means the placement of words out of their natural
grammatical sequence in order to impress. It leads to climactic
expectation. There are three particular applications of inversion.
One is the reversed epithet or the placement of the adjective after
the noun it modifies—*the house beautiful;* one is the placement
of the preposition after its object—*This is the man you tell me of*

has a much more emphatic ring than *You tell me of this man* or *Of this man you tell me;* the third is the placement of the subject after the predicate—*Great is Diana of the Ephesians* and the famous first couplet of Alexander Pope's *Iliad,*

> Achilles' wrath, to Greece the direful spring
> Of woes unnumbered, heavenly goddess, sing!

Sometimes effective inversion is made by means of interrogation, as in "Hath not a Jew eyes?" for "A Jew hath eyes." Poets sometimes use inversion for the sake of rime and rhythm, but this may be a flaw in poetical composition and the sign of a careless poet. Inversion, especially the kind here referred to, is an important device for emphasis and is justifiably used for it in numerous literary passages.

Irony is expression that says the opposite of what is really meant. In original Greek it means dissimulation. As the appearance of the word implies, it means hardness of attitude. It is ridicule transparently disguised as compliment. In ordinary conversation such ironic expressions as *A nice one you are! A pretty mess you've got me into!* are frequently heard. In literature it is made a most effective weapon, especially when it is sustained with proper dignity. Jonathan Swift used it mercilessly; Henry Fielding, merely with intent to impress; William Makepeace Thackeray, with cynical disillusionment. Marc Antony in his famous speech in *Julius Cæsar* began with "honorable men" as a compliment and gradually shaded it into irony and from irony into sarcasm (see page 118) until in the minds of the mob the expression became a kind of abuse. When Henry Fifth says (Act I, Scene ii)

> We are glad the Dauphin is so pleasant with us:
> His present and your pains we thank you for,

he is, of course, ironic, for the Dauphin had sent the tennis balls to Henry to indicate that the British king is fit only for the lighter forms of recreation and not for war. Continuing, however, Henry no longer disguises his reaction by irony but openly menaces the Dauphin's ambassadors as follows:

> When we have matched our rackets to these balls,
> We will in France, by God's grace, play a set
> Shall strike his father's crown into the hazard

In act IV of *The Merchant of Venice,* when Shylock's case is going sadly against him, Gratiano ironically taunts him with

> A Daniel, still a Daniel say I; a second Daniel!
> I thank thee, Jew, for teaching me that word.

thus resorting to one of the bitterest forms of irony, namely, turning a person's words in upon himself. Socrates, as a teacher and arguer, assumed ignorance of a subject in order to draw his student or his opponent out; hence, the term Socratic irony. Irony in speech is conveyed in large measure by tone of voice; in writing, the exclamation mark helps to enforce it.

Litotes (*miosis*) is affirmation made by the negation or belittlement or understatement of an opposite idea. Its use for emphasis is usually effective for the reason that the average person, on hearing something less than truth or justice done a subject, is quick to supply justice in his own mind at least. Litotes is a figure common to argument and oratory of all kinds. It is devised by means of negatives in one form or another, as witness

> The immortal names that were not born to die
>
> I am not unmindful of your great kindnesses
>
> I am a citizen of no mean city
>
> > *Acts xxi: 39*
>
> No words of mine can all your merits tell—
> I'm not forgetful that you served me well
>
> > Whereof in Hell
> > Fame is not silent
> >
> > > JOHN MILTON

Metaphor has long been defined as an implied simile (see page 121); *simile* as an expanded metaphor. The dictionary says that a metaphor is the application of a name or a descriptive term to something to which it does not literally apply. To call a fire "a great beard of flame," as Æschylus did, is to be poetically emphatic and picturesque thru the medium of metaphor. The expression, moreover, has the vigor of directness. To say "a fire is like a great beard of flame" is a simile; the comparison is made deliberately thru the use of a word to indicate the comparison. Metaphor appears in everyday usage in connection with any and every subject. Most of our abstract nouns and many, even, of our concrete ones derive in metaphor, tho the figurative quality in most instances has for so long been taken for granted that we no longer think of them as metaphors. *Golden hair, pearly teeth, iron muscle, tiger scratch, horse sense*, are but a few of the numerous ones that are in common use.

It is to be borne in mind that the implied comparison must be limited and unusual. It is no metaphor to say *the man is a hero* for the more or less ordinary thing is for heroes always to be men, even tho men may not always be heroes. This is, moreover, the merest conversational instance (see page 121). But to say *the man is a lion in the fight* implies something out of the ordinary in human experience and at the same time creates a special and unusual picture in the mind. The metaphor, like many other figures of speech, may be negative as well as positive, as

> You are not wood, you are not stones, but men
> WILLIAM SHAKESPEARE

Note that the metaphor may be expressed by verb as well as by noun:

> Now leaps the wind on the sleepy march,
> And tramples the grass with terrified feet
> JAMES RUSSELL LOWELL

> The periods are marshaled in due order of procession, bright and high-stepping; they never escape under an impulse of emotion into the full current of a brimming stream
> JOHN MORLEY

> The richest author that ever grazed the common of literature
> SAMUEL JOHNSON

Metonymy is a change of name, made for striking or economical or other figurative effect. The attribute or accompaniment or action of a thing is used instead of the name of the thing itself. Or something connected with the thing may be used for its name. As in the case of metaphor, metonymy is part and parcel of our everyday conversation. We speak of the *heart* of the matter, of the *kernel* of the question, of the *hand* of fate, of the *kettle's* boiling, of the *crown's* desire, of the *pen's* being mightier than the *sword,* of the *pastor* of a *flock,* and so on, each one of the italicized words standing as a sign for a thing signified, as a container for the thing contained, or as an instrument for an agent. Some authorities call metonymy a metaphor in which either the thing compared or the comparison is named, but never both. When, for instance, it is said that a man's muscle is iron, both the thing compared—*muscle*—and the comparison itself—*iron*—are named. This, then, is a full and direct metaphor. But in the following famous line from Thomas Gray's *An Elegy Written in a Country Churchyard,*

> Each in his narrow *cell* forever laid,

the comparison only is given, the reader being obliged to infer the thing compared, namely, *grave.* The author used another term for *grave;* he changed the name of grave to *cell;* he thus made use of indirect metaphor, according to these authorities.

It is probably simpler, however, to call *cell* a metonymy, as most books do. Metonymy is one of the most popular and effective figures of speech in literary usage.

> The scepter, learning, physic must
> All follow this, and come to dust
> WILLIAM SHAKESPEARE

> Princes and lords may flourish or may fade—
> A breath can make them as a breath has made
> OLIVER GOLDSMITH

> The robust heart of the nation laid aside its quarrels
> JAMES ANTHONY FROUDE

Onomatopœia or *echoism* means name-making. The child does this when he calls an engine a *choo-choo* or an airplane a *buzz-buzz*. In literature it means the adaptation of sound to sense— making words echo their sense or sound like what they mean. The so-called Bow-Wow theory of the origin of language, long since exploded, contended that language came into being by this method. Primitive man heard a short, sharp noise, and he grunted *bang;* he heard rain dropping and he said *patter;* he encountered a serpent and he learned to say *hiss;* he listened to the brook and said *babble.* And so such words as *cuckoo, bark, croak, shriek, murmur, splash, cluck, coo, chirp, tinkle, twitter, rustle, mutter, rattle, clatter, sprinkle, nestle, frizzle, guzzle, glitter, shimmer,* and a host of other sound words, came into being. Like alliteration (see page 83) echoism is artistically used only when it satisfies and pleases the ear without shocking. When it evinces a straining after sound effects, it is of course bad. Observe these excerpts:

> Dove of the fir-wood walling high our red roof
> Long the long noon coo, crooning through the coo
> GEORGE MEREDITH

> Fountains, and ye that warble as ye flow,
> Melodious murmurs, warbling tune His praise
> JOHN MILTON

Echoism is frequently devised in connection with other figures for the sake of heightening effects, especially with hendiadys and alliteration. And it is frequently secured by means of structural quality as well as by skilful choice of diction. Observe, for instance, the following excerpt from Alfred Tennyson's *Morte d'Arthur:*

> But, as he (Bedivere) walk'd, King Arthur panted hard,
> Like one that feels a nightmare on his bed

When all the house is mute. So sigh'd the King,
Muttering and murmuring at his ear, "Quick, quick!
I fear it is too late, and I shall die."
But the other swiftly strode from ridge to ridge,
Clothed with his breath, and looking, as he walk'd,
Larger than human on the frozen hills.
He heard the deep behind him, and a cry
Before. His own thought drove him like a goad.
Dry clash'd his harness in the icy caves
And barren chasms, and all to left and right
The bare black cliff clang'd round him, as he based
His feet on juts of slippery crag that rang
Sharp-smitten with the dint of armed heels—
And on a sudden, lo! the level lake,
And the long glories of the winter moon

The effects of echoism are secured, not only by such alliterative combinations as the hard-sounding "bare black cliff clang'd round him" and the alliterative hendiadys "Muttering and murmuring at his ear," but also by the long breathless sentence commencing "Dry clash'd his harness . . ." Bedivere here was keenly feeling the weight of his noble lord, and was making one final breathless effort to carry out his bidding, "Quick, quick!" Hence, the almost breathless monosyllabic sentence. Then, when the heights are attained and the lake appears in view, note the use of the soft, liquid, restful, mellifluous sounds of release, and the short evenly-accented phrases,

And on a sudden, lo! the level lake,
And the long glories of the winter moon

Perhaps, for sheer wealth of figurative force and pictorial beauty, this brief passage cannot be matched in English poetry. The King's loose, short-breathed "Quick, quick! I fear it is too late, and I shall die"; his loyal knight's periodic and climactic response of actions broken only by the balanced suggestion of pause, "He heard the deep behind him, and a cry before"; the comparison of simile and the suggestion of metonymy, and most of all the echo of hard *c* and *k* and *ng* sounds as the armed feet stride and clamp upward over the crags—all taken together constitute a vivid instruction for a painter's eye, and eloquent notes for the operatic ear.

Oxymoron is the use of contradictory epithet (see page 95), that is, the adjective contradicts the noun or vice versa. It is a close-up or concentrated form of paradox. *Cruel kindness, stupendous delicacy, harmless danger,* are familiar examples of oxymoron. Note also these:

... in this shrill hush of quietude
                              GEORGE MEREDITH
His humble ambition, proud humility,
His jarring concord, and his discord dulcet
                              WILLIAM SHAKESPEARE
His honor rooted in dishonor stood,
And faith unfaithful kept him falsely true
                              ALFRED TENNYSON
            ... and then there crept
A little noiseless noise among the leaves
Born of the very sigh that silence heaves
                              JOHN KEATS

Parallel or *correlative verse* is verse in which there is dictional
"match-up" or paralleling. The sequence of subject with predicate or of predicate with object, and so forth, is broken for the
sake of the parallelism. This is an example of triple dictional
parallelism or correlation.

                    Air, water, earth
      By fowl, fish, beast, was flown, was swum, was walked
                              JOHN MILTON
That is,

Air was flown by fowl; water was swum by fish; earth was walked
by beast

Such correlation frequently appeared in Elizabethan literature
and especially in a verse form known as *palinode*—poetic writing
in which there is deliberate retraction or recantation and in which
this return upon itself is aided by such arrangement. Note the
following palinode. Verses five, six, seven are correlative, and
enforce application of the comparisons set forth in the first four
verses. The eighth verse is the "clinch" verse. Verses nine, ten,
eleven, twelve vary the theme, and the couplet again concludes or
clinches. In the second stanza the four topics are again treated,
but in reversed order and varied theme, and the final couplet
summarizes by means of correlative or parallel verse.

            As withereth the primrose by the river,
            As fadeth summer's sun from gliding fountains,
            As vanisheth the light-blown bubble ever,
            As melteth snow upon the mossy mountains:
            So melts, so vanisheth, so fades, so withers,
            The rose, the shine, the bubble, and the snow,
            Of praise, pomp, glory, joy, which short life gathers,
            Fair praise, vain pomp, sweet glory, brittle joy.
            The withered primrose by the mourning river,
            The faded summer's sun from weeping fountains,

The light-blown bubble vanishèd for ever,
The molten snow upon the naked mountains,
Are emblems that the treasures we uplay,
Soon wither, vanish, fade, and melt away.

For as the snow, whose lawn did overspread
Th' ambitious hills, which giant-like did threat
To pierce the heaven with their aspiring head,
Naked and bare doth leave their craggy seat;
Whenas the bubble, which did empty fly,
The dalliance of the undiscernèd wind,
On whose calm rolling waves it did rely,
Hath shipwrack made, where it did dalliance find;
And when the sunshine which dissolved the snow,
Colored the bubble with a pleasant vary,
And made the rathe and timely primrose grow,
Swarth clouds withdrawn, which longer time do tarry:
O what is praise, pomp, glory, joy, but so
As shine by fountains, bubbles, flowers, or snow?

EDMUND BOLTON

Such verse reflects something of the artificial devices that were resorted to in Elizabethan times, and shows, indirectly at least, one of the many influences of euphuism (see page 97). It has all the challenging interest of the crossword puzzle, and young people have often found the attempted composition of correlative verse an excellent introduction to the writing of more difficult and more worthy verse.

The palinode is by no means always written in sonnet form, as here, nor is correlative verse confined to any such extended composition as this. It is frequently found imbedded in long poems, in plays, and in lyrics of various kinds. It usually does appear, however, in the palinode, and the word itself means "matching up" or repeating (*palin*, again and *ode*, song). It contains, moreover, both suspense and surprize elements in a mechanical sense.

Paradox is a statement that on first sight seems to be absurd or self-contradictory. The purpose of paradox is emphasis, but carried to excess it may make a work labored and confusing, and thus weaken the total impression rather than emphasize it. Happy paradox frequently becomes epigram or saying. As pointed out above, the terms of paradox are not so closely joined as are those of oxymoron. Excessive use of paradox causes attention to be fixed upon form rather than upon content. It is impossible sometimes to gather an author's thoughts for watching his pyrotechnical display of paradox, if he is given to extravagant indulgence in this style of writing.

> The coward dies many times before his death
>> WILLIAM SHAKESPEARE

> Good mother is bad mother unto me
>> ALFRED TENNYSON

> My wound is great because it is so small.
> Then 'twould be greater were it none at all!
>> JOHN DRYDEN

Parallelism is continued comparison made by means of similar expressions. It may be repetitive or synonymous, as

> And do you now put on your best attire?
> And do you now cull out a holiday?
>> WILLIAM SHAKESPEARE

It may be antithetical (see page 87):

> "Shoot if you must this old gray head,
> But spare your country's flag," she said
>> JOHN GREENLEAF WHITTIER

It may be resultant:

> Ten days and nights, with sleepless eye,
> I watched that wretched man,
> And since, I never dare to write
> As funny as I can
>> OLIVER WENDELL HOLMES

> The Lord is my shepherd:
> I shall not want
>> *Psalm xxiii: 1*

It may be constructive or reenforcing:

> Answer not a fool according to his folly,
> Lest thou also be like unto him.
>> *Proverbs xxvi: 4*

It may be deductive or illustrative:

> As the hart panteth after the water-brooks,
> So panteth my soul after thee, O God.
>> *Psalm xlii: 2*

The following gem from Abraham Lincoln is worthy of inclusion here as inimitably illustrative of parallelism and antithesis. He was twenty-three years old at the time he made the speech containing it, and was candidating for the Illinois legislature:

I presume you all know who I am. I am humble Abraham Lincoln. My principles are short and sweet, like an old woman's dance. I believe in the national bank and a high protective tariff. If I'm elected, good. If not, it's all the same

Paralipsis is an omission by means of which a speaker pretends to conceal what he really emphasizes by the device. One of the most eloquent examples of this device is the speech of Marc Antony to the mob in *Julius Cæsar*. He omits to mention the will until he is well along in his speech and is sure that he has the mob with him. He then deliberately forgets it again, as the mob of course does. In the same way, but to a lesser degree, he stages Cæsar's cloak, even Cæsar's body. In ordinary conversation paralipsis is by no means uncommon. "I say nothing of your bad marks, my boy, but your conduct is disgusting," said a father to his son in a report-card scene. "I accept your paralipsis as reprimand," replied the precocious progeny.

Paralipsis is an oratorical figure. Lincoln's famous "We cannot dedicate, we cannot consecrate, we cannot hallow this ground" is one of the great examples in American oratory. He really dedicated and consecrated and hallowed that ground for all time. The following excerpt from Daniel O'Connell's famous *Repeal of the Union* illustrates further:

> But I do not intend to detain you in the contemplation of those vulgar means of parliamentary success—they are within the daily routine of official management; neither will I direct your attention to the frightful recollection of that avowed fact which is now part of history, that the rebellion itself was fomented and encouraged in order to facilitate the Union

Paronomasia is a form of wit; it means a play on words, a pun. Punning is one of the oldest devices of literature for the sake of pointing and lightening effects. All great writers and speakers have made use of it. Joseph Addison declared that the seeds of punning are in the minds of all men.

> Now it is *Rome* indeed, and *room* enough
> When there is in it one only man
> WILLIAM SHAKESPEARE

> . . . at one slight *bound* high overleaped all *bound*
> JOHN MILTON

> They went and *told* the sexton,
> And the sexton *tolled* the bell
> THOMAS HOOD

Pastiche, strictly speaking, is a medley. But applied to literature it is conscious and deliberate imitation of somebody's style made either for purpose of ridicule or as result of admiring scholarship. George Meredith's *The Shaving of Shagpat,* for instance, is modeled after *The Arabian Nights,* as is also Robert Louis Stevenson's *The New Arabian Nights.*

Pathetic fallacy is the epithet applied condescendingly by John Ruskin to that practise among the romantic writers to attribute sensation and human feeling to inanimate things, especially to trees, flowers, moon, stars, earth. His contention was that they had overdone their supposed rapport with nature, especially when Wordsworth went so far as to suggest that the moon looked around her and was happy when the heavens were bare, and when he expressed himself further in *Lines Written above Tintern Abbey:*

> I have learned
> To look on nature, not as in the hour
> Of thoughtless youth; but hearing oftentimes
> The still, sad music of humanity,
> Nor harsh nor grating, though of ample power
> To chasten and subdue. And I have felt
> A presence that disturbs me with the joy
> Of elevated thoughts; a sense sublime
> Of something far more deeply interfused,
> Whose dwelling is the light of setting suns,
> And the round ocean and the living air,
> And the blue sky, and in the mind of man;
> A motion and a spirit, that impels
> All thinking things, all objects of all thought,
> And rolls through all things
>
> WILLIAM WORDSWORTH

Long before Wordsworth and his school, however, poets had made nature almost humanly sensitive and understanding, as witness the following from John Milton's *Lycidas:*

> But, oh! the heavy change, now thou art gone,
> Now thou art gone and never must return!
> Thee, Shepherd, thee the woods and desert caves,
> With wild thyme and the gadding vine o'ergrown,
> And all their echoes, mourn.
> The willows, and the hazel copses green,
> Shall now no more be seen
> Fanning their joyous leaves to thy soft lays.
> As killing as the canker to the rose,
> Or taint-worm to the weanling herds that graze,
> Or frost to flowers that their gay wardrobe wear,
> When first the white-thorn blows;
> Such, Lycidas, thy loss to shepherd's ear

Period, as far as composition is concerned, means the end of a sentence. But when you speak of an author's periods, you do not mean punctuation marks, but sentences as a whole. As a rule the word *period* used in reference to a sentence means a periodic sentence.

Periphrasis is composed of two words meaning to "talk around," that is, the use of more words and phrases than are really necessary to convey the full meaning of an expression. It is sometimes popularly defined as "beating around the bush." In general composition, periphrasis is a violation of the principle of economy. In literature, however, it may be not only permissible but desirable for the reason that it very often not only defines but explains and enriches as well. It is sometimes used for the sake of humor, as in calling a white lie "an intermittent and unpremeditated prevarication" or home-work "the pestiferous imposition by superannuated pedagogs upon the coveted freedom of adolescents." Edgar Allan Poe frequently wrote in the following periphrastic manner, usually but by no means always for the purpose of securing atmospheric effects:

> The people were in no bad humor at being now and then besprinkled with friendly showers of momentary duration that fell from large white masses of cloud profusely distributed about the blue vault of the firmament

This simply means that the people welcomed the showers. When Alfred Tennyson spoke of mathematics as "the hard-grained Muse of the cube and square" he characterized the subject from his own point of view as well as from that, doubtless, of numerous others. The word *circumlocution,* which also means indirect or roundabout expression, is commonly used for *periphrasis.* They really mean the same thing, the latter being more technical or specific in use than the former.

Personification is the attribution of personal life and understanding to inanimate things and abstractions, as in *The sun smiled* and *Procrastination is the thief of time.* It is human nature and especially child nature to attribute personal qualities to all kinds of things and activities. Primitive man almost invariably did this. Strictly speaking, the attribution of animal qualities to an object does not constitute personification; thus, *the ocean roared* is, to say the least, an imperfect personification if, indeed, it is personification at all, as some authorities contend. Moreover, the true personification should enable us to picture a person, to see personal characteristics demonstrated. In "The voice of thy brother's blood crieth to me from the ground" (Genesis iv:10), the human attributes of *voice* and *crying* are associated with no personal picture; hence, the personification is imperfect. Similarly in Macbeth's famous soliloquy, "Tomorrow and tomorrow and tomorrow, Creeps in this petty pace from day to day," there is nothing more than imperfect personification, if so much. But note in the following that the personification is elaborated until the picture approaches completion, and the figure is thus made perfect:

> But look, the morn in russet mantle clad,
> Walks o'er the dew of yon high eastern hill
>
> WILLIAM SHAKESPEARE

> Joy, whose hand is ever at his lips bidding adieu
>
> JOHN KEATS

Personification is expressed by the third person, that is, inanimate objects and abstractions are spoken *about* as if they had personal qualities. The apostrophe (see page 90), on the other hand, is expressed thru the second person. This, then, is apostrophe, not personification:

> What kind of God art thou, O ceremony?
>
> WILLIAM SHAKESPEARE

In formal literature personified words are usually capitalized—"printer's devil's personifications," Coleridge called them. This is a mechanical device that is not to be recommended. If the content of the personification is not sufficiently marked to carry it, then it is hardly to be helped by capitalization (see p. 39). In

> See how my sword weeps for the poor king's death
>
> WILLIAM SHAKESPEARE

the personification is direct or physical, and this represents its more common usage. But note that in the following examples it is indirect or suggested merely:

> Look, love, what envious streaks
> Do lace the severing clouds in yonder east
>
> WILLIAM SHAKESPEARE

> Oquendo had specially distinguished himself, being present wherever the danger was greatest, driving back into action vessels which were inclined to flinch
>
> JAMES ANTHONY FROUDE

Poetic license is the term applied to those privileges exercised by a poet in order to make his verse meet certain requirements or yield certain effects. He may shorten words; he may omit words; he may slur syllables, add syllables, thwart accent, change sounds, use archaic spellings and phraseology, invent words, invert sentences, deliberately commit solecism, and take still other liberties. As a matter of fact the good poet does not have to do any of these things, and usually does not. He is himself master of his meter and his diction; they are not or should not be master of him. It is well to remember, however, that what may sometimes seem to be license in a poem of a remote period may not have been license at all at the time the poem was written. The word *aspect*, for instance, was accented on the second syllable in Elizabethan times, and the second syllable is therefore stressed in Shakespearian lines. The double superlative and comparative, the double negative, the nominative case for the objective, and still other constructions that would be wrong today or that would constitute poetic license at least, were accepted as correct in earlier times.

Prolepsis is anticipation in the use of a word (usually an adjective) so that a future happening is indicated as being completed. Such everyday expressions as *Chop the apples fine* and *Strain the juice clear*, meaning *Chop the apples until they are fine* and *Strain the juice until it is clear*, illustrate this figure. Note these also:

> . . . to scatter plenty o'er a *smiling* land
>
> THOMAS GRAY

> So the two brothers with their *murdered* man
> Rode past fair Florence
>
> JOHN KEATS

In the former the scattering of plenty as result of which the land will smile is anticipated. In the second *murdered* really means about to be murdered—the act is anticipated.

In argument and oratory prolepsis frequently takes the form of question—interrogation (see page 103)—and answer, the latter sometimes being exclamation (see page 98).

> What is the evidence then on which the connexion of my noble client with the outrages of the mob is to be proved? Why that they had blue cockades. How absurd! Is he answerable for every man that wears a blue cockade? If a person commits murder in my livery, without my command, counsel, or consent, is the murder mine?
>
> THOMAS ERSKINE

Hence! home, you idle creatures, get you home!
Is this a holiday? What! Know you not,
Being mechanical, you ought not walk
Upon a labouring day without the sign
Of your profession?

WILLIAM SHAKESPEARE

Repetition that contributes to harmony and rhythm and general poetic effect is figurative. When words and phrases are repeated for the sake of enforcement the repetition is called *iteration;* when a thought is repeated in other phraseology the repetition is called *variation.* Repetition at the beginning of successive verses is called *anaphora* (for example see page 91). When it is run thru, it is called *epanaphora.* The following illustrate:

Thence simple bards, by simple prudence taught,
To this wise town by simple patrons brought,
In simple manner utter simple lays,
And take, with simple pensions, simple praise

CHARLES CHURCHILL

Oh villain, villain, smiling, damnèd villain!
My tables—meet it is I set it down
That one may smile and smile and be a villain

WILLIAM SHAKESPEARE

In these examples variety is used in the repetition, by way of new application of the word as well of idea.

To love bondage more than liberty,
Bondage with ease than strenuous liberty

JOHN MILTON

How beautiful, if sorrow had not made
Sorrow more beautiful than beauty's self

JOHN KEATS

The boundaries of space and time,
Of melancholy space and doleful time

WILLIAM WORDSWORTH

In the expression of grief repetition is customarily used, for the reason that it is natural for a person in grieving to dwell upon the name of the object of his grief. David's lament is well known:

O my son Absalom, my son, my son Absalom!
Would God I had died for thee, O Absalom, my son, my son!

II Samuel xix: 1

And repetition is par excellence the weapon of the orator in building periods for impression:

Let our age be the age of improvement. In a day of peace, let us advance the arts of peace and the works of peace. Let us develop the resources of our land, call forth its powers, build up its institutions, promote all its great interests, and see whether we also, in our day and generation, may not perform something worthy to be remembered. Let us cultivate a true spirit of union and harmony. In pursuing the great objects which our condition points out to us, let us act under a settled conviction and an habitual feeling that these twenty-four states are one country. Let our conceptions be enlarged to the circle of our duties. Let us extend our ideas over the whole of the vast field in which we are called to act. Let our object be, OUR COUNTRY, OUR WHOLE COUNTRY, AND NOTHING BUT OUR COUNTRY.

DANIEL WEBSTER

Repetition that results from awkwardness of structure or limited vocabulary is, of course, a blunder in oral and written composition.

Rodomontade is vainglorious swagger or bluster or boastfulness. The term is taken from the character *Rodomonte* in Ariosto's *Orlando Furioso* and the word literally means one who can roll mountains. Any highly exaggerated writing or speaking or acting is said to be rodomontade. Sir John Falstaff in William Shakespeare's *The Merry Wives of Windsor* is a rodomontade character, as is also, of course, the character of Braggodochio in Edmund Spenser's *Faërie Queene*.

Sarcasm means "flesh tearing." It is witty reproof or reprimand or abuse, always with intent to wound and without any such disguises as irony (see page 104) assumes. In everyday parlance such taunting exclamations as "Get a move on," "Where were you brought up?" "What do you know about this?" and "Does your mother know you're out?" constitute sarcasm. It has been defined as irony used with bitterness. One of the best examples in literature occurs in the quarrel episode between Brutus and Cassius in *Julius Cæsar* (Act IV, Scene iii):

All this! ay, more; fret till your proud heart break;
Go show your slaves, how choleric you are,
And make your bondmen tremble. Must I budge?
Must I observe you? Must I stand and crouch
Under your testy humour? By the gods,
You shall digest the venom of your spleen,
Though it do split you; for, from this day forth,
I'll use you for my mirth, yea, for my laughter
When you are waspish.

Satire in both prose and poetry is a more general and a more literary term than either irony or sarcasm. By means of wit it

FIGURES OF SPEECH 119

holds up to ridicule some cause or theory or individual or group of individuals. Its aim is usually to bring about reform and improvement rather than merely to hurt or embitter. The following excerpt from Oliver Goldsmith's *The Citizen of the World* illustrates:

> A mandarin, who took much pride in appearing with a number of jewels on every part of his robe, was once accosted by an old sly bonze, who, following him through several streets, and bowing to the ground, thanked him for his jewels. "What does the man mean?" cried the mandarin. "Friend, I never gave thee any of my jewels."— "No," replied the other; "but you have let me look at them, and that is all the use you can make of them yourself; so there is no difference between us, except that you have the trouble of watching them, and that is an employment I don't much desire"

Anatole France's *The Penguins,* Jonathan Swift's *Gulliver's Travels,* most of Bernard Shaw's plays (and especially *The Doctor's Dilemma*), Miguel de Cervantes' *Don Quixote* (satirizing chivalry), John Dryden's *Absalom and Achitophel* are a few of the great pieces of sustained satire in our literature. Satire usually exaggerates in the effort to get its effects; it concerns itself with one side—*its* side—of truth only; its mask of complete justice is always so thin that any discerning person can see thru it. But it has nevertheless done much good in the world and is very often the most entertaining of reading.

Sigmatism is the name given to the unconscious overuse of sibilant sounds in an expression, so that the hissing offends the ear. Used consciously, sibilants may, of course, contribute to echoism. But in these expressions the *s*-sound is not pleasant.

> . . . to whom soft sleep seems more secure and sweet
> EDMUND WALLER
> . . . whose kiss seems still the first; whose summoning eyes . . .
> DANTE ROSSETTI

In the following the ugly sound of the lines, as result of purposed sigmatism, characterizes the "singers":

> And when they list, their lean and flashy songs
> Grate on their scrannel pipes of wretched straw
> JOHN MILTON

Simile is an expression of similarity between two things that are in most respects unlike. In literature the simile should evoke play of the fancy and imagination; it should not treat of the familiar and the obvious. *Cold as ice, big as a barn door, mad as a March hare,* and other common conversational comparisons, are not to be regarded as similes in the literary sense. The first time they were used, however, they had the newness, the freshness, the naïveté that characterize to some extent the true simile. The telling merit of a simile is the unexpectedness yet perfect aptness of it by way of striking and beautiful comparison. The more unlike the two compared things are, the better the simile, because the one point of their similarity will then appear to have been undiscovered except in the special instance and will therefore be unique. The words *like* and *as* are the customary vehicles thru which the simile gets itself expressed, but *than* is sometimes used, as are still other terms (see below). But do not make the mistake of thinking that you have a simile every time that you use *like* and *as* or see them used. *John looks like an athlete* and *The apple looks like a ball* are not similes, for the reason that the comparisons have to do with persons and things respectively that are really much alike. They are, moreover, mere instances. These are good similes:

> How brilliant and mirthful the light of her eye,
> Like a star glancing out from the blue of the sky
> > JOHN GREENLEAF WHITTIER

> And as a bird each fond endearment tries,
> To tempt its new-fledged offspring to the skies,
> He tried each art, reproved each dull delay,
> Allured to brighter worlds, and led the way
> > OLIVER GOLDSMITH

> His words were shed softer than leaves from the pine,
> And they fell on Sir Launfal as snows on the brine
> > JAMES RUSSELL LOWELL

> > It were all one
> That I should love a bright particular star,
> And think to wed it, he is so above me
> > WILLIAM SHAKESPEARE

> But now the whole Round Table is dissolved,
> Which was an image of the mighty world
> > ALFRED TENNYSON

They had to meet the enemy, as it were, with one arm bandaged by their own sovereign
> JAMES ANTHONY FROUDE

Mirth is like a flash of lightning that breaks thru a gloom of clouds and glitters for a moment. Cheerfulness keeps up a daylight in the mind, filling it with a steady and perpetual serenity
> SAMUEL JOHNSON

A human soul without education is like marble in the quarry which shows none of its inherent beauties, till the skill of the polisher fetches out the colors

JOSEPH ADDISON

The simile may make a negative comparison and thus form a kind of litotes (see page 105) and it may be expressed in degrees of comparison (as in the third illustration above).

The sea enragèd is not half so deaf
.............as we to keep this city
WILLIAM SHAKESPEARE

O Spartan dog,
More fell than anguish, hunger, or the sea!
WILLIAM SHAKESPEARE

The Homeric simile (sometimes called *sustained, continued, Greek, classic*) is one that runs thru many lines and is expressed in the form of a mathematical proportion. Note in the following that the rich woman is to the poor drudge as Rustum is to the unknown youth:

As some rich woman, on a winter's morn,
Eyes through her silken curtains the poor drudge
Who with numb blackened fingers makes her fire—
At cockcrow, on a starlit winter's morn,
When the frost flowers the whitened window-panes—
And wonders how she lives, and what the thoughts
Of that poor drudge may be; so Rustum eyed
The unknown adventurous youth, who from afar
Came seeking Rustum, and defying forth
All the most valiant chiefs
MATTHEW ARNOLD

When the simile is expressed in appositive form it is sometimes called an *implied* simile, *like* or *as* being clearly understood. But some authorities insist that the so-called implied simile is sometimes metaphor (see page 105) and sometimes metonymy (see page 106), and not simile at all. Note the following:

The noble sister of Publicola,
The *moon* of Rome
WILLIAM SHAKESPEARE

Simile is likewise said by some authorities to be implied in such expressions as *the milk of human kindness in his heart, the bright song of heaven in her laugh,* and *Then her voice's music—call it the well's bubbling, the bird's warble.* But these are really not similes in the strict sense of the term. They are poetic expressions of similarity, but their figurative vehicle is metonymy in the first two and metaphor in the third. Since most figures of feeling and content are forms of comparison, then all figures may be reduced to simile and metaphor, and some authorities recognize but these two in the category of resemblance.

Slurring means hurrying over certain light or unaccented syllables in a line of poetry in order to produce the effect of equivalence. Thus in

No anger find in thee but pity and ruth

the next to last word *and* is slurred in the reading to make the last foot as much of an iambus as possible, the slurred sound being about this:

but pi|tyand ruth

Syllepsis is the use of the same word in two different senses in a single expression. Sometimes, especially in prose, it amounts to ill-advised economy. The word is usually a verb or a preposition (see pages 174 and 209). In strictly grammatical and idiomatic usage the word is wrong in one of the senses in which it is used. The simplest form of syllepsis occurs in such expression as

Neither he nor I have heard about it

wherein *have* is correct with *I* but not with *he*. But this is generally accepted as understandable if not strictly correct. The figure is sometimes used in literature to give point and humor to a sentence, sometimes for misguided economy.

Miss Bolo went home in a flood of tears and a sedan chair
CHARLES DICKENS

Questions and corks popped; laughter and silver rang
O. HENRY

Syncope is the elision of a vowel or a syllable from the middle of a word, as *ne'er, wat'ry, liv'ry, libr'y*. It is one of the commonest forms of poetic license. The running of words and syllables together or the slurring of letters and syllables "out of existence," as *Wensy* for *Wednesday, Satay* for *Saturday, wanna* for *want to, Wotchmeen?* for *What do you mean? Forsecstreet* for *Forty-second Street,* is really a form of syncope technically called *haplology*. It constitutes slovenly and illiterate speech and writing, whereas syncope proper may be an aid to purely literary form. (See *apocope,* page 94, and *apheresis,* page 88.)

Synecdoche makes use of a part for a whole or a whole for a part, an individual for a class or a class for an individual. *Hands* for *workmen*, *head* for *animal* (so many head of cattle), *sail* for *ship* are common conversational examples of synecdoche. These are from literature:

> My good blade carves the casques of men
> > ALFRED TENNYSON

> He stood alone amidst his land,
> Without one trusted heart or hand
> > GEORGE GORDON NOEL BYRON

> How easy dost thou take all England up!
> > WILLIAM SHAKESPEARE

> And cheeks of sorry grain will serve to ply
> The sampler
> > JOHN MILTON

> And a thousand thousand slimy things
> Lived on; and so did I
> > SAMUEL TAYLOR COLERIDGE

Vision is the description or narration or exposition of past or absent or imaginary scenes or happenings as if they were actually before the eyes of the speaker or writer. It is a continuous figure, usually a continued personification or apostrophe. One of the most noteworthy examples of this figure in literature is the following from William Shakespeare's *Macbeth* (Act II, Scene i), a few verses of which are here quoted:

> Is this a dagger which I see before me,
> The handle toward my hand? Come, let me clutch thee.
> I have thee not, and yet I see thee still.
> Art thou not, fatal vision, sensible
> To feeling as to sight? or art thou but
> A dagger of the mind, a false creation,
> Proceeding from the heat-oppressèd brain?
> I see thee yet, in form as palpable
> As this which now I draw

Wit is brief expression that is sharp or pointed or brilliant or sarcastic, or all of these and perhaps more. It is always intellectual and subjective, that is, it is always "highly pleasurable" to its author—he finds an inner satisfaction in a witty remark. This implies that wit is evoked by objective considerations—by some one to read or hear it. No small part of wit resides in the form of its expression; its form flashes as well as its content. It is as a rule not a sustained quality but, rather, brief and staccato and always sharp in its note of surprize. "Wit arises," said

Coleridge, "in detecting the identity in dissimilar things." It may rely for its effect upon any figure of speech, and especially upon irony, hyperbole, metaphor, and paradox.

Punning is a form of wit. Conscious ambiguity may be witty. Word inventions may be witty. The fundamental requirement in all manifestations of wit is that they be spontaneous. Once any studied quality enters, wit disappears. Its most natural place is in the run, the give-and-take of conversational and dialog repartee; hence, it belongs with particular fitness to drama, for here it may always be made to seem as if accidental, as if the time and the place and the conversational cue had somehow inescapably evoked it.

The height of word-play wit was once reached during the course of a speech by a wealthy and domineering employer of labor. He waxed eloquent now and again as he uttered the words "the rights of the laboring man." Presently the expression caused a snicker in the audience, and he stopt to ask whether there was anything objectionably singular in what he was saying. "Nothing but your plural," called a working man from the rear of the house.

The height of ironic wit was probably achieved one nineteenth-century morning in London when an aspiring British poet, meeting Oscar Wilde on the street, said: "I'm just taking my new poetic drama to the publisher." "How reckless of you," replied Wilde; "it would be stolen if you were not known."

Zeugma is a more remote or disconnected coupling than syllepsis. The coupling word in zeugma applies to only one of the terms placed together. In

> The sun shall not burn thee by day,
> Neither the moon by night
>
> *Psalm cxxi: 6*

while *sun* and *moon* are coupled, the word *burn* logically understood after *moon* cannot apply to *moon*. The word *harass* or *harm* or *destroy* must really be supplied after *moon* to make sense. Note also this:

> Forbidding to marry and to abstain from fruits
>
> *First Timothy iv: 3*

in which *commanding* or *ordering* or *exhorting* must be understood before *to abstain* in order to make a logical reading. A the passage stands *forbidding* seems to be understood before *to abstain* and this gives a meaning opposite to the one intended.

Keep figures appropriate. It is inappropriate and in bad taste to say, "The strains of music from the orchestra fall upon the ear like a soothing poultice." The resemblance is trivial and undignified and unworthy of the object for which it is drawn. It is a descending figure, that is, it grades resemblance downward. But be equally careful not to err in the opposite direction, on the side of high-flown or bombastic comparisons. The following is a bad *ascending* figure: "The strains of harmony from the orchestra were a heavenly symphony to my ears." Figures of inappropriate descent and ascent may sometimes be used with good effect for humor but not in serious expression.

Keep figures familiar. Do not draw comparisons that the ordinary reader will not be able to understand. Avoid, therefore, references to remote things, to purely local matters, to obscure places and objects, to technical or professional facts, and the like. To say, "This ink is like nebbiola" is to cloud the figure. Nebbiola is a sparkling red Italian champagne, but it is too local in its sale and use to have value in English figurative language. The figure that Longfellow used in the following is far-fetched as well as inappropriate:

> The day is done, and the darkness
> Falls from the wings of night,
> As a feather is wafted downward
> From an eagle in his flight

The coming on of nightfall has been likened by the poets to a cloak, to a tent of darkness, to a canopy or a mantle or a pall. But the falling of a feather is trivial in comparison with the cosmic phenomenon of nightfall. It is too great a strain upon a reader's imagination to ask him to see any resemblance between the two things compared. The resemblance is not only remote; it is strained and inappropriate as well.

Do not strain metaphors and similes. Do not carry them too far. Be satisfied when you have made them serve your purpose. It is good to say, "The golden crisp wafers with their creamy sweetened filling, veritable fairy sandwiches, appeal to the eye and the palate of every one," but this is sufficient. When the writer goes on to say, "Fragile as a frost flower in appearance, dainty as thistledown, and exquisite in taste as the ambrosia of the gods, they are the last word in dessert delights," we cannot help feeling that he has overdone the use of figurative language. Such figurative excess leads to bombast and insincerity, and thus sacrifices the striking effects that well-used figures of speech are so preeminently able to give expression. Here are two illustrations of the strained and excessive use of figurative language:

When the financial crash came in 1930 signaling what was to be the greatest financial depression the country had ever experienced, the stock market was all things to all readers. In a single newspaper it was required to run this metaphoric gamut: a storm-tossed ship; a towering but tottering skyscraper; a battlefield with papers crackling; a steam kettle; a steam locomotive and train of cars; a painting; a volcano; a stick of dynamite; a bit of earth which is first rocked by dynamite, then shaken by a tremor and finally smitten by a storm from a cloudless sky; a great lung into which oxygen is pumped; a sea beach and a rocky coast submerged by the surf and buffeted by the breakers; a mountainside down which the avalanche rushes.

A business house, undoubtedly "to poetry inclined," welcomed its "constituency" home from summer vacation with this exuberant message:

> May we express the hope that your anticipations for a delightful vacation found fulfilment in the strength and tenderness of Nature; that perplexities were cast aside for an untroubled world of undeniable charm. We hope that days were restful—zestful—whichever you preferred, but at any rate healthful and full of interest. May your reminiscences afford many pleasant hours thruout the coming winter

The following "flight of flowery fancy" was evoked by the retirement of a member of a large school organization, after his many years of association with it. One reportorial comment upon this farewell resolution expressed the feeling that the cultural future of the children of the community was evidently secure!

> One of our number is constrained to go ashore. We will miss his strength and skill at the oars and more than all else his sage advice and his unfailing solicitude. These qualities will be appreciated only when the bark of education majestically and serenely sails sunlit seas again. We bid heartfelt bon voyage to a seasoned mariner, ————. That the "Master of All Good Workmen" will paint his remaining days in the golden hues of the spirit even as a Rembrandt portrait is suffused with a golden radiance and that his soul will be cheered to the end with the memory and consciousness of a noble life magnificently spent in unselfish service is the wholehearted wish of his colleagues, who prize his friendship *

Do not use trite or hackneyed figures. Many figures have been used so much that they cease to have any forceful or pictorial

* Used by permission of *The New Yorker.*

value. They have become too colloquial and commonplace to be effective. A few of these worn-out figures are here listed:

a voice like a fog-horn	as round as the moon
alabaster brow	as shy as a deer
as black as a raven	as slim as a willow
as black as coal	as slow as molasses
as blue as the sky	as sly as a fox
as bright as a star	as soft as velvet
as brown as a nut	as stiff as a poker
as clear as a bell	as stubborn as a mule
as clear as crystal	as sweet as a nut
as dry as the desert	as sweet as sugar
as free as air	as swift as an arrow
as graceful as a bird	as tight as a glove
as green as grass	as tough as shoe leather
as happy as the day is long	as white as a sheet
as hard as a rock	as white as snow
as heavy as lead	fiery eyes
as high as the Alps	frowning night
as meek as a lamb	golden hair
as old as the hills	raven tresses
as pale as a ghost	rosy cheeks
as poor as a church mouse	ruby lips
as quick as a flash	silver moon
as quiet as a mouse	smiling dawn
as rich as Crœsus	teeth like pearls

Do not use figures of speech to excess. Language may be made too figurative. Piling climaxes too rapidly and too closely upon one another, for instance, will not only exhaust a reader or a hearer, but will really defeat the purpose of the figure. The theme will accordingly be weakened, the climax will lose its point and effectiveness. Figures are not a necessity of expression. Many writers and speakers do not use them at all. But they are recommended for use when they can be kept apt and restrained and when they really help to enliven it and make it graceful, to elucidate and ingratiate expression. Do not drag them in merely for ornament, or they will negative what you have to say. If your mind does not breed pictures in its thinking processes—if it does not feed thought with imagination and fancy—then do not try to make your expression figurative. Figures must be spontaneously thought of and applied; otherwise they are worse than useless.

You will do well in your use of figurative language to be guided by the following excerpt from Arthur Schopenhauer's *The Art of Literature* ("On Some Forms of Literature"). While he mentions similes and metaphors only, he uses these terms to include all figures of resemblance. They are taken by many authors (see page 122) as generic terms covering all such figurative expression metonymy, synecdoche, personification, and the rest being regarded as kinds of similes and metaphors.

Metaphors and similes are of great value, in so far as they explain an unknown relation by a known one. Even the more detailed simile which grows into a parable or an allegory, is nothing more than the exhibition of some relation in its simplest, most visible and palpable form. The growth of ideas rests, at bottom, upon similes; because ideas arise by a process of combining the similarities and neglecting the differences between things. Further, intelligence, in the strictest sense of the word, ultimately consists in a seizing of relations; and a clear and pure grasp of relations is all the more often attained when the comparison is made between cases that lie wide apart from one another, and between things of quite different nature. As long as a relation is known to me as existing only in a single case, I have none but an individual idea of it—in other words, only an intuitive or perceptive knowledge of it; but as soon as I see the same relation in two different cases, I have a general idea of its whole nature, and this is a deeper and more perfect knowledge

Since, then, similes and metaphors are such a powerful engine of knowledge, it is a sign of great intelligence in a writer if his similes are unusual and at the same time, to the point. Aristotle also observes that by far the most important thing to a writer is to have this power of metaphor; for it is a gift which cannot be acquired, and it is a mark of genius

CHAPTER SIX

BRIEF REVIEW OF GRAMMAR *

Grammar is the study of relationships among words in logical expression. The unit of expression is the sentence, tho there are shorter units that may be quite clear thru association or context. For the sake of convenience, and for this only, words are classified into eight different groups called parts of speech. These are not so very important either as groups or as names, but they are important as handles by which to maneuver certain words according to function performed. The words of any group are very often easily transferable to other groups. The transfer depends upon the function to be performed by a word or words. There is no such thing, then, as a grammar of words. But there is a grammar of word uses and functions in units of expression called sentences. Grammar really begins therefore with the sentence. And the only way to learn grammar is to study the functions that words perform in given sentences and longer contexts.

The word *he* is usually accepted as a pronoun. But use the expression *he man* and it takes on adjective nature immediately; that is, it now qualifies *man,* whereas its customary use is to substitute for such words as *man.* Adjectives become nouns in function without the slightest difficulty: *You omitted i from analytical, Generous is spelt with a u,* the *Sublime* and the *Beautiful,* the *Unknowable,* the *Just* and the *Unjust, the long and the short of it, the blacks and the reds, the whites of eggs, at sixes and sevens,* the *Liberals,* the *Conservatives,* and so forth. And nouns are equally versatile in performing the functions of adjectives: *night club, lawn tennis, office boy, linen sheets, insurance agent, bank manager, meat store.* In *It out-Herods Herod, Let's boycott them, He burked his man, He lords it over me, I shall school him in better manners,* nouns are parading as verbs. In *There is misplaced* and *Tomorrow creeps in this petty pace* adverbs are masquerading as nouns. In *We went outside, outside*

---

* This section is in no sense a complete and exhaustive treatment of grammar. It is for review or "recall" only.

129

is an adverb. In *The outside is covered with dust, outside* is a noun. Note further: *How much is it worth, Worth makes the man, Woe worth the day; I ride inside, He is an inside man, The inside is lined with Celotex, He lives inside the ramparts; Date everything you write, Your date is wrongly placed, Here is the date line, This play is dated; Don't regret the past, He has past me by, Past days are forgotten, He ran past the office; The count has arrived, Count the pupils, Keep count for me, That stroke doesn't count.* You may make a game of casting the parts of speech. They are most versatile, as the few illustrations here given prove.

This transference of function varies, to be sure. Fewer adverbs than adjectives perform noun functions; fewer verbs than nouns perform adjective functions. But any coinage by way of transferred function may be permitted thru the agency of italics or quotation marks (see page 217). So one word plays many parts of speech, and the eight terms that are defined and illustrated below must by no means be regarded as hard and fast within their classifications. But they must be thought of, rather, as versatile actors, if you will, each capable of varied casting. The labels or handles noted are simply useful for dealing with words. That is all.

As far as grammar is concerned, words may be grouped first of all into two main divisions. There are *ideational* words, that is, words the chief function of which is to contain and convey ideas or notions. Nouns and verbs are such words, for they denote and connote meanings that provoke or suggest thought even when they stand alone. As far as verbs are concerned, this classification does not of course include the verb *to be* and other auxiliaries that exercise merely the copulative function. Even when such verbs are used as principal verbs, they can scarcely be called ideational. And verbs do express relationships—time relationships and mood relationships. Yet they are primarily words of ideas and notions and concepts, and they are therefore in the main correctly classified as ideational.

All other words are *relational* or *qualifying* words. These show relationships between and among ideational words, and they qualify, that is, tone down or tone up or otherwise limit or expand ideational words. There are really two kinds of relational words: one qualifies and one connects. But since connection and qualification are usually contained to some degree in both connecting and qualifying words, we shall group them all loosely under the term relational or qualifying.

. . . .

Take the word *but*, for instance. This word is generally regarded as connective merely. And in *He is always willing but he always fails* it does connect the members of a double expression. But it also qualifies or modifies or limits, that is, it is to a degree a relational word as well as a connective word. It indicates that his willingness exceeds his ability, that his attitude is always perfect but his achievement is always deficient. So it may be said that *but* connects and also subtracts or reverses, that *and* connects and also adds, that *either-or* and *neither-nor* connect and also alternate or choose.

A sentence has long been defined as a group of related words having a subject and a predicate and expressing a complete thought. This means that the group of related words having subject and predicate is capable of standing alone as an expression. The words may draw certain shadings of meaning from what precedes in context and from what follows. But they are and must be inherently self-supporting to be a sentence. True, some important part may be left unexpressed—such as the subject in a command—but it must be clearly understood or the independence of the related group of words will be destroyed.

The subject of a sentence is that about which a statement is made or denied or asked. The predicate states or denies or asks something about the subject. In a *simple* sentence there is just one subject and one predicate: *The workmen report at the factory at eight o'clock.* Here *workmen* is the subject, *report* is the simple predicate, and *report* with its two modifying phrases is the complete predicate. Note now that either the subject or the predicate, or both, may be compound: *The workmen and the workwomen report at the factory and begin their work at eight o'clock.* Here there are two subjects—*workmen* and *workwomen*—and two predicates—*report* and *begin*. But it is still a simple sentence because the subjects both take the same action, that is, take the same predicates.

In *The workmen report at the factory at eight o'clock, but the workwomen begin work later,* the situation is changed. Here two different actions are specified, one for the men and one for the women. Hence, there are two sentences really linked by the connecting word *but*. If these two sentences were widely different in meaning and without any relationship whatever, it would be wrong to connect them with even so detached a word as *but*. There is, however, a common and homogeneous set of ideas expressed in the two parts and thus they may properly be put down as one *compound* sentence. Each member of this compound expression is called a *clause*, that is, a group of related words containing a subject and a predicate. These are independent or principal clauses, since one is neither more important nor less important than the other, and since either one might stand alone as a complete and self-subsistent sentence. A compound sentence may have more than two independent clauses.

Now suppose the sentence is made to read: *The workmen are at work in the factory before the workwomen arrive.* Here, again, two different actions are specified, one for the men and one for the women. There are two subjects and two predicates as there were before. There are likewise two clauses. The word *but* is missing, tho, and the word *before* is substituted. This substitution gives a different pitch entirely to the second subject-predicate group of related words. You cannot read the second clause capitalizing *before* and get the feeling of completion out of it. *Before the workwomen arrive* sounds as if it were hanging in the air, as it is. It sounds *dependent* or *subordinate* to something gone before, namely, the first clause in the sentence. This sentence, then, is made up of two clauses, one of which—the first—is principal or independent, and one of which—the second—is dependent. Such sentence is called *complex* for the reason that the relationship among words and phrases is more involved than it is in a simple sentence or even in a compound sentence. A complex sentence must have one independent clause and one subordinate clause or more than one.

Dependent or subordinate clauses are adjective clauses, adverbial clauses, or noun clauses. An adjective clause is one that is used as an adjective is used—to modify nouns and pronouns: *The car that won is beyond repair, He who would succeed must struggle.* An adverbial clause is one that is used as an adverb is used—to modify verbs, adjectives, and other adverbs: *He went because he wished to, She seems taller than I, They drive more carefully as night falls* (see page 159). A noun clause is one that is used in most ways that a noun is used. It is sometimes called a *substantive* clause, the word *substantive* being applied to any word or word group that functions as a noun.

That you are dishonest is quite apparent (subject)
It is quite apparent *that you are dishonest* (appositive)
I ask *that you go* (object)
The truth is *that you were speeding* (predicate nominative or attribute)
Her experience made her *what they call neurotic* (objective complement)
We are not certain about *what you said* (object of a preposition)

Tho noun clauses are usually introduced by *that,* expressed or understood, other words may be used in this office.

He inquired *whether* I would go
We don't know *where* you are going
He asked *why* we wanted him
We do not know *when* he will come
We do not understand *where* he is

A sentence that has two or more independent clauses and one or more dependent or subordinate clauses is known as a *compound-complex* sentence and also as a *multiple-clause* sentence.   In this sentence: *In the winter the workmen are at work in the factory before it is clear daylight, but the workwomen do not report for work until the sun is up,* there are two independent or principal clauses and two dependent or subordinate clauses.   *Before it is clear daylight* and *until the sun is up* are subordinate clauses, adverbial in nature, signifying time.   *In the winter the workmen are at work in the factory* and *the workwomen do not report* are principal or independent clauses connected by the coordinate conjunction *but.*

Sometimes predicates take certain terms after them to complete their meaning and thus add to the fulness of meaning in the sentence.   Such terms are quite properly called *complements* (that is, *completers*).   For instance, in *He did a good job* the word *job* adds completeness to the thought; it tells what he did; it receives the action of *doing* or *did* or of his energies.   It is called the *object complement.*

But sometimes the term that follows the predicate not only completes the predicate but describes or explains the object of the predicate.   In *The committee made him chairman* and *They thought her lazy* both objects—*him* in the first and *her* in the second—need clarification, that is, need to be explained to make the expression clear.   *Chairman* does it in the one case and *lazy* in the other—these words respectively help to complete the predicate and to clarify the object.   This construction used to give sense to the object is called the *objective complement* or *factitive object.*

Sometimes the term following a predicate not only completes the predicate but explains or describes, that is, clarifies the subject. This happens after such verbs as *be, appear, become, seem, feel* (see page 196). In *John is good, Bill is captain, The dog is cute, The cat seems foolish,* the last word in each case is functioning as completer of the verb and explainer or describer (or both) of the subject. It is called by many names—*subjective complement, predicate nominative* (when it is a noun), *predicate adjective, attribute complement.*

After certain verbs—*get, give, grant, hand, lend, offer, read, tell*— there is frequently a *secondary* or *indirect object* after the understood preposition *to* or *for.* This construction is called the *dative* in Latin. In *We read John a story* and *Lend him a hand* the preposition *to* is understood before *John* and before *him.* The direct objects are, respectively, *story* and *hand;* the indirect objects are *John* and *him. Get whoever wants it one of our catalogs* contains a noun or substantive clause—*whoever wants it* —as indirect object of the understood preposition *for* (tho *him* understood may be made the indirect object here and *whoever wants it* an adjective clause); and in *Do not give studying all your time, studying* is indirect object of *to* understood.

It is important to remember that the subject and the predicate and the complements in a given sentence are the "backbone" of that sentence. These elements are or should be so closely knitted together that the omission of any one will leave the sentence incomplete grammatically. But in many sentences there are other elements added to define or limit or qualify other words. In *The fifty hands in the factory produce these magnificent commodities, hands...produce...commodities* are subject, predicate, and object respectively—the backbone of the expression. The other words may be taken out, and while their elimination will be a loss to the meaning of the sentence and the richness of its detail, the sheer thought may nevertheless be conveyed without them. These extra words are called *adjuncts.* The expression *in the factory* is a special kind of adjunct called a *phrase.* A phrase is a group of two or more associated words not containing a subject and a predicate: *in the gloaming, running at will, a last faint glimmer, suddenly stricken, to be hurt badly.*

I   Nouns

A noun is a name word. Since persons, places, things, actions, conditions, qualities have names, these names are called nouns.

The word *boy* is the name of a class and is thus a *common noun*. The word *John* is the name of a particular boy and is thus a *proper noun*. The word *city*, then, is a common noun, and the word *Chicago* a proper noun. But note that a proper noun may be used to indicate a class or as the title of a class, and thus become a common noun in significance tho it must still be capitalized: *There are too many Johns in this class, We want no more John Wilkes Booths.*

Names of organisms and places and things that are perceived thru the senses are generally known as *concrete* nouns: *carpet, desk, Detroit.* Names of conditions—*orderliness, sickness*—and of qualities—*faithfulness, severity*—are called *abstract* nouns. *Sugar* is concrete; *sweetness* is abstract. *Mercy* is a common abstract noun; *Sister of Mercy* is a proper concrete noun. A *static* abstract noun is one that names a state or mani-festation or quality, as opposed to a *dynamic* abstract noun, which is one that names an action; thus, *drabness* is static; *running* is dynamic; *inertia* is static; *industry* is dynamic.

Names of groups or collections of people or places or things are called collective nouns—*army, crew, fleet, personnel, team, American Medical Corps.* Following is a list of some special collective nouns:

archipelago	group of islands
armada	fleet of men-of-war
band	of ruffians or robbers, musicians
batch	of loaves, of papers
bevy	of maidens, of quails
board	of directors, of trustees
brood	of chicks, of birds
bunch	of keys, of roses
cabinet	of ministers, of peers, of officers
cluster	of fruit
colony	of settlers, of ants
collection	of coins, of stamps, of books
company	of soldiers, of players, of stockholders
congregation	of worshipers, of nuns
constellation	of stars
covey	of partridges
crew	of train, of ship, of workers
crowd	of people
draft	of soldiers
drove	of cattle
faculty	of instructors
farrow	of pigs
fleet	of ships, of cars
flock	of chickens, of sheep

force	of policemen, of firemen, of workers, of office
galaxy	of learned people, of geniuses, of stars
gang	of laborers, of outlaws
gild	of craftsmen
hatch	of chickens
herd	of cattle
hive	of bees
horde	of barbarians
host	of angels, of locusts, of "daffodils"
jury	of citizens, of judges
league	of teams
litter	of pigs, of puppies
lot	of goods, of merchandise
menu	of eatables
muster	of recruits
nest	of drawers
pack	of cards, of wolves, of dogs
panel	of jurymen, of judges
regiment	of soldiers
senate	of representatives
shoal	of fish
school	of whales, of pupils, of thinkers, of artists
set	of dishes, of buttons, of croquet
suite	of rooms
swarm	of bees
throng	of pleasure seekers, of sightseers
troop	of horses, of children
troupe	of actors, of minstrels

The present participle—the *ing*-part of the verb—is often used as a noun. It is called *gerund* or *verb(al)-noun*. As a matter of fact the gerund is somewhat more of a verb than it is noun; the verb-noun is somewhat more of noun than it is verb. The verb-noun may not take an object, and it may be modified by an adjective but not by an adverb. The gerund, on the other hand, may take an object and it may be modified by an adverb, but not by an adjective. In *Typing a letter beautifully is an art*, the word typing is a gerund. In *The careless typing of letters is inexcusable* the word *typing* is a verb-noun. These noun-functional forms must not be confused with *participle*, which is also the *ing*-part of the verb. This functions primarily as an adjective, describing and explaining somewhat any noun or pronoun toward which it is directed. In *Typing her letters perfectly every day of the year she soon found herself first in line for promotion*, the word *typing* qualifies *she* and thus functions as an adjective tho it is the participial form of the verb. It may take an object—*letters*—as may also the perfect participle so used—*having typed her letters*. But the past participle may not take an object. It may, however, take a predicate adjective: *Struck dead by the shot, he rolled over and over down the hill.*

The term *gender* is used to indicate sex in respect to nouns and pronouns. The word *man* denotes male sex and is called *masculine* gender; *woman,* female sex, or *feminine* gender; *desk,* absence of sex, or *neuter* gender; *baby,* either male or female, or *common* gender.

The term *number* is used to indicate whether one or more than one is spoken of. English has two numbers: *singular* number, *girl;* plural number, *girls* (see page 141).

The term *person* is used to indicate the person, place, or thing spoken about—the *third* person; the person, place, or thing spoken to—the *second* person; the person speaking—the *first* person. (In a personified sense places and things may also be used in the first person.) In "John," said Mary, "please close the door," *door* is third person, *John* is second person, and *Mary* is first person.

The term *case* is used to indicate direct relationship between a noun (or a word used as a noun) and other parts of an expression. The *nominative* case denotes primary cause or basis of thought. A noun is said to be in the nominative case, therefore, when it stands in an expression as the center or the subject of some action. A noun is said to be in the *objective* case when it is object of a verb or a preposition, and indicates the object or receiver of some action, thought, or consideration. In *The garage is destroyed, The boy rows gracefully, This is William,* each noun is in the nominative case. Each is the center of thought in its given expression. Each is the "star" of its sentence, so to say. In *He likes carpentry, They provoked Thomas, He went to the shop,* each noun is in the objective case. Each is the object or focus toward which the accumulated thought of the sentence drives.

Possessive case denotes possession. It is indicated by the apostrophe, by the apostrophe and *s,* or by the preposition *of* (see page 478). Some possessives are *specific* or *particular* possessives. In *John's watch* John actually possesses the watch. But in the *divisional* or *partitive* possessive—*a pound of tea, a quart of milk, a box of raisins*—no real possession is denoted by *of.* Similarly, in the *descriptive* or *explanatory* possessive —*a man of parts, a field of lilies, the work of a lifetime*—the idea of ownership or possession is removed and indirect if, indeed, it exists at all. Some authorities call the first classification above the *direct* possessive, and the other two the *indirect* possessive.

The following listing shows in what numerous ways nouns may be used in expression:

Nominative case constructions

As subject	The *motor* stalled
As predicate nominative	That chap is a *chauffeur*
As exclamatory nominative	A *horse!* A *horse!* My kingdom for a horse!
As direct-address nominative (vocative)	Hand me the wrench, *Bill*
As absolute nominative	The *motor* being stalled we left the car and walked

Objective case constructions

As object of verb	He has rented a new *office*
As object of preposition	He goes to his *office* daily
As indirect object	He gave (to) his *son* a new car
As objective complement	They made him office *manager*
As subject of infinitive	I asked *James* to run slowly
As adverbial objective	He ran (for) ten *miles*

Possessive case constructions

By apostrophe	This is *John's* car
By preposition *of*	I am the friend of that *man*
By both preposition and apostrophe	He is a friend of *Mary's*

Nominative, objective, or possessive case construction

An appositive noun (a noun used as explanatory modifier) must agree in person, number, gender, and case with the noun or pronoun that it explains	Fred, the *agent,* has called twice (nominative)
	I have been visited twice by Fred, the *agent* (objective)
	Fred, *the agent's,* call has been reported to me (possessive)

II Pronouns

Pronouns are usually defined as substitutes for nouns. This is good as far as it goes, but it does not cover the entire use and purpose of pronouns. They are very often used to prevent what might be an awkward or monotonous repetition of nouns, and in this capacity they are most important. The pronouns *I* and *you*, for instance, are specific and directive. In many uses they are quite independent of noun reference or antecedence. In *I insist upon it* and *You pretend to be my best friend,* what nouns do *I* and *you* substitute for? None. They refer to actual people and not even to the names of people. In such expressions they are much more nouns themselves than substitutes for nouns.

Pronouns are likewise capable of emphasis quite independently of any external reference. *I myself insist* and *You yourself pretend* are now more emphatic than they are in the paragraph above for the reason that the *I* and the *you* are enforced by use of the reflexive form. Thus, the pronoun in this use performs a function quite apart from any similar function that any noun can perform and it does so without noun antecedent.

Pronouns, again, are far more than mere substitutes in such expressions as *It was late afternoon, It looks like rain,* and *You can never tell what may happen, We disagree with those who oppose the measure.* In the first two *it* is strictly generic and provisional. Nobody thinks of *time* as the antecedent in the first example, or *weather* in the second. In this usage *it* is independently established as a handle-word and substitutes for no other word. The other two pronominal subjects are likewise so general and scattered (or may be) in their reference as to make their reference indefinite to say the least. The *we* here used is sometimes called the editorial or royal *we* (see page 462) and also the *we* of affected modesty. *You, we,* and *they* in this kind of functioning—*They are erecting a new building, We (you) do not know what fate has in store for us (you)*—are sometimes called the conversational personal pronouns. The point here is, however, that they are not merely indefinite or generic in these uses, but that they are not substitutes for nouns that you can place the finger upon.

And this detached functioning of pronouns applies with even greater force to the relatives. What, for instance, are the antecedents of *who* and *which* (and of *what* in this sentence) when they are used interrogatively? In many cases they have none and require none. *Who, which,* and *that* in adjective clauses have greater conjunctive than pronominal nature, a quality not possessed by nouns. In *I gave the button to Arthur, who threw it away, who,* equivalent to *and he,* is much more important as connecter than as referrer. Nearly all non-restrictive clauses are reducible to a few words of modification, among which the relative pronoun does not appear. This seems to show that as a pronoun in the dependent clause its office is superfluous. *The cake which was home-made is delicious* is really *The home-made cake is delicious.*

Pronouns are classified as *definite* or *demonstrative, indefinite, interrogative, personal,* and *relative.*

Definite or demonstrative pronouns point out or distinguish— *this* and its plural *these* for persons, places, and things close at hand; *that* and its plural *those* for persons, places, and things less close. When they qualify or limit nouns or other pronouns they are called definite adjective pronouns. When they stand alone they are called definites or demonstratives: *This car is mine, This is my car.*

Indefinite pronouns are such as do not clearly point out or distinguish—*all, another, any, anybody, any one, both, each, either, every, everybody, every one, many, neither, none, other, several, some, some one, such.* When they qualify or limit nouns or other pronouns they are called indefinite adjective pronouns. When they stand alone they are called indefinites: *Every car has hydraulic brakes, Each must do his duty, All men must work, All men must do their duty.*

Interrogative pronouns are used in asking questions—*who, which, what,* and *whose,* the possessive of *who* (frequently used as the possessive of *which* and *what* also). *Whether* was formerly an interrogative but is rarely used as such now: *Whether of the two didst thou kill?*

Following are the personal pronouns with their various inflections: *I* and *we*—the first person—the person speaking; *you* (*thou* and *ye*)—the second person—the person or thing spoken to; *he, she, it,* and *they*—the third person—the person, place, or thing spoken of. The second paradigm is nothing more than a variation of the first.

Personal and relative pronouns are inflected for person, number, and gender, but pronoun case depends upon the construction of the clause in which the pronoun stands.

	Nominative Case	Possessive Case	Objective Case
First Person Singular	I	my *or* mine	me
Second Person Singular	you (thou)	your *or* yours (thy *or* thine)	you (thee)
Third Person Singular Masculine	he	his	him
Third Person Singular Feminine	she	her *or* hers	her
Third Person Singular Neuter	it	its	it
First Person Plural	we	our *or* ours	us
Second Person Plural	you (ye)	your *or* yours	you
Third Person Plural, All Genders	they	their *or* theirs	them

	First Person Sing.	Plu.	Second Person Sing.	Plu.	Third Person Sing. *Mas. Fem. Neu.*	Plu.
Nominative Case	I	we	you (thou)	you (ye)	he, she, it	they
Possessive Case	my mine	our ours	your yours thy thine	your yours	his, her, its hers	their theirs
Objective Case	me	us	you thee	you	him, her, it	them

Thou, thine, thy, ye are little used except in poetical expression. By far the greatest amount of speaking and writing done in the world has been done in the third person, and this will continue to be the practise. The third person is neutral and non-committal. It is used with greater security than first and second persons. It is less aggressive and therefore less provocative. It permits of more artful expression, is more modest than the other two persons, and objectifies expression desirably so that disinterested reactions may be provoked.

Relative pronouns refer or relate to nouns or other pronouns. They likewise connect or relate conjunctively, and are therefore sometimes called conjunctive pronouns. The relative pronouns are *who, which, that, what, as,* and (rarely) *but. Who* refers to persons only; *which* to animals and things; *that* to one or all of the three. *What,* as a relative, means *that which: He knew what I wanted,* that is, *He knew that which I wanted.* As an adjective and as an interrogative pronoun *what* modifies nouns and other pronouns. As a relative and as an interrogative it refers to places and things, not to persons. *As* is used as a relative with *same* and *such.* Such collective nouns as *company, firm, jury,* regarded impersonally, are always referred to by *that* or *which,* never by *who.*

I drive the same car as you do   I like such toys as are useful
(I drive the same car that you do)   (I like those toys that are useful)

But rarely occurs as a pronoun. When it does its meaning is *who not: There is hardly anybody but would like to be rich,* that is *There is hardly anybody who would not like to be rich.*

Who and *which,* as relatives used conjunctively, add new and really gratuitous ideas to an expression, that is, they expand and enlarge. *That,* on the other hand, restricts or confines the meaning within certain limits. In *The suitings, which were imported, were quickly sold* the *which* clause is not restrictive. The fact that the suitings were imported is thrown in, as the commas indicate. And the sentence means that *all* the suitings were imported. In *The suitings that were imported were quickly sold* the *that*-clause is restrictive and is so closely related to the principal clause that commas may not be used. Moreover, this sentence implies definitely that there were two kinds of suitings, imported and domestic, and that the imported ones sold well while the domestic did not sell so quickly. Tho *that* should always be used with restrictive clauses, this rule is sometimes eased for the sake of euphony. Repetition of any one pronoun, as of any other word, may become monotonous.

That is never used appositively with proper names. We cannot say *Torr Gate, that was erected in 1900* or *John Samson, that died in the war. Which* is required in the one case and *who* in the other. Nor is *that* used as object of a preposition: *The man of whom* not *of that I have heard.*

Relatives, with the exception of *that, as,* and *but,* may be compounded with *ever* and *soever: whatever, whoever, whichever, whatsoever, whosoever, whomsoever, whichsoever.* These additions make no difference whatsoever in the functioning of the relatives.

The antecedent of a pronoun should always be a noun or another pronoun. It may not be a word of another classification unless that word is functioning as a noun or a pronoun. It should not refer to a phrase or a clause, tho there is much general violation of this ruling. It is perhaps better to say that the relative pronoun that refers specifically to a word is likely to keep a construction clearer than one that refers to a whole clause, that it is indicative of somewhat clearer thinking to have the pronoun refer to a word and a word only rather than to any group of words. But the point cannot be pressed. Some authorities rule that *which* may be used to refer to a clause but *that* may not be.

The compound or reflexive or emphatic pronouns are *myself, ourselves, yourself, yourselves, herself, himself, itself, themselves,* (sometimes) *oneself. One* has both plural and possessive forms—*ones, one's*—and is treated by some authorities as a personal pronoun. *One's self* is a regular possessive form, like *one's heart* or *one's idea,* and should not be confused with the emphatic *oneself.*

Probably no other part of speech is so frequently omitted and left to be understood as is the relative pronoun: *The book (that) I own, The people I work with, The train I came in.*

Pronouns are used in all ways that nouns are used with the exception of one, namely, adverbial objective. Obviously pronouns do not indicate time, distance, measure, and the like.

Nominative case constructions

As subject	*They* steered carelessly
As predicate nominative	It is *I*
As exclamatory nominative	Even *you!* (Et *tu,* Brute!)
As direct-address nominative (vocative)	*You,* you are the one I mean
As absolute nominative	*He* having been delayed, they left without him

Objective case constructions

As object of verb	I love *him*
As object of preposition	He repaired it for *me*
As indirect object	Give (to) *him* the book
As objective complement	*What* did they elect him?
As subject of infinitive	I asked *him* to drive rapidly

Possessive case constructions

| By inflection (but *not* by apostrophe) | His hat is off
This is mine own
Our work is done |
| By preposition *of* | He likes this place of ours
I want that book of yours |

Nominative, objective, or possessive case construction

| An appositive pronoun (a pronoun used as explanatory modifier) must agree in person, number, gender, and case with the noun or pronoun that it explains | Thompson, *he* of the accounting department, has just been married (nominative)
I gave the box to that fellow, *him* with the red tie (objective)
This place is Mary's, *hers* forever (possessive) |

III Verbs

A verb is usually called an action word—a word that expresses or names or asserts action. We have become habituated to this definition, so let it stand. But sometimes verbs describe in addition. *Rustled, scrambled, struggled, wobbled,* and a host of other action words, carry with them a picture. They therefore have some adjective quality along with their verb quality. Again, the verbs *nosed, skulked, tiptoed, fawned* explain as well as assert action, and hence contain some adverbial nature and some adjective nature *and* some noun nature, along with the action they indicate. Such verbs are, of course, rightly called ideational (see page 130).

But in addition to describing and explaining and naming and asserting action, verbs express time, mood, habit, degree, continuity, and still other conditions and situations. Moreover, copulative verbs *connect.* In *John is ill, is* does nothing more than connect *John* and *illness.* Other "conjunctive verbs," besides *to be,* are *appear, become, grow, seem.* Sentences in which they are the principal verbs are nominal sentences only. The interrelationship between verbs and prepositions is pointed out on pages 160 and 210.

It appears, then, that verbs may be the most colorful, most exciting, most comprehensive part of speech, and that they may also be quite colorless and uninteresting. They are the former for the most part. The expression of thought can never be completed without the use of verbs. It may conceivably be expressed without other parts of speech. The verbs *go, come, answer, study* constitute sentences as they stand. They express complete thoughts without additional words.

As to form, verbs are classified as *regular* and *irregular,* and *defective* and *redundant.* As to quality and function they are classified as *auxiliary* and *principal, active* and *passive, transitive* and *intransitive.* The *copula,* mentioned above, is another kind usually listed along with these.

A regular verb is one that indicates past time, that is, forms its imperfect (past) tense by the suffix *ed: walked, rowed, tampered.* Those verbs that end with *e* and add *d* to form the imperfect tense are classed as regular: *saved, bathed, bereaved.* (For the final consonant rule applying to verbs ending with a consonant, see page 551.) Such verbs are increasingly forming their imperfect tense by the addition of *t* only: *dropt, slipt, stopt, wrapt.* Certain verbs in *ay* form their imperfect tense and past participle by the use of *d* only after changing the *y* to *i,* but they are still classed as regular verbs: *staid (stayed), paid (payed).*

An irregular verb is one that undergoes some other kind of change in the formation of its imperfect tense and its past participle: *speak, spoke, spoken; write, wrote, written; lead, led, led; sink, sank, sunk* (see list of irregular verbs on page 185). These verbs are usually the most troublesome for a stranger to our tongue to learn, just as the irregular verbs of foreign tongues cause us more trouble as a rule than any other part of those languages. Some sane person a little while ago devised a plan to make all verbs regular, that is, to make all verbs form their imperfect tense and past participle by the addition of *ed.* Like the plan for *thon* (see page 170) this one also failed, but there was nevertheless much to be said in its behalf. How convenient *speaked* and *writed,* and the others would be! Regular verbs are sometimes called *weak* verbs; irregular verbs, *strong* verbs.

A defective verb is one that is lacking in some of its parts or formations. The verb *shall,* for instance, has no *shalling* or present participle. It does have an imperfect form *should,* and it is used in present and imperfect tenses only, like *may* and *might* (it is possible to go *a-maying* but this is a different verb), *can* and *could* (fruit may be *canned,* but this, too, is a different verb), and *will* and *would* (with *willing* in a different category). The defective verb *must* has no other form. The lists on pages 185-187 show other irregularities. Some verbs, it will be noted, are the same for all parts, except for the present participle, which always adds *ing*. Here are a few such verbs: *beset, burst, cast, cost, cut, bit, hurt, put, let, read, rid, set, shed, shut, slit, split, spread.*

A redundant verb is one that has more than one form for a certain part (parts). One form in such cases tends to become archaic and thus falls out of use. The imperfect form of *speak* is *spoke* or *spake*, but the latter appears chiefly in the Bible. The past participle of *prove* is *proved* and *proven*, but the latter is no longer regarded as current, tho it is still used. The list on page 185 contains several other verbs that have redundant forms in either the imperfect tense or the participle, or both.

In *I have driven the car five miles, have driven* is the predicate. The verb phrase is *have driven;* in this phrase *driven* is the notional or principal verb and *have* is the helping or auxiliary verb—it merely helps to locate the time of the driving. The chief helping or auxiliary verbs are *be, can, do, have (had), may, must, shall, will.* In the following expressions the auxiliaries are italicized:

I *am* driving	I *shall* drive
I *can* drive	I *will* drive
I *do* drive	I *may* drive
I *had* driven	I *must* drive

Sometimes these auxiliaries stand alone as predicates, and when this is so they are usually connectives only, tho some of them have greater notional or ideational quality than others (see pages 130 and 144).

Auxiliary verbs function in a most important way in denoting the voice of verbs, that is, in indicating whether the subject of a given verb performs the action or is acted upon. A verb is in the *active voice* when its subject is the doer or proposed doer of the action; in the *passive voice* when its subject is the receiver or the focus of the action.

In all the above illustrations (wherein *drive* is the notional verb) the verbs are active. In these they are passive:

I am driven
I was driven
I shall be driven
I have been driven
I had been driven
I shall have been driven
I may he driven
I might be driven
I may have been driven
I might have been driven

Be driven

To be driven
To have been driven

Being driven
Been driven
Having been driven

Technically, the passive voice of a verb is formed by adding its past participle to every form of the verb *be* as auxiliary. The transference of object to subject, and of subject to object of a preposition is one of the important changes to observe in converting thought expression from active to passive form.

John drove the car
I gave John a car

The car was driven by John
A car was given to John by me
John was given a car by me

Thus the facility of voice forms enables one to express himself directly about the agent of action or the recipient of action. Note that in *I gave John a car, car* is the object. So it is also in one passive form: *John was given a car by me.* It is thus called the retained object. But the retained-object construction is preferably to be avoided whenever possible (see page 180).

Passive voice may very often be heavy and cumbrous, if used to excess. It is regarded as somewhat more polite and considerate than the active voice, less egotistical and aggressive. But the speaker or writer who habitually backgrounds himself thru the medium of the passive voice may by that very token get himself accused of pose and affectation. It is more direct, and a bit more honest perhaps, to say *I won the prize* than to say *The prize was won by me.* The subordination of self is sometimes highly commendable, but at other times—especially when it makes expression pedantic—it cannot be justified.

A transitive verb is one that requires an object—the action of the verb has a receiver of the action. In *He arranged the papers, arranged* is transitive because its action or the result of its action passes over to *papers.* An intransitive verb is one that requires no object—the action of the verb has no receiver of the action, at least, not in the expression itself. In *I shall go, The engine rumbles, It rains,* the verbs have no receivers of action and are therefore intransitive.

Authorities differ in regard to transitive verbs. Some hold that a verb in the passive voice cannot have an object or receiver of action. Others contend that in *The papers were arranged by him, papers* receives the action of the arranging, and that tho it is subject, it nevertheless receives the action of the verb. They call *were arranged* transitive therefore. Similarly in *The barn was made a garage* they contend that *barn* receives the action and that *was made* is transitive thru *barn* rather than thru *garage.*

The point is moot. In each of these—*The engine is called Diesel, The place was named Terrytop, The chauffeur was given warning, His story was told to the judge*—there appear to be two receivers of action. It should be noted that most verbs are capable of being either transitive or intransitive: *The car rattled, I rattled the car; The window slammed, I slammed the window.*

Sometimes the meaning of a transitive verb is enforced by the use of its corresponding form immediately after it as object, as in *I dreamed a dream, I voted a vote, Madame DeFarge coughed a cough.* Such an object is called a *cognate* (born with) object. It should be used sparingly. Again, transitive verbs are sometimes followed by reflexive or identical objects, as in *I asked myself, He tortured himself, We unintentionally imprisoned ourselves.* Note also that certain verbs likely to be intransitive have equivalents or near-equivalents that are likely to be transitive: *He stands there* but *He understands it, He runs slowly* but *He outruns me, He moans miserably* but *He bemoans his luck, He drinks deep* but *He drenches his shirt with water, He lies late in the morning* but *He lays his plans well, The plane sweeps down* but *We sweep the field, He falls hard* but *He fells his man.* These are but a few of the transitive and intransitive distinctions that may be drawn between certain pairs of verbs. Sometimes there is a prefix change; sometimes an internal-spelling change.

The copulative verbs (see pages 134 and 144) are regarded (1) as intransitive when used alone as notionals (2) as incapable of modification. Hence, in such sentences as *We are here, They were there,* the words *here* and *there* are regarded by most authorities as predicate adjectives rather than as adverbs of place.

Verbs have no gender and no case. A predicate must agree with its subject in person and number, and the verb must some-

times change its form to do this: *I drive, He drives.* We have
seen that most verbs change their forms (undergo inflection) to
indicate voice: *I catch, I am caught.* Verbs are inflected also
for tense and mode.

Tense means time. (It is from the Latin *tendo, tensus,* stretch.)
Time is first of all divided into present time, past time, and
future time, and tenses of the verb follow suit—present tense,
past tense (preferably called imperfect, as it is called in other
languages), future tense. *I go* is present; *I went* is imperfect;
I shall go is future. These all have interrogative and negative
forms:

Do I go?	Did I go?	Shall I go?
I do not go	I did not go	I shall not go

Note the use of the auxiliary *do,* and of *not* (see pages 183 and
195). In addition to these three simple and general indications
of time called tense, the verb may be used also to express degrees
of present, past, and future time.

The present perfect tense (sometimes called the perfect) denotes
action completed at present or near the present. *They have
gone away* means, for instance, that their going or their getting
off has been completed or perfected comparatively recently.
The present tense, *They go,* would imply nowness—they are just
getting off. Present tense passive voice, *They are gone,* would
indicate the action as more immediate than the present perfect
but not so immediate as the present. Note then:

They go (now), They are gone (just a little while ago), They have
gone (somewhat longer ago)

The past perfect or pluperfect tense denotes action completed or
perfected prior to some other action of the past. In *They had
gone when I arrived* the meaning is that their getting off was
completed or perfected before my arrival took place, but that
both their going and my arriving took place before the time at
which this remark is made. There is, in other words, a greater
degree of pastness in *They had gone* than there is in *I arrived.*
Consider the imperfect tense passive voice in this relationship:
They were gone when I arrived. Here *They were gone* means
that I missed them by fewer minutes or hours than was the case
in *They had gone.* So it will be apparent that the pluperfect
tense is correlated with the imperfect tense much as the present
perfect tense is with the present. Note also that *have* is the
auxiliary of the present perfect—the sign or token by which it

may be immediately recognized—and that its imperfect—*had*—is the sign or token of the pluperfect.

Both of these tenses may also be expressed interrogatively and negatively:

Have they gone?   Had they gone?
They have not gone   They had not gone

In the same way, the future perfect tense goes the simple future not only one—but many—better. It expresses not simply future action but future action as completed. It therefore becomes prophetic, as it were; it assumes that anticipations have become actual experiences and expresses them as such by means of the sign of the future—*shall* or *will*—and the sign of the perfect—*have*. In *I fancy that by the time you are twenty you shall have become a great financier* a hope or a wish or a prophecy or an interpretation of aptitude is expressed as a future fact. Note also *By this time tomorrow I shall have been graduated* and *The operation shall have been completed by the time we arrive at the hospital.* These two are passive voice—the signs of the future and of the perfect add the further sign of the passive—some form of the verb *be, been* in these examples.

It is pointed out on page 178 that the present tense may indicate future time: *The bus arrives at three, I go to the city tomorrow.* The present tense may also be used to vivify past happenings, and thus deliberately appropriate the function of the imperfect tense. This is sometimes called the *historical present: Napoleon now retreats. His men are in disorder and disaster. The day is won for Waterloo and for England.*

The present tense is customarily used to express habituated action or general truth. So used it is called the *gnomic* present. Other tenses may, however, be used for the same purpose (see page 178): *She loves Balzac, She wears red a great deal, Swift says Happiness is the perpetual possession of being well deceived, The square of the hypotenuse of a right-angled triangle is equal to the sum of the squares of the other two sides.* But *He used to like this place, He would stand by the gate and watch us depart.*

The tenses of two or more verbs in the same sentence must be gaged to the meaning expressed. As a rule they should represent the same time or a harmonized degree of time (see above). The tense of a subordinate clause, that is, should be the same as that of the principal clause. This rule is called the sequence of tenses. Note its application in these examples: *I know where he is going* (present), *I knew where he was going* (imperfect), *He will go if you will* (future). But note the gnomic present in these: *He told me that Columbus is the capital of Ohio, His parents assured us that he studies two hours every evening, It would be futile to deny that he is a very indifferent boy.* Note also in these that the meaning requires change of tenses: *They feel certain that he will be married in June, I think he has been here for two months.*

Mode means manner. Applied to verbs it means the manner of action indicated by a single or a phrasal verb. The *indicative mode* is used for positive and for negative assertions. But such assertions may be turned around into interrogative form, and thus become interrogative indicative: *He ordered a new car, He did not order a new car, Did he order a new car? Did he not order a new car?* The indicative is used also for action that is considered likely to occur: *He is coming if there is no sickness in the family, He arrives tomorrow if the train isn't held up.*

The *imperative mode* is used for positive and negative commands and requests, for advice and entreaty. Inasmuch as such expressions are addressed to others, the imperative mode is used only in the second person singular and plural, active and passive. The subject of a verb in the imperative mode—*you*—is usually not mentioned, but occasionally it is: *Go thou and do my bidding, Do as I say, Be approved of all if you can, Do not walk on the tracks, Do these problems first.*

The *subjunctive mode* is used for indicating concession, condition (contrary to fact), doubt, dread, fear, hope, likelihood, prayer, purpose, strife, supposition, wish, yearning, and after words of command. Illustrations of its commonest uses are given on page 182, and these are all that need concern us. In general the indicative may be called the realistic or the colorless matter-of-fact mode while the subjunctive is the fortuitous or likely-to-happen mode. It is the probable or possible mode. Some authorities separate the expression of probability or possibility by means of the defective verbs *can, may, must, ought* into a separate mode called the *potential* mode. Others group all such expressions under the subjunctive. The name *apodictive mode* is sometimes applied to *must* when it is used in a speculative sense, thus: *He must be asleep by this time, It must be snowing on that mountain, He must have arrived by this time, I should think.* It will be noted that such expressions have the quality of present or future time but lack certainty of fact.

Preceded by the conjunction *if* the subjunctive form of expression is usually non-committal and therefore indirectly on the defensive. Hypothetical examples, in the law for instance, are safe as parallels because they are subjunctive and thus non-committal. They permit of deadly analogies without endangering at all the cause of the one who draws them.

But *if* is by no means always the sign of the subjunctive. In *If I disagree with you about the importance of field athletics I nevertheless agree with you about the importance of health hygiene, if* merely introduces and has the meaning *just as.* Similarly *If it is important it is (will be) imperative a week from today* means that it is imperative at both times—equally imperative—and *if* merely emphasizes this equality. But say *If it be imperative today it will be imperative a week from today* and the subjunctive *be* after *if* keys the expression into negative inference, namely, *It is really not imperative today, but if it be made so, then we are committed to habitual action.* Note these further examples: *If I was a failure last term, that does not mean that I must fail this term.* The subjunctive is not used after *if* because the statement is not contrary to fact. *I was* a failure last term. The expression *I was successful in my last job and I wish I were a success in my present one* means that I am failing now; the subjunctive in the second clause makes this meaning inescapable. Observe this perfect subjunctive *if* from Matthew xv:14: *And if the blind guide the blind, both shall fall into the pit.*

Note that *Let every teacher pass her pupils* is equivalent to saying to teachers, *Pass your pupils;* but the former is subjunctive and the latter imperative in manner of expression. In *Help me,* addressed to God, the mode or manner is subjunctive, for it is a wish or a prayer. In *Help me,* addressed to a present individual, the mode or manner is imperative, for it is a command or request.

The infinitive is not a manner of action, not a mode of expressing action, but, rather, a *naming* of action. It is therefore partly verb and partly noun. It is usually introduced by *to* (see page 174). There are just two forms of the infinitive, present tense both active and passive and perfect tense both active and passive:

to take	to have taken
to be taken	to have been taken

It may be used in all the following ways:

To drive is exhilarating (subject)
He has learned *to drive* (object)
To work is *to live* (subject, and predicate nominative or attribute)
It is good for the morals *to work* (appositive)
He has no honorable course left but *to take* the case (object of preposition)
They helped him (to) *win* (objective complement)
They have tasks *to perform* (adjective modifying *tasks*)
His effort is not *to be taken* seriously (predicate adjective)
He is prepared *to answer* (adverb of manner)
He is too reckless *to drive* (adverb of degree)
He is training *to win* the race (adverb of reason)
He ought *to become* a good driver (adverb of result)
To tell the truth I think you are quite wrong (adverb of concession)

Time after that denoted by the principal verb of a sentence or time the same as the principal verb of a sentence is denoted by the present infinitive. But time completed supposedly before that of the principal verb of a sentence is denoted by the perfect infinitive (see page 181).

He asks to go	He was to have gone before
He asked them to reply	He was supposed to have known it

The gerund (see page 136) may be used as follows:

Driving the car has steadied my nerves (subject)
I do not like *driving* at night (object)
Working is *living* (subject, and predicate nominative or attribute)
His particular pride, *driving* on narrow roads, will sometime take a fall (appositive)
He is fond of *driving* a Cadillac (object of preposition)
We considered him *cured* (objective complement)
Barking dogs never bite (adjective)
Bill went *driving* (adverb)

The verbal noun (see page 136) may be used as follows:

Your *driving* will steady your nerves (subject)
Practise will improve your *driving* (object)
He has been forced to stop his *driving* (object of infinitive)
Their chief merit is their *listening* (predicate nominative or attribute)
That big job, your *practising*, must not be neglected (appositive)
He received a medal for his *driving* (object of preposition)
The judges consider his *driving* to be worthy of the medal (subject of infinitive)
They saw their son *chosen* (objective complement)

Note that in *freezing cold, wringing wet, blazing hot,* the participles are really adverbs; and that in *shooting star, blinking moon, ringing bells,* the participles are pure adjectives.

All. the possible forms of the verb, listed tense by tense, constitute what is known as *conjugation*. There are three particular conjugations—the *simple,* the *emphatic,* the *continuous* or *progressive.* The simple conjugation is the regular form of verbal expression. The emphatic conjugation exists in two tenses only, the verb *do* and its imperfect *did* being the emphatic auxiliary. The continuous or progressive conjugation indicates action as going on at the time of speaking or writing. A conjugation synopsis is the listing of all modes and tenses in one person and number only. Here are synopses of all three conjugations for the verb *walk* in third person singular number active voice:

	Simple	*Continuous*	*Emphatic*
Indicative			
Present	he walks	he is walking	he does walk
Imperfect	he walked	he was walking	he did walk
Future	he will walk	he will be walking	
Perfect	he has walked	he has been walking	
Pluperfect	he had walked	he had been walking	
Future Perfect	he will have walked	he will have been walking	
Subjunctive			
Present	if he walk	if he be walking	if he do walk
Imperfect	if he walked	if he were walking	if he did walk
Future	if he will walk	if he will be walking	
Perfect	if he have walked	if he have been walking	
Pluperfect	if he had walked	if he had been walking	
Future Perfect	if he will have walked	if he will have been walking	
Potential			
Present	he may walk	he may be walking	
Imperfect	he might walk	he might be walking	
Perfect	he may have walked	he may have been walking	
Pluperfect	he might have walked	he might have been walking	
Imperative	walk	be walking	do walk
Infinitive			
Present	to walk	to be walking	
Perfect	to have walked	to have been walking	
Participles			
Present	walking	being walking	
Past	walked	been walking	
Perfect	having walked	having been walking	

In idiomatic use the progressive commonly appears in such expressions as *The house is building, There's trouble a-brewing.* The passive voice is formed by inserting the corresponding forms of the verb *to be* in all tenses: *He is walked, He is being walked, He was walked, He was being walked, The horse has been walked a mile, The horse has been being walked all morning.* There is no passive voice of the emphatic forms.

IV Adjectives

Some one has said that adjectives dance attendance upon nouns as adverbs dance attendance upon verbs. This is a happy comparison. Adjectives expand or reduce the meanings of nouns and pronouns just as adverbs do of verbs, adjectives, and other adverbs. Adjectives specify nouns; they describe nouns; they explain nouns; they give tone and quality to noun usage. It is frequently pointed out by grammarians that the adjective is capable of ambiguity even when most closely adapted. This happens most frequently when nouns are themselves appropriated to do the work of adjectives. *A paper knife*—is it made of paper or for cutting paper? *A walking stick*—is it a stick to walk with or is it a mechanical device that walks automatically? And such figurative epithets as *round table, square deal, blue funk, triangular love affair* go even further to make the use of adjectives puzzling to those unacquainted with our English idiom. At the same time it is this very ambiguity that makes of the adjective a most versatile and colorful word instrument.

Adjectives are classified as *descriptive* (*qualifying* or *tonal*) and as *numeral* (or *limiting*). The former may be common or proper—*a* GOOD *engineer, a* ROMAN *holiday, a* RED *flower, an* IRON *decision.* The latter—limiting or numeral adjective—points out or limits or confines or states actual number or quantity—FIVE *hours,* TEN *men. Five* and *ten* and other numerals similarly expressed are *cardinals; fifth, tenth, twelfth, forty-ninth* are *ordinals.* The articles *a, an,* and *the* are limiting adjectives, as are such pronominals as *this, that, these, those, yonder, which, what, whose, my, your, their, each, some, such, few, every, many,* when they definitely limit or specify thru modification or reference. Participles that modify in an almost purely adjective sense are sometimes called *verbal adjectives* —*the* WHISTLING *advocate, a* BOUNCING *baby, a* FORGOTTEN *rendezvous, the* ENCIRCLING *gloom. What* is sometimes called an exclamatory adjective: *What a man! What rubbish this is!*

Own and *very* are emphatic adjectives: *The very idea! This is my own idea.*

Such adjectives as the following are called *quantitative: few, certain, enough, several, half, any, much.* These are called *multiplicatives—double, triple, threefold, quadruple, hundredfold.* A little book might be written about numeral adjectives alone, including the quantitatives and the multiplicatives. They grow and multiply almost beyond calculation. A *tripartite* thing is a thing made up of three parts; it is a *threefold* thing. *Trilateral* means three-sided, and *ternary* means proceeding or recurring in threes. A *biannual* publication is issued every half year, or *semiannually.* An *annual* publication is issued yearly; a *biennial* publication, every two years; a *triennial,* every three years; a *quadrennial,* every four years; and so, *quinennial* (5), *sexennial* (6), *septennial* (7), *octennial* (8), *novennial* (9), *decennial* (10), *centennial* (100), *sesquicentennial* (150), *bicentennial* (200), *tricentennial* (300), *millennial* (1000). These represent only very few of a single category. Start with *centenary* (hundredth anniversary), and follow with *bicentenary, tercentenary, quatercentenary,* and so forth; or with the algebraic terms *monomial, binomial, quadrinomial;* or with *quinquagenarian* (a person in his fifties), *sexagenarian, septuagenarian, octogenarian, nonagenarian, centenarian;* or with the *angle* category—*triangle* (3), *quadrangle* (4), *heptangle* (7), *octangle* (8), *decagonal* (10); or the *side* category—*quadrilateral* (four sided), *quinquelateral* (5), *sexilateral* (6), *septilateral* (7), *octolateral* (8), *nonilateral* (9), *decilateral* (10); and the limitless scope of limiting adjectives alone becomes apparent. Some one has said that the adjective is the most extravagantly and the most ruthlessly used part of speech there is. But somebody has replied that this is true only because there are so many more adjectives in the language than there are other parts of speech.

Note carefully the idiomatic use of *a* in connection with numerals. We say *a hundred, a thousand, a million, a billion, a dozen, a ream, a score, a gross;* but *half a gross, half a dozen, half a million.* We do not say *half a thousand* or *half a fifty.* We sometimes hear *half a hundred,* but strictly speaking this is incorrect even as idiom, *half hundred* being preferable. *One thousand four hundred and fifty* is better than *a thousand four hundred and fifty;* tho the latter is not wrong, the former is more idiomatic.

Adjectives are inflected for comparison (see page 588). They do not have person and number and gender, except such as are used as nouns and pronouns—*this, that, my, their, mine, ours,* and the like. Adjectives modify nouns and pronouns—*the little boy, poor little you.* They may modify nouns and pronouns as appositives—*The boys,* ALL *groomed for the fray, came running to the field.* They may explain the meaning of a subject and at the same time complete a predicate; they may explain the meaning of an object and at the same time complete the meaning of a predicate—*He is* STALWART, *He made the tramp* RESPECTABLE.

V Adverbs

The adverb is to the verb what the adjective is to the noun. It stretches or limits the significance of a verb and thus establishes the keynote of an expression. Any sort of question that may be asked regarding the predication of an expression the adverb is capable of answering—why, when, where, how much, how good, wherefore, consequence. The adverb answers all these and more. And it does so by the perfect elasticity of its functioning. It may modify adjectives, verbs, other adverbs, phrases (*quite in the open, terribly out of sorts*), and may both modify and connect as in such sentences as *He did the work while I was thinking about it* and *This is the direction whither they went.* To cap the adverbial climax, as it were, this part of speech may be used to qualify, limit, or "pitch" an entire sentence. Especially is this function true of *yes* and *no,* the so-called responsive adverbs.

> *Undoubtedly* you are aware of the time
> *Certainly* I shall have your booking reserved
> *Yes,* I think I shall be happy to go
> *Consequently* we started without our luggage

The following excerpt from *The Elements of Grammar* by Alfred S. West seems to be too cogent to be omitted:

> By the aid of adjectives we can distinguish different varieties of things, each of which distinctions would require a separate noun, if we had no adjectives. Thus, if we take *wine* as our noun, and *good, old,* and *red* as its limiting adjectives, with these four words we can mark eight distinctions: viz. (putting initial letters to represent the words) W, GW, OW, RW, GOW, GRW, ORW, GORW, and for these eight distinctions we should need eight nouns. This gives a very inadequate idea, however, of the economy of words which adjectives enable us to effect. For if we take the same three adjectives, *good, old,* and *red,* and change the noun from *wine* to *velvet,*

we shall need another eight nouns to express the varieties of *velvet;* another eight would be required to express the varieties of *curtains,* and so on. The three nouns *wine, velvet,* and *curtains,* in combination with the adjectives *good, old,* and *red,* would need twenty-four words instead of six.

The same point might be illustrated as regards verbs and adverbs. By combining *write, ride, walk,* with *gracefully, slowly, well,* we express by means of six words twenty-four distinctions. If we had no adverbs and wished to mark these distinctions, we should do so either (1) by using phrases composed of a preposition and a noun, e.g. "with grace," "in a slow manner," "in a good style," or (2) by adding twenty-one verbs to our vocabulary.*

As to mere form adverbs are classified as *simple, compound* or *derived,* and *phrasal. Happily, sadly, grandly* are simple adverbs; *furthermore, inside, nevertheless* are compound or derived; *by-and-by, inside out, back and forth* are phrasal. Phrasal adverbs may be formed *ad lib.: Explain the verb tense-by-tense, Hand it to me piece-by-piece, Read the figures to me column-by-column.*

As to meaning or qualifying and connective power combined, adverbs are classified as to *place* and *motion—here, there, in, upon;* as to *time* and *order—always, again, first, tomorrow, yesterday;* as to *manner—merrily, cruelly, ill, stupidly;* as to *negation—no, not, never;* as to *reason* or *cause—why, wherefore, whether* (archaic); as to *degree—too, very, quite, hardly, scarcely, enough, partly, altogether, already, almost;* as to *connection—however, because, moreover, therefore, inasmuch;* as to *interrogation—why, how, when, where, wherefore;* as to *responsiveness—yes, no, perhaps, verily, forsooth, undoubtedly* (these are sometimes called adverbs of affirmation and negation); as to *numbering (enumerative adverbs)—once, twice, thrice, often, seldom, secondly;* the adverb *there* is usually classified as an *expletive* (see page 197). There are of course many more illustrative adverbs that may properly be listed under each one of these headings. Adverbs of degree usually modify adjectives and adverbs; adverbs of the other classifications usually modify verbs or connect clauses adverbially.

Adverbs that merely modify verbs, adjectives, or other adverbs are called *modifying* or *qualifying* adverbs. Those that in addition connect clauses and show relationship between or among clauses are called *conjunctive adverbs* or *adverbial conjunctions* or *relative adverbs.* Note that the italicized words in

* By permission of The Macmillan Company.

the following sentences serve to connect and to establish relationships:

Come *when* you can (time relationship) *after, whenever, while, until, before*

Go *where* you will (place relationship) *whence, whither, wherever*

Drive *as* you like (manner relationship) *how, however*

Do the job *because* you love it (causal relationship) *for, since*

It will stall *if* the hill is steep (conditional relationship) *unless, provided*

Tho he deceive me, *yet* will I give him work (concession relationship) *altho*

He is a better driver *than* I (degree relationship)

I oil the car *in order that* it may run better (purpose relationship) *lest, so that*

The italicized words following the parentheses are the principal conjunctive adverbs in addition to the one used in the illustrative sentence. Note that each italicized word in the above sentences not only connects the principal thought of the sentence with the subordinate thought, but also establishes a specific relationship between the two. The clause following the adverbial conjunction is called an adverbial clause, and as a group of words it stands in the same adverbial relationship to the independent clause as a single modifying adverb stands to the word it modifies. Note *He came late* and *He came when it was late* and *He came at a time at which it was late.* The last two expressions are extravagant in wording. In all three sentences the inter-clause relationship is one of time, and therefore adverbial. The last sentence is ridiculously awkward and labored and would not be used by any careful writer or speaker. As it stands, however, the clause relationship has been resolved into an indirect adjective relationship. But this is probably not the intended meaning of the sentence. The same is true of *Here is the place at which he was born* for *He was born here, Here is where he was born,* or *Here is the place where he was born.* The intended meaning is *whereness* or *atness* of his birth. To call the subordinate clause adjective, as some authorities do, is to overlook the adverbial quality of the intended meaning. The adjective qualities of *when* and *where* in such sentences are so remote and strained that it is better usually to regard them as adverbs of time and place respectively.

The adverbs *how* and *why* are frequently used to introduce noun clauses. But they are usually more than mere introductory words in such usage. They invariably have in addition some modifying influence upon the predicate of the subordinate clause, as observe *He asked how I did it* and *He asked why I did it.* *How* and *why* bridge the gap between independent and dependent members of the expression. Each adverb in addition modifies the verb following it—*how* meaning *in what manner* and *why* meaning *for what reason.*

VI Prepositions

The preposition is both a relational and a connectional word. It has both adjective and adverbial quality with a little of the conjunction thrown in. Many prepositions may be adverbs; adverbs are to a certain degree their parents. But some prepositions are derived from nouns: *abroad, across, beside;* and some are derived from verbs: *during, notwithstanding, pending.* Prepositions for the most part mean position, location, direction, agent, instrument, accompaniment, purpose, condition. When they do not have any such signification they become mere connecters or relational links between one noun or verb and another. The verbal-prepositional combinations are numerous, and are likely to cause considerable trouble for him who is a stranger to the ways of the English tongue. The following sentences denote some of these misleading combinations:

> Please look over my work but overlook the errors
> If you overpay me I shall pay over my premium to the insurance company
> He climbed out thru the window and wandered thruout the night
> The garden is overgrown with weeds but they will not grow over the grass plot
> Come, play by the maple tree while I study the by-play in this drama
> You must undergo an operation, that is, go under the knife
> Take under your arm the parcel that I give you and undertake to deliver it promptly

The preposition is likewise capable of figurative use: *Will you stand by me? Will you see me thru it?*

The prepositional idiom has undergone great changes—greater perhaps than that of any other part of speech. The Elizabethan forms—*I have a suit to you, Prepare yourself to death, I stay here on my bond, I live with bread like you, We'll deliver you of your great danger, Have we eaten on the insane root*—are now archaic and sound very strange to us.

Prepositions, like adverbs, may be classified into *simple, compound* or *derived,* and *phrasal. At, by, for, in, on, with, of, from* are simple prepositions; *beside, beneath, without, within, upon, notwithstanding, concerning* are compound or derived prepositions; *because of, instead of, in spite of, on account of, out of* are phrasal prepositions.

Prepositional phrases are used in the following ways:

As Nouns

In high gear means first position (subject)
He called *"On your right, please"* (object)
He drove from *beyond that hill* (object of preposition)
They painted the car *in the same color* (objective complement)

As Adjectives

The car *in the next garage* is mine (limiting)
He is a chauffeur *of great courage* (descriptive)
She seems *in great trouble* (predicate nominative or attribute)
The city *of Denver* is the capital of Colorado (appositive)

As Adverbs

They have gone *to the factory* (place)
We shall arrive *in the morning* (time)
He drives *with great skill* (manner)
He was arrested *for speeding* (reason)
She pleaded *for mercy* (purpose)
I was helped *by my mother* (agent)
We shall go *with the party* (accompaniment)
The car was destroyed *by fire* (instrumentality)
He drove faster than I *by three miles* an hour (degree)

The prepositional idiom is one of the most difficult features of English. It is treated to some extent on page 211 *seq.* But no mere text-book treatment can do the work of the dictionary when you are in doubt as to the precise preposition to use after a given verb. Many true and tried speakers and writers make errors in the prepositional idiom. Practise and the dictionary —and a nice ear for correct usage—are the only preventives of error in this field. Here are twelve commonly used prepositions. Each one is briefly defined and briefly illustrated. Neither the list nor the illustration for each word is exhaustive. But the method of getting at correct idiomatic usage of the preposition is indicated:

at means definite and immediate time and position and also in or under given conditions
by means alongside, in direction of, agent of, instrument of
for means causation and purpose and time during
from means contrary condition or movement or position
in means position that is stationary in space or time or condition
into means movement or direction to a position from without to within

of means possession by way of accessory or adjunct
on means position of a thing as external to another or sustained by it
thru means working a way or discovering a route between or among
    things
to means connection or relationship or identity between terms
under means lower than or beneath something else or some condition
with means accompaniment and also similarity and instrumentality
    of reference between terms

Illustrations of the foregoing:

at this juncture, at any rate, at twelve, at once, at sixes and sevens, at dinner, at the end of my rope, love at first sight, at the least disturbance, at war, at peace, at work. In locations *at* designates the lesser and *in* the greater: *He is at school in Chicago, He works in New York City but lives at Westport*

stand by, forced by, helped by, meant by, flattered by, travel by sea, supported by, works by so-and-so, by leave, by request, by day, by hook or crook

a craving for drink, convenient for service, fitted for immediate use, ground for divorce, sufficient for the fare, a substitute for soap, suitable for summer wear, a taste for music, no use for it, reason for your stand, finished for all time, room for everybody, adaptable for many purposes

deduce from, desist from, differ from or with, *different from, part from* (with), *remove from, resign from, restrain from*

in crowds, in debt, in health, in liquor, in merriment, in mufti, in need, in nature, in opposition, in order, in perpetuity, in position, in partnership, in all probability, in Russia, in sorrow, in tights, in trouble, in youth, in support (but note *go into the office, jump into the water, walk into the forest, work long into the night, go into the affair, put yourself into a proper attitude*)

on advice of, approve of, conscious of, designation of, evidence of, forgetful of, ignorant of, jealous of, mindful of

on the table, on the shelf, on first thought, depend on (or *upon*) *what I say, on principle, on my word of honor, upon* (or *on*) *my word, on strike, on time, on the dot, on further consideration, on fire, on deck, on the carpet, on further notice*

thru a crisis, elbowing thru a crowd, failing thru over-eagerness, thru thick and thin, seeing thru somebody, winning thru sheer industry, looking thru the papers, getting thru an examination, running thru the woods, looking thru the window, passing thru the door

adjacent to, adjust to, adhere to, annex to, attentive to, appeal to, confine to, endeavor to, incomprehensible to, obvious to, obnoxious to, repellent to, repugnant to, similar to, try to, witness to

under special treatment, under these circumstances, under obligations, under the law, under the impression, under suspicion, under consideration, under false pretenses, under a delusion, under a misapprehension

associate with, acquaint with, affiliate with, combine with, compare with (to), *comply with, confer with, conform with* (to), *contend with, contrast with* (to), *incompatible with, inspire with, mix with, replete with, sated with, satiated with, satisfied with, saturated with*

VII Conjunctions

Conjunctions are connective words. But they are also, to some extent, relational words, as we shall see below. They connect in two general ways, collectively and distributively. In *He ate bread and butter* and *Two and two make four* the conjunction *and* is used collectively. In *Harry and Thomas won all the prizes* the conjunction *and* is used distributively. Each of the boys won some of the prizes. But in *Mrs. Smith and Mrs. Jones called during the afternoon* there is certain ambiguity. Whether they called together or separately the sentence does not say; hence, the conjunction *and* may be either collective or distributive.

Conjunctions are classified first of all as *coordinate conjunctions* and as *subordinate conjunctions*. The former connect words, phrases, and clauses of equal rank. The latter connect clauses of unequal rank.

Some coordinate conjunctions add ideas and are thus called *additive* or *copulative—and, also, then, moreover, likewise*. Other coordinate conjunctions, called *adversative*, subtract or reverse or contrast ideas—*but, still, yet, nevertheless, however*. Still other coordinate conjunctions, called *correlative*, correlate words, phrases, or clauses when these appear in pairs (see page 202). Sometimes they alternate ideas—*either...or, neither... nor, whether...or;* sometimes they perform addition—*both ...and, not only...but also, just as...so, and...therefore*. Coordinate conjunctions, again, may be *final* or *conclusive*, and they indicate inference after cause or result after effect—*hence, so, therefore, consequently, in fine, as a consequence, as a result*.

Subordinate conjunctions are those listed on page 159 as conjunctive adverbs or adverbial conjunctions. The word *that* is sometimes called the *expletive subordinate conjunction* inasmuch as it does not necessarily connect but, rather, introduces noun or substantive clauses: *He says that he can fly*. It frequently is omitted, but is always understood nevertheless as a pointer or signal of subordinate relationship to follow.

Obviously by this time it is evident that conjunctions, too, may be classified as simple, compound, and phrasal—*and, but, while, as* are simple; *inasmuch, therefore, moreover* are compound; *as soon as, as a result, in order that* are phrasal.

VIII Interjections

The interjection is usually dismissed with few words by grammarians. And it is true that this eighth part of speech is of little consequence in grammatical relationships. But tho interjections may be unimportant they are by no means uninteresting. For they are the emotional part of speech, and as such they have glow and warmth and color. It cannot be gainsaid, moreover, that the interjection was the first part of speech and that all other parts of speech have emanated from it as expansions in expression. It stands at the frontier of articulate language, at the crossroads, to change the figure, between articulate and inarticulate communication of thought and feeling.

The chirp of the robin, the screech of the owl, the scream of the eagle, the hiss of the snake, the neigh of the horse, the grunt of the pig, the bark of the dog, the purr of the cat, the lowing of the cow, the roar of the lion, the cackle of the hen, the crow of the rooster are nothing either more or less than interjectional expressions. The caveman had no oral forms of outlet and understanding except a few meager grunts and groans and calls or halloas, and our *Pooh! Pooh!* and *Oh! Oh!* are not so far removed as we probably like to think from the jargon of the jungle. And it is not at all unlikely that, when articulate speech disappears, the interjection will remain. For as with the lower animals, so with man, the interjection may not be a sound or an ejaculation at all, but a motion of some kind—a shrug, a gesture, a nod of the head, and the like. These are interjectional motions; they say much emotionally by means of very brief but very eloquent action.

Are you suddenly hurt? You say *Ouch! Oh! Alas! Dear me! Help!* Are you suddenly surprized? You say *Indeed! Really! Well I never! Never! For heaven's sake! Great Scott!* (Grandma said *Do tell! Sakes alive!*) Do you suddenly reprove some one? You say *Pooh! Fie! Pshaw! Bah!* Do you suddenly disagree with some one? You say *Nonsense! Rubbish! Rot! Bosh! Fudge!* Do you suddenly approve some one or something that is said? You say *Bravo! Hear! Hip, Hip Hurrah! Ah, yes! Atta Baby!* Do you suddenly desire some one's attention? You say *Hist! Hello! I say! Hi, there!* Do you interrogate some one suddenly? You say *And then? Well? What? Yes? No?* And so on. You evince agreement and disagreement, pain and pleasure, surprize and approval and admonishment and aversion and even prayer thru the interjection as an emotional medium. It expresses entire sentences and perhaps paragraphs for you by means of a word or a phrase. Slang and blasphemy are interjectional, that is, *thrown in* or *between (inter, between,* and *jacio, throw).* And so, while interjections have little or nothing to do with the mechanics of expression known as grammar, they have much to do with the flavoring of oral communication, and to dismiss them slightingly as insignificant is very much the same as to snub a friend or relative because he lacks proper social connections.

What constitutes an interjection is decided by its manner of expression. Any word, any phrase, any clause, any sentence may be interjectional in quality and thus in use, the exclamation mark very often being the deciding token: *Please. Please? Please!* The last *please* is an interjection. And observe this sequence: *Please leave the room. Please leave the room? Please leave this room! Leave! Go! Get out! I demand that you leave this room at once.* Now assume that the speaker says nothing but "looks much," and opens the door and then points decisively. The "pantomimic interjection" is effective—the intruder exits!

Indirect interjectional expressions, such as, *If this old chair could only speak, he mused, He was pondering what a sensation there would be if old Badger were to rise from his coffin and speak,* are evidenced by sentence tone and inference alone, not by punctuation.

IX Correct grammatical usage

A Nouns and Pronouns—Case

1 Nouns and pronouns modifying gerunds must be in the possessive case. It is at once obvious that there is an important difference between *I object to Mary's singing* and *I object to Mary singing.*

> I object to John's going
> We look forward to his coming

2 Except in a few special cases names of inanimate objects should not be expressed in the possessive case (see page 483).

> The corridors of the school were beautifully decorated
> *Not* The school's corridors . . .

In colloquial expression these are allowable:

> Three months' leave   Your money's worth
> One day's absence   My country's flag

3 The verb *to be* takes the same case after it as before it.

> It is I
> They took the man to be him
> I am to be he in the play
> Whom do you take me to be?
> Who did you say he is?
> I knew it was he
> I knew it to be him

There is controversy regarding this rule. Those who justify *It is me* would make majority usage the be-all and the end-all of grammatical requirement. But this is a dangerous policy to adopt, for it carries over *and down* to forms of speech and writing that its champions them-selves would never think of adopting. There is nothing to be gained by saying and writing *It is me.* Something very valuable may be lost in doing so. Facility or flexibility of word relationships will tend to be destroyed if we yield here to those grammarians who would "modernize," as they say, this common expression by substituting the objective for the nominative. Once the niceties of adjust-ments among word relationships are clipped by "popu-larizing" such expressions as this, precision will be a lost principle in speech and writing, and ambiguity will blur all communication.

4 The object of a verb must be in the objective case.

> Whom do you wish to follow?
> There is a man whom you can believe
> Whom did you give it to?
> Whom are you going with?

5 Likewise, the object of a preposition must be in the objec-tive case.

> Between you and me the job will be done
> The new era was brought about by us younger women
> The report was left here for him and me
> They distributed the papers among them, you, and us

6 The subject of an infinitive must be in the objective case.

> Permit him and me to accompany you
> He told them and us to make haste with the work
> Let her and me help you

7 The apostrophe is never used with the possessive case of pronouns (see page 484).

hers *not* her's or hers'
yours *not* your's or yours'
ours *not* our's or ours'

its *not* it's or its'
theirs *not* their's or theirs'
his *not* his' or his's or hi's

8 The corrupt forms, *youse, theirn, hern, hisn, hisself, meself, youself, theirself* or *theirselves* must not be used respectively for *you, their* or *theirs, hers, his, himself, myself, yourself, themselves.* They are vulgar and illiterate forms.

9 The contractions *you're* (you are) and *they're* (they are) must not be confused with *your* and *their.* The contraction *who's* (who is) must not be confused with *whose.*

10 Reflexive pronouns are not compounded with nominative forms and should therefore not be used as subjects of verbs instead of personal pronouns.

> John and I are done
> *Not* John and myself are done

But the reflexive pronoun may be used appositively in the nominative case.

> He himself has admitted it
> You yourself should do this thing

11 The objective case is usually not used after a comparative adjective.

> You are younger than I (am young)
> They were earlier than we

But note *He likes John better than (he likes) me* and *He likes John better than I (like John).*

12 A pronoun in apposition must be in the same case as the word it explains.

> We girls had a good time
> He gave it to us fellows

13 A noun or a pronoun in the possessive case should not be used as antecedent of a pronoun.

Not Harry's report was read by him, *but* Harry read his own report

Not His answer, who had come in late, was incorrect, *but* He who had come late answered incorrectly

Not Harry's report, who had worked night and day on it, was then read, *but* The report by Harry, who had worked night and day on it, was then read

14 Do not use the so-called group or "tandem" possessive. It is invariably an awkward and vague construction.

> The complaint of Bill's wife
> The answer of the boy's mother
> *Not* Bill's wife's complaint
> The boy's mother's answer

Even this construction: *Father, mother, and Mary's arrival* is labored. *The arrival of father, mother, and Mary* is to be preferred.

15 Similarly, the delayed or removed possessive is to be avoided.

> The two famous lamentations of the poem
> The insistent and justified demands of the manager
> *Not* The poem's two famous lamentations
> The manager's insistent and justified demands

16 The possessive *whose* is preferably not used in reference to inanimate things, tho there is much authoritative usage to controvert this rule (see page 166).

> This is a book the meaning of which I cannot gather
> *Not* This is a book whose meaning I cannot gather

B Nouns and Pronouns—Agreement

1 Two or more nouns connected by *and* and used as subject of a verb require the verb to be plural.

> The boy and the girl are going
> The depression and the rise in prices are incompatible

But if the two or more nouns so connected and so used mean the same person or thing or are commonly thought of as a unit, a singular predicate is correct. In *The star and author disappoints* the meaning is that the principal actor in the play is also the author of the play. The predicate is therefore singular. Note also

> The bread and butter is good
> The mortar and pestle is the sign of a pharmacy

2 Expressions linked to the subject of a sentence by the phrases *as well as, in addition to, together with,* do not change the number of the subject, and therefore of the verb, in any way. Theoretically in such cases a singular subject may be plural, but technically it remains singular.

> The dog, as well as the cat, refuses to drink the milk
> John, together with the other boys, is going swimming
> The truck, in addition to the limousine, is broken

3 A collective noun used as subject requires a singular verb when it is used integrally, that is, when it denotes unanimity of action or opinion on the part of the group indicated; a plural verb when it is used distributively, that is, when it denotes individual actions and opinions as differing one from another.

> The caste are nearly all married
> Jones, Porter, and Thompson is insolvent
> Jones, Porter, and Thompson are visiting me today
> The Excelsior Company has issued a statement
> The committee does not meet this week
> The jury is agreed on the prisoner's guilt
> The jury have failed to agree for two days and it is still in very argumentative session

4 The words *none, number, remainder, rest* may be regarded as either singular or plural. The context must decide. When they refer to a whole as a unit, they are singular and require a singular verb. When they refer to individuals in a group severally, they are plural and require a plural verb. Logically *none* is equivalent to *no one* and when it clearly means *no one* or *not one* it requires a singular verb. But the present tendency is to use *none* in plural number. When in doubt about its use, you will do well discreetly to avoid it altogether and resort to *no one.* There is an old rule to the effect that when *number* is preceded by *a* it is plural; when preceded by *the* it is singular. But the rule is greatly violated.

> None (not one) of the students is casting a vote
> None were expected and none have come
> The number present today was smaller than it was yesterday
> A number of people were unable to get in
> He is going, but the rest of us are remaining
> The remainder of life is going to be difficult
> The remainder of the ballots were thrown away
> None but the brave deserve the fair
> Beware that none touch the young man Absalom

5 The words *each, every, every one, everybody, anybody, either, neither, no one, nobody, some one* are singular and require singular verbs when used as subjects. They must be referred to by singular pronouns only. *Both, each, each other, either, neither, the other,* and the preposition *between* are used in referring to two persons, places, or things; *all, every, each, few, many, one another* and the preposition *among* in referring to more than two.

Each man is responsible at least to himself
Every one has great opportunities if he will but observe
Anybody is likely to be called to his supervisor
Neither of them is likely to pass his examination
Either of these answers is right
Every dog has his day
Everybody has his work done
Nobody is doing his duty
Neither Mary nor John has his work

The possessive pronoun *his* is common gender in constructions such as the last three, or may be so considered in order to avoid the labored form *Neither Mary nor John has done her and his work.* In 1858 Charles Crozat Converse proposed *thon,* a solidified form of *that one,* to serve as a third person common gender pronominal form. It has not been generally accepted, however, and so we still have three forms in the singular third person pronoun —*he, she, it*—and only one in the plural—*they.*

6 A verb separated from its subject by words or phrases or clauses must take its number from that subject, and not from any intervening noun or pronoun. Errors made in violation of this rule are known as errors of proximity. In

One of the fellows is going

the ear hears the plural *fellows* in immediate proximity to the verb, and the natural tendency is to be guided by the sound of plurality and supply a plural verb, but *one* is really the subject.

A clan of seven units has drawn up a petition
A group of twenty women is going to attend the meeting

Note this exception: When the subject is the singular part of a fraction and this is followed by a modifying phrase, the verb takes its number from the noun in the modifying phrase.

> One third of the shelves are filled
> One third of the shelf is filled
> Half of our days are wasted
> Half of our day is wasted

7 Singular subjects connected by *or* or *nor, either or* or *neither nor* require a singular verb.

> Either he or I am to go
> Neither you nor he has the time
> The hat or the cap was stolen

In all such cases the verb must be kept in agreement with the subject nearest it.   This sometimes requires an absurd reading if the first subject is read alone with the existing verb, and it is better to avoid such construction.   But theoretically the appropriate verb is always easily understood.

> Either he *is* or I am to go
> Neither you *have* nor he has the time

This, however, makes awkward reading, and the idiomatic form above is perfectly clear as it stands.   These are acknowledgedly better readings:

> Either he is to go or I am
> Neither you have the time nor has he

8 A pronoun must agree with its antecedent in person and number and gender, but its case depends upon its construction in the clause in which it stands.

> He whom you saw is the one
> They who are strong have to help him who is weak
> Many a man has seen himself held up to undeserved scorn

This rule applies to relative pronouns as well as to personal.

> He is the only one of my family who likes the country
> She is one of the few writers that have been able to interest me

9 Certain nouns that are plural in form but singular in meaning require a singular verb when they are used as subjects.   Certain nouns on the other hand are always plural and always require plural verbs when used as subjects (see page 463).

> What is his politics?
> What was the news yesterday
> Where are the scissors?
> The goods have arrived

Note also in this connection

Books is plural number
Eight bells means four o'clock
Gulliver's Travels was written by Jonathan Swift

10 Foreign plurals of course require plural verbs when they are used as subjects: *Data are, Phenomena have, Alumni were.*

11 When the predicate of a sentence precedes the subject, be sure of correct agreement in person and number between subject and predicate.

There are an old lady and a young gentleman in the room
In this book are all the rules of conduct you may ever need

12 Pronouns must refer to their antecedents clearly and unmistakably. It is best, therefore, to place them as closely as possible to the words to which they refer.

The man that won the prize went home happy
Not The man went home happy that won the prize

The dress that is soiled is displayed in the east window
Not The dress is displayed in the east window that is soiled

It is sometimes possible to depend upon the comma to clarify such lazy constructions as these. But this is a makeshift device. Place a comma before *that* in each of the *not* sentences above and the construction will still be bad.

Such ambiguous reference as this should be avoided: *Jones told him that if he could not come early he should not come at all.* Resort to direct discourse may always be depended upon to correct this error: *Jones said "If I do not come early I shall not come at all"* or *Jones said "Unless you can come early do not come at all."*

13 It is better not to use *which* or *that* to refer to an entire clause, for the reason that the construction will probably indicate thinking that is not strictly clear. Tho there is much excellent usage in direct violation of this rule, the young writer and speaker will do well to have his relative pronouns refer clearly and closely to individual nouns and pronouns.

His winning the prize pleased his parents very much
Not He won the prize which pleased his parents very much

14 A coordinate conjunction must not be used before a relative pronoun unless a pronoun of the same kind and construction has been previously used in the sentence.

> He is one who always appears to be idle but who nevertheless accomplishes a large amount of work
>
> *Not* He always appears to be idle but who nevertheless accomplishes a large amount of work

15 A plural pronoun must not be used to modify a singular noun: *this kind* or *these kinds,* not *these kind* or *those sort.*

16 The personal pronoun *them* cannot be used as a modifier. Say *these books* or *those apples,* not *them books* or *them apples.*

17 The personal pronoun *you* always requires a plural verb: *You were,* not *You was.*

18 It is preferable not to use *this* and *that* as adverbs of degree, tho there is much violation of this rule: *so much, so big, so tall, so little* are better than *this much, that big, this tall, that little.*

19 The superfluous use of the personal pronoun to double the subject (except in rare instances for the sake of emphasis) is studiously to be avoided. Do not say *John he stalled the engine,* but *John stalled the engine.*

C Verbs—Agreement and Function

1 The predicate of a relative pronoun must agree in person and number with the antecedent of that pronoun (see 8 on page 171).

> One of the men who are seated there may come in

The antecedent of *who* is *men* and its predicate—*are*—is plural.

> One of the men who has had experience may come in

The antecedent of *who* is *one* and its predicate—*has*—is singular.

2 The predicate always takes its person and number from that subject nearest it when such subject consists of two or more nouns or pronouns connected by *or* or *nor.*

Neither John nor the other boys are going
Either you or they or I am to go
Neither the horses nor the cow was able to escape

Remember that the correlatives *either...or, neither...nor*
are most correctly used when they connect nouns of the
same number and person.   Note also that in such colloquialism as *Not John but Bill is the boy I mean,* in
which *not* is used conjunctively in correlation with *but,*
the verb must agree with the closer subject—*Not this but
those are required, Not those but this is required.*

3 Tho the split infinitive is generally used in current as well
as in earlier literature, it is preferably to be avoided for
the reason that it is hardly logical.   The word *to* is a part
of the infinitive, that is, *to go* is logically one term, just
as *aller* (to go) is one word in French, *gehen* (to go) in
German, *ire* (to go) in Latin.   To separate the *to* from
the *go* by the insertion of an adverb is very much like
separating these three foreign words before the last
syllable of each for the insertion of a modifier—*al-rapide-
ler, geh-schnell-en, ir-celeriter-e.*   In only a few cases does
the split infinitive add anything by way of grace or
euphony or rhythm to expression.   In most cases it is
awkward and inchoate.   *To emphatically understand* and
to thoroly investigate may be accepted.   But *to hurriedly
achieve, to distinctly and unmistakably concur,* and *to
beautifully decorate* condemn themselves.   Macaulay's
free use of the split infinitive has apparently provided the
liberalists in English grammar with irrefutable argument
in its behalf.

The verbs *behold, bid, dare, feel, find, hear, know, let,
make, observe, please, see, watch* take the elliptical infinitive after them, that is, the infinitive with the *to* understood.   Do not supply the *to,* or your expression will
sound stilted and awkward: *Behold him run* (*not* to run),
Hear him sing (*not* to sing), *Bid him go* (*not* to go), *See
him jump* (*not* to jump).

4 The same principal or notional verb should be repeated
in compound verb phrases and in the clauses of compound
and complex sentences whenever its form varies in spelling (see page 209).

I never have done that and I never will do it
Not I never have and I never will do that

He told it better than I could tell it (*or* could have told it)
He told it better than I could do (*or* could have done) (British)
Not He told it better than I could

5 Predicates of different tenses within the same sentence require repetition of the subject, or, at least, this is preferable usage.

He arrived here in the summer, he has remained here ever since, and he will not leave until spring

Not He arrived here during the summer has remained here ever since, and will not leave till spring

6 Conversely, it is preferable—because it is more logical and more coherent—to make the predicates in two or more clauses of equal rank agree in conjugation, mode, and tense.

He is driving fast and is steering well
He drives fast and steers well
Not He is driving fast and steers well
Not He drives fast and is steering well

They have practised faithfully and have won promotion
They practised faithfully and won promotion
Not They have practised faithfully and won promotion
Not They practised faithfully and have won promotion

If you should get the prize and should thus surprize your parents they would be delighted
Not If you get the prize and should thus surprize your parents they would be delighted

7 The auxiliaries *may, can, shall, will* used in dependent (result) clauses follow present tenses; *might, could, should, would* follow imperfect tenses.

I think he may do it
I thought he might do it
He says he can do it
He said he could do it
I fancy he will come
I hoped he would come
He insists I shall go
He insisted I should go

After a verb in the present, the present perfect, or the future tense, *may* is used in a subordinate clause of purpose; after a verb in the imperfect tense *might* is used.

He has ruled that we may visit the zoo
He had ruled that we might visit the zoo

He decided that we might go
He says that we may go
He will decide that we may go

8 The primary meaning of *can* and *could* is power; of *may* and *might*, possibility or probability or permission; of *will* and *would*, wish or inclination or disposition; of *should* or *shall*, duty or obligation. *Should* is almost synonymous with *ought*. *Ought* is stronger and more compelling than *should; must* is stronger than either.

May and *might* indicate possibility or power or permission in respect to future action. They are, as a matter of fact, emotional verbs and are thus frequently capable of double meaning or misunderstanding. *Can* and *could* bear much the same connotation, but they are used principally in relation to power and *may* and *might* in relation to permission. However, *May I go?* while it asks permission implies power. *Can I go?* questions the permission of power. *How can I do it?* may mean that something is being done or that some action is proposed. The context must settle the problem. *I may go to the opera tonight* may mean that I have permission to go, that I am contemplating going and thus asking permission, that I am cogitating the subject. Again, the context must tell us.

9 The mere notion of future time is expressed by *shall* in the first person and *will* in the second and third persons.

I *or* we shall return next week
You, he, she, it *or* they will return next week

Now transpose the auxiliaries, and force, determination, and compulsion are added to the idea of futurity.

I *or* we will return next week
You, he, she, it *or* they shall return next week

Note this also: *Will* is internal or subjective; its use indicates decision from within the mind of the speaker. *Shall* is external or objective; its use indicates decision from without the mind of the person involved in the action. The expression *You shall do it* means that some one or something outside yourself is going to force you to do it. The expression *You will do it* means, in addition to simple future action, that something within your own makeup is the deciding factor. Note also that the emphasis brought to bear upon expressions having *shall* and *will* in them does much to convey the meaning.

Note again in *He shall go if I wish him to,* he has no say in the matter of his going. I am deciding for him and imposing my will upon him. He has no will about going. Thus, *shall* is correctly used. But in *He will go whether I oppose his doing so or not,* it is obvious that he is determining the matter for himself and that I do not count in his decision. *Shall* is customarily the correct auxiliary to use before an *if*-clause.

The Anglo-Saxon form from which *shall* is derived means *I am obliged.* It is always helpful to keep this in mind in case of doubt about its use. The Anglo-Saxon word from which *will* is derived means *will.* This will also be found worth remembering. *Will* is used in its original sense as an independent notional verb.

> He willed it so, that is, He wished it so
> He willed her one hundred dollars

The so-called "new school" of English grammar insists that the distinctions of usage between *shall* and *will* are pedantic and no longer to be observed. The author of this book disagrees with such policy of *laissez faire* or *laissez aller,* and believes that the clear understanding of such points in grammar helps not only to make speaking and writing more interesting and reliable but also to make thinking more logical. For all grammar is logic, and it may be added that all logic is grammatical.

The first person in questions always requires *shall: Shall I help? Shall we come along?*

The second and third persons in questions always require *shall* or *will* according as the one or the other is expected in the answer.

> How soon shall you come over again?
> I shall come again next week
> Will you carry my parcels for me?
> Certainly I will

In a dependent clause of concession, condition, purpose,, or doubt *shall (should)* is always correct.

If we shall pass, we must study
If he should fail, he would be heart-broken
Tho you shall pass, you will nevertheless not know
Tho you should succeed, you would not graduate
He has seen to it that nothing shall interfere

Should is sometimes used in the sense of obligation, and *would* in the sense of habitual or customary behavior.

You should do your duty as a citizen
She would pout at the slightest provocation

The present tense also carries this latter signification:

She pouts at the slightest provocation

In indirect statements *shall* or *will* is required exactly as it would be were the indirect expression given in direct form.

She says she shall be married in June
"I shall be married in June," she says

She said that she shall have twenty bridesmaids
She said, "I shall have twenty bridesmaids"

She insists that she will vote in spite of the long journey home

She said, "I will vote in spite of the long journey home"

Should and *would* follow the same rules as *shall* and *will*. The former are the imperfect forms, respectively, of the latter. This helps us to understand that the imperfect may sometimes have a future significance. This form is known as the conditional future or the imperfect future— *I should go if I were you.* There is likewise a present future—the present tense form with future significance— *Tomorrow I go to Hollywood.*

D Verbs—Form and Function

1 Avoid using such contractions as the following except in conversation and in reporting conversation: *I'll* for *I shall* or *I will*, *you'll* for *you shall* or *will*, *we'll*, *they'll*, *he'll*, *she'll*, *it'll*, *who'll*, and so forth. The same caution applies to *shan't* for *shall not* and *won't* for *will not*. Persons who are not sure of the correct usage of *shall* and *will* and *should* and *would* have been known to resort to these short forms to cover ignorance!

2 It is still imperative that you use *don't* and *doesn't* correctly in spite of the fact that there is a considerable school of thought(?) in favor of "letting down" here and sanctioning *He don't*. The correct forms are *He doesn't* and *They don't*, the former being singular and the latter plural.

3 Do not use the corrupt forms *ain't I* (*he, you, they,* and so on) and *aren't I*. There is no such word as *ain't*. The form *aren't I* is a British colloquialism, but it is not correct and is used in this country for affectation only.

4 Do not confuse the verb *ought* with the noun *aught* meaning anything or something owned. The former is sometimes spelled *aught,* tho this spelling is now archaic. The verb *ought* is not inflected for tense; hence, the expression *had ought* is non-existent. Do not use it. The closest inflection for time that *ought* is capable of is the present infinitive used after it to indicate present time, and the perfect infinitive used after it to indicate past time:

> He ought to work
> He ought to have worked

5 Confine your use of the present tense to the expression of present time. It should not be used to indicate time begun in the past and still going on in the present. But it should be used to express a permanent fact or truth. Observe these usages:

> John said to me that the road was very bad yesterday
> John said to me, "The road was very bad yesterday"
> *Not* John says to me that the road was very bad yesterday
> *Not* John says to me, "The road was very bad yesterday"
>
> We have been in Europe for three months
> *Not* We are in Europe for three months
>
> He said that Washington is the capital of the United States
> *Not* He said that Washington was the capital of the United States

6 The verb *have* is an important auxiliary and it should as a rule be used as such. It may and should be used, however, as an independent notional verb when possession is indicated. The expression *I have got* is tautological. Some authorities rule that *have* is used to indicate possession of abstract or intangible things only, as, *I have a*

theory and *I have a dread* and *I have an idea,* and that it should be followed by *got* when the possession and holding of a physical object is indicated, as, *I have got a hat* and *I have got a typewriter* and *I have got a new book.* This distinction is more nice than important. Do not use *got* after *have* except in rare cases where emphasis is desired as, *I've got you now* and *Have you got your man.*

7 The present perfect tense (sometimes called simply the perfect tense) should be used to indicate something that has recently happened or that frequently or continuously happens, without fixing the time definitely. The imperfect tense expresses definite past time.

> I did my work while I was waiting for the car
> I heard the great Paderewski when I was in Paris
>
> We have seen that play before
> She hasn't agreed to accompany us
> It has been raining for five days consecutively
> They have argued loud and long for the shorter day

Do not confuse the imperfect tense with the present perfect.

> Have you read the book yet?
> *Not* Did you read the book yet?

Note also the passive in both uses.

> My work was done while I was waiting for the car
> Has the book been read by you yet?

In regard to the latter it should be pointed out that a subject indicating the receiver of the action is preferably used with a verb in the passive voice.

> A car was given to me
> *Preferably not* I was given a car

8 Do not confuse the imperfect tense with the pluperfect.

> After we had finished our work we went to the field
> *Not* After we finished our work we went to the field

The past perfect or pluperfect tense indicates that the action of the predicate was completed definitely in past time.

> We had seen that play several times before
>
> Inasmuch as she had not agreed to accompany us, we waited no longer
>
> It had been raining for five days when we arrived

> Tho they had argued loud and long for the shorter day, they were doomed to disappointment
>
> I did not do that work
> I have not done the work yet
> I had not done the work when he called for it
> I have tried to do the work
> I had tried to do the work but I did not understand it
>
> I told him that I always had done my work and always would do it
> *Not* I told him that I always had done my work and always would

Since *done* (after *had*) is not the form of the verb required after *would*, the correct form must be supplied, as always in such constructions (see page 174).

> I never have failed him and I never will fail him
> *Not* I never have failed him and I never will

9 It happens frequently in conversation (and only less frequently in writing) that *of* is used for *have* after such auxiliaries as *had, ought,* and *must.* This happens in part because of "careless hearing"; in larger part because of ignorance or indifference, or both: *I must have failed,* not *I must of failed; You ought to have come,* not *You ought of come; If I had gone,* not *If I had of gone.*

10 The present infinitive must be used to indicate the same time as the predicate it follows or time future to that predicate.

> He wishes to see the report
> He wished to see the report
> We should have liked nothing more than to help you
> I have been meaning to write to you
> They would have desired to go had they been here
> I had intended to see him immediately on his arrival
> *Not* They would have desired to have gone had they been here
> *Not* I had intended to have seen him immediately on his arrival

Note in the foregoing correct examples that the present infinitive follows predicates indicating present time and past time, that the time indicated by the infinitive is the same as or later than that of the predicate.

Now observe these:

> They are said to have been seen entering the room
> It was rumored to have happened on the twelfth

and note that the perfect infinitive indicates action completed or perfected at the time indicated by the predicate. Observe these uses of the infinitives:

The Empire State Building is held to be the highest structure in the world

He declared that the petition was meant to be an expression of general feeling among the employees

The great southern generals of the Civil War are said to have been the best-trained military officers of their time

I firmly believe Napoleon to have been the greatest leader of men short of gods and goddesses

11 Tho the subjunctive mode is rapidly going out of fashion, there are still certain subjunctive forms required of the careful writer and speaker. The two most common uses of the subjunctive are those in the expression of a wish and in the expression of a condition contrary to a fact:

I wish I were (*not* was) an eagle
If I were (*not* was) he, I should do the work

These uses are generally observed today by the best speakers and writers. Those that follow are probably as often violated as they are observed, but they are nevertheless important.

Command: He orders that there be no disloyalty to duty
            (The order is merely a precaution; there is not likely to be any shirking or disloyalty)

Concession: Tho he hate me, yet I will refuse him
            (He probably will not hate me but I can quite understand that he might do so as result of my decision)

Doubt: If he be angry, I am sorry
            (He is probably not angry)

Fear: He is terrified lest some tragedy occur
            (His terror is probably quite unjustified, inasmuch as nothing tragic is likely to occur)

Likelihood: I had succeeded but for you
            (That is, if it had not been for you I should have succeeded)

Purpose: Answer the questions clearly that you be perfectly understood
            (The purpose of the questions is to get a clear and complete understanding for the benefit of the one questioned; he will therefore probably be at pains to make himself clear)

12 The verb *do* has so many uses that care must be taken to use it correctly (see page 149).

Question:	Do you intend to come?
Inversion:	Never did I see the like
Emphasis:	Do try to find the book
Substitute for other verb:	He studies harder than you do
Notional or principal use:	Do your very best
	You will do it well
With particles:	We shall do away with that (colloquial)
	I shall do up my dress today (colloquial)
	He was done in by the gangster (slang)
	He did me out of a dime (slang)

After *be, can, dare, have, must, need, ought* the auxiliary *do* is not necessary in negativing a verb. It is not necessary, moreover, in connection with negative words other than *not*, such as, *never, hardly, nowhere, scarcely, nobody, no,* or with prefixes that carry negative significance.

> He is dissatisfied with your answer
> We never saw a steeper hill
> He had no idea of going
> He dare not try it again
> He has no opportunity to practise
> He has hardly had time to return

Do is not necessary in such elliptical negatives as *I care not* and *They falter not,* sometimes called poetic negatives.

13 The *dangling* or *hanging* or *suspended* construction (usually participial) should be studiously avoided. It is one of the most commonly committed errors in the language. In *Running to catch the train the bus passed us* the participle is hanging because it is not properly related to the word it should be related to; it seems to modify *bus,* whereas it logically refers to *us.* The sentence should read *Running to catch the train we were passed by the bus.*

Note also this: *After running to catch the train it pulled out just before we reached the station.* The gerund phrase *After running to catch the train* is logically associated with *we,* for *we* did the running. But as the sentence stands it seems to be related to or to modify *it,* and this would be absurd. The correct reading therefore is *After running to catch the train we reached the station just after it had pulled out.*

In *There were plenty of raspberries in the garden, but not being very ripe I did not eat any,* the participial phrase *not being very ripe* is dangling—it seems to modify *I* but it obviously tells about *raspberries.* The sentence should read *There were plenty of raspberries in the garden, but since they were not very ripe I did not eat any.*

In *After pulling up the cabin steps the propellers began to buzz, and off went the plane,* the gerund phrase *after pulling up the cabin steps* is dangling—it seems to modify *propellers,* but it is obvious that the pulling was done by the attendants. The sentence should read *After the attendants had pulled up the cabin steps the propellers began to buzz and off went the plane.*

In *While experimenting in the laboratory a new cleansing solution was originated* the introductory dependent part is dangling—it has nothing to modify or be connected with. Who was experimenting? The sentence should read *While the chemist was experimenting in the laboratory he originated a new cleansing fluid,* or *While (he was) experimenting in the laboratory the chemist originated a new cleansing solution.*

14 Most verbs form their imperfect tense and their past participle regularly by the addition of *d* or *ed* (*t* in the simplified spelling form). The following list includes most of the exceptions called irregular verbs. Some irregular past participles, such as *bounden, cloven, drunken, graven, molten, shapen, stricken* have lost their verb nature almost entirely and are used now principally as adjectives. The imperfect tense formation sometimes changes the vowel sound—*deal* and *dealt, dream* and *dreamt* (but *dreamed*), *lean* and *leant* (but *leaned*), *leap* and *leapt* (but *leaped*), *mean* and *meant.* In *lay, pay, say, stay—laid, paid, said, staid*—the change to the imperfect is shortened, tho, like *delayed,* these used to be *layed, payed, sayed, stayed.* In these a vowel is dropt: *bled, bred, crept, fed, felt, fled, kept, knelt, led, left, met, shot, slept, sped.*

IRREGULAR VERBS

Infinitive	Imperfect Tense	Past Participle	Infinitive	Imperfect Tense	Past Participle
abide	abode	abode	dare	durst	dared
arise	arose	arisen	deal	dealt	dealt
awake	awoke	awoke	die	died	died
			dig	dug	dug
be	was	been	do	did	done
bear	bore, bare	borne, born	draw	drew	drawn
			dream	dreamt	dreamt
beat	beat	beaten	drink	drank	drunk
become	became	become	drive	drove	driven
befall	befell	befallen	dwell	dwelt	dwelt
begin	began	begun			
behold	beheld	beheld	eat	ate	eaten
bend	bent	bent			
bereave	bereft	bereft	fall	fell	fallen
beseech	besought	besought	feed	fed	fed
beset	beset	beset	feel	felt	felt
bespeak	bespoke	bespoken	fight	fought	fought
bestride	bestrode	bestridden	find	found	found
bid	bade, bid	bidden, bid	flee	fled	fled
			fling	flung	flung
bind	bound	bound	fly	flew	flown
bite	bit	bitten	forbear	forbore	forborne
bleed	bled	bled	forbid	forbade	forbidden, forbid
blow	blew	blown			
break	broke	broken	forego	forewent	foregone
breed	bred	bred	foresee	foresaw	foreseen
bring	brought	brought	foretell	foretold	foretold
broadcast	broadcast	broadcast	forget	forgot	forgotten, forgot
build	built	built			
burn	burnt	burnt	forgive	forgave	forgiven
burst	burst	burst	forsake	forsook	forsaken
buy	bought	bought	freeze	froze	frozen
			get	got	got
cast	cast	cast	gild	gilt	gilt
catch	caught	caught	gird	girt	girt
chide	chid	chid, chidden	give	gave	given
			go	went	gone
choose	chose	chosen	grind	ground	ground
cleave	clove, cleft	cleft, cloven	grow	grew	grown
cleave	clave	cleaved	hang	hung	hanged, hung
cling	clung	clung			
clothe	clad	clad	have	had	had
come	came	come	hear	heard	heard
cost	cost	cost	heave	hove	hove
creep	crept	crept	hew	hewed	hewn
crow	crew	crowed	hide	hid	hidden, hid
cut	cut	cut	hit	hit	hit

IRREGULAR VERBS—*Continued*

Infinitive	Imperfect Tense	Past Participle	Infinitive	Imperfect Tense	Past Participle
hold	held	held, holden	seek	sought	sought
hurt	hurt	hurt	seethe	seethed, sod	seethed, sodden
			sell	sold	sold
keep	kept	kept	send	sent	sent
kneel	knelt	knelt	set	set	set
knit	knit	knit	shake	shook	shaken
know	knew	known	shape	shaped	shapen
			shave	shaved	shaven
lade	laded	laden	shear	shore	shorn
lay	laid	laid	shed	shed	shed
lead	led	led	shine	shone	shone
lean	leant	leant	shoe	shod	shod
leap	leapt	leapt	shoot	shot	shot
leave	left	left	show	showed	shown
lend	lent	lent	shred	shred	shred
let	let	let	shrink	shrank	shrunk, shrunken
lie	lay	lain			
			shrive	shrove	shriven
light	lit	lit	shut	shut	shut
lose	lost	lost	sing	sang	sung
			sink	sank	sunk
make	made	made	sit	sat	sat
mean	meant	meant	slay	slew	slain
meet	met	met	sleep	slept	slept
mislead	misled	misled	slide	slid	slid
mistake	mistook	mistaken	sling	slung	slung
mow	mowed	mown	slink	slunk	slunk
			slit	slit	slit
outbid	outbid	outbidden	smell	smelt	smelt
outdo	outdid	outdone	smite	smote	smitten
overcast	overcast	overcast	sow	sowed	sown
overcome	overcame	overcome	speak	spoke	spoken
			speed	sped	sped
pay	paid	paid	spell	spelt	spelt
put	put	put	spend	spent	spent
			spill	spilt	spilt
read	read	read	spin	span	spun
rend	rent	rent	spit	spat	spat
rid	rid	rid	split	split	split
ride	rode	ridden, rode	spread	spread	spread
			spring	sprang	sprung
ring	rang	rung	stand	stood	stood
rive	rived	riven	stay	stayed	stayed
run	ran	run	steal	stole	stolen
			stick	stuck	stuck
saw	sawed	sawn	sting	stung	stung
say	said	said	stink	stank, stunk	stunk
see	saw	seen			

IRREGULAR VERBS—*Continued*

Infinitive	Imperfect Tense	Past Participle	Infinitive	Imperfect Tense	Past Participle
strew	strewn,	strewed, strown	thrive thrust	throve thrust	thriven thrust
stride	strode	stridden	tread	trod	trod, trodden
strike	struck	struck			
string	strung	strung			
strive	strove	striven	unbend	unbent	unbent
swear	swore	sworn	unbind	unbound	unbound
sweep	swept	swept	under-	under-	under-
swell	swelled	swelled, swollen	stand	stood	stood
swim	swam	swum	wear	wore	worn
swing	swung	swung	weave	wove	woven
			weep	wept	wept
tax	taxed	taxed	win	won	won
take	took	taken	wind	wound	wound
teach	taught	taught	wring	wrung	wrung
tear	tore	torn	write	wrote	written
tell	told	told	writhe	writhed	writhed, writhen
think	thought	thought			

E Adjectives and Adverbs

1 The article should be used before each adjective in a series when these adjectives modify different nouns, expressed or understood; otherwise it should be used before only the first adjective in the series.

> I have a black and gray overcoat (one overcoat)
> I have a black and a gray overcoat (two overcoats)

As a general rule a series of adjectives modifying the same noun should be so arranged that the shortest comes first and the longest last, except where idiomatic considerations make another arrangement desirable or where one particular adjective more closely modifies the noun than the others.

> A black, heavy, threatening cloud appeared in the west
> I have a new, felt-lined, double-breasted overcoat
> *But* A dilapidated old barn
> An aggressive young man

A and *an* are called the indefinite articles; *the* the definite article. The terms *a child* and *an apple* mean respectively *any child* and *any apple;* whereas *the child* and *the apple* refer, again respectively, to a particular child and a particular apple. In other words, *a* and *an* are genus modifiers; *the* is a species modifier. In some cases, however, the particularity or individuation of *the* may be practically lost and it may then have the signification of *a* or *an: The female of the species is more deadly than the male. The rose is a beautiful thing* is likewise correct under this signification of *the*. On the other hand *the* may outdo itself by way of particularizing, stress of voice in speaking and italics in writing indicating the special emphasis—*Is this* THE *Mr. Addison? This is* THE *thing nowadays.*

An is used before vowel sounds; *a* before consonant sounds (see page 618). Say *an heir, an heirloom, an heiress, an honest fellow, an honor, an hour,* because the *h* is silent and the pronunciation of these words begins with the vowel sound *e* or *o*. But say *a unique system, a university medal, a Europe divided,* because the pronunciation of these words begins with *y—yunique, yuniversity, yeurope.* There was once an old and a pedantic rule to the effect that a word beginning with *h* accented on the second syllable should be preceded by *an* rather than *a—an historical event, an heraldic design.* But this rule is rarely observed in this country. In England, where initial *h* is frequently dropt in pronunciation, the article *an* is used more frequently before words beginning with *h—an hotel, an hostelry.*

The article should be repeated before the names of two separate persons or objects written in a series, but when the names refer to the same person or object the article should be used before the first one only.

I employ a typist and a secretary (two different persons)
I employ a typist and secretary (one person renders two services)
We elected a secretary and a treasurer (two persons were elected)
We elected a secretary and treasurer (one person was elected)
She has a felt and a silk hat (two hats)
She has a felt and silk hat (one hat)

But *a* or *an* may be used in the sense of *any* as well as that of *one*. In this sense it indicates a typical specimen taken to represent a group.

A rose is a beautiful thing
A thing of beauty is a joy forever

That is, any rose—any thing of beauty.   (See pages 618 and 619 for additional instruction regarding *a* and *an*.)

2 Do not use *a* or *an* after *sort of* or *kind of*.   These articles are really abbreviations of *one*.   They should not be used, therefore, where the meaning of *one* would be absurd.

> This is a new sort of brake
> *Not* This is a new sort of a brake
> *But* This is a brake of a new sort

It could not very well be a new sort of one brake.   Since *a* and *an* mean *one,* observe the following.   All such expressions are more or less colloquial, even when correctly stated:

> You do not deserve the name of student
> *Not* You do not deserve the name of a student

> The beaver is their school emblem
> *Not* A beaver is their school emblem

Do not substitute *kind of* and *sort of* for the adverb of degree *rather,* even in colloquial conversation.   *I am rather sorry about it* is correct.   *I am kind of sorry about it* is incorrect.   The word *sorry* is the predicate adjective modified by the adverb of degree *rather.*

3 Some adverbs are compared as adjectives are, by suffixing *er* and *est: faster, fastest; sooner, soonest.*   But most adverbs are compared, as the longer adjectives are, by the use of *more* and *most: more quickly, most quickly; more severely, most severely.*   The comparison of adjectives is explained on page 588.   It is well to remember that comparison sometimes depends upon attributes that do not really exist.   Tho neither Bob nor Harry may be tall, we may say that Bob is taller than Harry.   Tho both Mary and Jane may be dishonest, we may attribute a degree of honesty to both of them for the sake of building such comparison, as *Mary is more honest than Jane.*

It is pointed out on page 589 that there are many intermediate degrees of comparison, such as, *His face grew whiter and whiter* and *His face became more and more dejected.*   There are, on the other hand, certain comparatives and superlatives that stop short and defy further intermediate degrees.   These words, for instance, may not

190

GET IT RIGHT!

be extended beyond the *er* ending: *elder, former, latter, outer. Outer than, former than,* and so forth, are absurd. *Elder than* should not be used. The extended form is *older than. Older* is general in use; *elder* refers to persons only and preferably to members of a given family in the sense of *senior. My elder brother has just arrived.* Moreover, both *elder* and *elders* are also nouns.

In using the adverbial *the* care must be taken to keep both terms of the expression uniform:

<blockquote>
the more the merrier
the sooner the better
the later the worse
Not the more the merriest
the sooner the best
the later the worst
</blockquote>

But in such progressive expressions as *if worse comes to worst* and *if good becomes better* naturally the latter word must represent a higher or a lower degree than the former.

Note in the list of irregular comparatives on page 589 that *farther* is the comparative of *far,* and *further* of *forth. Farther* therefore refers to distance, *further* to more forward position. *Farther* is more correctly used, therefore, in expressing the idea of distant or distance, real or figurative; *further* in expressing more or relative location or position. Note these:

<blockquote>
We are awaiting further orders
I shall aim at the farther mark
Do not help to further his plans
    (verb meaning to advance)
I have gone farther in Latin than he
    (implying that we have both gone a long way)
I'll see you farther before I'll further such a dastardly scheme
    as that
</blockquote>

Farther is generally an adverb; *further* an adjective.

4 It is commonly accepted that such adjectives as *circular, deadly, favorite, final, infinite, perfect, preferable, right, square, supreme, unique, universal,* and their adverbial derivatives do not admit of comparison, but in colloquial expression we hear much of *great favorites* and *special favorites,* and even of *squarer deals* and *perfectly circular layouts.* It is better, however, to accept these adjectives

in the same category as the demonstratives—*each, this, those*—and the cardinals and ordinals—*one, two, three; first, second, third*—which no one ever thinks of comparing. In biblical expression—the language of the Hebrews—both the comparative and the superlative were enforced and strengthened (not to say doubled) by such forms as *Holy of Holies, King of Kings, Lord of Lords.* Shakespeare used *mightiest in the mightiest* (*The Merchant of Venice*), and Tennyson *perfection's model* (*The Idylls of the King*).

So while it is technically wrong to use either the double comparative or the double superlative with either adjectives or adverbs—*more happier, most happiest; more faster, most fastest*—in ordinary workaday English, the poet (and the advertiser, who is akin) may go into such flights of doubling as *truer than truth, the past master of perfection, the end of the absolute.*

5 Do not use the adjective *first* to modify *beginning* or *commencement* in the sense of time. Be careful also in using such expressions as *the last three sections* and *the first three sections.* It is usually ridiculous to say *the three last sections* and *the three first sections,* unless, of course, the sections are arranged in groups of *three,* "abreast," so to say. In this event we might speak of *the three first sections, the three middle sections,* and *the three last sections.* But this would be unusual, to say the least.

Latter and *last* should be used to refer to space or to order in space or line; *later* and *latest,* to refer to time. *Later* is more frequently an adverb than an adjective; *latter* is an adjective. Note that *last* may be used also in the sense of extreme despair or least favorable as in the idiomatic expression *This is the last straw.*

Note again that idiomatic usage may sanction *the least of two evils,* when the strictly correct form is *the less* or *the lesser of two evils. Lesser* is more commonly used as a noun than is *less.* But while idiom may sanction colloquialism, it cannot stamp error with approval. The superlative degree must not be used in the comparison of two persons, things, or conditions, and the comparative must not be used in relation to three or more.

This is the better of the two
This is the best of the three
Mary is the tallest of the four
Not This is the best of the two
Not Mary is the taller of the four

6 Anything compared with a large group of similar things (or vice versa) must be excluded in expressing the comparison. This separation of the two terms of the comparison is usually made by the insertion of the word *other* in the second member of the comparison.

New York is larger than any other city in the country
Not New York is larger than any city in the country

The first term of the comparison is *New York;* the second is *any other city.* In the incorrect example *New York* is included in the term *any city* because it is among the cities of the country. This nullifies the comparison.

But in the comparison of more than two things, that is, in expressing the superlative, the thing compared must be included rather than excluded as above.

New York is the largest city in the country
Not New York is the largest of any other city in the country

In the incorrect form *New York* seems to be a part of "any other city in the country."

7 While most comparatives are followed by *than* when they are extended, those that have come down intact from the Latin or from the Latin thru the French are followed by *to* in extension. Some of these are not extended as a rule, but most of them are: *anterior to, exterior (to), inferior to, interior (to), junior to, major (to), minor (to), prior to, posterior to, senior to, superior to.*

8 In many of our idiomatic epithets the adjective follows the noun, and thus usurps the position of emphasis. This arrangement may well be borne in mind by any one who is interested in devising a firm name, title, or slogan: *mayor elect, beau ideal, letters patent, malice afore-thought, proof positive, Brown Brothers, Inc., house beautiful, fiend incarnate, goods galore, sales select, merchandising miraculous.* But note that some adjectives are confined almost exclusively to predicative or comple-

ment use and are rarely if ever used in the epithet sense. They are combinations of the preposition *in* or *on* (reduced to *a*) with other parts of speech, chiefly with verbs: *aback, abed, aboard, abroad, afoot, afloat, afraid, agape, agog* (*en* + *gogue*, old French, in fun), *ahead, akin, alive, aloft, amid, anew, around, ashore, asleep, astern, athirst, awake, aware, awry.* Owing to the fluidity of English grammar as a functional science (?) it is of course possible to say *He is an aware fellow* and *There is an asleep dog* without fear of being misunderstood. But such use of these adjectives is unconventional, to say the least. *He is aware, The dog is asleep, My hair is awry, Everybody was agog* are correct usage.

The difference between the adjective used as part of an epithet and the adjective used predicatively should be observed. The epithet *bad boys,* for instance, implies that more is to be said and that all boys in a given category are bad. In *The boys are bad* the implied meaning is that only certain boys in a given group are bad.

In this connection it may be helpful to note such other adverb combinations as these: *besides, betimes, beforehand, forsooth, overboard, together, today, tomorrow, tonight, withal*—combinations of prepositions (*be-by*) and other parts of speech to form independent adverbs.

9 The words *any, each, every,* and so forth (see 5 on page 170) are singular and thus, as adjectives or pronominal adjectives, set up singular relationships. *Either,* like *neither,* it must be remembered, refers to one of two; *any* to one of three or more. The term *many a,* the emphatic form of the old *a many,* is singular. Note these examples:

> Has any man a stamp?
> Has either of you two men a stamp?
> Many a man is going to rue this day
>
> *Not* Has any of you two men a stamp?
> *Not* Has either of you three men a stamp?
> *Not* Many a man are going to rue this day

10 Adjectives and adverbs must be placed as closely as possible to the words and phrases they modify.

> A cup of hot coffee is stimulating
> *Not* A hot cup of coffee is stimulating

The greatest offender against this rule is the adverb *only*. Some authorities have given up and thus yielded to the sheer momentum of the misplaced *only*. They say that *I only have one* may now be accepted as colloquial if as nothing more. But *I have only one* must still be insisted upon if we would be both logical and right. In such cases as *I have scarcely any, I have but two, I have hardly a hope* the adverb modifies the word following it. The following "variation of play" in the placement of *only* should be noted:

> Only he urged us to eat it
> He only urged us to eat it
> He urged only us to eat it
> He urged us only to eat it
> He urged us to eat only it
> He urged us to eat it only

11 Two negatives used in close connection or modification make an affirmative. Use a single negative only in any given statement.

> I have no books
> *Not* I haven't no books
>
> He doesn't want any paper
> *Not* He doesn't want no paper

The words *barely, but* (meaning *only*), *hardly, only, scarcely,* having negative inference, should not be used with other negative words in the same expression.

> I have scarcely any
> I have only one
> I have but one
> I have barely succeeded
> I have hardly a chance
>
> *Not* I haven't scarcely any
> *Not* I haven't only one
> *Not* I haven't but one
> *Not* I haven't barely succeeded
> *Not* I haven't hardly a chance

Note that under certain conditions *even* might be understood or implied in some of these, thus making the double negative logical. To say *I haven't even barely succeeded* may mean that I have failed disgracefully.

Two negatives may, of course, occur in the same sentence in case they modify different words or phrases: *You need not tell them that I did not go, Not only does he not know but he does not know that he does not know.*

The double negative is not to be confused with the figure of litotes, which is the affirmation of something by negativing its opposite. The two negatives are frequently used in this figure for emphasis or for oratorical effect (litotes is primarily a figure of oratory); one does not directly cancel the other (see page 105).

He is a young man of no mean, no insignificant caliber
I am not ungrateful for your many kindnesses

The adverb *also* gives an additive quality to the meaning of a sentence. It is preferable, therefore, not to use it in close modification with a negative word or phrase. *He is not going either* is better than *He is also not going.*

Care must be exercised in a sentence expressing negative comparison to use *no, none, nothing* to modify the comparative rather than *not,* which would modify the verb in all probability.

I can talk no more
Not I can not talk more

This coat is none the worse for wear
Not This coat is not the worse for wear

I am getting no younger
Not I am not getting younger

Similarly *Nothing better could be expected, None better made, No faster engine was ever made.*

The interrogative negative—*You are going to buy a new car, aren't you?*—implies an affirmative answer. In *You are not going to buy a new car, are you?* a negative answer is implied. The difference lies in the transposition of the negative word. But deliver the latter question with exclamatory expression—*You are not going to buy a new car, are you!*—and an affirmative reply is not only implied but certain. As a matter of fact, the car may already have been bought.

In the indirect form the implications are not similar. *He asked whether I was going to buy a new car* implies neither *yes* nor *no;* the answer may be either. But *He asked whether I was not going to buy a new car* implies that the purchase of a new car is at least being seriously considered by him.

12 Sense verbs, such as *feel, look, smell, sound, taste,* and copulative verbs like *appear, be, become, seem,* are usually followed by adjectives that denote quality or condition of their subjects. Adverbs should not be used after these verbs as a rule.

> He feels unhappy (*not* unhappily) about his failure
> She looks pretty (*not* prettily) in her new dress
> The rose smells sweet (*not* sweetly)
> The clarion sounds sharp (*not* sharply) in the morning air
> The berries taste delicious (*not* deliciously)

> He appears angry
> He is angry
> He became angry
> He seems angry
> He feels bad

There is some colloquial justification for *he feels badly,* but the expression cannot be said to be correct except in the actually tactual sense—feeling badly with the fingers.

But *well* may be either adjective or adverb; hence

> He looks well   She is not a well woman
> He sleeps well   How do you feel? Well, thank
> He is well   you
> The task is well   *But* He recited well (*not* good)
> done   His speech was good (*not* well)
> *Not* He looks good   All's well that ends well
> *Not* He sleeps good   *Not* All's good that ends good

Good is incorrect in reference to physical condition or well-being.

In *He feels unhappy* and the other examples in that group, the adjective explains or describes the subject and is thus a predicate adjective. It may likewise be used to explain or describe the object, and thus be an objective complement.

> He likes it *cold*
> He held the racket *tight*
> (You) Get it *right*

But note the adverbs here:

> He sat quietly in the seat
> He read the paragraph clearly
> I am nearly exhausted
> I have done it correctly

Not He sat quiet in the seat
Not He read the paragraph clear
Not I am near exhausted
Not I have done it correct

The adjectives *quick* and *sure* are also frequently misused as adverbs. It is correct to say *sure fire* and *quick change,* for here both words are used to modify nouns and are therefore adjectives. But it is incorrect to say *You sure are a remarkable fellow* and *How quick can you solve this problem?* for *sure* and *quick* are used respectively in adverbial sense and should therefore carry the adverbial ending *ly*—*You surely are a remarkable fellow* and *How quickly can you solve this problem?*

13 Adjectives do not modify verbs; adverbs do. The expressions *this here coat* and *that there hat* are therefore wrong. Moreover, they are repetitious. Used for emphasis or direction, as follows, *here and there* are locative adjectives or locative adverbs:

This coat here is the one I want
That hat there is the one I like

Note the adjective-adverb difference between

John's answer was sincere
John answered sincerely
His appearance was perfect
He appeared perfectly at ease

14 The adverb *there* is the cause of much grammatical confusion. Coming at the beginning of a sentence it is frequently mistaken as a kind of subject of the verb. This is wrong, of course. In such sentences the subject must be looked for *after* the predicate, which must be made singular or plural accordingly.

There are a young man and an old lady in the room
Not There is a young man and an old lady in the room

But There is the book you are looking for
Or There are the books you are looking for

In the former case *there* is expletive only; in the two latter cases *there* is regarded by some authorities as an attribute and by others as an adverb of place.

Meanwhile and *while* are adverbs and should be used strictly as such. *Meantime* and *time* are nouns, and should not be used for *while* and *meanwhile*. This rule is not

strictly observed in present-day speaking and writing, but
it is well worth bearing in mind by careful speakers and
writers.

>In the meantime I found my watch
>I am going to the library for a short time
>Meanwhile I shall read
>*Not* In the meanwhile I found my watch
>*Not* I am going to the library for a short while

Certain adverbs, such as *also, certainly, however, indeed,
nevertheless, now, so, therefore, assuredly, undoubtedly,
verily, both, either, neither* are linking adverbs; that is,
they invariably link the expressions in which they occur
with something gone before. They key the meaning into
harmony with scale. They are usually set off by commas.

>Certainly, I should like nothing better
>It is, indeed, a very serious misunderstanding
>Now, be it remembered that such was not the case
>Either, he will hate the one and love the other

15 Unnecessary repetition, in either word or sense, is called
tautology. All parts of speech are capable of causing
tautology in your writing and speaking, but adjectives and
adverbs are particularly to blame for tautological expression. Extravagance in their use should be studiously
avoided. If you hear some one say *It is the general con-
sensus of opinion* or *We supply all the information, official
and otherwise,* or *All unanimously agreed, An entire
monopoly of the whole business, It is ten years ago since
we were married, At three o'clock p. m. in the afternoon,*
you may be fairly sure that his thinking processes are as
wasteful and unregimented, as his speech indicates them
to be. Even worse, if possible, are such expressions as
*gorgeously grand, perfectly excruciating, determinedly
stubborn, awfully and wonderfully impressive.* The dictionaries have capitulated to *awfully.* It is now sanctioned,· if not accepted, in the sense of *very,* and *Thanks
awfully* of the Anglomaniac "passes muster." The overused adjective *nice* and the overused adverb *awfully* have
been happily named "general utility words" by Professor
Edward H. Grout. He classes them with the general
utility pronouns *gadget, what's-his-name, thing-a-bub,
what-you-call-m, thing-a-ma-jig,* and the slang *whosis.*

Do not use adverbs superfluously, especially after verbs
in which they are implied. Many verbs carry not only

their own meaning—action, that is—but also the inferred meaning of an adverb or a preposition. Thus, *start* is a verb meaning to move into action; the words *out, in, up, down* are implied in it. You do not have to say *start out* or *start in.* Eugene Field wrote a poem about the overuse of *up. Wake up, rake up, use up, drink up, kink up, do up, slack up, stack up, hold up, beer up, steer up, work up, talk up, chalk up, wet up, set up, let up, hang up, clear up, cheer up, back up, think up, make up,* are some of the *ups* he sings in dispraise of. In *returned back, back* is superfluous; in *repeat again, again* is superfluous; in *repeat it over, over* is superfluous; in *cooperate or collaborate together, together* is superfluous. In the words *hence, thence,* and *whence* the word *from* is implied; thus *from hence, from thence,* and *from whence* are wrong.

It must be remembered, on the other hand, that many verbs require more than one word for their complete expression. Such additional words (usually adverbs and prepositions) are sometimes called verbal particles. Note, for instance, *turn, turn in, turn out, turn up, turn down, turn off, turn on, turn right, turn back, turn slow, turn sharp* (see above), and so forth. Some verbs taking the verbal particle freely are *break, bring, carry, come, do, fall, get, go, hold, keep, look, pass, play, put, run, stand, stay, take, turn.*

Do not add the letter *s* to the adverbs *anywhere, nowhere, somewhere.* There are no such words as *anywheres, nowheres, somewheres.* But do not substitute for them *any place, some place, no place* as adverbial modifiers. These must be preceded by a preposition and used as adverbial phrases, if used at all with adverbial significance.

> I cannot find him anywhere
> I cannot find him in any place
> *Not* I cannot find him anywheres
> I cannot find him any place

16 Many words ending with *ly* are adjectives more frequently than adverbs: a *costly* experience, a *cowardly* act, a *deadly* enemy, a *deadly* parallel, a *friendly* fellow, a *gentlemanly* attitude, a *kindly* person, a *leisurely* journey, a *likely* story, a *lonely* road, a *lovely* girl, a *mannerly* boy, an *orderly* person.

Such words as *above, even, outside, off, thru,* customarily used as adverbs or prepositions, are sometimes used as adjectives: the *above* quotation, *even* John has failed (*even* you!), an *off* day, a *thru* train, an *outside* man.

Note that *even* always carries with it the implication of an idea gone before.

Many adverbs are formed by suffixing *ly* to adjectives—*accidentally, casually, incidentally, usually.* But some may or may not take *ly* and still be adverbs in both forms. Some adjectives are used colloquially or in a slang sense as adverbs, but the practise is not recommended. The following list is not exhaustive: *all* along, talk *big,* pay *dear(ly),* try *hard,* aim *high,* play *fair(ly), fast* bind, *deuced(ly)* tired, come *quick(ly),* lie *flat,* stay *late,* travel *light(ly),* speak *low, middling* good, *pretty* bad, go *slow(ly),* speak *ill,* sit *quiet(ly), plain* white, *right* about, look *sharp(ly),* sleep *sound(ly), stark* mad, hold *tight,* ring *true, wide* awake, *double* three, breathe *deep(ly),* "*clean* done," play *soft(ly),* "*soft* you now."

It will be noted that in some cases the adjective or the other word in the epithet takes on substantive quality. In *speak ill* and *plain white,* for instance, *ill* and *white* represent noun values.

Some adjectives and adverbs are similar in form, function in the sentence being the deciding factor as to their exact classification. The principal of these are *little, less, least, much, more, most, very, so, fast, just,* but the *ly* forms *mostly* and *justly* are commonly used.

> He has made a just decision
> He has decided justly
> He was most disturbed by the report
> He was mostly disturbed by the report, tho the coolness of friends and the loss of money upset him also

But note that adverbs, like other parts of speech, permit free transference of function. A man, for instance, who had just merely failed to win positions of leadership for which he had candidated for many years, came to be known as *an almost man.* Another who habitually used the word *somewhat* in his public utterances was dubbed *the somewhat candidate*—and the epithet had much to do with his defeat. In this connection it should be observed that adjectives may be used figuratively, as in *He is a white fellow thru and thru* and *He is true blue;* and that adverbs may appropriate this figurative use of adjectives to their own offices, as in such colloquial expressions as *He saw red* and *He came clean* (see 8 above).

17 Such distinctions as the following (they are but the minimum compared to those the dictionary will reveal to you) should be studied if you would be a polite, that is, a precise and accurate speaker and writer. When you say *This book is a quite interesting one* you do not care so much for the book as you do when you say *This is quite an interesting one.* Transposing the article with the adverb makes a difference in emphasis. *Quite an* is more emphatic than *a quite,* just as *many a* is more emphatic than the old *a many* (see page 193). When you say *There were few people in the room* you mean that the room was almost entirely unoccupied. When you say *There were a few people in the room* you mean that, while it was not altogether unoccupied, there were nevertheless more people in it than were indicated in the former expression. When you say *There were quite a few people in the room* you mean more people than in either of the two preceding cases.

Inasmuch as *off* is nothing more or less than the emphatic form of *of,* it is superfluous to repeat *of* after it: *Keep off the grass, The Marches are never let off anything. Too* is likewise the emphatic form of *to.* Care should be taken not to use it superfluously, except in colloquial or idiomatic expressions. To say that *Too much advice defeats the purpose* or *Too many cooks spoil the broth* is, strictly speaking, tautological, for even *much advice* defeats the purpose of all advice. and *many cooks* will spoil a dish.

The adverbs *so, too,* and *very* are primarily—and preferably—adverbs of degree. It is not strictly correct to use them, therefore, as direct modifiers of verbs. They should be used, rather, to intensify the degree of verb modification.

I am so much (or too greatly) overcome with this happening

I am too sadly affected by your account of the affair

I am very much pleased with your record

Not I am so overcome with this happening

I am too affected by your account of the affair

I am very pleased with your record

F Conjunctions and Prepositions

1 It is not at all wrong to end a sentence with a preposition —any preposition—much popular belief to the contrary notwithstanding. It is sometimes desirable to end a sentence with a preposition. It is often unavoidable to end a sentence with a preposition or a verbal particle (see page 199). But a sentence should never be ended with a preposition when such ending retards or confuses the thought expressed—when, that is, such ending requires the reader to look back to seek the prepositional relationship before proceeding to the next sentence.

It is similarly not at all wrong to begin a sentence with a conjunction—any conjunction—much popular belief to the contrary notwithstanding. The initial conjunction, indeed, may well be used for emphasis and variety and effective transition and the building of climax. It is not recommended for habitual use, as no single construction is, but it is illogical to assume that any word in the language may not be used at the beginning or at the end of a sentence.

2 Correlative conjunctions must be placed as closely as possible to the terms that they connect. The principal correlatives, that is, conjunctions used (or understood) in pairs, are *either...or, neither...nor, not only...but also, both...and, whether...or, and...therefore* (see page 163).

They play neither tennis nor golf

Checkers gives him not only pleasure but also training

Not They neither play tennis nor golf

Checkers not only gives him pleasure but also training

3 *Or* must not be used as correlative with *neither; nor* must not be used with *either* as correlative. Nouns modified in common by *no* should not be connected by *nor,* for *no* is not correlative with *nor* or *either.*

I have no books or papers
I have neither books nor papers
I shall take either books or papers
Not I have no books nor papers
I have neither books or papers
I shall take either books nor papers

4 Ideas connected by the coordinates *and* and *but* must be kept uniform in construction.

He was ill physically and mentally
He was ill in body and in mind
Not He was ill physically and in mind

5 The adversative conjunction *but* must not be used for the additive conjunction *and*. The caution applies also to the use of final or result conjunctions. The conjunction is not to be regarded as a word of connection only, but also as *the* part of speech for making subtle distinctions in the relationship of thoughts and ideas.

I was ill but I went to work
I was well and I therefore went to work
I was ill; nevertheless I went to work
Tho I was ill I went to work

Not I was ill and I went to work
I was well but I therefore went to work
I was ill; consequently I went to work
Tho I was well I went to work

But meaning *except* and used, therefore, as a preposition, very often takes the elliptical infinitive as object. In such instances do not supply the *to,* for this gives the expression an awkward note.

He does nothing but complain
We have done nothing but chatter all day

6 As a rule the infinitive *to try* takes an infinitive for its object. The two infinitives in this relationship should not, therefore, be connected by *and*.

I am going to try to meet you
Not I am going to try and meet you

7 After both of these comparative phrases the subject only of the following dependent clause is expressed as a rule:

He is as happy as I about it (as I am)
He is happier than I about it (than I am)

But note that the predicate of the dependent clause must sometimes be expressed to avoid ambiguity: *He likes Bill*

204   GET IT RIGHT!

better than John may mean one of two things: *He likes Bill better than he likes John* or *He likes Bill better than John does* or *likes Bill.* In the first example *John* is in the objective case; in the second, it is in the nominative. If personal pronouns are used, the inflection clarifies the meaning: *He likes Bill better than me* and *He likes Bill, better than I.*

8 The words *differ, difference, different, differently* should never be followed by *than.* The *er* in these words gives them the sound and appearance of comparatives. But they are not comparatives. *Differ* is the Latin prefix *dis* softened to *dif,* and the Latin root *fer.*

> This one is different from that
> They are different from me

9 Do not use *but* before *what* and *that* in such constructions as these:

> I do not doubt but that he can do it
> I do not doubt but what he will pass

They should read

> I do not doubt he will pass or that he will pass

But observe this:

> He sent me a message, but what it said I do not know
> He does nothing but what he is told

In the last example *but* is equivalent to *except* and the noun clause is object of it.

10 Be precise in your use of *that* and *whether.* Do not use *as* or *if* for *whether.* Do not use *as, how, because,* or *where* for *that.*

> He asked whether it is raining
> He doesn't feel that he is needed
> They told us that they intended to go to Europe
> The reason for her failure was that she was ill
> We read in the paper that wages are to be raised

> *Not* He asked if it is raining (*if* means on condition of)
> He doesn't feel as he is needed
> They told us how as they intended to go to Europe
> The reason for her failure was because she was ill
> We read in the paper where wages are to be raised

The word *if,* meaning on condition, should not be used for the conjunction *whether* to introduce substantive clauses. *Reason* and *because* express the same idea. (In some parts of the country this atrocious idiom persists: *He doesn't feel how as if he is needed.*) In each of these examples (correct) the subordinate clause is a noun clause. *That* and *whether* more frequently introduce noun clauses than any other words.

That, introducing indirect discourse, may or may not be expressed; introducing result clauses it must be expressed.

> He said he would go immediately
> He came early that he might get a good seat

In the former *that* merely introduces; in the latter it joins *and points.*

11 Do not use conjunctions superfluously. In *I do not know whether I shall go* the meaning is perfectly clear without the completed correlation *or not,* which is clearly understood. Some authorities urge that the emphatic form of this sort of expression is *I do not know whether I shall go or not.*

Similarly, *either* and *neither* are frequently superfluously used with their respective correlatives *or* and *nor*. *John or Bill is going. Either* is really unnecessary in this sentence, unless emphasis is desired. Then, according to the same authorities, the reading should be *Either John or Bill is going.*

Much confusion may result from a loose use of *or* when it is made to connect two words that are not alternatives. It should not be used to connect two words one of which is explanatory of the other. In *I shall come on Tuesday or Wednesday, or* is correctly used to connect alternatives. But in *I received a wireless or a marconigram* the second term of the *or*-connected pair is not an alternative of the first but is, rather, a repetition of it or an appositive. Suppose the reader or hearer does not know that a wireless is a marconigram. He may think of or visualize two different things, one of which he is able to identify but the other one of which he must look up in order to gather my meaning. It is better in such cases as this to place the second term in parentheses or to express the relationship by means of *that is.*

12 Do not use prepositions unnecessarily (see page 199). Note that the italicized prepositions in the following sentences are superfluous:

I fell off *of* the bridge
Where shall I take it *to?*
Where have you been *at?*
They are coming *at* (or *on*) about the twelfth
She does not remember *of* my arrival
You must prevent her *from* going
We are going *to* home tonight
They entered *into* the theater late
The house is too near *to* the lake
He was *of* about twenty years of age
He kept inside *of* the house

13 On the other hand, do not omit prepositions when they are necessary to the complete construction of a sentence (see rule 17, page 209).

Of what use is this mechanism	*not*	What use is this mechanism
On this side of the house is a wood	*not*	This side of the house is a wood
We are going either to Detroit or to Milwaukee	*not*	We are going either to Detroit or Milwaukee
His work is unworthy of mention	*not*	His work is unworthy mention
We shall be at home tonight	*not*	We shall be home tonight
The rain prevented me from attending the performance	*not*	The rain prevented me attending the performance
I shall restrain him from doing such a thing	*not*	I shall restrain him doing such a thing
Please refrain from speaking	*not*	Please refrain speaking
I have great fondness for and belief in the lad	*not*	I have great fondness and belief in the lad
The wall was two feet in diameter	*not*	The wall was too feet diameter
The boys of the school and of the club stood firmly together	*not*	The boys of the school and club stood firmly together
Try to do it in this way	*not*	Try to do it this way

14 *As* and *as* are generally used as correlatives in affirmative connections; *so* and *as* in negative ones. *So* intensifies that term of comparison which it precedes, while *as* merely indicates equality or similar extent or degree. This rule is probably violated quite as often as it is observed.

It is not so clear as it seems
I am not so ill as you think
John is as old as I
He did not come so soon as we expected
He came as soon as he could

But in *He was so angry that he left the room* result is expressed but no comparison—positive, negative, or parallel; hence, *as* would be wrong. In result clauses *so* and *that* are correlatives.

There are certain instances in negative comparative statements, however, where *so* would not only be incorrect but would really be ridiculous. Remember that it intensifies, and that *as* means to that extent or degree. Now suppose you have lost a very dear relative or friend. You should say *I am not as happy as I was,* that is, I am not happy to the degree to which I was happy before my friend died. But the use of *so* before *happy* implies a condition of happiness in excess of that denoted by the second term in the comparison.

The comparatives are capable of shades of meaning that call for precision of expression. Note the difference between these:

> He never sang so well as he did last evening
> He never sang better than he did last evening

15 *Except, like, without* are not conjunctions. They are prepositions in most English uses. *Like* must not be used for *as; without* and *except* (and *but* when it means *except*) must not be used for *unless*. *As* and *unless* are subordinate conjunctions used to introduce dependent clauses.

These are correct:

> He drives like me
> He drives as I do
> He won't go without me
> He won't go unless I go
> Everybody went but (except) me
> Everybody went except me
> He feels as if he wants to go

These are incorrect:

> He drives like I do
> He won't go without I go
> He won't go except I go
> He feels like he wants to go

Inasmuch as conjunctions not only connect, but specify something by way of relationship—time, condition, con-

cession, addition, and so forth—some authorities rule that
like may be used as a conjunction when, in addition to
connecting, it shows resemblance; when, in other words,
it has something of the simile in it. Inasmuch as *as* shows
equivalence without indicating similarity, it very often
causes ambiguity, and resort to *like* appears to be necessary. *He talks like a doctor* means that in his talking he
resembles a doctor, not necessarily that he is a doctor.
But in *He talks as a doctor* the decided implication is that
he is a doctor and is speaking professionally. Similarly,
in *I think you should dress as you promised you would,*
the meaning may be doubtful. Does the sentence mean
that you promised to wear a certain dress or to dress in
a certain manner or not to dress at all but appear in your
old clothes? *As* does not tell us; *like* would tell us, for
it would suggest manner or similarity or resemblance, and
thus imply that you had promised to wear a certain style
of dress.

The argument has plausibility certainly. The point to
emphasize in pressing *like* as a conjunction, is that it not
only connects but that it carries in it in addition a suggested resemblance to some person or place or thing
mentioned before. *The albatross dropt down like lead
drops into the sea,* that is, the dropping (gerund) of the
albatross was like the dropping of lead into the sea. This
is really a simile expressed by means of a *like*-clause
rather than thru a *like*-phrase, and a commonly accepted
simile. It may be better artfully to avoid the use of *like*
in such resembling connections—as a conjunction, that is
—until, at least, a preponderance of authority justifies
such use. There is now, however, much loose and un-
analytical usage of *like* as a conjunction, and in our
so-called best writers!

16 *Whence* means from where; *thence*, to there, away from,
elsewhere; *hence*, from here; *where*, at which or to which.
Do not, therefore, use superfluous prepositions or adverbs
with these words.

> Whence did you come?
> Go thence
> Where have you been?
> Get thee hence

Not Whence did you come from?
Go thence away
Where have you been at?
Get thee from hence

17 Avoid the use of the suspended prepositional phrase. This means that it is preferable not to connect two or more prepositions by a conjunction, reserving the common object of them all till the last preposition is given (see rule 13, page 206).

I am interested in the boy and curious about him
We believe in government of the people, by the people and for the people
Not I am interested in and curious about the boy
Not We believe in government of, by, and for the people

This kind of error invariably deters the grasp of an expression on the part of a listener or reader, for he usually has to stop after the final preposition to trace the relationship and to fix it as a unit in his mind. There is nothing grammatically wrong with the suspended prepositional phrase. This instruction is correlative with 4 under verbs (see page 209).

18 Avoid also the omission of the final word in the conjunctional phrases *as good as* and *better than.*

This is as good as if not better than mine
Not This is as good if not better than mine

But *This is as good as mine if not better* is good usage. As pointed out above, the suspended construction is likely to delay grasp of the thought expressed, and it is well always to avoid it, no matter what part of speech is chiefly involved.

19 The preposition *to* is understood before the word *home* but the word *at* is always exprest.

I shall be at home
I went home early

20 The preposition *of* should not be used superfluously after *off* (see page 201) or as substitute for *have* (see page 181).

You ought to have known
Not You ought to of known

Keep off the lot
Not Keep off of the lot

21 It is better not to make prepositions do the work of verbs,
tho in colloquial expression this rule is generally violated,
it is feared.

> I have no funds
> I am opposed to that point of view
> What are you doing?
> He has read the book thru
>
> *Not* I am without funds
> I am against that point of view
> What are you at?
> He is thru the book

22 There are nice distinctions to be made in the use of prepositions. *Among*, for instance, is used with more than two;
between with two only. You say *at* a thing but *with* a
person. You speak of a sale *of* shirts, not a sale *on* shirts;
of walking *beside* Josephine and taking Towser along
besides. You walk *on* the carpet, not *onto* it; you go
into the room, not *in* it; you place goods *upon* the shelves
or leave them *on* the counter. You look *behind* the piano
for the sales-slip that you lost, not *in back of* it. You
wait *about* an hour, not *around* an hour, but you may
walk *around* the block while you are waiting *for* (not *on*)
me. You may be in need *of* money *for* the necessities of
life. You stay *at* your friend's home, not *by* his home.
You differ *from* me and differ *with* my opinions.

23 It is obvious from such sentences as those below that
prepositional phrases must be placed as closely as possible
to the words they modify.

> He was sued for the crime of carrying a pistol by the grand
> jury
> The witness testified that a Ford ran into him on his cross-
> examination
> He is said to have been intoxicated by some reporters
> They are going to return to the land where they were born
> this summer
> This poem was written more than a century ago by a poet
> who has been sleeping for two decades in his grave for his
> own pastime

24 Be careful in regard to preposition-verbal idioms, that
is, in using the correct preposition after a verb to express
your true meaning. There are in our language more than
a thousand preposition-verbal combinations that are
capable of misuse. You must consult the dictionary

diligently whenever doubt arises regarding them. *This machine is adapted to hot-weather driving, This body type is adapted for five people, This body was adapted from the French by Fisher Brothers* illustrate correct combinations of *to, for,* and *from* with the word *adapt.* Note also the following list, which does not, of course, include more than a small fraction of these idiomatic combinations. The dictionary must be your guide to a large extent.

abhorrence of (I have an abhorrence of deviltry)
abhorrent to (Deviltry is abhorrent to me)
abide by (We must abide by his decision)
abide for (We shall abide for ten years in this place)
abide in (We shall abide in the city this winter)
abide with (She abides with her son-in-law)
accommodate to (Accommodate yourself to the new conditions)
accommodate with (He accommodated me with the necessary amount)
accompanied by (I was accompanied by my sister)
accompanied with (Accompany your letter with an announcement)
accord between (The accord between them is gratifying)
accord in (We accord in our judgments)
accord of (An accord of interests is important)
accord to (I shall accord to him what he deserves)
accord with (I am in accord with your statement)
account for (He shall account for his mistake)
account to (Account to me, please, for the error)
admit into (They will not admit us into the corridor)
admit of (This law admits of one interpretation only)
admit to (They admitted the theft to me)
advise of (He advised us of the danger)
advise with (We shall advise with him about the matter)
agree among (The members of the team cannot agree among themselves)
agree in (We agree in principle)
agree on (We agree on the undertaking)
agree to (They agree to our plan)
agree with (You will agree with me, I am sure)
aim at (Aim at a high accomplishment)
aim to (Aim to realize that accomplishment)
allied to (I am allied to his family by marriage)
allied with (The French are allied with the Russians)
ambitious of (He is ambitious of making a fortune)
ambitious to (He is ambitious to become rich)
apologize for (You must apologize for your mistake)
apologize to (You must apologize to her for your mistake)
apply for (He applied for the position)
apply to (He applied to me for the position)
apropos of (He spoke apropos of the centennial)
apropos to (His selection was not apropos to the occasion)

argue about (They argue too much about the fare)
argue for (He argued for increased tax rates)
argue with (He argued with me for an hour)
astonished at (I was astonished at his behavior)
astonished by (I was astonished by his achievement)
attend on (You must attend on your master)
attend to (You must attend to your business)
belong in (The tools belong in the car)
belong to (That car belongs to me)
belong with (The tools belong with the curtains in the car)
blush at (I blush at your insinuation)
blush for (I blush for your awkward behavior)
capacity for (She has great capacity for learning)
capacity of (The car has a capacity of one thousand tons)
center in (Center your interests in some worthwhile vocation)
center on (Center your efforts on a worthy cause)
(center around) (Do not use this expression. It is self-
    contradictory)
clear in (Clear this problem in your mind)
clear of (I shall clear you of any accusation)
clear to (The proposition should be clear to everybody)
clear with (He cleared the deck with his threat)
compare to (He compared New York to Chicago)
compare with (He compared Lincoln with Washington)
concerned about (I am concerned about your health)
concerned in (I am concerned in this undertaking)
concerned with (I am concerned with the alleviation of suf-
    fering)
confide in (He always confides in me)
confide to (Confide your proposal to me)
confirm by (The story is confirmed by the papers)
confirm in (They are confirmed in their theories)
connive at (I shall connive at tricking Harry)
connive with (Let us connive with each other to break out)
consist in (Character consists in stability of conscience)
consist of (The building consists of eight sections)
consult about (I consulted my lawyer about my bonds)
consult with (May I consult with you about my bonds?)
convenient for (Everything in the car is convenient for the
    chauffeur)
convenient to (The garage is convenient to the house)
correspond to (Your account corresponds to the actual hap-
    penings)
correspond with (I have corresponded with him for years)
defend against (I shall defend myself against thieves)
defend from (Defend me from my enemies)
defer to (I shall defer to your desires)
defer until (The meeting is deferred until tomorrow)
denounce as (He was denounced as a rascal)
denounce for (He was denounced for his rascality)
depend from (The lamp depends from the cornice)
depend upon (on) (Depend upon or on me for the loan)
descend from (I am descended from the Dutch)
descend on (The gangs descend on civilized society)
descend to (He has descended to a deplorable condition)

desirous of (I am desirous of winning the prize)
desirous to (He is very desirous to win the prize)
destructive of (Dissipation is destructive of health)
destructive to (Caterpillars are destructive to trees)
die of (He died of tuberculosis)
die from (He died from exposure to cold)
differ from (My watch differs from yours)
differ in (We differ in our policies)
differ on (We differ on the question of free silver)
disappoint by (He was disappointed by what he saw)
disappoint in (He was disappointed in love)
disappoint of (He was disappointed of his ambitions)
dispose of (They disposed of the old Ford)
dispose to (They are now disposed to buy another)
divert from (They diverted the funds from old investments)
divert to (They diverted their funds to industrial stocks)
divert with (She diverted the audience with stories of her
    travels)
eligible for (He is not eligible for the team this year)
eligible to (I am eligible to reelection this fall)
employ at (He employed me at a satisfactory wage)
employ in (Employ your energies in a worthwhile business)
encouraged by (I am encouraged by your record)
encouraged in (I shall encourage the boy in his work)
enter at (Enter at the rear door)
enter for (I shall enter for the finals)
enter in (Enter this charge in the daybook)
entertain by (We were entertained by professionals)
entertain with (They entertained us with imitations)
entrust to (The valuables were entrusted to me)
entrust with (I entrust you with these valuables)
exchange for (May I exchange this for that?)
exchange with (Will you exchange places with me?)
expect from (We expect a good return from this investment)
expect of (I expect nothing of you)
fail in (He failed in his promise to me)
fail to (Do not fail to come)
fail of (All his struggles failed of achievement)
feed into (He feeds the sheaves into the thresher)
feed on (The dog feeds on biscuits)
fitted for (He is ill-fitted for the job)
fitted to (This suit is nicely fitted to your figure)
free from (I am now free from any obligation to you)
free of (He was freed of the accusation)
free to (I am free to go where I will)
frighten at (I am frightened at his tone)
frighten by (The horse was frightened by the car)
glad at (We were glad at your success)
glad of (We are glad of a chance to accompany you)
guard against (You should guard against danger)
guard from (The officer will guard us from him)
identify to (Please identify me to the principal)
identify with (Do not identify yourself with bad company)
impatient at (He was justifiably impatient at error)

impatient with (He was justifiably impatient with her for her errors)
influence by (They were influenced by the speaker)
influence for (He has always influenced me for good)
influence of (The influence of a teacher is incalculable)
influence over (He has great influence over the members of his club)
insensible from (He was insensible from exposure to cold)
insensible to (He seems insensible to the finer influences of life)
intercede for (I shall intercede for you at headquarters)
intercede with (I shall intercede with the manager in your behalf)
invest in (He invested in city bonds)
invest with (He was invested with more authority)
join to (This layer of cement was joined to the board)
join with (Will you join with me in this new venture?)
labor at (He is laboring at another job in masonry)
labor for (They labored for hours without accomplishment)
labor in (Labor in the right)
labor under (They labored under adverse conditions)
labor with (Labor with conviction that you will achieve)
liable for (He is liable for damages)
liable to (He is liable to me for damages)
live at (He lives at the crossroads)
live by (He lives by doing odd jobs)
made of (This desk is made of hardwood)
made from (This pencil is made from large squares of wood)
martyr for (He was martyred for his patriotism)
martyr to (He was martyred to bigotry)
need for (There is need for improving the condition of the poor)
need of (The roof is in need of repairs)
occasion for (It was an occasion for great thanksgiving)
occasion of (It was the occasion of an unfortunate misunderstanding)
opposite of (Blunder Boy is the very opposite of Tabby-tab)
opposite to (His idea was opposite to mine *or* the opposite of mine)
originate in (The old custom originated in Spain)
originate with (The old custom originated with the bullfighters)
overcome by (He has been overcome by the adverse circumstances)
overcome with (Overcome evil with good)
plead for (I plead for him with all my heart)
plead with (Will you plead with the manager for me?)
possess of (He is possessed of great oratorical power)
possess by (He was possessed by devils)
possess with (They were possessed with panic)
present to (We present to you this watch)
present with (We shall present you with a watch)
preside at (Will you preside at this meeting?)
preside over (They presided over the prisoners with patience)
prevail against (The elements prevail against us)

prevail upon (Can't I prevail upon you to go?)
prevail with (Nothing but force prevails with him)
prohibit by (Shooting is prohibited by law)
prohibit from (You are prohibited from shooting on this property)
provide against (Thrift provides against poverty)
provide for (We shall provide for you always)
qualify for (He is preparing to qualify for a license)
qualify to (He is qualified to hold the job)
quarrel about (They quarreled about you)
quarrel with (They quarreled with the other boys)
reason about (They reasoned about the accident for hours)
reason together (Come, let us reason together)
reason with (Reason with me about this, won't you?)
reconcile to (I am reconciled to my loss)
reconcile with (This opinion cannot be reconciled with that)
regard as (I regard your remark as an insult)
regard for (Have more regard for your superiors)
resemblance between (There is a resemblance between the two)
resemblance to (Her resemblance to Martha is unusual)
resolve into (They resolved themselves into a committee)
resolve to (They resolved to push the matter)
respect for (Have respect for the rules)
respect to (He is talking in respect to the revision)
responsible for (You are not responsible for my actions)
responsible to (We are all responsible to God)
result from (Only remorse results from dissipation)
result in (Reduction of salaries results in dangerous discontent)
retire from (He has retired from the business)
retire to (He will retire to the hills)
scared at (I am scared at your appearance)
scared by (The chickens were scared by the motor)
secure by (Our position is made secure only by vigilance)
secure of (They are secure of mind and body)
sensible about (Be sensible about this negotiation)
sensible of (I am sensible of the great favor you show me)
serve for (This will serve for the purpose)
serve to (The medicine will serve to strengthen him)
serve with (Serve the biscuit with the salad)
skilful at (He is skilful at that sort of repartee)
skilful in (He is skilful in managing an office)
skilful with (He is skilful with machinery)
stand for (Stand for the cause)
stand upon (Stand upon your citizenship privileges)
stand with (Stand with me on this question)
supply by (This milk is supplied by the Blue Ribbon Company)
supply to (This milk is supplied to your home every day)
supply with (We supply you with milk every day)
surprize at (I am surprized at your behavior)
surprize by (I was surprized by all my friends)
talk to (The candidate talked to the audience)
talk with (I talked with my friend)

taste for (He has taste for the better things)
taste in (He has remarkable taste in color work)
taste of (The taste of honey sickens him)
thankful for (I am thankful for small favors)
thankful to (I am thankful to the employees for the gift)
tired of (We are tired of his complaining)
tired with (My feet are tired with walking)
trade in (We trade in leathers)
trade of (There is no trade of greater interest)
trade upon (They trade upon the high seas)
trade with (They trade with only the best firms)
translate from (Translate this from the Latin)
translate into (Translate this into English)
true to (Be true to yourself at least)
true with (This edge is not true with that)
unequal in (The cars are unequal in power)
unequal to (The car was unequal to the road)
unfavorable for (The weather is unfavorable for our proposed outing)
unfavorable to (The final goal was unfavorable to us)
unite by (Unite the threads by means of a ring)
unite with (Unite with me in this new organization)
useful in (This is useful in making boxes)
useful to (This will be useful to me)
vary from (This letter varies from that in makeup)
vary with (Letter writing varies with business offices)
vest in (The power is vested in that one man)
vest with (That one man is vested with entire power)
wait for (I have waited for you an hour)
wait on (She waited on me while I was ill)
write off (He will write off my indebtedness for me)
write out (Write the story out from your notes)
yield of (What yield of wheat had you per acre?)
yield to (I shall never yield to temptation)
zeal for (He has great zeal for his son's promotion)
zeal in (He evinces extraordinary zeal in his work)

CHAPTER SEVEN

ITALICS

I   Various uses of italics

Italic letters, in type, slope toward the right. The first letter—I—is pronounced short. Italics are used primarily to emphasize printed matter, to differentiate type faces, and to comply with printing usage.

In longhand and typewritten copy indicate italics by underlining once, small capitals by underlining twice, and large capitals by underlining three times. Other typographical variations must be indicated to the printer by means of direct written instructions.

A   Italics are used for emphasis—to call special attention to a sign, a word, a phrase, or a longer part, and to stress a word or other part used as a word or a phrase or a coinage. But in using italics thus care must be taken not to confuse a quoted word or phrase or sentence with one to which attention is called for reasons other than quotation. And it must be remembered that too much accentuation thru the medium of italics defeats the purpose of emphasis, as does the use of any other device to the same end—small capitals, large capitals, bold face, and the like.

> The word *trivial* has a very interesting origin
> He used that very meaningful phrase *embarras de richesses*
> Your % marks look like *8's*
> His style *annoys* me but his meaning *stimulates* me
> In college he was what is known as a *roisterer*
> As he sat down he used the grand old term "winning instance" first given popular currency more than a century ago

It may be pointed out here (see also page 529) that italics are being used increasingly to take the place of quotation marks where isolated bits of conversation are used and where contributions to conversation are to be stressed.

> *Never,* he stormed, *shall I permit my name to be used in such association*
> She replied calmly, *It will be used and you cannot stop them*

217

When this is done commas are really unnecessary to separate
direct from indirect matter.   But this style is somewhat in
advance of present-day usage.

Note how, in the following, the emphasis is changed at sight
by the use of italics and different meanings thus conveyed:

> *Mary* is beautiful in blue
> Mary *is* beautiful in blue
> Mary is *beautiful* in blue
> Mary is beautiful in *blue*

B   The terms *continued, to be continued, continued on page —,*
see page —, turn to page —, to be concluded, be it resolved,
be it further resolved, provided, whereas, see, see also, errata,
for —— read ——, ordered, and other such directive expressions in books, newspapers, magazines, circulars, catalogs,
library forms, are usually written in italics.   Individual house
style, however, is a justifiable exception to this rule.   Many
houses use other type faces for these terms.

> *Errata* (page 116) *for* JOURNEYS END *read* JOURNEY'S END
> *See also* Opdycke's *The Language of Advertising* (*pp.* 1-25)

C   Literary, music, art, and general printing titles of all kinds are
usually italicized.

> Beethoven's *Moonlight Sonata*
> Da Vinci's *The Last Supper*
> I liked Maxwell Anderson's *Mary of Scotland*
> He read it in the *New York Herald Tribune*
> He dramatized *A Tale of Two Cities*

Lesser titles, however, and titles within titles, are placed in
quotation marks, as are also titles of divisions, chapters, sections, cantos, parts, and the like.   Some authorities except
from italics the titles of toasts, sermons, papers, articles, and
lectures, but there would seem to be no good reason for such
exception unless, as above indicated, these are used within
greater titles or are themselves titles of parts of a larger
writing.

> In *The Language of Advertising* there is an interesting chapter on
> "From Parnassus to Publicity"
> Campbell Morgan's greatest sermon remains *The Hidden Years at*
> *Nazareth*
> I read "Tender is the Night" in *Scribner's Magazine*
> His toast "To the Ladies, God Bless'm," won applause
> or
> His toast *To the Ladies, God Bless'm,* won applause

Italics and quotation marks are preferably not used in referring to the books or other parts of the Bible or other sacred collections. It is likewise preferable not to use them in long bibliographies—of, say, a page or more—where their appearance would cause confusion and misunderstanding. Italics run to great length make reading difficult. In the writing of titles care must be exercised in regard to the articles *a*, *an*, and *the* according as they do or do not belong. There is much loose composition in regard to these.

D The titles of legal cases are written in italics as a rule, as are certain titles and subtitles in deeds, wills, contracts, and so forth. The *v.* or *vs.* used between names of plaintiff and defendant in legal citations may or may not be italicized. The terms *Party of the first part* and *Party of the second part* are sometimes written in italics, sometimes in large capitals, and sometimes in bold face. Usage varies.

> The *Sixth Avenue Railway* case
> *Jones* vs. *Smith*
> *Harrison, appellant* v. *Johnson, respondent*
> *In re Blaine vs. Williams* the court ruled
> *The State of New York* v. *The St. Lawrence Oil Company*

E There is much variation, not to say contradiction, of usage in the italicization of abbreviations, especially Latin abbreviations and Latin words used as such. Many authorities still list the following to be italicized except in those cases where they stand in italicized matter. Then they should be printed in body face.

> *ad lib.* (at pleasure)
> *ad loc.* (to the place)
> *ante* (before)
> *circa, ca., c.* (about)
> *et al.* (and others)
> *e.g.* (for example)
> *ibid.* (the same place or thing)
> *idem* (the same person)
> *i.e.* (that is)
> *infra* (forward or below)
> *in re* (in regard to)
>
> *loc. cit.* (place cited or given)
> *op. cit.* (work referred to or cited)
> *passim* (here and there)
> *post* (after, beyond)
> *sc.* (namely)
> *supra* (above, forward)
> *v.* or *vs.* (opposed, against)
> *via* (way, by way of)
> *vide* (see)
> *viz.* (namely)
> *vv.ll.* (various readings)

F The names of vessels, both air and sea, are usually italicized, tho style manuals are themselves contradictory in regard to this. Some newspapers both italicize and quote such names; some italicize only; some use quotes only.

> The sinking of the *Lusitania*
> The sinking of the "Lusitania"
> The sinking of the *"Lusitania"*
>
> The *U-9*
> The "Do-X"
> The *"Spirit of St. Louis"*

The first of these examples is still considered the preferred style. Some authorities rule that the names of ships are put in quotation marks when they are printed in faces other than italics, but this is probably too nice for general adoption.

G The following uses of italics are more or less optional, individual house style deciding the issue (if any) in most cases:

1 Italicize the symbols or letters for shillings, pence, and cents.

      2s. 3d.   *25 cts.*   *25¢*

2 Italicize scientific names, both species and genera. But the names of classes, families, or groups higher than genera are not italicized.

    Apocynum cannabinum

    Spinach (*Spinacia oleracea*) is a potherb of the goosefoot family

Note that the name of the genus is usually capitalized (see page 51).

3 Do not italicize chemical symbols, whether capitals, small capitals, roman; whether superior or inferior. But all such symbols are usually italicized in other connections. The first part of the rule is by no means closely observed in the use of chemical symbols.

$$Na_2CO_3 + H_2SO_4 = Na_2SO_4 + CO_2 + H_2O$$

$$C + 2.11V_x = H - 2^{m-4}$$

4 Address lines, introductions, and salutations in reports, speeches, and other similar writings are usually italicized. Titles following signatures to reports and letters that are issued in printed form are likewise usually italicized.

    To the Members of the House Committee

    Mr. Charles R. Townsend, *President*
    Miss Mary C. Treadwell, *Secretary*

    Ladies and Gentlemen

5 Punctuation marks that belong to italicized matter must be italicized. But brackets and parentheses enclosing and separating italicized matter are not italicized.

6 Italics are frequently used for subheads, sideheads, boxed-in heads, marginal heads, and still otherwise in displaying printed matter. In all such cases it is somewhat better to use an italic type face that is larger than the roman body

face. Italic lower-case (larger than the body-text type) and italic capitals are both excellent for such display work and also for emphasis, provided size-harmony of type faces is not violated. There are no general house rules, however, for such free-lance use of italics. Special house styles and special individual requests are the only guides.

II Italicizing foreign words

A Foreign words and phrases not yet definitely adopted into English should be italicized. Those that have been adopted by English, that is, that have been used in English speaking and writing for so long a time that they are generally understood, should not be italicized. There is wide variation and contradiction in the application of this rule, chiefly because people are by no means always able to tell whether a foreign phrase that they use is new to the language. As foreign words are adopted into English they tend to drop inflectional marks. This is especially true of words from the French.

Following is a list of most of the foreign words and phrases that are used in English today. Those printed in italics should, according to the best authorities, be italicized. Those not in italics have become so much a part of English as result of long usage that they need not be italicized. The names of the languages from which these terms come are in parentheses after the terms themselves. Free translation follows the parentheses.

abbé (French) a curate or other ecclesiastic
agrément (French) a pleasing characteristic or quality
à la carte (French) according to the card or bill-of-fare, each article of food being specially priced
à la mode (French) according to fashion
ad interim (Latin) in the meantime
ad infinitum (Latin) infinitely
ad libitum (Latin) at will, as much as one pleases
ad nauseam (Latin) to nauseation
ad valorem (Latin) according to value, as in levying duty
aide de camp (French) camp assistant, one who assists a general in carrying out orders
alias (Latin) another name, an assumed name
alma mater (Latin) literally *dear mother,* commonly applied to the college of which one is a graduate
ancien régime (French) the old order
anno Domini (Latin) in the year of our Lord
ante bellum (Latin) before the war
ante meridiem (Latin) before noon
appliqué (French) ornamented with a pattern cut from another stuff

a posteriori (Latin) proceeding from known facts to generalization, inductive

a priori (Latin) proceeding from an assumption to its detailed consequences, deductive

à propos (French) to the point, appropriate

atelier (French) studio, workshop

attaché (French) one attached to another person or thing, as to an ambassador or embassy

auto da fé (Spanish) public announcement and execution of sentence of the Inquisition with the attendant ceremonies

beau ideal (French) an ideal or faultless model

beau monde (French) the fashionable world

beauséant (French) standard or battlecry of Knights Templar

belles lettres (French) polite or elegant literature

bête noire (French) a bugbear, something especially dreaded or disliked

béton (French) concrete of lime, sand, and cement

billet doux (French) a love letter

blasé (French) sated or worn with pleasure

blessé (French) wounded

bona fide (Latin) in good faith, honestly

bon mot (French) a witty repartee or jest

bon ton (French) the height of fashion, fashionable society

bon vivant (French) a good fellow, a jovial companion

bouillon (French) a clear soup

bourgeois (French) the middle class of society

boutonnière (French) a buttonhole bouquet

cabaret (French) a restaurant in which music and entertainment are furnished

caïque (French) a long narrow boat having from two to ten oars

café (French) restaurant

calèche (French) a small carriage with folding top

camouflage (French) concealment by pretense of being something else

cañada (Spanish) a glade or narrow valley

canapé (French) bread fried in butter or fat, served with relishes

carte blanche (French) unlimited authority

carte de visite (French) visiting card

casus belli (Latin) cause of war

causerie (French) familiar or conversational criticism

centième (French) hundredth

chacun à son gout (French) every man to his taste

chargé d'affaires (French) an inferior diplomatic representative at a foreign court

chef d'œuvre (French) a masterpiece in art

chic (French) good form, style

chiné (French) dyed or woven or figured in Chinese fashion

clientèle (French) professional or business following

cloisonné (French) a form of ornamental design on walls, vases, etc.

coiffeur (French) a masculine hairdresser

comédienne (French) a comedy actress

comme il faut (French) correct, as it should be

communiqué (French) an official announcement

con amore (Italian) with love, heartily

concierge (French) superintendent or custodian of a building

confrère (French) intimate associate
congé (French) farewell, leave-taking
contretemps (French) hitch, mishap
cortège (French) train of attendants
coulée (French) a solidified stream of lava
coup d'état (French) a bold or brilliant piece of statesmanship
coup de grâce (French) the finishing or mortal stroke as in a duel
coup de maître (French) master stroke
couturier (French) dressmaker
crèche (French) a public day nursery
crédit foncier (French) a credit institution that makes loans on realty
crédit mobilier (French) a credit institution that places investments on personal property and conducts general financial operations
crème (French) cream
crêpe (French) a soft, gauzy, crinkled material
cul de sac (French) a passage with only one outlet, blind alley, trap
curé (French) a French parish priest
danseuse (French) a professional female dancer
débris (French) rubbish, fragments, waste
début (French) a first appearance or attempt
décolleté (French) leaving neck and shoulders bare in dress
de facto (Latin) actually, really existing or done
dégagé (French) indifferent, nonchalant
déjeuner (French) luncheon or to lunch
de jure (Latin) by right of law
demi tasse (French) half or small cup
dénouement (French) conclusion, solution
de rigeur (French) correct
de trop (French) superfluous
dilettante (Italian) a lover of the fine arts, an amateur who follows the arts for amusement only
distingué (French) distinguished
distrait (French) absent-minded, lost in thought, abstracted
divorcée (French) a divorced woman
dos-à-dos (French) back to back
double entente (French) double meaning
dramatis personæ (Latin) characters in a play
éclat (French) brilliance of effect or effort, glory, applause, strikingness
écru (French) color of hemp or unbleached muslin
élan (French) ardor, dash, an impetuous or brilliant rush of feeling
élite (French) the choicest part or group of society, the pick
embarras de richesses (French) embarrassment of riches
emigré (French) an emigrant, especially one who fled from France in 1789
employé (French) one who is employed
empressement (French) demonstrativeness, animated earnestness of tone and manner
en bloc (French) in the lump, in one lot
en masse (French) in bulk, in the mass
en route (French) on the road or way
ensemble (French) the whole, all the parts taken together
entente cordiale (French) cordial understanding

entourage (French) associates or followers collectively

entrée (French) entrance or permission or right to enter; a dish served early in a dinner

entre nous (French) between ourselves

entrepôt (French) a warehouse, a place where merchandise is deposited

entrepreneur (French) one who originates and manages, as entertainments or theatrical enterprises

ergo (Latin) therefore

errata (Latin) errors

esprit de corps (French) the common spirit pervading a body of persons

étage (French) floor

étude (French) a study or exercise, especially in music

ex cathedra (Latin) from the seat of authority

ex officio (Latin) by reason of office or power

exposé (French) formal exposition of facts, revelation

façade (French) the front elevation or chief face of a building

faïence (French) an earthen ware below the grade of porcelain

fait accompli (French) an accomplished fact

fauteuil (French) an upholstered armchair; hence, the seat of a presiding officer, as of the French academy

faux pas (French) slip, blunder, a false step

femme de chambre (French) chambermaid

fête (French) festival, to honor with a festival

feu de joie (French) a firing of guns to express public joy

fiancé (French) an affianced or betrothed man

fiancée (French) an affianced or betrothed woman

foyer (French) lobby of a theater; the crucible in a furnace

frappé (French) a water ice, a beverage served very cold

garçon (French) boy, waiter

gauche (French) awkward, clumsy, "lefthanded"

gendarme (French) a French policeman

genre (French) sort, style, type, genus

glacé (French) iced, frozen, served cold

habeas corpus (Latin) a writ to produce a prisoner before a court or judges—"You may have the body"

habitué (French) a habitual visitor, frequenter, customer

hors d'œuvres (French) a relish, a dish that does not form part of a regular meal

hors de combat (French) out of the combat, disabled by fighting

imprimis (Latin) in the first place

ingénue (French) a young, artless, or ingenuous character, or the one who plays such part on the stage

in propria persona (Latin) in one's own person

in re (Latin) in regard to

jardinière (French) an ornamental pot or stand, as for flowers

jeu d'esprit (French) play of mind, witticism

laissez aller (French) to allow to pass, to give safe conduct

laissez faire (French) go-as-you-please policy

lèse majesté (French) treason, or an offensive liberty taken against a reigning monarch

littérateur (French) a literary man

literati (Latin) literary men

literatim (Latin) letter for letter

longeron (French) supports, as of beams
maestro (Italian) master in any art, as in music
mandamus (Latin) a writ issued by some superior court directing
   some subordinate organization or person to do a specified thing
masseur (French) a male massagist
masseuse (French) a female massagist
matinée (French) an entertainment or reception held in the day
   time
mélange (French) a medley or mixture
meister (German) master
mêlée (French) a confused disorderly fight
mère (French) mother
mésalliance (French) misalliance; a marriage with one of inferior
   station
métier (French) trade, profession
milieu (French) medium, environment
mise en scène (French) a setting, as of the theater
moiré (French) waved or watered finish as of silk
motif (French) the leading feature in literary or other artistic work
nacre (French) mother of pearl
naïveté (French) unaffected simplicity, artlessness
née (French) born, used to indicate the maiden surname of a married woman
nisi (Latin) unless, if not
nisi prius (Latin) unless before
noblesse oblige (French) obligation deriving from aristocratic birth
nolens volens (Latin) unwilling or willing, willy-nilly
nom de guerre (French) an assumed war name
nom de plume (French) pen name, an assumed literary name
Nunc Dimittis (Latin) the canticle of Simeon (Luke ii, 29-32), a
   part of the liturgy of Greek, Roman, and Anglican churches
on dit (French) they say
onus (Latin) burden, obligation, responsibility
opéra bouffe (French) farcical comic opera
opéra comique (French) an opera in which the dialog is spoken and
   the story ends happily
opus (Latin) a work, especially in music
outré (French) odd, deviating from conventional form, far-fetched
papier mâché (French) pulped paper molded while moist into various forms
par excellence (French) preeminently, beyond comparison
parvenu (French) an upstart
passé (French) faded, out of date (used with masculine nouns)
passée (French) faded, past the prime, old-fashioned (used with
   feminine nouns)
passe-partout (French) a light picture frame of glass and pasteboard and paper; also a pasteboard mat for a picture
pâté de foies gras (French) a pasty made of fat goose livers
patois (French) provincial dialect
peccadillo (Spanish) a petty fault
peccavi (Latin) I have sinned
penchant (French) inclination, taste, bias
per annum (Latin) by the year
per capita (Latin) by heads, i.e., by units
per contra (Latin) on the contrary

père (French) father
pièce de résistance (French) the chief dish in a dinner; the principal work in a collection
piña (Spanish) the pineapple
pince-nez (French) nose glass
pléiade (French) a group of French poets headed by Ronsard; a constellation
porte cochère (French) a large doorway thru which carriages may drive or a carriage porch over an entrance
portière (French) a curtain for use in a doorway
poseur (French) one given to posing or attitudinizing
post meridiem (Latin) afternoon
pourboire (French) fee, tip
pourquois (French) why, wherefore
pousse café (French) layers of different colored cordials and brandy that do not mix
précis (French) summary, epitome, recapitulation
première (French) the first public presentation, as of a play
prie-dieu (French) a small desk arranged to support a book and having a foot-piece on which to kneel
prima facie (Latin) at first view, as it first appears
procès-verbal (French) a detailed statement in writing made by an official regarding the commission of a crime
pro rata (Latin) in proportion
protégé (French) a male cared for by another
protégée (French) a female cared for by another
raison d'être (French) reason for being
râle (French) a sound in addition to respiration heard in the chest and indicative of the stage of a disease
rapprochement (French) a state of harmony or reconciliation
rara avis (Latin) a rare bird, a wonder
recherché (French) choice, sought out with care
régime (French) administration
résumé (French) summary
reveille (French) morning summons by drum or bugle, as in the army
risqué (French) bordering on suggestiveness or impropriety
rôle (French) assumed character or function
rotisserie (French) a place where food is roasted and served
roué (French) a sensualist, a debauchee
salon (French) apartment for receiving company; fashionable society itself
sang froid (French) calmness, indifference
santé (French) health
savoir faire (French) knowledge of how to behave in society
savoir vivre (French) knowledge of how to live pleasantly
señor (Spanish) Spanish title for gentleman or Mr.
seriatim (Latin) one after another, serially
soi-disant (French) pretended, would-be, self-styled
soirée (French) an evening party
soufflé (French) a dish prepared with the beaten whites of eggs
soupçon (French) suspicion
table d'hôte (French) a complete meal in several courses regularly served

ITALICS   227

tabula rasa (Latin) an erased tablet upon which new writing may
  be set down
tant mieux (French) so much the better
tête-à-tête (French) private conversation, conference between two
  people; a sofa accommodating two people
Te Deum (Latin) an old Christian hymn sung at matins and on
  occasions of special thanksgiving
tour de force (French) a feat of remarkable strength or skill
tout ensemble (French) general effect of a work of art, the impression made by all parts taken together
tragédienne (French) an actress of tragedy
valet de chambre (French) man-servant, valet
verbatim (Latin) word for word
vice versa (Latin) reversal of an order of terms
vis-à-vis (French) person opposite, face to face
viva voce (Latin) by spoken word
Wanderlust (German) irrepressible impulse to travel
Zeitgeist (German) the spirit of the times

Note the capitalization of the last two, for the reason that all
German nouns are capitalized. But as words introduced from German tend to shake off italics, they tend similarly to "shed" capitalization. The German word *Blitzkrieg*, for instance, meaning
quick, sudden, aggressive attack in war, is increasingly appearing
in English without capital B and without italics. So, too, are
Ersatz and *Lebensraum*, the former meaning manufactured substitute (as coffee made from grain, or sausage made from fish),
and the latter meaning living room, that is, room for habitation.

But *Gestapo* and *Nazi* are properly regarded as proper nouns and
are therefore correctly capitalized even when they are not printed
in italics. Both of these are invented words—*Geheime Staats
Polizei* and *Nationalsozialistische*—Secret State Police and National Socialist (Party).*

* See *Don't Say It* by the same author, published by Funk and Wagnalls Company, for
other words in these categories.

CHAPTER EIGHT

LETTER WRITING *

I   The mechanics of letter writing

The parts of the business letter are as follows:

1 Heading
   Place
   Date
2 Inside Address
   Name and address of person written to
3 Salutation
   Greeting
4 Body
   The subject-matter of the letter
5 Complimentary Closing
   Courteous conclusion
6 Signature
   With official capacity in which letter is written
7 Reference Data or Annotations
   Annotation regarding enclosures and other matters
   Initials (or typed name) of the dictator, and of the typist

Part 7 and sometimes part 2 are omitted from friendly letters, tho the latter should not be omitted. Usually in friendly letters and in official letters the inside address is written at the lower left-hand corner of the letter, below the signature, where the annotations are usually placed. In official letters the annotations are placed below the inside address when it follows the signature.

* For extended treatment of the subject-matter of this chapter and the next see *Take a Letter, Please.*

228

EXCELSIOR LETTER SHOPS
BREWSTER CIRCLE
WASHINGTON
D. C.

October
Twelfth
0 0 0 0

The Bigsby Company
123 Market Street
San Francisco, Calif.

Gentlemen: *Attention Mr. Jay Bronson*

This, the so-called modified style of letter set-up, has been steadily gaining ground among business letter writers for many years. It is neither so conservative as the letter on page 231 nor so extreme as the letter on page 233.

Printed letterheads never have terminal punctuation, of course, no matter how conservatively punctuated the letters may be that appear beneath them. And in this form there is no terminal punctuation in either the date line or the inside address. But there is a colon after the salutation as well as a comma after the complimentary closing. And there is always a period at the end of a declarative sentence closing a paragraph.

As a compromise between the old and the new—as a sort of way-station between putting-off-the-old and putting-on-the-new—this letter style is both satisfying and beautiful. The blocked form gives it an agreeable uprightness and compactness that connote business practise and principle. Altogether it is to be recommended highly.

A caution is necessary, however: Many typists place the colon studiously after the salutation and forget the comma after the complimentary closing, or vice versa. Or sometimes they place a period after the date and then use no terminal punctuation in the inside address. These are slips—nothing more. But they are to be deplored because they violate the cardinal principle of the mechanics of business letter composition—*CONSISTENCY*. And perhaps they "show something" about an individual or a house—or both!

Balance, proportion, focus, movement—the four fundamental principles of Greek art—are beautifully illustrated in this letter. The placement of the letter is pictorially harmonious with the page size and shape. The margins, corresponding to the mat in a framed picture, are correctly proportioned. The paragraphs are of about equal length. There is no discordant note anywhere, no out-of-focus display, no irregularity in the procession of parts.

Very truly yours,

John B. Opdycke, President
EXCELSIOR LETTER SHOPS

O/8

THE BUSINESS LETTER BUREAU, INC.
138 State Street
CHICAGO

June   Tenth
00   00

Mr Irving Ravenscott
18 West Thirtieth Street
New York City 1

Dear Mr Ravenscott

After all, consistency is the one important thing in business letter copy. If you indent in some places and not in others, the recipient of your letters will decide that you have no positive letter policy, that you cannot make up your mind. He may conclude that you are yourself an undecided and perhaps vacillating person. And this would be unfortunate

You will probably not want to adopt a letter style and policy so "wide open" as this, with no period after *Mr* and no period at the end of a paragraph when its last sentence is declarative. This is considered altogether too advanced—too radical—for most business houses—yet. But I prophesy that the time is not far distant when everybody will see the wisdom of adopting this style. The letter picture is certainly the more beautiful for not being dotted here and there and everywhere with superfluous punctuation marks

Note especially the simplicity of margining in this letter. After your typist has centered the date (with which she will of course aline the complimentary closing) she has to think of only two margins— the left-hand and the right-hand. The former is automatically kept even by the typewriter. The latter she must take some pains with to keep it reasonably even, to prevent its looking like the hop, skip, and jump of a mountain cascade. But she can do this the more easily since she is relieved of managing numerous margins (see the letter on page 231) and of inserting much useless punctuation

Great unevenness in right-hand margining is also an indication of inconsistency. Since few syllables are longer than three or four letters, no line should be more than three or four letters longer than another. The trouble is that the average typist becomes so absorbed with the content of a line that she forgets to plan ahead mechanically to keep all lines even or nearly so

Very truly yours

John B Opdycke
Manager THE BUSINESS
LETTER BUREAU, INC.

JBO—mc

BETTER BUSINESS LETTERS
987 COLBY BOULEVARD
NEW YORK CITY

October 26, 0000.

Mr. Francis Kelehan,
  23 Warder Avenue,
    Denver, Colorado.

Dear Mr. Kelehan: *Re your query about style.*

This style of letter set-up is regarded by many people as being old-fashioned today. It is conservative, to say the least, just as the letter on the preceding page is radical. But many business houses still adhere to the indented form and to the terminal punctuation practise in all letter parts.

It is a perfectly good style to follow, but it calls for more detailed observation on the part of the typist. She has five or six margins to keep in line, and she has to be particular about the placement of commas and periods. But the letter picture can be kept consistent if she will exercise care and patience in looking after these details.

There is one inconsistency, however, that most of those who adhere to this style of letter must take responsibility for, namely, the use of two signs to indicate paragraphing. The paragraph indention alone is sufficient notice that a new paragraph is beginning. But the spacing after each paragraph constitutes a notice to the same effect. There are, therefore, two signals for paragraph divisions. One notice ought really to be sufficient for anything.

Indention harks back to the days when formality by way of engraved forms held sway. Those who wrote letters by hand felt impelled to imitate the work of the engraver as far and as well as they possibly could. The tradition carried over to the typewriter when it came into general use. It is now equipped with marginal adjusters, to be sure, but even they require manipulation by the typist, and unnecessary movements are the result. Moreover, the indented letter always carries with it an atmosphere of restlessness. It appears to be a more nervous and fatiguing style than the blocked set-up.

It is somewhat more consistent to use indented form and closed punctuation together. Both seem to belong to the same period and the same point of view. But there is nothing whatever wrong with using indented form and open punctuation together, and blocked form and closed punctuation together.

Very truly yours,

John B. Opdycke,
Educational Director,
BETTER BUSINESS LETTERS.

JBO...MC...bt

12 East Twelfth Street
New York City 3
April 18, 0000

Mr. Harrison Eastman
234 Madison Boulevard
Topeka, Kansas

Dear Mr. Eastman:

The business letter really consists of at least seven parts. The *heading* (1) consists of the address of the writer and the date on which the letter is written. The *inside address* (2) consists of the name and the address of the person to whom the letter is written. The *salutation* (3) is a formal greeting or "Hello" to the addressee. The *body* (4) is the message proper, and it is of course the longest and the most important part of the letter. The *complimentary closing* (5) is a formal adieu or "Good-by" to the addressee. The *signature* (6) consists of the writer's name signed by himself below the closing, and of his name and official position filled in by the typist. The *annotations* or *special data* (7) are the initials of the dictator and the typist and the notation of enclosures or of any other memoranda of importance to the firms concerned

On printed letterheads the first part or *heading* is divided into two parts—the address of the writer (with other matter perhaps, such as kind of business, telephone and cable addresses, names of company officials) printed at the top of the sheet, and the date line or block written in by the typist just below the printed heading or just below it and to the right. There may also be a letter title and an attention notice, either or both of which would be placed preferably a few spaces to the right of the salutation, one above the other in case both are used. But it is not customary to use both

In addition, there may be a filing notation at the upper left-hand corner of the letter page—above the inside address. This is for convenience of establishing letter sequence and for finding data pertaining to its contents. There may likewise be at this place a brief key to the letter, such as, To.............................. Date................
By....................... About......................... Mailed...................... And again, this part of the letter may contain a *prescript*, that is, an apology for tardiness of reply, an excuse for covering two subjects in a single letter, a word or two saying that a telegram or other message was received just as this letter was about to be mailed, and so forth. The prescript is no more to be commended than the postscript, but both have been known to serve valuable purpose now and again. It is well to remember that, generally speaking, data at the upper left-hand corner of the letter are for the convenience of the addressee; at the lower left-hand corner, for the convenience of the writer

Very truly yours,

John B. Opdycke

John B. Opdycke
CRS

BETTER LETTER SERVICE
777 WEST FIFTH STREET
NEW YORK CITY

From Murray Bates, Manager	*To* Mr. Clarence Witherspoon
Subject "The new letter"	*Address* Vinesboro
Enclosures Standard circular	New Jersey
Mailed 5p.m. 9/4/00	*Received* 9/5/00—9a.m.
Dictated by WWD	*Answer to* Inquiry of 9/2/00
Typed by AMV	*Reply* Open. Follow up
Pages 1	*File number* GW24365

This letter set-up is strictly twenty-first century! Many people feel that a really businesslike letter procedure, such as this, would be a great improvement over the present traditional letter form. And it is still traditional and conventional, no matter how much it is liberalized thru open punctuation and blocked paragraphing

These people regard *Dear Sir* and *Very truly yours* as superfluous and as parrotlike as *Pleased to meet you* and *Is it warm enough for you*. They would delete from business correspondence such mere formalities, and would concentrate all necessary data in brief tables either at the top of the letter (as here) or at the bottom. Their contention is that this plan enables the writer to concentrate upon the body of the letter—the real message—and places all filing and cross-reference items in one place where a perfect correspondence sequence and history may be easily traced

More important still, they contend, is the fact that the message in such a letter as this is much less likely to be harassed by hackneyed expressions. The minute the dictator says *Dear Sir* or *Gentlemen* he is automatically thrown into the old letter mood and atmosphere —into a "bromide" condition—and automatically he begins to speak in the cliché idiom, they say. This "new letter" will tend to counteract that deplorable tendency

Reforms similar to this have been tried occasionally by business houses, but owing to employee inertia or resistance they have always petered out after a short time. Never, I think, have they been abandoned because of adverse criticism. Some critics do insist, however, that such an impersonal letter smacks something too much of the robotism that is so greatly deplored today by ladies and gentlemen of the "old school," that it is lacking entirely in those little courtesies and considerations that do so much toward making the world run with even reasonable smoothness

There may be much to say on both sides. If the stereotyped salutation and complimentary closing tend to induce hackneyed letter language, so also may they be depended upon to take the edge off the temper of a business man when he has an unpleasant situation to treat in a letter. To hold to the old, however, just because "It's always been like this" is ridiculous. To refuse to put on the new just because "We've never done it like that" is ditto. A tailor once forgot to put the sleeve buttons on a customer's coat. The customer sued—and recovered them! Habit hallucinates

The Heading

On printed letterheads the typist writes in the date of the month and the year. Usually these items are centered under the letterhead itself or are placed to the right of it, thus establishing the right-hand margin. On plain stationery the place as well as the date has to be included in the letterhead, and it is usually written on the right-hand side as the topmost item of the letter. In friendly letters and sometimes (but rarely) in business letters the date is written at the lower left-hand corner of the letter. In social forms this placement is the rule. In all illustrations below the year is indicated by four ciphers. Zone number follows city name.

125 West 76 Street
New York City 23
May 15, 0000

———

Centerville
Bucks County
Pennsylvania
January 4, 0000

———

November 12, 0000

———

March 25
00   00

———

J U N E
23
0 0 0 0

———

125 West 76 Street,
New York 23, N. Y.,
May 15, 0000.

———

Airvale, Colorado,
June 25, 0000.

———

Coe Junction, Minn.,
May 3, 0000.

November Twelfth
0000

———

The Tenth of May
0000

———

December 12, 0000.

———

December
12
0000

———

There are many other variants of date placements, house practise and individuality deciding the issue in most cases.

The Inside Address

In business letters the inside address, consisting of the name and address of the one to whom the letter is written, is placed usually on a line below the date and at the left-hand margin directly above the salutation. In friendly letters and in official letters it is placed at the lower left-hand corner. It is frequently omitted in friendly letters, but it should not be, inasmuch as a letter that becomes separated from its envelop cannot thus be forwarded.

And if an exact heading has also been omitted it is unreturnable to the writer and is completely lost. In social forms it is always placed at the lower left-hand corner. The inside address should be the exact copy of the envelop address.

Mrs. Harrison Wentworth   Mrs. Harrison Wentworth,
181 Columbia Boulevard   181 Columbia Boulevard,
Harrisburg, Penna.   Harrisburg, Penna.

                                           Scott, Thomas, and Peabody,
The Merivale Company   534 Fifth Avenue,
Market and Calthorn Streets   Minneapolis,
St. Louis, Missouri   Minn.

           Market and Charnton Streets
           Market Street at Bale Boulevard
           Tenth Avenue at Thirteenth Street
           Fourth Avenue and Tenth Street
           Fifth Avenue at 38 Street
           345 Sixteenth Avenue

are better than
           Market & Charnton Streets
           Market Street—Bale Boulevard
           Tenth Avenue & 13th Street
           4th Avenue—38th Street
           345 16th Avenue

The former are clearer for the postman's eyes and are complete in form and statement. The latter are abbreviated forms, and in some cases the items may be run together by the eye at first glance. Serious mistakes have been made in handling letters so addressed that the street number and the house number ran together—*34 15 Street* should be *34 Fifteenth Street.*

It is permissible in business letters as elsewhere to place both personal and other title on the same line with the individual's name. But the business title may be placed one line below the name in case a more symmetrical arrangement results from doing so. The words *chairman, director, registrar, secretary, treasurer* are always used after names, never before them. Professional standing or rank of two different kinds may be indicated with the name, but two tokens for the same rank or standing may not be used. Lawyers and attorneys are sometimes addressed by *Esq.* after the name rather than by *Mr.* before, never by both. The former is commonly used in England as the general personal title instead of *Mr. Messrs.* should never be used before the name of a business organization or corporation. It may be used in connection with

DIGNIFIED AND ARTISTIC LETTERHEADS

TELEPHONE
9-9620 FRANKLIN

PARKMAN PICTURE CORPORATION

CABLE ADDRESS
PARPIC - CALIFORNIA

1334 Sunset Boulevard
Hollywood
California

Department CV
Number 33,176

April
Sixth
0000

WOOD OF EVERY KIND   WOOD FOR EVERY PURPOSE

THE LONG-RANGE TIMBER COMPANY
(ESTABLISHED 1875)

JAMES R. TILLING, *President*
SAMUEL MATTIS, *Vice-President*

2561 Hardman Avenue
Seattle, Washington

HOWARD ANDERSON, *Secretary*
WILLIAM BRAINERD, *Treasurer*

August Third
0000

GOOD FELLOWSHIP, Inc.
1820 Long Building
Kansas City, Missouri

•

In Replying Please
Refer to 93-2-AS

0000
July
10

THE HOWARD-WINTHROP COMPANY
18 STATE STREET
CHICAGO

EXECUTIVE OFFICES

May Fifth
0 0 0 0

PUBLISHED MONTHLY   •   THREE DOLLARS A YEAR

THE AMERICAN MERCHANDISING MAGAZINE

Direct-Mail Advertising

CHICAGO
25 Dearborn Street

SAN FRANCISCO
223 Market Street

19 West 19 Street
New York City

February 2, 0000

DIGNIFIED AND ARTISTIC LETTERHEADS

THE AMERICAN SPECIFICATION INSTITUTE
THE ENGINEERING BUILDING
205 WEST WACKER DRIVE
CHICAGO

BOARD OF DIRECTORS:
FRANK A. RANDALL
    CHAIRMAN
CHESTER L. POST
    VICE-CHAIRMAN
R. E. GILMORE
    DIRECTOR OF PUBLICATIONS
R. J. GAUDY
GARDNER C. COUGHLEN
    ACTING EXECUTIVE SECRETARY

February
10
0000

SHORTHAND . BUSINESS
VOCATIONAL

APT . TECHNICAL
SCIENTIFIC

PITMAN PUBLISHING CORPORATION
Two West Forty-Fifth Street
NEW YORK

20 March 0000

American Institute of Filing
Owned and managed by Library Bureau
Division of Remington Rand
Remington Rand Building
465 Washington Street
Buffalo, New York

N Mae Sawyer
Director

June 6, 0000

AMERICAN SOCIETY OF CIVIL ENGINEERS
AMERICAN SPECIFICATION INSTITUTE

WESTERN SOCIETY OF ENGINEERS

AMERICAN CONCRETE INSTITUTE
AMERICAN SOCIETY FOR TESTING MATERIALS

FRANK A. RANDALL
STRUCTURAL ENGINEER
205 WEST WACKER DRIVE
CHICAGO
TELEPHONE CENTRAL 5131

April Twenty-fifth
0000

Typesetting
Electrotyping
Printing
Binding
Editorial Service

J. J. Little & Ives Company
The Plant Complete
Printers and Bookbinders

New York
425-435
East 24th Street
Telephone
AShland 4-5220

Established in 1867  By Joseph J. Little

A Few Well-Addressed Envelops

BUSINESS LETTER SERVICE
CORRESPONDENCE ANALYSIS AND SUPERVISION
SALES, ADVERTISING, AND DIRECT MAIL COPY
JOHN B. OPDYCKE　∾　NEW YORK CITY

Stamp

Dr. Thomas Eggleston

25 East Forty-fifth Street

New York City

Hardinger Building
Sixteenth Floor

BLAIR PRINTING COMPANY
32 Grand Avenue
Buffalo
Idaho

Stamp

The Wilshire Company, Inc.

3112 Fordson Avenue

Chicago

Illinois

Attention:　Book Department

Return to
HARRISON-BLANKLEY, Inc.
1441 North Lake Avenue
Haddonfield, New Jersey

Stamp

Blains, Turner, and Company

Fifth Avenue at Tenth Street

New York, N. Y.

Credits

FUNK & WAGNALLS COMPANY
PUBLISHERS
354-360 FOURTH AVENUE
NEW YORK, N. Y.

Stamp

Messrs. O'Melia and Rand
Attorneys-at-Law
181 Chestnut Street
Philadelphia, Pa.

After Five Days
Return to
WESTERN GARAGE
Box 98
COLUMBUS, OHIO

Stamp

Mrs. James R. Blanton,
Fiske Building,
Broadway at 57 Street,
New York City.

Room 1831

Stamp

Mr. Maurice K. Landerman

324 Carrollton Boulevard

Minneapolis, Minnesota

c/o Lakewood Trust Company

Stamp

Lakewood Trust Company

324 Carrollton Boulevard

Minneapolis

Minnesota

Att. Mr. Maurice K. Landerman

legal or other professional partnerships. It is commonly used
before the names of a law partnership. The left-hand forms
below are correct; the right-hand forms are incorrect.

Mr. Thomas Brainard, Treasurer   *not*   Treasurer Thomas Brainard
The Blair Oil Company   The Blair Oil Company
    or
Mr. Thomas Brainard
Treasurer, Blair Oil Company

President James R. Treadwell
The Keedick Industrial College
    or
Dr. James R. Treadwell   *not*   Dr. James R. Treadwell, D.D.
President, The Keedick Industrial College
    or
The President of The Keedick Industrial College

Dr. Harrison Hunter   *not*   Dr. Harrison Hunter, M.D.
Dean of the Medical School
    or
Harrison Hunter, M.D.
Dean of the Medical School
    or
Dean Harrison Hunter
Blakeville Medical School

Mr. Joel Ellert Chanler, Registrar   *not*   Registrar Joel Ellert Chanler
North Mandeville College
    or
Mr. Joel Ellert Chanler
Registrar, North Mandeville College

Lawrence Hammersmith, Esq.   *not*   Mr. Lawrence Hammersmith, Esq.
    or
Lawrence Hammersmith, Attorney
    or
Mr. Lawrence Hammersmith
Attorney-at-law

Professor Samuel Dilman
    or
Dr. Samuel Dilman   *not*   Dr. Samuel Dilman, Ph.D.
Professor of History

Messrs. Tone and Zell   *not*   Messrs. Tone and Zell, Esqs.
Attorneys-at-law

The British combination forms—*Harold Janver, Jr., Esq.* and
Harold Janver, Sr., Esq.—are not used in the United States (see
pages 35-36).

THE SALUTATION

The salutation should be started at the left-hand margin, not
continued diagonally with the items of the inside address when

that is indented. It constitutes a new category or paragraph in itself. These are correct forms in business and official letters:

Dear Sir
Dear Sirs (not generally used or recommended)
Gentlemen (preferable form)
Sir
Sirs } (these two are primarily official letter salutations)
My dear Sir
My dear Sirs } (the three-word salutation is not generally used)
Dear Sir or Madam (used when letter is written to either a man or a woman, or when a writer cannot tell from the signature of the letter he is answering whether it is the signature of a man or of a woman)
Dear Sir and Madam (used in writing to both a man and a woman)
Dear Madam
Dear Ladies *or* Dear Mesdames (rarely used but correct)
Ladies
Mesdames
My dear Madam
My dear Mesdames (see above for three-word salutation)
Ladies and Gentlemen
Sirs and Mesdames (rarely used)
Sisters *or* Dear Sisters (in general convent address)
Brothers *or* Dear Brothers (in general monastery address)

These are used in friendly letters

Dear Mr. Jameson   Dear Mary
Dear Mrs. Thompson   Dear William

The attention notice is preferably written on the salutation line at the center of the letter page. But it is sometimes placed on the line below and sometimes (less wisely) between the inside address and the salutation.

The Erdman Company
Lancaster
Arizona

Gentlemen   Attention Mr. James R. Gill

The attention position in a business letter is sometimes used for the title of the message or for some other notation calculated to help the receiving house.

The Erdman Company
Lancaster
Arizona

Gentlemen   Re Accident Policy 11678

                   or

Gentlemen   The Jones vs. Adams Case

Both the title notice and the attention notice would rarely be used. But occasionally they are, and in such cases the attention notice should follow the general title.

Gentlemen   As to Invoice AF 657
                   Attention Mr. Elwell Bronson

It is good practise to underline the name of the person to whose attention the letter is called. It is correct for the salutation to be plural even with an individual attention notice, for the letter is addressed to the company and is called to the attention of Mr. Bronson as a member of the company.

The name of a single individual used as a firm name requires the plural salutation and does not take the personal title before it.

John Wanamaker   *not* Mr. John Wanamaker
                        not Messrs. John Wanamaker
Gentlemen   *not* Dear Sir

Madam is used for either a married or an unmarried woman. *Gentlemen* is the preferred salutation in all letters addressed to concerns, even when a partnership consists of a man and a woman or of men and women. *Sir* and *Sirs*, and *Mesdames* and *Ladies* are used in formal and official correspondence, but rarely in business. Such blunt salutations as *Gents, S'r, Messrs., Miss* constitute vulgarisms and should not be used.

The use of *My* in the salutation is gradually passing. The better form of personal salutation is *Dear Mr. Morrison,* not *My dear Mr. Morrison.* Where the latter is still used the word *dear* is preferably not capitalized.

In closed punctuation and in modified punctuation forms the salutation in business letters is always followed by a colon. In the open punctuation form it is not followed by any punctuation mark. In friendly letters a comma is preferably used after the salutation in the two former styles of set-up.

THE BODY

The body of a letter—business and friendly—must be regarded as a piece of regular composition, planned and paragraphed as any other kind of composition ought to be. In the main, however, the paragraphing in the letter should be briefer than it is in most other forms of composition. Care should be exercised to keep the paragraphing uniform with the style of set-up established by the other parts of the letter, that is, blocked consistently with those other parts, or indented like them, whichever the policy of the individual house or writer decides. A succession of paragraphs having very short last lines may give a lopsided appearance to the body of a letter, and it is nearly always possible to prevent such disproportional appearance. The right-hand margin can be kept far more even than most right-hand margins are kept as a rule. A little attention brought to bear upon it will work wonders. Since very few syllables are longer than three letters (four spaces in case the hyphen is counted) it follows that no line has to be more than four spaces longer than any other. Yet many letters have lines that are carried to as many as ten spaces beyond others on the right-hand side, and the appearance is ragged and inchoate as a consequence.

THE COMPLIMENTARY CLOSING

These complimentary closings are good:

> Truly yours
> Yours truly
> Very truly yours
> Yours very truly (these four are strictly business closings)
> Sincerely yours
> Yours sincerely
> Very sincerely yours
> Yours very sincerely (these are somewhat too intimate for formal business use)
> Cordially yours
> Yours cordially (these two have been called the "special acquaintance" closing)
> Yours respectfully
> Respectfully yours (these two are used in reports, in official letters, and in letters written to acknowledgedly superior authority)
> Yours faithfully
> Faithfully yours
> Yours as ever
> As ever yours (these four, and others of their kind, are friendly letter closings)

The complimentary closing should not be preceded by a participial phrase, such as *Hoping for an early reply* and *Trusting this will be satisfactory.* It serves no purpose whatever, and it may tempt into ungrammatical relationships. If used, it should always be followed by *I am* or *we are* in order that the participle may not dangle, that is, in order that the participle may have something to modify. This is correct:

Hoping to hear from you soon, I am
Very truly yours

These are incorrect:

Hoping to hear from you soon
Very truly yours

Hoping to hear from you soon, and oblige
Very truly yours

The terms *I am, I remain, and oblige* are hackneyed, and should not be used at or near the conclusion of a letter. Stop with the last necessary sentence of the body, and follow with the complimentary closing only.

It is customary to separate the complimentary closing from the last line of the body of a letter by double spacing. But in some cases single spacing only is permitted, especially in letters pertaining to credit. This prevents the insertion of any material that might invalidate the message itself. The first word only of the complimentary closing should be capitalized. In closed punctuation and in modified punctuation forms, it is followed by the comma. In the open punctuation form it is not followed by any punctuation mark. Such abbreviations as *Yrs., Res'y, Tly. yrs.* in the complimentary closing of a letter, are, of course, vulgarisms.

The Signature

Signatures to letters vary in form and placement. This is the one letter part that may be permitted to run riot against the principle of consistency in letter form. Individuality enters here. A person's signature is something strictly special to himself, and he cannot be denied the privilege of making it his very own. But every good business letter today carries—or should do so—the writer's name in type several spaces below the complimentary closing. The typist sees to it that it is typed here before she takes the letter out of the machine. In the wide space between the complimentary closing and the typed name of the writer he may individualize his signature to his heart's content and make it as customarily illegible as he pleases! The placement of the typed signature should correspond to the general letter form as to blocking or indenting. Observe the signatures below.

Titles and degrees should never be used with signatures. It is always preferable for the writer (dictator) of a business letter to indicate his position below his typed name. In case a secretary

A Few Model Letter-closings

Sincerely yours,

Ruth Wanger

(Miss)Ruth Wanger
Secretary to Mrs. Lee

RW
RF

Very truly yours

O'MEARA MOTOR COMPANY

p.p. *John M Casey*

Two Enclosures
John M.Casey/mc

Yours very truly,

Leon A. Walker

Eastern Advertising Manager

Leon A.Walker
TFG

Very truly yours,

Mabel Wentworth

Mabel Wentworth
Manager,Ladies' Department

Six Samples
Enclosed

MW.....cv

Yours very truly

Blaine Morgan

Blaine Morgan,Manager
Group Disability Division

M.....s

Respectfully yours,

Harold Twining

Secretary to the President,
American Artists' Association

JBA/HT/tu

A Few Model Letter-closings

Very truly yours,

Julian Harris

Eastern Manager

Enclosure
Julian Harris

Very truly yours,

R.H.Macy & Co.,Inc.

Per *R. P.*

Estimating Office

Job Number:U-1329
RP/cc

Yours very truly

THE FITCH-BROWN COMPANY

BY *George C. Bartley*

George C.Bartley

GCB—AF

Yours truly

John H. Smithson

John H.Smithson
Engineer of Location and Design

Three Enclosures
JHS::hto

Cordially yours

Adeline McGregor

Adeline McGregor
(Mrs.Charles D.)

Check($41.)enclosed
AMcG/GK

signs for him, said secretary may sign his own name and follow it with *For*, then adding his employer's name.   Or he may sign his employer's name, and initial or write his own after it, preceding either with the word *By*.

A man's name should be signed in full, or with two initials preceding the surname.   Never should the surname be preceded by a single initial.   *Harrison B. Smith* is a good form.   *H. B. Smith* is allowable, but not the best form.   *H. Smith* is bad.

A woman should always indicate whether she is Mrs. or Miss. Never should *Alice D. Wainwright* sign herself *A. D. Wainwright*, for the person who is called upon to address her cannot tell whether she is man or woman.   These are correct:

(Mrs.) Alice D. Wainwright	Alice D. Wainwright
(Miss) Alice D. Wainwright	(Mrs. Herbert K.)

Alice D. Wainwright is the woman's name.   *Mrs. Herbert K. Wainwright* is her "marriage title," and it is permissible and usually customary for her to retain this in case her husband dies. A divorced woman may assume and use her maiden name, but she usually retains her husband's name, even though this may lead to the confusion of having that name used by another woman.   Whether she signs herself *Mrs. Alice D. Sanderson* or *Miss Alice D. Sanderson* after she is divorced from Mr. Herbert K. Wainwright, is entirely a matter of her choice.   She may, however, keep the married surname and use her given name with it—*Miss* or *Mrs. Alice D. Wainwright*—but she may not follow this in her signatures with (*Mrs. Herbert K.*).   A married woman who keeps her own name for business or professional reasons may likewise use either *Miss* or *Mrs.*   If she desires to have her married name known also, then she must take the trouble to write two names.

In all legal papers, and especially in wills and deeds, a woman should use her name rather than her title.   In each case, however, she should sign the name used in the drawing of the legal paper itself.   It is wiser for a woman to use her name, not her title, in connection with a checking account at a bank.   But usage varies widely in this.   The individual woman sets up her own custom in such matters.   She may have *Mrs.* or *Miss* printed on her checks and may therefore endorse them with the personal title.   She may also dictate the form of name she prefers carried on programs, as a patroness, in publicity accounts, on sailing lists.   A business woman should indicate her position after her typed signature at the bottom of her letters.   She may sign herself *Mrs. James Hay, Mrs. Helen Hay,* or *Helen Hay* on hotel registers.   Husband and wife should always be registered under the form *Mr. and Mrs. Aaron Wentworth,* not *Mr. Aaron Wentworth and wife.*   The woman secretary follows the rules mentioned above in regard to signing for employer.   If her position as secretary is confined to a certain field she will indicate it, namely, *Executive Secretary, Secretary of Personnel, Corresponding Secretary.*

Special Data or Annotations

These belong at the lower left-hand part of the business letter— below the line on which the signature is typed and on the left-hand margin.   They are properly written after everything else has been included.   Last of all come the initials of the dictator and of the typist, and in this order.   This means two sets of initials written in various styles:

DR/CJ   DR—cj   DRcj   DR**CJ   DRxcj

In case three people are involved, three sets of initials may be used.   One may order a letter written; one may dictate it word by word; one (the typist) writes it.   The last may sometimes be designated by a number:

JBO/DR/CJ   JBO...DR...cj   JBO/DR/6

In much business letter writing today the typed name of the composer of the letter is written where the first initials above stand rather than under the complimentary closing.   This is also good. So long as the name is typed in somewhere clearly, it does not so much matter at which of these places it is put.

James B. Ogden/cj   James B. Ogden—CJ

At this location should be placed any other matter about which the house sending the letter wishes to guarantee or safeguard or verify action.   The initials above given are of no importance to the receiving house.   But to the sending house they may be valuable in tracing responsibility.   In the same way such notations as *Enclosure, Three Enclosures, Catalog Mailed, Stamps Enclosed* may later prove something or other for the house from which the letter goes.   These words, and others like them, should be placed on a line just above the initials above explained.   So also should the sign *Dictated by Mr........but signed in his absence.*   But this notice has now luckily fallen into such disrepute that it is rarely used any more. It was never anything more in business letter writing than an affectation, and a very discourteous one at that.

Data for the convenience or information of the receiving house should be placed at the beginning of the business letter. These are some of the many kinds of data that may be desirable in this position.

From........   To..........regaiding.......date......page....
To ....   Dictated to...........by..........date........
Subject ......   subject..........
Date.........

Dictated June 24, 0000
Mailed June 27, 0000
Held for importation invoice

In your reply please mention CF461

Please mention File Number 223ab when you answer this letter

And so forth. These are but few of the many devices that may be evoked by special conditions. The general principle of annotation of these and other kinds is important: for the recipient, annotations at the beginning of the letter; for the sender, annotations at the end.

FOLDING THE LETTER

The customary way of folding a letter—for both sizes of commercial envelop—is illustrated on page 249. A slightly different plan, however, now increasingly used, is as follows:

For the large commercial envelop, turn the paper up from the bottom somewhat less than one third of its length. Then turn it down from the top somewhat more than one third of its length. The top fold extends over the lower a little, affording a thumb-catch. It may also enable the receiver of the letter to see part of the firm name before the letter has been unfolded. There are two horizontal creases in the paper by this fold.

For the small commercial envelop, turn the paper up from the bottom somewhat less than one half of its length. Hold it before you so that part of the letterhead is visible. Then turn this once folded paper in from the right somewhat less than one third of its width, and turn it in from the left somewhat more than one third of its width. This last fold leaves a thumb catch. There are one horizontal crease and two vertical creases in the paper by this fold.

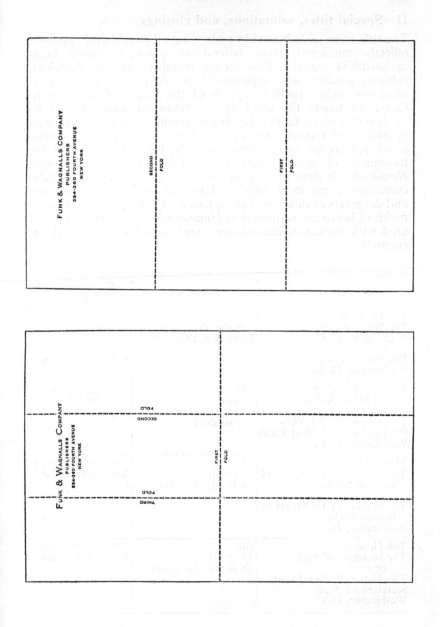

II   Special titles, salutations, and closings

The title Honorable is used in addressing all elected and appointed officials—municipal, state, federal—in whom is vested major authoritative power. This means members of the President's cabinet, senators and representatives, governors, ambassadors, ministers, judges (with exception of the judges of the Supreme Court for whom the word *Justice* takes on something of the quality of a given name), heads and members of important commissions and bureaus, mayors of cities, members of governing municipal bodies, and others who hold honorable place in any movement of public significance. *Right Honorable* (spelled *Honourable* in British usage, of course) is used in addressing privy councilors, commoners, knights, baronets, and the younger sons and daughters of dukes and marquesses. Children of peers and of maids of honor are addressed as *Honourable*. *Most Honourable* is used with marquess, marchioness, and sometimes with earl and countess.

Address	Salutation	Complimentary Closing
The President The White House Washington, D. C. *or* President Blankson Washington, D. C.	Sir To the President Dear Mr. President	Respectfully submitted Respectfully yours Sincerely yours Faithfully yours
The Vice-President United States Senate *or* The Honorable the Vice-President of the United States Washington, D. C.	Sir Dear Sir Dear Mr. Vice- President	Respectfully yours Very truly yours
The Honorable The Speaker of the House of Representatives *or* The Speaker of the House of Representatives Washington, D. C.	Sir Dear Sir Dear Mr. Speaker	Respectfully yours Very truly yours
The Honorable The Secretary of State *or* The Honorable Lee James Secretary of State Washington, D. C.	Sir Dear Sir Dear Mr. Secretary	Respectfully yours Very truly yours

Address	Salutation	Complimentary Closing
The Honorable The Secretary of Agriculture Washington, D. C. *or* The Honorable James Hall Secretary of Agriculture Washington, D. C.	Sir Dear Sir Dear Mr. Secretary	Respectfully yours Very truly yours
The Undersecretary of State Washington, D. C. *or* The Honorable James Dow Undersecretary of State Washington, D. C.	Sir Dear Sir Dear Mr. Dow	Respectfully yours Very truly yours
The Chief Justice of the United States *or* The Chief Justice *or* Chief Justice Conrad Washington, D. C.	Sir Dear Mr. Chief Justice	Respectfully yours Very truly yours
Mr. Justice Brand Department of Justice Washington, D. C.	Dear Mr. Justice Dear Justice Brand	Respectfully yours Very truly yours
The Honorable John Reed *or* Senator John Reed The United States Senate Washington, D. C.	Sir Dear Sir Dear Senator Dear Senator Reed	Respectfully yours Very truly yours

The Assistant Secretary of
   the Department of Agricul-
   ture
Washington, D. C.
or
The Honorable Henry Abbey
Assistant Secretary of the
   Department of Agriculture
Washington, D. C.
	Sir
	Dear Sir
	Dear Mr. Abbey
		Respectfully yours
		Very truly yours

The Honorable Thomas Lee *or* Representative Thomas Lee The House of Representatives Washington, D. C.	Dear Sir Dear Mr. Lee Dear Representative Lee	Respectfully yours Very truly yours

Address	Salutation	Complimentary Closing
The Honorable Harrison Roe Commissioner of the Bureau of Education Department of the Interior Washington, D. C.	Sir Dear Sir Dear Mr. Commissioner Dear Commissioner Roe	Respectfully yours Very truly yours
The Honorable James Brown Chief Judge, Court of Appeals Columbus, Ohio	Sir Dear Sir Dear Judge Brown	Respectfully yours Very truly yours
The Honorable Horace Fiske United States District Judge Chicago, Illinois	Sir Dear Sir Dear Judge Fiske	Respectfully yours Very truly yours
His Excellency The Governor of New York or The Honorable Alfred Blank Governor of New York Albany, N. Y.	Sir Dear Sir Dear Governor Blank Dear Governor	Respectfully yours Very truly yours
The Honorable Guy Spensler Lieutenant Governor of Ohio Columbus, Ohio or The Lieutenant Governor of the State of Ohio Columbus Ohio	Sir Dear Sir Dear Lieutenant Governor	Respectfully yours Very truly yours
The Honorable Mark Ordway or Senator Mark Ordway Senate Chamber The Capitol Albany, New York	Sir Dear Sir Dear Senator Dear Senator Ordway	Respectfully yours Very truly yours
The Honorable Aaron Smith or Representative Aaron Smith Assembly Chamber The Capitol Albany, New York	Sir Dear Sir Dear Representative Smith	Respectfully yours Very truly yours
The Mayor of the City of Chicago or The Honorable Anton Hollis Mayor of the City of Chicago City Hall Chicago Illinois	Sir Dear Sir Dear Mr. Mayor Dear Mayor Hollis	Respectfully yours Very truly yours

Address	Salutation	Complimentary Closing
His Excellency The Ambassador of Great Britain British Embassy Washington, D. C.	Sir Excellency Your Excellency Dear Mr. Ambassador	Please accept, Your Excellency, the renewed assurance of my highest respect and consideration *or* Yours respectfully
His Excellency The Ambassador of Italy Italian Embassy Washington	Sir Excellency Your Excellency Dear Mr. Ambassador	Yours respectfully *or* I have the honor to be, with the highest respect and consideration, Your Excellency's obedient servant
His Excellency The American Ambassador to Great Britain *or* The Honorable Alan Davis American Ambassador to Great Britain The American Embassy London England	Sir Your Excellency Dear Mr. Ambassador	Yours respectfully Very truly yours
The Honorable Pedro López Minister of Guatemala The Guatemalan Legation Washington, D. C.	Sir Dear Sir Dear Mr. Minister	Yours respectfully Yours very truly
The American Consul at Madras *or* Henry Treadwell, Esq. American Consul at Madras	Sir Dear Sir Dear Mr. Treadwell	Yours respectfully Very truly yours
The Rev. President Thomas Conrad	Dear President Conrad Dear Doctor Conrad	Yours respectfully Yours sincerely
The Rev. Professor Howard McGill *or* Professor Howard McGill *or* The Rev. Howard McGill	Dear Professor McGill Dear Dr. McGill	Yours respectfully Yours very truly

Address	Salutation	Complimentary Closing
Dean Harriet Black Grange College Boise City Idaho *or* Dean Black	Dear Dean Black Dear Dr. Black Dear Miss Black	Yours respectfully Yours very truly
His Holiness *or* His Holiness the Pope	Your Holiness *or* Most Holy Father	Dutifully yours Your dutiful son (daughter) Respectfully yours

His Eminence the Cardinal
  Archbishop Coe
or
His Eminence Cardinal Coe,
  Archbishop of Exeter
	Your Eminence	Obediently yours
		Respectfully yours

His Grace the Archbishop of
  Exeter
or
Most (or Very) Reverend
  Archbishop of Exeter
	Your Grace
	Most Reverend Sir
	Very Reverend Arch-
	  bishop
	Dear Archbishop
		Respectfully yours
		Sincerely yours

To the Right Reverend Harold T. Bass, Bishop of Cincinnati	Right Reverend and Dear Sir *or* Dear Bishop	Yours respectfully Yours sincerely
Rev. Father Cassidy *or* Rev. James J. Cassidy	Dear Father Cassidy Dear Reverend Father Dear Father	Sincerely yours Faithfully yours Cordially yours
Reverend Mother Superior, O.S.G.* Reverend Mother Rosaria	Reverend Mother Dear Reverend Mother	Yours respectfully Yours sincerely
Sister Alice Regardia	Dear Sister Dear Sister Alice	Yours respectfully Yours sincerely
Brother Bernardus	Dear Brother Dear Brother Bernardus	Yours respectfully Yours sincerely
Dean Albert Gray *or* The Very Rev. Dean Gray	Very Reverend Sir Dear Dean	Yours respectfully Sincerely yours Cordially yours

* Order of St. Gregory.

Address	Salutation	Complimentary Closing
The Reverend William Grew *or* Rev. William Grew *or* Rev. Dr. William Grew	Dear Sir Dear Mr. Grew Dear Dr. Grew	Yours respectfully Yours sincerely Yours cordially
Rabbi Horace Denken *or* Rev. Horace Denken	Dear Sir Dear Mr. Denken Dear Rabbi Denken	Yours respectfully Yours sincerely Yours cordially
The Most Reverend His Grace The Lord Archbishop of York *or* The Lord Archbishop of York	My Lord Archbishop Dear Archbishop	I have the honor to be, my Lord Archbishop, your faithful and humble servant *or* Your Grace's most obedient and humble servant
The Right Reverend the Lord Bishop of York *or* The Lord Bishop of York	My Lord My Lord Bishop Dear Bishop	I have the honor to remain your Lordship's obedient servant *or* I have the honor to remain, my dear Lord Bishop, sincerely and faithfully yours
The Very Reverend the Dean of York	Reverend Sir Very Reverend Sir Dear Dean	Sincerely yours Faithfully yours Obediently yours
The Venerable the Archdeacon of York *or* Venerable Archdeacon of York	Venerable Sir Dear Archdeacon	Respectfully yours Sincerely yours
Canon Armenton *or* The Reverend Canon Armenton	Reverend Sir Dear Canon	Yours respectfully Yours sincerely
The King's Most Excellent (*and/or* Gracious) Majesty	Sire May it please Your Majesty Your Gracious Majesty Your Majesty	Your Majesty's most obedient servant *or* I have the honor to be Your Majesty's most humble and obedient servant

Address	Salutation	Complimentary Closing
The Queen's Most Excellent (*and/or* Gracious) Majesty	Madam May it please Your Majesty Your Gracious Majesty	Your Majesty's most obedient servant *or* I have the honor to be Your Majesty's most humble and obedient servant
His Royal Highness the Prince of Wales *or* His Royal Highness Prince Alfred	Sir May it please your Royal Highness	Your Royal Highness's most obedient servant
Her Royal Highness the Princess Alice	Madam May it please your Royal Highness	Your Grace's obedient servant *or* I have the honor to be your Royal Highness's obedient servant
His Royal Highness the Duke of York	Sir May it please your Royal Highness	Your Royal Highness's most obedient servant *or* I have the honor to be your Royal Highness's obedient servant
Her Royal Highness the Duchess of York	Madam May it please your Royal Highness	Your Grace's obedient servant *or* I have the honor to be your Royal Highness's obedient servant
The Most Noble the Duke of Athol *or* His Grace the Duke of Athol *or* The Duke of Athol	Your Grace My Lord Duke Dear Duke of Athol	Your Grace's most obedient servant *or* Believe me, dear Duke, yours very sincerely
The Most Noble the Duchess of Athol *or* Her Grace the Duchess of Athol *or* The Duchess of Athol	Your Grace Madam Dear Duchess of Athol	Your Grace's most obedient servant *or* Believe me, dear Duchess, yours very sincerely

Salutations and complimentary closings for the following lesser degrees of nobility are similar to those given above, and are therefore not repeated.   In formal letters addressed to peers— earls, viscounts, barons, bishops, lord mayors—the feudal *My Lord* is still used.   But dukes, marquesses, archbishops are addressed formally as *My Lord Duke, My Lord Marquess, My Lord Archbishop*.   In informal correspondence *Dear Lord So-and-so* may be permissible, the style depending of course upon the relationship existing between the addresser and the addressee.

> The Right Honorable Lord Ashley Marmaduke
> The Right Honorable Lady Ashley Marmaduke
> The Most Honorable the Marquess Almansted
> The Most Honorable the Marchioness of Almansted
> The Right Honorable the Earl of Demscott
> The Right Honorable the Countess of Demscott
> The Honorable Harris Wenscote
> Lady Patricia Wenscote
> The Right Honorable the Viscount Shapland
> The Right Honorable the Viscountess Shapland
> The Honorable Robert Shapland
> The Honorable Alicia Shapland
> The Right Honorable Baron Bakersfeld
> The Right Honorable Baroness Bakersfeld
> Sir Hamilton Bartonfield, Bt. (*or* Bart.)
> Lady Bartonfield
> Sir Alfred Ferguson, K. C.
> Lady Ferguson
> The Worshipful the Mayor of Exeter
>   *or*
> The Lord Mayor of London

III   Social forms and announcements

Formal notes, announcements, invitations, and the like, are expressed in the third person and are usually given the decorative (irregularly indented) set when engraved.   Salutation and complimentary closing are omitted.   Dates are written out.   The inside address is placed at the lower left-hand corner, as is also the date of sending when included.   A reply to a formal invitation always repeats the date and hour mentioned in the invitation.   The initials *R.S.V.P.* or *R.s.v.p.* (*Répondez s'il vous plaît* or *Reply if you please*) are placed in the lower left-hand corner of such formal messages as require replies.   Announcements follow events. Invitations precede events.   Invitations to church weddings do not as a rule require replies, but to home weddings they do. Separate cards should be used to invite guests to a reception following a wedding.   Impersonal invitations and announcements are engraved in full; personal ones have blank spaces in which to write names. Details of such forms may well be left to the engraver or stationer, who is able to give expert advice as to style and fashion in such forms. He will know whether roman, gothic, script writing should be used, will be able to relate all the social forms of a family typographically, and may be depended upon to indicate correct forms of address.

The difference between a formal and an informal invitation may be illustrated by comparing some of the following forms with the two delightful "regrets" by Sydney Smith on page 282.

SPECIAL CHURCH INVITATIONS

The Reverend Joseph Donaldson
Ordained to the Holy Priesthood
by the
Most Reverend Thomas Machern, D.D.
Sunday, November eighteenth
nineteen hundred and forty five
Archiepiscopal Chapel, Cleveland
invites you to be present at his
First Solemn Mass
on Sunday, December thirtieth
at eleven o'clock
Church of Saint Joseph
Cleveland
Ohio

The Reverend Patrick Gillan
cordially invites you to be present at
his Ordination to the Holy Priesthood
to be conferred by the
Most Reverend Francis Kehoe, D.D.
on
Saturday morning, March the twenty-second
nineteen hundred and forty five
at eight-fifteen o'clock
Cathedral of Saint Ignatius
Wayne
Ohio

Announcements of Engagements

Engagements are generally announced verbally or by private letters to friends, but formal announcements such as these are sometimes used:

Mr. and Mrs. Horace Winterburn
announce the betrothal of their niece
Miss Eva Frances Carl
to
Mr. Charles Vanderpool
Ensign, United States Navy

Lensanoako
April Twelfth

Mr. and Mrs. Montague Montalvo
have the honour to announce the
betrothal of their daughter
Maud Elizabeth
to
Mr. Henry Haverill

Stony Ridge
Hartsville
Pennsylvania

Announcement of Engagement and Reception by Mother and Stepfather

Mr. and Mrs. Julius Eisemann
announce the engagement of their daughter
Miss Jane Levy
to
Mr. Moe Rosenbaum
Reception
Sunday, February tenth
from four until seven o'clock
at the
Hotel Copley-Plaza
Boston

ANNOUNCEMENTS OF THE BREAKING OF ENGAGEMENTS

Mr. and Mrs. Horace Winterburn
announce the annulment of the engagement of their niece
Miss Eva Frances Carl
to
Mr. Charles Vanderpool
Ensign, United States Navy

Lensanoako
November Third
Nineteen Hundred Forty Five

You are hereby notified
that the engagement of
Miss Jane Levy
to
Mr. Moe Rosenbaum
has   been   broken
June Twelfth

IMPERSONAL INVITATION ISSUED BY A WIDOW FOR HER DAUGHTER'S WEDDING

Mrs. Henry Harrison Blanchard
requests the honour of your presence
at the marriage of her daughter
Martha
to
Mr. Howard Lawson Chamberlain
on the evening of Friday, January the Fifth
at seven o'clock
at the residence of her brother Mr. James Harrison
Fifty-five Maple Avenue
Doylestown   Pennsylvania

RECEPTION INVITATION ENCLOSED IN THE ABOVE WEDDING
INVITATION

Mrs. Henry Harrison Blanchard
requests the pleasure of your company
at the wedding reception of her daughter
Martha
and
Mr. Howard Lawson Chamberlain
on the evening of Friday, January the Fifth
at half after seven o'clock
at the residence of her brother Mr. James Harrison
Fifty-five Maple Avenue
Doylestown   Pennsylvania

R.S.V.P.

INVITATION ISSUED BY A WIDOW FOR HER WEDDING

The honour of your presence is requested
at the marriage of
Mrs. Howard Thompson Kneeland
(*née* Brinton)
to
Mr. Floyd Raymond Fitch
on the afternoon of Tuesday, December Third
at four o'clock
Westminster Presbyterian Church
Exeter, New Hampshire

INVITATION TO A DOUBLE WEDDING

Mr. and Mrs. Richard Blake
request the honour of

presence at the marriage of their daughters
Mary Elizabeth
to
Mr. Paul Torregiani
and
Evelyn May
to
Mr. William Anderson Pye
on Thursday, the twentieth of September
at seven o'clock in the evening
at 251 South Kensington Avenue
Denver, Colorado

—————————

ILLUSTRATING THE USE OF TITLES

Reverend (or Doctor or Captain) and Mrs. Thomas Binns
request the honour of your presence
at the marriage of their daughter
Jane Katheryn
to
Mr. Stanley Lee Thanor
Lieutenant, United States Army
on Wednesday afternoon, June Twenty-third
One thousand nine hundred and forty five
at half after three o'clock
The Collegiate Church
Haverford, Pennsylvania

Invitation to the Wedding Reception of Daughter by Divorced Couple

Mr. Maurice Wertheim
and Mrs. Paul Lester Wiener
request the pleasure of

company at the marriage reception of their daughter
Josephine Alma
and
Mr. Ralph Pomerance
on the afternoon of Friday, the eighth of June
at four o'clock
33 East Seventieth Street
New York

R.S.V.P.

Wedding Invitation Issued by the Bride's Brother

Mr. Spencer Traymore Briggs
requests the honour of your presence
at the marriage of his sister
Mrs. Thomas Briggs Jay
to
Mr. Anthony Manson
at high noon, April Fifteenth
Nineteen Hundred Forty Five
St. George's Chapel
Exeter   England

WEDDING INVITATION ISSUED BY CONTRACTING PARTIES, THE BRIDE'S
PARENTS BEING DEAD

The honour of your presence is requested
at the marriage of
Mrs. Thomas Gray Radnor
formerly Grace Sylvia Conard
to
Mr. James Buckner
on the afternoon of May twenty-third
at half after four o'clock
Trinity Chapel
Ogdensville Maryland

WEDDING ANNOUNCEMENT

Mr. and Mrs. Hanneford Renée La Montagne
have the honour to announce
the marriage of their daughter
Elise
to
Mr. Lee Laidlaw Stevenson
on the tenth of April
one thousand nine hundred forty five
in Housatonic, Massachusetts

TYPICAL BIRTH ANNOUNCEMENTS

Birth announcements are by no means in general use, but the
following illustrate the forms that are sometimes sent out. Sometimes a tiny card, bearing the baby's name, is attached by ribbon
to the visiting cards of the parents.

It's a BOY Eight Pounds
Harold Brewer Erickson
Born May Fifth

Mr. and Mrs. Thomas Ray Erickson

Harold Brewer Erickson
Born May the Fifth
Nineteen Hundred Forty Five
Mr. and Mrs. Thomas Ray Erickson

Mr. and Mrs. Thomas Ray Erickson
have the honor to announce to

the birth of a son
Thomas Ray Erickson, junior
on Monday, June the Eighth
Nineteen Hundred Forty Five

INVITATION TO MEET A PARTICULAR PERSON

Mrs. Mary Frances Dearborn
requests the pleasure of your company
on Tuesday, May Fifteenth
at three o'clock
Thirty-two Lenox Avenue
New York City
To meet Miss Adelaide Grainger

INVITATION TO BREAKFAST

Doctor and Mrs. Jonas Appleby
invite you to join them
at Breakfast
at half after twelve o'clock
May thirtieth
The Pines

Please Respond

SPECIAL AT-HOME ANNOUNCEMENT AND INVITATION

Major and Mrs. Reginald Thompson
will be at home
on Tuesday evening, April first
from eight-thirty
to
eleven o'clock
Three hundred twelve Beacon Street
Boston   Massachusetts

GENERAL AT-HOME ANNOUNCEMENT AND INVITATION

Reverend and Mrs. Benjamin Bartley
At Home
after February first
Twenty Park Avenue
New York City

ANNOUNCEMENT OF SEPARATION

The announcement is made
of the complete separation
of Mr. and Mrs. John DeForest
and the custody of her

two children, Margarite and Alice

Mrs. Agnes Marion DeForest

Houston, Texas
June 3, 0000

ANNOUNCEMENT OF DIVORCE

By authority of the decree of divorce of the
Supreme Court of the State of New York
granted to me, dated July the seventh,
one thousand nine hundred forty five,
I have elected to resume my maiden name
and to be known as Mrs. Jane Mattison
(Formerly Mrs. Jane M. Collings)

34 East Thirtieth Street
New York City
July the eighteenth

Mr. and Mrs. Harold Lee Bronson accept with pleasure
Mr. and Mrs. Charles Rogers' kind invitation for dinner,
Thursday evening, March fifteenth, nineteen hundred forty five,
at seven o'clock.

Greylock Lodge
March second

Mr. Stanley Rayburn accepts with pleasure
Mrs. Arnold Gluck's kind invitation for the evening
of Thursday, May fifteenth, from eight until ten o'clock

Queens Hall
May tenth

Doctor and Mrs. Willard Lee Finney
accept with pleasure

kind invitation to meet

on Thursday afternoon, June the tenth
at Thirty Park Place
Brooklyn   New York City

Captain and Mrs. Roger Blumenstein
regret that a previous engagement
makes it impossible to accept

kind invitation to attend the

in honor of

on
at

Evergreen Lodge
Littledale, Maryland

Mr. and Mrs. Harold Lee Bronson regret that they are unable to accept Mr. and Mrs. Charles Rogers' kind invitation for dinner, Thursday evening, March fifteenth, at seven o'clock, owing to a previous engagement.

Greylock Lodge
March second

Miss Thomasina Smith regrets her inability to accept the invitation of Mr. and Mrs. Harry M. Shook to be present at the marriage of their daughter Margery to Mr. Leon Mollet, on Tuesday evening, June the seventh, nineteen hundred forty five, at seven o'clock.

Dragolinden Chambers
May thirteenth

Mr. Harrison Mabie gratefully acknowledges your expression of sympathy in his recent bereavement

Mr. and Mrs. Thompson Ellis thank you for your expression of sympathy in their recent bereavement

The members of the family of the late James Boardman gratefully acknowledge your kind expression of sympathy

Please accept my grateful acknowledgment of your congratulatory greeting

____

____

____

ENCLOSED IN A WEDDING INVITATION

Reception immediately following the ceremony at the Hotel Adlon

____

____

Reception from eight-thirty until ten o'clock at thirty-one T Street

will please present this card at the Chantry of St. George's on Friday, the thirteenth of June

Please present this card at St. Paul's Chapel

Seat number——

AT-HOME CARDS

At Home

after March first
Twenty-four Park Avenue
New York City

At Home

Tuesdays after March first
at
Thirty-nine   Clark Street
Baltimore   Maryland

MISCELLANEOUS SOCIAL CARDS

Miss Mary Hartley Anderson
acknowledges with thanks your wedding gift
and will write you personally at an early
date to express her appreciation of your
kindness

Announcing the Death of
Robert   Trainor   Archibald

Born

May Third
1881

Died

February First
1945

Services at his Late Residence
12 Witherspoon Avenue
Philadelphia, Pa.
Thursday Evening, February Third, at Eight O'clock

Relatives and Friends of the Late
Robert Coe Benson
Are Invited to Attend Religious
Services in his Memory
at
Grace Church
Grant and Wycombe Avenues
Friday Afternoon at Three O'Clock
October Tenth

Owing to the death of the sister of
Miss
the invitations issued for Friday
afternoon, October twenty-first, are
recalled by
Mrs.

Owing to the sudden death of
Miss   sister
Mrs.   recalls
the invitations issued for Sunday
afternoon, October twenty-first

BUSINESS ANNOUNCEMENTS OF THE DEATH OF A MEMBER OF A FIRM

Jameson, Lee, and Company
announce with profound sorrow
the death of
Mr. Harrison Compter
for twenty-five years a loyal and beloved
Member of this Firm
on Tuesday, June twentieth
at his late residence
Wilmington   Delaware

It is with deep regret
that The Wechsler-Adams Company
announces the death of its President
Charles Towner Adams
at Springfield, Illinois
on Tuesday, January twenty-seventh
For thirty years he has served this
company in official capacity with
unwavering faithfulness and uncompromising loyalty

We announce with deep regret
the death of
Mr. Martin Bronson
Vice-President of our firm
on Friday, June twenty-fifth
at his home
Radnor   Pennsylvania

Penn Mutual Insurance Company
Philadelphia, Pennsylvania

Owing to the sudden death of
James Henderson
Senior Member of this firm
on Thursday, June the tenth
at his home in Philadelphia
these offices will be closed
until Monday, June fourteenth

Brown, Henderson, and Alderschott
Attorneys-at-Law

IV Miscellaneous business announcements

HAROLD BANKFORT
MODERN DESIGNER
Announces his removal to
321 Green Avenue, Chicago,
on September first 0000
TELEPHONE
RA-6-4108

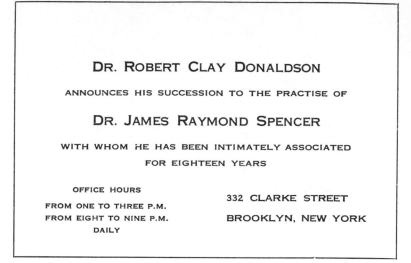
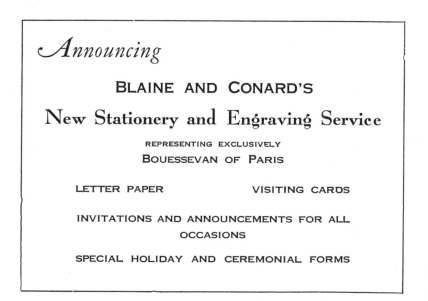

Radio City Music Hall

Rockefeller Center   New York

FOR YOUR CONVENIENCE

¶ ALL SEATS in the first mezzanine of the Music Hall are reserved for all performances. Patrons may telephone, write, or call, and may thus be assured the choicest seats, afternoon and evening.

¶ THIS CONVENIENCE especially appeals to those who wish to attend the theater after a leisurely dinner. The Music Hall is the only New York playhouse where reserved seats may be secured for a performance beginning at nine fifteen p.m.

¶ SMOKING is permitted.   Columbus 5-6535.

AINSWORTH AND HARRISON

Clothiers

25 GRAND AVENUE   DENVER

invite your inspection
of their

NEW FALL AND WINTER SUITINGS

A completely new line of patterns in woollen goods under varied lightings and in combination with haberdashery coloring and make-ups

. . . . . .

Saturdays all day
Wednesdays until nine

The Hale Community House Sculpture Committee

requests the honor of your presence

at the

TWELFTH ANNUAL SHOWING

of

Sculptures Done in Soap, Clay, Putty, and Cement

by the

CHILDREN OF THE HOUSE
18 Foraker Square

June Third to June Eighth Inclusive
Nine to Five Daily

The Janes Company

REQUESTS THE PLEASURE OF YOUR PRESENCE

AT THE

PREMIER PERFORMANCE

OF

Better Than Gold

THE FIRST FULL-LENGTH DRAMATIC COMPOSITION WRITTEN
FOR EXCLUSIVE BROADCAST PRODUCTION

THURSDAY EVENING, SEPTEMBER TENTH, AT HOME

THROUGH THE FACILITIES

OF

The International Radio Distribution Company

BOOK BY ANDREW J. BRAINERD
DIRECTION BY STEPHEN DAND
CAST INCLUDING MARY STEWART,   8:30 EASTERN STANDARD TIME
ROGER WORTHING, LEE TRAINOR,   7:30 CENTRAL STANDARD TIME
WILLIAM SIMPSON, AND RAY RAY   6:30 MOUNTAIN STANDARD TIME
                                    5:30 PACIFIC STANDARD TIME

SUBSEQUENT RADIO PRESENTATIONS
WILL BE BROADCAST AT THE SAME
HOURS EVERY THURSDAY EVENING
UNDER THE SPONSORSHIP OF
THE JANES COMPANY

V Visiting cards

MRS. HAROLD RANDOLPH CURTIS
THE MISSES CURTIS

MRS. HAROLD RANDOLPH CURTIS
MISS CURTIS
MISS HARRIET BROWN CURTIS

(The forms above may be used when a mother introduces her two daughters to society at the same time. The older daughter's first name is not used)

MRS. CURTIS

MR. HAROLD RANDOLPH CURTIS

(This simple form of the woman's card is used when she is recognized socially as the senior social leader of her family)

BUSINESS, OFFICIAL, AND PROFESSIONAL CARDS

With the compliments of
MR. JOHN CALLAN O'LAUGHLIN
Dean, Oñativia, and Company
Woodward Building
Washington, D. C.

Telephone Main 2040

LORD & TAYLOR
Founded 1826

L. E. Weisgerber

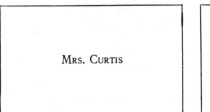

MR. STEPHEN TYNG MATHER

Director
National Park Service
Department of the Interior

CLAUDE E. GUYANT
Consul of the United States
of America

Lima, Peru

CAPTAIN MARK ELDREDGE
Quartermaster Corps
National Army

MAJOR JAMES MARCELLUS HOBSON
United States Infantry
Military Attaché
Legation of the United States
of America

Havana

THE RT. REV. WILLIAM T. RUSSELL, D.D.
The Bishop of Charleston

SHŌITCHI NAKAYAMA
Third Secretary of the Japanese
Embassy

Washington

VICE ADMIRAL
SIR LOWTHER AND LADY GRANT

H.M.S. Warrior

LORD LEE OF FAREHAM

Admiralty House
Whitehall

ADOLFO BALLIVIÁN
Envoyé Extraordinaire et
Ministre Plénipotentiaire
de Bolivie

ERNEST GREENWOOD

American Representative
International Labour Office
Geneva, Switzerland

618 Seventeenth Street
Washington, D. C.
Telephone Main 333

VI Friendly letters

The body of a friendly letter is just informal conversation in written form. Its quality should be a fair index of the character and personality of the writer. The gentle art of personal letter writing is said to be a lost one. The intrusion of telephone and radio and talkie and the thousand-and-one other complications of modern life has to some extent crowded out the leisurely and artistic pursuit of friendly correspondence. And it was a pursuit in the old days. The letters of the great in literature and history and painting, and other fields, prove that it was. Their friendly missives throw much light, not only upon their characters, but also upon the times in which they lived. It has long since been shown that there can be no better chronicle of times past than that presented in the friendly letters of those who lived full lives and wrote fully about them to their friends.

It has been pointed out under *The Mechanics of Letter Writing* that there is hardly any limit upon the liberties that may be taken in friendly letters by way of ignoring the conventions. The college lad may write—sans heading, sans closing, sans everything but the actual message itself:

Dear Dad

SOS——$$$$——R.S.V.P.

Your loving son

And to the informal invitation "Will you dine with me on Thursday?" the ready guest-to-be may reply even less informally, "Won't I!" It is, indeed, the understandable tone that constitutes the be-all and the end-all of friendly correspondence. While exactness of form may be by no means so important here as in business correspondence, certain rules of organization should nevertheless be observed. Merely as a matter of safety, friendly letters should always contain complete heading and inside address. So much precision is wise in order to facilitate the return or forwarding of a letter that may accidentally be lost from its envelop. But this rule is by no means always observed in friendly letters, as witness some of those that follow. These are all friendly letters in tone and quality. In addition, most of them treat of some particular business matter. They are valuable, therefore, in that they show how personal characteristics may be brought to bear upon business detail, and how even the great of bygone days have recognized the importance of writing engagingly about routine subjects.

Charles Dickens (1812-1870) wrote this letter of claim to a John Bennett, clocksmith, about a timepiece "with something on its works." How interesting the daily routine of business would be if all business letters were written in such delightful vein!

Gad's Hill Place, Higham by Rochester, Kent,
Monday Night, Fourteenth September, 1863.

My dear Sir,

Since my hall clock was sent to your establishment to be cleaned it has gone (as indeed it always has) perfectly well, but has struck the hours with great reluctance, and after enduring internal agonies of a most distressing nature, it has now ceased striking altogether. Though a happy release for the clock, this is not convenient to the household. If you can send down any confidential person with whom the clock can confer, I think it may have something on its works that it would be glad to make a clean breast of.

Faithfully yours,
CHARLES DICKENS.

Thomas Babington Macaulay (1800-1859) wrote the following adjustment letter to Leigh Hunt in reply to one from Hunt making claim for a pension from the government. Macaulay was at the time Secretary of State for War. Note the caution and restraint that characterize the letter; yet it nevertheless carries a positive note of sincerity and good grace. It has been called a "diplomatic masterpiece."

War Office, March 6, 1841

Dear Sir,

Your letter of February 16 has this moment been put into my hands. It finds me surrounded with estimates and pay lists—things much less agreeable than the comedies of Congreve or than your criticisms on them. I am afraid that my answer must be short. I will only say that the goodwill which I expressed towards you was perfectly sincere, and that if I used any expression which could either give you pain, or affect your interests unfavourably, I am exceedingly sorry for it. If I should be able to find a few hours in the midst of official and parliamentary business, for Vanbrugh and Farquhar, assure yourself that I will bear your wishes in mind.

I am quite sensible of your claims on the party to which I belong; and I will say, without any circumlocution, that I have a real desire to serve you. At the same time, my power is very small. My patronage is confined to clerkships, which would suit only boys; and district paymasterships, which can be held only by military men. The demands of a hundred and forty thousand constituents also press heavily upon me. The power of granting pensions resides with Lord Melbourne, who is not so much of a Mæcenas as might be expected from his fine understanding, his numerous accomplishments, and his kind nature. To get anything from him for a man of letters is almost as difficult as to get a dukedom. But if a favourable opportunity should offer, I will see whether anything can be done.

In the meantime I should be really glad if you could point out any mode in which any interest which I may possess might be of use to you.

Believe me, my dear sir,
Your faithful servant,
T. B. Macaulay.

Charles Kingsley (1819-1875) wrote this informal invitation to his old Cambridge friend, Rev. Peter Wood. Needless to say, Wood paid him a visit on receipt of the letter, and he found Kingsley "roughly lodged" but quite happy nevertheless. Christ gave the name *Boanerges* to the two sons of Zebedee (Mark iii:17). It means "vehement preacher" or "thunderer," as Kingsley humorously uses it here.

Eversley, 1842.

PETER!—Whether in the glaring saloons of Almack's, or making love in the equestrian stateliness of the park, or the luxurious recumbency of the ottoman, whether breakfasting at one, or going to bed at three, thou art still Peter, the beloved of my youth, the staff of my academic days, the regret of my parochial retirement!—Peter! I am alone! Around me are the everlasting hills, and the everlasting bores of the country! My parish is peculiar for nothing but want of houses and abundance of peat bogs: my parishioners remarkable only for aversion to education, and a predilection for fat bacon. I am wasting my sweetness on the desert air—I say my sweetness, for I have given up smoking, and smell no more. Oh, Peter, Peter, come down and see me! O that I could behold your head towering above the fir trees that surround my lonely dwelling. Take pity on me! I am like a kitten in the washhouse copper with the lid on! And, Peter, prevail on some of your friends to give me a day's trout fishing, for my hand is getting out of practice. But, Peter, I am, considering the oscillations and perplexing circumgurgitations of this piece-meal world, an improved man. I am much more happy, much more comfortable, reading, thinking, and doing my duty— much more than ever I did before in my life. Therefore I am not discontented with my situation, or regretful that I buried my first-class in a country curacy, like the girl who shut herself up in a bandbox on her wedding night (*vide* Rogers' *Italy*). And my lamentations are not general (for I do not want an inundation of the froth and tide-wash of Babylon the Great), but particular, being solely excited by want of thee, oh Peter, who art very pleasant to me, and wouldst be more so if thou wouldst come and eat my mutton, and drink my wine, and admire my sermons, some Sunday at Eversley.

Your faithful friend,
Boanerges Roar-at-the-Clouds.

Nathaniel Hawthorne (1804-1864) wrote this letter to his friend G. S. Hillard, who had been instrumental in helping the author in a "pinch." Hawthorne was United States Consul at Liverpool from 1853 to 1857, hence the date line. Never successful in a financial sense, Hawthorne was more than merely successful in the character sense (as this letter so abundantly proves) and in fine literary achievement.

Liverpool, December 9, 1853.

Dear Hillard,

I herewith send you a draft on Ticknor for the sum (with interest included) which was so kindly given me by unknown friends, through you, about four years ago.

I have always hoped and intended to do this, from the first moment when I made up my mind to accept the money. It would not have been right to speak of this purpose before it was in my power to accomplish it; but it has never been out of my mind for a single day, nor hardly, I think, for a single working hour. I am most happy that this loan (as I may fairly call it, at this moment) can now be repaid without the risk on my part of leaving my wife and children utterly destitute. I should have done it sooner; but I felt that it would be selfish to purchase the great satisfaction for myself, at any fresh risk to them. We are not rich, nor are we ever likely to be; but the miserable pinch is over.

The friends who were so generous to me must not suppose that I have not felt deeply grateful, nor that my delight at relieving myself from this pecuniary obligation is of any ungracious kind. I have been grateful all along, and am more so now than ever. This act of kindness did me an unspeakable amount of good; for it came when I most needed to be assured that anybody thought it worth while to keep me from sinking. And it did me even greater good than this, in making me sensible of the need of sterner efforts than my former ones, in order to establish a right for myself to live and be comfortable. For it is my creed (and was so even at that wretched time) that a man has no claim upon his fellow-creatures, beyond bread and water, and a grave, unless he can win it by his own strength or skill. But so much the kinder were those unknown friends whom I thank again with all my heart.

N. H.

The following letter was written by James Russell Lowell (1819-1891) to Nathaniel Hawthorne, as an introduction-recommendation for William Dean Howells. Lowell's facetious reference to the famous Roman consul Plancus refers to Hawthorne's consulship abroad (see preceding letter):

Cambridge, August 5, 1860.

My dear Hawthorne,

I have no masonic claim upon you except community of tobacco, and the young man who brings this does not smoke.

But he wants to look at you, which will do you no harm, and him a great deal of good.

His name is Howells, and he is a fine young fellow, and has written several *poems* in the *Atlantic*, which of course you have never read, because you don't do such things yourself, and are old enough to know better.

When I think how much you might have profited by the perusal of certain verses of somebody who shall be nameless—but, no matter! If my judgment is good for anything, this youth has more in him than any of our younger fellows in the way of rhyme.

Of course he can't hope to rival *Consule Planco* men. Therefore let him look at you, and charge it

To yours always,

J. R. LOWELL

Sydney Smith (1771-1845) was an English clergyman and humorist *and* delightful letter writer. The "regrets" below may be compared to their incalculable advantage with such formal social notes as are reproduced on pages 267 and 268. The first of the following notes was written to Mrs. Meynell, the second to Miss Berry. Both women were prominent in social and literary circles in Sydney Smith's time.

Thy servant is threescore-and-ten years old; can he bear the sound of singing men and singing women? A Canon at the Opera! Where have you lived? In what habitations of the heathen? I thank you, shuddering; and am ever your unseducible friend,

SYDNEY SMITH

Engaged, my dear Miss Berry, up to the teeth on Saturday, or should be too happy. It gives me great comfort that you are recovered. I would not have survived you. To precipitate myself from the pulpit of Paul was the peculiar mode of destruction on which I had resolved.

Ever yours,

SYDNEY SMITH

Robert Louis Stevenson (1850-1894) "deeds over" a birthday in the proper legal manner. There is to be no nonsense about the transaction—no loophole thru which the bequest may be avoided. The letter* is addressed to H. C. Ide, father of the "legatee."

Vailima, June 19, 1891.

Dear Mr. Ide,

Herewith please find the DOCUMENT, which I trust will prove sufficient in law. It seems to me very attractive in its eclecticism; Scots, English, and Roman law phrases are all indifferently introduced, and a quotation from the works of Haynes Bailey can hardly fail to attract the indulgence of the Bench.

Yours very truly,

ROBERT LOUIS STEVENSON

I, Robert Louis Stevenson, Advocate of the Scots Bar, author of *The Master of Ballantrae* and *Moral Emblems*, stuck civil engineer, sole owner and patentee of the Palace and Plantation known as Vailima in the island of Upolu, Samoa, a British subject, being in sound mind, and pretty well, I thank you, in body:

* Used by permission of Charles Scribner's Sons. New York City.

In consideration that Miss Annie H. Ide, daughter of H. C. Ide, in the town of St. Johnsbury, in the county of Caledonia, in the state of Vermont, United States of America, was born, out of all reason, upon Christmas Day, and is therefore out of all justice denied the consolation and profit of a proper birthday:

And considering that I, the said Robert Louis Stevenson, have attained an age when O, we never mention it, and that I have now no further use for a birthday of any description;

And in consideration that I have met H. C. Ide, the father of the said Annie H. Ide, and found him about as white a land commissioner as I require:

Have transferred, and *do hereby transfer*, to the said Annie H. Ide, *all and whole* my rights and privileges in the thirteenth day of November, formerly my birthday, now, hereby, and henceforth, the birthday of the said Annie H. Ide, to have, hold, exercise, and enjoy the same in the customary manner, by the sporting of fine raiment, eating of rich meats, and receipt of gifts, compliments, and copies of verse, according to the manner of our ancestors;

And I direct the said Annie H. Ide to add to the said name of Annie H. Ide the name Louisa—at least in private; and I charge her to use my said birthday with moderation and humanity, *et tamquam bona filia familia*, the said birthday not being so young as it once was, and having carried me in a very satisfactory manner since I can remember;

And in case the said Annie H. Ide shall neglect or contravene either of the above conditions, I hereby revoke the donation and transfer my rights in the said birthday to the President of the United States of America for the time being:

In witness whereof I have hereto set my hand and seal this nineteenth day of June in the year of grace eighteen hundred and ninety-one.

SEAL

ROBERT LOUIS STEVENSON

Witness, LLOYD OSBOURNE,
Witness, HAROLD WATTS.

Charles Lever (1806-1872) wrote to his lifelong friend and sponsor, Alexander Spencer, for sympathetic as well as material support. Lever's novels are too little read today. The one referred to in the letter and the once popular *Con Cregan* are highly worth reviving. The first chapter of the latter is a masterpiece in character humor and has been widely used in public readings.

Brussels, January 17, 1840.
A MOST absurd blunder has induced a certain Charles O'Malley, Esq., barrister-at-law, and leader of the Western Circuit, to suppose that my new book under that name is meant to be his Life, etc. And the consequence is that a meeting of the bar has taken place at Litton's and resolutions entered to compel a change of title.

Now as I never heard of this gentleman, nor with a very wide-spread acquaintance do I know of one single Mr. O'Malley, I have refused pointblank. My book is already advertised in all the London papers, and if I changed the name for another, any individual bearing the newly-adapted one would have—what Mr. O'Malley has not—just and sufficient ground of quarrel with me.

All my friends here—military, diplomatic, and literary—agree in this view, Lord Lennox, Ranelagh, Suffield, etc., saying that it would be a very weak thing indeed to yield, and one which would undoubtedly reflect both upon my courage and judgment.

I write these few hurried lines to put you *en courant* to what is going on.

For God's sake send me some gilt. I am terribly hard up just now.

CHARLES LEVER

Elbert Hubbard (1856-1915) almost invariably wrote master-pieces, and when he turned his hand to business letters he was a supermaster, as this short collection message* proves.

THE ROYCROFTERS
DEVOTED TO PRINTING AND ARTS AND CRAFTS
EAST AURORA, NEW YORK
MAY 1, 1909

Dear Friend:

This is a pretty blunt question. But its answer is one of vital importance to us—

Are you going to settle for Volume One of the Complete Works, or are you not? Ten Dollars, you know.

Hope still crimsons all the East, and we await your reply by return mail.

Yours very sincerely,
ELBERT HUBBARD

P.S. Volume Two is ready.
Shall we send it along?

Tobias Smollett (1721-1771) was a Scotch physician and novelist, author of *Roderick Random, Peregrine Pickle,* and other novels written in letter form. He had a gift for phrase-making, and his "great Cham of literature" has been famous ever since he coined it. This letter was written to John Wilkes, a member of Parliament, and a politician of great power—and some scandal! Johnson disliked Wilkes, but Boswell tells amusingly how Wilkes overcame this dislike. The letter speaks for itself, evincing as it does, the world-old custom of seeking political influence or "pull" from those who are able to wield it. The letter is nevertheless written in a worthy cause, for an estimable person, and with consummate dignity and tact. Francis had "joined up"

* Used by permission of Elbert Hubbard II, President, The Roycrofters, East Aurora, New York.

quite on his own and had not been pressed into service. But he was discharged and returned to his master.

Chelsea, 16 March, 1759.

Dear Sir:

I am again your petitioner, in behalf of that great CHAM of literature, Samuel Johnson. His black servant, whose name is Francis Barber, has been pressed on board the Stag frigate, Captain Angel, and our lexicographer is in great distress. He says the boy is a sickly lad, of a delicate frame, and particularly subject to a malady in his throat, which renders him very unfit for His Majesty's service. You know what matter of animosity the said Johnson has against you: and I dare say you desire no other opportunity of resenting it, than that of laying him under an obligation. He was humble enough to desire my assistance on this occasion, though he and I were never cater-cousins; and I gave him to understand that I would make application to my friend Mr. Wilkes, who, perhaps, by his interest with Dr. Hay and Mr. Elliot, might be able to procure the discharge of his lacquey. It would be superfluous to say more on this subject, which I leave to your own consideration; but I cannot let slip this opportunity of declaring that I am, with the most inviolable esteem and attachment, dear Sir, your affectionate, obliged, humble servant,

TOBIAS SMOLLETT

Abraham Lincoln (1809-1865) wrote firmly and pointedly, yet simply, in "refusing credit" to his foster-brother, John D. Johnston. The letter bristles with common-sense and positiveness, but it is not unfriendly.

January 2, 1851.

Dear Johnston:

Your request for eighty dollars I do not think it best to comply with now. At the various times when I have helped you a little you have said to me, "We can get along very well now"; but in a very short time I find you in the same difficulty again. Now, this can only happen by some defect in your conduct. What that defect is, I think I know. You are not lazy, and still you are an idler. I doubt whether, since I saw you, you have done a good whole day's work in any one day. You do not very much dislike to work, and still you do not work much, merely because it does not seem to you that you could get much for it. This habit of uselessly wasting time is the whole difficulty; it is vastly important to you, and still more so to your children, that you should break the habit. It is more important to them, because they have longer to live, and can keep out of an idle habit before they are in it, easier than they can get out after they are in.

You are now in need of some money; and what I propose is, that you shall go to work, "tooth and nail," for somebody who will give you money for it. Let father and your boys take charge of your things at home, prepare for a crop, and make a crop, and you go to work for the best money wages, or in discharge of any debt you owe, that you can get; and, to secure you a fair reward for your labor, I now promise you that for every dollar you will, between this and the first of May, get for your labor, either in money or as your own indebtedness, I will then give you one other dollar. By this, if you hire yourself at ten dollars a month, from me you will get ten more, making twenty dollars a month for your work. In this I do not mean you shall go off to St. Louis, or the lead mines, or the gold mines in California, but I mean for you to go at it for the best wages you can get close to home in Coles County.

Now, if you will do this, you will soon be out of debt, and, what is better, you will have a habit that will keep you from getting in debt again. But, if I should now clear you out of debt, next year you would be just as deep in as ever. You say you would almost give your place in heaven for seventy or eighty dollars. Then you value your place in heaven very cheap, for I am sure you can, with the offer I make, get the seventy or eighty dollars for four or five months' work. You say if I will furnish you the money you will deed me the land, and, if you don't pay the money back, you will deliver possession. Nonsense! If you can't now live with the land, how will you then live without it? You have always been kind to me, and I do not mean to be unkind to you. On the contrary, if you will but follow my advice, you will find it worth more than eighty times eighty dollars to you.

Affectionately your brother,

ABRAHAM LINCOLN

Charles Lamb (1775-1834) wrote to Samuel Taylor Coleridge in recommendation of roast pig. The *O* refers to Charles Ollier, a publisher who issued many of the works of Shelley and Keats and a collected edition of Lamb's works. Lamb's essays are all personal letters, and his letters are all personal essays. Perhaps you can best understand the meaning of this statement by reading this letter and the next one together with his *A Dissertation on Roast Pig.*

Dear C.,

It gives me great satisfaction to hear that the pig turned out so well—they are interesting creatures at a certain age—what a pity such buds should blow out into the maturity of rank bacon! You had all some of the crackling—and brain sauce—did you remember to rub it with butter, and gently dredge it a little, just before the crisis? Did the eyes come away kindly, with no Oedipean avulsion? Was the crackling the colour of the ripe pomegranate? Had you no cursed complement of boiled neck of mutton before it, to blunt the edge of delicate desire? Did you flesh maiden teeth in it? Not that I sent the pig, nor can form the remotest guess what part O—— could play in the business. I never knew him give anything away in his life. He would not begin with strangers. I suspect the pig, after all, was meant for me; but at the unlucky juncture of time being absent, the present somehow went round to Highgate. To confess an honest truth, a pig is one of those things I could never think of sending away. Teals, widgeons, snipes, barn-door fowl, ducks, geese—your tame villalio things—Welsh mutton, collars of brawn, sturgeon, fresh or pickled, your potted char, Swiss cheeses,

French pies, early grapes, muscadines, I impart as freely unto my friends as myself. They are but self extended; but pardon me if I stop somewhere—where the fine feeling of benevolence giveth a higher smack than the sensual rarity, there my friends (or any good man) may command me; but pigs are pigs, and I myself therein am nearest to myself. Nay I should think it an affront, an undervaluing done to Nature who bestowed such a boon upon me, if in a churlish mood I parted with the precious gift. One of the bitterest pangs I ever felt of remorse was when a child—my kind old aunt had strained her pocket strings to bestow a sixpenny whole plum-cake upon me. On my way home through the Borough, I met a venerable old man, not a mendicant—but thereabouts; a look-beggar, not a verbal petitionist; and in the coxcombry of taught-charity, I gave away the cake to him. I walked on a little in all the pride of an Evangelical peacock, when of a sudden my old aunt's kindness crossed me; the sum it was to her; the pleasure she had a right to expect that I—not the old imposter—should take in eating her cake; the cursed ingratitude by which under the colour of a Christian virtue, I had frustrated her cherished purpose. I sobbed, wept, and took it to heart so grievously, that I think I never suffered the like—and I was right. It was a piece of unfeeling hypocrisy and proved a lesson to me ever after. The cake has long been masticated, consigned to dunghill with the ashes of that unreasonable pauper.

But when Providence, who is better to us all than our aunts, gives me a pig, remembering my temptation and my fall, I shall endeavour to act towards it more in the spirit of the donor's purpose.

Yours (short of pig) to command in everything,   C. L.

Here he continues the recommendation in a letter to a farmer and his wife. The message bears directly upon the essay above referred to.

Twelfth Day, '23.

The pig was above my feeble praise. It was a dear pigmy. There was some contention as to who should have the ears; but in spite of his obstinacy (deaf as these little creatures are to advice), I contrived to get at one of them . . .

He must have been the least of his race. His little foots would have gone into the silver slipper. I take him to have been a Chinese, and a female.

He crackled delicately.

I left a blank at the top of the page, not being determined which to address it to: so farmer and farmer's wife will please divide the thanks. May your granaries be full, and your rats empty, and your chickens plump, and your envious neighbors lean, and your laborers busy, and you as idle and as happy as the day is long.

Yours truly,
CHARLES LAMB

Percy Bysshe Shelley (1792-1822) wrote to Horatio Smith. himself a poet and friend of Shelley and of Hunt, asking him to lend money to William Godwin, Shelley's father-in-law. Smith was unable to do this. Godwin had already approached him. Why Godwin's friends should assume responsibility for his legal expenses, could not be made clear to Smith, in spite of such moving appeals as this. The novel that Shelley refers to is *Frankenstein*.

Lerici, May 1822.

My dear Smith,

It is some time since I have heard from you; are you still at Versailles? Do you still cling to France, and prefer the arts and conveniences of that over-civilized country to the beautiful nature and mighty remains of Italy? As to me, like Anacreon's swallow, I have left my Nile, and have taken up my summer quarters here, in a lonely house, close by the sea-side, surrounded by the soft and sublime scenery of the gulf of Spezzia. I do not write; I have lived too long near Lord Byron, and the sun has extinguished the glow-worm; for I cannot hope, with St. John, that *the light came into the world, and the world knew it not.*

The object of my present letter is, however, a request, and as it concerns that most odious of all subjects, money, I will put it in the shortest shape: Godwin's law-suit, he tells us, is decided against him; and he is adjudged to pay £400. He writes, of course, to his daughter in the greatest distress: but we have no money except our income, nor any means of procuring it. My wife has sent him her novel, which is now finished, the copyright of which will probably bring him £300 or £400—as Ollier offered the former sum for it, but as he required a considerable delay for the payment, she rejected his offer. Now, what I wish to know is, whether you could with convenience lend me the £400 which you once dedicated to this service, and allow Godwin to have it, under the precautions and stipulations which I formerly annexed to its employment. You could not obviously allow this money to lie idle waiting for this event, without interest. I forgot this part of the business till this instant, and now I reflect that I ought to have assured you of the regular payment of interest, which I omitted to mention, considering it a matter of course.

I can easily imagine that circumstances may have arisen to make this loan inconvenient or impossible. In any case, believe me,

My dear Smith,
Yours very gratefully and faithfully,
P. B. SHELLEY

This request was made by William James (1842-1910), the great American teacher, psychologist, and philosopher. The human-interest note in this letter is important in comparison with the businesslike and forceful tone of the letters on pages 335 to 338. It was written to Henry L. Higginson, Boston banker and philanthropist.

Cambridge, Mass., Nov. 1, 1902.

Dear Henry,

I am emboldened to the step I am taking by the consciousness that though we are both at least sixty years old and have known each other from the cradle, I have never but once (or possibly twice) traded on your well-known lavishness of disposition to swell any "subscription" which I was trying to raise.

Now the doomful hour has struck. The altar is ready, and I take the victim by the ear. I choose you for a victim because you still have some undesiccated human feeling about you and can think in terms of pure charity—for the love of God, without ulterior hopes of returns from the investment.

The subject is a man of fifty who can be recommended to no other kind of benefactor. His story is a long one, but it amounts to this, that Heaven made him with no other power than that of thinking and writing, and he has proved by this time a truly pathological inability to keep body and soul together. He is abstemious to an incredible degree, is the most innocent and harmless of human beings, isn't propagating his kind, has never had a dime to spend except for vital necessities, and never has had in his life an hour of what such as *we* call freedom from care or of "pleasure" in the ordinary exuberant sense of the term. He is refinement itself mentally and morally; and his writings have all been printed in first-rate periodicals, but are too scanty to "pay." There's no excuse for him, I admit. But God made him; and after kicking and cuffing and prodding him for twenty years, I have now come to believe that he ought to be treated in charity pure and simple (even though that be a vice) and I want to guarantee him $350. a year as a pension to be paid to the Mills Hotel in Bleecker Street, New York, for board and lodging and a few cents weekly over and above. I will put in $150. I have secured $100. more. Can I squeeze $50. a year out of you for such a non-public cause? If not, don't reply, and forget this letter. If "ja" and you think you really can afford it, and it isn't wicked, let me know, and I will dun you regularly every year for the $50.*

Yours as ever,

WM. JAMES

* Used by permission of Little, Brown, and Company, Boston, Mass.

CHAPTER NINE

LETTER WRITING (Continued)

I Business letter composition

Business English must be clear, concise, correct, and dignified. It must be nicely adapted to the uses made of it. The musician expresses himself in terms of tone, movement, beat, melody, harmony, scale, minor or major key, and the like. The doctor employs such terms as temperature, pulse, fever, diet, mastication, tonic, metabolism, digestion, physic, congestion. The electrician talks of volts, watts, ohms, currents, charge, positive, negative, insulation, meter, and so forth. And the business man uses turn-over, overhead, profit, loss, balance, ledger, delivery, sales, clerk, credit, debit, collection, adjustment, per cent, and hundreds of other terms particular to his pursuit.

Since business is a very general activity, most people being engaged in business in one way or another, the language that belongs to it is widely used and deserves some consideration on the part of those who study English speaking and writing. There could be no better training for them in attaining to expression that is crisp, strong, and specific. For business expression *must* be kept brief and pointed; other expression should be, but often is not and nothing is lost. So much depends in business dealings upon saying exactly what one has to say, no more and no less, that training in business speech and writing should be made training in directness and forthrightness of conduct and manner. Loose expression pertaining to business may have serious results —much more serious results than loose expression in other fields of speaking and writing.

Sentences and paragraphs in business expression are as a rule shorter than in other composition. Every sentence and every paragraph should be made to *achieve* something. There can be no accidental notes, as in music; there can be no entertaining experiment, as in the laboratory; there can be no decorative lighting, as in electrical exhibitions. Ideally, every syllable and every punctuation mark must be made to count definitely toward the accomplishment of a desired end.

Business expression is primarily objective, that is, it is directed specifically to "the other fellow," to some one beyond the mind of the writer or speaker. It is *you*-directed. Sometimes, however, a writer or a speaker must use the subjective attitude, but he must never do it aggressively or conceitedly or otherwise objectionably. Tone in any sort of expression is of the utmost importance, but especially in business speaking and writing. A high tone, a dignified tone, a polite tone, a tolerant tone, an understanding tone, a genial tone—all these are to be cultivated by him who would talk and write to men and women in business. Any manifestation of smartness, flippancy, irritability, brusqueness, superiority, weakness, vacillation, unreliability, inertia, triteness is certain to defeat.

It is frequently said that a business letter should never treat of more than one subject. This good rule is sourced in the principle of concentration, and this in turn means unity of expression. It is wise in writing and speaking of any kind to concentrate upon one subject at a time, and it is especially wise in business expression for the reason above given, namely, the consequences of a business message that is not unified or concentrated may be very serious. If it is weakened by diffuseness and incoherence it will not only mis-convey meaning but it may also convey actually wrong meaning. There is another reason for the rule. Many business establishments are highly departmentalized; letters have to be routed to those departments to which they belong; it is obviously awkward to route a letter that has something in it for the consideration of two or three departments.

But like most rules, this one has logical exceptions. A letter that the writer is certain will go to one person and one person only, may be written seriatim about two or more subjects. An applicant for a position would not write one letter telling about his education, another about his experience, another about the salary he wishes, and so on. It very often happens that two or more subjects may be perfectly well handled in one letter. But the letter situation in each individual case must be the deciding factor.

In spite of all that has been said and written in regard to business English, it is still very far from what it should be, even in the most highly organized quarters. One business house of considerable prominence still feels it imperative to issue the following circular to all its employees every little while. Its trenchant style may be pardoned in view of the importance of the message itself:

BE SINCERE—SAY WHAT YOU MEAN—
OMIT THE MILLINERY

When you write to a person, you are really talking to that person from a distance, aren't you? You do not *say* "Your esteemed remark of a moment ago is hereby acknowledged and contents duly noted," do you? And you do not follow up with "Beg to advise that shipment went forward on tenth instant, and hoping same will be found to your entire satisfaction, we remain . . ." At least I hope you don't. But if you do, then your speaking and your writing and probably your thinking also need to be debunked! Perhaps you will do well to begin the intellectual vacuum-cleaning by consigning the following to the H. B.

1 BEG TO ADVISE

All right, beggar! Beg if you must, but get out to the pavement and do your begging. Don't reduce any self-respecting business office to the underground levels of beggary! And please do not be so generous and flippant with your advice, for it is always a superfluous and gratuitous procedure, this one of giving advice. Say what you have to say, and don't preface it with any such paleozoic slime as BEG TO ADVISE!

2 CONTENTS DULY NOTED

Certainly you have noted the contents of the letter that you are answering, or you are in no condition whatever to reply to it. Besides, it would be downright insulting not to read a serious letter that comes to you, wouldn't it? If your letter in response to another constitutes a real honest-to-goodness response, then you won't have to tell anybody that you have "noted" the message you are responding to. Was there ever an expression more idiotic and asinine and feeble-minded!

3 ESTEEMED FAVOR

This is *not* a synonym or an alibi or an alias for the good old Latin word *letter!* Moreover, the two words mean the same thing to a great extent. They are hoary with age—moldy, mildewed, fungous! Get them out of your speech, out of your writing—OUT OF YOUR SYSTEM! In addition, they are as a rule downright dishonest, as used in business letters. Probably fifty per cent of all business letters ask favors rather than grant them. Call a spade a spade, and have done with it—unless, of course, you always wear a false face and dress for business as people do for a masquerade!

4 YOUR KIND AND APPRECIATED LETTER

Come on, now. Get this one out too! Such saccharine palaver gets you and the other fellow just exactly nowhere! What's the use of giving the gears more oil than they can hold? Courtesy? Yes, of course. Always and everywhere, evince courtesy. But don't paste it on so thick, or there will be more icing than cake, if you'll pardon this quick-change figure of speech. Courtesy speaks for itself in numerous ways in conversation, and therefore in business writing. The total composition tone must convey kindness and consideration and appreciation. But just as soon as you signpost or fingerpoint courtesy, you run the risk of getting yourself accused of insincerity and artificiality.

5 ATTACHED HERETO, ENCLOSED HEREWITH

Ye gods and little fishes! If a thing is attached it is very likely to be hereto. If a thing is enclosed it is very likely to be herewith. The heretoness and the herewithness of the attachedness and the enclosedness, respectively, constitute a toomuchness of letter-writing hackneyedness and stereotypedness! All of which is to say that such expressions cap the climax of superfluity, tautology, redundancy, and verbosity. You may, of course, attach something to something in an envelop besides the letter proper, but it would not be good to do so. And I suppose you may say that you enclose something herewith in contradistinction to therewith, meaning by the latter another envelop or parcel. But this would be precious and far-fetched. So don't quibble. Just dynamite these bromides with all the wim, wigor, and witality you can summon.

6 ULTIMO and INSTANT and PROXIMO

Never mind these. They went out with bustles and hoopskirts and buggies. You date your letters, don't you? You date and sign everything you write, don't you? And the other fellow does too, I hope. Well, then, can't you and he read the date line and fix time by the calendar? These words are used nowadays only by those morons who cannot count beyond ten and who do not know their a-b-c's. They were used in epistles five or six centuries ago just to show off Latin learning, and to impress the recipient of letters with the fact that the writer could calculate time by the calendar, then a new and complicated document. Don't be an exhibitionist—unless you are a moron! Besides, haven't you in your office an up-to-date filing system?

7 PERMIT US TO INFORM YOU

Inasmuch as you are at some distance (or you wouldn't be writing to me) I am helpless about this business of permission. If you attempted to talk this expression to me—in the flesh—you may bet your life that I would *not permit you!* But in a letter you have me at a disadvantage and you'll probably abuse your privilege! Anyhow, why must you give me notice that you are going to inform me? Why not go ahead and do it, without saying, "See here, now, I'm going to do some informing"? When you go about writing a letter, do you say "Permit me to inform you that I am now going to write a letter"? When you apply your habitual quid of chicle (I hate the filthy weed!) do you say to your friends, "Beg to be permitted to inform you that I am now about to bite off considerably more than I ought to attempt to chew"?! Now, in the name of all that's prolix, pleonastic, paraphrastic, wordy, diffuse, and embroidered, I ask you WATDYEMEAN!

8 I WOULD STATE

O would you, now? Would it be just too painful to give the unassuming little Anglo-Saxon word *say* a chance sometimes in competition with the highfalutin *state?* Politicians and legislators state things—and where do they get us? And why use *would?* You fully intend to say something, don't you, to which this three-word persiflage is preface? Well, why don't you say it? Why beat about the bush? Moreover, this fossilized piece of phraseology is deceptive: When you write this to me my first impression is that you would like to say something to me but that you have somehow or other been prevented. Then—lo and benold —in the next breath or the next pen-stroke I find that you are going straight ahead to say it, or—pardon me—to *state* it. In other words you get me all prettily set for a disappointment, and then you undisappoint me! So there is a Santa Claus after all, I find! Will you, for heaven's sake, stop WOULD STATING, WOULD SUGGESTING, WOULD APPRECIATING, and all the rest of the WOULD works!

9 HAND, MATTER, PLEASURE, PER (and the end is by no means yet)

Just renege on these at the very outset of our letter writing, and a thousand and one (more or less) others like them. Or do you prefer to say—TO STATE—"In regard to the matter of your esteemed favor we take pleasure in handing you herewith as per your request," and so forth? If you do, then you're built like the original whatyoumaycallim who still rambles on to whatshisname about thingamajigs and whosis. And if all your mail is at hand after coming *to* hand, and if you are forever taking pleasure in referring to every last business detail as per matter, better see a doctor at once and ask him to put you to sleep by means of a sure-fire anesthetic. Pleasant dreams! Believe me when I say that there are some very good people who will not take pleasure in reading your letters when they come to hand, if you still persist in juggling such jargon. May the typewriter snarl at you and bite you if you dare to use these dictional vermin in my business office! They are OUT— O-U-T! Gather me?

10 WISHING, HOPING, TRUSTING, ANTICIPATING (and all this sort of rot)

If you insist upon using the participial getaway in this enlightened(?) day and age, I hope you take a banana-peel slip upon it and suffer a compound fracture of every tonsil in your cosmos! So there! And if you go in for the SINCERELY-HOPING and IMPLICITLY-TRUSTING junkability, why then, better hand in your resignation, lay in a stock of juicy red apples, and set up on some street corner as a super salesman of the emblem of original sin! When your letter is finished, it is finished, isn't it? Don't frame it off with such ancestral blather as OPEFULLY HANTICIPATIN' YOUR FAVORABLE REHACTION TO THIS HUNHUSUAL HOPPORTUNITY. Such nonsense is a waste of everybody's time! Write what you have to write as hopefully and as trustingly, as lucidly and as honestly, as concisely and as courteously as you possibly can, and have done with the job. In trying to clinch a message with a grand and elaborate participial getaway, you may knock out all the underpinnings of your composition—and it will serve you jolly well right, say I!

The first excerpt below is not well adapted to the requirements of business expression. The second one is. And in this comparative illustration lies the principal difference between business writing and general writing. The unbusinesslike excerpt is taken from a weekly review for general reading. The second is adapted to the columns of a business weekly.

The style of the following is extravagant and elaborate, and unsuitable for business purposes:

Though the depression has now achieved a literature which begins to rival that of the World War, few of the books about it have been widely read. The reasons for this are perhaps not difficult to understand. The course of events in the last three years has changed so rapidly that it has been difficult for contemporary interpretations to keep pace with new developments. Moreover, the conflict with which this literature deals is essentially impersonal. There are no heroes and no villains in the slow, ruinous decline of commodity prices and the inexorable contraction of bank credit. There are scapegoats. But it is less easy to feel certain that any one of them brought about the depression single-handedly than that the Kaiser brought about the war, and more difficult to make economics interesting to a large audience, even in a period of misfortune, than to dramatize diplomacy and battle. (150 words)

Here is the above excerpt adapted to business use—the style is direct, economical, and businesslike:

Books about the depression are becoming as numerous as those about the World War. Few of them, however, are widely read. Events have moved too rapidly for interpretation to keep abreast. Depression is less personal than war. It has scapegoats but they are not individualized. Economics is not good theater. (50 words)

NOTE

Inasmuch as business letter writing is neither an exact science nor a finished art, it is impossible to submit letters in a book of this kind that are unanimously approved. A letter thought by some to be excellent will be considered by others unsatisfactory; a letter that is highly effective in one sort of business may not do at all in another. The letters submitted in the following pages are letters that have served well the purposes for which they were originally composed. They have been taken from actual, successful correspondence, tho names and places have naturally been disguised. The body only is given of these illustrative letters inasmuch as this is the part that actual letter composition is concerned with. The reader is to frame in his imagination the complete letter picture, and he must not allow the omission of dates to beget a bad habit. *Date and sign everything* is the invariable rule of all good business writing. Note also that, owing to the exigencies of the printed page, the shorter letters here presented are "out of shape." All letters should be longer than wide if the artistic principles of placement and proportion are to be satisfied. The two boxed letters on page 317 illustrate.

Study the two following solutions. The first two letters are extremely badly written. But they are not exaggerated. There are many so-called business letters in the mails at this very moment that are quite as bad as these. There are also, it is comforting to note, many business letters in the mails at this very moment that are quite as good as the rewritten ones below (perhaps better).

A bad reply to an inquiry-claim letter:

3 February,

James R. Griffen, Esq.,
   25 Madison Square 10
   New York City

My dear Sir:——
     I am in receipt of your communication of even date and in reply would say that I am enclosing booklets asked for, I list them in order that you may check up,—
Foreign Trade Outlook
Recommended Investments
Trust Funds and their Management
Liberty Bonds below Par
China as Undeveloped Financial Territory
The Executor and his Work
Our South American Branches
     I am sorry that you have been displeased with our monthly statement forms. I will have duplicate of your last statement examined, and corrected form forwarded to you. Trusting this will prove entirely satisfactory,
          Truly yours,
          TAVISTOCK TRUST COMPANY

A bad adjustment letter:

181 Lenox Av16
June 25th
New York

Misses Jones and Everett;
   222 Broadway—N.Y.7
Dear Ladies,—We beg to acknowledge yr. esteemed favor of 20th inst and in reply would say that errors in acct. for May are deeply regretted by us. I have taken immediate steps to have same corrected and enclose herewith another statement which we hope will meet with your entire satisfaction.
     We crave your parden, and beg to inform you that mistakes are made as result of circumstances over which I had no control, namely and to wit, illness on part of many employees, removal into new building, disturbed and fluctuating market conditions, incomplete equipment due to removal, transference of certain employees from

one dept. to another in order to help us overcome the disadvantages of our situation and ect.

Hoping you will forgive us this time, regretting our shortcomings in connection with and pertaining to your monthly statement, and trusting you have not been seriously inconvenienced thereby

Yrs. Resp'y
Commercial Trust Company
p.p.James Wickersham
CD/JW/VN

The foregoing reply written as it should be. It would be better in all such cases as this to write two letters, since two entirely unrelated subjects are treated. When this is not done, however, some clear-cut partition should be made, as here:

February 3, 0000

Mr. James R. Griffen
25 Madison Square
New York City 10

Dear Mr. Griffen

I

The duplicate of your last statement is being corrected and it will be sent to you today, or tomorrow at the latest. We are very sorry indeed that our monthly forms have not been satisfactory to you. Please always let us know at once whenever our transactions and correspondence are not right in every way, and we shall do everything possible to make them so, especially in your case.

II

The booklets requested are enclosed, arranged as here listed for your convenience of check-up.

A

Foreign Trade Outlook
Our South American Branches
China as Undeveloped Financial Territory

B

The Executor and his Work
Trust Funds and their Management

C

Recommended Investments
Liberty Bonds Below Par

We think you will find these both useful and profitable. Many of our customers have transferred funds to their advantage after studying these publications and conferring with us.

Very truly yours
TAVISTOCK TRUST COMPANY

/ enclosures

CS/hg

The foregoing adjustment letter as it should be:

June 25, 0000.

Misses Jones and Everett,
222 Broadway,
New York 7, N. Y.

Dear Ladies:

Your statement, revised and corrected, is enclosed. It comes to you under special delivery because we fear that you may be delaying important transactions pending its receipt.

According to our records you have been a highly valued customer of ours since 1920, and you have never before, we think, been obliged to call our attention to error in our reports to you.

This fine relationship covering more than fifteen years simply reacts now to make the present lapse of ours all the more culpable. We have neither alibis nor excuses. We would not impose them upon you if we had. We are very sorry, and we are appreciative of your indulgent attitude toward us.

Yours very truly,

COMMERCIAL TRUST COMPANY
p.p. James Wickersham

P.S. By the way, have you seen our new ladies' wallets of damascene cloth? We shall be happy if you will accept the two that we are sending to you by parcel post. These are made up in various tints and shades to match ensembles, and we shall be glad to give you others in different tones. They are to be distributed to certain customers of long standing on the tenth of next month when we celebrate our sesquicentennial, and you might as well have yours now.

CD/JW/VEN

II Letters of application

The good business letter begins with the subject to be discussed. It makes immediate connection between the prospective reader and the thing the writer has to say to him. Remote introductory matter is distinctly out of place. This applies nowhere with greater emphasis than in letters that have to do with selling personal efficiency, making introductions, and recommending one person to another.

Age, nationality, purpose in writing, education, experience, salary expected (if requested), references, copies of recommendations, arrangement for interview (if suggested) are the principal content of a letter of application. It must be made to look well and to look important. This means that good stationery should be used.

preferably of the larger commercial size, and that the letter should be typewritten. Care should be exercised to avoid an aggressive I-tone, but at the same time the writer should write in a strong and confident vein, otherwise he may be thought weak, timid, and inferior. He should be most thoro in analyzing the situation which evokes his letter, be it a help-wanted advertisement or an opportunity of which he has heard thru a friend or other source. He would do well to analyze himself in relation to the kind of opportunity that is offered, to the end that he may be able to write a letter that will "dovetail" with the requirements of the job. He should say nothing that he cannot support; that is, proof of education mentioned, proof of experience claimed, proof of achievements listed to further his chances, should be borne out by references or copies of enclosed recommendations, or both.

Two particular kinds of recommendation are usually considered important. One pertains to character and reputation; one to education and experience. The former kind is general; the latter should be made special to the position for which the application is made. The letters of application reproduced below vary in form and content but bear out in general these principles. The seriatim letter is usually considered better than the one that is set solid, but either style is permissible and the latter may be quite as good as the former. References should be listed in the order in which the writer desires them considered, and all enclosures should be firmly clipped together so that the whole communication will constitute a unity and nothing will be lost. In practically all applications automatic reply should be arranged for —stamps or, better, a stamped, addressed envelop. (Do not use the term *self-addressed* in reference to an enclosed addressed envelop.)

In introductions, the introduction proper should come first. This should be followed with the reason for making it, with a word or two about the person introduced, and with whatever request the introduction entails. In recommendations it is customary to list a few qualities first, and then to treat each one individually but briefly.

In reply to this advertisement

WANTED—A well trained, experienced stenographer, one with some legal knowledge preferred, tho work to be done is strictly commercial. State education, experience, age, nationality, present employment and salary, reason for application, and references. Twaddell and Cousins, 1233 Market Street, Philadelphia.

one applicant wrote as follows:

> It would be a mistake to overlook me in filling the position you advertise in the morning *Inquirer*.
>
> I am A1 in every respect. It would almost seem that you must have had me in mind when you penned that little masterpiece for the Help-Wanted column. Give me a ring—MT 0-0000—and I shall make it possible for you to see me.
>
> My photograph is enclosed. Salary of $50. weekly will be considered.

and another did this:

> My achievements in the realm of Pitmanization have been noised hither and yon, and I am accordingly indelibly impressed with your restrained solicitation in the morning publications for a stenographical secretarial amanuensis.
>
> Fortunately I am at the present juncture a member of the regimentation of unemployed, and am therefore at liberty to consolidate my interests with your own at a moment's notification. Both by educational attainment and experiential service I am preeminently qualified to render you superlative performances in the acknowledged artistry of abbreviated communication.

but a third wrote this and got the job:

> May I ask you, please, to consider the following in connection with your advertisement for a stenographer in this morning's *Inquirer:*
>
> 1 My average rate of speed is one hundred words a minute in straight copy, accuracy guaranteed
>
> 2 At the time I was graduated from high school I held the record in the State for speed and accuracy
>
> 3 After leaving high school I attended Blair College for two years, where I served as part-time secretary to the President, thus earning my tuition
>
> 4 For two years I was chief stenographer to the Court of Special Sessions in this city, and for the past two years I have been serving in the same capacity with the well-known law firm of Brown and Inglesby, 25 Market Street
>
> I am twenty-five years of age, American born, and live at home with my family. My present salary is thirty-five dollars a week
>
> 6 My application is made to you because your advertisement indicates that you are a commercial house. I do not want to continue longer now in legal stenography, for the reason that I feel I know it well enough. It is excellent training for a young stenographer but my aim is to be a generalist in my field, not a specialist
>
> 7 You may address my present employers to ask any special questions about my qualifications and efficiency. You may also write to President Cummings of Blair College, Brookston.

Penna., and to the Principal of Calvin High School in this city.
I enclose, however, copies of recommendations from all of
them

Inasmuch as my present employers are aware that I am looking for
an opportunity to broaden my training and service in stenography
they have very kindly arranged to permit me to absent myself from
the offices for a short time on any day that I may be called for interview. If therefore you care to talk with me, please let me know and
I shall be able and glad to call at your convenience. A stamped
addressed envelop is enclosed

This application is frank and honest without being aggressive:

Re your advertisement in the morning *Bee*
The following data will serve to show that my training and experience tally with the requirements of your advertisement

Age	Twenty-four
Family	American for five generations, living with parents
Education	Wells High School graduate, commercial course Towne Industrial College, B.C.L. degree
Employment	Since graduation from college, with the corpora- tion law firm of Carstell and Barnaby, 181 Walsh Avenue, in the capacity of consultant on records
References	Dr. Andrew Borden, Principal Wells High School, this city President Charles R. Marston, Towne Industrial College, New Brunswick, New Jersey Archibald Carstell, Esq., senior partner of the law firm above referred to
Salary	I have been receiving fifty dollars a week straight in addition to monthly commissions on work that I have been able to bring in to the firm. These have amounted to about fifteen dollars weekly
Reason for Application	My present connection holds little promise for the reason that three of the members of the firm have sons who are nearly ready to enter it. I am one who will be automatically supplanted, and I am simply looking ahead—and hoping

It is possible for me to call to talk with you briefly at almost any
time, day or evening. I enclose copies of both scholastic and service
recommendations, and you are at perfect liberty to consult the
writers of these further in regard to me. Their addresses are enclosed, and I attach to each recommendation a stamp for your use

*This is a good application written in reply to a personal letter
rather than to a newspaper advertisement:*

Thank you for your letter. It is very kind of you to remember my
telling you that I should some day like to work for you. Father

thinks it is a great oportunity you offer me, and, needless to say,
I do too

You want to know my qualifications. I shall give them to you
seriatim

1 My tastes and aptitudes	All of my instructors have told me that I am "mechanically inclined." I hope they are right, for I love a workshop and machinery and the handling of tools
2 My education	I finished the machine-shop course at Dakin High in three years, and was graduated from Dale Technical Institute last June. At both places I was first honor man, and at the latter I perfected the water-hot device that you mention in your letter and that has just this week been patented. For these reasons I think I shall fit into your factory especially well
3 My ambitions	Well, I should first like to "make good" with you, I suppose. Then I want to work out another idea or two of my own in the line of water heating and heat retention. If and when this comes to pass, I shall give you dignified notice and set up for my-self! But this is a long way off, I assure you, so please don't allow it to make any difference in the present situation
4 My wages	Whatever you say will be satisfactory to me. As you know, I have worked for the past four summers in the Graves Laboratories and received thirty dollars a week. The important thing is to have steady work at an open job. I mean at a job that consists of something more than blind routine. I am not mentioning this for selfish reasons, but because I know I can give you better service in such a job

I *think* this answers your letter fully. And I do hope I haven't
said anything wrong, for I am looking forward with enthusiasm to
being a workman in overalls in your big and important place

This letter is what the theater would call CASTING AGAINST TYPE.
*It is unusual, certainly, to apply for a job for which an advertise-
ment tells you you are not wanted. But this is a winning example,
and deservedly:*

Your advertisement in today's *Leader* calls for a road sales*man* to
sell children's wear. I hope you won't mind my answering it—and
applying for the job—especially if I am able to prove to you that
I can hold my own with any man on the road? If I am able to
do this, will you give me a trial?

I have sold children's wear for the Transblower Company for the
past five years. Each year my sales have shown an increase of at
least fifteen per cent over those of the preceding year. This year
I lead the sales force of twelve women and eighteen men

This record has been made on long hard road trips up and down the country, in all sorts of weather, in face of all kinds of competition, and with never a day's illness or a penny's loss in old trade. I ask no concessions in this business of selling shoulder to shoulder with men on the road. It's hard, I admit. But all work is. And I've studied the road as I've studied men and their methods of selling, and if you think that, just because I'm a woman, I expect concessions, then please just give me a chance to try to prove to you that I don't

Perhaps your advertisement reads as it does because you have never yet hired women. This is a day when traditions just have to come down off their pedestals, isn't it? Isn't a woman just as quick and intuitive about getting a buyer's point of view as a man is, especially when the article for sale is children's wear? Can a man talk color and quality and price and smartness and values better than a woman, think you, when it comes to selling anything *for children?* I don't believe he can, and all I ask is a chance to prove to you that I am right about this

Perhaps I want to make a change just because your advertisement got under my skin a little. I don't know. And this isn't important. What is important tho is this: I have studied the business you conduct. I doubt whether you yourself have studied it any harder than I have, and you are a boss and I'm merely a "roadster." But I see in your business a great opportunity for a live sales*woman*. I have a burning ambition to be that woman. I have just about exhausted all the resources that my present job can ever yield. Will you please subordinate your convictions a little and give me a trial?

Here is an application that shows a fine sense of fair play:

Your advertisement in the *Times* today interests me particularly because it seems to call for exactly the qualifications that I have and for exactly the service which I hope to be able to render to some house on my graduation from high school next month when I shall be eighteen years of age. I am American born and live with my parents

During the last two years of my high school course I have been employed on the cooperative plan, that is, one week in school and one week out of school, working in a business office. For approximately seventy-five weeks now I have been the general office assistant at Blaine and Gertner's Emporium, Chelsea Avenue and Pearce Boulevard. Mr. Horace G. Winterburn, my immediate supervisor, will recommend me to your satisfaction I am sure, and I enclose a stamped envelop addressed to him for your convenience in consulting him about me

My office work during this period has consisted of answering telephone calls, filing letters and other papers, keeping the office daybook, and, during the past year, taking dictation and typing letters. Just at present I am acting as Mr. Winterburn's private secretary also, because of the serious illness of his regular secretary

I have for the past two years been an honor student at high school and have had two official designations as head boy—once in commercial law and once in stenography and typewriting. I enclose a copy of a letter from Principal Harry S. Wood in which he writes of both my character and my scholarship record

The position that I hold, cooperatively with an alternate, at Blaine and Gertner's is really a position belonging to the school and not to me, you understand. On my graduation it automatically goes to another cooperative student in the school. It is for this reason that I am now seeking a position. It would not be fair for me to try to hold my present tryout job (tho I think Mr. Winterburn would probably like to have me) for by doing so I should be interfering with some other student's commercial training

This introduction ought to merit respect—and action:

Miss Jennie Fairman, who brings this letter to you, is a good friend of mine. She is spending the present academic year in Chicago doing graduate work at the University

She wants to gather some information about highly organized filing systems, and she and I together have decided that a large mail-order concern such as yours is probably the best place to study filing under the most extensive and intensive conditions

Will you therefore help her a little, please? In so doing you will make a new friend and prove—again—your unfailing loyalty to an old one

The gentleman will probably be well received and perhaps even entertained:

This will introduce to you Mr. Charles Cadman who is considering your city as a possible location for a branch of his large sewing-machine factory here in Tulsa

I have known Mr. Cadman for the past twelve years, and I cannot speak too highly of his business integrity, civic spirit, and personal worth

If you can find it possible to help him a little in getting his bearings in your home town, I shall be very grateful to you

This is a formal introduction of a general kind usually written on a card:

Introduction of
    Mr. Arthur R. Brock
to
    Mr. Harrison Foley
by
    James B. Ogden

Any courtesies that Mr. Foley can extend to Mr. Brock will be appreciated by his old friend

                   JBO

May 3, 0000

This reference note is in part a form and in part a personal letter:

Mr. George Chapman (photograph attached) has applied to us for a position as general office assistant

It is our custom to require all applicants to supply us with references who can vouch for their character and ability

Mr. Chapman has mentioned you as one who will probably be willing to do this. May we therefore trouble you to answer the following questions regarding him?

1 Are his habits correct?

2 Is he able and industrious?

3 Do you think he can fill satisfactorily the position for which he has applied?

4 Can you add anything else in his behalf that will help us in making our decision?

This is a combined introduction and recommendation:

The bearer of this note—Miss Alice Fox—is seeking a position with some good long-established business concern

She is particularly qualified to render efficient service as private secretary in view of the fact that she has for the past two years been employed in this capacity by a college president

While her training and most of her experience have been academic, she is nevertheless a graduate of a business school as well as a bachelor of arts from Cole College. She is therefore somewhat better qualified than the average applicant for the position of private secretary in business. She is quick, accurate, intelligent, and easily adjustable to new conditions. She holds, I believe, certain records and medals for speed writing. She will tell you about these

I hope that you will be able to give Miss Fox employment in your office. There will be no regrets on either side of the house, I am sure

Note in this general recommendation the special salutation form and the absence of a complimentary closing. The general recommendation is always so written:

To whom it may concern

Mr. Henry Ketterer is a young man of sterling character, unusual ability, and indefatigable industry. He has been employed in our offices for the past five years in a variety of capacities, and he has never evinced anything but the greatest possible confidence in his employers and in their business, and has never rendered anything but the most faithful and efficient service. We are extremely sorry to lose him, especially at this time when work is heavier than ever before and when therefore his help is more necessary than ever

But a death in his family makes it imperative that he move to Kansas City and make it his home probably for many years to come. Since this is so, we are very much concerned about his finding satisfactory employment there. We are likewise eager to see some excellent concern in Kansas City avail itself of the rare loyalty and industry that he has to offer. To this end we shall always be ready and punctual in making this recommendation special and individual to any man or woman or company that desires us to do so

CHARLES BUTTERFIELD
President
Leather Products, Inc.

This is a special recommendation, that is, it is a personal letter written in reply to one. The tone of recommendation is somewhat more restrained than it is in the preceding recommendation:

The subject of your inquiry has been employed by us for the past two years and a half. He has always been conscientious in discharging whatever duties were assigned to him, and he is honest and loyal in every way, as far as we are able to judge

Unfortunately we are obliged to dispense with his services, not at all because he is not satisfactory to us, but because we do not feel that we can longer continue the position that he is occupying. By assigning his work fractionally here and there among other *older* employees, we shall be able to subtract one more item of cost from our budget, which will still be too heavy for these strenuous days. There is nothing personal whatever in his dismissal. It is just one of those misfortunes that are so inextricably linked with the general depression

We shall do anything that we can to help him find congenial work. You will make no mistake, we think, in assigning him in the manner you propose. But if you do not see your way clear to do this, we shall make effort to place him elsewhere His domestic situation is said to be rather desperate. But his father and his older brother both secured positions last week after unemployment for over a year

III   Letters of general everyday transactions

The principle of directness, important in all kinds of expression, is of paramount importance in letters of inquiry and information, and order and acknowledgment. Too often regarded as mere routine, these letters are neglected, written without proper attention and care, and thus neither say the little they have to say in the proper form nor express it in the proper tone. A question should be asked and answered precisely; an order should be placed explicitly and in detail, or the one who writes it cannot expect satisfactory acknowledgment of it by way of delivery of goods. Every letter, it has been said, is really a selling letter. It should more frequently be borne in mind that so-called routine letters, since there are more of them than of any other kind, constitute business gain or business loss in proportion as their sales values are or are not realized by writers.

This inquiry is a good one:

> As an employee of the .... Company I have been appointed chairman of a committee to study form-letter plans with view to recommending the adoption of some form system for use of the Company
>
> So many good things have been said about your system that I should like to know about it in detail. Will you please—at your leisure—explain its salient features to me and let me see a few sample forms?
>
> I shall be very much obliged to you

But this reply is not an answer at all. It is merely a filled-in form, and does not fit the query at that:

> In reply to your esteemed favor of May 17th beg to state we have a very complete line of letter forms and are prepared to serve your every wish. Hoping to be honored with your orders
>
> Very truly yours

This reply, however, evinces personal attention on the part of the writer and the spirit of "nothing-can-be-too-much-trouble-in-your-behalf":

Re your inquiry about our form paragraph system

For many years we had no such thing as a form paragraph in our correspondence practise. But as business increased, especially in our mail-order department, we found it necessary to devise certain forms for the saving of time and expense

Our first step was to have a clerical assistant assort the carbons of our letters for a given week into such groups as acknowledgment of order, inability to fill order promptly, inability to fill order at all, and replies to certain claims—damage, shortage, exchange of goods, and the like. These carbons revealed many other situations as standard, that is, as sufficiently general to justify form treatment. The best treatment of any one was taken as model for our form paragraph. Sometimes the form paragraph was a composite of several good excerpts. Our derived form for complete, normal, unmodified acknowledgment is this

> Thank you for your order of .... for ......
> .... with ....
> ...... enclosure for ....
> ....
>
> The goods will be sent immediately by ....
> ....
> and you should have them not later than ....

Exact duplicate of your order will be found in the parcel. Please tally against this when you unpack the goods

The enclosed leaflet will explain to you some very attractive offerings AND PRICES. We hope that you will look it thru carefully and avail yourself of some of the many opportunities presented

The file designation for this form is AU—acknowledgment *un*modified. In case we are short of stock and cannot therefore send goods immediately, the second paragraph is changed to read

The goods will be sent to you in a few days by ......
.... You should have them not later than .... The brief delay is caused by a temporary stock shortage owing to the unprecedented demand for these goods. Depend upon us to do our very best to get them to you in advance of the date indicated above if we possibly can

The file designation for this form is AMss—acknowledgment *m*odified *s*tock *s*hortage. The correspondent writes these initials in the lower right-hand corner of the customer's order letter and his stenographer understands that she is to substitute this paragraph for paragraph two of AU

There is a paragraph filed under AMos—the small letters meaning *o*ut of *s*tock and not to be renewed

Unfortunately these goods were all sold before your letter came to us, and we cannot now tell you when they will again be available. You will recall that our advertising warned that only a very limited number of orders could be filled inasmuch as these were end stocks. We are sorry to disappoint you. We are returning your check to you—and we thank you just the same

Our forms for the adjustment of claims are filed under C. Cd is claim made against damaged goods; Cs is claim against shortage on receipt of goods—less or fewer than ordered were received; Cz is claim against sending wrong size, and so forth. Paragraphs one and three for all adjustments are as follows

Thank you for your promptness in informing us about the ....
of the .... we sent you on ....
Only by the speedy action of the customer in such cases can the merchandiser do justice to himself. You must believe us when we say that we are more eager to adjust claims such as yours than we are to fill initial orders
....
Please accept with our compliments the enclosed flexible leather order booklet. Note the half-dozen claim forms at the end. May you never have to use one of them! But in case something should go wrong again, this will make your end of the correction easy and our end will have to do all the work—and this is as it should be!

Suppose the Cz paragraph is to be inserted

We are sending to you at once ....
of the size you require, and we are enclosing postage refund
for the return of those you cannot use. We have no explanation to make as to how or why the mistake was made—
and it would not be important. The really important thing
is, do you get the .... by .... the date on
which special delivery should bring them to you according
to the promise of the post-office here

These few details regarding our form-paragraph system will make
clear to you its fundamental workings. Ours is not an elaborate
system, yet our plan is elastic enough to permit of tremendous expansion. We have never cared to go in for an elaborate system of
form correspondence. We do not believe in it to an extended degree.
But to meet a few standard situations we have found the foregoing
plan invaluable

It is important to tell you that we never use any form paragraph
for more than a year. Our present forms will be scrapped at the
end of the year and fresh new ones will be devised. We are firmly
convinced that such forms have earned the disrepute that they
"enjoy" because business houses do not overhaul them often enough.
The tendency is to use the same forms year in and year out—to be
inert and indifferent and to let "well enough alone." We think this
a great mistake. New wording, new format, new stationery forms
even have much the same effect upon a form-paragraph and a new
form-letter system as a good coat of paint has upon an old house

*The following note was written in reply to an inquiry about a
certain locality in a state that has long been a favorite summer
vacation land:*

Replying to your esteemed favor take
pleasure in sending you booklet describing
.... in the State of ....

The booklet gave much general information about the place, but
it did not answer one question that had been asked in the inquiry.
The legislature of this particular state has never gone to the
trouble or expense of establishing a publicity bureau. It main-
tains merely an information desk in the capitol. A similar
inquiry about a resort was sent to the capital of another state
equally famous as a summer vacation land. This is the reply
that was made by the Summer Vacation Bureau of the State
of .... :

We shall be delighted to have you spend the summer with us here
in .... While your inquiry does not, of course, commit
you to do so, we hope that our reply will make you decide in
favor of ....

.... is a beautiful mountain village skirted but not disturbed by the new cement road between .... and
.... The townspeople saw to it that the road went around
rather than thru their little beauty spot. It is about three thousand
feet above sea level; the air is always cool and clean; and the natural
spring waters are unsurpassed anywhere in the country

In the neighborhood of .... are some of the most striking
scenic attractions to be found in the United States. Mount Blerner
and Knife Notch and the region surrounding them are said to be
the wildest and most thrilling views in American scenery. Hunting,
tennis, golf, riding, driving, bathing—every summer sport—are all
excellently provided for at .... And the participation in
any kind of sport is made doubly exhilarating, isn't it, when it is
enjoyed where Nature herself has made sport out of mountains and
music out of brooks and waterfalls

A list of hotels is enclosed, with exact locations, prices, special offerings for the season, and so on. There are also lists of our prominent summer residents and of the several state and national sports
meets to be held here during the next six months. Under other
cover a de luxe booklet comes to you. The color photography is by
the famous .... who lives at .... the year round

Enclosed is a stamped, addressed envelop for your use in writing us
further. We feel sure that you will want to know more about
.... than we have been able to tell you in this short letter,
especially after you have examined the booklet. Please consult us
freely about all the things that we have forgotten. AND PLEASE
COME TO ....

These four acknowledgment forms are courteous in tone:

Thank you for your order of December third. The goods are being packed, and delivery will be made at your country home by the time you specify	The samples you requested are enclosed. It may be a wise pro-cedure to indicate a second choice as a substitute for your first in case that fabric has been sold out by the time we hear from you. All mailable pack-ages are forwarded free of charge to the customer
Re Red Cavaliers, size 11½ Sorry, but the third item on your order of October tenth is completely out of stock and we fear it will not be renewable for a long time. Won't you please check a substitute on the en-closed prepaid card?	Your order is appreciated. The merchandise will reach you in a day or two. It has been neces-sary to have our store stocks re-plenished by transfers from our warehouse. This means a delay of possibly twenty-four hours at the most. We shall hasten de-livery for you in every way

This letter shows that a mere form covering numerous similar cases may have tone and quality:

Thank you for your order of ....

We do not appear to have an account with you and to open one for a small amount would mean a detail and expense we must try to avoid, but we do want to be of service to you. We therefore fill the order, and enclose the bill which we shall carry on memorandum only. If you will kindly remit now and return the bill with your payment, this will help us very much in keeping down the detail

If it is your expectation to buy with some frequent regularity in the future and you desire the convenience of a monthly account, you will understand, of course, that we shall be very glad to arrange for this. If, however, this memo account arrangement suits your purpose, we shall be very glad to continue it

We should like to hear from you often

This acknowledgment goes out of its way to make everything satisfactory:

Certainly. Come right along, and bring as many students as you care to bring. We always welcome school visitors, and we have made special arrangements for their accommodation

When you arrive at the Eighteenth Street entrance of our plant, send in your card and our Mr. Willard will see you at once. He will place your party in charge of a guide who will show you everything and who will tarry with you as long as you want him to in the press room where you will see some of the largest printing presses in the world in operation. He will welcome any questions that you may have to ask, and will answer them "with interest"

If by any chance something happens to necessitate the postponement of your proposed visit, will you please let us know as far in advance of cancelation as you can? We make this request so that we may be helped in the routing of other parties and in the assignment of guides

The enclosed card-map shows you the easiest and quickest ways by which to reach our building

This letter is none the worse for its violation of the two-subject rule:

We acknowledge your letter of March 27, and regret there has been some delay in replying to it because of oversight

Our salesman understood that you wished us to use the woman's figure for one side of each link; and therefore we estimated for only the two masks in the design submitted

To make a pair of links with two masks on each link will cost approximately $200. We shall have to see the design again to estimate the price exactly

The allowance for the old cuff links will be $12.25

Thank you for your favorable comment on our policy of open punctuation in our correspondence, which we adopted about fifteen years ago

We did not use typewriters for correspondence until 1910

Our correspondence has for a great many years been centralized and passed on by trained supervisors

The bookkeeping form cannot be too highly recommended for a letter of order:

Will you please send me the following and charge against my monthly account? Perhaps the quickest and most convenient delivery can be made by way of American Railway Express, since deliveries are made by this company twice a day in the suburbs

Item Number	Number Ordered	Title or Description	Item Price	Total Price
2441	10 reams	Blue-White Gobbler Bond	$ .50	$ 5.00
2763	12 reams	Mauve Water-marked Bond	.85	10.20
2772	4 boxes	Ever-Grip Fasteners	.20	.80
3001	1 gross	Self-sharpening Pencils	1.00	1.00
3111	5 gross	Mechanics Measures	1.25	6.25
			Total	$23.25

The Gobbler Bond is an experiment. I am ordering it as result of the strong promotion letter you sent to me last month. If it "measures up" I shall adopt it for permanent use in place of the Kurtner, which, you will recall, I have ordered in large quantities for the past half-dozen years

This letter of confirmation could not evince better tone and cooperation:

Confirming our telephone conversation of this morning I am writing to remind you that your wagon is to call for one four-drawer filing cabinet and one four-drawer card cabinet

The former is to be delivered to our downtown office at 131 Mason Street, and the latter to our midtown office at 18 Grand Avenue

To replace these pieces at the above address, you are to deliver one two-drawer cabinet on a stand and four four-drawer card cabinets

I am sorry that a mistake was made in these deliveries. It is my fault entirely

Note again the tabular arrangement and the consistent set-up:

Please send me the following articles listed from your special sale announcement in the morning papers

One Dozen Arrow Collars, size 15½.......$ 1.80....$ 1.80
Three Pairs Silk Socks, size 11............. 1.50.... 4.50
One Dozen Supreme White Handkerchiefs,
half-inch hem, initial K.................. 3.00.... 3.00
Three Manhattan Shirts, size 15, sleeve
length 35............................. 1.25.... 3.75
Three Black Ties (special sale advertised to-
day—clipping attached)................. 1.00.... 3.00

Total $16.05

A money order for sixteen dollars and five cents ($16.05) is enclosed.
I shall be pleased if your wagon can deliver these things before six
o'clock tomorrow evening

*This order is a tie-up with a previous one on a credit arrangement.
Note that catalog numbers should always be listed from low to
high:*

Will you please deliver the following five items as soon as you can
do so. They are listed from your January catalog, which, I think,
is your latest. In case you have revised listings since then, however, the list numbers will have to be verified against the item
description

Item	List Number	Description	Price
I	52	Typewriting Machine One Underwood narrow carriage Number five with rubber cover Underwood Typewriter Company	$ 70.00
II	5210R	Manila Folders One thousand manila folders legal size Library Bureau (per 1000)	$ 16.00
III	6250H	Metal Tip Pressboard Guides One hundred metal tip pressboard guides, legal size in fifths Library Bureau (per 100)	$ 10.25
IV	8220	Vertical File One legal size vertical file antique oak with two 8080 antique oak ends (with lock) Library Bureau	$ 51.30
V	18956	Low Roll-top Desk One desk fitted with low roll type- writer drop in center, antique oak Library Bureau	$145.00
		Total	$292.55

This order brings the total for the month to something over five
hundred dollars ($500.). My check will be remitted promptly on
receipt of your formal bill

314   GET IT RIGHT!

This is an excerpt from a letter of general specifications preparatory to working on the job:

SPECIFICATIONS

OF LABOR AND MATERIAL TO BE FURNISHED FOR THE ALTERATION OF BUILDING KNOWN AS 1282 ARLINGTON BOULEVARD, WASHINGTON, D.C.

JAMES GOULD
OWNER

IN ACCORDANCE WITH THE PLANS, AND THESE SPECIFICATIONS
FURNISHED BY

HOWARD GRAY, ARCHITECT

AND UNDER HIS SUPERINTENDENCE

GENERAL CONDITIONS

The contractor shall furnish all material labor, transportation, scaffolding, utensils, and so forth, of every description required for the full performance of the work herein specified. He shall lay out his work and be responsible for its correctness, and shall keep a competent foreman on the premises or shall be in attendance himself; shall not sublet any part of the work without written consent of the owner, and shall obtain all and any permits necessary to carry out his work, paying the lawful fees therefor; shall give the proper authorities all requisite notices relating to the work in his charge; shall afford the architect every facility for inspection; shall be responsible for any violation of law or damage to property caused by him or his employees; and shall properly direct his work during its progress

All materials are to be the best of their several kinds as therein specified; and all labor is to be performed in the best manner, and to be subject to the approval of the architect. All work and material must conform to the laws, rules, regulations in force in the locality in which the building is to stand, anything herein specified to the contrary notwithstanding

MASON WORK

The mason shall do all the mason work hereby required in connection with the alteration, plastering, concreting, furring, lathing, fireproofing, brick and terra cotta work, and patching included, and also all 4" and other terra cotta blocks. Furring and lathing shall be of metal. Mason shall do all cutting of bricks, terra cotta, and other work apportioned to himself or his sub-contractors that may be required by other contractors to carry on their work

HALLS

Halls are to be cemented with proper height of bed, and are to have ceramic tile furnished. Style of tile is to be selected by the owner or architect

OUTSIDE BRICK WALLS

Foundations of concrete, of size and depth as shown in plans, are to be built. Contractor is to repair all breaks of plaster, etc., caused by himself or his workmen, whether in new or old portion of the building. When directed by the architect the contractor shall remove all rubbish left by himself or his workmen

Atlas or Whitehall Portland Cement is to be used for all foundations

CARPENTER WORK

The carpenter is to do all the carpentering required in this alteration

The timber to be used is to be white pine, which must be sound, dry, well seasoned, and free from all defects, such as sap, knots, etc.

The official letter is an occasional letter. It is not a letter written every day in connection with the routine of business, nor yet the informal chatty letter that is written to a friend. It is, of course, less formal than engraved announcements and invitations, but more formal than either the business or the friendly letter. Its salutation is usually *Sir, Sirs, Dear Sirs,* or, in less formal official letters, Dear Mr. Thompson; its complimentary closing is *Respectfully yours, Sincerely yours,* or *Cordially yours.*

The official letter is usually written as result of some special event:

Briarcliff Springs, Inc.
New Harmony
Kansas

October First
00   00

Dear Mr. Donaldson

The report of our organization for the last fiscal year is a most gratifying one

The Board of Trustees has every reason to be proud of the management that you have brought to bear upon the enterprise, and as a member of that body I thank you most heartily for all that you have done

At our next stated meeting I shall make it a point to move you a vote of thanks, and to recommend your permanent appointment to the position you now hold temporarily

Cordially yours

GRAHAM MASON
Second Vice President
Briarcliff Springs, Inc.

Mr. Jay Donaldson
231 Linden Avenue
New Harmony, Kansas

GM/CF

Invitations of this kind belong primarily to the category of official letters:

The Curtis Club
Gray College
Chicago

May Twelfth
0000

Dear Senator Tellsen

Your record in Congress during the past winter has made such a tremendous impression the country over that I fear you have demands upon your time that justify your declining invitations from comparatively unimportant organizations

Yet the Curtis Club of Gray College is made up of young men and women who are about to enter upon public careers, and there are probably few organizations, therefore, that could be more profitably addressed by you as far as the future of Chicago and of the United States is concerned

Will you please come to us on Wednesday evening, May nineteenth, when you will be in Chicago on your way to Washington? The Mayor has promised to be present, as has also the President of the College. We want them to meet you and you to meet them. Chiefly, we want you to talk to us if you will on the significance of the special session in relation to the war feeling in the country

The enclosed telegram, completely made out except for your name at the end, must be sent collect, of course. We are hoping that you will add your name to this message and send it straight back to us

Respectfully yours

BLAINE WORTHINGTON
President, Curtis Club
Gray College

Senator Jay Tellsen
181 Pearl Street
Minneapolis, Minn.

BW...REF

IV   Letters of claim and adjustment

When letters of claim were called letters of complaint they not infrequently contained bitterness and defamation. When letters of adjustment were called "grouchgrams" they were similarly epistles of unpleasantness, to say the least. But human beings have learned—all too slowly perhaps—that good manners are as contagious as bad manners, and so letters of claim and adjustment are today written in agreeable and constructive tone and business transactions are accordingly speeded and facilitated.

There are so many things that may lead to dissatisfaction in the field of merchandising alone that it is impossible to cover all of them here. Orders may be wrongly or incompletely filled as result of misunderstanding. Deliveries may be delayed or goods may be damaged or not as advertised. Misunderstandings may arise in regard to charges and bills and exchanges, or employee discourtesy. Claims should always be specific about any of these or other causes. And adjustments should dovetail exactly with the specific claims made. This means for one thing that the writers of claim and adjustment letters should be at pains to note reference data and make use of them in any claim-adjustment correspondence that requires several letters on each side, as is often the case.

This is a considerate and courteous claim:

And this adjustment brings courtesy and consideration to match:

The furniture that I bought of you on May twelfth was delivered in satisfactory condition with the exception of a single piece—the gate-leg table

This has a deep scratch on the top, and the finish on one leaf is badly rubbed. Will you kindly call for it and have it made right, or deliver another one in its stead?

I shall be very much obliged to you

We are very sorry indeed to learn that your gate-leg table was damaged in wrapping and delivery

Our men will call for it tomorrow and will at the same time leave a duplicate which, we hope, will be satisfactory

Even tho we allow no piece of furniture to leave our shipping department without thoro inspection, an occasional piece that is not perfect will slip thru. It is unfortunate that you had to be inconvenienced by the exceptional case, and we hope you will pardon us.

There is usually one claim department in a business house to look after all claims that come in; hence, Madam is not wrong in making two different claims in the same letter:

Friday last I bought at your store five yards of georgette crepe. This is Tuesday and the goods have not yet been delivered. The delay has caused me great inconvenience

If this were the first time that you had been careless in sending out goods, I should feel less impatient. But three times within the last four weeks I have been similarly annoyed

On April second I returned my bill to you for correction, goods sent back to you not having been credited to my account. On April fifteenth you submitted the bill to me again in its original form, bearing the notation *Please remit*

I am sorry to ask for two corrections in the same letter, but I feel that I have been so unlucky recently in my dealings with you that a little return of bad luck is deserved by you just in the cause of discipline!

And her justifiable annoyance is kindly and considerately met:

You certainly have every reason to be annoyed with our delays in deliveries and our errors in monthly statements. We are entirely at fault, and we shall make it our special business to see that such annoyances do not occur further

The georgette crepe was by mistake sent to Mrs. *James* Graves and taken in by her maid in her absence. She returned it to us this morning with a note saying she had ordered no such material

The error in the bill is quite inexcusable. Please accept our apologies for the annoyance. The corrected bill will be sent you June first

We appreciate your custom, Mrs. Graves, and thank you for calling our attention to these errors. They shall not be repeated!

A fair and frank but uncompromising way of putting an adjustment is always the best procedure:

Thank you for your check for $55.32

You probably intended this to cancel our July first statement

In doing this, however, you have included an express charge of $1.66. Before we can give you credit for this we must have the original receipt or a copy of it

Then you have deducted $2.92 cash discount, although the discount period has already expired

In fairness to our dealers who remit on the specified date, we cannot allow your deduction.

While we are very careful not to give you any advantage over other dealers in terms of payment, you may feel sure that we are just as careful to give them no advantage over you

So if you will send us a check for $2.92 and a copy of the express receipt we can balance your account to July first

This is a good exposition of the case to make the claimant understand the reasonableness of the stand taken:

We are returning your links, having soldered the ring which opened, and they should now withstand any ordinary pressure used on such an article

You have evidently forgotten that you insisted upon our using the swivel connection, which we put on at your request. In a pair of links of this character there must be some hook so that you can detach one side from the other. This may be a swivel, like the present one, or a figure-eight hook, which is sometimes used in an ordinary pair of links

∞

It would not be possible to use a straight bit connection, as the round button would not pass through an ordinary button-hole

We gave this order a great deal of attention and we consider the work is well done and in accordance with your orders. And the price is very reasonable and correct

A manufacturer anticipates, and thus probably forestalls, claim from a dealer later in the season:

According to our records we have a bulk order for your house, but we have not yet received your itemized follow-up

In view of the large volume of business that is promised us for the new season, we must ask you to let us have details regarding this order—sizes, colors, qualities, dates for deliveries—not later than May fifteenth. It will be to your advantage, of course, to send them in even before this date if you can, inasmuch as we fill all orders in rotation of receipt

You will understand that we cannot plan our manufacturing intelligently until all definite details are supplied us. As matters now stand with us, it will take us almost three months after orders are detailed to make shipments ready. Because of this pressure on our manufacturing plants we shall have to make it a rule to void all bulk orders for which we do not receive complete itemized follow-ups by the date above mentioned

Thank you very much for the general order you have sent us. We hope that you will find it possible to send us on the very date on which you receive this letter, the details that we are asking for. This cooperation with us will guarantee the continuance of the fine relationship that we have enjoyed with you for more than a dozen years

Many claim-and-adjustment situations call for detailed and astute study and analysis. It is by no means always easy to meet a complicated claim at every point and at the same time build constructive tone. The first thing for the adjuster to do is to discover if he possibly can the correct opening to his letter—the opening that will placate and disarm the claimant at the same time, and then lead to some definite plan of action that will be satisfactory to him. This calls for good judgment and keen strategy in many cases. The adjustment letter must not place blame upon somebody in the establishment against which claim is made, for this is unsportsmanlike as well as illogical. And the adjustment manager need not waste his time devising forms to meet such cases, for they are special and require personal treatment.

The employee assigned to answer the following letter was instructed to be firm but courteous in covering these points:

The policy of the firm with respect to return of goods is indicated on its invoice; namely, no goods may be returned or claims made later than five days after receipt of goods. The goods referred to in this correspondence were shipped by express on April twelfth. Mr. Stuart has apparently overlooked the condition stipulated in the invoice. Indicate willingness to make the exchange in view of the fact that he is a new customer and is apparently unaware of this return policy.

                          590 Franklin Avenue
                              C A M D E N
                              New Jersey

                                          May Tenth
                                          00   00

Colonial Fixture Company
1835 Euclid Avenue
Cleveland
Ohio

Gentlemen

Three pewter lightoliers (catalog number 335) included in your shipment to me last month were received in a damaged condition as result of faulty packing

I am returning these today by express and am expecting you to send me three others in exchange

I must insist upon prompt delivery as these fixtures are needed for an installation that I am under contract to have completed by May thirteenth

                              Very truly yours
                              JAMES R. STUART

    JRS/rv

You regret very much the inconvenience caused by damage and you are shipping today (date of your letter) by express three perfect lightoliers:

Three perfect lightoliers are sent to you immediately on receipt of your letter, by way of American Railway Express special service. You will receive these, we hope, in ample time to meet your contractual demands. If you do not, please let us know, and we shall reimburse you for any loss that you may sustain

That you should have suffered annoyance and inconvenience in your initial dealing with our company, is a cause of great embarrassment to us—the more so since we have been anticipating a continuous and increasing business relationship with you. Like the rest of the world we were anxious to make a good first impression! We hope we haven't failed too badly

This sort of thing happens only two or three times a year—a by no means bad showing when you consider that our merchandise is delicate, and that packing can never be guaranteed as infallible in cases where goods have to be shipped for great distances and transferred several times from one carrier to another. This is the first time, however, that we have ever had such bad luck with a new customer

Breakage or other damage in the shipment of our goods is adequately covered by transit insurance. But it is imperative that we enter claim always within a fortnight of the occurrence of such damage. It is for this reason that all customers are requested to notify us promptly in the event that merchandise is received in damaged condition. The marked regulation on the enclosed invoice form is called to your attention. You are not to be blamed at all for not seeing this. It should be printed in bold face or in red, and it is going to be in the next issue. But may we ask you, please, to keep it in mind in connection with further orders, which, we hope, will be large and frequent!

Our new de luxe catalog is mailed to you with this letter. Please observe that it is something decidedly more than a mere catalog. PART ONE, for instance, shows you the geographical distribution of our goods, and gives you the names of leading firms in all parts of the country that look to us for supplies. PART TWO is really a separate booklet in itself, containing detachable order and receipt forms, the receipts having a column for notes on the condition of goods as received. PART THREE explains, pictorially and in writing, our numerous styles of merchandise. PART FOUR details the special terms and facilities that we are able to offer dealers everywhere

May you find our catalog useful—and may we have better luck next time!

The president of the Federation of Women's Clubs of —— —— wrote an irate letter to a premium publishing concern because she felt she had been cheated in a transaction with it. She had understood that the magazine for which she subscribed was to come to her twice a week (tho the salesman had emphasized *biweekly*) and that the premium was to be much larger and more impressive. The company had her signature on the salesman's receipt form. She was an important and influential person, and the company was therefore desirous of keeping her name on its mailing lists. This is the adjustment reply that was sent to her:

The solution meets her more than halfway:

Certainly we shall cancel your subscription, if you really wish us to. We hope, however, that after you have read this letter you will feel differently about it. A stamped addressed envelop is enclosed. Please use this to send to us a revision of your decision to discontinue. But if you are still of the same opinion after reading this letter, then please return in it the complimentary copy of the *Handy Informational Dictionary* and we shall immediately return to you your two dollars and the receipt that you kindly signed for our representative

Here is an excerpt from the sticker that is pasted on the inside front cover of the dictionary. (The complete content of the sticker you will find used as a full-page advertisement on the outside back cover of *Live and Learn*.) Will you please read this excerpt very carefully?

Live and Learn will come to you biweekly, i.e., *every two weeks*. Our feeling is that the engaging quality of its content requires at least two weeks for thoro reading and enjoyment

The *Handy Informational Dictionary* contains almost twice as many terms as the regulation desk dictionary, yet it is only one-tenth as large. It is not only handy; it is, indeed, the most beautiful and decorative piece of printing and binding ever issued

You see now, do you not, Mrs. Ferguson, that our representative in no way took advantage of you. He gave you full value received, and MORE. You will realize this two years hence if you do not now. And just to show you how firmly we believe in *Live and Learn* and IN YOU, we are going to ask you to accept the remaining issues for the two-year period without any obligation whatever. To this highly desirable end we enclose a receipt covering your instalment payments for the next twenty-two months. We are especially happy to make this arrangement with you because we want you to be one of our thousands of satisfied readers, and because we shall value your opinion of the publication when, a little while later, we make a collection of testimonial copy from our subscribers for further promotional work

By the way the April issue of *Live and Learn* is going to contain on those pages devoted regularly to domestic science a section headed *Distinguished State Recipes,* with photos of those good housewives who have devised and tried them out. Won't you please send us one of your very own favorite dishes—one that is bound to become the kind that mother used to make? Accompany it with a small photograph of yourself, and it shall have assured place in this special-feature issue of the magazine

How about using the enclosed stamped addressed envelop for the recipe and the photo, Mrs. Ferguson, and allowing bygones to be bygones?

V Letters of credit

A person's Character, a person's Capital, and a person's Capacity are the three basics upon which that person is commonly judged in the business and industrial world. These are the three points that are generally taken into consideration when financial reports are made upon his standing and fitness. There are other points, of course, but they are minor by comparison. The person or the company asked to report on the credit of another should tell something of the length and the kind of relationship, the kind of business the subject is engaged in, his standing in the community and in his business field, his local credit rating, and whatever other special details (favorable or unfavorable) it may be possible and helpful to point out. These added to the three C's above mentioned, will be used by the one requesting the information in deciding whether full credit privileges shall be granted, whether they shall be refused, or whether certain limited or modified credit considerations shall be extended.

This brief outline summarizes the procedures in connection with opening and maintaining a credit account:

I Prospect makes four kinds of request
   A Initial request
   B Extension request
   C Renewal request
   D Discontinuance request

II References of at least three kinds are offered
   A Individual
   B Bank
   C Mercantile

III Responses vary as
   A Favorable
   B Unfavorable
   C Reserved
   D Neutral
   E Modified

IV The sales department may approach the prospect with
   A Invitation
   B Assumption
   C Revival

V The collection department keeps prospect's record by
   A Files
   B Charts

VI Questionnaires regarding the creditor may be renewed from time to time

VII Dun-Bradstreet ratings may be periodically consulted

VIII Other agencies specializing in credit may also be consulted

IX Credit personnel may call at creditor's home or office and at the homes or offices of references

There are many different styles of credit forms. They vary among houses, among different kinds of business. Here are a few of the more usual ones:

324   GET IT RIGHT!

This form is for the use of the personal credit interviewer:

REPORT
ON
APPLICATION FOR ACCOUNT

Date.......................19

Name ....

Address ....

....

Business Address ....

REFERS TO

REPORT

This is a form request for credit information, used by a large department store:

....

....

....

In making application for a charge account, we have been referred to you

by ....

of ....

....

We shall appreciate and consider confidential any information that you may furnish us concerning the financial responsibility of the applicant

Very truly yours,

PLEASE ANSWER HERE

Gentlemen:

This is a department shop form used to notify bookkeepers that an account has been opened:

...............................19

Name ....

Residence ....

Business Address ....

Limit $....................

This is a department shop form to be filled out by the collection department for the credit department:

Date.........................

Name ....

Address ....

House or order only

C.O.D.— Failed
       Too slow
       By request
       Dispute

Close Account—Owes, and slow
           Returns goods
           Small, and pays on account
           Death
           Revises when buys

Have understanding before charging
Stop and revise
Reopen account by request
Keep to terms

....

This is a department shop form to be filled out by the book-keepers, notifying that the account limit has been reached:

LIMIT NOTICE

Date.........................

Name ....

Address ....

Amount of Limit.............. ...Amount of Account.............

PURCHASES BY MONTH
MAKING UP PRESENT INDEBTEDNESS

Jan.	May	Sept. ....
Feb.	June	Oct. ....
March	July	Nov. ....
April	Aug.	Dec. ....

LAST PAYMENT

Date..Am't....................

This form is devised for special use in covering a temporary situation

This form carries the subject's name or number at the top of the body of the letter

We refer to your.............. ....establishing credit in favor of.................... covering a shipment of.......... .... A communication from the beneficiaries has now come to us. They will avail themselves of this particular credit. Your further instructions will be carried thru

We should like to have your expert opinion regarding the above subject Your estimate of his financial responsibility, his ability, his reputation, and his methods of borrowing heretofore, will be especially helpful to us. Anything additional that you may be able to give us will likewise be appreciated

It is customary for financial concerns, giving credit information regarding a person or a company, to protect themselves with some such printed form as the following. It is usually printed on the stationery of the credit department, either at the top or at the bottom of the page:

It is understood that the information contained in this letter is given in absolute confidence, and entirely without prejudice or the assumption of responsibility by us

or

All persons are informed that any statement on the part of this bank, or any of its officers, as to the responsibility or standing of any person, firm, or corporation, or as to the value of any securities, is a mere matter of opinion, and given as such, and solely as a matter of courtesy, and for which no responsibility, in any way, is to attach to this bank or any of its officers

There are important legal considerations to be taken into account in writing credit letters. Tact and restraint must be exercised in making unfavorable credit reports. False statement must not, of course, be made. But under the law there are certain qualified privileges that may be exercised confidentially and judiciously for the good of a common interest. Names of people or concerns are sometimes blanked in letters in which unfavorable reports are made. Such reserved or modified phraseology as "it is said," "it is rumored," "to the best of our knowledge," "the impression prevails," is sometimes used for the sake of security. No definite credit information should be given that is not accurate, that is not provable by facts. This applies to letters of recommendation, too, which are credit letters really. Too frequently these err on the side of "inflation," that is, they overstate a case without the substantiation of facts.

Credit revival or stimulation forms such as this are not to be recommended, however expensively devised they may be:

> We cordially invite you to use your charge account with ......
> and Company
>
> Although the account has been inactive it remains open and available for your convenience
>
> We shall welcome an opportunity to be of service to you

Credit revival is preferably attempted in courteous and effective language:

It has been a long time since we have had the pleasure of serving you. Your credit account has been inactive so long, indeed, that we fear something has happened to displease you? Won't you make use of the enclosed stamped addressed envelop to let us know whether our service has been unsatisfactory to you?

This is an especially good time of year to take advantage of our stock-clearing operations. In all of our fifty years of merchandising we can truthfully say that never before have we been able to dispose of such superior values at such ridiculously low prices

Our thought—our *hope*—is that you will feel disposed to resume relationship with us on the old-time credit arrangement. We feel sure that you will do so once you have looked over the enclosed folder. Credit customers of long standing—both active and inactive —have the privilege of four advance special days to avail themselves of these offerings before the general public is privileged to take advantage of them

The following model letters in credit information should be studied for the sake of tone, guardedness of content, and special nature of credit correspondence.

The report is indefinite and reserved, but more will probably follow:

We understand that the company to which you refer in your letter of May 27 is a limited one

It was organized in 1928, in succession to an old established firm

It has a declared capital of $25,000., and we are informed that it is regarded as safe for a fair credit. Its principal capacity of operation appears to be as agent for manufacturers

We regret that our report must be so brief, but we shall communicate with you further in case we are able to secure additional information

This credit information is now somewhat out of date, but immediate renewal is promised:

The company referred to in your letter of April eighteenth is engaged in the wholesale drug business

We are informed that this company has an excellent reputation, and is generally considered safe for regular business engagements

Our information, however, is a year old. We are therefore writing to our correspondents for an up-to-date report on the name. As soon as we receive a reply, we shall communicate with you further

Meager as the information is, the letter is nevertheless helpful, and it is well written:

The subject of your inquiry of September twelfth, Mr. Isaac J. Mordak, has maintained an account with this bank, as well as with its branch in Shanghai, China

We understand that he is a young agent of some means, and that he is active and reliable

Inasmuch as he has never requested any credit favors, we have never had occasion to investigate his affairs exhaustively

He represents the Shanghai Platinum Company and the Hankow Trading Corporation, and his visit to this country at present is occasioned by the interests of these two concerns

We hope this information will be of some value to you

Some valuable information is presented about a "third party," and in terms that are confidential and dignified:

M.B.O. and Co. is not a customer of ours, but from such investigations as we have been able to make we have found the business to be well-established and well-officered

Tho the company has occasionally required extra time for making payments, it is generally regarded as safe and satisfactory and has never been refused credit for its requirements

We are not in possession of any financial details, but the responsibility of the company is apparently unquestioned, and the risk is viewed as desirable by those whom we have consulted

This information is, of course, extended in strict confidence. We hope it serves your purposes

330 GET IT RIGHT!

The legal protective note comes at the beginning, but in this favorable case it is hardly required:

> *This letter is confidential and written without prejudice, as a matter of business courtesy, with the understanding that its source and content will not be divulged, and that no responsibility therefor is to attach to this company or any of its officers or agents. It contains information and expressions of opinion subject to change without notice, and, while obtained from sources deemed reliable, the accuracy of any statement herein made is not vouched for in any way*

> Regarding your inquiry about ...., Inc., of Boston, Mass.

> This company does not maintain a deposit account with us but we have had considerable relationship with it in connection with some of our custody accounts for which it acts as investment counsel

> We have gained the impression that the members of the firm are most satisfactory people with whom to deal, always alert and reliable, and invariably schooled in the nothing-is-too-much-trouble policies of good business

> The company has branch offices in Hartford, New York City, Philadelphia, Washington, Detroit, Chicago, and Los Angeles. It has also more than a dozen foreign affiliates

> When last we checked the company thru friends of ours in Boston, we were given nothing but the best possible reports in regard to its services and its customers. It is regarded as one of the most responsible and resourceful organizations in the investment advisory business

A letter pertaining to credit may be intimate and almost "gossipy" and yet it may be written with restraint and safety:

> The subject of your inquiry was formerly one of our depositors, but he closed his account with us the early part of this year. While he was a depositor here, we made him substantial advances on a collateral basis, and when these loans were finally liquidated, the balance was withdrawn. For a time he appeared to be more or less hampered by lack of working capital and was compelled to lean rather heavily upon his bankers

> We have naturally not been in close touch with his affairs since he left us, and are consequently not in a position to say what his invested capital amounts to at present. The latest figures we have are those of February 27, and these show a net worth of $195,000.

> The opinion is expressed in some quarters that ....
> is one of the real principals in the Lewiston concern; in others, it is said that he is connected in only a subordinate capacity

> We are sorry that we cannot give you a "close-up" on this situation. But you are right in identifying him with the Wakeman affair

Refusal of credit privilege is based upon sound and sufficient argument, and the cash arrangement is made attractive:

It has become necessary for us to limit new credit accounts to a certain number each year. The quota for this year has long since been filled and the credit books are accordingly closed. We are obliged to say this to many credit prospects every year, and it is never an easy thing to do. But we almost invariably find that these good people deal with us on a cash basis, and that this relationship with them proves to be so satisfactory that nothing whatever is lost and much is gained by both of us. We feel sure that such will be the case between you and us, and we are thus reconciled to saying *no* to your kind credit request. You will be reconciled, too, we prophesy, once you have availed yourself of our merchandising opportunities

Newcomers to this community are always welcome to the CHIC SHOP. And this means real hospitality with no strings attached. You, as a new resident in Heartville, are at liberty to come in and use our general guest rooms at any time—our writing room, our library, our auditorium (where interesting programs are usually in progress), our parlors, and the rest. In the exercise of this privilege you are to feel no obligation whatever to buy. But our hope is, of course, that the sight of our offerings, the touch of them, even the smell of them will very often tempt you to buy—and that you will as often yield to temptation!

And while our merchandise is always a temptation to our shop guests, our price policy is even a greater one. It is because our top-notch qualities are procurable for so little money that ninety per cent of our business is conducted strictly on a cash basis. This it is, in turn, that enables us to give our regular customers such extraordinary values. The majority of them have come to prefer the cash relationship with us

For many years now we have made it a point to invite new residents in Heartville to our private pre-showings, along with our long-standing credit customers. They are permitted to buy at these events on a cash basis. We enclose, for instance, two special permission tickets for your personal use—the white one will admit you to the spring-hats opening next Tuesday; the pink one, to the showing of our new lingerie importations on the following Tuesday. You will find both of these events (and others that will follow during the year) un-usually interesting socially as well as economically. Music, dancing, and refreshments are always incidental to these affairs. We shall look forward to seeing you in attendance.

The second part of the following problem is solved. This is the more difficult part of the two solutions called for. The first you should work out for yourself:

Mr. George P. Rodney, 249 Main Street, Pawtucket, Rhode Island, has sent in an initial order to the Imperial Pen Company, 315 South Street, Rochester, New York, requesting that the goods be sent on credit. He gives the name of Gregory and Wilder, 608 State Street, Ithaca, New

York, as reference. Mr. James Fuller, credit manager of the Imperial Pen Company, sends an inquiry to Gregory and Wilder concerning Mr. Rodney, with assurances, of course, that any information given will be treated confidentially. An unfavorable reply is received from Gregory and Wilder, based upon the following memoranda:

—Unreasonable demands for delivery of goods
—Unwarranted deductions on several remittances
—One check returned marked *insufficient funds*
—Account overdue

I   Write Mr. Fuller's letter to Gregory and Wilder under date of January twelfth
II Write Gregory and Wilder's reply under date of January fourteenth

A frank and fair solution:

Mr. George P. Rodney

or

Credit Prospect 10445 is now an unsatisfactory account. He has dealt with us for many years, and up to 1929 was in all respects a good and sometimes highly profitable credit customer. Since then, however, he has been increasingly difficult and troublesome, and we have within the past year been reluctantly obliged to tell him that we can no longer continue the credit privilege to him

Chief among our difficulties in dealing with him of late has been his insistence upon deliveries within dates that could not reasonably be met. When these were not made on the impossible dates he specified with his orders, he voluntarily and entirely without justification made deductions on his tardy remittances. On June fifteenth 1933, his check for $53.27 was returned to us marked *insufficient funds*. This amount represented about one-third of his actual indebtedness to us. Up to the present we have been trying to get this bill settled but without success, tho we have offered unusual (for us) concessions in order to close with him

This is by no means the sort of report that we like to make in reply to credit-information requests, and we are extremely sorry that it has to be so adverse in this particular case because the subject was for so many years one of our most highly respected and appreciated accounts. Our feeling is that he has been caught—we hope not irrecoverably—in the depressing financial and industrial events of the past three or four years

VI   Letters of collection

Personal attention is essential in making collections. Form letters should not be used for the purpose. Collection letters should be kept within the scope of the commercial letter (8 x 10½) page. Long letters of collection defeat their own purpose. It is not wise in a collection letter to suggest that you need the money or that you are to be pitied because you have not been paid. Such statements are superfluous. And it is a mistake to refer to indebtedness

as "bad debt." There is no such thing as a bad debt. The term
is sometimes wrongly used to refer to a debt of long standing. A
person who has owed money for a long time or for a number of
times should not be referred to as a delinquent. (See page 391.)

The tone of a collection letter should be constructive, up to the
point certainly where it is clear that the situation has to be turned
over to a lawyer or a collection agency. Sales and advertising
matter may well be enclosed in letters to let the debtor know that
you are still thinking of him as a customer rather than as a debtor.
Always enclose automatic reply devices, such as a stamped
addressed envelop, or a coin card, or an unusually devised postcard. It may be possible to indicate in the lower left-hand corner
of each letter some striking device to serve as serial number and
at the same time encourage payment. A picture of a batter on
the baseball field to whom the umpire is calling "Three times and
out!" has been successfully used. Short, live sentences and plain-
as-day diction should be used, without any attempt at smartness
or aggressiveness. Nowhere are hackneyed expressions more
deadly than in collection letters; nowhere are freshness (in the
right sense) and congeniality of tone more important.

The following serial steps are sometimes indicated in collection
work. The diagram that follows them is self-explanatory. No
such cut-and-dried schemes as these can be applied rigidly, of
course. But they may be effective when skilfully adapted to
special cases. All collection serialization must be adjusted even
among risks coming under general classifications. The terms commonly used to indicate degrees of risk—poor, fair, gilt-edge—are
themselves most variable. There are many different kinds of poor
risks, of fair risks, of gilt-edge risks. Naturally, then, collection
sequences must be varied to meet individuals. Fourteen appeals
or more may be used in one case; two or three in another. Intermittent reactions on the part of the debtor may cause intensive
application of one step or the omission of the remainder of a
sequence. But for general guidance in understanding the philosophy of collections, the student should ponder both the serialization below and the analytical chart following it.

First Letter

NOTIFY

Say how long the account has been standing
Say how many bills have been sent
Say that promptness on former occasions makes the present delay
    puzzling

Second Letter

REQUEST

Ask reason for non-payment to date
Ask whether delinquency is due to illness, change of address, absence, etc.
Suggest that bills may have been overlooked
Suggest that the terms of the account may have been misunderstood or misinterpreted
Request notice if any error has been made in presenting bill

Third Letter

APPEAL

Appeal to the sense of sportsmanship and fair play
Appeal to pride, prestige, regard for reputation, standing in the community
Invite comparison of your methods with debtor's own in similar situation—"Put yourself in our place"
Inquire what you shall say if you are called upon for credit information regarding the delinquent
Ask for suggestion for better or more agreeable course of procedure than the one you are taking

Fourth Letter

EXPLAIN

Explain the endless chain system of business debit and credit
Show that one broken link impairs the whole machine
Make the comparison specific and personal to the present case
Say that the prompt payment of bills keeps prices down for future orders
Point out the bad effect upon the debtor as well as upon you
Offer and explain inducements, such as
    —payment by instalment
    —acceptance of note with security
    —enclosure of coin card, or check filled out except for signature
    —extension of bill by thirty, sixty, or ninety days
    —suggestion that your agent call personally
Again ask for any criticism of the course you are taking
Insert note of finality thruout

Fifth Letter

INSIST

Recall past satisfactory transactions and insist that they be repeated
Suggest limited possibilities of future transactions
Require logical reasons for receiving goods gratis
Give warning that patience is exhausted
Interrogate as follows
    —"Have we been fair?"
    —"Do you insist upon trouble?"
    —"Have we not served you well in the past?"
    —"Can you afford to return the compliment?"
Reenforce note of finality

Sixth Letter
SUMMARIZE

Review your entire action
Cite number of letters sent, with dates
Give contents of letters, in brief
Give contents of replies, in brief, or say what debtor's attitude has been
Contrast the two groups of letters, or the two attitudes
Call attention to the fact that every possible consideration has been extended
Say finally that only one course remains open to you unless account is settled by certain date

Seventh Letter
DEMAND

Inform that the time has expired
Inform that the matter has been turned over to your attorney
Inform that all further communications must be addressed to him and that he is in possession of all the correspondence to date
Give the name and address of your attorney. (In case the matter is turned over to a collection agency, the letter may be revised accordingly)

The following collection serialization does not exactly tally with either of the foregoing exhibits. But the letters represent the average deviation from prescription that is necessary in meeting

VARYING DEGREES OF PRESSURE IN COLLECTIONS

	1	2	3	4	5	6	7
Poor Risk							
Fair Risk							
Gilt-Edge Risk							

Numbered Columns Represent Months — Formal Notices or Bills — Personal Letter Appeals — Threat Letters — Other Steps Taken to Collect

given cases. They are "taken from life," and they settled the account. The important thing is that they were written according to a plan or a system, completely thought out to meet a case before the letters were composed. Every house must have some system—it matters not which or what kind so long as it is logically followed thru and is adapted to specific situations.

1 Enclosed is a memorandum of your overdue account. An early settlement of this balance is requested

Re $75. still owing

2 The amount of seventy-five dollars ($75.) remains open on our books against your name

No adjustment is necessary, we think, in regard to this bill. Will you remit, therefore?

3 On February tenth we wrote you calling your attention to a bill of seventy-five dollars ($75.) that you owe us. We have not heard from you, to our surprize, and we must ask you now to send us your check at once, or, at least, to explain when we may expect settlement of this account

Customers who pay their bills promptly make it possible for us to sell our goods as reasonably as we do. We should like you to help this worthy merchandising cause along. You yourself have benefited by our low prices, and we hope that you may continue to do so

Won't you, please, in justice to us, pay us what you owe us in order that we may meet our obligations? Please use the enclosed stamped addressed envelop for mailing your check to us—now

4 Why have our letters of February tenth and March first brought no reply from you? You do not want us to feel that you are trying to evade payment, do you? You can at least "pay" us an explanation, can't you?

By meeting your bills promptly you keep your credit clear and reputable. To default in a small amount, such as your indebtedness to us is, means just as much against your credit standing as to default in a large amount. And if all our customers were to fail us in the small amounts they owe us, as you have thus far done, we should have to go out of business

Just sign the enclosed check *now*, won't you please? It is filled out for the correct amount. And here is a stamped addressed envelop—another one—for your use

5 We shall be extremely sorry to resort to forcible measures to collect the seventy-five dollars you owe us

Mild measures, however, appear to leave you cold. We feel that we have been very patient and courteous. Won't you agree?

But—unless your remittance is in our hands by March twentieth, we shall be obliged to take legal action for the collection of your account. Sorry!

6 Harrison Brothers have placed in our hands the enclosed statement of the amount they claim you are under contract to pay. They say that they have met their part of the agreement, but that in spite of repeated urging, you have failed thus far to meet your part

As intermediaries of many years' experience in adjusting differences among business men, we have found that frequently there is a misunderstanding of the terms of agreement; and in taking this case up for our clients we hope that you will trust us to act in your behalf also (without charge to you) and thus assist in bringing about a settlement on a basis of friendship and good-will

We believe it is their intention to treat you with the utmost fairness, for they are long and favorably known in the business world; and we infer that it is your intention to treat them honorably, for it seems hardly likely that, for so small an amount, any one would wish to forfeit his self-respect and the respect of those with whom he deals

Please write us fully and frankly. If there is any reason why the account should not or cannot now be paid, tell us why and your reason will have the utmost consideration

If, however, this account is correct and has not been paid simply because of oversight, we urge that you at once send to the publishers, or to us, the amount of the enclosed bill

7 Can it be possible that we were mistaken in supposing, as we did in our recent letter, that you would respond to an appeal to your sense of fairness? Must we believe that you are so indifferent to the requirements of customary business usage as to ignore the good offices of a third party, tendered (without charge to you) in the interest of mutual good-will?

We have given you the opportunity to make to our clients, Harrison Brothers, any explanation you desire with regard to your indebtedness, but you appear to have treated our offer with contempt. Perhaps you did not receive our previous letter? Very well—we take the precaution to call your attention again to your obligation

Our business is to collect or to adjust accounts. We believe, on the statement of our clients (which you have not denied), that you owe the money claimed and that you are able to pay your debts. However, before starting further proceedings we wish you to know that we are ready to consider all the facts with a view to a friendly settlement. But we must reach an adjustment quickly

Unless we hear from you within ten days, we shall be compelled to place this claim in the hands of the attorney representing us in your locality, with instructions to proceed to the collection of the amount due by every legitimate means at his command

The following four collection letters represent units from collection sequences. The single unit may make the collection and the sequence thus be stopped, or the entire system may have to be used:

A short and pointed note very often brings results:

Please send us the ten dollars that you owe us

We have written to you about this before, but in the rush and tumble of affairs you have probably overlooked our letters—and the bill

Please—this time—put the check into the enclosed envelop this very minute and get the thing off your mind—and ours

This attempt at collection places the responsibility fairly and squarely:

Is there anything wrong with the five dollars we have charged against your account?

If there is, please just write us frankly and say so

We're always glad to correct any errors. We're not perfect. We don't pretend to be

Our records tell us that you owe us five dollars. They may be wrong. They may not be. The point of the matter is that you have neither paid us nor answered our letters which we have tried to keep fair in argument and pleasant in tone. We think we have succeeded in this. What do you say?

Please use the enclosed addressed stamped envelop and write YES or NO on the card it contains

A claim-and-adjustment collection is often trying on the patience of both parties. There is a note of restraint in this letter:

You would not have made a claim, we know, for discount on your recent remittance unless you honestly felt that there was some good reason for doing so

In our letter of June ninth we tried to explain what our records show concerning your account with us. Now, won't you please go over your record of your dealings with us, Mr. Roberts, and write us whether we are really in error to the extent to which your note indicates?

If you still think that we are in error, then please write us what you wish us to do. We are open to any sort of compromise that seems to you to be reasonable and fair. We want to settle the account satisfactorily to you, so that we may still retain your custom and therefore your good-will. Nothing else matters so very much, does it?

There could not be a kindlier handling of a collection situation than this:

Our bookkeeper has called our attention tc the fact that your account has been overdrawn. We are sorry about this and we feel perfectly certain that there is some mistake somewhere

It is always our desire, as you must know by this time, to give depositors the very best service possible. But you will realize of course that we must, out of fairness to our other depositors, call your attention to this overdraft

Won't you please deposit seventy-five dollars ($75.) to your account immediately? This will cover everything, and reestablish our fine old relationship more firmly than ever

Please give us the privilege of greeting you personally when next you call at the bank

Here is a problem that calls for combination sales-collection solution. It must have promotional or house-organ quality together with collection appeal:

You are chairman of the employees' welfare committee of your firm Each employee pledged himself for five dollars one month ago for the annual outing. The outing has come and gone, and still many members have not paid the promised fee. Some have paid only one dollar "on account." A few, who paid "cash down" at the time the pledge was given, were unable to attend the outing, but they have loyally refused to accept any refund, preferring to let their contributions go toward employee relief insurance. The majority of the employees, however, paid the outing fee and attended the outing, at which a "pleasant time was had by all." Write *one strong* letter calculated to reach and impress all four classes of employees above defined, namely:

1 Those employees who have as yet paid nothing, but who nevertheless enjoyed the outing
2 Those employees who still owe your treasurer four dollars, but who nevertheless enjoyed the outing
3 Those employees who could not attend the outing, but who nevertheless paid you in advance and refused reimbursement
4 Those employees—the largest group of all—who paid in full and who enthusiastically attended the outing

Your letter should be so written as to collect from groups one and two. It should express grateful acknowledgment to groups three and four. It should make in general for greater *esprit de corps* among all classes of employees. And it should begin now to "sell" next year's outing to every employee in the firm.

And the "solution solves"!

THE GREATEST EVER YET! That's what they said about our last annual outing. And they were right—with one possible exception, of which more anon

What made it the greatest ever yet—until next year? Why, our fine old company spirit—and nothing else but! LENSCO is and has been for years the envy of other industrials the country over because of superior product, because of superior service, and primarily because of the single-thoughted, close-knitted body of happy working people unanimously bent upon BIGGER AND BETTER LENSCO as the days, months, and years go trippingly by

The vast majority of employees this year paid for the outing in advance and participated with gusto. A few—thirty-three to be exact—paid in advance, but owing to some last-moment occurrence were prevented from attendance. Your committee sent refund checks to these thirty-three disappointed people. And what do you think happened? Every check came back with a note to this effect: ADD THIS TO THE RELIEF INSURANCE FUND. ANYHOW I HAD MORE THAN FIVE DOLLARS' WORTH OF ANTICIPATION FUN OUT OF IT! To a man, they did this! Seemed like a conspiracy in altruism. Your committee was "too full for utterance." Good old LENSCO esprit de corps was never more eloquently manifested!

But now—that minor note: A few employees—twenty-one to be exact again—enjoyed the outing but have not yet paid the promised fee. A few others—just fourteen (you expect your committee to keep figures straight and names dark, don't you?)—paid the original deposit of one dollar but have not yet paid the other four dollars. They too enjoyed the party—we saw 'em doing it! Both of these groups are requested to regard this letter as a collection appeal. The recreation committee of LENSCO freely admits that it doesn't

know how to write collection letters—it has never had any experience
in this field. This is, indeed, the very first time it has ever had to
ask for overdue outing funds, and it finds the task awkward and
embarrassing. It would refuse to go in for expert collection serialization if it knew how, for it knows that these comparatively few—
thirty-five out of 781—will pay up now—right now! A bill envelop
is enclosed for the convenience of these signed and solvent thirty-
fivers

Next year it's to be a two-day and three-night cruise! We embark
Friday p.m. and disembark Monday a.m. And where, and when,
and how? It's all in the bag—yet! But you may feel justified in
saving your pennies now and looking forward, for it's going to strike
a new high in industrial recreational undertakings. And the fee will
be no more than it was this year, namely and to wit, five dollars.
Think of that!

VII Letters of sale

Sales letters are written to sell commodities, services, and ideas.
A letter that is written with the aim to expand an old business or
industry or to establish a new one, or to gain adherents to policies
and enterprises, by the sale of stocks perhaps, is sometimes called
a sales promotion or a promotional letter.

Sales literature may be either inductive or deductive, that is, it
may begin with details and build to a general fact, or it may start
with a big claim idea or a general statement or command or question and work thru to more and more detailed expression. The
first example below is deductive; the second, inductive.

Everybody needs a radio these days. You are no exception, are you?

Well, then, there is just one particular set for *you*—and for everybody else, as a matter of merit as well as of fact

The *Sonoclear* is guaranteed. It is used by all the important people
(see list of owners in the enclosed leaflet). AND it is equipped with
the new tone-scale adjustment that enables you to enjoy all the
radio pleasures and privileges without annoying your neighbors

It is, moreover, a decorative piece. It will not dominate your other
furniture, but it will add quietly and unaggressively to the furnish-
ing of any kind of room. It is made in all styles and periods, and
in all sizes

The prices are so nominal as to be trifling, and the service guaranties
are phenomenal

The price of the new *Sonoclear* is—almost nothing at all, comparatively speaking

As a piece of furniture it is beautiful. Made in all styles, sizes, and
periods, it fits nicely and unobtrusively into the furnishings of any
room without causing a riot

The *Sonoclear* is guaranteed, and our service vigilance guarantees our guaranty. It is used by famous people the world over (see enclosed leaflet). AND it is equipped with the new tone-scale adjustment that enables you to use it freely whenever you wish, without exposing your neighbors to its intrusion

There is just one particular set for *you*—and for everybody else, as a matter of merit as well as a matter of fact

And everybody needs a radio these days. You are no exception, are you?

Writing or speaking that appeals primarily to the emotions is sometimes called human-interest expression or human-interest copy. Other names for it are character copy and short-circuit appeal. Writing or speaking that appeals primarily to the reason and judgment and general intelligence is sometimes called reason-why or long-circuit copy (see page 73). Writing or speaking that appeals primarily to the five senses is sometimes called sense-appeal copy. These three kinds of copy do not by any means always appear as strictly isolated styles. Many appeals in sales literature make use of all three, and all three may be adapted to almost any sort of commodity. It is possible that women yield more easily to human-interest appeals; men to reason-why appeals; children to sense appeals. It is possible that luxuries are sold best thru human-interest appeals; that the idea of thrift is sold best thru reason-why appeals; that foodstuffs are sold best thru sense appeals. But these are unreliable generalities. Vitamins have brought reason-why into the sale of foods; thrift—savings banks, insurance, safety devices—may be sold quite as well thru human-interest as thru reason-why, especially since it has become fashionable; the luxury of travel may be presented thru the most logical of reasoning. One man's human-interest may be another man's reason-why, and vice versa.

This is human-interest appeal for class circulation:

"Beauty," said Henry Ward Beecher, "is God's trademark"

He was doing some advance advertising for our beauty products when he said this—or at least, so it would seem

Our face powders, soaps, hair tonics, dentifrices, lip rouge, nail preparations, and the rest, are all made from the purest natural products gathered from God's landscapes—field and highway and mountain and meadow. They make for beauty, if used according to our prescriptions. And in this day and age to be beautiful has become an obligation

Beauty gets you entrée. Beauty gets you distinction. Beauty gets you position and power. Who can gainsay any of these propositions?

AND—our products make you beautiful *with safety*. There is not an atom of poisoned chemicals in a single one of them. So use them and be safe as well as beautiful

This is reason-why appeal for class circulation:

There are men here in our own city—in your own neighborhood— who are getting their automobile insurance for twenty per cent less than you are probably paying for it, in a good sound company, mind you, with no sacrifice in service

You are one of very few in your city to whom we are sending this invitation to become a .... policyholder. We select our policyholders very carefully and try to insure only those whose good loss records will enable a saving cost to all

Since the company was organized nearly fifty years ago, we have returned to policyholders twenty cents on every dollar of premium paid us by them—a total of more than forty-one million dollars returned as dividends

Don't decide *now* about buying your insurance from us

Simply return the enclosed card and we shall tell you what the cost for your auto insurance will be and how much you may save by placing it with us. There is not the slightest obligation on your part. It simply gives us the chance to submit figures that you can check against the price you have been paying. If you are interested in our budget payment plan, we should like a notation to that effect

So don't file this away to think over. There is nothing to puzzle you because you don't have to send one penny or promise anything. Just fill out the card and mail it now

In this appeal, note how reason-why and human-interest are combined to make a skilful pleading:

Comfort was a strange and foreign word to Horace Blanford, until he owned a Millmobile. He takes pride in giving this testimony personally. "Riding on air," he says, "doesn't begin to do it justice. It's more like riding *thru* air to the music of some heavenly host! It gives me, after a hard day's work, the peace that passeth understanding, and the comfort that never was on sea or land

"And not the least of its comfortable merits is the fact that it leaves nothing for the chauffeur to do but just to sit close at the wheel and—*go*. There's no new part to be repaired every hour or so; no engine trouble every time you get out on a pleasure trip fifty miles from nowhere; no hallelujah chorus of blow-outs whenever we strike rough goings, and none of the thousand and one other motor miseries

"No, sir! It just goes and goes and goes. And we go with it. There hasn't been a single case of ill-health or ill-temper in the family since the Millmobile was brought into our midst. Even the chauffeur keeps well, and he used to be far from a well man whenever Saturday nights and Sundays came around! You've made us all happy"

Reason-why plus human-interest must make an irresistible combination in such a letter as this:

> You have written to me so many times—and I to you—that it seems to me we must be personal friends by this time, even tho we have never met
>
> And, now, I am going to ask you to write to me again to tell me just exactly why you haven't resumed your courses this year. You can be frank with me. I shall understand, no matter what you say. I understand you—I have learned to do so thru the fine papers you sent in last year and the year before. So be perfectly frank—by return post—and be assured of a sympathetic reader
>
> You know that you ought not to drop the work now, don't you? You're right in the middle of things, with an excellent record on our books and with great promise as a student. There must be a reason for your dropping the work—and a good one. But I want to know what it is—I feel that I have a right to know it. And I'm positive I can help

There are certain specific instincts and feelings upon which sales appeals may well be based in connection with given commodities and services and ideas. Insurance of all kinds, safety devices, burglar alarms, banks, for instance, may be sold thru appeals to the instinct of fear; correspondence courses, civic improvements, contests and competitions—anything that has to do with self-improvement, ambition, ultimate success and achievement—thru appeals to the fighting instinct; foods of all kinds thru appeals to the feeding instinct; charitable institutions, hospitals, sailors' funds, and the like, thru appeals to sympathy; slippers, house robes, comfortable chairs, beds, cushions, thru appeals to love of ease and luxury; soap, preserved foods, vacuum cleaners, moth killers, thru appeals to the sense of cleanliness; sports, recreational opportunities, journeys, hotels, thru appeals to the play sense.

This appeal to the fear instinct is calculated to provoke serious thought on the part of the prospect: *

> As you will see by the card, we have set aside for you one of our useful little memorandum books—gilt-edged, leather-bound, and very attractive
>
> We take this means of getting before you our new INCOME-FOR-LIFE PLAN
>
> Some day you hope to retire from active work. But WHEN? And HOW? Have you a plan? Or is it only a hope?
>
> Retirement is a comforting thought or it is a nightmare, depending upon what we make of our working years. *Which will it be for you?*

* This letter and the following are taken from *The Literature of Letters* by the same author, and are used by permission of the publishers, Lyons and Carnahan.

Most men are confident of accumulating a snug sum before they grow old. But, strangely enough, few men at sixty have anything to show for their life's work. Their saving is all done "tomorrow"

Our INCOME-FOR-LIFE PLAN will assure you absolute independence. Through scientific cooperation it does for you that which you could not do for yourself

You'll find it intensely interesting. JUST FILL THE ENCLOSED CARD. No obligation

This appeal to the fear instinct is logical and convincing:

Dread of the rainy day has been known to bring on paralysis and heart disease. Fear of evil days to come has been known to super-induce nervous breakdown and even death. Panicky and palpitating temperaments have been thrown entirely out of balance by the tragic contemplation of "over the hill"

And it is all so unnecessary! Our new savings-insurance policy takes all the terror and all the horror out of the latter half of life. What's more to the point, it takes all the risk out of the evil and ruinous days that are "always to come"

Just fill in the enclosed stamped return card, and you will receive, without the slightest obligation of any kind, definite information as to just how, through a little reasonable saving as the days go by, you may set your mind and heart at rest about future dangers that the gods may seem to be holding awesomely before you

There is never any such thing as being down and out—never, that is, where this savings-insurance policy is permitted to do its work. There is never anything but being *up and in* hereafter for you, if you avail yourself of the generous terms of this antidote to latter-day dangers

Pianissimo the poverty panic, and be an *up-and-inner*, not a down-and-outer

The fight instinct, especially at election time, can usually be depended upon to reveal itself if it is properly appealed to:

Are you an intelligent voter, or just an automatic one? Has your mental and character right to vote ever been challenged at the polls? Has any one ever yet dared to call you a ballot-box slacker? Is your political citizenship characterized by grit and stamina, or are you apathetic and cowardly in matters that pertain to good government?

Oh, don't trouble, please! We know the answers to all these questions, for we've taken the trouble to look *you* up. We know how you voted last time. We can prophesy how you will vote this time. We know that you'll feel compelled bright and early next Tuesday morning to go to the polls and cast a vote that tokens genuine forethought and concern about good government

That is to say, we are positively sure that your preelection reading and listening and thinking will obligate you to vote constructively for those men and women on the ticket who stand for the very best things by way of good government—fair taxation adjustments, good schools, efficient police, unequivocal Americanism, and all the rest

And this means that you will be obligated to vote destructively— to vote *out* of office all those pretenders to statesmanship and community spirit who have brought us to such sorry pass in these political fundamentals

This is not a partizan letter. If it were, we should say very different things indeed

It is a *good citizenship* letter—a fortissimo letter

THINK, MAN, THINK! AND THEN—VOTE!!

The food instinct is here linked with human-interest clearly and rationally, without sentiment:

The milk and cream of the Baby-Brand Conservatories have time and time again stood the hundred-per-cent qualification test of the Rockefeller Institute

This means that the Baby-Brand Conservatory products possess the highest possible caloric and vitamin food values for the members of your family, and especially for the kiddies

And this is all true because Baby-Brand milk and cream come from cows that are not only contented but happy and even enthusiastic about their work. They are fed on siloed clover and corn the year round. In summer they browse in meadows knee-deep in rich weedless grass, and drink at the brink of pearly gurgling mountain streams. In winter they are groomed mornings and evenings in white-tiled sanitary stalls, and are served by white-suited, white-gloved attendants

From the time our milk comes from the cow until it is delivered at your door, its temperature, as it passes through the various processes of cooling, setting, creaming, skimming, pasteurization, and so forth, is carefully guarded. You are aware, of course, that milk that is permitted at any step of its processing to remain too warm or too cool for any length of time, loses its life and becomes flat and stale to the taste. Temperature is not a whit less important to milk than it is to wine. Every department in our establishment is likewise standardized in the matter of cleanliness. From vat rooms to bottling closets all our employees are uniformed from top to toe in purest and cleanest white. Where the food of babes is concerned, surely cleanliness is godliness

The satisfying flavor; the creamy texture; the foody substance; the fresh, life-giving quality; the rich, tasty frothiness; the savory, saccharine smack of summer greenery; the mellow, wholesome, appetizing body tone—of the Baby-Brand Conservatory Products— all derive from the breeding and the treatment of the cows as well as from the handling of their milk, once they have given it over

Some poet or other has called our output

The nectar of the milkmaids—
The ambrosia of the dairy

Perhaps he was overenthusiastic. But we should like to know what YOU think

In order to impress any one and make him act as you wish him to, it is necessary, first, to catch his attention, then to develop this into interest or desire, then to build interest into belief or conviction, then to get him to resolve to do something, and then to induce him to act. Interest is attention grown up; belief is interest made decisive; resolution is belief in action.

These steps are sometimes set down as the developmental steps in sales talking and writing. They are by no means always usable in quite such cut-and-dried fashion as the following formula would seem to indicate. But they are good to know and to think about, especially if you have to treat with business men and with things for sale. After all, it is personality in selling as in everything else that counts for most in writing forceful sales letters. The person who can write strong, dignified, persuasive sales letters—letters that *talk* strongly, dignifiedly, and persuasively—is a good salesman, whether or not he bothers about patterned procedures.

ATTRACT ATTENTION
  by arousing curiosity
  by appealing to and featuring YOU
  by catch-word, phrase, or sentence
  by hint of news, trade or general
  by line, color, diagram, arrangement
  by avoiding all intimation of command, superiority, self-reference, excessive advertising tone

DEVELOP INTEREST
  by appealing to fundamental emotions and sentiments
  by referring to conditions and happenings of general interest
  by playing up certain types and classes of people
  by local and special human-interest appeals
  by stimulating an interrogative attitude in the prospect
  by featuring some unique or novel detail about the commodity

ESTABLISH BELIEF
  by complete knowledge of commodity
  by ability to tell all about commodity
  by connecting commodity with needs and desires of the prospect
  by description, exposition, argument, and good stories
  by illustration of all kinds
  by stressing superior points with superior argument
  by concretizing the sales situation
  by enclosures, such as charts, samples, catalogs

INSTIGATE RESOLUTION
  by showing that nothing is too much trouble
  by evincing no impatience or irritability
  by failure to recognize any antagonism on part of prospect
  by ready recognition of merits of competing commodity
  by respectful attention to and interest in anything prospect may say
  by honest, strictly-as-represented inducement, such as guaranties, cou-

pons, stamps, "last chance," "closing out," "money refunded if not satisfied," "special offer"

INDUCE ACTION

by unfailing optimism as to making sale
by autosuggestion thruout the sale
by summing up the principal selling points
by being ready with order blank and other sales-closing machinery
by requesting verification of name and address and other shipping data
by telling good wind-up story

· ·

FOLLOW-UP

by following up purchase and purchaser
by frequent inquiry as to how the purchase has pleased
by evincing readiness to adjust anything that is not satisfactory
by missing no opportunity to call attention, in a postscript perhaps, to new stock, improvement on old lines, changed policy, and other opportunities for further dealings

This is calculated to catch and hold attention:

Have you seen the New Burton Twelve?

We cannot send you a sample by mail, unfortunately. But if we could you'd be so delighted with it that you'd pay cash to keep it, and ignore our unusual payment plan

More anon. But will you please keep the enclosed photograph, and read two or three times the note on the back of it about trading in your old car for a New Burton Twelve

This car and this opportunity were made for YOU

The prospect's interest is invited here:

Here's another photograph—somebody's wife and kiddies who are enjoying the country of a Sunday afternoon in a New Burton Twelve

Did you read about its appearance at the automobile show last week, and about the sensation it made? There were feature stories in all the papers about the shiftless and starterless car-miracle

But unique as these things are, they are nevertheless nothing more than details in comparison with the tout ensemble—the body grace and poise, the artistic Greek proportions, the nose height and impressiveness from the front, and all the rest of it

Really, they would appeal to your wife and kiddies, wouldn't they?

This makes assurance doubly sure:

It's a great business car. It's a great pleasure car. It can be run by any member of the family—from the sixteen-year-old to the octogenarian grandma. As a matter of fact it runs itself

There is no gearshifting to bother and confuse. There is no starter—the accelerator starts and runs and regulates. The hydraulic brakes make safety a foregone conclusion. And the general comfort and adaptability and convenience of the inside of the New Burton Twelve are the ultimate diction in body novelty and elaborateness

Here's a diagram that may help to justify our enthusiasm and confirm our faith in this newest of motor vehicles. We hope it will make the workings of this marvelous car clear and simple to you. Note that the machine is really cut straight thru lengthwise and crosswise, so that you can see every possible bit of machinery at work or ready for work. Follow the arrows from the wheel, from the accelerator, and from the brakes, and you will see exactly what happens when you press any one of them

Whoever said that the simplest things are the most beautiful (or was it the other way around?) must have been thinking of the New Burton Twelve—in advance

Let it now be resolved that a new car is sold!

Your old car may be traded in at an unbelievable allowance. Your New Burton Twelve may be "taken away with you" on an unbelievable arrangement. Indeed, this whole business of introducing the New Burton into the family circle is incredibly easy and satisfactory —and delightful

Just drive up to our place tomorrow—any time. Bring the family along. Take all your togs out and come right in and settle yourselves and everything in one of the New Burtons standing on the sales floor. And then—glide out and in and thru and among—and the car is yours for keeps. There'll be no mention of money or anything, if you will just fill out and sign the enclosed questionnaire—a perfectly harmless permit-sheet authorizing you to drive this car for one day just to test it and get the feel of it

Note the service clause especially, and also the substitute privileges at the end of your first year with Burton. Please check up on your first day to see that everything that is claimed for this marvelous new car is true. Test it everywhere—up hill and down dale, thru traffic tangles and out on the straight and level—and then come in and tell us what you think of its performance

Then, if you want to, you may leave Burton with us and take your old car back! But you "won't wanna." . . .

Delay is but the darkness before the dawn of sale:

You found everything strictly as represented, did you not?

You liked the automatic shifting and the accelerator starter and the hydraulic brakes, did you not?

And you must admit that the riding values of the car surpass anything you have ever known in automobile history—what?

So now, here's the closing "machinery" for the deal—your old car plus so much (very little really)—and the New Burton Twelve left at your door with its multitudinous equipment and blessing

By the way, don't decide for yourself. Ask Madam. And whatever she says we'll accept as law!

The blue is the service guaranty; the white is the transference of insurance; and the pink is the graduated bill just awaiting our Thank You

The service follow-up must be vigilant and sincere:

Why haven't we heard from you?

You have been Burtoning, now, for exactly four weeks. You must have run four hundred miles and you should let us look the machine over carefully

No news is good news, we are sure. Yet, there are doubtless adjustments to be made, and it's just like a Burton never to let you know—never to cause a bit of trouble

Bring the car in as soon as possible and avail yourself of our expert servicing free of any charges whatever—according to contract

Sales letters did much some years ago to bring business expression into disrepute. Their tone was often so flippant or "smart-alec" and their form so loose or irresponsible that the term *commercial English* was scorned in many quarters. But persistent campaigning for better business letters and for better business writing and speaking in all fields has changed this. Today the best business houses turn out much writing that is even better than that to be found in many of the novels, biographies, poems, and books of general literature heralded in advertisements and reviewing columns.

The following model letters should be carefully studied, especially those that are solutions of set problems.

This letter attempts to revive a service. The marginal notes mark the steps in its organization:

BASIC DATA
{ It has just been brought to our attention that you have recently closed your account with this bank

YOUR REASONS
{ Have we made any mistake in handling your business, or failed in any way to render you the best possible service?

Please use the enclosed stamped, addressed envelop, won't you, to tell us just why you felt obliged to withdraw?

OUR SERVICE ATTITUDE
{ We feel a strong personal interest in every one of our customers as well as in every one who has ever been one of our customers. A renewal of your account will be more than welcome at any time, and we sincerely hope that in your case that renewal will be made in the very near future. If we can do anything to hasten it, please say *what* in your reply to this letter

Good-will is not only maintained but expanded by such a message as this:

> This letter has nothing to do with any financial transaction between you and us. It is an acknowledgment of a happy relationship that has existed and is accompanied with the hope that this relationship has been as pleasant to you as to us
>
> Everywhere about us we see signs of distrust and hear notes of discord. Our relations, however, have been more closely cemented this year. Perhaps it is because you and we have kept something of the Christmas spirit in our attitude toward each other thruout the year. Perhaps if more of this spirit were shown in meeting the large problems of the day, those problems would begin to disappear
>
> We wish you a Merry Christmas and a Happy New Year

This is a strong human-interest appeal that few women would wish to resist even if they could:

> When you are shopping in ———— hardly a day passes that you do not wish for some place to leave your bundles—some convenient corner that you can look upon as your personal headquarters
>
> You do not like the nervous haste of the interurban waiting-room or the lobby of a hotel. It is too hard there to find your friends or for them to find you in the crowds
>
> Your personal preference points to a central location where you can meet your friends or rest quietly and comfortably for a few minutes at odd times during the day
>
> We considered these things very carefully when we planned the arrangements of this new store. We want to make it convenient and "homey" for every woman who chooses to enter the store. It is but one of the many helpful services that we hope to make pleasing to every woman who shops in ————
>
> Many avail themselves of the conveniences of our rest room every day. They find the congenial surroundings restful, the refined atmosphere pleasant. Please accept this as an invitation to make our store your home when you are in ————
>
> The central location of The Ossry and Company Store makes it easy to find. [Here add distance and direction from interurban station; distance and direction from nearest well-known building or public point]
>
> You will receive a cordial welcome here. The helpful service and convenience will be our welcome to you. If you choose to look at merchandise in any department, you will receive courteous attention and considerate suggestions by salespeople who are thoroly acquainted with the goods they handle

This is sound reason-why appeal addressed to the "woman of the house":

> In New York City last year over two and a half million electric light, gas, and merchandising bills were paid by means of checks

This resulted in an incalculable saving of time and trouble for the women who pay the regular monthly bills

We fancy that Chicago women, too, would find this method of payment safe, economical, and convenient. And so we are opening several neighborhood agencies, the one nearest to you being at ———. This particular agency is open now, and if you care to make use of it, just stop in some day and ask for our Mr. Ogden

The charge for this service is only one half of one per cent on every one hundred dollars' worth of checks used. Almost trivial, isn't it?

The wholesaler writes a strong cooperative appeal to the dealer:

Forty per cent of the motorists in this country ride on Tampter Tires. Many of these wise people live right in your own town. That dealer who is prepared to service them is on the way to fame and fortune

You run a service station. You sell tires. And you have written to ask intelligent and promising questions about Tampters. We think your inquiry is important enough to justify our sending one of our men up to see you. He will be there on Thursday of this week. If this is not convenient for you, please wire us collect and we shall try to make a date that is more convenient for you

Incidentally he will bring with him a batch of letters from your community, all of them asking questions about these new tires and all of them revealing between the lines an interest that can soon be kindled into enthusiasm by your expert salesmanship

We enclose a telegraph blank properly executed for you to use in case you have to postpone our agent's visit. But we are hoping that you won't have to ask for a postponement

A change of policy is skilfully used for the enforcement of a genial sales talk:

We have counted you as a good friend and valued customer of our store during the many years that we sold exclusively for cash and during the few years when we carried a limited number of charge accounts

During the past few months, we have experienced a growing demand for cash savings instead of credit privileges, and we are therefore returning to an all-cash policy on May 28 of this year

It is our plan to conduct a series of private sales which will be limited by invitation to those who, like yourself, have previously been accorded charge-account privileges. With your permission we shall notify you of these events as they take place

We are hoping, of course, that this policy will be approved by you, and that you will find the added savings to be a welcome substitute for your former charge-account privilege

We write to you personally because, while this change of policy affects but a small number of our patrons, it happens to affect those whom we regard as our most valued customers

The bank sends out this promotional copy to a selected list and gets the deserved profitable returns:

We are extending an invitation to representative merchants and manufacturers thruout the United States to avail themselves of the numerous facilities we offer. Our reason for doing this is that we want to cooperate with them in increasing their present business, and to assist them in developing new business at home as well as abroad

In this connection we have considered the value of our service with reference to your particular business, and we believe that a relationship between .... and our institution will be mutually advantageous. Please bear in mind that this suggestion is not made with the idea of disturbing your present banking connections in .... but rather to supplement them for the purpose stated above

We feel that our facilities are such that you will find more than satisfaction in any connection you may wish to form with us. We shall consider it a privilege to serve you

Number three of the following problem is solved just below. You should try numbers one and two yourself:

The new Janus Fountain Pen is so constructed that it may be used for red ink and for black. The cylindrical ink holder is partitioned. By pressing a small button in the top, the side containing black ink begins to flow and the black pen is pressed down into place. Automatically the red flow is closed, and the red pen pulled up within the frame. There is a gage to adjust the flow in case red and black are needed in rapid alternation. And in this event both pens may be left down at the same level. Inasmuch as the pens are round, they operate as well on the one side as on the other. (1) Write a letter to stationers, selling this new idea in fountain-pen manufacture, and urging them to include it in their fall orders. (2) Write a letter to be sent to district sales managers, explaining to them that you have sent a letter to dealers, and telling them to follow up. (3) Write a letter to be sent to the homes of school children, selling the new pen to them. Assume that school is about to open for the fall term

And the first pin-money of the school year is spent in the twinkling of an eye!

You will be interested, we think, in the new Janus Fountain Pen, especially at this time of year when you are taking up your studies again

The filling cylinder of this pen is partitioned so that one side may carry black ink, let us say, and the other side red ink. Instantaneous alternation of flow may be made by means of a press-button at the top of the pen which not only releases the ink on one side or the other but also at the same time lowers the pen required for use at paper level and lifts the one not required. These pens, by the way, are round like the leads in a pencil, and are usable from any side and from any angle

All Janus pens are made up in hexagonal form to prevent rolling, and in a number of colors and artistic designs. Prices range from two dollars all the way up to fifty dollars. Instalment arrangements may be made with your cooperative shop. And you may even trade in your old pens at a substantial allowance, as we are able to re-process them and thus convert them into the double-flow Janus style

You will see at once the advantage of this new school utensil. You do not have to carry two pens. You do not have to switch from one pen to another clumsily when you wish to write two-color copy as you increasingly do. In your own private account book—and all students are keeping such books in these difficult days—you may automatically differentiate credits and debits by color and see at a glance where and how you stand! Incidentally, Janus sales to finan-cial institutions have been phenomenal, and for obvious reasons

Most of our prospects, indeed, become customers once they have been privileged to write a single sentence with Janus. The enclosed folder, with addressed stamped envelop attached, tells you how you may secure one of these pens on trial with subsequent easy payments. This very letter, by the way, is a photostat of a letter that was written with a Janus straightaway in five minutes with all the red trimmings

This problem calls for unusual treatment. It suggests a new idea in cigaret merchandising:

There may be room for another cigaret on the market. We shall say so, at any rate. It is a blend of Old World and New World tobacco. Not only is it "smooth" and "satisfying" and "oriental" and "Virginia," all in one, but it is also a "savory smoke." It is made in a variety of sizes, and with straw, cork, plain, gold, and Russian tips. There is, in addition, a special rose-leaf tip made up in special boxes for clubs, colleges, and certain hotels. As this rose-leaf tip is perishable in about twenty-four hours, only such quantity is prepared for daily consump-tion as advance orders justify. Let us assume that you are trying to get haberdashers to take up this new cigaret as a side line. Write a strong introductory letter to the highest-class haberdashers in a city, setting forth the special features of the new cigaret, offering to furnish an especially attractive display case for introductory purposes, and making especially liberal terms. The old spelling—*cigarette*—probably would be desirable in such a letter.

The solution sells both a new policy and a new commodity:

If a druggist may sell everything from fly-swatters to libraries, there would appear to be no logical reason why a haberdasher may not sell cigarettes—especially smart, unique, exclusive cigarettes

You will be interested, we think—*and hope*—in this idea. Certainly cigarettes are today well-nigh a component part of the costuming of the well-dressed man and woman. Shirts and blouses, pajamas and suitings, top coats and lounge coats are always provided with ciga-rette pockets. It would seem the natural thing, therefore, for the high-class haberdasher to make the innovation of a subsidiary offer-ing to his customers by way of a distinctive cigarette with accessories

Science has achieved a tasty, foody blend of Turkish and Virginia tobaccos that is likely to appetize the smoking world to the point of prejudice. We are privileged to be the sole distributors of this new *TURKVIR* brand, and we are extremely eager to develop the new haberdashery field of cigarette retailing because it seems to us to be a logical—if not the most logical—source of supply to the individual customer

TURKVIRS are made up in all seasonal and fabric tints and shades and with every sort of tip. In particular there is a new experi‑ mental roseleaf tip which perishes, it is true, in twenty-four hours, but which during the twenty-four hours is rapidly becoming *the* cigarette of the élite to whom you preeminently cater. In keeping, there are, of course, packaging in a variety of modernistic tones and display stands and cabinets to harmonize with salesroom furnishings. But more of these later

As you well know, a cigarette is frequently the agent par excellence of sales induction. It very often puts a customer at ease, relieves of hurry and reticence, and establishes natural and congenial relation‑ ship at once. Moreover, our grandmothers used to say, didn't they? that tobacco smoke is sanitary—keeps moths away and eats dust. Certain of our brands, however, are slightly scented for those of your customers who prefer delicate aromas to *naturelle*

You have been selected by us as the sole dealer in your community for this new cigarette and for this new departure in tobacco mer‑ chandising. You are our choice because our investigators have found that you represent top-notch quality in goods, in custom, and in policy. It is our sincere hope that you will fall in with the idea, and permit us to send our representative to see you regarding instal‑ lation and terms. We enclose a sample package containing various styles of TURKVIRS, together with a stamped addressed envelop which we hope you will be prompted to use after you have taken your first puff

The problem requires dignified and persuasive promotional appeal —and gets it:

With the completion of a new wing to the building of an express com‑ pany, the opening of three branch offices in different parts of the city, and the enlargement of service to include travel, storage, banking, and insurance, the company is ready, let us say, to make a campaign for increased business. Write a letter making a general appeal to indi‑ viduals—men and women—setting forth the special opportunities, both new and old, that the express company is able to offer. Aim to make your copy strong and convincing in appeal without being aggressive or directly competitive.

New accounts will probably "form a line" in the morning:

Your investments require banking facilities that are progressive as well as reliable

For thirty-five years the Brewster National Express Company has had the honor of rendering such service to men and women who have found in the bank the encouraging human element necessary for the creation and maintenance of confidence

The uniformly satisfactory history of this company for the past generation testifies to the reliable payment of interest and of the principal on maturity. This quick turnover increases the volume of business and reacts in the form of increased facilities for our customers

Credit experts make searching investigations of all securities and investments, so that we can offer you a service protected by every safeguard. The knowledge thus gathered is at the disposal of every one whom the company serves. A personal visit, a letter of inquiry, or even a telephone call will bring you the counsel of the department concerned

You will find our services even more reliably available in the future, for not only have we completed a new wing to our building, but we have opened three new branches in different parts of the city. This will bring us in closer touch with thousands of busy men and women who have been waiting for a conservatively progressive house like ours

The enclosed card bears a brief statement of the present financial condition of the Brewster National Express Company and indicates the location of the new branches

If we are strangers to you, talk with any of our customers, or come in and consult our officials. Let us apply our experience to your personal needs

Information is supplied from the sales or promotional angle in answer to the inquiry.

Mr. George J. Stebbins, 18 Herkimer Street, Scranton, Pa., writes the following letter to your bank. Answer Mr. Stebbins' letter in such a way as not merely to satisfy his queries, but also to build agreeable and possibly permanent relationship. Assume that Mr. Stebbins' business connections are known to your house, and that his business will be highly desirable.

Owing to business expansion, it has become necessary for us to have extended banking facilities in New York City. Will you please let us know, therefore,

(1) Whether you pay interest on daily balance, and, if so, at what rate?

(2) Whether you have branches or close agency connections in Colombo, Hongkong, and Hankow?

(3) Whether you are prepared on occasion to make short-time loans of forty or fifty thousand dollars, security and other guaranties being satisfactorily furnished?

We shall be very much obliged for this courtesy

The answer may be in this manner:

Thank you for referring your questions of March first to us. We are glad to be able to furnish you with this information

The rates of interest that we allow on daily balances are as follows:

2% on balances from $ 1,000. to $ 10,000.
2½% on balances from   10,000. to   50,000.
3% on balances from   50,000. to   250,000.
3½% on balances over   250,000.

Itemized statements showing the transactions that have occurred and the balance on hand are sent to depositors every three months, or more frequently, if they wish

Thru our affiliations with the Asia Banking Corporation, we negotiate direct banking transactions at its Hongkong and Hankow branches. In Colombo we are served by the Mercantile Bank of India, Ltd. Information concerning these banks and concerning other foreign service is at your disposal thru our international trade department, which we maintain for the use of our customers and other friends

Accommodation in the matter of loans is a part of our regular service. We are ordinarily prepared to make secured loans for any amount up to $250,000. for a period not exceeding thirty days. But in the case of old and established firms such as yours, we customarily extend this time to suit conditions

The steady growth of your foreign trade may give you a bit of interest in the booklet that we have sent you. It will supply specific information regarding the prospects for the sale of American goods in foreign markets

Mr. Walter Chadwick, our Philadelphia representative, will be in Wilkes-Barre on Thursday. We have informed him of your inquiry. In case you would like to have a talk with him, please feel at liberty to telephone him—380 Market—between ten and twelve, and he will call at your convenience. If we can be of further service to you, please let us know

This problem makes opportunity, and the promotional copy it evokes is to the point:

A letter has come to your bank from the Central Bank of Sydney, New South Wales, Australia. The salutation is, "Honoured Sirs"; and the complimentary closing is, "I have the distinguished honour, sirs, to be your humble and obedient servant." The letter is signed by William Jarvis Brown, Cashier

The letter asks what facilities your bank has and what terms it makes for the handling of foreign accounts and the investigation of American firms dealing in Australia. The writer explains that, owing to the rapid increase in its American business, it is becoming imperative that his bank establish an affiliate in New York City, and it requests a statement from your bank as to its attitude about this. The Central Bank is, in turn, ready to act as representative for your bank in Australia, provided you are not already represented there. The various London and other European connections of the Central Bank are given in the letter, as a gratuitous evidence of good faith

Answer the letter. Your reply should be favorable to an arrangement with the Central Bank for the transaction of its business in America and the transaction of your business in Australia. You should incorporate some little sales copy in your reply; give London and, perhaps, other references; and most of all aim to keep the general tone and makeup of your letter polite, formal, and dignified.

This solves the problem and makes for continued amity between nations:

Your letter of March 31 is as timely as it is welcome; *timely*, because we are just now finding it necessary to establish Australian banking connections in order to facilitate our rapidly increasing business in Australia; and *welcome* especially, because we already have many favorable reports on the Central Bank of Sydney and also because the London banking firms that you mention are correspondents of ours

To leave no doubt, therefore, that we are entirely willing to fall in with your complimentary suggestion, we are instructing the Provincial and Union Bank of London (one of our mutual references) to remit to you £50,000. and we are notifying our various Australian connections that this relationship has been established. We understand from your letter that your rate is three per cent, and that you cable statements bimonthly

On the sheet attached to this letter you will find three particular annotations that have been arranged for convenience of reference. The first explains to you graphically our organization, our capitalization, and our interest and other rates. The second lists our foreign connections in all countries of the world, including references, three of which you will hear from regarding us. The third elaborates the special services we are in a position to render you as American affiliate

One of these services, we think, may need some further explanation, namely, the one listed under Credit Industrial Files. We carry in these files, subject to constant revision and reassortment, exhaustive data regarding all the principal American industrial firms engaged in foreign trade. As far as we know we are the only American banking house that specializes in this particular kind of service. We have a corps of one hundred workers constantly employed on these files, and an equal number in the field making investigations and analyses. This service alone, we think you will agree, should enable us to take a unique position in your wide and deservedly-expanding American business. It is unqualifiedly yours to command

In a few days you will receive several of our publications. These will henceforth, of course, come to you periodically as issued. Certain of these, as you will note, are dated forward in order to meet discrepancies in calendar time necessitated by the distance among our various connections

Thank you very much indeed for initiating the movement that will assuredly result, not merely in more convenient banking facilities for you and for us, but in deeper understanding and broader sympathy between your great country and our own

CHAPTER TEN

LIBRARY SELF-SERVICE

Every intelligent person should be able to answer such questions as the following in order that he may use the library to the best advantage for general as well as for special purposes. If he cannot do so, and easily, he will be obliged to waste much of his own and other people's time, and, what is worse, he will be nothing more than a "browser" as far as his visits to the library are concerned. By a study of these questions and others like them, and by familiarizing himself with the various kinds of cards used by libraries for cataloging books, he will equip himself to use large collections of books confidently and expertly—to command them to serve him rather than be overwhelmed and confused by them.

—Would the unabridged dictionary or the *New International Encyclopedia* give you the better material for a theme on Florence Nightingale?

—Could you find in *Who's Who* a brief biography of William Shakespeare?

—If there were no book on Mussolini in your high-school library catalog, could you find material about him in current magazines? What index would you use to locate this material quickly?

—Under what word or words would you look in Bartlett's *Familiar Quotations* for the quotation, "The quality of mercy is not strained"?

—If you wanted to find the name of the novelist who won the Pulitzer prize for 1931 would you consult the *World Almanac* or *Who's Who in America?*

—Either *The Reader's Handbook* or *The Century Cyclopedia of Names* will give you a short account of the character Peggotty from *David Copperfield*. Would *Who's Who* (English edition) also give you this information?

—What do the Dewey Decimal Classification numbers, as used on the backs of the books and on the catalog cards, really stand for?

—If you knew that "I wandered lonely as a cloud" was the first line of a poem, in which of the following books would you be able to find the complete poem: Hoyt's *New Cyclopedia of Practical Quotations* or Stevenson's *Home Book of Verse?* Under what words would you look in the index?

The fundamentals of library cataloging according to the Dewey Decimal Classification, used generally in libraries thruout the country, are given in brief below—in the reformed spelling of the original.*

I The ten main classes, with explanation

By this system, all knowledge is divided into 9 main classes, numbered 1 to 9, as follows: 1 Filosofy, 2 Religion, 3 Social sciences, 4 Filology, 5 Pure science, 6 Useful arts, 7 Fine arts, 8 Literature, 9 History. General works, dealing with several classes, such as general cyclopedias and periodicals, are markt 0 (naught, meaning *not* limited) and form a 10th class. Each class is divided into 9 parts or divisions, with 0 indicating general works on that subject, and each division is divided into 9 sections with 0 again used for general material. Each section may be similarly divided into subsections, and this principle of division into 10 groups, which gives to the system the name "Decimal," may be carried on indefinitely to any extent needed, as a collection grows and requires, for convenient consultation, more and more detail division by topic; e.g. with a small amount of economic material 331 might be sufficient for all works on Labor and capital (class 3 Social sciences, division 3 Economics, section 1 Labor and capital) but as the material accumulates it becomes desirable to have it distributed under more detail headings, as by adding 7, with result 331.7 Classes of workers; by further adding 6, with result 331.76 Workers in special industries; 8, with result 331.768 Workers in mechanic trades; 7, with result 331.7687 Clothing makers; 4, with result 331.76874 Economic condition of hat makers. In a small collection, a short number may, as shown above, be used at first and, if growth of collection makes it desirable, this number may be extended figure by figure, as seems best, without altering work already done, while in larger collections fuller numbers, with more specific meanings, may be preferd from the first.

To cite a 2d illustration, class 3 Social sciences, division 7 Education, section 2 Elementary = 372 Elementary education. This number may be further extended, e.g. 372.2 Kindergartens, 372.21 Kindergarten methods, 372.215 Songs and games in kindergarten work. As a 3d illustration: class 6 Useful arts, division 7 Manufactures, section 7 Textiles = 677 Textile manufactures. This

* Reprinted from *Decimal Classification and Relativ Index* by Melvil Dewey, by permission of the copyright holder, Lake Placid Club Education Foundation, Lake Placid Club, N. Y.

may be extended as follows: 677.2 Cotton and similar fibers, 677.21 True cotton, 677.216 Cotton industry products, 677.2164 Products of weaving, 677.21648 Printed cottons.

II The one hundred divisions

SECOND SUMMARY

DIVISIONS

000	**General works Prolegomena**		**400**	**Filology**
010	Bibliografy		410	Comparativ
020	Library economy		420	English
030	General cyclopedias		430	German
040	General collected essays		440	French
050	General periodicals		450	Italian
060	General societies Museums		460	Spanish
070	Journalism Newspapers		470	Latin
080	Polygrafy Special libraries		480	Greek
090	Book rarities		490	Other languages
100	**Filosofy**		**500**	**Pure science**
110	Metaphysics		510	Mathematics
120	Special metaphysical topics		520	Astronomy
130	Mind and body		530	Physics
140	Filosofic systems		540	Chemistry
150	Psychology		550	Geology
160	Logic Dialectics		560	Paleontology
170	Ethics		570	Biology Ethnology
180	Ancient filosofers		580	Botany
190	Modern filosofers		590	Zoology
200	**Religion**		**600**	**Useful arts**
210	Natural theology		610	Medicin
220	Bible		620	Engineering
230	Dogmatics Theology		630	Agriculture
240	Devotional Practical		640	Domestic economy
250	Homiletic Pastoral		650	Communication Business
260	Church Institutions Work		660	Chemic technology
270	General hist. of the church		670	Manufactures
280	Christian churches and sects		680	Mechanic trades
290	Nonchristian religions		690	Bilding
300	**Social sciences Sociology**		**700**	**Fine arts**
310	Statistics		710	Landscape gardening
320	Political science		720	Architecture
330	Economics Political econ.		730	Sculpture
340	Law		740	Drawing Decoration Design
350	Administration		750	Painting
360	Associations Institutions		760	Engraving
370	Education		770	Fotografy
380	Commerce Communication		780	Music
390	Customs Folklore		790	Amusements

DIVISIONS—*Continued*

Literature		History	
000 Literature		900 History	
810	American	910	Geografy and travels
820	English	920	Biografy
830	German	930	Ancient history
840	French	940	Europe
850	Italian	950	Asia
860	Spanish	960	Africa
870	Latin	970	North America
880	Greek	980	South America
890	Other languages	990	Oceania and polar regions

(950–980 marked "Modern")

A   A general sub-division of biografy

BIOGRAFY

920   Biografy

Including autobiografy, diaries, personal narrativs, eulogies, biografic diction-aries, etc. All biografy is here groupt together under the main classes, and sub-divided in the same way with the variations indicated below for Filosofy, The-ology, and Sociology, i. e. the biografy of science is divided like science itself, see 500–599. Lives of chemists ar 925.4; of botanists, 925.8; of sailors, 926.56; of actors, 927.92; of the inventor of hard rubber, 926.78, etc. The rule is to giv each life the number of the subject it illustrates most, or to the student of which it wil be most useful

Lives which wil not go under any hed without 'forcing' ar best put in a single alfabet under the 3 figures 920 for men and under 920.7 for women

Another plan is to scatter biografy with the other books, using 920–928 only for general works, cross references, etc. This simply omits the first 2 figures 92, and the life of a botanist is 580 instead of 925.8, and goes with botanic books. This plan may be carried out more specificly where 9 has been used for the his-tory of a subject, by adding for biografy the figure 2, making the life of a botanist 580.92

A 3d plan, specially adapted to public libraries, is to arrange all individual biografies in a single alfabet under 92 (better than B, which is often used but which has no logical position in a numeric arrangement). Group 92 may be shelvd before 920, under which all collectiv biografies may be arranged in a single alfabet, but it is generally better to distribute these under more specific numbers 921–928 printed below

GENERAL AND COLLECTIV BY LOCALITIES

Including only collected lives too general to go under any subject heding

.01	Universal
.02	Partial collections not limited to any special country or subject
.03	Ancient
.04	Of Europe
.05	" Asia
.06	" Africa
.07	" North America
.08	" South America
.09	" Oceania

B Elaboration of a divisional unit

(*English Drama, under Literature*)

From 822   ENGLISH DRAMA

822.2	Pre-Elizabethan	1400–1558
.21	Heywood, John	1506–65
.22	Udall, Nicholas	1505–64
.23	Bale, John	1495–1563
.3	**Elizabethan**	**1558–1625**
.31	Greene, Robert	1561–92
.32	Marlowe, Christopher	1564–93
.33	Shakspere, William	1564–1616
.34	Jonson, Ben	1574–1637
.35	Beaumont, Francis	1584–1616
	and Fletcher, John	1579–1625
.36	Webster, John	1582–1652
.37	Massinger, Philip	1584–1640
.38	Ford, John	1586–1639
.39	Minor writers	
.4	**Post-Elizabethan**	**1625–1702**
.41	Davenant, Sir William	1605–68
.42	Etherege, Sir George	1637–88
.43	Crowne, John	1644–99
.44	Wycherly, William	1640–1715
.45	Otway, Thomas	1651–85
.46	Congreve, William	1670–1729
.47	Vanbrugh, Sir John	1666–1726
.48	Farquhar, George	1678–1707
.49	Minor writers	
.5	**Queen Anne** Early 18th century	**1702–45**
.51	Dennis, John	1657–1734
.52	Southerne, Thomas	1660–1746
.53	Centlivre, Mrs Susannah (Freeman)	1668–1723
.54	Cibber, Colley	1671–1757
.55	Rowe, Nicholas	1674–1718
.56	Gay, John	1688–1732
.57	Lillo, George	1693–1739
.58		
.59	Minor writers	
.6	**Later 18th century**	**1745–1800**
.61	Garrick, David	1716–79
.62	Foote, Samuel	1721–77
.63	Colman, George, the elder	1732–94
.64	Home, John	1724–1808
.65	Cumberland, Richard	1732–1811
.66	Sheridan, Richard Brinsley	1751–1816 See also 825.64
.67	Inchbald, Mrs Elizabeth (Simpson)	1753–1821
.68		
.69	Minor writers	

.7	Early 19th century	1800–1837	
.71	Baillie, Joanna		1762–1851
.72	Knowles, James Sheridan		1784–1862
.8	Victorian period	1837–1900	
.91	Early 20th century	1901–	

The system is frequently summarized and simplified as follows by small branch circulating libraries:

HOW TO FIND A BOOK *

The books in this library are arranged on the shelves in numerical order according to the Dewey Decimal Classification System, which separates all books into ten classes with numbers as follows:

000-099 GENERAL WORKS: books that deal with no particular subject such as encyclopedias, periodicals, newspapers

100-199 PHILOSOPHY: psychology, ethics, etc.   Example: 150 is the number for psychology.

200-299 RELIGION: Christian and non-Christian beliefs.   Example: 220 is the number for the Bible.

300-399 SOCIOLOGY: government, economics, law, education, etc.   Example: 331 is the number for labor and capital.

400-499 LANGUAGE: readers, grammars, dictionaries, etc., in all languages. 423 is the number for dictionaries of the English language.

500-599 SCIENCE: mathematics, astronomy, geology, botany, zoology, etc. Example: 598.2 is the number for bird books.   520, the number for astronomies, is arranged on the shelves after 510, the number for mathematics and before 530, the number for physics.

600-699 USEFUL ARTS: medicine, engineering, home economics, etc.   Example: 641 is the number for cook books.

700-799 FINE ARTS: architecture, needlework, painting, music, amusements, etc.   Example: 770 is the number for photography.

800-899 LITERATURE: poems, dramas, and essays in all languages.   822.33 is the number for books by and about Shakspere.

NOVELS: may be grouped on the shelves separately and are arranged alphabetically by the authors' surnames.   Example: Dickens, Scott, Thackeray.

900-999 HISTORY: travel, biography, histories of all countries and all ages. Example: 973 is the number for a history of the United States.

TRAVEL: in all countries has the number 910-919; a book explaining life in the United States is numbered 917.3.

The librarian will be glad to help you, if you cannot find the book you want.

* Used by permission of Gaylord Brothers, Inc., Syracuse, N. Y.

III Library catalog cards

Following are a few specimen library catalog cards made out in keeping with the Dewey system. There are many other variations than the ones here shown. But these are sufficient for illustration of general principles. They proceed from simple to complex, it will be noted, and they reveal clearly the fluidity of the system. It makes it difficult not to find the book you want, as some one has said of it.

1 Author card for a book of fiction. In some libraries it carries also the name of the publisher and the date of publication:

M	Morley, Christopher Haunted bookshop

2 Title card—the reverse of the foregoing—title first and author last:

M	Haunted bookshop Morley, Christopher

3 Author card for non-fiction book.   Publisher is given and the
year of copyright:

915.3
T
	Thomas, Lowell Jackson.
	      With Lawrence in Arabia. Century, c1924.
	      408p.
	
	○

4 The reverse of the foregoing—title card for non-fiction book:

915.3 T	With Lawrence in Arabia. Thomas, Lowell Jackson. ○

5 Subject card bearing both general and special subjects, with name of publisher and date of copyright:

915.3
T
	European War, 1914-1918,—
	                       Arabia.
	Thomas, Lowell Jackson.
	    With Lawrence in Arabia. Century, c1924.
	    408p.

6 Sample analytic card. Under subject or author some special treatment is indicated. The entire book is not referenced by this card:

920 C	Conrad, Joseph. Cooper, Frederic Taber. Joseph Conrad. (In his Some English story tellers. p.1-31)

7 A typical cross-reference "see" card:

	Wireless telegraphy, see Radio
	◯

8 A so-called "full card" from the Library of Congress:

| 822
G | **Galsworthy, John,** 1867–
    Plays, by John Galsworthy. New York, London, C. Scribner's sons, 1928.
vi, 698 p. 20^{cm}.
Contents.—The silver box.—Joy.—Strife. — The eldest son. — Justice. — The little dream.—The pigeon.—The fugitive.—The mob.—A bit o' love.—The foundations.— The skin game.—A family man.—Loyalties. —Windows.—The forest.—Old English.— The show.—Escape.—Six short plays: The first and the last. The little man. Hallmarked. Defeat. The sun. Punch and go.

                    28—25469
           PR6013.A5A19 1928
Library of Congress
————Copy 2. ◯
Copyright A 342   [30z²5] |

IV   Bibliography

Since the library is a place where books are kept, it is naturally the place where bibliographies may most easily be made. Distinction must be made between *bibliography* and *book list*. The latter may be merely a listing of nothing but titles of books, or of titles with accompanying names of authors. A bibliography in the real sense of the term is considerably more than this. It gives or should give at least three additional things—the place of publication, the name of the publishing firm, and the date of publication. These five items regarding a book constitute the minimum requirement for each entry in a bibliography. But an exhaustive bibliography will contain much more regarding each entry, namely, the number of pages, the kind of binding, the price of the book or other publication, a list of chapter headings, the outstanding dates in an author's life, a summary of reviews of certain types of literature.

The average catalog card rarely gives all of these items or even half of them. But in compiling bibliographical subject and analytic cards for his own special use in surrounding a subject, the research worker will see to it that references are made to all books (chapter, page, paragraph), articles, speeches, periodicals, brochures, reports, diagrams, photographs, maps, museum exhibits, field operations, and to whatever else may be required to make his study complete. His bibliographical cards will be used for both immediate purposes and future consultation. Very often all the resources of a great library are insufficient to supply the necessary contents of the perfect bibliography, and the bibliographer may be obliged to make exploratory travels and to pry into the hidden books and corners of rare collections to make his work complete.

Here is a simple five-entry bibliographical card or slip:

> Deland, L. F. *Imagination in Business.* Harper and Brothers, New York City, 1909.

The five items above mentioned—author, title, publisher, place, date—are given in this order. The name of the author and the title of the book are always placed first (see cards 1 and 2). The other three items vary in placement. There is no hard-and-fast rule about them, as there is no fixed rule regarding punctuation. Note the changes in order and punctuation here:

> Scott, Walter Dill, *Influencing Men in Business*, New York City: Ronald Press 1916.

The title itself is always italicized in a bibliography of books. In a bibliography of articles the title of the article is placed in quotation marks and the title of the periodical in which it is to be found is italicized (see page 218).

> Opdycke, John B. "The Murder of the Mother Tongue," *New York Herald Tribune*, December 11, 1932.
> ———"On Calling a Spade a Spade," *Printers Ink Monthly*, vol. 15, no. 8, pp. 138-142. August 1931, New York City.

Note that in the listing of periodical articles additional items for specific location are given. Note also that the repetition of author's name is not necessary when consecutive listings are by the same person. In consecutive references to the same book or periodical, the abbreviation *ibid.* (*ibidem*, the same place) is usually used in the second and following items.

> Opdycke, John B. "On Tearing a Passion to Tatters," *Printers Ink Monthly*, vol. 15, no. 9, pp. 167-171. September 1931, New York City.
> ———"On Begging to State," *ibid.*, vol. 15, no. 10, pp. 224-227. October 1931, New York City.

In the following, note the subtitle, the price, the reference to special chapter, and the additional explanation of contents:

> Larwood, Jacob, and Hotten, John Camden, *History of Signboards: From the Earliest Times to the Present Day*, with one hundred illustrations in facsimile by Jacob Larwood. Published in London by John Camden Hotten, 1866, and in New York City by Charles Scribner's Sons, 1899. Pages 532. Price 10s 6d in London; $2.50 in New York City. Heraldic and Emblematic signs, pp. 101-149.

The placement of special subject-matter reference is variable in such extended entries as this one. Still other items that are frequently listed, especially in connection with rare volumes, are: *out of print; reprinted in   ,   ,   ; rare, one copy in British Museum, one in possession of private collectors; chapter on trademarks reprinted in Encyclopedia Britannica, vol. XX, 1928 edition, pp. 882-945,* and so forth. Bibliographies compiled for research only need not carry such items as price and date of issue of various editions, but while one is about the business of running down all information regarding a book it pays to omit nothing. The time so frequently comes when information thought to be useless turns out to be most useful.

In listing bulletins, reports, commission findings, the rules above explained should be applied. Volume, number, month, year, and page numbers are imperative, and if different authors have contributed to the compilation, the name of the author of any special article referred to should be given.

> United States Foreign and Domestic Commerce, Bureau of, *Advertising American Goods in New Zealand,* by A. S. Sweetzer. No. 10 in series of reports made by United States Foreign and Domestic Commerce Commission, 1919. Superintendent of Documents, Washington, D. C. Twenty-five cents.

V Reference

The reference department of a library is, as a rule, open to every visitor, and the card catalog does not have to be consulted in order that a reader may find books of general information. There are many different classes of reference books and general literature on the "open shelves," of which the following are the most commonly found:

A The great dictionaries of the English tongue:

> *The New Standard Dictionary of the English Language,* published by Funk and Wagnalls Company, New York and London
> *Webster's New International Dictionary of the English Language,* published by G. and C. Merriam Company, Springfield, Mass.
> *The Oxford English Dictionary,* published by the Oxford University Press, London, England
> Winston's *Simplified Dictionary,* published by The John C. Winston Company, Philadelphia, Pa.
> *The Century Dictionary* (no longer issued)

B   The large encyclopedias, some of them general and some special:

The Encyclopedia Britannica
The New International Encyclopedia
The New Standard Encyclopedia of Universal Knowledge
The Catholic Encyclopedia
The Jewish Encyclopedia
The Lincoln Library
Ridpath's Library of World Literature
Warner's Library of the World's Best Literature

C   The general biographical collections:

Congressional Directory
Living Authors
Authors Today and Yesterday
Dictionary of National Biography
Dictionary of American Biography
Who's Who

There is a *Who's Who* for most countries of the world and for most professions—*Who's Who in America, Who's Who in Medicine, Wer Ist's* (German), *Qui Êtes Vous* (French), *Who's Who in New England, American Labor's Who's Who,* etc. The original *Who's Who* (published by The Macmillan Company) pertains to England for the most part. Others usually designate differentia after the two genus or principal title words.

Other general reference books belonging to the field of biography are *The Social Register,* containing the names of men and women of prominence and wealth living in and near New York City and giving their family connections, colleges, clubs, distinctions, and so forth, and *The Blue Book,* issued in many cities and following in general make-up and purpose *The Social Register.*

Corresponding to these "social guides" in England are *Burke's Peerage, Kelly's Handbook to the Titled, Landed, and Official Classes,* and *Whitaker's Peerage, Baronetage, Knightage, and Companionage;* and in Europe *The Almanach de Gotha* which attempts to cover the world of titles, genealogical family trees of royalty, and general officialdom.

D   Almanacs, yearbooks, directories, and the like:

The World Almanac
The Chicago Daily News Almanac

Whitaker's Almanac (British)
New Standard Encyclopedia Year Book
Bradstreet and Dun's Directory (financial)
American Jewish Year Book
Official Catholic Directory
United States Government Manual (Revised currently)
Official Congressional Directory for the Use of the United States Congress
Statesman's Year Book
American Year Book
United States Bureau of Education Publications
United States Bureau of Census Publications
Official Gazette of the United States Patent Office
New International Year Book: A Compendium of the Year's Progress
Handbook of American Private Schools
Yearbooks in various fields of industrial and professional activity

E Guides and indexes of special value to the research worker:

The Reader's Guide to Periodical Literature
Stories and articles that have appeared in the leading periodical publications from 1900 to the present. (It was preceded by *Poole's Index*, covering the period from 1800 to 1900. The *International Index*, first issued in 1907 as *The Reader's Guide Supplement*, indexes scientific and technical articles in foreign periodicals not listed in *The Reader's Guide*)
The Cumulative Book Index
Issued monthly except August, and containing titles of all book publications of the year. The annual supplements are bound in annual volumes
The United States Catalog
A bibliography of books in print in the United States up to 1928. This has been supplanted by *The Cumulative Index*, which now carries in one summary volume the books published in the United States from 1928 to 1932
Mudge's Guide to Reference Books—a guide to reference shelves
The Publishers' Weekly—new and prospective publications

Most important publications issue periodical indexes. These are likewise compiled of the principal issues in given fields of literature, history, science, art, and so forth, and are in many cases followed with supplements. There are, for instance, the *Book Review Digest* (H. W. Wilson Company), *Index to One-Act Plays* (1924) with *Supplement* (1932) by Hannah Logas and Winifred VerNooy (F. W. Faxon Company), *Essay and General Literature Index* (revised to 1934) by Minnie E. Sears and Marian Shaw (H. W. Wilson Company), *The New York Times Index* (listing the important or major articles in *The New York Times*).

F Collections, manuals, general literature:

Good collections of synonyms, such as Crabb, Allen, Fernald
Dictionaries of phrase and fable such as Allibone, Bartlett, Brewer,
Douglas, Hoyt, Stevenson, Sully, Walsh
Roget's *Thesaurus of English Words and Phrases*
Style Manual of the Government Printing Office
The Manual of Style of the University of Chicago
Lippincott's *Pronouncing Gazetteer*
Century *Dictionary of Proper Names*
The Bible, both Authorized and Revised Versions
Boas and Hahn's *Social Backgrounds of English Literature*
Brewer's *The Reader's Handbook*
Bulfinch's *The Age of Fable*
Chambers' *Book of Days*
Fernald's *English Synonyms, Antonyms, and Prepositions*
Fowler's *Modern English Usage*
Garnett and Gosse's *Illustrated History of English Literature*
Gayley's *Classic Myths*
Krapp's *Comprehensive Guide to Good English*
Larned's *History for Ready Reference*
Mencken's *The American Language*
Sabin's *Classical Myths that Live Today*
Stevenson's *Home Book of Verse* and *Home Book of Modern Verse*
Traill's *Social England*
Vizetelly's *Essentials of English Speech and Literature*

Special collections and editions, such as *The Dollar Library* (D. Appleton-Century Company), *Companion Classics* (W. J. Black, Inc.), *Everyman's Library* (E. P. Dutton and Company), *The Five-Foot Book Shelf* (P. F. Collier and Son), *The Home Library* (A. L. Burt Company), *Modern Library* (Modern Library, Inc.), *Modern Readers' Series* (The Macmillan Company), *Modern Students' Library* (Charles Scribner's Sons), *Novels of Distinction* (Grosset and Dunlap), *Riverside Library* (Houghton Mifflin Company), *Star Books* (Garden City Publishing Company), *Modern Eloquence* (Modern Eloquence Corporation).

G Atlases and general geographical guides:

Cram's *Unrivaled Atlas of the World*
Hammond's *World Loose-Leaf Atlas*
Literary Digest Atlas of the World
Rand-McNally's atlases
The London Times Atlas
Railway guides (in British libraries)
International Postal Guides
United States Official Postal Guides

CHAPTER ELEVEN

MINUTES—REPORTS—CITATIONS

I Minutes

Minutes are brief notes or records of the proceedings of a meeting of any kind. They are a report of a meeting. The old word *minute* means jotting or note, and in the plural it has come to mean a collection of such jottings or notes all pertaining to sessional proceedings. They summarize primarily for the sake of fortifying memory, safeguarding against misunderstandings, and (unconsciously) supplying history of legal or corporate or other actions. Minutes should be written in the order of the events they report, and they should be accurate to minutiæ. Unless they are precise to a nicety they will be invalidated for consultation, for verification of facts, and for proof or evidence in case of disputes. Annual and interim reports of a company are sometimes little more than a reworking of collected minutes over a given period, sequentially arranged and displayed by means of running plan so that the salients may be easily gathered by the reader.

A permanent or temporary secretary takes notes or minutes at a meeting and preserves them in an official minute-book. Name of organization; place, date, hour of meeting; names of absentees (optional); reading of the minutes of the preceding meeting; unfinished business (business left unfinished at preceding meetings); reports of committees; new business taken up at the present meeting; record of action taken on both old and new business; report of debate on proposed action (if especially important); place, date, hour of next meeting (unless these are prescribed permanently by constitution or by-law); time of adjournment; signature of secretary and president—these are the principal points to be covered by the secretary of an organization (or his representative) in his composition of the minutes of a stated meeting. On their being read at the next meeting, they will be approved, or amended and then approved, by vote of those concerned. Whether all of these points—or fewer or more—will be reported depends upon the kind of body in session and the kind of business transacted.

MINUTES OF THE MEETING OF THE EXECUTIVE COMMITTEE OF THE YOUNG MEN'S PROTECTIVE LEAGUE

Time of Meeting Thursday evening, March twelfth, at 8.30

Place of Meeting Auditorium, Granville High School

Preliminary Procedures The meeting was called to order promptly at 8.34 p.m. by the chairman of the committee

The committee roll was called by the secretary, and all members were present with the exception of Harold C. Judd and Horace M. Carforen. The former was obliged to be in Washington; the latter was detained by illness. The nine other members of the committee conducted the business of the evening seriatim as follows

Old Business Reports Supervision The committee on supervision of League activities reported twenty important projects under way, and requested postponement of detailed procedures until such time as full attendance could be guaranteed

Publicity The committee on publicity reported $981.23 spent since the last meeting for the purpose of instructing the general public as to aims and methods of League reforms. Every cent of this money was accounted for by way of space in the daily newspapers, on local billboards, and direct-by-mail circularization. (An itemized statement of disbursements is attached to these minutes.)

Functions The dinner committee reported that the Louis Four-teenth Ballroom of the Hotel Fronterre has been taken for Saturday evening, April second, at seven-thirty, for the annual dinner-dance. The Honorable Charles L. Simons and Mrs. Simons have promised to attend as guests of honor. Tickets will be five dollars a plate. Dancing will begin at ten o'clock

New Business Legislative (pro) It was unanimously voted to sponsor the following bills now pending in the State legislature

The Weis Bill providing for a more equitable distribution of police funds

The Naylor Bill extending leaves of absence more liberally to officers who have served efficiently for twenty years or more

The Harris Bill exempting certain of the higher-class neighborhoods from the extra city protec-tive tax

Legislative (con) The following bills were disapproved by unanimous vote following motion and discussion

The Crawford Bill that would make the posses-sion of a pistol a five-year-penalty offense

The Rinehart Bill that would remove all metal buttons, badges, medals, and the like, from official uniforms, and supply these in other materials

New committee   A motion was unanimously passed to investigate the
                       recent outbreak of the unemployed in the Shore Inlet
                       district. The chairman appointed Messrs. Donaldson,
                       Gillan, and Springer a committee of three to make
                       a report on this subject at the next meeting

Vote of   A motion was made and seconded to extend to Mr.
felicitations   Harrison Butler the felicitations of the executive
                       committee upon his appointment by the Governor to
                       the State Tax Commission. The motion was enthusi-
                       astically supported by every one present

Vote of thanks   A vote of thanks was extended to the reception com-
                       mittee for its perfect arrangements for the welcom-
                       ing of the foreign visitors last month (February
                       tenth)

Adjournment   Adjournment was taken, on motion, at 10.45 p.m.

                       Respectfully submitted

                       CONRAD RAPHAELSON
                       Secretary

Signed by _____

                       Chairman, Executive Committee of the Young Men's
                       Protective League

II Reports

Reports in the business and industrial sense are summarized
statements of proceedings, findings, data, statistics, terms, conditions, achievements, operations, and the like, compiled for the
purpose of record, reference, information, or any other. Changes
or modifications of policies are usually based upon reports. Needless to say, a report, like any other piece of responsible writing,
should be thoroly organized and the materials of organization
should be clearly regimented by way of marginal or internal
headings, or both. The main divisions, with the related subdivisions, should serve as table of contents for the completed report.

Reports may be made in the form of letters, in the form of
neutral briefs, in the form of general working theses. In its general organization a report may most conveniently be divided
perhaps into the three common divisions of documentary composition—introduction, discussion, conclusion—tho these terms themselves do not necessarily have to be used. The introduction should
contain first of all a statement of just what the subject of the
report is and what its scope is, that is, whether it is a report of an
entire enterprise or of only one section or phase or undertaking.
The introduction should further inform as to the aim of the report,
its authorization, the necessity or desirability for it, the period of

time that it covers, the sources from which its content is drawn, a complete classification of its material (relevancies and irrelevancies), the order of treatment followed, and the values it is calculated to bring to bear upon the enterprise or section thereof.

The conclusion of a report should enumerate findings definitely, succinctly, and sequentially. If the report is made to decide a course of action or to modify a line of policy, this list of findings should be followed with specific recommendations. In a public report the conclusion may be drawn in such a way as to make it usable by the press without change. Sometimes, however, a press summary is drawn off the complete report to be handed to newspapers for publication intact. This should follow the general principles of newspaper composition (pages 385-424).

The discussion or general body of a report should be strictly inductive in its development, that is, the accumulation and presentation of materials should precede the generalization of individual sections and of the conclusion. Intermittently, in this part of a report, there should be brief summaries for the sake of holding content closely together, for convenience of reference, and for building cumulative impression. Reports that pertain to public matters and that are made for the betterment of community service, let us say, should be written in general terms, usually in the third person, and in the simplest of language and construction. Reports that have to do with private enterprise, made for special or technical groups in such enterprise, may, of course, be written in the technical language of such groups. These latter may be formal or informal, the choice depending upon the situation that evokes the report. If it is the outcome of strained relationships of any kind or of legal necessity, it should be written in formal language and in the third person. If it is evoked by internal relationships that are congenial and agreeable, it may be written informally and in the first person. In no event, except in strictly confidential reports, should company secrets (if any) be revealed or used as the basis of findings and recommendations.

Reports should, whenever and wherever possible, be elucidated by means of photographs, graphs, tabulations, drawings, and whatever other visual devices may be brought to bear. They invariably concretize and impress. If one picture is worth a million words, then a graph that is logically conceived and clearly worked out is worth a billion, especially in a report upon the findings of which momentous action may hinge. Moreover, it is well always in report-making to present a complicated issue in more than one way, so that those who find one form perplexing may find another pertaining to the same thing quite clear. Tabulations as a rule are not especially interesting to most people. But a live graph drawn accurately from a tabulation may save the day for those readers who have difficulty understanding compilations of figures (see pages 437-444).

When a report is finally presented to the person or group of persons by whom it was authorized, it is usually accompanied by a brief letter of transmittal. This should, as a rule, be kept as brief as possible. There may, however, be conditions that require a somewhat long letter of transmittal—original authorization may have been changed, aims may have been modified, members may have resigned and new ones may have been assigned, economic outlook may have been disturbed by unforeseen events, and the like. For the average report some such letter of transmittal as the following will be found sufficient.

February 19, 0000

Hon. Horace C. Burns, Governor
State Capitol
Santa Fé
New Mexico

Honorable Sir

The Special Commission on Desert Reclamation appointed by Your Excellency on October twelfth last, has made a thorogoing investigation of all phases of desert conditions and of reclamation possibilities in the State of New Mexico, especially as these possibilities pertain to increased agricultural opportunities, and it reports findings and makes recommendations as contained in the accompanying statement

Respectfully submitted
HARRIS W. CONNOLY
Chairman

HWC/bb

A blanket outline for a report is one that is flexible and adjustable, so that it may be adapted to many different parts or phases of a given subject. It is, in reality, a miniature filing arrangement under the principal headings of which much or little may be listed, as investigation warrants. It makes for convenience and uniformity in a firm of many different departments, to have departmental reports follow such a general or blanket plan, provided, of course, the plan is broad and elastic enough to permit of wide variations of adaptation. The plan reproduced below, for instance, is ideally devised for use in the survey of almost any industry of major significance. The headings, both major and minor, are sufficiently broad and comprehensive to include practically everything that it would be desirable or possible to bring under survey, no matter what the specific end of such survey. Some of the headings would have to be omitted entirely, perhaps, in framing the final report; some would bulk large; some slight. The important thing, however, is that those who engage in making the survey or investigation, have a comprehensive guide to start from and to focus upon, a gage wherewith to make selections and rejections of materials.

BLANKET OUTLINE (TABLE OF CONTENTS) FOR SURVEY OF VARIOUS INDUSTRIES IN RELATION TO EDUCATION

(The following should be used for the general development of surveys, tho in individual cases deviations will naturally have to be made at the dictation of subject-matter)

INTRODUCTORY

    I Personnel of the report—section committees, acknowledgments, and so forth

    II Recommendations, general and specific, cross-referenced to findings hereunder

    III Objectives of the survey, with substantiation

FINDINGS PERTAINING TO THE INDUSTRY

    IV Importance of the .... industry—history, progress, analyses, trends

    V Modern processes in the .... industry, including changes in trade practise and the ramifications of the trade

    VI Employment organization in the .... industry—employer and employee; race, sex, nationality

    VII Employment welfare in the .... industry—health, hygiene, sanitation, hazards, compensation, insurance, organs, morale

EDUCATIONAL IMPLICATIONS AND RECOMMENDATIONS

    VIII Educational facilities at present—public, private, shop apprentice —their development and degree of adequacy

    IX Educational expansion proposed and recommended in light of trade study—supervision, centralization, departmentalization; a central school and annexes as geographically required or justified

    X Courses of study—types of students, classification of subject-matter, correlation with trade practise

    XI The instructional corps—training, licensing, grades, salaries, trade experience allowance

APPENDIX

    Bibliography and other supplementary materials

The average business or industrial report is too long to include in its entirety in a book of this scope. But the following three pages represent a section development (a part of point V in the blanket outline above) of a report made on the printing industry by the Vocational Survey Commission of New York City.*

* Used by permission of the Commission.

V PLANOGRAPHIC PRINTING

A *Lithography*

The name lithography originated about 1796 at a time when original designs were placed on stone (hence the name, from *lithos* stone and *grapho* I write). The present extensive and ever increasing use of zinc and aluminum in place of stone as a printing surface makes the term somewhat of a misnomer when applied to modern processes of planographic printing.

The underlying processes of lithography are relatively simple and are fundamentally based upon the principle of the mutual antipathy of grease and water. In the simplest terms they may be explained as follows: The design to be lithographed is drawn or otherwise made on the specially prepared printing surface, which may be stone, aluminum, or zinc. The plate or stone is then etched with a suitable acid solution (see counter etching and etching under the caption *Preparing the Printing Surface*). The surface is next dampened with water and printing ink applied by means of a roller. The portions of the surface which carry the greasy crayon repel the water but it adheres to the non-crayon-carrying portions, whereas the greasy ink adheres only to the portions carrying the greasy crayon. This is the necessary printing condition. A sheet of paper is put in contact under pressure with the inked side of the stone or plate, thus transferring the pattern or design to the paper.

Through the development of mechanical devices and modification of methods these fundamental principles are today applied in a variety of ways to produce a range of product running from the fine line detail of a postage stamp to the large solid color areas of a twenty-four-sheet poster. This has resulted in a relatively high degree of specialization. Very few lithographing plants are equipped to produce the complete range, tho some of them produce more than one of the following products: art reproductions, booklets and circulars, commercial papers, decalcomanias, display matter, greeting cards, labels, magazine covers, metal (sheet metal or tinplate), package inserts, posters, and wrappers.

The extent of the industry is indicated by the following figures taken from the 1929 census of manufactures:

```
Number of establishments   ...........................        367
Number of wage earners   ...........................      18,202
Wages   ..................................................$ 30,818,490.
Cost of materials   ....................................   36,771,321.
Value of products   ...................................  114,315,430.
Value added by manufacture   .........................   77,544,109.
```

These figures represent a minimum because they do not include combination printing and lithographing establishments.

Regardless of the specialty which is being produced, the procedure includes some method or methods of (1) getting the desired outline, picture, or sketch (known as *copy*) on a prepared glass, stone, or metal surface—this is making the original; (2) transferring one or more impressions from the original to the plate which is to be run on the press; (3) securing the desired number of impressions from the press plate. If the subject is to be produced in more than one color this procedure is repeated for each color.

Some of the methods most widely used in each step of the foregoing procedure are set forth briefly in the following explanations:

1 Making originals
  a Stone engraving
    An outline of the copy is transferred to the stone. (There are many different ways of doing this.) Then, with the use of a diamond-pointed tool and sharp-pointed steel needles, the engraver cuts the design into the surface of the stone. This method is used principally in the production of fine detail, one color, commercial paper, such as letterheads and banknotes.

  b Crayon and color art work
    The artist, using greasy crayons, reproduces the copy on stones or metal plates, one for each color. In doing this the artist must analyze the copy in his mind so that the several drawings when printed in their respective colors, one on top of the other or superimposed, will produce a facsimile of the original copy. In order to guide the artist and to insure exact proportions in outline, a key is made by tracing the outlines of the copy. This is usually done by pinning a sheet of gelatin firmly on top of the copy and tracing the latter by scratching the gelatin with a steel point. This outline is then transferred to the surface of the stone or plate to be filled in by the artist. In poster houses a stereopticon is sometimes used to enlarge the copy to the required size in order that a key may be made by tracing the outline thus projected. Stippling, Ben Day, and air-brush spraying are different methods used by the artist for securing special effects such as fine graining, lining, or shading.

  c Photographic methods
    During the past fifteen or twenty years the camera has become an important factor in the lithographic industry. Several different methods have been developed. The range of their application and their comparative usefulness depends upon the class of work to be done. The process consists of photographing the copy on to a glass plate called the negative. For multi-color jobs a separate negative is made for each color. Color filters are used with the camera lenses to keep out all but the desired color. This process is called color separation and the resulting negatives are called separation negatives. In some methods glass positives are then made from these negatives while in other methods the positives are made on stones or metal plates. If glass positives are used negatives are next made on glass, stone, or metal plates.

In order to break the solid color where tones and shades are desired, a screen is used in making either the negative or the positive. This screen consists of two plates of glass having parallel lines etched on one surface of each glass. These plates are faced with the etched sides in contact, so that the lines on one are perpendicular to the lines on the other. The resultant effect of photographing through the screen is a collection of microscopic dots instead of a solid mass. These dots produced by the photographic process correspond to the graining of a stone or metal plate which catches the particles of greasy crayon applied by hand.

While photographic methods produce accuracy of outline and sharpness of detail, the camera has not yet been able to make entirely satisfactory color separations. It is therefore necessary at some stage, to retouch or amplify the work of the camera. This is done by hand tooling or by means of chemicals. The particular stage at which this is done and the means of doing it account for the variety of methods used in the photographic processes.

The following chart shows the major steps taken in the different photographic methods used in lithography and the comparative steps in four-color process printing and gravure.

MAJOR STEPS TAKEN IN DIFFERENT PHOTOGRAPHIC METHODS
USED IN PRINTING

Planographic
(Lithography)

Photo Litho		*Photo Mechanical*	
Hand Tooling	Staining	Hand Tooling	Staining
1 Make separation negative	1 Make screened separation	1 Make separation negative	1 Make screen separation negative
2 Make screened positive on stone or plate	2 Correct values on negative by staining	2 Make positive	2 Correct negative by staining
3 Correct positive (submarine)	3 Make positive on stone	3 Correct positive	3 Make positive on press plate
4 Pull transfer	4 Correct positive (submarine)	4 Make screen negative	
5 Place transfer on press plate	5 Transfer to press plate	5 Make positive on press plate	

Deep Etch	Relief Printing (Four-color process)	Intaglio (Gravure)
1 Make separation negative Correct negative	1 Make separation negative	1 Make separation negative
2 Make screen positive	2 Make negative on sensitive plate	2 Correct negative
3 Print positive on press plate (reverse)	3 Etch slightly	3 Make positive
	4 Paint out sections not to be printed	4 Correct positive
	5 Etch	5 Make screened print on carbon tissue or film
	6 Repeat 4 and 5 for each gradation of values until values are O K	6 Lay down carbon tissues on cylinder
		7 Etch cylinder

III Citations

A citation of distinction may be made when honors are bestowed upon some outstanding person, by an association or society of some kind or by a college or university. It consists of a list of honorable deeds or of distinguished services or of achievements in scholarship and research accredited to the person who receives social, civic, or educational recognition in public by way of medal or diploma or degree or other reward of merit.

POLICE VALOR CITATION *

THE MARTIN J. SHERIDAN MEDAL FOR VALOR

Patrolman William J. Ryan, Shield No. 5645, 27th Precinct. At about 8:30 a.m., January 10, 1931, off duty in civilian clothes, jumped into the west channel of the East River at Welfare Island, and despite the temperature and treacherous currents Patrolman Ryan rescued a woman who had attempted suicide by drowning.

HONORABLE MENTION *

Patrolman John J. Dunleavy, Shield No. 15387, 90th Precinct, **William R. Loeffler,** Shield No. 13155, and **William I. Somerville, Jr.,** Shield No. 17798, Motorcycle Squad No. 2. At about 9:45 a.m., June 24, 1932, Patrolman Dunleavy, on patrol duty, encountered two men who had held up a collector at Broadway and Lorimer Street, Brooklyn. He exchanged shots and arrested one of them as they were about to board an automobile operated by an accomplice. Patrolmen Loeffler and Somerville, on motorcycle sidecar duty, pursued the automobile and after an exchange of shots disarmed and arrested another of them.

ACADEMIC CITATION †

John Henry MacCracken, A.B. 1894, A.M. 1897, Ph.D. 1899, LL.D. 1915. Associate director of the American Council on Education, former President of Westminster College and of Lafayette College, former Syndic of New York University and Administrative Assistant to his father, Chancellor Henry M. MacCracken—"Son of a father distinguished for creative vigor in the annals of this university, you have worthily carried on the tradition of your family both in your career within New York University and in your later public service outside its walls. This tribute we give you in recognition of your continuing loyalty to the University and its great tradition."

* Used by permission of the New York City Police Department
† Used by permission of New York University.

384 GET IT RIGHT!

CARNEGIE HERO FUND CITATION ‡

No.	ACT	AWARD
2703	**William H. Willis, Jr.,** aged sixteen, schoolboy, helped to save Arthur B. Rivers, aged thirty-three, farmer, from drowning, Swansboro, N. C., August 13, 1931. While wading in the Atlantic Ocean at Bear Beach, Rivers lost his footing in rough water and a strong undertow and was carried to a point nine hundred feet from the shore. Willis ran a mile to the shore. After other swimmers delayed to attempt to render aid, Willis, who was not accustomed to ocean-swimming, removed his outer clothing and then swam, pushing a life-preserver ahead of him, toward Rivers. Newton S. Guiley swam beside Willis, and he also pushed a life-preserver ahead of him. After swimming seven hundred feet, Willis and Gulley reached Rivers and placed one of the life-preservers under him. Almost immediately Willis and Gulley, who were about exhausted, were tossed by a wave; and they swam a few feet to the other life-preserver, which had been tossed out of their reach. Feeling unable to render Rivers further aid, they then swam toward the shore. Progress was difficult, and Willis soon left the life-preserver and with great exertion swam more than seven hundred feet to wadable water. He then waded to the shore. He was temporarily exhausted. Gulley also swam to the shore. Rivers held to the life-preserver and drifted closer to the shore and then was rescued by another man.	Bronze Medal and $500. for educational purposes or other worthy purpose as needed.

‡ Used by permission of the Carnegie Hero Fund Commission.

CHAPTER TWELVE

NEWSPAPER COPY

I Stories and interviews

Almost everything that is written for the newspapers is called a story. The "straight news story," so-called, is an account that holds rigidly to facts. Opinion or criticism or comment of any kind by the news writer or reporter must not be expressed. He may not use the first-person pronoun, either singular or plural, in reference to himself. But he may refer to Congress, to the United States, to American custom and tradition, and so forth, by *our*. Special feature writers whose names appear at the head of the column which they write (their name line is called *by-line*) do not come under this rule. Nor do British newspaper writers. It is not at all uncommon to find in British news stories comment made here and there by the reporter.

The straight news story opens with what is known as a lead (pronounce as *leed*). This is a short summary of the salients of the story—the who (or what), the how, the when, the why, the where, of the events set down. From this the casual reader or the hurried reader is enabled to gather the whole story in a nutshell. Some librarians summarize the news of the day by clipping the leads of important news stories from the paper and posting them on a bulletin board. It is not to be understood that all of these questions just enumerated are answered in all leads. Most of them should be, however, and most of them usually are. There are frequently more than one answer to each question, that is, two places, two times, two persons may be mentioned in a lead. And it is not to be understood that the news writer sets himself the task of writing a good lead immediately he starts his story. He may do so, but more than likely he draws this summary climax of facts thru his completed story, and places it at the top of his writing.

It is ruled by some newspapers that leads are not to begin with *a, an, the, there*, but this rule is widely violated. Leads are preferably begun, however, with concrete nouns, with phrases, with clauses, and with the nominative absolute. This means that wide

*The six-part lead and the detached paragraphing (see
pages 385 and 387) make grasp easy for the reader*

STEEL MEN ACT TO BLOCK STRIKE

Johnson and Richberg to Fly from Washington Today to Join Conference.

Leaders of the steel industry [who] conferred in the offices of the American Iron and Steel Institute in the Empire State Building [where] today [when] in regard to heading off the threatened strike [why] of 120,000 men [who] by making a fractional grant of the demanded wage increase [how].

General Hugh S. Johnson, accompanied by Donald Richberg, NRA counsel, and possibly other government representatives, planned to fly from Washington this afternoon to meet with the steel men.

Those sitting in the session this morning were the thirty-two directors of the Iron and Steel Institute, who with Mr. Richberg and Kenneth M. Simpson, NRA Deputy Administrator, compose the code authority.

President Roosevelt kept in close touch with the developments and was reported to believe a settlement could be reached along the lines of the agreement that recently headed off the automobile strike in Detroit.

General Johnson, sponsor of the Detroit compromise, was severely criticized by union representatives who gathered in large numbers in Washington awaiting word both from the White House and from the Empire State Building meeting here.

The union leaders have sent back word to their members that the Detroit motor settlement is not satisfactory, and that the steel workers will be ill-advised to accept any such agreement.

The steel industry leaders, meanwhile, insisted there was no change in their policy as outlined in a statement issued Monday on demands submitted by the Amalgamated Assn. of Iron, Steel and Tin Workers.

In that statement the strike possibility was minimized and the union leaders were described as representing "only a small minority of the workers."

"The industry believes," the statement read, "that a general walkout of employees from the mills is not in prospect.

"There is only one point at issue —'the closed shop.' The great majority of employees in the steel works do not want to strike and the companies will cooperate in every way possible to enable them to remain at work."

When the President moved in on the auto crisis he forced postponement of a strike by demanding time to negotiate. The President's prestige was enough to hold off the threat.

But the steel workers have given nearly a month's notice. They have already brought the issue out into the open. They say "no auto board. We'll strike in mid-June."

range is given by way of initiating the lead. But such indefinite terms as *recently, sometime tomorrow, a day or two ago* should be given no place in factual news reports. Verbs in the lead, as elsewhere, should be active. Proper names should be given in full the first time they are used. Thereafter, the surname only or some other reference may be used.

That part of the news story following the lead is made up in what is called detached paragraphing. Thus the story may be concluded at the end of any paragraph and still stand as what appears to be a complete unit of writing. In case some big news breaks just as the paper is going to press, many of the prepared stories may have to be cut. Or the writer may have written more than will go into his allotted space. In any case the story is cut from the bottom up. This means that the least important details are customarily placed at the end of the story and that their loss is not serious. Note the news story on page 386 and measure it by the facts just stated.

In stories that run in the news for several days, all leads after the first one should summarize previous happenings briefly and then give the very latest developments in the chain of happenings.

I

Entering the apartment house at 382 Blair Boulevard [where] from the roof [how] thieves ransacked the home of Harrison Andrews [who] early yesterday morning [when] and escaped with jewels and other valuables estimated at more than $10,000.

II

Sleeping calmly beside a tank on the roof of the large apartment house adjoining 382 Blair Boulevard [where] Hy Barom and William Galvano [who] were taken into custody late yesterday afternoon [when] as suspicious characters [why]. Harrison Andrews [who], whose apartment at 382 Blair Boulevard had been entered the previous night, identified the men at police court [where] in connection with the Andrews robbery as former employees [who] on his country estate [where]. Andrews also identified certain tools left in his apartment by the thieves in their hurry to get away, as coming from his country place. The two men were held for further hearing.

III

Hy Barom and William Galvano [who], questioned by the police regarding the robbery of the Andrews apartment [where] early Thursday morning, confessed their guilt last night [when] after pawn tickets found in their pockets had been used against them [how]. Both admitted the motives of poverty and revenge [why], claiming that they had not eaten for days and that Andrews had underpaid and abused them during the summer while they worked for him on his country estate. Barom confessed to having served a prison sentence in Ohio in 1934 and Galvano is at present on parole from Sing Sing.

The elements of the straight news story above discussed do not apply closely to the feature story. In this the reporter is not held to the strict treatment of facts, but he is at liberty to let his imagination play; for a feature story consists of a basis of fact fringed with fancy and imagination. The writer makes it colorful or grotesque or whimsical or humorous or sometimes even tragic. He takes a fact or an occurrence as his starting point and plays with the ideas that it suggests. Thus a feature story has no clear-cut lead, tho the elements of the lead will be found at its beginning; and it does not follow the rule of detached paragraphing. It stands, as a rule, as it is written—a complete treatment of some actual happening, from the human-interest and character-featured angle.

It sometimes happens that a good feature story is developed from special treatment of an ordinary news item. It has been said many times that it is the out-of-the-ordinary happening that constitutes news, that if a dog bites a man this event is not news because it is the expected and ordinary thing. But if a man bites a dog, that IS news. Now, suppose that shortly after being bitten by a man the dog develops rabies. Not only is there news here, but a particular phase of news that calls for special featuring. This is quite a ridiculous example, of course, but it differs in degree only, not in kind, from the following lead written from a special feature angle:

TEA FORTIFIES HIM
IN POLITICAL FIGHT
While defending himself against a four-hour bombardment of questions from oppocition members in the Chamber of Deputies yesterday, Minister of Finance Federico Pinedo drank twenty-three glasses of Russian tea.

The important serious news in the lead is, of course, Pinedo's being required to face the opposition for four hours in a grueling political cross-examination. But the tea is permitted to bring in a new and unusual feature angle. Occasionally this special play-up or featuring of something that constitutes news but that is nevertheless comparatively unimportant, causes annoyance. A certain society leader gave an elaborate party. It was attended by a European notable of title. The news reports of the party the next day minimized the party itself and featured the foreign guest. In the same way a high school commencement report played up or featured a fourteen-year-old graduate as a prodigy, with the consequence that lengthy accounts of him were printed while the commencement procedures were afforded comparatively small space. Short feature stories are frequently set in rules, as is the first one on the next page. In newspaper language it is said to be "boxed."

If an important business man arrives in some city, reporters interview him in order to gather his opinion on current economic and industrial problems. If an important politician arrives they interview him on the political situation in the country. If a well-known actress comes to town, they interview her in all probability for her views on art in the theater, and for whatever other human-interest discussion they may be able to feature.

It is necessary for the interviewer to make up his mind in advance as to just what kind of materials he should attempt to develop from any prospective interview. He must not question the actress on international finance, unless there are unusual reasons for his doing so. He must not expect the financier to answer questions on the latest styles in millinery. His questions, made up in advance and wisely chosen, must be adapted to the interests of the person interviewed. He must be especially careful to report exactly what is said, to get the name of the person interviewed exactly right, to play up that person and subordinate himself entirely, and to know when the interview is logically and tactfully to be brought to an end.

The *I* and the *we* are not used here, either in reference to the reporter or to the paper that he represents. It is better to say "Miss Coe, asked about the new play in which she is to appear during Christmas week, said that . . ." than to say "I (we) asked Miss Coe about the new play . . . and she said . . ." or "Inquiring about her new play reporters were told by Miss Coe . . ." The latter play up the newspaper men; the former plays up the person interviewed. The content of an interview should, for the sake of variety and reality, make some use of direct quotation as well as of indirect. But, as in all other writing, both direct and indirect quotation should preferably not be used in the same paragraph. This is a fundamental rule of unity. It is not strictly observed by all papers.

The excerpt on page 391 illustrates in part the foregoing exposition. It is varied in style; it subordinates the mechanics of reporting;

*Short feature stories (see pages 388 and 389) add
piquancy to newspaper content*

World's Oldest Man Cheats Death at 160

ISTANBUL, Turkey, June 7 (U. P.).—Wrinkled, toothless Zaro Agha, reputed to be the oldest man in the world, sat in the sun before his little home today and planned his future.

The 160-year-old Zaro left yesterday the hospital at which he had been under treatment for several weeks. He had fooled the doctors, because they said when he entered, muttering deliriously of events of a century ago, that he could not live.

Zaro Agha had come nome showering blessings on the doctors and nurses who had treated him.

SPLIT INFINITIVES

Guilty Princeton Students Must Take New Course.

PRINCETON, June 12.—An eight weeks' compulsory course in oral and written English composition for all undergraduates who are addicted to the grammatical errors of split infinitives and dangling participles will be inaugurated by Princeton University at the beginning of the new academic year, it is announced.

Dr. Robert Kolburn Root, dean of the faculty, said that the university will require those students who "do not pass a satisfactory examination in the use of correct and idiomatic prose" to take the course, for which they will receive no academic credit, but which they must have before being eligible for the junior class.

'Thank God Tonight' Brings Wire Error Suit

Plaintiff Says His Message Was 'Sank Died Tonight'

MEMPHIS, Tenn., Oct. 8 (A. P.).—J. B. Robinson, a contractor, today asked $1500 from a telegraph company because, he charged, the funeral of his nephew, Robert Owens who died recently, had to be postponed as a result of an error in the transmission of a telegram.

Mr. Robinson's Circuit Court suit said he telephoned to the local office of the telegraph company and dictated a message reading, "Sank died tonight, wire me." When delivered, he charged, the message read, "Thank God tonight, wire."

Owens's uncle in Vicksburg, Miss., to whom it was addressed, answered, "What happened, let me know. I am always thankful."

it emphasizes two or three salients that are certain to be of interest to the general public; it opens with a good news lead; it follows the rule of detached paragraphing; it combines news values with feature presentation; it is headlined according to rule, and so on. At the same time it bears upon letters of collection (see page 333).

'BAD DEBT' LETTER BRINGS INDICTMENT

Westchester Man is Accused Under Old Law of 'Intent to Cause Annoyance'

Special to THE NEW YORK TIMES.

WHITE PLAINS, N. Y., Feb. 18. —A bright red automobile, a law believed not to have been used in twenty years, and a letter allegedly written "with intent to cause annoyance" caused the indictment today of Harry Y. Moyer, of 49 Central Avenue, White Plains, over an $8.80 debt.

Mr. Moyer, who conducts a collection agency here and in Jamaica, L. I., was indicted by the Westchester grand jury for allegedly writing the letter to C. Elmer Talley, attorney and former president of the White Plains Board of Education.

For some time the collection agency has used red cars bearing in large white letters, the information that "We Collect Bad Debts." The cars have created a stir among Westchester's residents and home owners.

Collectors use the spectacular vehicles to visit persons slow in paying bills and the presence of one of the cars in front of a home is believed to add to the ease of collection.

The action against Mr. Moyer was taken, according to Assistant District Attorney Frederick Jameson, because of a letter sent by the collection agency last July 8 to Mr. Talley. The letter, the Assistant District Attorney said, referred to an $8.80 debt owed by the attorney.

Mr. Jameson said the letter threatened to "advertise the account for sale" and warned that "our collectors are furnished with red cars to call on debtors who ignore indebtedness after courtesy has been extended."

"If this indebtedness is not paid within ten days," the letter said, "our collector will make a call upon you at your residence, place of business or employment to collect what is due. We trust it will not become necessary to place this account in the hands of our attorney or to advertise the account for sale."

Mr. Jameson said the debt was paid by Mr. Talley and a few days ago the case was brought before the grand jury. The indictment was based on Section 551 of the penal laws, which makes it a misdemeanor to write letters "with intent to cause annoyance." District Attorney Walter R. Tinney said he believed the law had not been used in at least twenty years.

If convicted Mr. Moyer could be fined $500. and sentenced to a year in jail. County Judge Horace Brown set bail at $500.

II Editorials

The editorial is comment upon news, exposition of news, interpretation of news, or general expression and presentation of views calculated to be helpful and inspiring and cultural for readers. It aims most largely, perhaps, to frame opinion among readers without making the readers aware that it is doing so. It is, therefore, very often argument in disguise. All the dammed-up comment that reporters would express in their news stories but dare not, may be loosened under the reins of dignity and restraint upon the editorial page of the newspaper.

The editorial has no lead as such, but it may have a kind of "opener" corresponding to the lead, in which the circumstance that evokes the editorial is explained. It then proceeds in step-by-step logic, and makes a deduction at the end—sometimes a sweeping deduction. It must be specific and logical and authoritative. It must not be superior or condescending, dictatorial or domineering, undocumented or inflaming. Editorials are usually impersonal, that is, third-personal. But sometimes the first-personal plural —the editorial *we*—is used to represent the paper or the chain of papers in which the editorial appears. Seldom is the second person used in the better journals.

Occasionally a paper publishes an editorial that is not specifically connected with the news, but has bearing upon life in general. It is sometimes called an uplift editorial. This does not mean that it is preachy in the annoying sense, but that it is cultural and makes its appeal to the so-called finer things—to good taste and refinement and intelligence. Newspapers, it is frequently said, do as much to raise the general cultural standards of a community as do the schools and the churches and the homes. They do this primarily perhaps thru their editorials. But they do it also to no small extent thru their news columns. In almost any issue of a large metropolitan daily you may read such allusions as these:

Mary's lamb is roasted
Solomon's glory outdone
Morpheus cures the King
A modern Dorothy Vernon
Prodigal returns third time
Mars is on the march again
Mercury loses a winged foot
Black sheep turns pure white
David and Goliath shake hands
The Pheidippides of the Olympics
The blushing bride was sober, stedfast, and demure
Tomorrow and tomorrow comes creeping into his life
They tripped the light fantastic until the wee sma' hours
The quality of mercy was decidedly strained in his court
Modern Lochinvar motors across country to wed daughter of Crœsus

Editorials such as these have permanent cultural value

GOUDY

A MAN like Goudy in the Middle Ages would have been an adornment of a century. In this remarkable era of mechanical advance he is scarcely known to the general public. Frederic W. Goudy—ask the man in the street who he is. Ask a school child. A doctor, lawyer, merchant. They likely will not know him. Ask book publishers, printers, artists, craftsmen—they will know him as the greatest designer of types now living and one of the greatest the world has ever produced and by far the most prolific.

Just now Frederic W. Goudy, with his wife and collaborator in printing, is being accorded his most important public glory in an exhibition of the best of the eighty and more distinguished fonts of type he has designed. The exhibit is at the Museum of Science and Industry at 220 E. 42nd St., under the auspices of the American Institute of Graphic Arts.

Craftsmanship generally — in wrought iron, stained glass, cabinet work and various other mediums—is now achieving a remarkable rise in America. With those few at the very head of the procession of great American craftsmen walks Goudy, maker of beautiful yet useful type.

Thoroughly immersed in the history of type and printing, a spiritual friend of all the great printers and type designers of history, he yet creates for large-scale use.

He says:

"I haven't had time to devote to letters for the sake of beauty alone. The only beauty that can be of any good to the bulk of humanity from this time on is the beauty that can be utilized."

Here is a solidly philosophical as well as great artizan.

At 68 Frederic W. Goudy ought to be just beginning to work. He \s of this new era, even as he is of \ll time.

New York World-Telegram

Variety in Speech.

New Yorkers whose ears are offended by the variety of pronunciations and colloquialisms heard on the city streets may be comforted to know that in London the sensitive are similarly annoyed. A letter to the London *Times* records these anecdotes:

" 'What shype is the world?' asked a teacher in a London school, and the children answered in chorus 'It's raound! It's raound!' 'Where do you live?' demanded a teacher in a Home Counties school of a new infant, and the reply was 'In the co'age a' the bo'om of our ga'en.' "

The same correspondent says he has heard school girls call one another Lellay and Ivay for Lily and Ivy; that in some districts field is pronounced "fade" and bulb "borb." The dropping of the h is a common flaw. In comparison with some of these examples the usual perversions observed here, such as "thoid" for third and "Noo Yawk" for New York seem almost acceptable.

In our own city the public schools struggle constantly against mispronunciation. It is desirable, however, that those in charge of the campaign for better speech should differentiate between slovenly language and permissible individuality in diction and locution. Variety in speech is not an unmitigated evil.

London, like New York, is using its schools in an effort to improve the spoken word, but it has an important ally which, because radio broadcasting is a commercial, not an official, enterprise in the United States, can be used to only a limited degree here. The British Broadcasting Corporation in cooperation with the Central Council for School Broadcasting has made a study of the use of wireless lessons for the improvement of speech. The experiment, carried on since 1930, has shown that broadcasting of instruction in speech has produced marked improvement among teachers as well as pupils.

The (New York) Sun

III   Reviews

In writing a sports review give the exact data of the sport or game
—teams, players, place, and so forth.   The result will be told in
the lead; then the point-by-point or play-by-play will follow.
Since the halves or the innings or the rounds or the sets have to
be run thru if the report is to be complete, the paragraphing
cannot be cut as explained on page 387.   In case notables attend
or there is an old and bitter rivalry between the contestants or
the contest is an anniversary event, there is opportunity for
feature elements in the write-up.

In all reviewing, fair and unprejudiced reporting is imperative.
Any attempt to evaluate a play or a book or a game from a
personally biased point of view is dangerous and unworthy of a
reviewer.   Honest personal judgment and opinion may be expressed, the more so in writing about books and plays inasmuch
as there is no conventional measurement to be followed in such
writing.   The so-called masterpieces may of course be taken as
standards for comparative purposes.   But this is by no means
always a valid method of comparison, inasmuch as "times change"
and they have changed very much since many of the classics were
written.   The nearest approach to a code for reviewing is "I know
what I like."   Perhaps one of the most important aims in reviewing a book or a play is to make the review helpful to those who
are interested in books and in the theater.

As in the write-up of a game, give first the requisite preliminary
data—place, title, author, producer, director, scenic designer,
character cast, in the case of a play or a film; title, author, publisher, price (optional), size (optional), in the case of a book.   In
neither case should the reviewer reveal the complete story, for this
will negative the best selling point.   To "let the cat out of the
bag" in regard to a new play or a new novel is not considered
quite the professional thing on the part of a reviewer.   But he
may tell parts of it—enough to appetize the reader if he thinks it
a worth-while production.   And in both book and play he may
discuss the author's achievement, the realization of aim, the
progress or carry-thru of the original design, the comparative
importance of the work placed side-by-side with other works of
the same kind by the same author or by other authors.

The play reviewer may also discuss acting, diction, settings, cos-
tumes, direction, casting, reactions of audience, outstanding per-

formances of individual actors, and still other particulars. In reviews of both legitimate plays and films the actual program is usually reproduced at the top, and the reviewer's summary of impression at the end. In case either the film or the play is a dramatization of a book, variations from the original may be discussed. In reviewing a film a reviewer may speak of the synchronization of sound with action. If it is a picture adapted from a play formerly produced, comparison of the one with the other may be made.

After complying with the preliminaries above mentioned in connection with book reviewing, the reviewer should define the book —novel, travel, treatise, biography, and so on. He should further define within these and other headings—romantic novel, mystery novel, sea story, character study, and the like. Some idea of the action should be presented, with the cautions above pointed out; some discussion of the leading characters is always in order; comment upon the history and locale, if they are important features of the book, will come in for paragraph or longer treatment; the author's style, sense of reality, power in making characters alive, comprehension and sweep in handling situation and movement —all these and many more elements in a story may be treated in the book review. Different kinds of books call, of course, for different treatment. A review of a biography and a review of a novel have many points in common, as have a review of an anthology and a review of a period or historical volume. The general method is to define and classify first, then to discuss analytically, and then to summarize impression.

Do not confuse reviewing with criticism. Reviewing is ninety per cent reporting and ten per cent evaluating or judging. Criticism is the expression of discriminating judgment. It is ninety per cent evaluation and ten per cent (or less) reporting. Reviewing merely tells you what happened last evening in the theater and how the writer liked the play, or it reports the publication of a new book and how the writer likes it. Criticism measures the play or the book or the musical composition or the painting by rules and principles long accepted for standardizing works of art. These are illustrated in so-called masterpieces, and the critical measurement inevitably takes on some degree of comparison. There can be but little trustworthy criticism of contemporary works for the reason that all artistic output has to have time to season. The reviews below are good succinct examples.

These reviews, and the sports review on the next page, are concise, informing, and interesting

An Edgar Allan Poe Thriller.

THE TELL-TALE HEART, a film presentation of an Edgar Allan Poe short story, with Norman Dryden, John Kelt, Yolande Terrell, Thomas Shenton and James Fleck; directed by Desmund Hurst; a Clifton-Hurst production. At the Fifty-fifth Street Playhouse.

Another of Edgar Allan Poe's eerie stories has been brought to the screen, nearly a century after his death, for the delectation of admirers of combinations of psychological studies and camera efforts.

In "The Tell-Tale Heart," just arrived at the Fifty-fifth Street Playhouse, the British producers have clung almost literally to the original tale, and in so doing have supplied further evidence that it is not absolutely necessary to distort a great author's work in order to create a fascinating motion picture. Through the use of a prelude and a finale located in an asylum, and the interpolation of a couple of brief love scenes, Desmund Hurst, the director, has managed to spin the brief story into a film running for about fifty minutes without imposing upon the spectators' patience.

In fact, at no time is there any slackening in interest. Even persons familiar with the gripping pen portrait of the unhappy youth driven mad by his obsessions regarding an evil eye and a thunderously beating heart are bound to be entertained by the remarkable manner in which the camera reproduces the early nineteenth-century atmosphere. The light effects are particularly impressive. The very sparseness of the dialog adds to the illusion.

While all the actors are excellent, the honors naturally go to Norman Dryden as the insane young man and to John Kelt as the aged victim of the youth's delusions. It is hard to imagine any actors making their parts more real.

The New York Times.

Anno Domini 1934

FUNK & WAGNALLS NEW STANDARD ENCYCLOPEDIA YEAR BOOK FOR 1934. Prepared Under the Editorial Direction of Frank H. Vizetelly. Illustrated. 544 pp. New York: Funk & Wagnalls Company. $1.50.

THIS Year Book for 1934 brings down to date entries of continuing and developing interest in the Funk & Wagnalls New Standard Encyclopedia and can be used as a supplementary volume for that work. But it is also planned for separate use solely as a year book and as such makes a convenient and efficient reference volume. Its small format (18mo) renders it especially easy to handle, carry about and consult. The arrangement of contents is wholly alphabetical, without classification of subjects, but with subdivisions within the subject.

The editors and collaborators comprising the editorial staff include almost forty men and women of special knowledge and expertness in the subjects they handle. Among them are a number of members of the editorial boards of the Funk & Wagnalls New Standard Dictionary and New Standard Encyclopedia and several members of university faculties, newspaper staffs and government departments. In its handling of the important events and trends of the dealings of the administration with the depression the mood of the Year Book is hopeful and its outlook encouraging.

The New York Times.

DARTMOUTH ROUTS NORWICH BY 39-0

Newest Edition of Big Green Eleven Rolls Up Six Touchdowns in a Pouring Rain.

155-POUND BACKS EXCEL

Chamberlain and Conti Go Over Twice—Rand Sprints 48 Yards for a Marker.

Special to THE NEW YORK TIMES.

HANOVER, N. H., Sept. 29.— The newest edition of a Dartmouth football team rolled up six touchdowns to defeat Norwich, 39—0, today in a pouring rain, which kept the big Green chiefly to fundamentals.

Despite the uncertain footing of the field, the two new 155-pound halfbacks of the Indians, Eddie Chamberlain and Phil Conti, each scored two touchdowns after long drives by the team, which used only the simplest of off-tackle plays, and no passes.

Best Dash of Day.

Norman Rand, a former scholastic great of Massachusetts but overlooked until this, his senior, year, reeled off the best dash of the day, cutting through the left side of his line for 48 yards and a touchdown. Tony Geniawicz, sophomore back, scored the last Dartmouth touchdown on a charge through the line.

The big Green, starting the year under Coach Red Blaik, presented an almost entirely new front, and few were the familiar faces of last year. Much further advanced than at this time in 1933, the two sophomore tackles, Don Otis and Gordon Bennett, did impressive work, while Carl Ray, a bulky center, was a standout in the line.

Single Wing-Back Used.

The Green operated from a single wing-back formation unbalanced with no shift. Don Hagerman and Herb Stearns, the veterans who were shifted to guard from tackle and center, respectively, looked well on interference. Habicht and Hicks were stars of a Norwich team which played eight men of the eleven the entire game.

IV Headlines

Headlines advertise the news. They should do this by attracting attention and creating interest. They pull out of the news story the most important elements in it and take them to the reader; that is, they take the copy to the reader, whereas the advertising headline (see page 65) attempts to take the reader into the copy.

The headline is, then, even a briefer and more heavily charged summary of the news than the lead is. This means that judgment and precision are essentials to good headlining. The mechanical requirements given below will be seen to make even greater demands upon skill in word choice and adjustment to space.

Headlines should be composed of short simple words. Verbs, nouns, adjectives, and adverbs should be depended upon to convey the headline message. Do not use articles in headlines; use titles seldom; even *Mr.* and *Dr.* are usually omitted. Break by sense (see page 67) must be the rule wherever possible. This means that words and phrases are not to be divided at the ends of lines. As nearly as possible make each line express a complete phrase. All parts of the verb *to be* are usually omitted from headlines. Other verbs should be active always and present tense as often as sense or meaning will allow. The present tense should be used to indicate both past time and future time. It is best to use a pictorial or panoramic verb at the very beginning of a headline. Single quotation marks are usually used in headlines in order to save space, and figures may be used for the same purpose, even tho they would be wrong in customary usage.

Note the following mechanics of headlining:

This is a single headline	YANKEES' GAME OFF
This is a double or two-part headline. It is sometimes called *stept* because of the indention of the second line. Another name for it is *dropt-line*	COURT SENTENCES 17 FOR PARK LITTER
This is a pyramid or inverted pyramid headline	SCHOOL BOARD SANCTIONS COMMENCEMENT DATE SECOND TIME

This is a decked headline—there are four decks in all; hence it is called quadruple deck. Each part between rules is called a deck. The first one is the key or title deck

SAILORS OF FLEET
FLOCK TO DANCE

The second deck is sometimes called a *bank* headline. It is specific while the key deck is generic. It is pyramided in most papers, while the title or key deck is stept

5000 Bluejackets Are Guests of the City at Chief Event of Warship's Stay Here.

This is the third deck but the second key or title deck. Here, as usual, it is a single-line or *cross-line* deck

70,000 THRONG WARSHIPS

This is the fourth deck but the second bank. It details the second key deck just above it, and like the first bank it is pyramided

Admiral Sellers Has Reunion With Aged Nurse—Kiwanis Hosts at Luncheon.

Headlines may run to more than four decks, especially when big news breaks. When they are run over more than two-column width they are called *spread* headlines (see page 417). Their arrangement is in general the same in all papers—keys and banks alternating—but individual styles still persist in some localities. The leading paper in one large American city still carries the *blind headline* at the top of every major column. It just labels the news in most generic terms: *GREAT GAME—SERIOUS ACCIDENT—GROSS MISUNDERSTANDING.* Such headlines were common in the old journalism, but they have for the most part passed.

HEARTLESS!

Pretty Yankee Girl

Saves Italian Count's Life on Condition That He Cease To Pop the Question

Cold Water and Threatening Breakers Force Quick Compliance with Terms

"PULL"

Of Letter Amazes.

Replies Reach 50 Per Cent, Delegates Hear,

Discussing Merits of Mail Advertising.

Missive Offered Stock of Bootlegger Wares.

Every deck used should add a new element to the news. As a rule the bank constitutes a subordinate heading to the main or key headline preceding it, and may be linked to it by grammatical construction. The principal words in a key headline should never be repeated in a bank except in specific form. Feature story headlines should contain some colorful words in order to convey to the reader the character of what is to follow. The semicolon is still used in headlines, primarily for the reason that it stands for a word or more than one word, and counts as a half unit only. For the same reason the comma is usually used instead of *and* or *but*. Dashes are used in banks, if at all, but sparingly even there.

Headlines are devised by a specialist known as the headline editor. His task is one of precise measurement of letter spaces. Most letters are counted as one unit, but *i* is a half unit and *m* and *w* are one and a half units each. Every figure represents one unit in his count, with the exception of *I*, which is a half unit; and most of the punctuation marks likewise are half units. Dashes, interrogation marks, and quotation marks, however, count as one unit each. The period is a half unit but it is rarely used except after pyramids and by no means always there. Space between words is one unit. For the sake of symmetry the editor tries to get the same number of units in each line of a stept headline. This cannot always be done, of course, for he must work rapidly, and his copy is not sent back for revision. It is set immediately in molten lead. Note the count in each of these:

Each line has twelve and a half units according to the above specifications	**BELGIUM HAILS** **A NEW ALBERT**
The first line has fourteen units and the dropt line thirteen and a half. Note the figure 2 to economize the count	**2 SHIPS TIED UP** **BY DOCK STRIKE**
The first two lines here have thirteen and a half and thirteen units respectively, and the third has fourteen. Stepping or dropping is therefore impossible. Note the use of single quotation marks	**HOOVER PRAISES** **NEW PLATFORM** **AS 'COURAGEOUS'**
Note the use of *six* and the use of *8* in order to facilitate the unit count	**Six to 8 Thousand Jobs** **Approved by Congress**

These two lines in the key line are exactly even—seventeen and a half units—and cannot be stept therefore. Note the single quotation marks and the double ones around the same word in the first line of the lead

'INFLUENCE' CHARGED IN CITY PARK AWARD

Asphalt Concern Sues to Cancel Rival's Bid on Contract.

Note the bad hyphenation in the bank

Note the participial opening of the lead

Charging that "influence" caused the city's Department of Purchase to ignore the charter provision which requires awarding of contracts to lowest bidders, the Empire Asphalt Products Co., Inc., of Brooklyn, today filed a motion in Supreme Court for a mandamus ordering canceling an award to Limestone Products Co., Inc., of Westchester, second lowest bidder, for 20,000 tons of asphalt for park use.

V Copy (see pages 54-77)

Copy for newspaper and magazine publication should be prepared so carefully that misunderstanding is impossible. Proper names and difficult or unusual words should be spelled most carefully and *follow copy* should be written above them or on the margin opposite them. Never should single-spaced copy be submitted for printing. Double spacing is the rule, and it is often preferable to triple-space. This last arrangement makes it possible for editing to be done between lines and renders less likely the repeating or the skipping of lines by the linotyper. Copy should be folded horizontally thru the middle with written side out. This makes it possible for the linotyper to start work at it with the least possible rehandling. Generous margins should be left on all sides of copy, and at least one third of the first page should be left blank for the insertion of any general directions or titling that it is desirable to make when it goes out for setting.

Copy should of course be submitted in typewriting, but in those rare cases where it cannot be, the writer should take more than usual pains to write clearly and in a large open hand. It is possible so to adjust typewritten copy that it will equal line by line the printed column. The amount of copy can thus be almost exactly calculated in terms of print. Count the number of words in each of six lines, say, in the ordinary newspaper column. Add the total and divide by six. This will give you the average number of words to the line. Now adjust your typewritten margins so that each line of copy contains this number of words, and it will be easy to see when you have written a column or half column or other fraction.

Every leading newspaper has its own style book—a book in which are summarized the rules and regulations regarding the technique of copy preparation, typographical set-up, and other like matters. The contents of *Get It Right*, especially Chapters 1, 3, 6, 7, 16, 17, 18, give a fair idea of what such manuals contain. He who prepares copy for a newspaper should know the requirements set down in the style book of that paper. Much of the editing that is done in newspapers consists of adjusting copy to the regulation style of the paper, such, for instance, as the following:

—say *persons*, not *people* [this is a general newspaper rule]

—say *bridegroom*, not *groom; body*, not *remains*

—say *widow of Horace Brown*, not *of the late Horace Brown*

—say *abolition* instead of *abolishment; begin* instead of *commence; woman* instead of *lady* or *female; give* or *gave* instead of *donate* or *donated;* and generally Saxon words are better than Norman-French. Where a word has a shorter or longer form, as *jeopard* and *jeopardize*, use the former. *Beside* is strictly a preposition, while *besides* has the additional adverbial idea of moreover. Distinguish carefully between *claim* and *assert, take* and *bring, describe* and *explain*

—use *&* between personal names only; use *and* between names of materials and places—*Brander & Colson Manufacturing Company, Steel and Nickel Plating Company, Hatboro and Germantown Refining Company* [a most arbitrary rule]

—capitalize [or do not capitalize] *jr.* and *sr.* following surnames, and use [or do not use] comma before them

—use three asterisks to indicate ellipsis either in the body of your copy or at the end of it

—place quotation marks before *&c.* or before an em-dash or a two-em-dash when they follow unfinished quotations

—indent and single-space quoted excerpts rather than place them in quotation marks

—place in brackets any term inserted to indicate an omission from copy, or an explanation or clarification of copy:

> "The charges are absolute lies. I never struck anybody. Very definite instructions have been given to cottage fathers not to use force. [The boys live in cottages, each of which is in charge of a master or 'cottage father.'] Why, only a month ago a cottage father was discharged when a hearing showed he had struck a boy."

—use quotation marks at the beginning of each line of an editorial when such quotation runs to more than two lines:

> Several years ago Senator Gore asked unanimous consent to have Magna Carta printed as a Senate document, saying that he had found it impossible to secure a copy in the Senate Library and that he wished to make it "generally available." He referred to it as "the foundation of English lib-"erty and jurisprudence, and the "cornerstone of American liberty "and jurisprudence" as well. He called Section 39 the "finest fruit of sixty centuries of human struggle of evolution." It reads:
>
>> No free man shall be seized, or imprisoned, or dispossessed, or outlawed, or in any way destroyed; nor will we condemn him, nor will we commit him to prison, excepting by the legal judgment of his peers, or by the laws of the land.

These typical rules taken at random from as many different style books illustrate the kind and the scope of stylistic details covered in the ordinary book. While the contents of all of them are very much alike, there are nevertheless differences—some very arbitrary ones sometimes. The use of "side-quote" marks, for instance, as illustrated in the editorial excerpt above, is by no means generally followed. One of the most famous democratic papers in the country ruled that Theodore Roosevelt, when he was running for the presidency the third time, should never be mentioned by name, but should always be referred to, rather, as The Third Term Candidate or as Theodore the First. The owner of this paper thus added another little note to its opposition on the grounds that Roosevelt was imperialistically inclined and wished to make himself monarch of an American Empire. Shortly after the Carnegie Committee on Simplified Spelling issued its first propaganda for the simplification of the spelling of certain words, the style books of practically all papers carried in bold face a rule ordering the retention of conservative spelling. Some papers and some publishing houses still do so in their style manuals.

In the main, however, the newspaper style book is an excellent guide and compendium in the technique of writing and printing, and it may profitably be used as a classroom text from time to time. Most business houses, and especially publishing and printing establishments, likewise issue style books for guidance in preparing company copy and in setting up company printing.

Every school should have certain well established rules in regard to note and letter set-up. And one of the very first steps to take in connection with a school paper should be that of deciding upon specific details of copy and printing forms—how copy must be submitted, how the title of the paper is to be set, how standing heads are to be harmonized, how variations of type face are to be made. These and other questions like them should be made subject of discussion by the board of editors, in conference with the departments of art and English, and as result a simple and explicit style sheet or folder should be issued to all students in the school.

VI Make-up

The most important news is found on the first page of the daily newspaper. The most important article in a magazine is usually placed first. In British newspapers, however, the first page may be given over entirely to classified advertisements, and this was once the case with some of the leading papers in the United States. The most important news position on the first page is the extreme right-hand column—the eighth column in most make-up. The eye generally "trails" to the right. The newspaper fold on the news stands is so made that this column or the upper right-hand quarter of the paper is seen most easily. It is here, too, that spread headlines are most frequently used. The next spread-line position is usually the corresponding left-hand columns. "Full position" is the name given to the two middle columns at the very top of the page. In pages following the first this space is coveted by advertisers. In case of streamer or scare headlines newspapers are usually folded only once horizontally so that the entire head may be seen by the passer-by. This fold also makes visible all decked headlines above it.

In order that the most important national and international news may be grouped on the first page, it is necessary to run *break-overs* to the second page if the news is especially important, to subsequent pages in descending scale of importance. News tends in most papers to become more and more local as paging progresses. But the last page of the newspaper is rated as second in importance to the first in many organizations. The editorial page usually comes somewhere near the middle of the paper. Advertising is never carried on the first page with the exception of brief agate notes at the bottom of a column now and then. In most papers it begins on the second or third page and increases in space up to the editorial page. Following the editorial page closely come news records of various community interests. Following these come classified advertisements—as many as seventy-five different classifications in some papers.

Note, in the reproduction on page 406, the symmetrical balance achieved by the make-up editor in the arrangement of news. The headlines themselves in correlative columns are harmonized as well as the boxed items. The orderly and sedate placement of parts makes for good impression and sales attractiveness.

Sunday editions are exceptions to these specifications. There are many more sections in these editions, and full-page and double-spread advertising copy is much more commonly placed. Preferred positions in newspaper advertising are as follows:

1 Full position—top of page middle, completely surrounded by reading matter
2 Next to reading matter at top of column
3 Next to reading matter at bottom of column
4 Second, third, and last pages
5 Opposite editorial page (when available)
6 Women's and other special pages

A number of small advertisements carried on a single newspaper page are frequently wedged diagonally into the reading matter as

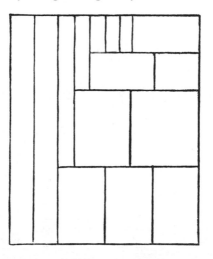

illustrated above. This intrudes them upon the attention of the reader. News make-up has to be adjusted accordingly. The

The symmetrical balance (see page 59) not only pleases but invites

"All the News That's Fit to Print."

The New York Times.

LATE CITY EDITION

VOL. XC....No. 30,428. NEW YORK, FRIDAY, MAY 16, 1941. THREE CENTS

ROOSEVELT CAUTIONS VICHY, APPEALS TO PEOPLE; U. S. HOLDS FRENCH SHIPS; SEIZURE BILL PASSED; GERMAN PLANES ENTER SYRIA TO ASSIST IRAQ

STRIKE PEACE PLAN ACCEPTED BY G. M.; WAGE DEMAND MET

Corporation Accepts Proposal of Mediation Board, as Union Waives the Closed Shop

WALKOUTS HAD STARTED

35,000 Men Had Quit Work for Day at Plants in Flint Despite Officers' Appeals

The International Situation

FRIDAY, MAY 16, 1941

NAZIS AT AIR BASES

Clash Believed Imminent as British Act to Parry Thrust at Suez

GERMANS IN BAGHDAD

Axis Leaders Reported Awaiting Men and Arms to Help 'Rebels'

SENATE VOTE 59-20

Ban on Transferring Axis Vessels to Britain Is Beaten, 43 to 38

100 SHIPS INVOLVED

Stimson Holds to Stand for Convoys—Lee Asks Seizure of Dakar

Normandie in U. S. Custody; 10 Other Ships Are Boarded

Coast Guard Acts Quickly on Orders of the President—Watches Placed Over Engine Rooms—Crews Are Not in Custody

OUR PACE WON'T DO, SAYS OPM OFFICIAL

Hours Must Be Longer, Civil Output Cut and Business Bolder, Batt Asserts

PETAIN ASKS UNITY ON DEAL WITH NAZIS

Tells the People to Follow Him Implicitly in Outcome of Talks With Germans

PRESIDENT MOVES

Declares 'Collaboration' With Reich Is Menace to This Hemisphere

PLEA IS SHORT-WAVED

Petain's Assurances to U.S. Cited—Status of Fleet Is Watched

CARREL BELIEVED DETAINED BY NAZIS

Forced to Stay in the Occupied Zone of France, Friend in This City Fears

BRITISH TO ATTACK GERMANS IN SYRIA

Eden Tells Commons Breaking of French Pledges Invites 'Appropriate Action'

Hess's Inquisitors Submit Report; Hitler Said to Have Known of Flight

narrow vertical spaces in the diagram on page 405 indicate read-ing matter; the large spaces, advertising.

Full-page newspaper copy is not to be recommended, except for holiday publication when people have more leisure to devote to daily reading.   As a rule the two-interest page is more profitable than the single-interest page.   In some magazines and newspapers advertisements of a kind are grouped together.   In such cases the advertiser knows beforehand what his advertising company is to be, and he may thus be able to construct his copy more advan-tageously as a result.

The following diagram represents relative immediacy of attention-value for the placement of copy, advertisement, or picture on any

rectangular golden proportion (see page 58), and summarizes what has been said above regarding the placement of news upon a page.   Let the entire graph represent any newspaper page or any magazine page.   Let the quarter labeled *c a b d* represent any quarter-page in the newspaper or the magazine.   Then *A* is the most valuable position on the page; *a* the most valuable point in the quarter-page copy.   *B* and *b* are the next most important positions, and so forth.   It will be noted that in both cases the portion that covers the optical center has first visibility.   There is very little difference between *C* and *B* in "pulling" power. The upper half of the page is better page position than the lower half; the upper right quarter-page is better than any other quarter.

Certain terms particular to newspapers and newspaper writing have already been explained. There are some others that students and office workers who have to do with printing and publishing, should know and be able to use intelligently. The first list of terms below is used in connection with copy—all manuscripts are referred to as *copy*. The second list contains terms that pertain to printing; the third list, to terms peculiar to newspaper make-up.

I

add, insert, kill, more written in copy mean respectively that something is to be added, inserted, canceled, and more is to follow

art is the term applied to any pictures, drawings, graphs, illustrations used to accompany copy

article is the general or layman's name for a "piece in the paper." It refers to something special rather than to the regular newspaper content

classified advertisements are advertisements that are printed in agate type (see page 414) and run in almost uniform style in given classifications, such as *Help Wanted, Situations Wanted, Lost and Found, Automobile Exchange, Furnished Rooms, Apartments Wanted, Houses for Sale, Houses for Rent, Country Estates, Business Opportunities, Investment Opportunities.* These are typical. The indention of the second line is one of the traditional mechanisms of set-up.

UNUSUAL OPPORTUNITY to secure bargain office, outside, high up, in one of finest office buildings in downtown financial district. Purdy Management, COrtland 7-2483.

MORTGAGES — Certificates bought and sold; all company issues. Frank M. McCurdy Co., 158 Remsen St., Brooklyn.

ANACONDA Van Service—New England, Western, Southern to Florida; return load rates; insured. 250 West 57th. CIrcle 7-7243.

60TH ST., 145-147 EAST—Attractive 2 rooms, bath, kitchenette, 2d floor; convenient all transportation; immediate, Oct. 1st possession; $40-$50. Supt. or Wm. A. White & Sons. VAnderbilt 3-0204.

close up means to ignore or cancel space and set upper part of copy consecutively with lower

copy-cutter, copy-holder, copy-reader mean respectively the one who cuts a long piece of copy into parts called *takes* for distribution to typesetters or linotype operators so that the composition into type may be hastened as well as equalized; one who holds copy and reads it to a proofreader or proof-checker; one who revises stories, edits them, arranges to have them cut or lengthened, and suggests or writes headlines for them

date line is the line used at the beginning of stories that are about happenings in places other than local. The technique should be noted. The initials AP or UP following the date line refer to the two leading American news agencies—Associated Press and United Press

LOS ANGELES, Sept. 5 (A.P.). —The community chest system of administering to the needy was praised by former President Hoover in an address here today.

TORONTO, Sept. 6 (U.P.).— Accused under a statute framed in the year 1360 which provided, among other things, cutting off of the ears as a penalty upon conviction, eight strikers were dismissed today in court here.

dead is written on copy that has been completely killed (see below) and cannot therefore be used

dead line is the last possible admissible date for getting copy in

end or ♯ or *"30"* or *H* is written at the conclusion of a piece of copy to indicate that there is no more to follow

fillers are notes or pieces of copy used for filling space but having little or no real value as news

follow written at the top of a piece of copy means that the story is a continuation of a story gone before. It is usually followed by a key word to indicate the connection to make-up and headline editors

ghost or *shadow writing* is the name given to copy that has been written by a reporter or some other writer for a person under whose name the story appears

hold written on copy or proof means that it is to be kept for future printing, that it is being held pending break of additional news, or that it will be just as good later as now

it is reported, it is rumored, it is said, it was announced, according to, it is generally believed, and other similar forms of expression are commonly used by newspapers, especially in cases where the statement of news as a fact has not been legally substantiated and may cause trouble on its being printed as such. It is likewise customary for a paper to identify some one authoritatively in case a news story is likely to cause doubt or its authenticity is questioned, as *Harold Johnson,* EXPERT ADVISER TO THE ———— COMPANY, *is authority for the statement that pliable glass is to be a reality within six months*

COMPOSING STICK

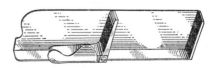

item, that is, *news item* is a short news note about two inches in depth. It is sometimes called a *stickful* in printers' parlance. The printing tray, called a *composing stick,* is adjustable in size so as to fit comfortably into the typesetter's left hand while he sets type into it with his right. The completed set is called a stickful, or a news item. The stick is usually metal (sometimes wood)

justify means to fill exactly the space allotted, that is, to make your copy fit exactly the lines or half column or column that you were assigned

kill, written across matter or on the margin, means that it is to be deleted, and, as a rule, that the space thus left is to be closed up

must is sometimes written on copy to show that it must be used at once if it is to have any value. Postponed it will become stale

n.b. is sometimes written at the bottom of one page and at the top of the next when matter is to be carried on without a break—*no break*

periods, commas, and other marks of punctuation are sometimes put in a circle when their exact use is of special importance. A circle around an abbreviation or a figure means that it is to be spelled out

railroad is to rush a piece of copy thru to the press without detailed editing, because of haste

record or *news record* is birth or death or marriage or weather announcement, or any other form of announcement that appears regularly and in set form

release written at the top of copy followed by a date indicates when it should be printed

revise may be written on copy to mean that it should be revised. Written on a proof that is full of corrections, it means that a new, corrected proof is desired

rewrite is a rewritten account of a story that has previously appeared. A rewrite man is one who writes stories that are told crudely or hastily, either in person or by telephone, or who edits or rewrites unsatisfactory copy. He is first cousin to a shadow or ghost writer

run in means that tabular matter, for instance, is not to be set as a table but is to be run in line by line; it may also mean that sections of copy sent in after the major portion has been received are to be run in to the main copy at places indicated

space man or *space writer* is one who is assigned and paid according to the space his writing fills

teaser is a short bit of copy—a line or two or a short paragraph—used to fill in spaces, column ends, and the like. It is calculated to please or amuse the reader and to stick in his memory. Teaser writers or paragraphers are in many newspaper and magazine organizations highly specialized writers

II

body type or *body face* is the style of type in which a story is printed— the main or principal print

boiler plate is the stereotyped sheet of lead with the type imprint upon it. It is sold by syndicates to publications. Country papers make large use of such ready-set articles and illustrations. They are sometimes called *patent insides*

bold face (b.f) is type in especially heavy inking—heavy black (see p. 471) *chase* is a frame of steel into which type pages, groups of pages, or other units of set type are locked for running off printed matter or for making plates. This locked or fastened type is called a form

FORM LOCKED IN CHASE

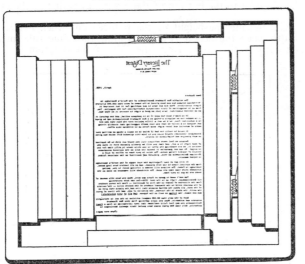

composition of type means the setting of type in readiness for printing

condensed type or *face* is type that is narrowed; *expanded type* or *face* is type that is broadened. In the first of the following

JOHN
JAMISON

John is expanded; in the second *Jamison* is condensed, in order to get a perfect blocking (see page 233)

cut is the metal reproduction of a picture or illustration, from which the picture is to be printed. It is tacked on a type-high piece of wood or type metal. The word is also used to mean the actual picture when printed

The manner of estimating what the height of a cut or an engraving will be after it is reduced to a given width, or vice versa, is based on a simple principle, illustrated by the following diagram

Draw a diagram the same length and width as the photograph, drawing, or subject-matter to be reduced; draw also a line diagonally from the upper left corner to the lower right corner

If, for example, the engraving is to fit a standard newspaper column of two inches in width, move a ruler horizontally from the bottom line of the diagram upward, until a point on the diagonal line is reached where the distance from the right of the diagram is two inches. Draw a horizontal line here and also a vertical line from this point on the diagonal to the bottom of the diagram parallel to the outer edge.

This will indicate the height of the reduced cut when made. To find the width when the height is given, follow the same rule, meeting the diagonal line with a ruler from the side of the diagram

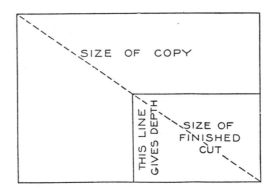

strip cut is a long narrow cut calculated to run across an entire page. A *slip cut* is any small cut that may be "slipped in" anywhere in a story, marginally or squarely in the body of copy

dash is the line or rule between parts of a display head and at the ends of stories

display type or *face* is type that is larger and more striking than body face, or type that is variously and strikingly arranged

displayed advertisement is one that is made to constitute a picture as result of large and decorative type faces, illustrations, striking and unusual arrangement, and the like

font is the name given to a complete set of letters of one style or size of type (see page 414), including small letters and capitals, punctuation marks and figures

form is a set of type composed and ready for printing, locked in a chase

job case is a single case in which lower-case letters and capitals are together. Italic and job fonts are kept in job cases

lead (pronounced as *led*) is a narrow strip of metal placed between lines of type to give the printing a more open appearance. Double leading, triple leading, quadruple leading mean that two, three, four, or more such strips are placed between lines. Wide spacing may be made a form of display. When leads are placed between lines the printing is called leaded matter; when no leads are used it is called solid matter. To *set solid* means to omit leading

linotype is a typesetting machine operated by a man sitting before it and fingering a keyboard much like the typewriter keyboard. The machine casts type line by line solidly in molten metal

lower case (*l.c.*) means small letters as opposed to capitals. The name comes from the case in which small letters are kept in the printing bank, lower than the case in which capitals are kept. Capitals are therefore called *upper case* (*u.c.*). Figures, punctuation marks, and other characters are included in these classifications

metal furniture is the name given to the wide metal pieces used for separating type pages in a form, or for spacing out parts that are to be left blank. It comes in various lengths and widths

pi means a mixed-up lot of type. Type becomes pied when it falls out of the form (because the chase was not securely locked) and scatters. A *pi-line* is one in which type is mixed so that the letters make nonsense or no sense

pica is a standard of measurement used for indicating the widths of columns or pages, the sizes of printing material, and the like. Six picas are an inch. One-twelfth of a pica is a "point," the modern unit for the measurement of all type

PICAS 6   1|2   1|8   2|4
INCHES   1   2   3   4

point means punctuation mark. *Pointing* is punctuating. A *point* is also the unit of measurement of letter height—one twelfth of the height of a pica letter

SIZES OF BODY TYPE IN COMPARISON WITH ONE INCH SPACE

A point is $\frac{1}{72}$ of an inch. The standard width of a single column (newspaper) is $2\frac{1}{12}$ inches ($12\frac{1}{2}$ pica ems). The standard width of a double column (newspaper) is $4\frac{1}{4}$ inches ($25\frac{1}{2}$ pica ems). An *em* is a unit square of any type body, which is the dimension required for the face of a lower case *m*. A pica *m* (*em*) is 12 points wide, and 12 points in depth, or a sixth of an inch each way

POINTS		LINES TO INCH
5½	(Agate)	14
6	(Nonpareil)	12
8	(Brevier)	9
10	(Long Primer)	7
12	(Pica)	6
14	(English)	5
18	(Great Primer)	4

A FEW BODY TYPE FACES

5½ Point (Agate) Solid

Make every word count in writing your copy. Omit no essential phraseology, but strip your message to minimum conciseness and directness consistent with adequacy and courtesy. Aim to say a part wholly rather than a whole partly.

5½ Point (Agate) Leaded

Make every word count in writing your copy. Omit no essential phraseology, but strip your message to minimum conciseness and directness consistent with adequacy and courtesy. Aim to say a part wholly rather than a whole partly.

6 Point (Nonpareil) Solid

Make every word count in writing your copy. Omit no essential phraseology, but strip your message to minimum conciseness and directness consistent with adequacy and courtesy. Aim to say a part wholly rather than a whole partly.

6 Point (Nonpareil) Leaded

Make every word count in writing your copy. Omit no essential phraseology, but strip your message to minimum conciseness and directness consistent with adequacy and courtesy. Aim to say a part wholly rather than a whole partly.

8 Point (Brevier) Solid

Make every word count in writing your copy. Omit no essential phraseology, but strip your message to minimum conciseness and directness consistent with adequacy and courtesy. Aim to say a part wholly rather than a whole partly.

8 Point (Brevier) Leaded

Make every word count in writing your copy. Omit no essential phraseology, but strip your message to minimum conciseness and directness consistent with adequacy and courtesy. Aim to

10 Point (Long Primer) Solid

Make every word count in writing your copy. Omit no essential phraseology, but strip your message to minimum conciseness

10 Point (Long Primer) Leaded

Make every word count in writing your copy. Omit no essential phraseology, but strip your message to minimum conciseness

12 Point (Pica) Solid

Make every word count in writing your copy. Omit no essential phraseology, but strip your message to

12 Point (Pica) Leaded

Make every word count in writing your copy. Omit no essential phraseology, but strip your message to

14 Point (English) Solid

Make every word count in writing your copy. Omit no essential phras

14 Point (English) Leaded

Make every word count in writing your copy. Omit no essential phras

18 Point (Great Primer) Solid

Make every word count in writing your copy. Omit

18 Point (Great Primer) Leaded

Make every word count in writing your copy. Omit

A FEW DISPLAY TYPE FACES

72 Point Cheltenham Bold

ABJ

60 Point Cheltenham Bold

ABEI

60 Point Scotch Roman

APB

48 Point Cheltenham Bold

ABDG

48 Point Caslon

ABCJ

48 Point Cheltenham Condensed

ABCEFJ

42 Point DeVinne Italic

Abcdif

36 Point Kennerley

ABCDN

36 Point Bodoni

ABCDEFJ

36 Point Garamont

ABCDEF

36 Point Caslon Open

ABCDI

36 Point Cheltenham Bold Italic

Abcdefg

36 Point Caslon Italic

Abcdefgh

36 Point Goudy Italic

Abcdefgh

24 Point McMurtrie

ABCDEFG

quad is a square or block of blank metal used for spacing between letters and for filling out blank lines. It is lower than the top surface of letters, that is, it is not type high, and it is made in various widths

quoin is a wedge used to tighten type in a frame or form by pressing or hammering in

rule is a thin piece or strip of metal used for making lines (dashes) and for enclosing boxes. Rules are type high, of different lengths and thicknesses, light or shaded. Boxes are enclosed in light rules; displayed special death notices, in heavy rules

set means placed in position, when used in reference to the setting of type

slug is a thick strip of solid lead made by the linotype machine; also such a strip with type set on one side of it. Slugs are leads larger than two-point

solid is a term used of type when it is set without spacing or leading between lines. Here are a few solid lines of six-point type:

> In the main, however, the newspaper
> style book is an excellent guide and
> compendium in the technique of writ-
> ing and printing, and it may profitably

stone is the table upon which the compositor or the make-up man arranges the type matter into page forms and later takes the forms apart

stick (*composing stick*) see illustration on page 409

III

box or *boxed head* or *boxed item* is the square or rectangular display of a heading or piece of news, light or heavy rules being used to enclose it

break is said of any event that constitutes news, at the time that it happens. "When do you expect the news to *break?*"

break-over or *jump-over* is the continued part of a story on another page from the one on which it starts

caption is the title of a cut. It customarily appears beneath it but is increasingly being used above. When the latter is the case it is called *overline* (see pages 62, 66, 411, and elsewhere in this book)

credit line is a line given over to acknowledgment of permission to print— from another publication, an organization, an individual, and so forth

ears are parallel boxed matter, balanced on the two sides of a title or heading or other similar unit in make-up

extension or *hanging* means the extending of the first line of matter further to the left than the other lines

flush means even with—two or more lines that begin on exactly the same margin are said to be flush

Monday, May 12, 1941

Owned and published daily by New York Tribune Inc., a New York corporation. Ogden Reid, President; Helen Rogers Reid, Vice-President; Howard Davis, Second Vice President; Stanley D. Brown, Secretary; A. V. Miller, Treasurer Address 280 West Forty-first St., New York City.

MAIN OFFICE—230 West 41st Street. Phone PEnnsylvania 6-4000. Open daily 8 A. M. to 12 P. M.; Sunday, 10 A. M. to 12 P. M. for the receipt of advertisements and sale of newspapers. DOWNTOWN OFFICE—132 Nassau Street. Phone PEnnsylvania 6-4000. Open daily 9 A. M. to 7 P. M.; Saturday to 3:30 P. M. Closed Sundays and holidays.

WASHINGTON................National Press Building
BOSTON.....................Statler Office Building
CHICAGO...............360 North Michigan Avenue
DETROIT...............General Motors Building
LOS ANGELES...............448 South Hill Street
ST. LOUIS.................Globe Democrat Building
SAN FRANCISCO................5 Third Street
SEATTLE....................1004 Second Avenue
PORTLAND, Ore............Terminal Sales Building
LONDON ....Bush House, Aldwych
PARIS ....21 Rue de Berri
BERLIN ....80a, Wilhelmstrasse
ROME ....54 Via della Mercede
SHANGHAI ....34 Avenue Edward VII

SUBSCRIPTION RATES—By Mail, Including Postage.

THE UNITED STATES, POSSESSIONS AND TERRITORIES

	One Year	Six Months	Three Months	One Month
*Weekday and Sunday.	$17.00	$8.50	$4.25	$1.50
†Weekday only........	12.00	6.00	3.00	1.00
Sunday only	6.00	3.00	1.50	.75

*One week, 50 cents. †One week, 40 cents.

CANADA AND NEWFOUNDLAND

Daily and Sunday.....	$22.00	$11.00	$5.50	$2.50
Daily	15.00	7.50	3.75	1.50
Sunday	8.00	4.00	2.50	1.25

SOUTH AND CENTRAL AMERICA AND SPAIN

Argentina, Balearic Islands, Bolivia, Brazil, Canary Islands, Chile, Colombia, Costa Rica, Cuba, Dominican Republic, Ecuador, El Salvador, Guatemala, Haiti, Mexico, Nicaragua, Panama, Paraguay, Peru, Republic of Honduras, Santo Domingo, Spain and its colonies, Uruguay, Venezuela.

Weekday and Sunday..	$20.00	$10.00	$5.00	$2.00
Weekday only........	13.00	6.50	3.50	1.25
Sunday only.........	7.00	3.50	2.00	1.00

OTHER FOREIGN COUNTRIES

Weekday and Sunday..	$50.00	$25.00	$12.50	$4.25
Weekday only........	32.00	16.00	8.00	2.75
Sunday only.........	18.00	9.00	4.50	1.50

Entered at the Postoffice of New York as Second-Class Mail Matter.

MEMBER OF THE ASSOCIATED PRESS

The Associated Press is exclusively entitled to the use for republication of all news dispatches credited to it or not otherwise credited in this paper and also the local news of spontaneous origin published herein. All rights of republication of all other matter herein also are reserved.

heading or *head* is used to mean headline or any other form of titling

indention means setting a line or lines in from an established margin, such as paragraph indention

jump-head is the heading or headline of that part of a story that is continued from a preceding page

make-up is the cutting and arranging of galleys (see page 470) into the positions in which it is desired to have matter appear page by page. A make-up editor may have complete charge of this work

masthead is that part of the paper, usually at the top of the first column of the editorial page, which lists its officers, terms, etc., as in the *Herald Tribune* masthead on this page

morgue is the name given to the place—file and filing room —where information is kept on tap for emergency consultation—biographies of notable people, important statistics, and the like

pull means to take off on paper an impression of the set type properly inked. Proofs are "pulled" from the type

scoop or *beat* is the printing and circulation of a piece of news by one paper before another has been able to get it

spreadhead is a headline that runs over two or more columns. If it runs the full width of the paper it is called *streamer head* or *headline*. If it is printed with colored ink and its lettering is extremely large it is called a *scare head* or *headline standing head* is a head or headline that is used regularly in every issue and is therefore kept standing for constant use. It is never killed

subhead is a sectional title or headline inserted here and there thruout a long story to make reading easier by way of periodic summaries

VII   Letters to the editor

Letters to newspapers are somewhat special in form. The salutation is different from that in other types of letter (see below) and the date is usually placed at the lower left-hand corner. The name of the writer (or the assumed name) goes in the customary position, tho some newspapers give the names of letter authors a by-line. In case an assumed name is used, the writer must, as a matter of good faith, enclose his real name and his correct address. The latter will, of course, not be printed. Newspaper letters should be worth while, that is, they should be written about some question of immediate or permanent public interest, and they should—it goes without saying—be well organized and not too lengthy.

Daniel Defoe (1659?-1731) wrote this letter to the editor of *Applebee's Journal,* in which it appeared on July 21, 1722, following the death of John Churchill, Duke of Marlborough, and during the period of obsequies. It is, in reality, a reflective essay on the "futility and instability of human glory"—the phrase that is sometimes given it as a title. *Hic jacet* is Latin for *Here lies,* a commonly used epitaph in the early centuries.

Sir,
    I have employed myself of late pretty much in the study of history, and have been reading the stories of the great men of past ages, Alexander the Great, Julius Cæsar, the great Augustus, and many more down, down, down, to the still greater Louis XIV, and even to the still greatest John, Duke of Marlborough. In my way I met with Tamerlane the Scythian, Tomornbejus the Egyptian, Solyman the Magnificent, and others of the Mahometan or Ottoman race; and after all the great things they have done I find it said of them all, one after another, AND THEN HE DIED, all dead, dead, dead! *Hic jacet* is the finishing part of their history. Some lie in the bed of honor, and some in honor's truckle bed; some were bravely slain in battle on the field of honor, some in the storm of a counterscrap and died in the ditch of honor; some here, some there; the bones of the bold and the brave, the cowardly and the base, the hero and the scoundrel, are heaped up together; there they lie in oblivion, and under the ruins of the earth, undistinguished from one another, nay, even from the common earth.

Huddled in dirt the blust'ring engine lies,
That was so great, and thought himself so wise.

How many hundreds of thousands of the bravest fellows then in the world lie on heaps in the ground, whose bones are to this day plowed up by the rustics or dug up by the laborer, and the earth their more noble vital parts are converted to has been perhaps applied to the meanest uses!

How have we screened the ashes of heroes to make our mortar, and mingled the remains of a Roman general to build a hogsty! Where are the ashes of a Cæsar, and the remains of a Pompey, a Scipio, or a Hannibal? All are vanished, they and their very monuments are moldered into earth, their dust is lost, and their place knows them no more. They live only in the immortal writings of their historians and poets, the renowned flatterers of the age they lived in, who have made us think of the persons, not as they really were, but as they were pleased to represent them.

As the greatest men, so even the longest lived. The Methuselahs of the antediluvian world, the accounts of them all end with the same. Methuselah lived nine hundred sixty and nine years and begat sons and daughters—and what then? AND THEN HE DIED.

> Death like an overflowing stream
> Sweeps us away; our life's a dream.

We are now solemnizing the obsequies of the great Marlborough; all his victories, all his glories, his great projected schemes of war, his uninterrupted series of conquests, which are called his, as if he alone had fought and conquered by his arm what so many men obtained for him with their blood—all is ended, where other men, and, indeed, where all men ended: HE IS DEAD!

Not all his immense wealth, the spoils and trophies of his enemies, the bounty of his grateful mistress, and the treasure amassed in war and peace, not all that mighty bulk of gold—which some suggest is such, and so great, as I care not to mention—could either give him life or continue it one moment, but he is dead; and some say the great treasure he was possessed of here had one strange particular quality attending it, which might have been very dissatisfying to him if he had considered much on it; namely, that he could not carry much of it with him.

We have now nothing left us of this great man that we can converse with but his monument and his history. He is now numbered among things past. The funeral as well as the battles of the Duke of Marlborough are like to adorn our houses in sculpture as things equally gay and to be looked on with pleasure. Such is the end of human glory, and so little is the world able to do for the greatest men that come into it, and for the greatest merit those men can arrive at.

What then is the work of life? What the business of great men, that pass the stage of the world in seeming triumph as these men we call heroes have done? Is it to grow great in the mouth of fame and take up many pages in history? Alas! that is no more than making a tale for the reading of posterity till it turns into fable and romance. Is it to furnish subject to the poets, and live in their immortal rimes, as they call them? That is, in short, no more than to be hereafter turned into ballad and song and be sung by old women to quiet children, or at the corner of a street to gather crowds in aid of the pickpocket and the [poor]. Or is their business rather to add virtue and piety to their glory, which alone will pass them into eternity and make them truly immortal? What is glory without virtue? A great man without religion is no more than a great beast without a soul. What is honor without merit? And what can be called true merit but that which makes a person be a good man as well as a great man?

If we believe in a future state of life, a place for the rewards of good men and for the punishment of the haters of virtue, how [many] heroes and famous men crowd in among the last! How few crowned heads wear the crowns of immortal felicity!

Let no man envy the great and glorious men, as we call them! Could we see them now, how many of them would move our pity rather than call for our congratulations! These few thoughts, sir, I send to prepare your readers' minds when they go to see the magnificent funeral of the late Duke of Marlborough.

DANIEL DEFOE

This letter written by John Ruskin (1819-1900) to *The London Times* is an appreciation, an exposition, and an art criticism all in one. Note in particular the excellent organization of the letter content. The first paragraph is introductory—it gives a reason for writing the letter. The second paragraph is an analysis of the public reaction to the picture. The third short paragraph is merely transitional to paragraphs four, five, six, seven, which are explanatory or interpretative. Paragraphs eight and nine summarize the explanation and justify it. Paragraphs ten and eleven constitute technical criticism with a view to informing the public of the difference between the true and the spurious in a certain school of painting. This letter—it is, indeed, a short essay on Holman Hunt's masterpiece—is an excellent example of art analysis and criticism.

To the Editor of the *London Times:*

Sir—

I   I trust that, with your usual kindness and liberality, you will give me room in your columns for a few words respecting the principal Præ-Raphaelite picture in the Exhibition of the Royal Academy this year. Its painter is traveling in the Holy Land, and can neither suffer nor benefit by criticism. But I am solicitous that justice should be done to his work, not for his sake, but for that of the large number of persons who, during the year, will have an opportunity of seeing it, and on whom, if rightly understood, it may make an impression for which they will ever afterwards be grateful.

II   I speak of the picture called "The Light of the World," by Holman Hunt. Standing by it yesterday for upwards of an hour, I watched the effect it produced upon the passers-by. Few stopped to look at it, and those who did almost invariably with some contemptuous expression, founded on what appeared to them the absurdity of representing the Saviour with a lantern in his hand. Now, it ought to be remembered that, whatever may be the fault of a Præ-Raphaelite picture, it must at least have taken much time; and therefore it may not unwarrantably be presumed that conceptions which are to be laboriously realized are not adopted in the first instance without some reflection. So that the spectator may surely question with himself whether the objections which now strike every one in a moment might not possibly have occurred to the painter himself, either during the time devoted to the design of the picture, or the months of labour required for its execution; and whether, therefore, there may not be some reason for his persistence in such an idea, not discoverable at first glance.

III   Mr. Hunt has never explained his work to me. I give what appears to me its palpable interpretation.

IV   The legend beneath it is the beautiful verse: "Behold, I stand at the door and knock. If any man hear my voice, and open the door, I will come in to him, and will sup with him, and he with me" (Rev. iii: 20). On the left-hand side of the picture is seen this door of the human soul. It is fast barred; its bars and nails are rusty; it is knitted and bound to its stanchions by creeping tendrils of ivy, showing that it has never been opened. A bat hovers about it; its threshold is overgrown with brambles, nettles, and fruitless corn— the wild grass "whereof the mower filleth not his hand, nor he that bindeth the sheaves his bosom." Christ approaches in the night time—Christ, in his everlasting offices of prophet, priest, and king. He wears the white robe, representing the power of the Spirit upon him; the jeweled robe and breastplate, representing the sacerdotal investiture; the rayed crown of gold, inwoven with the crown of thorns; not dead thorns, but now bearing soft leaves, for the healing of the nations.

V   Now, when Christ enters any human heart, he bears with him a twofold light: first, the light of conscience, which displays past sin, and afterwards the light of peace, the hope of salvation. The lantern, carried in Christ's left hand, is this light of conscience. Its fire is red and fierce; it falls only on the closed door, on the weeds which encumber it, and on an apple shaken from one of the trees of the orchard, thus marking that the entire awakening of the conscience is not merely to committed, but to hereditary guilt.

VI   The light is suspended by a chain, wrapped about the wrist of the figure, showing that the light which reveals sin appears to the sinner also to chain the hand of Christ.

VII   The light which proceeds from the head of the figure, on the contrary, is that of the hope of salvation; it springs from the crown of thorns, and, though itself sad, subdued, and full of softness, is yet so powerful that it entirely melts into the glow of it the forms of the leaves and boughs, which it crosses, showing that every earthly object must be hidden by this light, where its sphere extends.

VIII   I believe there are very few persons on whom the picture, thus justly understood, will not produce a deep impression. For my own part, I think it is one of the very noblest works of sacred art ever produced in this or any other age.

IX   It may, perhaps, be answered, that works of art ought not to stand in need of interpretation of this kind. Indeed, we have been so long accustomed to see pictures painted without any purpose or intention whatsoever, that the unexpected existence of meaning in a work of art may very naturally at first appear to us an unkind demand on the spectator's understanding. But in a few years more f hope the English public may be convinced of the simple truth, that neither a great fact, nor a great man, nor a great poem, nor a great picture, nor any other great thing, can be fathomed to the very bottom in a moment of time; and that no high enjoyment, either in picture-seeing or any other occupation, is consistent with a total lethargy of the powers of the understanding.

X   As far as regards the technical qualities of Mr. Hunt's painting, I would only ask the spectator to observe the difference between true Præ-Raphaelite works and its imitations. The true work represents all objects exactly as they would appear in nature, in the position and at the distances which the arrangement of the picture supposes. The false work represents them with all their details, as if seen through a microscope. Examine closely the ivy on the door in Mr. Hunt's picture, and there will not be found in it a single clear outline. All is the most exquisite mystery of colour, becoming reality at its due distance. In like manner examine the small gems on the robe of the figure. Not one will be made out in form, and yet there is not one of all those minute points of green colour, but it has two or three distinctly varied shades of green in it, giving it mysterious value and lustre.

XI   The spurious imitations of the Præ-Raphaelite work represent the most minute leaves and other subjects with sharp outlines, but with no variety of colour, and with none of the concealment, none of the infinity of nature. With this spurious work the walls of the Academy are half covered; of the true school one very small example may be pointed out, being hung so low that it might otherwise escape attention. It is not by any means perfect, but still very lovely—the study of a calm pool in a mountain brook, by Mr. J. Dearle, No. 191, "Evening, on the Marchno, North Wales."

I have the honour to be, sir,
Your obedient Servant,

THE AUTHOR OF *Modern Painters*.

Denmark Hill, May 4, 1854.

TELEVISION FORECAST IN VERSE YEARS AGO

To the Editor of The New York Times:

The article in The Times Magazine last Sunday entitled "Poets Who Were Prophets," quotes Stephen Phillips' poem entitled "Midnight," published Dec. 31, 1900, in which television is predicted. I would call your attention to another rhyme that was printed long before that date, satirizing the trend of modern invention:

A long haired scientific crank once
  lived on Murray Hill,
The march of science failed to march
  with his gigantic will.

And his very last invention, which increased his fame by half,
Was the poly-chromo-tele-panto-photo-phonograph.

This instrument so wonderful was
  fitted by degrees
With a sounding board, a diaphragm,
  and many rows of keys,
Besides electric wiring and complete
  harmonic staff
As a polychromotelepantophotophono-
  graph.

The professor called upon me and in
  manner shrewd and keen
Explained the salient features of his
  intricate machine.
He seemed so much in earnest that I
  did not dare to laugh
At his polychromotelepantophotophono-
  graph.

We set to work next morning to test
  the new machine,

Having first secured connection with
  the cable submarine.
And we studied Western Europe from
  the Tiber to the Taff
Through his polychromotelepantophoto-
  phonograph.

DANIEL CAVANAGH.

New York, April 19, 1927.

DEAR ATLANTIC,

Are typewriters people? When
my little Rem (Remington Portable), first came to me, it was like
adopting a baby. He weighed just
eleven pounds, he had to have his
little mat to play on, he must be
carefully covered, he needed new
ribbons, he came down with
childish disorders. It used to
seem to me sometimes that he
needed everything but a bottle
and a gocart—as it was, I carried
him. He has been doing very
badly lately, and yesterday he
grew worse and worse, so there
was nothing for it but to telephone to the Service Office. In
an hour or two an automobile
drew up, and a young man, with
a bag, stepped out and walked
briskly to my door. I introduced
the patient, described the symp-
toms, and hung around with all
the solicitude of a mother, while
the young M.D. (M. can stand for
mechanics as well as medicine)
poked and prodded, just as it has
been done to me a hundred times.
Then he did something, somewhere, and the little invalid was a
cure. But what made it all so
human was that, when I asked
anxiously, 'What was the trouble?'
(I *think* I said 'Doctor') he looked
grave and said, 'It was the lever.'

ALICE GRAY TRUSLOW.

April 1934

"STANDARD" ENGLISH.

ESSENTIALS IN SPEECH.

To THE EDITOR OF "THE DAILY
  TELEGRAPH."

SIR—Your correspondent Mr. H.
Drummond asks if there is such a
thing as standard English. Surely
what we are all unconsciously
aiming for is a standard resulting
from three factors: (1) A true
physiological standard in the production of the four factors of
speech—breath, note, tone (that is
to say, vowel sound), and articu-
lation. (2) Much less important,
a general agreement within certain limits in the selection of the
sounds we use. For example,
"Ither" or "Eether." (3) The establishment of a central æsthetic
standard from which song, lyric
and dramatic diction, and public
speaking can naturally grow.

No. 1 is a standard of formation,
since speech has developed from
the movements of the organs
which produce it. It will give us
the voices sighed for in your
leader of to-day, the true resona-
tor shapes of the vowels, and no
speech sounds formed so that they
interfere with musical tone or
individual clarity. It is the
absence or presence of these factors which really makes us like or
dislike speech far more than
agreement with a conventional
social standard.

Number 2 is a matter of general
convenience. The majority of dis-
crepant phonetic standards would
soften and disappear under proper
physiological training; noticeably
the perverted "r's" which trouble
your correspondent in Cornwall.

A sense of beauty and musical
tone, of significance and control in
lyric diction, and a freedom and
audibility in public speaking
would eliminate another great
part of our phonetic differences.
What remains could be safely left
to comfort local patriotism. One
method of teaching will never do
any good; it is that based on the
order, "Stop talking your way and
talk my way," whether the authority invoked be academic,
phonetic, or merely social.—Yours,
&c.,

ELSIE FOGERTY.

Kensington, S.W. 7, August 3.

Longfellow on Reading Aloud.

To the Editor of The New York Times:

To show another point of view on "Reading Aloud," may I ask you to print Longfellow's "Sonnet on Mrs. Kemble's Readings from Shakespeare"?

O precious evenings! All too swiftly
    sped!
Leaving us heirs to amplest heritages
Of all the best thoughts of the greatest
    sages,
And giving tongues unto the silent
    dead!
How our hearts glowed and trembled
    as she read,

Interpreting by tones the wondrous
    pages
Of the great poet who foreruns the
    ages,
Anticipating all that shall be said!
O happy Reader! having for thy text
The magic book, whose Sibylline leaves
    have caught
The rarest essence of all human
    thought!
O happy Poet! by no critic vext!
How must thy listening spirit now re-
    joice
To be interpreted by such a voice!

JANE MANNER.

New York, July 13.

CHAPTER THIRTEEN

NUMERALS AND NOTATIONS

1 Numerals spelled out

A In straight copy, that is, books, magazines, newspapers, and the like, numerals should be spelled out except in those cases where they are so highly involved as to require the writing of four or five or more words. Round numbers should always be spelled out in solid, connected-sentence copy. Exception is made, however, in reference to the four digits used to indicate the year. Observe this taken from a recent novel:

> In 1933 he had earned as much as fifteen thousand two hundred dollars. In 1934 his income had shrunk to a mere five hundred. And what he had to expect—all-told—in 1935 was a paltry twenty dollars a month.

But $181,322,411.31 should, of course, be expressed by figures. Too many words are required to write it out in full.

B Numerals of distinction and those customarily identified as titles or part titles should be spelled out in both literary and official copy:

> the sixty-eighth Congress of the United States
>
> in the year of our Lord, seventeen hundred and seventy-six
>
> millions for defense but not one cent for tribute
>
> the thirteen colonies
>
> Dickens wrote "It was the year of our Lord one thousand seven hundred and seventy-five"

C Numerals used indefinitely or approximately are usually spelled out:

> about three or four hundred
> in the late nineties
> a thousand obstacles to overcome
> almost a hundred errors

D Ordinals detached and isolated from other matter of the same kind are preferably written out:

> the fifth of April
> the tenth of May
> received on March eleventh

But this does not necessarily apply to date lines or to matter in which many dates are listed serially. It refers to the occasional mention of a date in letter and other copy.

E It is increasingly the custom to omit *and* in the writing of numerals, tho usage is variable in this.

> six hundred eight dollars   six hundred and eight dollars
> twelve hundred twenty dollars   twelve hundred and twenty dollars

Many manuals prefer the former to the latter in each case. Usage is divided also in respect to

> twelve hundred twenty dollars
> or
> twelve hundred and twenty dollars
> and
> one thousand two hundred twenty dollars
> or
> one thousand two hundred and twenty dollars

Usage, that is to say, is disputed as to whether a numeral of four figures should be expressed thru the word *thousand* or thru the word *hundred*. Some humorist has insisted that if he were writing he would say *twelve hundred twenty dollars,* but if he were speaking he would say *one thousand two hundred and twenty dollars.* The latter sounds like a much bigger amount! (See K below)

F Numerals should be written out at the beginning of a sentence. Otherwise they may appear confusing in relation to preceding solid matter.

> He came trudging home from the sale. Fifty cows followed broodily in his wake

This rule should be observed even tho odd numbers are expressed by means of figures in the same copy.

> He came trudging home from the sale. Fifty cows followed broodily in his wake. He had paid $18.27 for the youngest heifer, and $269.75 for the blooded bull that swung his head from left to right with the regularity of a pendulum

G Numbers of one reference or designation should not be
written consecutively with numbers of a different reference
or designation.

> *Good:* In 1933 sixty companies agreed to the codes
>
> *Bad:* He received $319.11; $214. fell to me
>
> *Permissible but*
> *not recommended:* In 1934, 34 boys won the scholarships

In the date line of a letter the comma is used to separate
the date of the month from the year, and some firms wisely
spread the spacing even when the comma is used.   In extreme cases of open punctuation the spacing takes the place
of the comma.

> September 15, 1900
> September 15 1900

H Different kinds of numbers or amounts should be expressed
similarly in a consecutive piece of writing.

> Twelve boys for three weeks at twelve dollars and fifty cents
> a week
>
> 12 boys for 3 weeks at $12.50 a week
>
> *not* Twelve boys for 3 weeks at 12 dollars and fifty cents a week
>
> *not* Twelve bys. for 3 wks. at twelve $'s and 50¢ a wk.

J Fractions written out should be hyphenated if they are
linked as an adjective to modify a noun.   They should not
be hyphenated if they stand alone as nouns.

> a three-quarter rule   three fourths of a yard
> a three-eights measure   one eighth of a mile
> one-half inch   half an inch

K Except in date lines and in special technical work, ordinals
are preferably spelled out.   Some authorities say that in
street and avenue addresses ordinals up to and including
twelve should be written out and those above should be
expressed by figures.   But this is an arbitrary ruling that is
not sanctioned by the best practise.

> twentieth century
> Forty-fifth Street
> One Hundred Sixteenth Street

> or

> One Hundred and Sixteenth Street
> my eighty-first birthday

Even in the date line of letters it is by no means uncommon to find monosyllabic (and sometimes dissyllabic) date ordinals spelled out.   In formal invitations and announcements this style is the rule, as is also the cardinal reference to the time of day.

> July Eleventh 1800   August Twenty-first 1832
> June tenth at three o'clock
> May twenty-first at half-past two
> October fifteenth at quarter after five
> January eighteenth, nineteen hundred thirty-six

In legal documents dates are purposely elaborated for the sake of indisputable accuracy and also for imposing emphasis:

> *on this the fifteenth day of March, in the year of our Lord, nineteen hundred thirty-five, one thousand six hundred and forty-one dollars have been transferred*

In few other connections, however, should the four digits indicating the year be written out.   Note also that in legal documents the word *thousand* is preferable in such sums as the one indicated.   To express the amount as *sixteen hundred forty-one dollars* would be neither so impressive nor so legalistic (see E above).

II   Numerals not spelled out

A   In all kinds of technical or mechanical or tabular work, numerals should be expressed by means of figures, for the sake of clarity and convenience.   This applies to groups of tabular matter covering more than two items.

> 8 women
> 6 men
> 12 children

But in an isolated citation

> six persons to the compartment
> a three-year-old child

numerals, as indicated above, should be spelled out.

B   Serial numerals of all kinds used primarily for reference, whether in footnotes or in the body of technical composition, should be expressed in figures.   This rule applies also to distance, degrees of latitude and longitude, money (especially market quotations), measurements of all kinds,

amounts of commodities, tallying for games and votes, and
so forth.

pp 181-322	4 qts.	Ch. IX
circa 17	6 pts.	ll. 31-40
col. 5-2763	1 m	pls. 5, 6, 7
Ex. xx: 16	2 ft.	vols. II & III
¶'s 10-13	3 yds.	nos. 8, 9, 10
3¼% RR bds.		12 Fahr.
1000 4¼'s @ par		8x12 inches
Pa. RR @ 84¾		$8.20 per cord
1917 Libs. @ 4%		£2. 4s. 6d.

Single spacing is customarily used in enumerations that
have to do with measurements, such as *8x12*. This protects against insertions of any kind. Note that the letters
indicating shillings and pence follow the numeral, and that
the sign for pounds precedes the numeral.

C Whole sums of money expressed by figures should invariably
be followed by periods. This rule applies to an isolated
statement of money by figures in, say, the body of a letter.
In general practise this rule is frequently ignored, but it
is being increasingly observed. Some business firms have
learned by sorry experience that it is comparatively easy
for an extra figure to be inserted between the last digit of
an amount and the word that follows, and so they now
"place a period with precision" after the last digit in the
total sum. Not so long ago there was a case in the courts
pertaining to this very point. The amount indicated in a
letter was $40. The typist's machine roller had slipped on
two or three spaces after the figure and she did not trouble
to adjust it. Some unprincipled employee slipped two zeros
into the picture, making $40 read $4000. A great deal of
trouble followed, but the important thing is that a certain
company was taught an unforgetable lesson. This is correct:

> We are asking $65,000. for the property

These are incorrect:

> We are asking $65,000 for the property
> We are asking $65,000   for the property

The comma is used in all tabulations of figures for the
purpose of separating them into units of three digits each.
It is used also for the same purpose in isolated numbers of
five digits or more in straight copy. Numbers of four
digits in such copy do not require the comma after the first

digit. It would look absurd to write *1,775*, in referring to the year, or to place a comma after the first digit of the current year in the date line of a letter. But observe

$ 1,644.16	$ 1 644.16
21,100.17	21 100.17
181,000.00	181 000.00
2,111.40	2 111.40
12.32	12.32
$205,868.05	$205 868.05

Note that the dollar sign in the total amount is single-spaced to it in order to prevent any falsification without erasure. Note also that the dollar sign is carried before only the first of the individual items and is single-spaced to the longest entry (see pages 437 and 440). If there are two or more rows or columns of dollar listings, the dollar sign is required with the top entry of every such column.

D In writing decimals it is preferable to provide a zero before the decimal point in case there is no independent sum. Zeros do not have to be supplied to the right of the decimal point in straight copy in case there is no fractional amount to be indicated. In tabulations they should be provided for the sake of aiding the eye in making additions or other summaries (see above). Like independent numerals, decimals should be spelled out when they stand at the beginning of a sentence:

Four and a half per cent is the customary interest
It fluctuated about 0.25 of an inch
He has $613. in the bank
The specific gravity is 0.8999

In indicating amounts under a dollar it is preferable not to use the dollar sign, unless, of course, such amounts appear in a tabulation.

I am reduced to exactly 17 cents

Do not write

$.17   or   17cts.   or   17¢

But in financial statements of any kind the sign ¢ is customarily and properly used.

E In business letters in which sums of money are specifically mentioned, and in legal documents generally, it is good practise for the sake of safety to indicate exact amounts by means of both words and figures. The figures should be placed in parentheses and the parenthetical expression should follow the word dollars. It should likewise be placed at the lower left-hand corner of the letter, below the signature, in case the money mentioned is enclosed in the letter itself.

Enclosed is a check for thirty dollars ($30.)

III Miscellaneous cautions

A Do not use figures in connection with the words *number* and *per cent*. Conversely, do not write out an amount when a sign or an abbreviation is used to indicate it.

	number eleven	ten per cent
	no. 11	10%
not	no. eleven	*not* 10 per cent

B Dates and figures that belong in the same category should not be divided between lines.

> Lincoln's birthday was February 12, 1809
> *not* Lincoln's birthday was February 12,
>   1809

C Two or more numbers used to indicate pages or addresses should, for the sake of clarity, be given in full. It is better also to connect them by means of words rather than dashes.

Pages 334 to 389	*not*	Pages 334-89
122 and 124 Fifth Avenue	*not*	122-4 Fifth Avenue
	not	122-4 5th Avenue

> Between Fifteenth and Sixteenth streets
> *not* Between 15th & 16th streets
>   Between 15-16 streets

Numeral references of more than three figures, in footnotes and technical matter, do not come strictly under this rule. The following are allowable:

> arts. 1156-61   the winter of 1917-18

D A fraction that is used as unit modifier of another word should be hyphenated to make it a single adjective modifier. This applies to all kinds of matter.

one-half inch tubing	½-inch tubing
a three-quarter rule	a ¾-rule

When fractions stand alone without any following word to modify they should not be hyphenated:

> He accepted two thirds of the original amount

E When the time of day is indicated by figures, hours are separated from minutes by the colon and the complete statement is single-spaced (see page 486).

> He came at 12:30 p.m. tho we did not expect him before 3:15

But it is better usage to write out the hours and fractions thereof in regular copy.

> He came at twelve-thirty today tho we did not expect him before three-fifteen
> He arrived at ten a.m.
> He arrived at three in the afternoon

Note that the use of *o'clock* is superfluous in these expressions. Statements pertaining to the time of day are frequently unnecessarily repetitious. Do not say

> He arrived at ten o'clock a.m. in the morning
> He arrived at ten a.m. in the morning

The abbreviations *a.m.* and *p.m.* are preferably lower-cased. They should be capitalized only for emphasis.

F In textual matter and preferably in addresses spell out numbered avenues, streets, boulevards, and places up to the hyphenated numbered names. Even these latter are spelled out by some business houses in all letter writing. The same rule applies to house numbers in strictly formal composition (see page 265).

> Ten Forty-second Street
> 10 West Thirty-fourth Avenue
> 112 Thirteenth Street
> 124 East 47 Street
> 76 Tenth Boulevard

G It is preferable to refer to age by writing out numerals, but there is considerable variation of usage in regard to this detail. These

> He is between six and seven years of age
> He is sixty-six years old
> He is seventy-five years and three months old

are better than

> He is between 6 and 7 years of age
> He is 66 years old
> He is 75 years and 3 months old

Note the hyphenation in such cases as these (see page 510):

> a four-year-old boy
> a 3-months-old baby
> a 2½-year-old colt

H In making biblical references, or references to other books and compilations that are highly divided and subdivided, both Roman and Arabic numerals are generally used. The Roman numerals indicate the principal reference, the Arabic numerals the subordinate reference. The two may be separated by either the colon or the dash in those cases where there is but one subordinate reference. Where there are two or more subordinate references, the Roman numeral is separated from the first Arabic numeral by means of the colon, and the Arabic numerals are separated by dashes or commas. Capitals may be used for further differentiation.

> Exodus x-2   Exodus xi: 2-8
> Exodus X: 2   Section X, Article ix, Paragraph 12
> p. 1—col. 2   sec. XI, art. x, ¶ 13

It is sometimes ruled that a word referring to a part should be abbreviated when it is followed by a number or letter referring to a definite item in that part (see page 10). The better ruling would appear to be, as far as authoritative usage is ascertainable, to capitalize and spell out the word —article, figure, section—the first time it appears and at all later points to lower-case and abbreviate it.

This follows from a generally accepted usage in connection with italics and quotation marks and any other token of attention. They are used formally in the first instance; thereafter when the same material is repeated they are omitted or suggested merely.

IV Notations

A Any system of marks, figures, signs, or other characters used marginally or medially, or both, to partition a piece of writing into its logical parts for the convenience of both reader and writer, is called a system of notation. The system in commonest use for this purpose is made up of a combination of letters—both capitals and small letters—and figures—both Arabic and Roman. In scientific papers— reports, statements, analyses, and the like—Greek letters

are likewise used for notation of parts. Roman numerals
and the Greek alphabet are here given.

Arabic	Roman
1	I
2	II
3	III
4	IV *or* IIII
5	V
6	VI
7	VII
8	VIII *or* IIX
9	IX *or* VIIII
10	X
11	XI, etc.
20	XX
30	XXX
40	XL *or* XXXX
50	L
60	LX
70	LXX
80	LXXX *or* XXC
90	XC *or* LXXXX

Arabic	Roman
100	C
200	CC
300	CCC
400	CCCC
500	D *or* IↃ
600	DC *or* IↃC
700	DCC *or* IↃCC
800	DCCC *or* IↃCCC
900	CM *or* DCCCC *or* IↃCCCC
1000	M *or* CIↃ
2000	MM *or* CIↃCIↃ
3000	MMM
4000	$M\overline{V}$
5000	$\overline{V}$
1925	MCMXXV
1928	MCMXXVIII
1930	MCMXXX
1,000,000	$\overline{M}$

Characters		Greek name	Characters		Greek name
A	α α	Alpha	N	ν	Nu
B	β б	Beta	Ξ	ξ	Xi
Γ	γ	Gamma	O	o	Omicron
Δ	δ	Delta	Π	π	Pi
E	ε	Epsilon	P	ρ	Rho
Z	ζ	Zeta	Σ	σ s	Sigma
H	η	Eta	T	τ	Tau
Θ	θ	Theta	Υ	υ	Upsilon
I	ι	Iota	Φ	φ φ	Phi
K	κ	Kappa	X	χ	Chi
Λ	λ	Lambda	Ψ	ψ	Psi
M	μ	Mu	Ω	ω	Omega

The better modern usage omits periods after letters and
figures used in making notations, as well as after the statements they classify. In simple copy one of the following
forms may suffice for regimenting matter by notation:

I Animals
  1 Domesticated
  2 Undomesticated

II
  1
  2
etc.

A Residences
  a Houses
  b Cottages

B
  a
  b
etc.

For more complex organization of materials in which there must be more detailed subordination and assortment, these two simple plans are combined into what is generally accepted now as the Harvard system of notation:

```
I Animal
  A Quadruped
    1 Domesticated
      a Dog
        (1) Pigmy type
          (a) Spaniel
            1' Japanese
              a'
                1"
                  a"
```

The first point under the leading or principal point above —A—is called the first degree of subordination. The last point—a" or a double prime—is the ninth degree of subordination. Seldom would any notational scheme be carried so far, with the possible exception of that in legal briefs. Highly articulated composition, calling for complicated degrees of subordination with their corresponding notations, are not to be recommended. But the foregoing illustrates the step-by-step process, and it is apparent that it may be carried still further by adding triple prime, quadruple prime, quintuple prime, ad infinitum. Moreover, if the first subordinate point A were to be carried thru the alphabet to Z without exhausting that degree, then recourse could be had to AA, BB, CC, as well as to 11, aa, (1)(1), and so forth. The letter I or J is usually omitted in such tabulations (observe the notation of matter in the sections of this book) and one or the other is always omitted from the lettering of rows of seats in an auditorium or theater; sometimes both are. This is done because they are so much alike that one may easily be mistaken for the other. Moreover, J is a late variant form of the Latin I, and up to the end of the fifteenth century these two letters and their sounds were represented by the same symbol.

The following scheme clarifies the divisions and subdivisions by parallel columns to the third degree of subordination:

```
I First major point
  A First degree of subordination
  B First degree of subordination
    1 Second degree of subordination
    2 Second degree of subordination
      a Third degree of subordination
      b Third degree of subordination
```

II Second major point
  A First degree of subordination
    1 Second degree of subordination
      a Third degree of subordination

B The above is marginal notation, so called because the symbols of notation are used on the left-hand margin of each degree of subordination, the number of margins depending entirely upon the degree to which subordination is carried.

But there are many other styles of partitioning subject-matter and there are many other symbols. Sometimes notation is made in the middle of the page between statements.

Chalk this plus +

_____

_____

Chalk this double plus + +

_____

_____

Sometimes it is implied by extending the first line of the content further to the left than the other lines.

_____

  _____

  _____

Sometimes it is implied by means of underlining, once for italics, twice for small capitals, three times for large capitals. This device makes it possible to indicate two degrees of subordination in solid matter:

In the first place, it is readable. More important than this, however, is the fact that it is useful. Most important of all— it is the one and only reliable book on the subject

Sometimes notation is implied by means of a symbol— mathematical or other—at the beginning of each unit of material.

    —a liberal education in business principle and procedure

    # an adaptable and entertaining text that the entire family will want to read

    _ a ready-reference book of reliable information on credits, collections, claims, sales, direct-mail

C Whatever the systems of notation or implied notation employed (and those here indicated are but comparatively few), it must always be remembered that the one purpose of notation is to indicate degrees of assortment and arrangement of subject-matter, and that it must do this in some such manner as to convey immediacy of impression to the eye. To this highly desirable end typography is being increasingly depended upon for differentiation and subordination of contentual matter. As a general rule it is not good to employ too many type faces in reading matter, because it confuses the mind of the reader by calling his attention to the form rather than to the content. But in listings and formulæ and in diagrammatic materials, type variation may well be used for indicating main heads and subheads and other divisions. Note how clearly the following stands out as result of the implied notation in the typography:

Agate   Clique
Roman   Company
Italics   *Clan*
Small caps   ARMY
Old English small   𝕮𝔬𝔱𝔢𝔯𝔦𝔢
Bold-face caps   **HOST**

D A few additional graphic and tabular devices are shown below. To materials usually regarded dryasdust, the methods of display bring immediacy of grasp and uncover a new kind of interest. Dates and figures are of little consequence when, as here, the object is to illustrate pictorial treatment.*

GROWTH OF THE PRINTING AND PUBLISHING INDUSTRY IN NEW YORK CITY AS COMPARED WITH THAT IN THE UNITED STATES FROM 1919 TO 1929

	United States	Per cent Increase	New York City	Per cent Increase
A Increase in number of establishments..	4 738	21.1	699	24.6
B Increase in number of wage-earners ..	74 337	26.5	8 059	15.3
C Increase in amount paid in wages	$ 199 524 093	46.3	$ 36 260 347	39.3
Increase in cost of materials	$ 100 883 065	15.3	$ 23 023 172	(17.)
D Increase in value of products	$1 080 135 032	52.3	$248 553 181	52.4

* Pages 437-441 used by permission of the Vocational Survey Commission, New York City

INCREASING IMPORTANCE OF THE PRINTING AND PUBLISH-
ING INDUSTRY IN THE UNITED STATES 1921-1929

BY NUMBER OF ESTABLISHMENTS

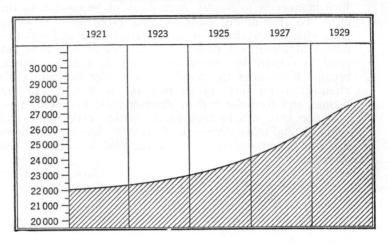

| 1921 | 1923 | 1925 | 1927 | 1929 |

BY NUMBER OF WAGE EARNERS

1919	1929
52,425	60,484

Increase 8059 or 15.3 per cent

GROWTH OF THE PRINTING AND PUBLISHING INDUSTRY
IN NEW YORK CITY 1919-1929

C By Amount Paid in Wages

1919	1929
$92,169,838.	$128,430,185.

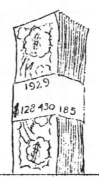

Increase $36,260,347. or 39.3 per cent

D By Value of Product

1919	1929
$474,076,186.	$722,629,367.

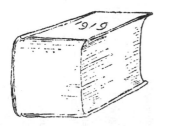

Increase $248,553,181. or 52.4 per cent

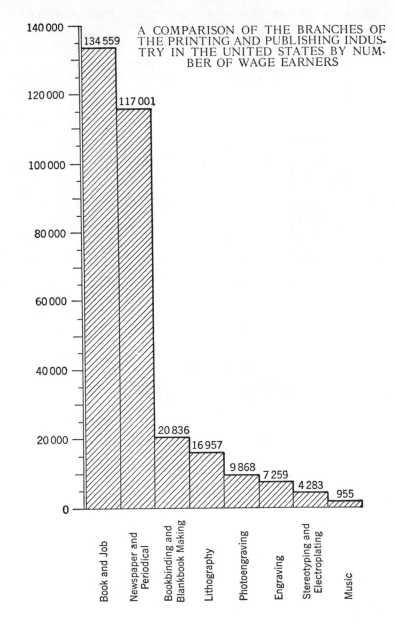

A COMPARISON OF THE BRANCHES OF THE PRINTING AND PUBLISHING INDUSTRY IN THE UNITED STATES BY NUMBER OF WAGE EARNERS

EXECUTIVE BRANCH OF THE GOVERNMENT

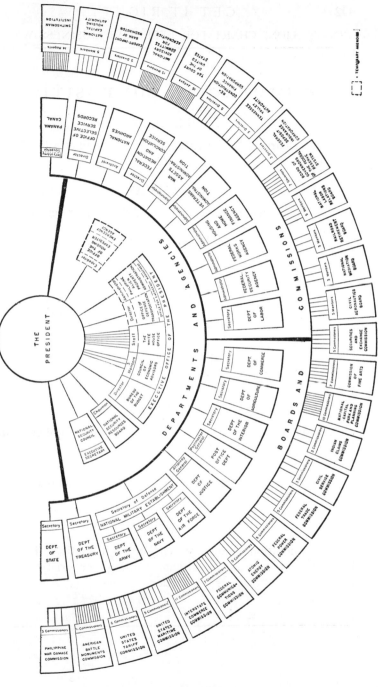

THE PRESIDENT

EXECUTIVE OFFICE OF THE PRESIDENT

DEPARTMENTS AND AGENCIES

BOARDS AND COMMISSIONS

National Security Council — Executive Secretary

National Security Resources Board — Chairman

Bureau of the Budget — Director

Council of Economic Advisors — Members

The White House Office — Staff

Office of Defense Transportation — Director

Philippines War Damage Commission

War Mobilization and Reconversion

Office of the Housing Expediter — Expediter — Office of the Housing Expediter — Temporary Agency

DEPT. OF STATE — Secretary

DEPT. OF THE TREASURY — Secretary

DEPT. OF THE ARMY — Secretary

DEPT. OF THE NAVY — Secretary

DEPT. OF THE AIR FORCE — Secretary

NATIONAL MILITARY ESTABLISHMENT — Secretary of Defense

DEPT. OF JUSTICE

POST OFFICE DEPT. — Postmaster General

DEPT. OF THE INTERIOR — Secretary

DEPT. OF AGRICULTURE — Secretary

DEPT. OF COMMERCE — Secretary

DEPT. OF LABOR — Secretary

Federal Security Agency — Administrator

Federal Works Agency — Administrator

Housing and Home Finance Agency

National Military Establishment

Veterans Administration — Administrator

War Assets Administration — Administrator

Federal Mediation and Conciliation Service

National Archives — Archivist

Office of Selective Service Records — Director

Panama Canal — Governor

SMITHSONIAN INSTITUTION — 14 Regents

NATIONAL CAPITAL HOUSING AUTHORITY — 5 Members

EXPORT-IMPORT BANK OF WASHINGTON — 5 Directors

NATIONAL ADVISORY COMMITTEE ON AERONAUTICS — 15 Members

TAX COURT OF THE UNITED STATES — 16 Judges

RFC RECONSTRUCTION FINANCE CORPORATION — 5 Directors

TENNESSEE VALLEY AUTHORITY — 3 Directors

FEDERAL DEPOSIT INSURANCE CORPORATION

BOARD OF GOVERNORS FEDERAL RESERVE SYSTEM

NATIONAL LABOR RELATIONS BOARD — 5 Members

RAILROAD RETIREMENT BOARD — 3 Members

NATIONAL MEDIATION BOARD — 3 Members

CIVIL AERONAUTICS BOARD — 5 Members

SECURITIES AND EXCHANGE COMMISSION — 5 Commissioners

COMMISSION OF FINE ARTS — 7 Commissioners

NATIONAL CAPITAL PARK AND PLANNING COMMISSION — 10 Commissioners

INDIAN CLAIMS COMMISSION — 3 Commissioners

CIVIL SERVICE COMMISSION — 3 Commissioners

FEDERAL TRADE COMMISSION — 5 Commissioners

FEDERAL POWER COMMISSION — 5 Commissioners

ATOMIC ENERGY COMMISSION — 5 Commissioners

FEDERAL COMMUNICATIONS COMMISSION — 7 Commissioners

INTERSTATE COMMERCE COMMISSION — 11 Commissioners

UNITED STATES MARITIME COMMISSION — 5 Commissioners

UNITED STATES TARIFF COMMISSION — 6 Commissioners

AMERICAN BATTLE MONUMENTS COMMISSION — 11 Commissioners

PHILIPPINE WAR DAMAGE COMMISSION — 3 Commissioners

[ ] = TEMPORARY AGENCIES

"INVITATION" CHART FOR EFFECTIVE BUSINESS WRITING

COMMERCIAL COMPOSITION

ELEMENTS

clearness   coherence   emphasis   organization
proportion   unity

GRAMMAR

agreement   connection   modification   reference

PARAGRAPHS

development   form   sequence

PICTURE

date   harmony   margining   neatness   signature
title   typography

PUNCTUATION

exactness   internal marks   terminal marks   policy

QUALITIES

ease   energy   figure   logic   progress   range   simplicity   tone

SENTENCES

balance   compactness   completeness   length   periodicity
rhythm   variety

WORDS

connotation   economy   euphony   formation   idiom
invention   precision   spelling   propriety
syllabication   usage

GRAPHIC REPRESENTATION OF THE OUTLINE ON PAGE 346

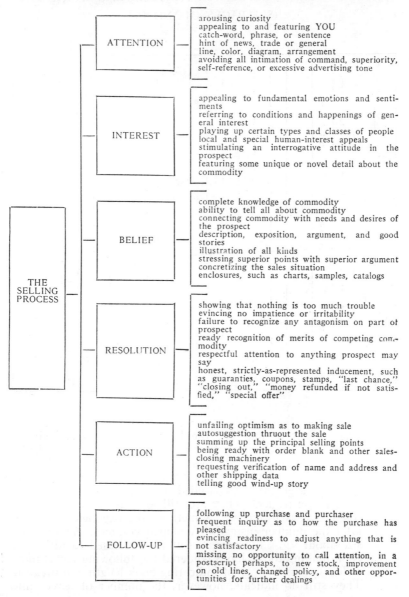

NOTATION GRAPHS FOR PARTITIONING WORK
(SEE PAGES 434 AND 436)

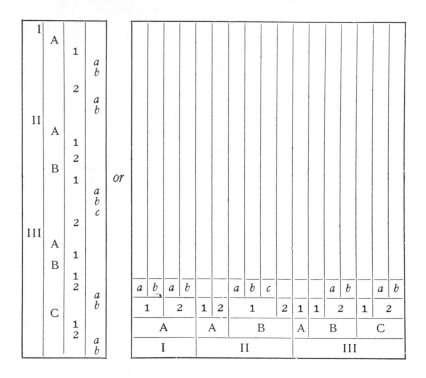

E The suffixes *to* and *vo*, the last syllables respectively of
quarto and *octavo*, together with the suffix *mo*, the Latin
ablative ending of *decimus*, were formerly used with
numerals to refer to the number of leaves or pages into
which a large sheet was folded in order to present printed
matter to a reader. They are still so used today, but not so
commonly as formerly. Sometimes the exponent ° is used
after the number instead. A quarto volume meant a book
size about 9½ x 12 inches. But the increased facilities for
book making today have rendered the following terms more
or less useless by way of indicating book length and breadth.
They still do indicate, however, the number of leaves into

which a large sheet of paper is folded. Take a sheet of paper
and fold it once each way and you have four leaves or eight
pages—eight pages of any surface size. Octavo (a book size
of about 6 x 9 inches) means that the sheet is folded into
eight leaves or sixteen pages. Each one of the book sizes
below indicated is expressed in the three ways:

quarto	or	4to or	4°	four leaves ....eight pages
octavo		8vo	8°	eight leaves.......sixteen pages
duodecimo		12mo	12°	twelve leaves .....twenty-four pages
sextodecimo		16mo	16°	sixteen leaves.....thirty-two pages
octodecimo		18mo	18°	eighteen leaves....thirty-six pages
twenty-fourmo		24mo	24°	twenty-four leaves.forty-eight pages
thirty-twomo		32mo	32°	thirty-two leaves..sixty-four pages
thirty-sixmo		36mo	36°	thirty-six leaves...seventy-two pages
forty-eightmo		48mo	48°	forty-eight leaves..ninety-six pages
sixty-fourmo		64mo	64°	sixty-four leaves ..hundred-twenty-eight pages

V Signs and symbols

Every line of human endeavor and thought develops its system
of signs or symbols. The sciences in particular have an intimate language of their own. Chemistry, physics, astronomy,
botany, biology. and the rest, even in their elementary forms,
make use of signs and symbols. A few of these highly special
signs have crept into everyday usage—have become generalized
to a large extent—and for one not to know what they stand for
is as remiss as not to know how to spell and pronounce the
words in the average conversational vocabulary. The signs
listed below are a few of the common ones that have outgrown
the boundaries of the original fields to which they had been
adapted and are now in common circulation:

′   acute accent; stress of voice in pronouncing, or primary accent; also minutes or inches or feet when
used in expressions of measurement of time or distance; one of the signs of subordination in outlining

&   and

&c.   and so forth

‖   archaic (in dictionary sense); but this so-called parallel
sign is used to indicate lines that are parallel or that
ought to be made so (as in printing); "is parallel
to" (as in geometry)

: :   as, equal—the middle term in expressing a proportion

*   asterisk—used in writing and printing for footnote or
other references

⁎ ***   asterism—asterisks used collectively for the same purpose as the asterisk and also (in the latter form) to
indicate omissions

@	at, about
∵	because or since
{ }	braces—used for much the same purpose as brackets, tho usually for matter that is even more remotely connected with copy than that placed in brackets. Braces are used also to unify words or figures—to indicate that they are homogeneous
[ ]	brackets or crotchets—used tc enclose interpolated words or other matter independent of body copy
˘ ˘	breve—placed over a vowel to show that it is short in pronunciation (the opposite of macron)
^	caret—a sign placed below the line and pointing between words or letters to indicate that there has been an omission at that point
¸	cedilla—used under the letter c (ç) to indicate that it is pronounced like s
¢	cent
ˆ ˆ	circumflex—placed over a letter to indicate the combination in pronunciation of a rising with a falling tone, or to mark a contracted or expanded vowel
†	dagger; before or after a name, died; after a word in the dictionary, obsolete
‡	double dagger; also used to signify archaic or variant as to diction
°	degree (see also book-paper sizes on page 445)
<	derived from, as word derivations in the dictionary
¨	diæresis (dieresis)—placed over the latter of two consecutive vowels to show that they are to be pronounced separately
÷	division; divided by
$	dollar (capital U written thru capital S)
ℨ	dram
* * * . . .	ellipsis
1^1 1^2 1^3	exponents written in this way are interpreted to mean fourths, thus, one and one fourth, one and two fourths, one and three fourths, and so on
`	grave accent, used to distinguish different inflections of voice
∴	hence, therefore
-	hyphen—according to the Webster Dictionary
⸗	hyphen—according to the Standard Dictionary
☞	index or "fist"
:	is to

...... leaders (see above and also page 48)

‒ macron—placed over a vowel (ō, ā) to show that it is long (the opposite of breve)

M minim or drop (chemist's term)

— minus

× multiplication; by, as in 8×10; the mark made for the signature of a person who cannot write

♂ northeast

◹ northwest

\# number

℥ ounce

¶ paragraph

‖ parallel sign (see above)

℔ per

% per cent

⊥ perpendicular

π pi—the sixteenth letter in the Greek alphabet. It stands for the relation of the circumference of a circle to its diameter—3.14159+

+ plus; mark made before the signature of a bishop; in heavy face, placed in some prayer-books to indicate that the sign of the cross is to be made at that point

± ∓ plus or minus; hence, ambiguous

£ pound

§ rare; section

℞ recipe; prescription; used to indicate the part read by the congregation in a responsive service. Derived from the symbol of Jupiter used to propitiate the king of the gods

√ root of (algebraic term)—the radical sign meaning square root. If a figure is written above it, as ∛ then the figure indicates the root—cube root in the illustration

S Latin *signa;* used to indicate seal; also to indicate directions on package of medicines

◺ southeast

◿ southwest

″ secondary accent; double prime, as a″ in an outline; read as double prime. This sign is also used to indicate measurement of time and distance—1′ 2″ may be one foot two inches, one hour two minutes, one minute two seconds, and so forth (see acute accent above); used also as ditto mark

~   tilde—this diacritical mark is placed over *n* in Spanish words to show that it carries the sound of *y* with it, as, *cañon,* canyon

℣   versicle—used to indicate the part read by the priest in a responsive service

>   whence is derived

CHAPTER FOURTEEN

PETITIONS—PROCLAMATIONS—RESOLUTIONS

Petitions, proclamations, and resolutions are conventional written forms allowing of but slight variations no matter how the situations that occasion them may differ. Petitions and resolutions are usually written by many to one; proclamations are usually written by one to many. As a rule petitions anticipate change; resolutions follow change; proclamations initiate change. A petition is a collective request; a resolution, a collective decision; a proclamation may be both.

I Petitions

In writing a petition you should state first the reasons for making it. These should be arrayed in order of importance, each being preceded by the expression *Inasmuch as* or *Whereas* or *Owing to* or *In view of the fact that*. Then the request or petition proper should be made. This is usually introduced by some such expression as *We therefore petition, We hereby request, We shall appreciate your granting, We respectfully urge upon you the desirability of.*

PETITION FOR SPECIAL SESSION OF THE LEGISLATURE
TO BE PRESENTED TO THE GOVERNOR

To His Excellency, Herbert H. Lehman
Governor of the State of New York
Albany, New York

Sir:

Whereas, the budget of the State of New York for the fiscal year of 1934-1935 does not provide for the full quota of State Aid for education, and

Whereas, such deficiency in State Aid may cause the closing of the schools of New York State for at least a part of the school year and will probably cause a further consolidation of classes and additional curtailment of necessary extension activities, and

Whereas, the results of the deficiency in full State Aid will in turn cause further retardation among school children, increase juvenile delinquency and maladjustment, and lessen educational opportunities

for the children of the State of New York, at the same time adversely
affecting both employed and unemployed teachers, and

Whereas, such consequences are contrary to the tradition of free public
education in a state, the richest in the Union, which prides itself on
its high educational standards;

Therefore, we, the undersigned, citizens of the State of New York,
respectfully petition Your Excellency to call a special session of the
State Legislature to provide for the full appropriation for State Aid
for education in accordance with the Friedsam Act and the Porter-
Hewitt Bill.

[Date]   [Signatures of group or officials]

II Proclamations

A proclamation is a formal statement or declaration made usually
by some individual or organization of assured authority having
powers of enforcement. Any public authoritative announcement
may be called a proclamation. In form it is similar to the
petition and the resolution. A declaration of war may, indeed,
be a combined resolution and proclamation.

THE FAMOUS WORLD WAR PROCLAMATION

Whereas, The Imperial German Government has committed repeated
acts of war against the Government and the people of the United
States of America; therefore, be it

Resolved, by the Senate and House of Representatives of the United
States of America in Congress assembled, That the state of war between
the United States and the Imperial German Government, which has
thus been thrust upon the United States, is hereby formally declared;
and

That the President be, and he is hereby, authorized and directed to
employ the entire naval and military forces of the United States and
the resources of the Government to carry on war against the Imperial
German Government; and to bring the conflict to a successful termina-
tion all the resources of the country are hereby pledged by the Congress of the United States.

THE EMANCIPATION PROCLAMATION
JANUARY 1, 1863

Whereas, on the twenty-second day of September, in the year of
our Lord one thousand eight hundred and sixty-two, a proclamation
was issued by the President of the United States, containing, among
other things, the following, to wit:

"That on the first day of January, in the year of our Lord one
thousand eight hundred and sixty-three, all persons held as slaves
within any State, or designated part of a State, the people whereof
shall then be in rebellion against the United States, shall be then,
thenceforward, and forever free; and the Executive Government of the

United States, including the military and naval authority thereof, will recognize and maintain the freedom of such persons, and will do no act or acts to repress such persons, or any of them, in any efforts they may make for their actual freedom.

"That the Executive will, on the first day of January aforesaid, by proclamation, designate the States and parts of States, if any, in which the people thereof respectively shall then be in rebellion against the United States; and the fact that any State, or the people thereof, shall on that day be in good faith represented in the Congress of the United States by members chosen thereto at elections wherein a majority of the qualified voters of such State shall have participated, shall in the absence of strong countervailing testimony be deemed conclusive evidence that such State and the people thereof are not then in rebellion against the United States."

Now, therefore, I, Abraham Lincoln, President of the United States, by virtue of the power in me vested as commander-in-chief of the army and navy of the United States, in time of actual armed rebellion against the authority and government of the United States, and as a fit and necessary war measure for suppressing said rebellion, do, on this first day of January, in the year of our Lord one thousand eight hundred and sixty-three, and in accordance with my purpose so to do, publicly proclaimed for the full period of 100 days from the day first above mentioned, order and designate as the States and parts of States wherein the people thereof, respectively, are this day in rebellion against the United States, the following, to wit:

Arkansas, Texas, Louisiana (except the parishes of St. Bernard, Plaquemines, Jefferson, St. John, St. Charles, St. James, Ascension, Assumption, Terre Bonne, Lafourche, St. Mary, St. Martin and Orleans, including the city of New Orleans), Mississippi, Alabama, Florida, Georgia, South Carolina, North Carolina, and Virginia (except the forty-eight counties designated as West Virginia, and also the counties of Berkeley, Accomac, Northampton, Elizabeth City, York, Princess Ann, and Norfolk, including the cities of Norfolk and Portsmouth), and which excepted parts are for the present left precisely as if this proclamation were not issued.

And by virtue of the power and for the purpose aforesaid, I do order and declare that all persons held as slaves within said designated States and parts of States are, and henceforward shall be, free; and that the executive government of the United States, including the military and naval authorities thereof, will recognize and maintain the freedom of said persons.

And I hereby enjoin upon the people so declared to be free to abstain from all violence, unless in necessary self-defense; and I recommend to them that, in all cases when allowed, they labor faithfully for reasonable wages.

And I further declare and make known that such persons of suitable condition will be received into the armed service of the United States to garrison forts, positions, stations, and other places, and to man vessels of all sorts in said service.

And upon this act, sincerely believed to be an act of justice, warranted by the Constitution upon military necessity, I invoke the considerate judgment of mankind and the gracious favor of Almighty God.

III Resolutions

Resolutions are usually somewhat more legal in their format than are petitions. The reasons for offering them are first set down, as in petitions, in order of importance. Each special reason stated is formally preceded by *Whereas* as a paragraph beginning, tho the word preceding it, at the end of the preceding paragraph, is frequently *and*. A semicolon is usually placed before *and*, and a comma after *Whereas*. After the reasons are all thus formally stated, the resolution proper is made in a paragraph beginning *Be it resolved*. If additional resolutions are to be made, this introductory expression reads: *Be it further resolved, Be it still further resolved, Be it finally resolved*. In case a series of resolutions is to be made, sequential numbering may be included, as *Be it resolved first, Be it resolved second*, and so forth.

The old plural of *present—presents*—meaning present writing(s) is still used in very formal resolutions and in legal documents —*Know all men by these presents, To all for whom these presents are intended, To all to whom these presents shall come*. In all such documents the resolution has much the nature of a proclamation.

There is a wholesome modern tendency to get away from the formal type of resolution that is drawn up in connection with social or semi-social matters. The omission of the formal note gives a more intimate and sincere tone to the expression, and adds to its simplicity and dignity. Regrets of any kind may quite properly be expressed in regular composition form, without the technical terms that earmark them as resolutions. But in resolutions pertaining to any kind of collective organization action —commemorations, honors, congratulations, approvals, and the like—the conventional form is still generally adhered to.

RESOLUTIONS AND PROCLAMATION COMBINED

To the People of the City of New York:

Whereas, Benjamin Franklin was born January 17, 1706; and

Whereas, this is the bicentennial year of the beginning, late in 1732, of the publication by Franklin of *Poor Richard's Almanac,* which was also written by him; and

Whereas, in 1732 Franklin established *The Philadelphia Zeitung,* the first American newspaper to be printed in a foreign language; and

Whereas, on March 31, 1732, the first books were ordered by the Library Company of Philadelphia, founded by Franklin, thereby starting the first circulating library on the North American Continent; and

Whereas, 1932 is the 150th anniversary of the negotiation by Dr. Franklin of the preliminary treaty of peace with Great Britain which helped to assure victory to the United States; and

Whereas, Benjamin Franklin is called a "patron saint" by many groups, including printers, publishers, advertising men, music dealers; electrical, optical, cartoonist, labor, and numerous other organizations; and

Whereas, National Congresses of both the Daughters of the American Revolution and the Sons of the American Revolution have recommended celebration of Franklin's birthday, especially in the schools, as has the International Benjamin Franklin Society:

Therefore, I, James J. Walker, Mayor of the city of New York, call upon our citizens this week-end of January 17 to pay tribute to the name and fame of Benjamin Franklin, requesting that the Stars and Stripes be well displayed on Sunday and Monday. Let the schools on Monday honor Franklin as a patriot and advocate of many worthwhile projects. As President Coolidge well stated: "No American career more deserves the gratitude and reverence of the nation than does that of Franklin. He was one of that marvelous group of Revolutionary leaders, each of whom seemed in his particular department to be a supreme genius. His life's story is replete with illumination for the problems of our time."

Attention is further called to the fact that Franklin's birthday this year is "Share with Others Sunday" of National Thrift Week. As Franklin was not only an unselfish patriot but was a great philanthropist, it is especially appropriate that in 1932 his natal anniversary be thus doubly commemorated.

In witness whereof, I have hereunto set my hand and caused the seal of the City of New York to be affixed this fifteenth day of January, 1932.

JAMES J. WALKER,
Mayor.

By the Mayor:
THOMAS J. McANDREWS,
Secretary to the Mayor.

SIMPLE RESOLUTION FORM

Whereas, Section 15 of Chapter 178 of the Laws of 1934, an act to effect economies, provides:

"If furloughs shall be imposed thereunder and savings of $11,000,000. effected thereby, and if the actual receipt of moneys by the City of New York from tax collections and all general fund revenues shall exceed $540,000,000. (including the tax reserve of $23,950,000.), then the city shall refund proportionately to the employes subjected to such furloughs the excess of such moneys over and above $540,000,000. which has been collected by the city between January 1 and December 31, 1934," and

Whereas, the collection of taxes already has far exceeded that anticipated for the year 1934, and

Whereas, the receipts of the General Fund have already exceeded the estimate by upward of $11,000,000., and

Whereas, it is evident that the receipt of taxes and that of the General Fund will exceed the $540,000,000. provided in Chapter 178 of the Laws of 1934, and

Whereas, it is apparent that a refund of the furlough will have to be made as provided for in Chapter 178 of the Laws of 1934, be it therefore

Resolved, That the resolutions heretofore adopted by this board and by the Board of Education relative to imposing the furlough be rescinded.

IV Constitutions

The first business of any newly formed organization is to draw up a constitution or, to use the accustomed phraseology, to *frame* a constitution. The plan of a constitution consists of major divisions called *articles,* and of minor divisions under these called *sections.* The sections may be subdivided into *items.* Each article should carry a title. In order of composition these titles are usually: name of organization, aims of organization, names of offices to be filled, duties of officers, standing committees, dates and rules of elections, regulations for amending the constitution. Minor rules for conducting the business of an organization are called by-laws. These are added as time and event prove their necessity, and as the practise and application of the constitution reveal that provision should be made for covering subjects not covered in detail in the constitution proper. All expressions in these various parts of a constitution must be kept legally exact and formal. A complete constitution is a long document as a rule. Space here permits of the inclusion of but a few excerpts.

FIRST FIVE AMENDMENTS TO THE CONSTITUTION OF THE UNITED STATES

ARTICLE I

RELIGIOUS ESTABLISHMENT PROHIBITED, FREEDOM OF SPEECH, OF THE PRESS, AND RIGHT TO PETITION

Congress shall make no law respecting an establishment of religion, or prohibiting the free exercise thereof; or abridging the freedom of speech or of the press; or the right of the people peaceably to assemble and to petition the Government for a redress of grievances.

ARTICLE II
RIGHT TO KEEP AND BEAR ARMS

A well-regulated militia being necessary to the security of a free State, the right of the people to keep and bear arms shall not be infringed.

ARTICLE III
NO SOLDIER TO BE QUARTERED IN ANY HOUSE, UNLESS, ETC.

No soldier shall, in time of peace, be quartered in any house without the consent of the owner, nor in time of war but in a manner to be prescribed by law.

ARTICLE IV
RIGHT OF SEARCH AND SEIZURE REGULATED

The right of the people to be secure in their persons, nouses, papers, and effects, against unreasonable searches and seizures, shall not be violated, and no warrants shall issue but upon probable cause, supported by oath or affirmation, and particularly describing the place to be searched, and the persons or things to be seized.

ARTICLE V
PROVISIONS CONCERNING PROSECUTION, TRIAL AND PUNISHMENT—PRIVATE PROPERTY NOT TO BE TAKEN FOR PUBLIC USE, WITHOUT COMPENSATION

No person shall be held to answer for a capital or otherwise infamous crime unless on a presentment or indictment of a Grand Jury, except in cases arising in the land and naval forces, or in the militia, when in actual service, in time of war or public danger; nor shall any person be subject for the same offense to be twice put in jeopardy of life or limb; nor shall be compelled in any criminal case to be a witness against himself, nor be deprived of life, liberty, or property, without due process of law; nor shall private property be taken for public use without just compensation.

From the

CONSTITUTION AND BYLAWS OF THE UNITED TYPOTHETAE OF AMERICA, INC.*

International Association of Master Printers

ARTICLE I   The name of this Association is the UNITED TYPOTHETAE OF AMERICA, a Corporation.

ARTICLE II   *Objects of the Corporation*

Section 1

To effect a thorough organization of the employing printers and allied employing trades of the United States, Canada, and Mexico, into a trade association

* Used by permission of the United Typothetae of America. Inc.

ORGANIZATION   with branches, district federations, and locals, in order constantly and continually to improve and maintain the best possible conditions in the printing industry in every proper and lawful manner.

Section 2

MEETINGS   To meet at stated periods for the discussion and dissemination of reliable information relative to the best methods of conducting business from the standpoint of practical experience and of approved business ethics.

Section 3

TRADE   To foster and protect trade and commerce in printing
AND   and to reform abuses relative thereto; to promote uni-
COMMERCE   formity and certainty in trade customs and usages; to uphold just and equitable methods of conducting business; and to devise ways and means for advancing the interest of the industry in general.

Section 4

COOPERATION   To encourage and foster friendship and cooperation between employing printers, allied employing trades, and the business world; to promote the settlement of differences among its members and between its members and others, to the end that the relationships in the entire printing trades may be harmonious; and in general to cooperate in such other ways as may be found necessary and convenient.

CHAPTER FIFTEEN

PLURALIZATION

I Pluralization

A The plural of most nouns is formed by adding *s* to the singular form: *bay, bays; tree, trees; shah, shahs; train, trains; woe, woes; zephyr, zephyrs.*

The plural of nouns ending with *ch, s, sh, x,* and *z* is formed by adding *es* to the singular; *brush, brushes; chintz, chintzes; church, churches; fox, foxes; kiss, kisses; marquis, marquises; waltz, waltzes.*

The letter *s* does not unite in pronunciation with these sounds; hence, its addition to form the plural makes another syllable. This is true also of words ending with soft *ce* and *ge: age, ages; lace, laces; place, places; ridge, ridges; sedge, sedges; wedge, wedges.*

The plural of proper nouns is formed in accordance with this rule: *Alices, Henrys, Johns, Joneses, Lentzes, Mattises, Vauxes, Zitters.*

B The plural of common nouns ending with *y* preceded by a consonant (or by *u* pronounced *w*) is formed by changing the *y* to *i* and adding *es: colloquy, colloquies; lady, ladies; mercy, mercies; sky, skies; soliloquy, soliloquies.*

The plural of nouns ending with *y* preceded by a vowel (except *u* with the power of *w*) is formed by adding *s* only to the singular form: *alley, alleys; attorney, attorneys; guy, guys; key, keys; valley, valleys.*

The irregular plural *monies* still sometimes occurs in the sense of sums of money.

C The plural of many nouns ending with *f* and *fe* is formed by changing *f* or *fe* to *ves*.

beef	beeves	loaf	loaves
calf	calves	self	selves
elf	elves	sheaf	sheaves
half	halves	shelf	shelves
knife	knives	thief	thieves
leaf	leaves	wife	wives
life	lives	wolf	wolves

But note these exceptions:

beliefs	reefs
briefs	roofs
chiefs	safes
cliffs	scarfs (*also* scarves)
dwarfs (*formerly* dwarves)	serfs
fifes	surfs
griefs	staffs (meaning officers)
gulfs	staves (meaning sticks)
handkerchiefs	turfs (*formerly* turves)
hoofs (*formerly* hooves)	waifs
proofs	wharfs (*also* wharves)

As language evolves and becomes simplified, the tendency increasingly is to make all such words conform to the regular formation of plural (rule A above).

It may be helpful to note that the third person singular, present indicative active, undergoes the same formation as the plural of nouns in many instances.

He brushes	He halves
He buys	He slays
He coaxes	He tries

D The pluralization of words ending with *i* varies. As a rule, however, such words are pluralized regularly under A above.

alibi	alibis	macaroni	macaronis
alkali	alkalis	Maori	Maoris
antiscii	antisciis	rabbi	rabbis
cadi	cadis	Sufi	Sufis

E The plural of nouns ending with *o* tends to be formed regularly, that is, by adding *s* only. Some nouns ending with *o* preceded by a consonant are pluralized by the addition of *es*. Most nouns ending with *o* preceded by a vowel are pluralized by the addition of *s* only. Some nouns ending with *o* are pluralized in either way.

bamboo	bamboos	Lothario	Lotharios
cameo	cameos	oratorio	oratorios
folio	folios	portfolio	portfolios
gigolo	gigolos	ratio	ratios
impresario	impresarios	punctilio	punctilios
dado	dadoes	mulatto	mulattoes
domino	dominoes	negro	negroes
echo	echoes	no	noes
embargo	embargoes	potato	potatoes
hero	heroes	tomato	tomatoes
hobo	hoboes	tornado	tornadoes
jingo	jingoes	torpedo	torpedoes
manifesto	manifestoes	veto	vetoes
mosquito	mosquitoes	volcano	volcanoes

These final-*o* words, however, form their plurals regularly:

albino	albinos	lasso	lassos
alto	altos	magneto	magnetos
auto	autos	merino	merinos
archipelago	archipelagos	octavo	octavos
armadillo	armadillos	octodecimo	octodecimos
banjo	banjos	piano	pianos
bronco	broncos	piccolo	piccolos
burro	burros	proviso	provisos
canto	cantos	quarto	quartos
casino	casinos	radio	radios
chromo	chromos	salvo	salvos
contralto	contraltos	sexto	sextos
curio	curios	sirocco	siroccos
dido	didos	silo	silos
duodecimo	duodecimos	solo	solos
dynamo	dynamos	sombrero	sombreros
electro	electros	soprano	sopranos
embryo	embryos	stiletto	stilettos
Eskimo	Eskimos	tobacco	tobaccos
Filipino	Filipinos	torso	torsos
inamorato	inamoratos	two	twos
junto	juntos	tyro	tyros
kimono	kimonos	virtuoso	virtuosos

These may be pluralized in either way:

bravo	bravos	bravoes
buffalo	buffalos	buffaloes
calico	calicos	calicoes
cargo	cargos	cargoes
flamingo	flamingos	flamingoes
fresco	frescos	frescoes
grotto	grottos	grottoes
halo	halos	haloes
innuendo	innuendos	innuendoes
memento	mementos	mementoes
motto	mottos	mottoes
portico	porticos	porticoes
zero	zeros	zeroes

F The plural of certain nouns is formed by an internal vowel change or by the addition of *en* or *ren*. Such irregular plurals were once much more numerous.

child	children	louse	lice
brother	brethren (see N below)	man	men
foot	feet	mouse	mice
goose	geese (but *gooses* for tailoring irons; also *mongoose* and *mongooses*)	ox	oxen
		tooth	teeth
		woman	women

Compounds of these words are pluralized similarly: *workman, workmen; dormouse, dormice*. But words ending with *man* that are not compounds are pluralized regularly: *desmans, Germans, Normans, Ottomans, talismans*.

G The plural of some nouns is the same as the singular: *cannon* (also *cannons*), *cattle, cod, deer, fish, gross, grouse, heathen, quail* (*quails*), *rye, salmon, sheep, swine, trout, vermin*. These identical plurals, along with such as *barley, corn, wheat*, take a regular plural in *s* or *es* when they are used to indicate a number of different species.

The wheats of Siberia
The trouts of Canada

Athletics, meaning various sports, is plural: *Athletics are his only interest* (i. e. He is interested in many different kinds of sport). *Athletics*, meaning a system of training, is singular: *Athletics has developed his body remarkably*. The plural is the more general and preferable use.

The singulars of such words as *couple, dozen, foot, fowl, gross, head, hundred, mile, pair, sail, score, stone* (and most others listed under this rule) may be used colloquially with plural significance without pluralization of form when they are preceded by numeral adjectives:

a hundred fowl	an eighty-mile run
a six-foot rule	fifteen stone
five dozen	five score
fifty head of cattle	five hundred heathen
thirty hundred	six pair
three couple	twenty sail
twenty gross	two hundred trout

When, however, the number words are indefinite, pluralization is necessary: *hundreds of fowls, scores of sails, tens of miles*.

Certain proper nouns ending in *ese* (sometimes *is*) likewise have the same form in the plural as in the singular: *Chinese, Japanese, Portuguese, Singhalese, Tyrolese, Iroquois.*

The plural of solid compounds is formed regularly or in accordance with the foregoing modifications: *airships, birthplaces, cupfuls, handfuls, spoonfuls, stockholders.*

But the plural of hyphenated compounds is placed according to rule on the principal or fundamental part of the compound: *aides-de-camp, courts-martial, cousins-german, editors-in-chief, go-betweens, hangers-on, jacks-in-the-box, knights-errant, lookers-on, maids-of-honor, men-of-war, mothers-in-law, passers-by, poets-laureate.*

A few compounds are pluralized in both parts: *knights bachelors, Knights Templars, men servants, women servants.*

The foregoing rule applies to titles consisting of two or more words but written as neither solid nor hyphenated compounds (but see page 503 *seq.* on the puzzling uses of the hyphen): *attorneys general, chargés d'affaires, deputy judges, lieutenant colonels, major generals, notaries public, ocean liners, postmasters general, sergeants at arms, surgeons general, under secretaries, vice chairmen.*

H The plural of figures, letters, signs, words, phrases, and characters mentioned without regard to their meaning is formed as a rule by *'s: 2's, g's, $'s, &'s, *'s, and's, don't's, if's, as-it-were's.* But *the two os in good* is gaining in usage in preference to *the two o's in good,* as are also *the pros and cons* and *the ins and outs.*

J The plural of titles is formed regularly. The pluralization of a title pluralizes the name following it. There is no plural for *Mrs.* The plural of *Mr.* is *Messrs.* The plural of *Miss* is *Misses;* of *Master, Masters.* Note the following forms:

> Messrs. James and Kingsley
> the Misses Ackerson   or   the Miss Ackersons
> Masters Jones   or   the Masters Jones
> Drs. Blaine and Corey
> Profs. Arthur Hunt and Hugh Kelly
> Professors Hunt and Kelly
> Attorneys Richardson
> the Mrs. Hurlburts

The Misses Ackerson and *the Messrs. Green* are preferable to *the Miss Ackersons* and *the Mr. Greens*. The word *the* may or may not be used to precede a plural title. Both title and name are never pluralized. The pluralization of either makes both plural.

K   The so-called editorial plural—*we, our, us, ourselves*—is used when a speaker or writer is expressing himself for a group rather than as an individual. It is called the editorial plural because it is commonly used in editorial writing. But the spokesman of a group such as a board or a committee likewise uses it. It is affectedly used when a speaker or a writer, referring to himself as an individual, indicates himself as *we* in order to avoid using *I*. He is sometimes (and rightly) accused of false modesty.

L   The so-called royal plural—*we, our, us, ourselves*—is used by kings and queens and other similar rulers to indicate plurality of domain, power, and station, as when Cæsar says: "What touches us ourself shall be last served," and Macbeth: "Yet, when we can entreat an hour to serve, We would spend it in some words upon that business."

M   The so-called indefinite plural or plural of approximation is a pronominal plural used without definite reference— *They say, You never know, We all want this*—and such cardinals as *sixties, thirties, twenties, He is in his early forties, It happened back in the eighties*—which indicate general periods rather than definite ones.

N   Some nouns have two plurals of different meanings:

brother	brothers (family)	brethren (church or society)
cloth	cloths (kinds of cloth)	clothes (wearing apparel)
die	dice (for games)	dies (for stamping or making screws; the cubical base of a pedestal)
fish	fish (collective)	fishes (distributively; varieties)
genius	geniuses (men)	genii (spirits)
index	indexes (books)	indices (figures, signs, symbols, as in mathematics)
pea	peas (the seeds)	pease (in bulk or collection)
penny	pennies (coins severally)	pence (amount collectively)
shot	shot (collective)	shots (distributively)

The following are "singular plurals"—plural in form but singular in meaning and use. They usually require singular verbs. They have no singular forms with the same meaning:

acoustics	hydromechanics	phonetics
aeronautics	hydrostatics	phonics
alms	linguistics	physics
analytics	magnetics	pneumatics
civics	mathematics	poetics
conics	means (way to end)	politics
dynamics	measles	rickets
economics	metaphysics	spherics
esthetics	molasses	statics
ethics	mumps	statistics
hydraulics	news	tactics
hydrodynamics	optics	United States

◯ The following "plural plurals" are plural in form and also in meaning and use. They are rarely used in the singular and usually require plural verbs:

annals	entrails	pliers	suds
ashes	goods	pincers	thanks
athletics (see G	lees	proceeds	tongs
above)	links	remains	trousers
billiards	nuptials	riches	tweezers
clothes	oats	scissors	victuals
dregs	obsequies	shears	vitals
eaves	pants	spectacles	wages *

ℐ Following are a few additional words that are commonly used in the plural form. Some of them have no corresponding singular form. They are usually used with plural verbs, tho a few are occasionally singular in both use and agreement. They are sometimes called "mixed plurals":

aborigines	breeches	grounds	mnemonics
antics	chaps	gums	odds
antipodes	commons	hangings	outskirts
archives	compasses	headquarters	pains
arms	corps	Hebrides	pantaloons
assets	credentials	hindquarters	polemics
auspices	creeps	hysterics	premises
bagpipes	doings	Indies	pyrotechnics
barracks	drawers	intestines	quarters
bellows	dumps	knickers	quoits
belongings	environs	leavings	scales
bitters	falls	lodgings	shambles
blues	fetters	manacles	sharings
bowels	forceps	manners	shivers
braces	fries	matins	snuffers
brains	gallows	middlings	stables

* Used biblically in the singular—*The wages of sin is death*—but rarely so today.

stairs	sweepings	tights	woods
straits	teens	trappings	works
summons	theatricals	vespers	yards
suspenders	tidings	winnings	zippers

Q   Certain words may have a very different meaning in the plural from what they have in the singular—*blues, eatables, greens, sweets, valuables,* for instance; and

beef (meat)	*beeves* (cattle)
compass (extent)	*compasses* (measuring instruments)
draft (air, plan, check)	*draughts* (checkers—British)
effect (result, modification)	*effects* (property)
ground (basis, earth)	*grounds* (cemetery, recreation field)
iron (metal)	*irons* (fetters or implements)
leaving (going away)	*leavings* (leftovers)
mean (middle, medium)	*means* (plan, money)
pain (suffering)	*pains* (care, diligence)
paring (cutting down)	*parings* (scraps, refuse)
part (portion)	*parts* (qualities, talents)
return (coming back)	*returns* (statistics, or goods returned)
salt (table salt)	*salts* (smelling, or Epsom)
shroud (of a corpse)	*shrouds* (of a ship)
spectacle (a sight)	*spectacles* (for clarifying vision)
stay (continuance in a place)	*stays* (props, support, "mast stays")
stock (line, trunk, goods)	*stocks* (investments)

R   Many foreign words that are used in English still retain their foreign plurals and thus cause considerable difficulty in spelling. The tendency is, however, for all such words to take on the regular English plural forms as they are increasingly used in English. The list below indicates some of those that have become "naturalized" by dropping the foreign *æ, i, a,* or *es:*

Foreign Singular	Foreign Plural	Regular Naturalized or Adopted Plural
addendum	addenda	
alga	algæ	
alumna	alumnæ	
alumnus	alumni	
amanuensis	amanuenses	
analysis	analyses	
antenna	antennæ	antennas
antithesis	antitheses	
apex	apices	apexes
appendix	appendices	appendixes
arcanum	arcana	

Foreign Singular	*Foreign Plural*	*Regular Naturalized or Adopted Plural*
automaton	automata	
axis	axes	
bacterium	bacteria	
bandit	banditti	bandits
beau	beaux	beaus
bureau	bureaux	bureaus
candelabrum	candelabra	
château	châteaux	chateaus
cherub	cherubim	cherubs
crisis	crises	
criterion	criteria	criterions
cumulus	cumuli	
curriculum	curricula	
datum	data	
desideratum	desiderata	
dilettante	dilettanti	
dogma	dogmata	dogmas
effluvium	effluvia	
ellipsis	ellipses	
erratum	errata	
focus	foci	focuses
folium	folia	
formula	formulæ	formulas
genius	genii	geniuses
genus	genera	genuses
gladiolus	gladioli	gladioluses
gymnasium	gymnasia	gymnasiums
hippopotamus	hippopotami	hippopotamuses
index	indices	indexes
larva	larvæ	
madam	mesdames	
magus	magi	
matrix	matrices	
maximum	maxima	maximums
medium	media	mediums
memorandum	memoranda	memorandums
minimum	minima	minimums
minutia	minutiæ	
monsieur	messieurs	
monsignor	monsignori	monsignors
nebula	nebulæ	
oasis	oases	
parenthesis	parentheses	
phenomenon	phenomena	
plateau	plateaux	plateaus
procès verbal	procès verbaux	
radius	radii	
referendum	referenda	referendums
septum	septa	
seraph	seraphim	seraphs
spectrum	spectra	
stadium	stadia	stadiums

Foreign Singular	Foreign Plural	Regular Naturalized or Adopted Plural
stimulus	stimuli	
stratum	strata	stratums
syllabus	syllabi	syllabuses
synopsis	synopses	
tableau	tableaux	tableaus
tempus	tempora	
terminus	termini	
thesis	theses	
trousseau	trousseaux	trousseaus
ultimatum	ultimata	
vertebra	vertebræ	
vertex	vertices	vertexes
vortex	vortices	vortexes
viscus	viscera	

CHAPTER SIXTEEN

PROOFREADING

Before any piece of printing is issued in final form—as book, pamphlet, circular, publication of any sort—it should be and usually is carefully looked over in order that it may come from the press "clean," that is, in order that there may be no errors in it. To this end the printer runs off samples of the printed matter for the author (or his deputy) to scrutinize. The first of these samples to come from the printer is called *galley proof,* usually shortened to *galleys* (the name comes from the long trays in which composed type used to be placed).

These galleys are long narrow slips of paper, as a rule, with wide margins on all sides to give room for corrections and comments. The person who reads these galleys is the proofreader. He must necessarily have a keen eye and a precise knowledge of English. Sometimes—in newspaper offices and large job-printing establishments—a copyholder reads the original manuscript to the proofreader for check-up.

A second set of galleys—called *revises*—may be requested, in case the changes to be made by the printer are so numerous and so involved as to justify such request; and sometimes a third set may be considered necessary. Very often galley proofs are not sent to authors at all. They are read and checked against copy in printing or editing offices by expert proofreaders, and page proofs only are sent to authors.

When the galleys are done, the printer divides them into pages, and the proofreader again reads these to see whether all galley changes have been accurately made. Changes made in page proofs are likely to be both troublesome and expensive, so it is well to ask for as little change as possible at this stage of the printing. As a rule only one set of page proofs is sent out for proofreading. But if extensive revision is required in the first set, making it necessary, for instance, to renumber pages, a second set of page

468   G E T   I T   R I G H T !

proofs may have to be read. After these proofs are regarded as perfect in form and set-up, they are "locked up" for the electro-typer or for the printing-press.

At this stage the printer may send what are called *foundry proofs*, but these are seldom required if galleys and pages have been care-fully done. The final proofs are called *plate proofs*—proofs run off from electrotype plates which duplicate the type-face of each page in a solid block or plate. Books are nearly always printed from these copper-faced plates. It is evident that changes made in this proof are expensive, as they are likely to require the casting of new plates. But plate proofs are seldom sent to any one outside the publisher's office. One reason why simplified spelling was so strongly opposed by publishing houses is that to change all the accumulated plates in their storage rooms would be such a laborious and expensive undertaking.

Proofs are examined, then, for two important reasons—correction or adjustment of any slips that may have occurred in printing, and verification of copy against printed matter. Unfortunately a third thing is sometimes considered necessary in proofreading, namely, revision of copy. It may happen, of course, that new materials are unearthed between the time copy goes to press and the time that the first galleys are run off. In such case revision more or less extensive may be pardonable. But too frequently revision in galleys and even in page proofs has to be made because copy has been carelessly and inaccurately prepared and is thus not clear to the type-setter.

By the word *copy* is meant the manuscript that is prepared to be sent to the printer for printing set-up. Needless to say, it should be typewritten neatly and clearly, double-spaced for the indication of body face in the final printing, and single-spaced for any parts that should be set in smaller type. A good wearable quality of paper should be used. Pages should be numbered consecutively, and inserted pages should be lettered after the numbers. Three pages, for instance, to be inserted between pages 8 and 9 should be paged *8a, 8b, 8c*. Insertions briefer than page size should be pasted in. New chapters and other divisions in the work should be started on new pages.

Footnotes should be accurately identified with reference in copy by placement at the bottom of the page on which such reference is made. If the footnotes are numerous they should be numbered, beginning with [1] at the commencement of each chapter and running as high as desired. The asterisk and other signs used for footnoting are not easily handled when there are many notes. Great care should be exercised to get titles and names of authors accurately written for footnote use, and conscientious scholarship demands that page numbers be given for quoted matter, as well as edition and publisher of books from which quotation is made, and year, month, and volume of magazine. Even more important, if possible, is precision in crediting these notes—when from copyrighted books—in accordance with the requirements under which permission to quote is given. Publishers vary in their requirements in permission phraseology, as do authors. Carelessness in embodying permission notice in copy exactly as required may be the cause of much trouble and unpleasantness.

Illustrations should be clearly placed. Sometimes these are too large to be inserted among the sheets of the manuscript proper. In such case a blank sheet should be inserted with instructions to printer as to the exact kind and use of illustration required at a given place in the book. Illustrations may thus be segregated in a separate envelop, and accurate cross referencing be made. The caption (legend), that is, the descriptive or explanatory statement belonging to an illustration, is preferably written on the back of the picture or on a slip of paper pasted to the top or bottom of it. Captions still appear in the majority of cases at the bottom of the illustration, but there is a growing and wholesome tendency to place them at the top. This is where they are most conveniently placed from the reader's point of view. It is a mistake to write these captions on the inserted blank illustration reference sheet, inasmuch as this sheet may so easily be lost or mixed up in position. Of course, when the illustration is easily fitted into the manuscript itself, it should always be so placed.

Illustrations that must be run at right angles to printed matter should be so placed that the bottom of the picture comes at the inside lower part of the page, tho there is a persistent printers' tradition that militates against such placement, just as there is in regard to the placement of the caption at the bottom of the picture rather than at the top. It is easier for a reader to turn to the inside of a book than to the outside, and there is some evidence at hand to indicate that the longitudinal illustration will some day always be focused inward.

In case a blank space is left on a page of copy which it would be wrong to leave in the finished printing, the author should write the words *CLOSE UP* on it. The printer will understand this to mean that the matter above the space and the matter below it are to be joined solid. In case something is to be omitted from the copy the author should cross it out and write *KILL* across it or on the margin of it. A manuscript should be sent flat, not folded, and the sheets should be securely held together by some temporary binding device rather than by string. Safety demands that the author keep a carbon copy for himself. Original copy always goes to the publisher or printer.

A few other terms special to copy and proofreading should be understood by the layman. A *cut* is the block or plate from which an illustration is printed. It is a reproduction in metal tacked upon a block of wood that is type-high in thickness. And the term is used loosely to refer to any sort of reproduced picture or graph. A *dummy* is blank paper folded and bound in exact size and appearance of a proposed finished print job. Used in connection with booklet or magazine (school paper) publications the dummy may be made to indicate the precise placement of material by cutting the galleys into page sizes and pasting them in it as desired. When the dummy is used for this purpose it becomes what is called the *layout* of the printing job. Care must be exercised in doing this to get the continued parts of articles accurately keyed. (See pages 408 to 417.)

Front matter is the term used to include all the items in the front part of a publication before the actual printed content is commenced. The *half title* or *bastard title,* usually the first of the front matter, is the title of the work standing alone in the middle or at the optical center of an otherwise blank page; then follows the *frontispiece* (picture or other illustration), the title page proper, the dedication (if any), the preface, the table of contents, the table of illustrations, the introduction (if any, in addition to the preface), and the title above the actual beginning of the book. The copyright notice is on the reverse of the title page. Books are usually copyrighted in the name of the publisher, who merely holds the copyright for the author under the contract which both have signed. Sometimes the name of the manufacturer or printer is placed at the bottom of the copyright-notice page. More frequently it is placed on a flyleaf at the end of the book. The title page should contain the exact title, the subtitle (if any), the full name of the author, the name of the publisher, and the date, in this order. In addition it sometimes carries the number of the edition and the house symbol or colophon of the publisher.

The *running head* or *title* of a publication is placed across the top of the page. Usage varies in its composition. If it is long, one part may be run on the left-hand page and one on the right-hand. If it is short, it is now usually run on the left-hand page, and the chapter titles are run on the right-hand.

Books are always started on a right-hand page, that is, the right-hand pages always carry odd numbers and the left-hand pages even numbers. Page margins should in the main correspond with those indicated for letters on page 229 *seq*. The outside margins are wider than the inside—usually about twice as wide. The bottom-page margin should be about one-third wider than the top-page margin. But these are variables. The proportions are, however, important artistically. By *head margin* is meant the space above the running title, that is, above the first line on a page. A *flyleaf* is any blank sheet (two pages) in a book. It is always to be found at the beginning and at the end of a book, but sometimes fly-leaves are inserted at intervals thruout a book for notetaking or other convenience. The *bulking* of a book refers, really, to its thickness without covers; but the term is used loosely to refer to its thickness over all, that is, with covers included. Remember that the thickness of paper used in manufacturing a book decides its bulk, not the number of pages necessarily.

As far as possible the author of a manuscript should indicate in his copy such points of typographical makeup as he is able to. Many authors are naturally unacquainted with the technicalities of type faces, type setting, and printing traditions. But every author, it is hoped, knows what can be done with type by way of mechanical emphasis, and he should, as far as he can, indicate what he wants in arrangement of material and variation of type face. This he can do in marginal notes in longhand. But it will be better for him to make use of the regular trade signs and symbols, for instance:

underlining copy once	———	means *italics* to the printer
underlining copy twice	═══	means SMALL CAPITALS
underlining copy thrice	═══	means LARGE CAPITALS
the wave	∼∼∼	means heavy or **boldface**
the wave under a single line	∼∼∼	means *heavy italics*
the wave under two lines	≋≋	means HEAVY SMALL CAPITALS
the wave under three lines	≋≋	means **HEAVY LARGE CAPITALS**

If something in copy or proof has been crossed out by mistake and has to be restored, place a line of dots under the deleted words\ and write *stet* on the margin. This is the Latin verb meaning "Let it stand." If a capital letter has been used where it should not have been, the author should draw a diagonal line thru it and write *l.c.* on the margin nearest it. These letters mean *lower case,* the compartment in the old hand-printing bank where small letters were kept. Other proof-marking signs are given below. They should be used, as a matter of fact, by teachers of English in marking compositions, for they have values that carry over into life. They are used from time to time in all business and industry. It is a waste of time for students to be required to learn a set of arbitrary marks that have no use whatever beyond the school or college walls.

Proof should be read letter by letter in order that even the smallest errors in spelling, punctuation, spacing, type faces, alinement, and general appearance may be checked. Good proof readers, it is said, are born, not made. But the average person can do much to train his eye to the minutiæ of proofreading. The house proofreader, that is, the person (persons) employed by a printing or a publishing house to look over proofs before they are sent out to the author, makes corrections in uniform color. The author should, therefore, consistently use another color. All corrections should be made on the right-hand or the left-hand margin nearest the place where the correction is to be made by the printer. In case a period is to be inserted it is customary to place it in a circle on the margin, thus ⊙ ; if a comma, it is placed in a caret; if quotation marks, they are placed in inverted carets. If the house proofreader places question marks on galleys or page proofs, they mean that there are some doubts to be cleared up by the author, and he must be sure to heed these queries and answer them on the margin of proofs.

PROOF-READERS' MARKS *

Signs indicating alterations to be made in the type are placed in the margin of the proof, corresponding to marks placed where the corrections are to be made, and may be explained as follows: ⊥, push down space or quad showing with type; *center*, bring the opposite line to the place indicated by ⌐; #, insert space where caret (∧) is made; ℐ, take out letters or words canceled; ᴑ, turn inverted letter underscored; *stet*, restore word or letter inadvertently canceled (literally, "let it stand"); ∨, insert apostrophe; other superior characters are similarly indicated by being placed in an inverted caret, as \¹/, */, and for inferior characters the caret is made in its usual position, as ∧; □, indent line an em; ⌐, bring matter to the left; the mark is reversed (⌐) when it is desired to move matter to the right; a correction is suggested to the author by an interrogation-point, as ?/ℐ; ⌐___⌐, lower word or letter; to raise a word or letter the sign ⌐‾‾⌐ is used; ⊙, insert full point; change of a word or letter is indicated by a line drawn through the faulty matter, the word or letter to be substituted being written opposite in the margin; omitted words or letters are indicated in the same manner, a caret being placed where the insertion is to be made; ‖, justify the lines—that is, space so that the margin will appear even and straight; ⊶, broken letter; a logotype character is indicated by a tie, as ﬀ; *caps*, change matter underlined to capitals; *tr*, transpose words or letters underlined; ᴑ, draw together matter indicated by a similar mark in type; *No* ¶, run on matter without break; ℐ̂, a combination of ℐ and ᴑ, signifying "take out canceled character and close up"; *l. c.*, change matter underlined to lower-case; ≡, straighten lines; *rom.*, roman type; *ital.*, change to italic type; < *lead*, insert a lead that the space between the lines may be uniform throughout; ∨, space more closely; if too much matter has been omitted by the compositor to be conveniently written in the margin of the proof, "Out, see copy" is written, and the place for insertion indicated as shown. Other marks in the following example are practically self-explaining.

* From the *Funk & Wagnalls Standard Dictionary*. By permission.

Typographical Signs and a Marked Proof-Sheet

⌐ center ══ ⌐ THE LOST ARTS.⌐ *caps/⌐*

ital Ladies and Gentlemen :

I am to talk to you to-night about⌐The Lost Arts⌐—a
⌐ lecture⌐which has grown under my hand year after year⌐
~~after year,~~ and which belongs to that first phase of the
lyceum system, before it undertook to meddle with polit-·
ical duties or ⟨angry⟩and⟨dangerous⟩ questions of ethics ;
⌐ when it ⌐as merely an academic institution⌐ trying to
win busy men back to books, teaching a little science,
stet ~~or~~ repeating some tale of foreign travel, or painting
Run back some great representative cha⌐acter, the symbol of
his⌐ age. I think I can claim a purpose beyond a *objectionable feature*
⌐ moment⟨s⟩ amusement in this glance ~~at early~~ civilization.
× ⌐I, perhaps⌐ might venture ⌐o claim that it was a medi⌐
⌐ ?/⌐ cine for what is the most⌐of our nation⌐l character ;· and
⌐—that is self⌐conceit⌐—an undue appreciation of our-⌐
selves, an exaggerated estimate of our achi⌐ve⌐ments, of
⌐ur inventions, of our contributions to popular comfort,
⌐ and of our place, in ⌐fact,⌐ in the great pro⌐ession of the
⊙ ages⌐ We seem to imagine that, whether knowledge will
die with us, or not, it certainly began with us.⌐

estimates/ ⌐We have a pitying ~~esteem~~, a tender compassion, for
the narrowness, ignorance, and ⌐arkness of the bygone
ages. We seem to monopolize not ⌐nly to our⌐selves⌐ but
over/ to have begun, the era of light. In other words, we
are all running⌐with a fourth⌐day⌐of⌐July spirit of self-
content. I am often reminded of the german whom the
English poet Coleridge met at Frankfort.⌐ It seems to
× me, the ⌐merican people might be painted ⌐n the chro⌐nic
⌐ attitude of taking o⌐ its hat to itself⌐and ⌐herefore it c⌐n
⌐ be no waste⌐of time, with an audience⌐in such a m⌐ood⌐
to take their eyes for a moment from⌐the present civ⌐z-
⌐ation, and guide them back to that⌐ earliest possible era⌐
that ⌐history ⌐describes ⌐for us, ⌐t ⌐it ⌐were only for the
⌐lead purpose of asking whether ⌐e boast on the right line.
⌐I might despair of curing ⌐he habit of boasting, but I
!/ might direct it better⌐

Wendell Phillips.——⌐ *s. caps/⌐*

e/⌐ ⌐[1] This lectu⌐ was ne⌐er ~~revised~~ by Mr. Phillips, and is⌐perfect in
#⌐/ form and⌐x⌐ression. ⌐But⌐is the best report in existance.

Out. See copy.

The Same Galley After the Corrections Have Been Made

THE LOST ARTS.[1]

Ladies and Gentlemen:

I am to talk to you to-night about "The Lost Arts"— a lecture which has grown under my hand year after year, and which belongs to that first phase of the lyceum system, before it undertook to meddle with political duties or dangerous and angry questions of ethics; when it was merely an academic institution, trying to win busy men back to books, teaching a little science, or repeating some tale of foreign travel, or painting some great representative character, the symbol of his age. I think I can claim a purpose beyond a moment's amusement in this glance at early civilization.

I, perhaps, might venture to claim that it was a medicine for what is the most objectionable feature of our national character; and that is self-conceit—an undue appreciation of ourselves, an exaggerated estimate of our achievements, of our inventions, of our contributions to popular comfort, and of our place, in fact, in the great procession of the ages. We seem to imagine that, whether knowledge will die with us, or not, it certainly began with us. We have a pitying estimate, a tender compassion, for the narrowness, ignorance, and darkness of the bygone ages. We seem to ourselves not only to monopolize, but to have begun, the era of light. In other words, we are all running over with a fourth-day-of-July spirit of self-content. I am often reminded of the German whom the English poet Coleridge met at Frankfort. He always took off his hat with profound respect when he ventured to speak of himself. It seems to me, the American people might be painted in the chronic attitude of taking off its hat to itself; and therefore it can be no waste of time, with an audience in such a mood, to take their eyes for a moment from the present civilization, and guide them back to that earliest possible era that history describes for us, if it were only for the purpose of asking whether we boast on the right line. I might despair of curing the habit of boasting, but I might direct it better!

WENDELL PHILLIPS.

---

[1] This lecture was never revised by Mr. Phillips, and is imperfect in form and expression. But it is the best report in existence.

CHAPTER SEVENTEEN

PUNCTUATION

Punctuators, like spellers, are divided into two schools. One insists upon strict adherence to the old conservative rules formulated two centuries ago, long before such a thing as versatility in typography was known. The other would reduce punctuation to a minimum—would use it only where it is imperative for the clarification of thought expressed on paper. Those in the former group are called closed punctuators; those in the latter, open punctuators. Both are most strikingly revealed in the two types of business letters illustrated on pages 229 to 233.

The tendency today in all kinds of writing is definitely toward the simplification, that is, the minimization, of punctuation. This is a wholesome tendency, for the evolution of language should and does mean the elimination of all excess baggage by way of signs and symbols above, below, or between letters. If typography can make a sentence clear without any punctuation whatever, then the open punctuators would have typography do it. If word and phrase and clause can always be so set down on paper that there can be no doubt whatever about relationships and modifications, then the open punctuators would have them so written and would thus not belabor sentences with comma and semicolon, and the rest.

Unfortunately word and phrase and clause cannot always be so written, especially when thoughts become involved and complicated. But clear thinking presupposes simplicity of expression. And the will to be simple in expression places upon us the obligation to be clear and concise in our thinking. So, then, the open punctuators would have us think and write with such clarity as to make many punctuation marks unnecessary. What gesture and pause and inflection and even facial expression are to speech, marks of punctuation are to writing. But that person is probably best understood when he speaks, who makes use of the minimum of "effects" to clarify, who depends upon the choice and arrangement of words chiefly to this end.

476

Some open punctuators would go so far as to omit the period at the end of a declarative sentence. They say that the capital with which the next sentence begins is sufficient signal that there is an end of one sentence and a beginning of another, and that to use both period and capital is to repeat—to use two bumpers to stop the engine. Some advertising copy has adopted the no-period policy, and so far there have been no reports of misunderstanding. But such a step may be as yet a little too advanced for general adoption.

Take this sentence, however, punctuated according to the rules of our forefathers:

> Last night, when I reached home from the factory, after a hard day's work, I found my mother sitting by the window, crocheting those beautiful red woolen socks for the important head of the house.

According to the modern school all the commas would be omitted. And certainly the meaning is quite clear without any punctuation, for there is no doubt whatever about modification; the phraseology moves ahead coherently regimented; every word and phrase and clause stands closely enough to the word or phrase or clause modified to leave no misunderstanding as result of ambiguous modification.

It is a regrettable fact that many young people are trained to lean upon punctuation as a matter of course. This leads them to let weak constructions pass and to depend upon marks (usually the comma and the semicolon) to make their meaning clear. They should, rather, rewrite and rewrite until they get their sentences so closely knit in construction that no punctuation (or at least very little) is required. And it will surprise them to find how very frequently just a little replacement of sentence parts will do this for them.

The following pages explain both conventional and unconventional usage in regard to punctuation. Note that thruout this book punctuation is used as sparingly as possible without sacrificing anything (it is hoped) to clarity.

Marks of punctuation used at the ends of sentences are called *terminal* marks; those used within sentences are called *internal* marks. Marks that are written on the line or that are in part on the line or above or below it are called *line-level marks;* those that appear above the line entirely—the apostrophe and the quotation marks—are sometimes called *upper-range marks*. Many high school children, having a penchant for slang, call the apostrophe and the quotation marks sky commas!

I The apostrophe '

A The apostrophe is used with *s*—'*s*—to form the possessive case of singular nouns.

boy's	John's book
girl's	the chairman's gavel
man's	the princess's carriage
secretary's	the doctor's arrival
worker's	the chauffeur's skill

The rule applies likewise to compound and hyphenated **nouns.**

my son-in-law's car
the letter-carrier's route
the baggage-master's duties
her step-mother's shawl

B The apostrophe is used after the *s* to form the possessive of plural nouns ending with *s*. If the plural does not end with *s* the '*s* is used to form the possessive.

boys'	chairmen's
girls'	chauffeurs'
men's	children's
secretaries'	doctors'
workers'	princesses'
youths'	women's

The rule applies likewise to compound and hyphenated nouns.

my sons-in-law's cars
the letter-carriers' routes
the major-generals' journey
their step-mothers' shawls
the workmen's hours

A good general working principle for the use of the apostrophe in the formation of possessive case is this: *The sign of possession comes nearest the thing possessed.*

C The sign of possession on two or more consecutive words possessively modifying a word or words is carried on the last, provided joint ownership is indicated. But if individual rather than joint ownership is indicated when two or more consecutive words possessively modify a word or words, then the sign of possession must be carried on each modifying word.

> Wanamaker and Brown's store (one store)
> Wanamaker's and Brown's stores (two stores)
> men's, women's, and children's clothing
> John and Mary's mother
> John's and Mary's mothers
> John's and Mary's parents
> John and Mary's parents
> Byron's and Wordsworth's poems
> Eliot's and Brontë's fiction
> Beaumont and Fletcher's plays (collaboration)
> The Governor's and the President's policies
> The Governor and the President's policies

D In terms and titles consisting of more than one word, used to modify possessively a word or words, the 's is added to the last member of the term or title (thus following the rule under B above).

> John Brown, Jr.'s record
> George the Fifth's reign
> George V's reign
> the steel magnate's mansion
> the Prince of Pilsen's estate
> the Bank of England's policy (see F below)

It is customary for authors of textbooks to point out that the apostrophe has two particular functions: the function of indicating possession and the function of indicating elision. In *John's hat* possession is indicated. In *ne'er* elision is indicated. But the function of the apostrophe to indicate the possessive case of nouns was originally the function of elision. Possessives were formerly indicated by *es*— Chaucer's *The Clerkes Tale, The Milleres Tale.* It later became the style to elide *e* and use the apostrophe in its stead. This made it easy to distinguish the possessive singular of such words as *dog's, crow's,* from their regular plurals— *dogs, crows*—exactly the same letters being used. To the ear, however, ambiguity is certain to exist. The *dog's scent* and *the dogs scent* are immediately clear to the eye but they can never be to the ear except thru context (see E below). Even for the convenience of the eye some printers follow the practise of extra spacing before apostrophes when they represent elision only—*girl 's, it 's*—and of close-up single spacing when they represent possession—*girl's, boy's.*

The apostrophe is not used when actual ownership is not indicated. There are many instances in present usage where it is omitted, especially in place and institutional names, in case nothing is sacrificed to clarity by its omission. This is a hopeful and logical usage, and it deserves to grow for it is a simplifying one. It facilitates set-up and reduces tendency to error. Thus, the following are written without apostrophe:

All Souls Church	St. Albans Course
Governors Island	Teachers College
Owens College	Citizens League
Johns Hopkins University	Millers Dale
St. Ives Hotel	Somers Point
Actors Equity	American Bankers Association

But

St. John's (Newfoundland)	Women's Auxiliary
St. John's Wood	St. Michael's Mount
Queen's College (Oxford)	St. Thomas's
Queens' College (Cambridge)	*Printers' Ink*

E   It is held by conservatives that proper names ending with *s, x, ʒ* should add—regularly—the *'s* to form the possessive singular:

H. G. Wells's works	Keats's *Endymion*
Dickens's *Bleak House*	Jones's *Year Book*
Diaz's régime	John Knox's prejudices

And in view of what was said above (under D) in regard to eye and ear understanding of the apostrophe, this conservative usage has much to recommend it. But there is no denying the fact that modern practise is increasingly adopting the use of the apostrophe only to indicate the possessive case of singular nouns, both common and proper, ending with *s, x,* and *ʒ*. This is a forward movement also, for it makes for simplification in both writing and pronunciation. It is no trivial task for the average person to pronounce distinctly such tongue ticklers as *The princess's slippers are to be seen in Coss's shop window* and *Brooks's sermons seem strange set up in Sanford Press's style.* There is much good authority for

H. G. Wells' works	Keats' *Endymion*
Dickens' *Bleak House*	Jones' *Year Book*
Diaz' régime	John Knox' prejudices
St. Thomas' Church	Knox' hats
Richards' Almanac	Burns' poems
Heinz' pickles	Harris' stories

Note that the apostrophe may often be automatically dropped when possessive expression is preceded by an article. In this case the noun takes on the function of an adjective.

> a Prince of Wales mannerism
> the Duke of York estate
> the John Brown, Jr. record
> the Jones *Year Book*
> the Burns poems
> a Wells work

Time out of mind it has been set down by textbooks that "for the sake of avoiding unpleasant sound the apostrophe without the *s* is used by most authorities in these two expressions" (sic):

> for conscience' sake   in Jesus' name

It is not at all clear why these two expressions should be singled out for special pronunciation favors, why so many other innocent ones should be required to carry the *'s*.

In all cases where the repeated sibilant is troublesome to eye or ear (and this is especially likely to be the case with words of two or more syllables accented on the last) it is decidedly preferable to use the apostrophe only, especially if the next word begins with *s*.

> Ulysses' son   Moses' sayings   Wilkins' stories

The following list contains many names in the pronunciation of which confusion might result, however, were the simplified form of possessive used:

Abraham	Ayers	Bower	Carstair
Abrahams	Ayres	Bowers	Carstairs
Abram	Beal	Boyer	Coate
Abrams	Beals	Boyers	Coates
Adam	Beard	Brand	Crewe
Adams	Beards	Brands	Crewes
Ade	Beatty	Bridge	Dietrich
Ades	Beattys	Bridges	Dietrichs
Alter	Beaver	Britt	Everett
Alters	Beavers	Britz	Everetts
Andrew	Becker	Brook	John
Andrews	Beckers	Brooks	Johns
Askin	Beer	Brun	Key
Askins	Beers	Bruns	Keys
Atkin	Beyer	Burn	Larkin
Atkins	Beyers	Burns	Larkins
Ayer	Bowe	Byrne	Law
Ayre	Bowes	Byrnes	Lawes

Mark	Olds	Rollin	Ulrichs
Marks	Owen	Rollins	Vincent
Master	Owens	Roper	Vincents
Masters	Power	Ropers	Walter
Matthew	Powers	Searle	Walters
Matthews	Pyle	Searles	Water
Meyer	Pyles	Tabor	Waters
Meyers	Quayle	Tabors	Young
Nichol	Quayles	Thom	Youngs
Nichols	Robert	Thoms	Zeller
Old	Roberts	Ulrich	Zellers

F   For the sake of euphony the *of-phrase* equivalent to *'s* may be used:

Sinclair Lewis's stories   the stories of Sinclair Lewis

Note that both the *of-phrase* and the *'s* possessive may easily be subject to misunderstanding thru ambiguity, the *of-phrase* the more frequently perhaps. *My brother's story,* for instance, may mean a story that he owns, a story that he has written, a favorite story of his, a story about him, or the story of his life. *The story of my brother* probably means a story about my brother, tho there are other possible interpretations. *A picture of Mary* means a likeness of Mary herself. But *a picture of Mary's* may mean one that Mary painted or one that Mary owns, or both. The context must always be depended upon to make the meaning clear. In the same way *Brown's epitaph* may mean the epitaph on Brown's tombstone, an epitaph that Brown composed, an epitaph that Brown designed, an epitaph that Brown carved, an epitaph that Brown composed for another or carved on another's tombstone. Again, the context must be depended upon to clarify. If Mary painted the picture or if Brown composed or designed the epitaph, the construction is known as *subjective possessive*. If Mary merely owns the picture or if Brown is lying beneath the tombstone and had nothing whatever to do with the epitaph, the construction is called *objective possessive*.

In *Bill's pinching of Arthur was vicious, Bill's* is subjective possessive and *of Arthur* is objective. In *the love of pleasure* there is objective possessive only, for *pleasure* is inanimate and therefore incapable of loving.

The double possessive (sometimes called the idiomatic double) may clarify the use of the possessive case to some degree, yet by no means always. In this form the sign of possession is carried by both *'s* and the *of-phrase—a picture of Bessie's, a story of my brother's, a favorite horse of Bill's, this old hat of Mabel's.* All are capable of more than one meaning. The idiomatic double is customary in British proper names—*the court of St. James's, the steeple of St. Thomas's.* The noun understood after the *'s* in such expressions is usually the noun used before the *of-phrase* or a modification of it—*a horse of* or *among Bill's horses, a hat of* or *among Mabel's hats, the steeple of St. Thomas's church* or *of St. Thomas's (many) churches, the court of St. James's palace.*

It is preferable to indicate the possessive of animals and of inanimate objects by means of the *of-phrase* rather than by *'s.* This rule is sometimes modified to admit domestic animals to the *'s* class, and it is sometimes applied to inanimate objects only. Usage is by no means unanimous in observing the rule or its modifications. But there can be no doubt that *the top of the desk* is better than *the desk's top, the heel of my shoe* than *my shoe's heel.* The personification of an inanimate object carries with it the *'s* privilege —*the morning's eye, the thunder's curse, the ocean's chant, the ship's grace* (*ship* usually being spoken of as *her*). Examples under D above would be better expressed by the *of-phrase.*

Exception is customarily made to this rule in the case of colloquial expressions referring to time, distance, and value.

a dollar's worth	a day's trip
a week's work	a month's salary
a stone's throw	the world's work
thirty days' notice	ten days' grace
a half-day's walk	a five-minutes' run
a few minutes' quiet	an hour's delay
at arm's length	a couple of days' work
for pity's sake	in harm's way

G The following more or less mechanical uses of the apostrophe should be noted:

1 A noun or a pronoun modifying a gerund should be in the possessive case.

> Lily Pons' singing delights me
> I object to Mary's going to the party
> There can be no doubt about his coming

2 The apostrophe and *s* are used with abbreviations.

> He OK's the bill
> The G. A. R.'s are marching
> The D. A. R.'s convention is held this week
> James Blaine, Sr.'s house was destroyed by fire

3 The plural of letters, figures, signs, and words *as words* (as well as larger units of expression) is formed by *'s* (see page 461).

> Open your *e's*
> Write two *4's*
> Observe these *Don't's*
> You don't know your *a-b-c's*
> You have too many *by-and-large's* in your paragraph
> Watch your ¶'s

There is, however, much excellent authority for the pluralization of letters, figures, signs, and words by the mere addition of *s*.

> They marched by *fours* (or *four's*)
> The *1900s* (*1900's*) were the grand old times
> Let's return to the three *Rs* (*R's*)
> He was born in the *20s* (*20's*)
> *3x6s* (*3x6's*)   *ps* and *qs* (*p's* and *q's*)

4 The apostrophe is used to denote the omission of letters and figures.

can't	o'er	o'clock	mustn't	isn't
didn't	'38 (1938)	ne'er	e'er	spirit of '76
I'd	you'd	he'd	she'd	it'd
I'm	you're	he's	she's	it's
I've	you've	he'll	she'll	it'll
I'll	you'll	they're		'tis
we'd	who'd	they've		'twill
we're	who's	they'd		'twere
we've		they'll		
we'll		there'll		

But note that no apostrophe should be used with the possessive pronominal forms: *ours, yours, his, hers, its, theirs, whose*. It is used, however, with possessive adjectives: *one's, other's, either's, some one's, everybody's, somebody's*, but *somebody else's*. George Bernard Shaw has for many years inconsistently omitted the apostrophe in contractions. In practically all of his books, *dont* is to be found for *don't*. And this is good. But his *cant* for *can't* is not so good, because the context may not always be depended upon to clarify at once whether the noun *cant* is meant or the contraction for *cannot*. This confusion may occur in writing *wont* for *won't*. Strangely enough Mr. Shaw writes *he's* and *she's*, not *hes* and *shes!*

5 The apostrophe is sometimes used for dialect, poetic, and other contractions.

    fishin'   mornin'   ass't   ass'n   dep't   'neath

It is preferable to abbreviate with period than to contract with apostrophe—*asst., assn., dept.*—in all commercial and general short-cutting. But in dialect and poetic short-cutting the contracted form is preferable. Do not use the apostrophe with words that are frankly shortened in compliance with the rules of simplified spelling—*tho, thru, thoro.*

II The colon :

A The colon is used to precede a long formal quotation, one that is taken usually from written matter.

> The writer had this to say about the word *précis:* "It is from the French, and, of course, academic people like nothing better than to parade their superiority by way of injecting foreign terms into their expression. It has consequently become a sort of furore just because of foreign birth. Time out of mind in English classes everywhere it has been the custom to have pupils exercise their expressional powers by writing summary or résumé or epitome or recapitulation or—what have you. Well, now we have *précis*, and this eclipses them all"

B The colon is used to introduce a clause that supplements or restates a preceding clause.

> The work of the class continued unchanged in any way while the instructor was out of the room: an additional proof, if any were needed, that the good teacher can inspire fine disciplinary responses from his students whether or not he is always with them in the flesh

C The colon is used before a detailed explanation or a "bill of particulars."

> The formula for writing good copy is very simple: in the first place have a thought that is worth recording; then organize that thought into logical sequences; and then write it down in a few, plain, unaffected, well-chosen words, and the result cannot help being *good copy*

D The colon is used before a list or a table when the items are begun on the same line as the colon. Where this is not the case the colon is really not necessary. In other words, no colon is necessary where spacing and arrangement make the content perfectly clear. It is sometimes ruled that the colon must be used after the word *following*, but this in modern usage varies according to the above-mentioned modification.

The Montgomery District	The Hardwicke District
Hospitals	Hospitals
Parks	Parks
Prisons	Prisons

No colon is required after the word *district*. But note these:

We bought the following: chairs, tables, desks, rugs, dishes, trays
We bought the following

chairs	rugs
tables	dishes

E The colon is often used before a query or a statement.

He asked: What is to become of the nations of the world if they are periodically to be involved in devastating warfare?
He answered: Mankind will be wiped off the face of the earth, and the precious handiwork of humankind will become the prey of animal life

F The colon is used in such technical forms as the following:

1 To separate units of different categories when the indicating words, abbreviations, or symbols may be omitted because they are understood by the context; thus, $2:30$ *p.m.* or $1:45:27$ as elapsed time in a race. The period is also used in the same way (see page 523). But the colon should not be used to separate degrees or hours and minutes and seconds in such forms as $89°27'31''$ and $7^h05^m26^s$ and $1'10''$. It should be noted in this connection that the colon is not used in the metric system which is a pure decimal system and always takes the decimal symbol after the digit denoting unity, as 4.25 meters equals 42.5 decimeters or 425 centimeters.

2. To signify mathematical proportions, as $1:3$ and $1:3::5:15.$*

3 In biblical and other literary citations, as

Mark xi:3 and *Canto 1:16*

A short dash is used to extend the minor reference,

Matthew xi: 3–8 and *Canto 1: 16–144*

* Inasmuch as there is no easy way to express the equals sign on the typewriter, the double colon is often used for it; and the printer, except in the case of a complete ratio expression, should substitute the conventional equals sign.

After a first citation or reference has been written out or abbreviated, those following may be indicated by numerals only and these may be separated by the colon.

> Vol. XX, sec. 12, col. 2; also XXI:14:1 and XXII:23:2

4 To separate generic from specific references.

> Boston: Little, Brown, and Company
> Macmillan: New York City

5 After the salutation in a business letter and after any other form of group or individual address.

> Dear Sir: Ladies and Gentlemen:
> Mr. Chairman: Kind Friends:
>   Dearly Beloved Brethren:

6 After the word *Resolved* in the statement of a proposition for debate.

> Resolved: That the business letter writing of the average firm does more to prevent or retard business than to build it

G There is wide variation of usage in regard to the capitalization of the word that follows a colon. The best usage seems to be (see also page 46) to capitalize the word following a colon when it is the beginning of independent material, not to capitalize when the material following is merely supplementary to and expansive of material gone before. There is much general practise, however, in observance of the rule to the effect that the word following a colon is capitalized when what follows constitutes a complete subject-and-predicate expression, not to capitalize when the material following constitutes a single item or a group of words, phrases, or clauses dependent upon a major construction that is implied.

> We were discussing the possibility of death caused by fright. Doctor B said that he was pretty well convinced that death is never caused in that way. Doctor A took issue with him and cited his unusual experience in India during the summer of '17 to justify his disagreement: A young interne, it seemed, had developed a rather notorious fear of cobras. Sitting by the window of his club one day, he fell into a doze with his arm extended on the outer, ivy-covered window-sill. When he lazily opened his eyes after a brief nap he was startled to see a cobra winding its way up his arm and diagonally down across his body. Doctor A, who was sitting a few feet away, whispered softly, "Sit still. Don't move. It will soon run away." And it did. But the young interne was nevertheless dead—dead from fright!

Loyola had two sides, of so different an aspect that it seems
almost incredible that they belonged to one man: the mystical
Loyola, who fixed his eyes on heaven, beheld visions, dreamt
dreams, was subject to ecstasy; and the intensely practical
Loyola, who kept his eye on the earth, estimated human capacities and weaknesses with the nicety of a diamond cutter, knew
how to play upon hope, ambition, desire, and fear, was patient,
laborious, contriving, and full of resources

It follows from all that has been said regarding the colon
that it is wrong to use a conjunction immediately after it.
unless, of course, you are writing a quotation that begins
with a conjunction or are discussing a conjunction as a word
or a part of speech.

The correct use of the colon, more than of any other mark
of punctuation, perhaps, signals a writer as a master of
precision and terseness in his expression of thought.   There
is probably no mark about which greater doubt exists in the
mind of the average individual.

III   The comma ,

A   The comma is used to separate the members of a series of
similar expressions similarly exprest—letters, words, phrases,
clauses, figures, signs—whether the members of the series be
single or in pairs or in larger units.   When the last two
members of such a series are connected by a conjunction, the
comma is preferably used before the conjunction.   It
follows, conversely, that if the members of such a series are
all regularly connected by conjunctions, then no commas
are necessary.

He mused upon yesterday, today, and tomorrow
The vowels of the alphabet are a, e, i, o, and u
He wrote his 7's, his 9's, and his 12's illegibly
Mary and John, Rose and Bill, and Jane and Harry are coming

In summer, in winter, in fall, or in spring
The glories of Switzerland let us sing

Dot your i's, cross your t's, open your o's, and close your e's
The common mathematical signs are $+$, $-$, $\times$, and $\div$
The common mathematical signs are $+$ and $-$ and $\times$ and $\div$

B   Related closely to the foregoing rule is this: Place a comma
after each of a series of coordinate modifiers—adjectives, for
instance—of equal qualifying force.   But discernment is
necessary in the application of this rule.   It very often
happens, for instance, that the last adjective in a series

modifying a noun is so closely identified with its meaning
as really to be a part of it. When such is the case the last
two or more adjectives before the noun are not separated by
the comma.

> Clear, sparkling, frolicsome brooklets were skipping down to
> the sea
> They paddled away in their long, narrow, comfortable canoe
> They paddled away in their long, narrow green canoe
> He is a hard, serious, contented worker
> They asked for a cake of pure white Ivory soap

The three adjectives in the last example are not really
coordinate. Their order could not be changed without
making the meaning absurd, and the insertion of *and* between *pure* and *white* would change the meaning. The three
adjectives, in other words, build cumulatively toward a
single modification of the word *soap*. Likewise in *a careful
young man* and *a dilapidated old barn* the omission of the
comma between the qualifying adjectives leaves no ambiguity.

C A comma is sometimes needed after an introductory modifying phrase or between such phrase and the subject of the
sentence, for the sake of clarification of meaning.

> Harassed by enemies everywhere, he sought peace
> With no one to look to, Helen waged her own good fight
>
> Beset by insuperable difficulties he deserved great credit for his
> success
>
> To achieve happiness he knew what he must do and what he
> must not do

D Introductory independent phrases—including the ablative
absolute—are preferably set off by the comma, as are also
adjective and adverbial phrases out of their natural order or
following the words they modify.

> The election being over, he again settled down to work
> In every sense of the word, honors he won were amply deserved
> The lad, shaking with fear, ran straightaway to his mother
> In the last analysis his findings, he knew, were right
> By and large, a man comes into his merited own
> This being true, I shall therefore remain at home
> He was inclined to be vacillating, yielding to this whim and to
> that without any provocation whatever

E The comma should be used to separate a dependent adverbial
clause from a principal clause when the former precedes the
latter and is likely to cause misunderstanding if it is not

so set off. But this rule must be applied with reason, as all
rules must be. It very often happens that a sentence in
which the dependent clause precedes the independent clause,
is perfectly clear without any internal punctuation. This
rule brings us to the parting of the ways between the old
and the new in punctuation practise, between the conservative and the modern. This sentence is perfectly clear and
needs no comma:

> When I reached home yesterday I found my mother ill

The conservative will insist upon a comma after *yesterday;*
the modern will not. The construction of this sentence is
so closely knit that every word and phrase follows closely
the word or the phrase modified. The omission of the
comma is more likely to be permissible in a complex sentence of this kind in which each clause has the same subject.
In this sentence the comma is preferable tho not, strictly
speaking, necessary:

> Altho my mother was ill when I reached home yesterday, she
> insisted that there was nothing I could do for her

Here again, the construction is so coherent that no misunderstanding is likely if the comma is omitted. But the sentence
is somewhat long and there is a definite breathing break after
yesterday; hence, the comma may be used. Note in the
following sentences, however, that the comma is necessary
for clarity:

> While men, women, and children crowded around the gates, and
> the doors were being forced inward by those with special tickets,
> the policemen were making arrests right and left
>
> When they swooped down upon the castle, gates were broken
> thru and the courtyard soon filled with people
>
> When he saw John, Ferguson gave up all hope

When the independent clause comes first, however, in
such complex sentences as those above, the comma is not
always necessary:

> Ferguson gave up all hope when he saw John
>
> Gates were broken thru and the courtyard soon filled with people
> when they swooped down upon the castle

F Adjective clauses that are non-restrictive are usually set off
by the comma, for they really have parenthetical or appositive quality. But restrictive adjective clauses are not set

off by the comma, inasmuch as they are too closely related to the general content of a sentence to be set apart in any way. This rule applies also to restrictive and non-restrictive phrases (see page 142):

> Every boy who enters this school must sign the pledge of good citizenship
>
> Good business letters, which must be composed thoughtfully and typed with accuracy and beauty, are an asset to any business
>
> The book that I want is not here
>
> The man who wanted to see the exhibit was not admitted
>
> The man, who was not admitted, wanted to see the exhibit
>
> Frank, seeing the danger, shifted his position quickly
>
> Books pertaining to correct usage are always in demand

The comma very often distinguishes the coordinate use of *who* and *which* from their subordinate uses:

> The officer who was close at hand must have heard the shot

This implies that there were other officers present but that the one referred to was closer than the others to the place where the shot was fired. Set off the relative clause by commas and you give it coordinate distinction:

> The officer, who was close at hand, must have heard the shot
> The officer—and he was close at hand—must have heard the shot

G There are two or three old-fashioned rules in regard to the use of the comma in compound sentences. Some of these are being discarded gradually by modern usage. Here, as elsewhere, when the meaning is perfectly clear without the comma and the grammatical relationships are coherent and closely knit, it is foolish to insert the comma simply as result of respect to tradition. No comma is required in such compound sentences as these:

> We hurried home after the party but they had already left
>
> John was determined to go and Mary was equally determined to accompany him

The old grammars prescribed a comma before *but* in the first example and before *and* in the second, and this punctuation is still observed to some extent. The rules were: Use a comma between clauses of equal rank connected by *and, but, or, nor;* use a comma between clauses that are set in contrast one to another; use a comma between coordinate clauses that have different subjects. So there would seem to be a triple-proof reason for placing a comma before *but* in the foregoing sentence.

An additional rule was applied to the second sentence above: The conjunction between the clauses of a compound sentence must be preceded by the comma when the matter immediately before it is not coordinate with that immediately following it, otherwise the conjunction will appear to connect two coordinate members. There seems, however, to be little likelihood that the words *to go and* presuppose or even suggest an infinitive immediately following *and.* The meaning is quite clear as the sentence stands.

Even in simple sentences expressing contrast the comma is by no means always necessary to set off the contrasted members.

> Unlike the old daguerreotype the present-day photographic plate has no silver wash
>
> To all appearances a shirker he nevertheless achieved wonders in his field

But note these:

> True worth is in being, not seeming
>
> Reading, in the worth-while sense, means getting the spirit of a book, not skimming its mere surface values
>
> Work, not mere words, is what we need

H Short informal direct quotations are set off by the comma. Words that interrupt a quotation are set off by the comma. Indirect quotations, however, are not set off by the comma. Under the last provision of this rule it follows that noun clauses coming after the simple predicate of a sentence and beginning with *how, that, what,* or *whether,* are not preceded by a comma.

> "Let me go," cried Bill, "or I'll get even with you"
>
> "Do not compromise with error to the minutest degree in your letter writing," said the supervisor
>
> He said that the letters sent out by his firm constituted its greatest asset—or its greatest liability
>
> He asked what we thought of the future of the gyroscope

Note, however, that when the indirect matter is not preceded by an introductory word it may be preceded by the comma.

> The question is, will he go
> The answer is, he will not

J A comma is used to separate a principal clause from a dependent clause beginning with *as, because, for, since.* These words are causal conjunctions when they introduce dependent adverbial clauses. But they have other uses and one use may be confused with another unless care is exercised to clarify by means of the comma. But here again, in the event of a short and coherent complex sentence containing these words, the comma may be omitted.

> We were late because we had tire trouble
> (We were late because of tire trouble)
> He came as I was leaving
> Keep to this side of the road, because the other is under repair
> He works untiringly, for his family is in dire need
> I shall go with you, since you say you are afraid
> He has worked untiringly since he came here

K The comma is used in many merely mechanical connections.

1 To prevent words, figures, phrases, or clauses from running together and thus conveying wrong or ambiguous meanings. The commas in these sentences (and the quotation marks in the first) cannot be omitted without obscuring the meaning:

> "Harold," said his father, "is always ready to work"
> Boy accused of cheating, bears ordeal bravely
> Waiting for John, Smith became bored
> When I was about to start, the engine stopped
> He wrote the letter on March 12, 1862
> Long after, she received the telegram

2 To separate similar or identical words running consecutively.

> Whoever wins, wins nobly
> Whatever is, is right
> Yield to John, John will yield to you

3 To set off figures in groups of five or more (see page 430). In columnar tabulations commas are used to mark off hundreds, thousands, millions, and so forth, but not in straight copy unless the number is one too detailed to be written out.

There were 50,000 in the stadium	$1,444,231.
We have $1600. in the bank	1,114.
Assets were estimated at $1,877,365.	606,120.
I saw him last in 1933	32,141.

It is ridiculous to place a comma after the first of a four-digit number in straight copy, tho many books and newspapers still follow this usage. Note the confusion caused by the unnecessary comma in the following headline:

BUCHMAN, AT SEA, TALKS TO 3,100 HERE

It should be noted in this connection that neither serial numbers nor exponent figures or letters used for footnote references follow this rule.

14133 Brewster Avenue   See examples 1 2 3
Saratoga 50604 (telephone)   See below a b c d
page 14333   Eng. ed. i p. 216

4 To set off light and inconsequential exclamations.

> Alas, I cannot go!
> Oh, if he were only here!
> And oh, the difference to me!

5 To separate the surname of an individual from the Christian name when the surname comes first, as in catalogs and directories.

> Jansen, Joseph R.
> Matthews, Hilda Jane

6 To separate the name of an individual from a title that follows it (tho there is some authoritative violation of this rule in regard to *Jr.* and *Sr.*).

Harrison Ainsworth, President of Chatsworth College
Harold Bronson, LL.D.   Blaine Gardiner, M.D.
Bronson, Harold, LL.D.   Rabbi Aaron Stein, Ph.D.
Matthews, Hilda J., A.M.   Thomas Donaldson, S.J.
John Blagden Jr.   John Blagden, Sr.
John Blagden, jr.   John Blagden sr.

7 To set off expressions, used in connection with personal names, denoting residence and position. There is, however, much authoritative violation of this rule, especially in cases where names have become so closely appositive with place or position designation that the two have become identified as one.

Harrison Wentworth, of Collegeville, Ohio, will address us

Harrison Wentworth, chairman of the board of managers, will address us

Miss Alice Graben of Oberlin will attend the meeting

My sister Jane will come along
My friend Bill will come to dinner
King Henry of Navarre
William the Conqueror
Richard the Lion-Hearted

The reflexive pronouns—*myself, yourself, himself, herself, itself,* and their plurals—are not set off by the comma when they are used appositively with the noun.

John himself knows better
They themselves are to blame
I am speaking to you yourself
We ourselves take all the responsibility

It is well to recall again that typographical variation is increasingly eliminating punctuation. Nouns in apposition, printed in italics or in small capitals, by very token of typography need not be set off by commas:

The word *panic* is from the Greek word Pan

8 To set off volume, page, and line references following titles of works, and other similar data.

Tennyson's *The Princess,* Canto II, Page 9, Line 4
Encyclopædia Britannica, volume III, page 654, column 2

9 To set off suspended parts of compound phrases and clauses (tho such constructions should not be used—see page 209).

He asked about, not for, the book
He walked into, not out of, the room
What he does, and when, is none of my affair

10 To separate repeated words.

It's a long, long way to Tipperary
He's a truly, truly great man

11 To indicate omitted words or phrases, unless the meaning is quite clear without the comma.

I have three; John, four; Mary, five
The former is beautiful; the latter ugly
Patience is a virtue; procrastination, a vice
Reading maketh a full man; conference, a ready man; writing, an exact man

12 To set off any expression that is independent by direct address.

> I wish, sir, to ask just one question
> Cheer up, my boy, summer is almost here
> I hope, Mr. Chairman, that the motion will be lost
> Yes, Anderson, I shall want the large trunk

13 To set off words and expressions used in a purely trans-itional or parenthetical or thrown-in manner. This rule refers also to adverbs and adverbial phrases and clauses that modify entire clauses and sentences, sometimes called "omnibus modifiers." Such words as *absolutely, certainly, indeed, positively, however,* not infrequently are built into constructions as definite modifiers, and in such cases they are therefore not set off by commas.

> He is indeed a lucky boy
> I shall certainly take him to task
> Afterwards, we went to the library
> In the first place, his figures were wrong
> I think, therefore, that I shall go
> My opinion, then, carries no weight
> Certainly, I shall be glad to go with you
> You must, of course, be respectful in your arguments
> He said, moreover, that he took no interest in it
> He will try, however, to meet us half way
> This plan, as I shall explain, is the best of its kind ever offered
> Study, we are informed, is the be-all and the end-all of full and complete living

14 Before *and so forth, and so on,* and *and the like;* and before such introductory expressions as *as, for example, for instance, such as, namely, that is, e.g., i.e., viz.,* when they introduce parenthetical explanations. When, how-ever, these latter terms introduce lists, they are preceded by the comma and followed by the colon or comma (see page 486). In brief simple constructions they are both preceded and followed by commas:

> Many of our students, for example, finish the course in three years
>
> This, for instance, is out of tune
>
> You know that February twelfth, namely, Lincoln's birthday, is the day of our party
>
> He bought a large variety of things, for example: axes, toys lamps, suits, seed, ale, what-not
>
> If you walk in this direction, that is, straight down the avenue, you will find stores, theaters, hotels, and so forth
>
> He has many names, such as *Jack, Jock, Red, Steady,* and he apparently likes them all (See 7, page 494)

15 To set off *yes, no, surely,* and other such words used as
expletives.

Yes, I shall go
No, he has not come yet
Surely, you may have it all

L In letters in which closed punctuation is used, commas are
placed between place names of different categories, between
dates of different categories, at the ends of lines (except the
last, which is followed by a period), in headings and inside
addresses, and after the complimentary closing (after the
salutation also in friendly letters). On printed letterheads
the comma is used as internal punctuation only, never as
terminal (see pages 235 and 236).

In letters in which completely open punctuation is used,
commas are placed only as required in the body of composition of the letters, spacing being depended upon to keep
dates and places of different categories from being misunderstood.

In letters in which modified punctuation is used, commas
are placed internally in the heading and the inside address
and after the complimentary closing; and a colon is placed
after the salutation. The comma is preferably not used
after the salutation in a business or in an official letter. It
should be used after the salutation in a friendly letter.

Business Letter—Closed

HAGAN-BRAINERD EXPORT COMPANY
897 Westchester Avenue
New York City

May 12, 0000.

Mr. Alexander Drew,
24 State Street,
Boston, Mass.

Dear Mr. Drew:

Yours very truly,
ARCHIBALD TREMAINE,
Manager.

AT—DR

Business Letter—Open

BLAINE HARRISON AND COMPANY
Importers and Exporters
332 Fox Street
Detroit

December 10 0000

Mr Harrison Baer
35 Janeway Street
Chicago

Dear Mr Baer

Very truly yours

WARDER HARRISON
Assistant Manager

WH/cc

Business Letter—Modified
(The most popular form)

THE EXCELSIOR COMPANY, INC.
382 Ordway Avenue
St. Louis
Missouri

January 24, 0000

Mr. Charles Higgins
25 Market Street
San Francisco
California

Dear Sir:

Very truly yours,

ARNOLD REID
Vice-President

AR:CV

¶ A few cautions about the use of the comma may prove helpful.

1 Do not use the comma when spacing and arrangement of copy render it unnecessary.

Columbus Ohio	July Fourth
1936	17 76
Eleventh of June	

2 Do not use the comma after the word *following*. When this word precedes a list or a complete sentence it should be followed by a colon.

3 Do not separate subject and predicate by a comma.

> *Wrong* The young people, danced gracefully
> *Right*   The young people danced gracefully

4 Do not place a comma after the name of the month when it immediately precedes the year.

> *Wrong* February, 1930
> *Right*   February 1930

5 Do not separate an adjective from its noun by a comma.

> *Wrong* He is an able, fellow
> *Right*   He is an able fellow

6 Do not place a comma before the first of a series.

> *Wrong* Last summer he went to, Paris, London, and Rome
> *Right*   Last summer he went to Paris, London, and Rome

7 Do not place a comma after the last of a series.

> *Wrong* Good, bad, and indifferent, were the classifications
> *Right*   Good, bad, and indifferent were the classifications

Authorities differ as to this rule, some contending that the comma is correct after a series of three or more.

8 Do not place a comma before or after the words *that, whether, how, what* used to introduce noun clauses.

> *Wrong* He said, that he would go
> *Wrong* He asked whether, we would accompany him
> *Right*   He said that he would go
> *Right*   He asked whether we would accompany him

9 Do not overuse the comma, that is, do not use it trivially and unnecessarily.

> *Wrong* In the room, we saw the instructor
> *Right*   In the room we saw the instructor
> *Wrong* I shall be ready, when you come, if you care to have me, go with you
> *Right*   I shall be ready when you come if you care to have me go with you

10 Do not connect or "splice" two independent clauses with a comma.

> *Wrong* He came yesterday, he went today
> *Right*   He came yesterday. He went today
>
> *Wrong* We telegraphed, we telephoned, we finally sent a messenger

| *Right* | We telegraphed; we telephoned; we finally sent a messenger |
| *Right* | We telegraphed. We telephoned. We finally sent a messenger |

11 Do not use the comma or the dash with any other mark of punctuation. It was customary in the old days to use the comma and dash in combination after the salutation in a letter and after the word *following* preceding a list. Modern usage does not sanction such double punctuation. Single punctuation or one mark of punctuation at a place is the better present-day practise.

IV The dash —

A The dash is sometimes used to mark off appositive or parenthetical expressions.

> The man that I mean—he of the red hair and the freckled face— is evidently not the one you refer to
>
> I shall never forget that letter—a letter as perfect as a work of art and as moving as a great play

B The dash is used to indicate a sudden change of thought and the consequent break of sequence in a sentence. The abrupt stoppage may come at the end of a sentence and the sentence may thus terminate with a dash. Stammering or hesitation in speech is indicated by the dash between letters or words when such speech is set down in writing.

> "I'd rather go with you than with ——," she said with some reticence but we all knew whom she meant
>
> "I thought—well—a—I thought perhaps you'd not mind lending me a half dollar—or—well—if that's too much—maybe—a quarter," he said embarrassedly while his pals outside kept whistling and calling for him to go to the circus
>
> They haven't heard their marks yet, but—there's the postman's ring and that probably means a letter from the school
>
> "Heh-Heh-Henry," he stammered, "c-c-come with me"

C The short dash is used to separate dates, page numbers, reference notations, and the like, as a substitute for the words *to* and *and*.

1914-1918	chaps. X-XII
pp. 29-131	parts 3-4
cols. 3-4	lines 14-24

D The dash is used to precede surname of author or source of quoted matter.

The world is still deceived with ornament
—SHAKESPEARE
The earth is the Lord's, and the fulness thereof
—*Psalm xxiv:1*

E The dash is frequently used to separate questions and answers of run-in testimony when these units are brief. When they are long they are, of course, paragraphed.

> Q. Have you ever been a spy yourself?—A. No. I scorn the base insinuation

F The dash is sometimes used (tho this use is not recommended and is rapidly being discontinued) after signs of notation in an outline and after a main topic when subordinate topics follow below. It is likewise used before points in an outline when notation is omitted altogether.

> We suggest—   I—We suggest
>   a play   A—a play
>   a debate   B—a debate
>   a festival   C—a festival
>   an exhibition   D—an exhibition

>   —We suggest
>   —a play
>   —a debate
>   —a festival
>   —an exhibition

G The dash is sometimes used after a question mark when what follows elaborates the question itself.

> What have you to say to this item?—"Tennis rackets $25."

H A series of dashes amounting to a solid line is placed before titles or other entries in catalogs, to take the place of ditto marks. Note, however, that in the first item listed the name must be written out.

> Shakespeare *As You Like It*
> —————— *Twelfth Night*
> —————— *Macbeth*
> —————— *Othello*

] The following more or less automatic or mechanical uses of the dash should be noted. The first two are derivatives from B and C respectively.

1 To indicate the omission of letters or words, very much as leaders and asterisks are used.

> The d–v–l you are!
> Take it, —— you, and go!

2 To separate a running list of terms and to some extent to display them.

> Coal—Ice—Wood
> Comfort—Satisfaction—Happiness: That's a Packard

3 To emphasize a word or a phrase following a statement.

> Never speak to me again—never!

4 To separate a brief summarizing enumeration from the general statement to which it belongs.

> She possessed that triune of starriness that makes all men astronomers—health, wealth, and beauty
>
> Health, wealth, and beauty—that triune of starriness in a woman that makes all men astronomers

K Do not use the dash habitually with other marks of punctuation. It was formerly the custom to use the dash with the comma and with the colon, but modern usage has wholesomely discontinued the practise. Do not depend upon the dash to "cover a multitude of punctuation emergencies." Some young people develop the habit of using it carelessly for commas and periods and still other marks. This is a serious abuse of punctuation privilege.

It will be noted that there is a similarity in the use of the colon and that of the dash. Both, in general, indicate additional development of thought to follow. In the case of the colon that addition is continuance and expansion; in the case of the dash, it is more likely to be tangent or backfire. The dash reflects sadly upon mental processes, for it emphasizes their tendency to ramble off into the incoherencies of ordinary conversation. The colon, on the other hand, is a credit to the thought power of him who uses it correctly, for it proves his ability to focus and point his expression. Charlotte Brontë is frequently referred to as the author who used the colon with greatest nicety.

V The exclamation point ! (*ecphoneme*)

A The exclamation point is used after an expression that evinces feeling—admiration, appeal, dissension, incredulity, irony, surprize. The feeling may be evinced by a single word, by a phrase, or by a whole sentence. The exclamation point follows that unit of expression by which it is evinced.

The idea!	Alas! I shall not see him again
Great!	I don't believe a word you say!
Westward Ho!	What a beautiful new car!
How dare you!	He has finally confessed!
Oh, I say!	What a day I've had!
I'll say so!	He is wearing a real (!) diamond

B The exclamation *O* is used in direct address. It is never
   followed by either an exclamation point or a comma. In
   case it is used in a sentence expressing strong feeling, the
   exclamation point is placed at the end of the sentence.

> O Lord, have mercy upon me!
> O no, my lad, you can't do that

C The exclamation *oh* is not used in direct address. It expresses pain, sorrow, anxiety, shame, disapprobation, long-
   ing. It is preferably followed, not by the exclamation
   point, but by the comma.

> Oh, it is raining again
> Oh dear me, here comes the train

The distinction between *O* and *oh* is by no means strictly
observed by writers. Some writers capitalize *oh* within a
sentence; some do not.

D The exclamation point is not used after mild or unemphatic
   expressions of feeling.

> Well, I am glad to see you
> Alas, I fear we shall have more snow

VI The hyphen - =

A There are two kinds of compound words as to form—SOLID
   COMPOUNDS like *something* and HYPHENATED COMPOUNDS
   like *son-in-law*.

Our leading dictionaries are by no means always in agreement about compounding by hyphenation. The two best-
known ones do not even use the same mark to indicate the
hyphen. In Webster's *New International Dictionary* it is
the first mark above; in the *New Standard Dictionary* it is
the second. Because of disagreement among authorities, the
subject of hyphenation is one of the most confused and
tantalizing departments of word-study. Since language tends
to become simpler as time goes on (or so it is hoped) you
will do well to err on the side of under-hyphenating rather
than over-hyphenating. When in doubt, don't hyphenate

—unless you have time to look up the doubtful cases in at least two dictionaries, a research that may do nothing for you but confirm your doubt!

Below are a few words that are hyphenated in the Standard and not in Webster:

Webster	Standard	Webster	Standard
basketball	basket-ball	living room	living-room
blue print	blue-print	motorcar	motor-car
camp followers	camp-followers	notebook	note-book
camp meeting	camp-meeting	note paper	note-paper
camp stool	camp-stool	parcel post	parcel-post
candle power	candle-power	parcels post	parcels-post
countinghouse	counting-house	postcard or	post-card
dress goods	dress-goods	post card	
dwelling house	dwelling-house	post office	post-office
everyday (adj.)	every-day	postpaid	post-paid
everyone	every one	reading room	reading-room
good will or	good-will	savings bank	savings-bank
goodwill		secondhand	second-hand
halfway	half-way	steam boiler	steam-boiler
house boat	house-boat	textbook	text-book
house fly	house-fly	upkeep	up-keep
lead pencil	lead-pencil	water color	water-color
life belt	life-belt	waterproof	water-proof
lifeboat	life-boat	waybill	way-bill
life buoy	life-buoy	well to do	well-to-do

And *up to date—up-to-date—uptodate* is a wayward child indeed, appearing with sanction in all three forms.

B   There are, again, two kinds of compound words as to meaning or conveyance of idea—LITERAL like *alongside, brother-in-law, childlike, drydock, everybody, forethought, good-looking, hearsay, hereby, looker-on, moreover, nowadays, on-looker, stepmother, today, tomorrow, tonight, whitewash,* and NONLITERAL like *carpetbagger, dumb-bell, hold-up, jack-in-the-box, ladyfinger, man-of-war, ne'er-do-well, newsprint, redcoat, starboard, tipstaff, whippersnapper.*

C   A still further classification of compound words divides them into PRIMARY COMPOUNDS and SECONDARY COMPOUNDS, the former being made up of simple parts, such as *barnyard, blackboard, homesick, southeast;* the latter being made up of three or more word units two of which have been previously compounded, such as *unladylike, beforehand, midshipman, whatsoever, warehouseman.*

Compound words are formed in various ways without very much system or rule. Most of them have come into use as result of the convenience and facility of expression they afford. Sometimes a noun and a verb (subject and predicate) are compounded, as *machine-made, pigeon-toed, teamwork, waylay;* sometimes a verb and object, as, *cross-question, make-believe, helpmate, carryall;* sometimes a preposition and object, as, *tonight, upstairs, overhead, beforehand;* sometimes verbal or other phrases, as *has-been, happy-go-lucky, insofar, up-and-up, ne'er-do-well.*

D Below are three groups of words—solid compounds, hyphenated compounds, and two-word combinations unhyphenated —that are likely to give a writer pause when he comes to use them. These groups are not exhaustive—cannot be, for obvious reasons. But they include most of the words in everyday use about which question most often arises. These are accumulated from the leading dictionaries and style books, and are therefore authoritative *at present.* It must not be forgotten that as new issues of dictionaries and style books come from the press revisions in hyphenation are made, the tendency being to graduate words from hyphenation into solid compounds as rapidly as usage will permit. The following lists represent weight of authority at the time of compilation:

SOLID COMPOUNDS

aircraft	bedspread	boathouse	bookstore
airman	bedtime	boldface	bookworm
airship	beechnut	bombproof	brakeman
antechamber	beefeater	bonbon	breadwinner
antedate	beefsteak	bondholder	breakneck
antislavery	beehive	bonfire	breastbone
anybody	beeswax	bookbinder	breastpin
armchair	beforehand	bookcase	brickmaker
autotruck	behindhand	bookcraft	brickmaking
backdoor	biannual	bookkeeper	brickyard
background	billposter	booklore	bridesmaid
barberry	birthday	bookmaker	broadside
baseball	birthmark	bookmaking	brotherhood
bathhouse	birthplace	bookman	businesslike
bathroom	bittersweet	bookmark	busybody
bathtub	blackboard	bookplate	bygone
battleship	blackmail	bookrack	bylaw
bedcover	blindfold	bookseller	byplay
bedridden	bloodhound	bookshop	bystander
bedroom	bloodthirsty	bookstall	byword
bedside	blunderbuss	bookstand	cabinetmaker

SOLID COMPOUNDS—*Continued*

candlepower	dreadnought	headline	meanwhile
cardboard	dressmaker	headlong	midday
cardcase	earache	headquarters	middleman
caretaker	earthquake	headstrong	midsummer
careworn	eastbound	headwaters	milestone
carryall	elsewhere	heartache	motorcycle
cashbook	evergreen	heartbreak	nearby
castaway	everlasting	heartrending	network
causeway	everybody	helpmate	newspaper
cellarway	everywhere	henceforth	nevertheless
childlike	eyeglass	henceforward	nobody
churchgoer	facsimile	hereafter	noncombatant
churchman	farmhouse	hereby	nonconformist
churchwarden	faultfinding	herein	nondescript
churchyard	fellowship	herewith	nonessential
claptrap	ferryboat	highball	nonpareil
classmate	firearms	highway	nonplussed
classroom	fireplace	homesick	nonstop
closefisted	fireproof	horseback	nonsuit
clotheshorse	flagpole	horsepower	noontime
clothesline	flagstaff	hotbed	northeast
clothespin	flaxseed	household	notebook
clubhouse	flywheel	housekeeper	oneself
coeducation	foghorn	housetop	onlooker
commonplace	foolhardy	hundredweight	onrush
commonwealth	foolscap	iceberg	onslaught
companionway	football	inkstand	onward
copperplate	foreclosure	innkeeper	otherwise
copybook	forever	ironmonger	outgoing
copyholder	foursquare	jawbone	outside
copyright	freethinker	juryman	outlawry
corkscrew	frontiersman	keyboard	overdue
councilman	gainsay	keyhole	overhead
courthouse	gangplank	keynote	pawnbroker
courtyard	gaslight	kinsman	paymaster
craftsman	gatekeeper	ladyfinger	penholder
crossbow	gentlewoman	landholder	piecework
crosspiece	godchild	landlord	pigeonhole
crossroad	godfather	lawgiver	pineapple
crossway	godmother	lawmaker	pocketbook
crosswise	greenback	layman	pocketknife
cupboard	griddlecake	layout	policeman
curbstone	gristmill	letterpress	policyholder
customhouse	guardsman	lifeboat	postgraduate
dashboard	guesswork	lifelike	postmark
daybook	handbook	lifetime	postscript
daybreak	handclasp	mainland	praiseworthy
daylight	handiwork	mainsail	pressroom
daytime	handmade	mainspring	presswork
doorway	handshake	makeshift	quartermaster
downhearted	handwriting	mankind	quitclaim
downpour	hardware	masterpiece	railroad
downtrodden	hardwood	mealtime	railway

SOLID COMPOUNDS—*Continued*

roadside	signboard	teaspoon	whatever
roadway	signpost	tenfold	whatsoever
roommate	slaughterhouse	textbook	whenever
runabout	snowball	thousandfold	whereabouts
safeguard	snowflake	timekeeper	wherefore
sailboat	snowstorm	timesaver	wherein
salesman	somebody	tiptoe	whereof
salesroom	something	today	whereon
saleswoman	sometimes	tomorrow	wheresoever
schoolbook	somewhat	tonight	whereto
schoolboy	somewhere	toothache	whereupon
schoolfellow	songbook	toothbrush	wherever
schoolhouse	southeast	transatlantic	whichever
schoolmaster	spoilsman	transoceanic	whirlpool
schoolmate	spokesman	transship	whitewash
schoolroom	spoonful	tricolor	whosoever
schooltime	standpoint	turnover	widowhood
schoolyard	stockbroker	typesetter	windmill
scrapbook	stockholder	typewriter	windstorm
seacoast	stockjobber	undersell	wintergreen
seafarer	storehouse	upkeep	wintertime
seaman	storekeeper	upstairs	womanhood
searchlight	storeroom	viceroyal	wonderland
seashore	straightforward	viewpoint	woodwork
selfless	subdivisions	warehouse	workaday
selfsame	subnormal	warship	workingman
semiannual	subtreasury	waterproof	workman
semicircle	sunshine	wayfare	workroom
semicolon	switchboard	wayfarer	workshop
semiofficer	tablecloth	waylay	wrongdoer
shipboard	taxicab	weatherman	yachtsman
shipbuilder	teacup	weatherproof	yearbook
sideboard	teakettle	weathersail	zigzag
sidewalk	teamwork		

HYPHENATED COMPOUNDS

able-bodied	broad-brimmed	cross-banded
absent-minded	broad-minded	cross-country
after-dinner	built-in	cross-examination
all-round	by-product	cross-examine
awe-stricken	check-book	cross-eyed
awl-shaped	chicken-hearted	cross-fertilize
baggage-master	clean-cut	cross-fire (v)
bald-headed	clear-cut	cross-grained
base-burner	clear-headed	cross-interrogate
base-minded	clear-sighted	cross-purpose
bell-shaped	coal-black	cross-question
big-eyed	coarse-grained	cross-reading
bird-cage	cold-blooded	deep-dyed
bird's-eye	cold-hearted	deep-rooted
book-learned	color-blind	double-faced
brand-new	cream-colored	double-spaced

HYPHENATED COMPOUNDS—*Continued*

drawing-room
dry-as-dust
dry-eyed
dull-eyed
dull-sighted
eagle-eyed
ear-minded
ear-splitting
easy-going
egg-shaped
ex-soldier
eye-minded
faint-hearted
fair-minded
far-fetched
far-reaching
far-seeing
far-sighted
feeble-minded
first-born
first-class
first-rate
flat-bottomed
flat-footed
flat-headed
follow-up
forty-four
foul-mouthed
foul-spoken
four-footed
four-in-hand
four-wheeled
free-born
free-for-all
free-handed
free-hearted
free-spoken
gilt-edged
go-between
God-fearing
gold-filled
golden-eyed
good-by
good-humored
good-looking
good-natured
great-hearted
half-and-half
half-breed
half-hearted
half-hourly
half-mast
half-moon

half-witted
half-yearly
hard-favored
hard-headed
hard-hearted
hawk-eyed
heart-easing
heart-shaped
helter-skelter
high-flown
hit-and-miss
hit-or-miss
honey-tongued
hot-tempered
ill-advised
ill-humored
ill-mannered
ill-natured
iron-bound
iron-gray
jack-in-the-box
kind-hearted
knife-plaited
labor-saving
large-hearted
law-abiding
left-handed
letter-perfect
life-giving
light-fingered
light-footed
light-headed
like-minded
lion-hearted
long-distance
long-lived
long-suffering
loose-jointed
low-lived
low-spirited
lower-case
machine-made
mail-carrier
make-believe
make-up
man-eating
man-made
middle-aged
middle-class
middle-sized
money-making
moss-backed
moss-grown

moth-eaten
mother-in-law
motor-driven
muddle-headed
namby-pamby
narrow-minded
neat-handed
noble-minded
non-commissioned
non-contagious
non-interference
off-color
old-fashioned
old-maidish
old-womanish
old-world
on-coming
one-horse
one-sided
open-hearted
open-mouthed
parti-colored
pepper-and-salt
pigeon-toed
post-mortem
poverty-stricken
powder-blue
quick-witted
rain-proof
rattle-brained
rattle-headed
red-breasted
red-handed
red-headed
red-winged
rose-colored
safe-deposit
second-class
second-rate
self-assured
self-conceit
self-confidence
self-control
self-explanatory
self-governing
self-made
self-reliance
self-respect
self-starter
self-taught
self-willed
sharp-witted
shock-headed

HYPHENATED COMPOUNDS—*Continued*

short-handed	thick-and-thin	unlooked-for
shrill-tongued	third-class	vine-clad
side-splitting	third-rate	warm-blooded
silver-haired	three-bagger	warm-hearted
simple-hearted	top-heavy	whole-souled
sky-high	two-decker	wind-blown
slow-burning	ultra-violet	wonder-working
square-built	uncalled-for	worn-out
take-off	unheard-of	wrong-headed
tender-hearted	unhoped-for	

TWO WORDS

abiding place	cash account	grass seed
account book	cast iron	ground floor
alarm clock	civil service	half dollar
all aboard	clearing house	hard finish
all right	coal field	hard labor
ant hill	commission merchant	high mass
a posteriori	common sense	high priced
a priori	concert hall	home rule
apple pie	cream cheese	ice cream
apple tree	cross action	ill at ease
ash heap	cross bill	ill health
assembly hall	cross fire (n)	ill humor
attorney general	cross grain	ill temper
auction bridge	cross reference	ill will
back door	cross section	income tax
back rest	cross street	insurance office
back stairs	crown glass	laissez faire
back step	cup valve	lattice window
balance book	cylinder press	letter paper
ball bearing	day labor	letter press
ballot box	dining room	license plate
bank book	dress goods	lieutenant colonel
bank note	dress parade	life sentence
barber shop	dress suit	live stock
basket weave	en route	mail box
bay window	ex cathedra	mail man
beef tea	ex dividend	major general
bell boy	ex officio	meat market
bench mark	fellow citizen	mother tongue
bill book	fire commissioner	mutton chop
binding tape	fire escape	navy yard
birth rate	fire insurance	*noblesse oblige*
black bass	form letter	no one
black damp	fountain pen	notary public
book learning	free trade	ocean greyhound
box car	good afternoon	ocean liner
by and by	good evening	parcel post
candle power	good morning	pen name
card index	good night	plate window
car fare	government employee	poll tax

TWO WORDS—*Continued*

post card	return fare	ticket office
post office	safety match	title page
postal card	safety valve	trade name
postal service	sales letters	training camp
price list	school board	water works
printing office	spark plug	wave length
pro tempore	stage door	working day
profit sharing	street car	wrought iron
proof reader	ticket agent	yeast cake

E The hyphen is used to improvise a compound term of two or more words for the conveyance of a new or combination idea and for making a unified modifier out of the group so compounded. The first word in all such cases is not only descriptive but definitive as well, and this is a fundamental rule of such hyphenation.

house-to-house canvass	greenish-gray suit
dyed-in-the-wool prohibitionist	out-of-the-way inn
up-and-doing young man	down-in-the-mouth Jane
two-way avenues	step-on-it generation
fifty-year-old trees	out-of-date hat
devil-may-care attitude	navy-yard assignment
three-fourths vote	honorable-mention graduate
matter-of-fact look	three-ply weave
above-mentioned rule	holier-than-thou editorials
New York-Atlanta route	one-half interest
well-known explorer	bride-to-be Betty
never-to-be-forgotten drive	five-o'clock coffee
long-distance telephone	ten-foot pole
2-inch pipe	12-foot rail

But note that foreign expressions so combined do not take the hyphen.

laissez faire policy	ex cathedra procedure
a priori argument	*noblese oblige* spirit
a posteriori reasoning	à la carte luncheon

Note also that proper names so used are not hyphenated but that proper adjectives are likely to be.

North America furs	French-American alliance
New England greenery	Anglo-German feeling
Euclid Avenue shops	Indo-European outlook
Bond Street shopping	Greek-Italian feud
North Carolina scenery	British-Scandinavian friendship

An adverb ending with *ly* is not hyphenated to the adjective that it precedes in forming a unit modifier, inasmuch as this constitutes a normal grammatical relationship. But some authorities rule that *well* so used should be hyphenated to the adjective.

wonderfully fine weather	well-known author
beautifully polished silver	well-versed teacher
highly provocative sermon	well-expressed thought
unnecessarily aggressive tone	well-dressed woman

This hyphenation of *well* is, however, increasingly disregarded by both books and periodicals. It is sometimes ruled that when *well* and the word it accompanies to form a unit modifier follow the word modified, the hyphen should be omitted.

The commodity has shown itself to be well worth the money
He is a man well suited for the work you have to do

F Compound numbers from twenty-one to ninety-nine are usually hyphenated, but there is much variation of usage in this connection—*forty-three, seventy-eight,* but *one hundred twenty, two hundred eighty-one.* Written as modifiers, the parts of a fraction (numerator and denominator) are hyphenated; used as nouns, they are not—*six sevenths, twelve twenty-eighths, three-quarters new, one-third rate.*

He is fifty-six
We have twenty-five acres
She asked for one-half pound
He invested three fourths of his fortune in realty

G The words *today, tomorrow, tonight* have evolved to the unhyphenated stage of their careers. There is still a little good authority for their hyphenation, but the best modern usage does not hyphenate them.

H The syllable *self* used in reflexive pronouns is never hyphenated—*myself, yourself, himself, herself, itself, ourselves, yourselves, themselves.* The words *oneself, selfsame,* and *selfless* are likewise unhyphenated. But *self* in other compound uses usually is hyphenated (see list on page 508).

I The words *anybody, everybody, nobody, somebody* are not hyphenated. When *anyone, everyone,* and *someone* refer respectively to *anybody, everybody,* and *somebody* they are written as solid compounds. But when they refer to individuals or a group severally with the phrase *of them* understood to follow, they are written as two words—*any one, every one, some one.* The expression *no one* is always written as two words.

K *Anyway* used as an adverb meaning *in any way* or *in any case* is written as a solid compound, but used as part of a prepositional phrase wherein *way* is object of the preposition, *any* and *way* are written as two separate words—*I shall not help in any way, I'm going anyway.*

L Two nouns put together for the conveyance of a single idea should be written as solid compounds in case the first member is monosyllabic—*sailboat, stockbroker, penknife, paymaster, cupboard, penholder.*

M *Ex, elect, quasi, self, ante, anti, mid, pseudo, pan, neo, un, pro, pre, ultra* used with names and titles are usually hyphenated. The word *vice* may or may not be hyphenated, with the exception of *viceroy* and *viceregent,* which are always solid compounds. Civil and military titles are, however, preferably not hyphenated.

ex-governor	pan-Asiatic
president-elect	neo-Platonism
quasi-corporation	un-American
self-interest	pre-Galilean
ante-bellum	pro-Ally
anti-aircraft	ultra-modern
mid-September	vice consul or vice-consul
pseudo-Egyptian	vice president or vice-president

In the main, however, prefixes and suffixes do not form hyphenated compounds, for they constitute an important derivative element in word composition. *Like* is never hyphenated except in word inventions and then only until the novelty wears off.

antedate	foolish	preferment
businesslike	friendship	southward
bylaw	interview	superfine
childlike	landwise	threefold
dotage	passionless	transmigration
excommunicate	postscript	womanhood

Note also

biennial	monopoly	therefore
circumscribe	nonofficial	thorogoing
downward	offset	toward
extraordinary	overdo	transmit
forehanded	retrograde	tricolor
introduction	semiannual	understand
intramural	subway	upward

N The hyphen is used to prevent the doubling of a vowel and the tripling of a consonant. When a prefix ends with the same vowel with which the root of a word begins, then it may be separated by a hyphen, or a *dieresis* may be placed over the first letter of the root. The *diæresis* (*dieresis*) consists of two dots over the second of two vowels to indicate the independent pronunciation of each: *aërial, ʒoölogy*. But the tendency is to simplify this usage and use neither hyphen nor dieresis. Thus some authorities still write *pre-eminent* or *preëminent, co-operate* or *coöperate,* but the preferable forms now are:

preeminent	coworker
cooperate	reorganize
coeducation	anti-imperial
coagulate	micro-organism
coequal	bell-like

O Note that the hyphen should be used to prevent misinterpretation and mispronunciation.

non-junior-high-school positions
non-civil-service jobs
a large green house
a large green-house
a retreat
a re-treat
my morning recreation
my re-creation of the scene
I recovered my lost umbrella
I re-covered my umbrella
a square paper-box (a box to hold paper)
a square paper box (a box made of paper)

P The hyphen is used to join a letter or a figure or a sign with a word (usually a noun or a participle).

U-boat	T-rule	X-ray	V-shaped	X-section
¶-indention	$-mark	⊥-line		∟-angle

Q The hyphen is used to indicate the syllabication of words —*sin-cere-ly, in-ter-mit-tent*. The hyphen is omitted, however, in the dictionary listings after the syllables on which primary and secondary accents are indicated—*de-vel'op, gov″ern-men'tal*—but the spacing beneath the accent mark implies the syllabication.

R Two or more hyphenated compounds connected with another part expressed but once take the hyphen after them even tho conjunctions are used between them:

3- and 4-foot rules
common- and preferred-stock rates
6- and 7-ply widths

but   six-ply and seven-ply widths
long-term and short-term bonds

S   A solid compound and a hyphenated compound remain solid and hyphenated respectively when their form is changed from one part of speech to another:

He is a hard-hearted man
His hard-heartedness is inexcusable
He acted most hard-heartedly
The ship is in drydock
They are drydocking the ship

T   The hyphen is used in most compounds pertaining to distance, direction, measurement, estimate, and in repetition or accentuation of the first term of a solid compound:

north-northeast	great-grandmother	secretary-treasurer
light-year	forty-second cousin	horsepower-estimate

U   Terms indicating color combinations are usually hyphenated, but an adjective preceding the name of a color is not hyphenated with it:

red-orange	dark blue
beige-brown	greenish yellow
coal-black	brownish red
yellow-green	middle red

V   A hyphen is customarily used (1) between a noun and an adverb following (2) between an adjective and a participle following (3) between a noun and a prepositional phrase following, when such combinations are used to express unit ideas.

passer-by	ill-advised	son-in-law
looker-on	light-fingered	man-of-war
hold-up	cold-blooded	stick-in-the-mud

W   Multi-worded idioms are not hyphenated:

ups and downs	come by
rack and ruin	bee line
hammer and tongs	hook or crook
by and large	thick and thin

X   The hyphen is used to indicate the division of a word between lines of writing and printed matter.

1 A word of one syllable (monosyllable) must not be divided between lines—*dip-ped* and *fou-ght* are wrong.

2 A word of two syllables (dissyllable), of three syllables (trisyllable), of four syllables (quadrisyllable), of five or more syllables (polysyllable), should be divided between lines strictly according to pronounceable syllables. The word *walked* (like *dipped* above) is monosyllabic according to pronunciation and it must not therefore be divided between lines by placing *walk* on the first line and *ed* on the second. Such words as *chaos, chasm, given, heaven, rhythm* should never be divided between lines.

3 Never place the hyphen at the beginning of the second line before the second part of the word division. The division hyphen between lines always goes at the end of the line on which the first part of the word appears.

4 A word should never be divided between lines by a single letter or even by two letters if this can be avoided. Dissyllables of four or five letters should not be divided between lines—*i-tem, ver-y, un-do, in-dex.*

5 Avoid dividing a word between lines so that a last syllable signifying agent or tense or gender or number is separated from the principal part of the word—*advis-er, preced-ed, prin-cess, church-es.*

6 A solid compound should be divided between lines according to its component make-up—*self-same, help-mate.*

7 A hyphenated compound should be divided between lines at the place of hyphenation in the compound. Do not add a line-division hyphen to a word already hyphenated, for it may thus take on a peculiar and unrecognizable appearance.

8 Do not divide words between lines for more than two consecutive lines. If you do, your right-hand margin will appear ridiculous.

9 Do not divide a word between lines by a contracted part or by a syllable without a vowel—*would-n't, Vandewater-'s.*

10 Do not hyphenate between two or more letters that are pronounced as one—*be-autiful, quenc-hable* are wrong, but *di-er-e-sis* is right.

11 Do not divide proper names of any kind between lines. Do not divide initials standing for organizations or titles or degrees, dates, abbreviations, homogeneous numerals, and the like, between lines.

12 Do not divide between lines the last word of a paragraph and do not divide words between pages.

13 The hyphen is sometimes used to convey hesitation and deliberation in expression and for suiting the appearance of a word somewhat to its meaning.   In advertising copy it is sometimes used to give distinction and attraction and unification of trade-name.

> T-a-k-e y-o-u-r t-i-m-e——————g-i-n-g-e-r-l-y n-o-w!
> It s-t-r-e-t-c-h-e-s, Kiddie-Koop, Coca-Cola, Aetna-ize

14 Words may be divided between lines at prefix or suffix breaks, provided the former is not a single letter and the latter has more than two letters in it and does not determine agent, tense, gender, or number—*pre-dilection, acknowledg-ment.*

15 Two or more consonants at a syllabic break are themselves divided, as a rule—*com-mis-sion, en-ter-prise, cor-rec-tion;* not *comm-iss-ion, ent-erpr-ise, cor-rect-ion.*

16 Following the rule above, verbs forming their imperfect tense and present participle by doubling the final consonant should be divided between the consonants—*plan-ning, com-pel-ling, rat-tling.*

17 A single consonant at a syllabic break usually belongs to the following syllable, unless the preceding vowel is short and the syllable in which it occurs is accented—*inti-mate, intimi-date, col-umn, bal-ance, pleas-ure;* not *intim-ate, intimid-ate, co-lumn, ba-lance, plea-sure.*

18 Pronunciation sound must, therefore, be the guide in much splitting of words between lines.   It will be found an especially good guide in words having such suffixes as *able, ible, ent, ant, ance, ence*—*provi-dent, cap-able, assist-ant, reluc-tant, despon-dent, reli-ant.*

19 When two vowels come together but are separately pronounced, line division of a word may be made between then—*hero-ically, recre-ation, di-er-e-sis.*

20 The *shul, shun, shus* suffixes are preferably not carried over from the root of a word to stand alone on the following line—*spe-cial, par-tial, dimen-sion, gra-cious, outrag-eous.*

21 In spite of rules, do not divide a word so that one part or the other will look ridiculous or may be taken for an independent word and thus confuse the context—*goril-la* is better than *go-rilla; cate-chize* than *cat-echize; Helles-pont* than *Hell-espont.*

22 The parts of a word divided between lines should be mutually suggestive of the entire word, and the suggestion should come thru sound as well as sight. A queer-looking, queer-sounding division is probably wrong. Note that such consonant combinations as *th, sh, ph, ng, gn, tch, gh, gt, hn, nst* separated from other letters have a strange and forbidding appearance. Place them between sounded vowels, however, and the word picture at once falls into syllabic parts. They should not be divided, of course, when they are used to convey one sound—*leng-then, remon-strate, tech-nocracy, fur-ther, lan-guage, rhyth-mic, wretch-edly, judg-ment.*

23 Keep word division between lines at an absolute minimum. In dividing words, however, keep an eye upon the evenness of the right-hand margin of composition. It is always well to divide words between lines as nearly in the middle as the foregoing rules will permit. But some unevenness of division is naturally inevitable.

The chaos existing in the use of the hyphen must by this time be not only apparent but impressive. It may be some comfort to remember that the hyphen is after all merely a sort of halfway house in the evolution of a solid compound. Hyphenation represents a timid step taken with a gentle hope that the general public will recognize the desirability and the convenience of wedding two certain words. Once accustomed to seeing them linked by hyphen it will very

soon (it is always hoped) accede to their permanent association as a solid compound. The words *wheel barrow* were
once two perfectly independent words. They came to be
used together so much that the hyphen between them was
soon acknowledged to be not only helpful but imperative.
Eventually the well-known G. P. said to itself, "O, what's
the use!" And so *wheelbarrow* became a solid compound.
It is typical of hundreds of other words.

VII   Parentheses ( ) Brackets [ ] Braces { }

A   Use parentheses to mark off supplementary and interpretative matter related to the main thought of a sentence but
not necessary to its grammatical construction. Parenthetical
matter is too remote in relationship to be set apart by mere
commas and yet too important to be omitted altogether:

> Witness (after examining photograph): Yes, this is he
>
> The President (addressing Mr. Jones): What do you think of it?
>
> Mr. Jones (with some hesitation): I think it's wrong!
>
> The prevailing and (as we hold) the correct view is this
>
> The words *fancy, idea, ecstasy, pathos, sympathy* (medieval
> Latin and French in their origins) have long had place in the
> popular vocabulary

As indicated by the first three examples, dramatic asides
and character portrayal are frequently indicated briefly thru
parentheses. Almost any page of a printed play will
illustrate this general use of the parenthesis in dramatic
literature.

B   Letters, figures, signs, and combinations of them in references and citations, are enclosed in parentheses. Letters
and figures used before topics in outline subordination are
likewise sometimes placed in parentheses. Roman numerals
and capital letters, however, are not properly placed in
parentheses when they are used in outlining. References to
time and place for the purpose of accuracy may likewise be
put into parentheses.

> This example (no. 2 of p. 56) is not clear to me
>
> The Paris (Ill.) *Sentinel* carried the story
>
> The *Sentinel* of Paris, Illinois, carried the story
>
> During the second year of the war (1915) we moved to Erie
> (Pa.)

He addressed us on (1) the importance of education (2) the continuance of education thruout life (3) the uses of education

These (plates 12 and 13, between pages 11 and 14) give a very clear idea of the growing plant

Abraham Lincoln (1809-1865) was assassinated by John Wilkes Booth

He paid each of three (3) men four dollars ($4.) a day

It is important that confirmatory figures, letters, signs, symbols used parenthetically, as in the last example above, be placed after the word or words that they confirm or verify. This is wrong:

He paid each of (3) three men four ($4.) dollars a day

C The word *sic,* meaning *thus it is put,* is usually enclosed in parentheses. In American usage this word is used frequently with some degree of scorn or irony or surprize or doubt, but in British usage it stands for verification or for throwing responsibility for an expression upon source

He told us, among other things, that however hardly (*sic*) the world treats us, we shall invariably find lasting compensations in good books

D The following technicalities should be noted in connection with the use of other marks of punctuation with parentheses. Rule 11 on page 500 is being increasingly applied by newspapers, magazines, and publishers generally, and it is a wholesome sign. This means that single punctuation is always preferable to double punctuation, that is, only one mark of punctuation should be used at a place. Parentheses themselves indicate sufficient stoppage in printed matter without the addition of any other mark. Thus in the example under B above

He addressed us on (1) the importance of education (2) the continuance of education thruout life (3) the uses of education

it is quite superfluous to place a comma or a semicolon before (2) and before (3). Some authorities still insist, however, upon doing so. The omission of the comma and the semicolon in all such cases is recommended for the reason that nothing whatever is to be gained by way of clarity. Neither should the period be used in the places indicated, even tho the word immediately following the parentheses may be capitalized. And this modern ruling should be applied to all run-in parenthetical expressions, that is, to all parenthetical matter that occurs somewhere between the beginning and the ending of a sentence.

> Take a boy like John, for instance, who goes to both day school and night school (and to Saturday and Sunday school, for that matter) and evaluate for me the spontaneous youthful pleasures he is denied by the enslavement of his ambition

No comma is necessary before *and evaluate* really, tho the conservative authority will insist upon one.   The break of the parenthesis before these words constitutes a sufficient break.

Parenthetical matter at the end of a sentence is placed before the period unless it constitutes a complete sentence.   If the latter is the case, then the period belongs within the parenthesis.

> Only a part of this need be studied (pars. 2-5 on pages 45-47).
>
> The book proves beyond all peradventure that the man was an undiscovered genius. (See especially chapters eight and nine.)

In case a sentence has two or more parenthetical references of the same character they should be similarly stated.

> This ring (cat. Y, page 7) is more beautiful than the other (cat. Y, page 12)
>
> *Not* This ring (cat. Y, page 7) is more beautiful than the other. (See cat. Y, page 12.)

The following illustrate the use of the question mark and the exclamation point in connection with parentheses:

> I was surprized (who would not have been?) but I managed to conceal my feelings
>
> She carried those three parcels (as heavy as lead they were, and as large as a young hemisphere!) all the way to the top of the mountain

When the question and the exclamation come at the end of a parenthetical expression, itself at the end of an otherwise declarative sentence, then the period may be carried after the parenthesis, tho strictly modern usage does not regard it as necessary.

> Then and there I decided to go (and why not?).
>
> Learning of my sudden decision she swooned on the spot (O my god!)

E   Do not enclose an expression in parentheses for the purpose of emphasizing it.   An exclamation point or a question mark may be placed in parentheses after an expression for the sake of emphasis, however, or for conveying irony or scorn or doubt or surprize.

> You gave it to Tom (!) of all people
> You're an expert (?) with a capital E

Likewise, special words in parentheses may be italicized, as they may be in straight copy, but parentheses themselves have no significance whatever as signs of emphasis. It will often be found that italics in straight copy are explained by the parenthetical expression (*the italics are ours*) but this is a protective and clarifying device, not an emphasizing one.

A signal instance of the foregoing may be indicated in the second line of Hamlet's most famous soliloquy (Act III, Scene i, Line 57):

> Whether *'tis* nobler in the mind to suffer (the italics are ours)

There is only one acting edition that carries the italicized *'tis* with the parenthetical clarification to indicate that *'tis* should be accented in rendering this line, the implication being that Hamlet has many times before meditated the subject of suicide. The accent therefore connotes much. (The acting profession in general, let it be noted in passing, has remained ignorant of the subtlety here involved.)

F Do not use parentheses for numbers or signs or words unnecessarily. It is ridiculous to write

> Bunyan's masterpiece (*The Pilgrim's Progress*) is seriously in need of renewed popularization

for the italics both emphasize and set apart and the parentheses are therefore quite superfluous.

G Do not use parentheses to indicate deletion or cancelation. A horizontal line thru the delated part or the delete sign on the margin, or both, should be used for this purpose.

H It is obvious that parenthetical expression should be avoided at the very beginning of a piece of composition.

J Brackets are generally explained as necessary for indicating omissions, corrections, interpolations, totally independent and gratuitous comment, and the like. The truth is that they are used almost interchangeably with parentheses in most modern writing but are becoming extinct in literary copy tho still necessary in mathematical text. Most of the illustrations given above under C, D, and E are quite as allowably placed within brackets as within parentheses. It may be well, however, to remember the old two-part ruling for their use, namely, material in brackets is interpolated from outside—from another author—by the author using them or by the person editing the manuscript, and material in brackets is more remotely related to the general subject matter than material in parentheses. Neither is observed today with any degree of nicety.

> In spite of the many changes which this system [the complicated system of strong verbs] has undergone, the author insists that it remains just as complicated as it ever was in the days of Old English and of Middle English
>
> He came at four p.m. [three p.m. standard]
>
> We shall never yield on that basis [Applause.] no matter what torture you may bring to bear
>
> And when he saw he conquered. [Laughter from the galleries.] And when he conquered he became . . . [Prolonged applause.]

K A single bracket is placed before words and figures that overrun linage and that are placed either above or below the line.

> [king
> So like a shattered column lay the
> Try the following codes tomorrow—76m, 44s2,
> [516T

L Brackets are frequently inserted in copy for the inclusion of matter still to come.

> On the day of sale ladies' wraps will be marked down to [   ] ladies' street shoes to [   ] ladies' sport dresses [   ]

M There are many special uses of brackets in connection with legal and official papers and also with special commercial undertakings. In general the rules of punctuation that apply to parentheses apply also to brackets. The one exception would seem to be that matter in brackets is independently set apart by capitalization and by placement of period within the bracket, even tho no complete statement is made.

> [Laughter.]   [Applause.]

N Braces are used for grouping materials and for showing relationship among groups. They are not used in straightaway writing, but in outlining and graphing and equational arrangements (mathematics) and in tabular work generally they are necessary for indicating unified and coherent partitioning.   It should be noted, perhaps, that parentheses show a comparatively close relationship to copy; brackets show a remote relationship to copy; braces a still more remote (foreign) relation to content.   In general usage the point of the brace should stand toward the fewer points, that is, the brace should be so used that the idea of expansiveness will be indicated—from lesser to greater.

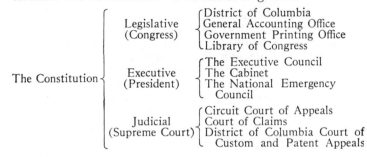

VIII   The period .

A   The period is placed at the end of a declarative sentence, at the end of an imperative sentence, and at the end of an interrogative sentence that makes a request, that is, in cases where the interrogative form is a matter of courtesy rather than purely interrogative.

> He asked me to close the door.
> Will you please close the door.
> Close the door, please.

This is an old conventional rule that is now being violated with justification wherever spacing and arrangement make it evident that the end of a statement has been reached. Business houses are increasingly omitting periods at the ends of paragraphs in letters, statements, and reports that end with obviously periodic expressions.   There is a wholesome tendency likewise to omit the period after such conventional abbreviations as *Mr* and *Mrs*

B   The period is sometimes used between figures that indicate two distinct classifications of time in the same category. The colon is, however, preferably used in this connection.

> 11.45 a.m.   *better*   11:45 a.m.

C The period is used before a decimal, immediately after whole numbers representing dollars, and by some firms after *s* and *d* for shillings and pence (not after £). The second provision holds in both tabulated matter and in run-in or straight copy (see page 429). The period should be single-spaced to the last digit in a group of figures representing dollars.

$157.85
   .20
 66.00 He lent me $300. for one month   £12 3*s*. 4*d*.

D In parenthetical expressions—declarations, commands, and courtesy questions—place the period inside the parentheses when they are independent of other matter, that is, when they are not grammatically connected with the content in which they appear, and when they thus begin with capital letter. Conversely, place the period outside the parentheses when the content contained within them is closely connected with what goes before or after, or both, and does not therefore begin with capital letter.

> He contradicted me fiercely when I accused him before the judge (tho he knew perfectly well that I had seen him snatch the bag).

> I accused the culprit positively. (He knew that I had seen him snatch the bag.) But he nevertheless contradicted me fiercely.

E The period should be placed inside quotation marks. This is a convention of printing and is generally observed in both longhand and typewritten copy. It is, however, quite illogical sometimes, as a little reasoning will clearly indicate.

> He asserted with some precision and much conviction: "It is foolish to contend that culture is to be inculcated only in the school and college classroom."

Strictly speaking, the foregoing sentence ends simultaneously with the quotation, or, at least, the speaker completes his statement *with* his quotation. Hence, the quotation marks should be written directly above the period, or should precede the period. Either arrangement would look awkward. The latter would leave awkward spacing also.

> "...........and the college classroom."
> "...........and the college classroom".

F Successive periods like those just above are called leaders. Omitted matter in sentences is usually indicated by either leaders or asterisks. This rule applies also to omitted letters in words. Note that a quotation broken somewhere at the beginning begins with a small letter in case the break comes in the middle of the expression. The quotation marks, however, are placed before the leaders to show that quoted matter is omitted:

H..ry   Marg***t   You sc....rel!

"......the last to lay the old aside," he muttered as he saw me wearing my three-year-old suit

G   The period is used at the end of the last line of the heading and of the inside address of a letter that is written with closed punctuation (see page 497). Printed letterheads, however, do not take the period at the end of the last line, or any other terminal punctuation, for that matter, even in letters written in the closed style.

124 Lenox Avenue,
New York City,
June 24, 0000.

Mr. Martin Ferguson,
33 Columbia Avenue,
Sandusky, Ohio.

But note the following letterhead:

Telephone 3-0123   Oil Department

THE GRAINGER FUEL COMPANY
Coal and Fuel Oils
144 Blair Street
Sacramento
California

April
First
0000

H   The period is not used at the end of last lines in letter headings and inside addresses when the open style of punctuation is followed. It should never be used after signatures, titles (or subtitles) of writings, running headlines, captions, boxed headings, items enumerated in lists, and so forth. The custom of our forefathers was to hold rigidly to the use of the period after all such matter. Old visiting cards reveal the fact that the period was carried after the engraved name. There has been a wholesome evolution in this respect. There are a few instances, however, in which the period is still carried in compliance with the old fashion,

The New York Times.

being one of the most important. Few other newspapers hold to this style, and no books and magazines do.

J   There are certain abbreviated forms that do not take the period after them. It is being increasingly omitted (as A above indicates) after *Mr* and *Mrs*. It is likewise omitted after *M, Mme,* and *Mlle* when they are used in French text, after OE (Old English) and MHG (Middle High German) in their glossarial uses, after the initials indicating points of the compass, after initials indicating well-known societies and their publications. Some authorities rule that the period should be omitted after *ms.* and *mss.* when capitalized, thus: *MS* and *MSS*

K   It follows from the foregoing that the period is omitted after chemical symbols, after the shortened forms of words indicating the size of books (see page 445), and, according to increasing practise, after *percent* and *per cent*.

H_2O 12mo   3 percent

L   It was once the custom to hold rigidly to the placement of periods after the numbers and letters of a system of notation, but as pointed out on page 434 this usage is being rapidly discontinued. Periods are likewise omitted from the ends of words, phrases, clauses, and sentences that follow notation figures and letters. No matter in what connection Roman numerals may be used, the better form today is not to follow them with a period. This applies particularly to Roman numerals used as ordinals.

Volume XX
William II

I   Publishers
II Printers
III Distributors
IV Retailers

I Introduction
A The circumstances
1 Definition
a Horse
b Carriage
c Driver
2 Time
3 Place
B The conditions

M   The period should be used after an initial that stands for the name of an actual person referred to. It should not be used after a letter used to indicate a fictitious or supposed individual.

> Mr. A. owes me fifty dollars
>
> Let it be assumed that A has five dollars and that he lends three to B for two weeks

N   The period is used after any single expression that stands alone in consecutive matter and that thus makes sense in relationship to what goes before and comes after. Other marks such as the question mark, the exclamation point, the dash may likewise be so used. The sense of the entire passage decides. It is more and more the fashion among those who write in what is apologetically called the "modern idiom" to give words and phrases and clauses independence of position.

> He was tired. Yes. Very tired. Why, then, should he sacrifice himself to the fuss and botheration of putting on his dinner coat and spending the evening with those perfect bores? Not he! No, sir. He would call up his pal, Frank, and treat him to a good dinner. Then—poker. No social fol-de-rol for him tonight.

O   The period should not be used after numerals or letters that are used to indicate the sequence of pages in a thesis or a book of any kind.

IX   **The question mark or interrogation point   ?**

A   The question mark is used after a direct question and also after a definite statement that is intended to be conveyed and taken as a question.

> How did you do it?
> Can you find your way?
> Who inquired, "What time is it"?
> He inquired, "What time is it?"
> Do you mean to say he stole it?
> He stole it?
> He asked, "Did he steal it?" with an I-told-you-so tone

B   The question mark is sometimes used in parentheses to indicate doubt or irony.

> She says she is sixteen (?) years old
> He is wearing a real (?) diamond

C   The question mark is used after each unit in serial queries, tho there is some authority for separating the different units by commas and placing the question mark at the end only.

What is its location? its population? its chief industry?
Can you see it? or feel it? or touch it? or hear it?
What is your name, your age, your nationality, your address?

D The question mark is placed after a parenthetical question
even tho it appears in the middle of a declarative sentence.

They convicted "Leftie" Louis (did he wish he were "Rightie"
now?) of murder, and sent him to jail for life

E The question mark is put within or without quotation
marks according as it belongs or does not belong to the
quoted matter. Here it belongs within because the quotation
is a question:

"Where are you going, Tom?" he asked

Here it belongs without because the quotation is not a
question:

Who shouted, "I'm cold"?

Note also:

Has *Business Letter Practice* an excellent chapter in it on "Selling Solvency by Letter"?

(See pages 531 and 532)

F Indirect questions do not require the question mark (see
pages 492 and 527). Requests, technically in question form,
are nevertheless followed by the period as a rule.

X Quotation marks " " ' '

A Quotation marks are used to enclose direct quotations. They
are not used with indirect quotations.

"The best part of every effort," said the speaker, "is its beginning"

"Are you going, John?" she asked
"Certainly not," replied John

The speaker said that the best part of every effort is its beginning

John replied that he was certainly not going

Note that the first word of the continued part of a broken
quotation, such as the first example above, is not capitalized.
This is also true of any broken or fragmentary quotation
wherein a person is not necessarily represented as speaking

but his exact words are quoted for purposes of emphasis and accuracy.

> The speaker said, "The best part of every effort is its beginning"
>
> Harrison commended the soldier for his "promptness of response, sobriety of conduct, and efficiency of action"

B A quotation within a quotation is set off by single quotation marks. If a third quotation is expressed within the matter between single quotation marks, then the double marks are again used. Quoted matter should rarely go beyond the "third degree" of quotes.

> She said, "John replied, 'Certainly not' "
>
> "What you mean to say," commented the professor, "is, 'For a long time I have been unable to understand the Shakespearean line, "The quality of mercy is not strained" ' "
>
> { "   ['   ("   ")   ']   " }

Single quotation marks are being increasingly used in modern writing in place of double for straight single-quoted matter or conversation. In British usage the quotation-within-quotation system is commonly reversed: ' " " '

C Consecutively quoted paragraphs take the quotation marks at the beginning of each but at the end of the last only. This rule applies also to consecutively quoted stanzas.

> "Plans are valuable in proportion as they are workable, and in proportion as they are fluid and flexible enough to be adapted to a variety of situations
>
> "They invariably represent ideals, as they should do, and they invariably serve as guides if they do not completely solve
>
> "The best plans, like the best rules, sometimes fail"
>
>> "A muffled ear, a filmy eye,
>> A mimicry of mirth,
>> A little groping for the sky—
>> And that is birth!
>>
>> "A blinded sight, a deafened sound,
>> A heaviness of the breath,
>> A little groping for the ground—
>> And that is death!"

D Typographical variation is being increasingly used to obviate the necessity for quotation marks, especially in cases where their use would become involved and would thus tend to confuse both mind and eye. Small capitals, italics, variations in type faces, and other changes in type style are recommended in such matter as this:

The true life of a man is in his letters said **John Henry Newman.** Taking this as cue some professor or other has said facetiously in bold face *Letters are the literature of blab, the literature of tattletale, the literature of giveaway, and inasmuch as the best letters have always been written by women, epistolary literature is naturally no respecter of secrets*

Book titles, magazine titles, newspaper titles, words and phrases that are emphasized as words and phrases (that is, used in "conscious reference") are preferably underlined in copy and, thus, italicized in print. But there is wide variation of usage in the observation of this rule. When two titles are referred to in the same writing, a greater and a lesser, the greater is printed in italics and the lesser is placed in quotation marks, the whole in italics and the part in quotes.

He is reading *The New York Times.*

The word *muslin* is from the name *Mosul,* a city on the Tigris in Mesopotamia where the fabric was first made

I read Edna Ferber's "American Beauty" while it was running in *The Ladies' Home Journal*

But note the quotations around *conscious reference* above. They are there because the expression was commonly used by a famous professor of English and is here quoted from his spoken language as well as from his books. In the same way any familiar speech or writing—from single words to entire sentences—is customarily placed in quotation marks. Slang, nicknames, misnomers, any deliberate misusage made for effect, malapropisms, and the like, come under this ruling.

He belongs to the "lame-duck" régime

You must be what they call a "down and outer"

What do you think of my new "allegory" bag?

The government is said to be "playing with fire" in its new monetary policy

Don't let your business letters "stereotype or freeze the business man's gray matter"

Such prefatory terms as *entitled, so-called, known as, termed, specified as, endorsed, indicated as, mentioned as, marked* are usually followed by matter that belongs either in quotes or in italics.

He signed himself *Patrick Hillegas, Esq.*

The act definitely specified "all doors closed on Sundays"

After this, parcels marked *hold* will be kept in that drawer

E   According to a printing tradition quotation marks are always placed outside the comma and the period; and as a rule (some authorities say *always*) inside the colon and the semicolon. The best usage seems to be to place the colon and the semicolon inside or outside the quotation marks according as these marks do or do not belong to the quoted matter, as is the unvarying usage with the question mark and the exclamation point. This, too, is the rule with the dash and with the parentheses—when the dash stands for something left unsaid or unquoted, the quotes belong outside; when it does not, that is, when it is used as a mark of punctuation rather than a fill-in for quoted matter, the quotes belong inside. When matter within parentheses is quoted, the quotes belong within the parentheses; otherwise outside.

The rule applying to the period and the comma is mechanical purely and by no means always logical. The placement of these marks where they usually logically belong—after the quotes—makes for awkward spacing, and on printed pages where there is much use of quotes, diagonal "trickles" of space are likely to mar the typographical picture. The following illustrations may help to clarify a little this complicated issue. Practise and observation are the keys to success in this as in other phases of punctuation. But here, too, typographical variation may solve difficulties sometimes.

> Can you tell me what is meant by "taxation without representation is tyranny"?
>
> "What," he asked, "is the meaning of 'taxation without representation is tyranny'?"
>
> "What," he asked, "is the meaning of *taxation without representation is tyranny?*"
>
> "What is the meaning," he asked, "of non-representative taxation ('taxation without representation is tyranny') when it is applied to real estate?"
>
> He asked, "What is the meaning of 'taxation without representation is tyranny' (the grand slogan-climax of every socialist soap-box orator)"?
>
> "Blessed," said Lowell, "are the horny hands of toil"; but the more I see of toil the more I pity hands!
>
> Said the orator of the evening, "Not what you have or what you can do or even what you think, will make very much difference;" then stepping to the very edge of the platform he shouted in climactic tones, "It's what you are that counts!"

As I stood there silent as the stars I heard some one mutter "Heaven forbid!"

"Heaven forbid!" she muttered, as I stood there silent as the stars

"Oh, well, I suppose one must yield to ——"

She couldn't finish. There wasn't time. For at that very instant he sprang deliberately to his death, shouting "Farewell everybody"——

F Quoted matter that has long ago become a part of our everyday expression, such as, *a house divided against itself cannot stand* and *a Daniel come to judgment,* is not set off by quotes. Such presently accepted one-time slang as *up to you* and *take it from me* comes under the same exemption.

Some authorities object to the use of quotation marks by a writer to label his own humor. But the objection is by no means always well taken. Quotation marks in this connection correspond somewhat to the tongue-in-cheek expression of the punster, and they cannot be entirely condemned as a distinguishing mark of humor. Care must be taken, of course, to see to it that the humor is worthy of distinction! It is certainly well that young people who lapse into slang in their writing should use either italics or quotes or some prefatory phraseology in order that their elders may not accuse them of having no better equivalent in reserve. Such signal or label is recommended in young people's speech— tone inflection, pause, or facial expression may be depended upon to offset misjudgments. Perhaps irony is the one type of humor that is most justifiably set off by quotes.

This is the "umpty-umptieth" time I've tried to pass

You made "quite a hit" with your gangster costume

What this term "air-stifler" in the first paragraph means, I do not know

He is here using the word "esquire" in the British sense of country gentleman

He goes here and there posing as a new "savior of womankind"

Don't hide behind "owing to an error in our so-and-so department" or "owing to circumstances over which we had no control" in writing your adjustment letters

G Few other marks of punctuation require such nicety of mechanical adjustments in writing as do the quotation marks. The following points should be carefully noted:

1 When a quotation is broken by such interpolated expressions as *he said, he replied, cried she, they called,* the first part must be closed and the second part opened again. Usually such interpolations are set off by commas, but the meaning and construction of the quotation may make other marks of punctuation necessary.

> "I confess," he said, "that I did it"
>
> "I confess it," he said; "I did it"
>
> "Will you confess?" asked the officer, "or shall we have to resort to the third degree?"
>
> "Good God, no!" he cried. Then with his head between his hands, he wailed, "If you hurt me I shall confess to any crime you care to accuse me of"

2 The first word after a broken or interrupted quotation is not capitalized. But the resumed section of the quotation may or may not be, according to the meaning (see page 525 under period).

> "It is a great novel," he said. "More fiction of this sort is what the American public needs"
>
> "It is a great novel," he said, "and the kind that the American public needs"
>
> "It is a great novel," he said. Then perusing its pages gently, he continued, "More fiction of this sort is what the American public needs"

3 When quotations are followed by footnote exponents— letters, figures, signs—the citation reference should follow quotes.

> He closed with: "Let us then be up and doing, With a heart for any fate——" *
>
> * Henry Wadsworth Longfellow's *The Psalm of Life.*

4 Do not use quotation marks around a proper name (place, person, or thing), around the title of a theme, around a firm name or slogan, in formal dramatic dialog where the name of each speaker precedes his speech, for two different kinds of designations in a unit of expression. In regard to the last, note the following:

> The famous *An Elegy Written in a Country Churchyard*, by Thomas Gray, begins "The curfew tolls the knell of parting day".

This is correct set-up. It is wrong to put both the title and the quoted line in quotes. The terminal punctuation is logically correct but not technically so according to universal usage (see E above).

XI   The semicolon   ;

A   The semicolon is used to separate the clauses of a compound sentence when their relationship is not close and when the conjunctions are omitted. In this use the semicolon is closest to the period.

> We started early in the morning; it had taken us practically all night to get our goods and chattels all collected and packed for the journey; the consequence was that before noon of the first day of our long trip we were exhausted

B   The semicolon is used to separate the clauses of a compound sentence when these clauses are themselves long and when they consequently are likely to require commas within their own constructions. This rule applies to any consecutive expressions—listings, enumerations, references—wherein two or more kinds of entries are necessary. In such matter the semicolon is used to separate the major groups and the comma to separate the minor groups or the units between semicolons.

> If bad business letters are the result of carelessness and ignorance, then their writers ought to be sent to school; if they are the result of the I-don't-care spirit and of a lack of respect for addressees, then their writers ought to be arrested; if they are the result of the feeling that the kind of letters our forefathers wrote are good enough for us, then their writers ought to be buried

> Those entertained at the Embassy were Lord and Lady Thomasdale, of Throckmorton Lodge; Major and Mrs. Randolph Edderson, of Madras, India; Dame Terrirson, sojourning here from the Isle of Wight; and Professor and Mrs. Cyril von der Muethe, of Vienna, Austria

> See Taintor and Monro's *The Secretary's Handbook,* pages 84-91; Blaine's *Handbook of American Usage,* page 34-67; Douglas' *Forty Thousand Quotations* (Sully), page 1112

> See Proverbs xxiii:3-6; xxiv:10-12

C   The semicolon is used to separate a series of phrases and clauses that are themselves cumulatively dependent upon a general or summarizing construction.

> To be exact without being finicky; to be artistic without being freakish; to be proper without being prudish; to be gay without being hilarious, and to be serious without being gloomy—these were the attitudes he tried to inculcate

> We hold these truths to be self-evident: that all men are created equal; that they are endowed by their Creator with certain inalienable rights; that among these are life, liberty, and the pursuit of happiness

Note that either the dash or the colon may be used to set off the general statement; note also that when the series precedes the general statement the last two members of the series may be separated by a comma, especially when *and* is supplied, as in the first example above.

D The semicolon is used to separate expressions that are not closely enough related to be separated by commas and not sufficiently independent of each other in meaning to justify their separation by periods.

> He came; he saw; he conquered
> He reads to live; he lives to read
> It is true of Jim; it is true of Bill; it is true of Mary

This has been called the epigrammatic use of the semicolon, for the reason that two-part epigrams, especially those that are antithetical in nature, are usually divided by this punctuation mark. But usage is by no means unanimous in regard to its use in this connection. Much written material has commas where the semicolons are in the above examples; much has periods.

E The semicolon is used before *as, for example, for instance, i.e., namely, to wit, viz.,* and the like, when they precede enumerations or classifications or bills of particulars of some length. When these words come before merely a simple item or two, the comma is preferably used both before and after (see page 496). When they are preceded by the semicolon they are customarily followed by the comma.

> Only two boys were there, namely, Bill and Frank

> Much dramatic literature so called is merely the rewriting of other literature; for instance, all of Shakespeare's plays but one; nearly all of the comedies of the eighteenth century; at least seventy-five per cent of nineteenth-century drama

> There are certain rules and regulations that every member must strictly observe; to wit, always be prompt at meetings, always participate in discussions, always pay dues on time, always help to preserve good order, and always volunteer services for those in need

It not infrequently happens that these terms are imbedded in the matter that follows the general statement and are not prefatory to it. In such cases they are set off by commas (both before and after) and the general statement is followed by a colon or a dash.

> Your new organization should begin with one of two procedures: it should, for instance, appoint a committee to draw up a constitution, or it should adopt certain general administrative policies

F The semicolon is used before *accordingly, besides, consequently, hence, however, moreover, nevertheless, otherwise, still, then, therefore, thus* when they are used to show relationship between independent and dependent clauses. In such use they are usually followed by the comma (see K 13, page 496, under the comma).

> I had come to regard the old man with a good deal of suspicion; besides, he was becoming more and more curious in his actions, I found, according to the opinion of my neighbors
>
> He had failed in both examinations and was very much discouraged; however, he still had a good job to fall back upon
>
> It is pretty generally agreed that honesty is an excellent policy; therefore, you would do well to adopt it

But note, in compliance with the second part of E above, that *therefore* may be placed later, taking on more of the adverbial nature than of the conjunctive, and thus may be set off by commas.

> It is pretty generally agreed that honesty is an excellent policy; you would do well, therefore, to adopt it

The first rule under the semicolon is thus followed, and *therefore* is punctuated under the comma rule K 13.

G The semicolon is sometimes used for the purpose of securing greater emphasis than is possible with commas. This is a practise that applies to writers of advertising copy as well as to writers in other fields.

> He thought of her the day she had first come to him; of those deep inquiring eyes; of her soft yielding ways
>
> We had visions of green fields and running brooks; of rapidly passing scenery; of ribbon roadways winding before us; OF THE JOYS OF THE CADILLAC

H The semicolon is used to prevent misunderstanding or ambiguity when words, phrases, or clauses would run together and convey a meaning not intended.

If I were a prince of high estate, I should mingle with laborers, with white-collar workers, with employers, with professional people, with engineers and other technicians; and all mankind would benefit by my example

J The semicolon is sometimes used before terminal *and* in sections of resolutions when the word *whereas* follows on the line below. The comma is, however, sometimes used in this connection:

; and
Whereas, he was invariably loyal to his duty in our behalf, etc.

Do not use the semicolon after the salutation in a letter or between a related clause and phrase or between a dependent clause and the independent clause to which it belongs. *Use the semicolon as sparingly as you can.* There are wholesome signs that, in the evolution of language, it is gradually disappearing—more rapidly, probably, than is the little toe in the physical evolution of man!

CHAPTER EIGHTEEN

SPELLING

I Some helpful rules

It was once almost fashionable to pose as a bad speller and to throw the burden of responsibility upon the unphonetic quality of English words. But this is fortunately no longer the case. People have learned how to learn to spell—how to study spelling. First of all they have learned that bad spelling is largely the result of bad seeing or bad looking at words. They now know that bad hearing is another fundamental cause. And they know that careless and inaccurate pronunciation is to blame for much bad spelling. Loose speakers frequently add letters or syllables to such words as *advice, advise, athletics, cruelty, desirous, Elizabethan, emigrant, finally, formally, formerly, library, mischievous, possibly, probably, realty, several, similarity, tremendous.* They frequently omit letters or syllables from such words as *accidentally, arctic, accompanying, convenience, curiosity, delivery, familiar, governor, history, incidentally, interesting, laboratory, memory, Niagara, original, particularly, perhaps, poem, popular, regular, sarsaparilla, superintendent, singular, veterinary, vulnerable.* Thus, a kind of contagion of misspelling is spread thru mispronunciation.

Bad spelling is the first and most obvious symptom of illiteracy. The fact that English words are by no means always spelled as they are pronounced, is a challenge to the person who cares, rather than a discouragement. Practise is important, as are also special lists of troublesome words—*your* special words. Group these latter with similar words that you are sure you can spell, and learn from the association. Trace your spelling bugbears out in the air with your forefinger or your pencil. Discuss them. Argue about them. Make a hobby of them. Develop a defense complex about them, rather than a frustration inferiority. Visualize words carefully. Pronounce them aloud slowly and accurately. Syllabize them, and clinch the first and last letters of syllables. Use some stunt to play up troublesome letters or syllables—*stationAry.*

A stands for adjective; thus, for *principAl*, intrinsically an adjective. Study word derivations. Own a dictionary and be a slave to it. Know a few of the best spelling rules, and play with them and their exceptions until you have lists of your own illustrative of both.

The following terms are necessary in the study of spelling, either from the following pages or from the dictionary:

Monosyllable—a word (prefix) of one syllable—*dis*
Dissyllable—a word of two syllables—*credit*
Trisyllable—a word of three syllables—*discredit*
Quadrisyllable—a word of four syllables—*discredited*
Polysyllable—a word of many (five or more) syllables—*discreditable*

A prefix is a unit of one or more letters added at the beginning of a word to modify its signification—*dis*.

A suffix is a unit of one or more letters added at the end of a word to modify its signification—*ed, able*.

A root is the fundamental or original word element to which prefix and suffix may be added to change its meaning—Latin *credo* (*creditus*) meaning trust, faith, believe, is the root of the English word *credit*.

A digraph is a group of two letters representing a single simple speech sound—*ea* in *lead* is a vowel digraph or diphthong; *th* in *cloth* is a consonant digraph.

A silent letter is one that is not meant to be heard when a word is properly pronounced (see page 557).

For acute accent, breve, double acute accent, macron, and other terms pertaining to pronunciation and spelling see pages 445, 580-586.

A   Pertaining to vowels:

1 Words ending with silent or unpronounced *e* usually drop the *e* before suffixes beginning with a vowel.

argue	arguing	arguable
arrive	arriving	arrival
blame	blaming	blamable
bribe	bribing	bribable
bride		bridal
come	coming	
deplore	deploring	deplorable

desire	desiring	desirable, desirous
dine	dining	
force	forcing	forcible
give	giving	
grieve	grieving	grievance
guide	guiding	guidance
hope	hoping	
love	loving	lovable
move	moving	movable
note	noting	notable
please	pleasing	pleasant
plume	pluming	plumage
sale		salable
separate	separating	separable
subdue	subduing	subduable
true		truism
use	using	usable

2 The final silent *e* is retained after soft *c* and *g* before adding *able* and *ous* so that the *c* and *g* will not be pronounced hard.

advantageous	disadvantageous	outrageous
allegeable	enforceable	peaceable
changeable	manageable	pronounceable
chargeable	marriageable	serviceable
courageous	noticeable	traceable

3 The final silent *e* is retained, however, in *hoeing, shoeing, toeing*, to prevent mispronunciation. But it is dropt when *er* is added—*hoer, shoer, toer*.

4 Final silent *e* is retained also in *dyeing, singeing, springeing, swingeing, tingeing* to distinguish them from *dying, singing, springing, swinging, tinging*. Note that *e* is retained also in *hingeing* and *mileage* but is omitted in *linage* meaning the lines in a piece of writing. It is retained in *lineage,* meaning descent in race or family line, in *lineal,* the adjective form, and in *pineal,* referring to the gland. Note the irregular *mortgagor.*

5 Final silent *e* is usually retained before a suffix beginning with a consonant.

appropriateness	lonely
baleful	lovely
chastely	movement
encouragement	paleness
excitement	respectively
hateful	sincerely

6 Certain words ending with silent *e* immediately preceded by *u* drop the *e* in forming the derivative.

	argue	argument
	blue	bluish
	due	duly
	true	truly
but	rue	rueful

7 These words are also exceptions to 5 above: *abridgment, acknowledgment, judgment, lodgment, nursling, wisdom, wholly.* Many writers, however, still write the first four with the *e* after *g*.

8 Verbs ending with *ie* usually drop the *e* and change the *i* to *y* when adding *ing*, in order to prevent doubling of *i*.

die	dying
hie	hying (sometimes *hieing*)
lie	lying
tie	tying (sometimes *tieing*)
vie	vying

But note that *pi*, meaning disarranged or confused type, is *pied* and *pieing* in the imperfect tense and present participle respectively.

9 Words ending with *y* preceded by a vowel usually retain the *y* before suffixes.

buy	buying	buyer
enjoy	enjoying	enjoyable, enjoyment
gay	gayety	gayly
	(*also* gaiety)	(*also* gaily)
gluey	glueyness	
joy	joyful	joyous
obey	obeying	obeyer
play	playing	player
sway	swaying	swayed
stay	staying	stayed (*also* staid)

Note these definite exceptions, however:

day	daily	
lay	laid	laid
pay	paid	paid
say	said	said
slay		slain

But *colloquies* and *soliloquies* are not exceptions inasmuch as the *u* in *colloquy* and *soliloquy* is really equivalent to the consonant *w* (see page 457).

10 Following the second part of rule 3 above, derivatives of such words as *agree, free, hoe, oversee, owe, see, sue* drop the last vowel when adding a syllable beginning with *e*.

	agreed		hoed		seer
	agreer		hoer	*but*	
but		*but*			seeing
	agreeable		hoeing		sued
	agreeing		overseer		suer
	freer	*but*		*but*	
	freest		overseeing		suing
but			owed		suable
	freeing		ower		
		but			
			owing		
			owable		

Note these, however:

beau		beauish
coo	coos (*also* cooes)	cooed, cooer
echo	echoer	echoed
huzza		huzzaed
woo	woos (*also* wooes)	wooed, wooer

11 As to *ie* and *ei* there is one rule (with many exceptions) expressed in three ways:

In words spelled with *ie* or *ei* (pronounced *ee*) *e* follows *c*, and *i* follows all other letters.

> *i* before *e*
> Except after *c*,
> Or when sounded like *a*,
> As in *neighbor* and *weigh*

In words that are spelled with *ie* or *ei* (pronounced *ee*) the *i* comes first if the letter immediately preceding the diphthong in the word stands nearest *i* in the alphabet; the *e* comes first if this letter stands nearest *e*.   To illustrate:

A B C D E F G H I J K L M N O P Q R S T U V W X Y Z

believe	(*l* is nearer to *i* in the alphabet than to *e*)
chief	(*h* is nearer to *i* in the alphabet than to *e*)
deceive	(*c* is nearer to *e* in the alphabet than to *i*)
grieve	(*r* is nearer to *i* in the alphabet than to *e*)
niece	(*n* is nearer to *i* in the alphabet than to *e*)
piece	(*p* is nearer to *i* in the alphabet than to *e*)
receive	(*c* is nearer to *e* in the alphabet than to *i*)
siege	(*s* is nearer to *i* in the alphabet than to *e*)
wield	(*w* is nearer to *i* in the alphabet than to *e*)
yield	(*y* is nearer to *i* in the alphabet than to *e*)

The same is true of

achieve	frontier	relieve
apiece	grief	reprieve
ceiling	mischief	shield
conceive	perceive	shriek
deceit	pierce	shrieve
fiend	receipt	sieve

But note these:

feign	neighbor	their
freight	reign	weigh
heinous	sleigh	weight
	sleight	

Note also these:

counterfeit	height	seize
foreign	leisure	weird
forfeit	neither	

12 The older or British spelling of the last syllable in the following words would in each case be *our:* arbor, ardor, armor, behavior, candor, clamor, clangor, color, demeanor, endeavor, favor, fervor, flavor, harbor, honor, humor, labor, misdemeanor, neighbor, odor, parlor, rancor, rigor, rumor, savior, savor, splendor, tenor, tremor, tumor, valor, vapor, vigor. These would also be spelled with *u* before the *r: clamorous, discoloration, humorous, invigorate, laborious, odorous, rigorous, vigorous.*

The words *gage, mold, molt,* and *stanch* are preferably spelled without the *u,* tho in England the *u* is still retained. The *u* has long since been dropt, even in England, from *bold, bolt, cold, colt, gold,* and so forth.

13 The dictionary must be consulted in regard to words beginning with *en* and *in.* These are the same prefix but the Latin *in* became *en* thru the French. Either spelling is correct in such words as *inclose, indorse, inquire, insure,* tho the British spelling leans more definitely to the *en* and the American to the *in.*

14 Much the same distinction holds in regard to words ending with *er* and *re,* preferred American spelling placing the vowel before the *r* and British spelling doing the opposite: *caliber, calibre; center, centre; fiber, fibre; maneuver, manœuvre; meter, metre; theater, theatre.* But these spellings are still followed in American usage: *acre, chancre, nacre, massacre*

ogre to preserve the hard sound of *c* and *g*. We nevertheless spell *eager* and *meager,* not with *re* but with *er.*

15 The following word lists should be studied. Troublesome suffixes beginning with vowels or containing key vowels cause spelling errors very often.

-ance, -ence, -ant, -ent, -ince

abundance	abundant	credence	credent
accordance	accordant	deference	deferent
acquaintance		dependence	dependent
admittance		diffidence	diffident
annoyance		eminence	eminent
arrogance	arrogant	excellence	excellent
circumstance		impertinence	impertinent
contrivance		independence	independent
distance	distant	indolence	indolent
elegance	elegant	inference	inferential
finance		influence	influential
importance	important	innocence	innocent
maintenance		insistence	insistent
observance	observant	insolvence	insolvent
perseverance		magnificence	magnificent
pittance		obedience	obedient
predominance	predominant	opulence	opulent
reliance	reliant	precedence	precedent
remembrance		preference	preferential
repentance	repentant	presence	present
resistance	resistant	prevalence	prevalent
resonance	resonant	prudence	prudent
significance	significant	reference	
sustenance		reminiscence	reminiscent
		residence	resident
abhorrence	abhorrent	reticence	reticent
adherence	adherent	reverence	reverent
cadence	cadent	sentence	
circumference	circumferential	subsistence	subsistent
coherence	coherent	violence	violent
competence	competent		
concurrence	concurrent	convince	
conference	conferential	evince	
confidence	confident	province	

-al, -el, -le

brutal	mental	recital	universal
central	moral	ritual	vital
coral	mortal	rival	vertical
fatal	naval	rural	
feudal	neutral	sandal	apparel
interval	pedal	scandal	cancel
jovial	penal	total	expel
legal	petal	trivial	flannel

grovel	repel	dimple	simple
jewel	shovel	drizzle	single
model	tunnel	double	sizzle
novel		fickle	thimble
parcel		jingle	tremble
quarrel	assemble	rifle	trifle
ravel	bubble	ruffle	triple
rebel	bungle	scuffle	

-or, -er, -ar

abhor	labor	developer	trotter
contractor	odor	disaster	
creator	orator	eager	calendar
demeanor	predecessor	fitter	dollar
dishonor	protector	inner	familiar
distributor (or *er*)		laborer	grammar
editor	reflector	lecturer	muscular
elevator	suitor	poster	polar
equator	survivor	plotter	popular
factor		premier	regular
governor	adviser	provider	scholar
harbor	believer	reciter	similar
honor	debater	refer	solar
humor	defender	rubber	tabular
inventor	defer		

-ious, -ous, -uous

ambitious	obnoxious	gratuitous	vigorous
anxious	obvious	grievous	villainous (or
conscientious	odious	jealous	villanous)
conscious	ostentatious	ludicrous	zealous
contagious	pernicious	luminous	
copious	precarious	marvelous	ambiguous
curious	religious	miraculous	arduous
delirious	spacious	mischievous	assiduous
disputatious	superstitious	momentous	conspicuous
dubious	suspicious	monotonous	contemptuous
efficacious	tenacious	monstrous	contiguous
envious	vicious	poisonous	incongruous
fastidious	vivacious	preposterous	ingenuous
ferocious		ravenous	innocuous
fictitious	blasphemous	ridiculous	perspicuous
glorious	circuitous	rigorous	presumptuous
gracious	credulous	scrupulous	promiscuous
illustrious	desirous	scurrilous	strenuous
infectious	dexterous	solicitous	superfluous
ingenious	disastrous	stupendous	tempestuous
injurious	fabulous	tremulous	tortuous
luxurious	famous	treacherous	tumultuous
malicious	garrulous	venomous	vacuous
mysterious	generous		

-ay, -ey

defray	repay	chimney	money
delay	yesterday	donkey	monkey
dismay		galley	prey
display	abbey	jockey	tourney
pray	alley	journey	turkey
relay			

-ary, -ery

auxiliary	necessary	brewery	flattery
contrary	obituary	bribery	mockery
dictionary	stationary	cemetery	monastery
hereditary	subsidiary	distillery	stationery
monumentary	summary	finery	thievery

-ible

accessible	deductible	fencible	incorrigible
addible	defeasible	flexible	incorrodible
adducible	defectible	forcible	incorruptible
admissible	defensible	fusible	incredible
affectible	depressible	gullible	indefeasible
apprehensible	descendible	horrible	indefectible
audible	destructible	ignitible	indefensible
bipartible	diffusible	illegible	indelible
coercible	digestible	immersible	indeprehensible
cognoscible	dirigible	impartible	indestructible
cohesible	discernible	impassible	indigestible
collapsible	discerptible	impedible	indiscernible
collectible	dissectible	imperceptible	indivisible
combustible	distensible	impermissible	indocible
committible	distractible	impersuasible	inducible
compactible	divertible	implausible	ineffervescible
compatible	divestible	impossible	ineligible
compossible	divisible	imprescriptible	inevasible
comprehensible	docible	impressible	inexhaustible
compressible	edible	imputrescible	inexpansible
conducible	educible	inaccessible	inexpressible
conductible	effectible	inadmissible	infallible
confluxible	effervescible	inapprehensible	infeasible
connectible	eligible	inaudible	inflexible
contemptible	eludible	incircumscriptible	
contractible	evasible	includible	infractible
controvertible	evincible	incoercible	infrangible
conversible	exhaustible	incognoscible	infusible
convertible	exigible	incombustible	inscriptible
convincible	expandible	incommiscible	insensible
corrigible	expansible	incompatible	instructible
corrodible	explosible	incomprehensible	
corrosible	expressible	incompressible	insubmergible
corruptible	extendible	inconcussible	insuppressible
credible	extensible	incontrovertible	insusceptible
decoctible	fallible	inconvertible	intactible
deducible	feasible	inconvincible	intangible

intelligible
interconvertible
intervisible
invencible
invendible
inventible
invertible
invincible
invisible
irascible
irreducible
irrefrangible
irremissible
irreprehensible
irrepressible
irresistible
irresponsible
irreversible
legible
mandible
negligible

nexible
omissible
ostensible
partible
perceptible
perfectible
permiscible
permissible
persuasible
pervertible
plausible
possible
prehensible
prescriptible
producible
productible
protrusible
putrescible
receptible
redemptible
redressible

reducible
reflectible
reflexible
refrangible
remissible
renascible
rendible
reprehensible
resistible
responsible
reversible
revertible
risible
seducible
sensible
sponsible
suasible
subdivisible
submergible
submersible
subvertible

supersensible
suppressible
susceptible
suspensible
tangible
tensible
terrible
traducible
transfusible
transmissible
transmittible
transvertible
tripartible
unadmissible
unexhaustible
unexpressible
unresponsible
vendible
vincible
visible

-able

appreciable
approachable
arable
available
bailable
believable
blamable
bookable
bounceable
breakable
bribable
bridgeable
burnable
buyable
calculable
capable
chargeable
clubbable
cognizable
comfortable
commendable
companionable
conformable
conversable
creditable
culpable
customable
debatable
delectable
demonstrable
deplorable

despicable
dispensable
distinguishable
durable
educable
effable
equitable
eradicable
estimable
exceptionable
excitable
excusable
execrable
expiable
farmable
fashionable
favorable
formidable
gettable
governable
habitable
hailable
hatable
honorable
hospitable
ignitable
impassable
implacable
imponderable
impregnable
impressionable

indefatigable
indomitable
inevitable
inexorable
inviolable
irreparable
irritable
judicable
justifiable
knittable
knowable
knowledgeable
lamentable
laudable
laughable
leasable
lendable
lettable
leviable
liable
likable
limitable
liquefiable
livable
locatable
lovable
mailable
malleable
manageable
marriageable
measurable

memorable
merchantable
miserable
movable
mutable
navigable
notable
noticeable
notifiable
objectionable
offerable
orderable
palatable
palpable
pardonable
passable
peaceable
peccable
penetrable
perishable
permeable
personable
persuadable
perturbable
pitiable
pleasurable
pliable
plowable
poisonable
potable
practicable

preferable	reputable	solvable	transposable
presumable	respectable	squeezable	treasonable
printable	restorable	stable	unconscionable
probable	retrievable	storable	unimpeachable
profitable	returnable	subscribable	unmistakable
pronounceable	revocable	substitutable	unnamable
questionable	ridable	sufferable	unspeakable
quotable	salable	suitable	usable
readable	salvable	superable	valuable
reasonable	satisfiable	surmountable	variable
reclaimable	scalable	tamable	vulnerable
reconcilable	scrutable	tenable	warrantable
recoverable	seasonable	terminable	washable
redeemable	seizable	traceable	wieldable
registrable	separable	tractable	wishable
reliable	serviceable	transferable	workable
remarkable	sizable	translatable	writable
remediable	sociable	transportable	yieldable

B Pertaining to consonants:

1 When a prefix ends with the same letter with which a root begins, both letters are usually retained.

dissatisfy	dissolve
dissent	misspell
dissimilar	misstatement
dissyllabic	misstep

When the two letters concerned are vowels they may be separated by a hyphen, or a dieresis may be placed over the second vowel. Such device indicates that both letters are to be pronounced. But usage is increasingly eliminating both the hyphen and the dieresis (see page 513).

co-operation	coöperation
pre-eminent	co-ordinate
reorganization	readjustment

2 When a suffix begins with the same letter with which a root ends, both letters are usually retained.

accidentally	keenness
barrenness	occasionally
casually	plainness
coolly	really
exceptionally	stubbornness
finally	suddenness
incidentally	usually

3 Prefixes and suffixes ending with *ll* usually drop one *l* in combination.

almighty	fulfil (*also* fulfill and fulfillment)
almost	skillful (*also* skilful)
alone	tearful
also	useful
although	welcome
altogether	welfare
already	withal
always	woeful (*also* woful)
awful	wonderful
helpful	willful (*also* wilful)

Note that the term *all right* is still two words, and should be so written, tho its persistent misspelling as one word with one *l* may ultimately make *alright* acceptable, as has been the case with certain other *al*-words in the foregoing list.

4 Most words ending with a double consonant retain both consonants before a suffix.

assessment	recklessness
embarrassment	stiffness
dullness (*also* dulness)	stuffer
fullness (*also* fulness)	shrilly (see below)
oddity	successful
purring	yelling

The words *enrolment, instalment, thraldom,* and *allotment* are preferably spelled, as here, with the single consonant before the suffix, but they are still spelled with the double consonant by many authorities. Both spellings are usually given in the dictionaries.

Note, however, that one *f* is dropt in forming the derivative *pontifical* from *pontiff*. One *l* is likewise dropt in certain cases when *ly* is added to a word ending with *ll*, in order to prevent tripling the *l*.

dully	fully	illy

The three *l*'s may be retained, however, when an unusual hyphenation is made to a suffix beginning with *l* (see page 513).

skill-less	trill-less
smell-less	will-less

5 Conversely, words ending with a double consonant, to which a prefix is added, usually retain both consonants.

befall	overall
distill	rebuff
emboss	recall
enroll	refill
foretell	tipstaff
fulfill (*see* 3 above)	undersell
instill	unroll

But there is an increasing tendency to simplify these spellings by dropping the final consonant, especially in the case of

befal	instil
enrol	recal
distil	rebel
foretel	refil

The word *until* is always written with one *l*.

The suffix *mass* drops one *s* in such compounds as *Christmas, Michaelmas, Candlemas.*

Hyphenated compounds usually retain all original letters: *well-bred, wide-eyed, stiff-necked, dull-eyed.*

6 Many words ending with *c* require the addition of *k* when a syllable is added beginning with *e, i,* or *y,* to indicate that the *c* is not to be pronounced like *s.*

colic	colicky	
frolic	frolicking	*f*rolicker (*but* frolicsome)
panic	panicky	
physic	physicked	physicky
picnic	picnicking	picnicker
traffic	trafficked	trafficker
zinc (*variable*)	zincked	zincking zincky

When *c* follows a vowel in monosyllabic words *k* usually follows. This is true also in longer words provided the vowels preceding *c* are not *i* or *ia: back, black, buck, clack, click, cluck, fleck, hack, knock, rack, rock, sock, tack; buttock, cassock, hammock, hassock, hemlock, hillock, mattock, padlock, shamrock, wedlock.*

There are some exceptions to both of these provisions: *arc, disc, talc, zinc* (see above). As is implied, words of more than one syllable ending with *ic* and *iac* are less likely to carry the *k: arctic, athletic, arithmetic, cambric, cubic, elec-*

tric, elegiac, maniac, music, public, ʒodiac. It is interesting to note that *almanac* and *havoc* are still very often written with final *k*, especially in England. Likewise, in England, hard *c* followed by *tion* may become *x*: *connexion* for *connection; deflexion* for *deflection; inflexion* for *inflection; reflexion* for *reflection.*

7 Words ending with *y* preceded by a consonant change *y* to *i* before a suffix unless the suffix begins with *i*.

busy	busier	business
carry	carrier	carried
cleanly	cleanlier	cleanliness
easy	easily	easiness
holy	holiest	holiday
likely	likeliest	likelihood
mercy	merciful	merciless

carry	carrying
defy	defying
fancy	fancying
hurry	hurrying
study	studying

Note, however, that before *like* and *ship y* is retained:

citylike	ladyship
countrylike	secretaryship
ladylike	suretyship

The *y* is likewise retained at the end of an adjective of one syllable when a suffix is added:

dry	dryly (*also* drily)	dryness
shy	shyly (*also* shily)	shyness
sly	slyly (*also* slily)	slyness

8 Monosyllabic words and other words accented on the last syllable, ending with a single consonant (except *h* and *x*) preceded by a single vowel, double the consonant before a suffix beginning with a vowel.

bag	baggage	refer	referred
begin	beginner	regret	regrettable
bid	bidden	repel	repellent
commit	committal	rob	robbery
control	controlling	rub	rubbish
hot	hotter	sad	sadden
hurrah	hurrahing	sit	sitting
impel	impelled	swim	swimmer
man	mannish	tax	taxing
plan	planning	win	winner
occur	occurrence	wit	witticism

In *squat* and *squatting u* is equivalent to *w* in pronunciation.

Note these exceptions:

gaseous	(*but* gassed, gassing, gassify)
inferable	(*but* inferred, inferring)
transferable	(*but* transferred, transferring)

When the accent is thrown forward by noun formations the final consonant is usually not doubled: *caballed, cabalism; deferring, deference; inferring, inference; preferred, preference.*

Metallurgy follows its Greek origin in escaping the rule, and *chancellor* and *crystalline* their Latin origin, and they are therefore not really exceptions.

Note that the provisions of the rule cover both the following lists:

beating	appareling
ceiling	banqueting
concealing	benefiting
congealing	broadening
dealing	canceling
feeling	carbureting
joining	conquering
needed	developing
purloining	meriting
reeled	offering
retailed	reddening
revealed	rendering
sealed	suffering
soaked	summoned
stealing	traveled (*see* below)
toiled	worshiped

The following words are preferably spelled with one *l,* according to the rule (most are accented on the first syllable). British spelling, however, and some American spellings double the *l* in them. While only one form of each word is given, the *l* would be single in all other forms.

appareling	counseling	kenneled	medalist
barreled	cudgeled	impaneling	metaling
beveling	dialing	imperiled	modeler
canceled	disheveled	jeweler	paneler
caroling	dueling	labeled	paralleling
caviled	enameled	leveling	parceled
channeling	equaling	libeled	penciled
chiseled	gamboled	marshaling	periling
councilor	graveling	marvelous	pommeling

quarreled	shoveled	stenciling	trammeling
raveling	shriveling	tasseled	tranquilize
reveling	signaling	tinseling	traveling
rivaling	sniveling	toweling	tunneled

In the following words the consonant is still frequently doubled in all forms. The simpler spelling is, however, the better.

equaled	or	equalling
equiped	or	equipping
groveling	or	grovelling
jewelery	or	jeweller
kidnaped	or	kidnapping
modeled	or	modeller
rivaled	or	rivalling
traveler	or	travelled
woolen	or	woollen (British)

Words ending with *w* preceded by a vowel do not double the *w*.

blowing	flowed	growing
mowed	rowing	sowed

By inference it follows that final consonants are not doubled when the word ends in more than one consonant.

boundary	helped	reforming
fording	hoarded	standing

9 The following points and lists pertaining to consonant spellings should be carefully noted:

-ce, -se

> *defense, expense, offense, pretense* are preferred spellings. The *ce* endings are more commonly used in England for these words

> In a few cases the *ce* ending denotes the noun form and the *se* ending the verb form. The distinction in spelling is made, if made at all, only in those words that are accented on the last syllable, as *device, devise; advice, advise. Practice* is still used as the noun form, but *practise* is increasingly used as both noun and verb

·f, -l, -s

> These consonants at the ends of monosyllables and of many longer words are usually doubled: *all, call, cliff, cuff, grass, off, pass, puff, staff, tell, toll, well*

> The consonants *b, d, g, m, n, p, r, t, ʒ* are the only others that are ever doubled at the ends of words: *ebb, add, egg, lamm, inn. Lapp, burr, butt, buʒʒ*, and many of these in rare case only

After a diphthong or digraph a consonant is rarely doubled
(see rule 8 above). The word *guess* is an apparent exception but not a real one, for it is a rule of English phonetics
to make *c* and *g* soft before *e* and hard before *a, o,* and *u.*
The *u* is therefore inserted in *guess* to keep the *g* hard—*go,
gave, gallant, guttural; change, nice, notice, siege.* But *get*
is an exception.

-cede, -ceed, -sede

There is only one *sede* word—*supersede*

There are three troublesome *ceed* words—*exceed, proceed, succeed*

There are five troublesome *cede* words—*accede, concede, precede,
recede, secede*

-sion, -tion

ascension	convulsion	accommodation	intention
condescension	derision	attention	interrogation
confession	excursion	collection	occupation
confusion	explosion	denunciation	resurrection
conversion	persuasion	inspiration	satisfaction

-ty, -ity

anxiety	poverty	authority	laxity
casualty	property	capacity	majority
cruelty	royalty	community	necessity
dynasty	society	complexity	oddity
frailty	specialty	credulity	rapidity
guaranty	variety	curiosity	reality
loyalty		equality	severity
mighty	ability	equity	stupidity
modesty	absurdity	humanity	velocity
penalty	audacity	impunity	vitality

-ise, -ize, -yze

The last is unusual, *analyze* and *paralyze* being the two
most commonly found. The increasing tendency is to extend
the use of *ize* to all words having *ise* and *yze* endings.

advertise	demise	excise	otherwise
advise	despise	exercise	premise
affranchise	devise	exorcise	prise (to force)
apprise (to inform)		franchise	reprise
arise	disenfranchise	improvise	revise
	disfranchise	incise	rise
circumcise	disguise	likewise	sidewise
chastise	emprise	merchandise	supervise
comprise	enfranchise	misadvise	surmise
compromise	enterprise	mortise	unwise

aggrandize	emphasize	mercerize	scandalize
agonize	energize	mesmerize	scrutinize
anatomize	epitomize	metamorphize	signalize
anglicize	equalize	methodize	solemnize
apologize	eulogize	minimize	soliloquize
apostrophize	evangelize	modernize	specialize
appetize	extemporize	monopolize	spiritualize
apprize (to appraise)		moralize	standardize
authorize	familiarize	nationalize	sterilize
baptize	fertilize	naturalize	stigmatize
brutalize	fossilize	neutralize	subsidize
canonize	fraternize	organize	summarize
capitalize	galvanize	ostracize	surprize
catechize	generalize	oxidize	syllabize
catholicize	gormandize	particularize	syllogize
cauterize	harmonize	pasteurize	symbolize
centralize	hellenize	patronize	sympathize
characterize	humanize	penalize	synchronize
Christianize	idolize	philosophize	systematize
civilize	immortalize	plagiarize	tantalize
classicize	italicize	polarize	temporize
colonize	jeopardize	prize	tranquilize
criticize	journalize	professionalize	tyrannize
crystallize	legalize	protestantize	utilize
demobilize	liberalize	pulverize	vaporize
demoralize	localize	realize	visualize
deputize	macadamize	recognize	vitalize
dogmatize	magnetize	reorganize	vocalize
dramatize	materialize	revolutionize	vulcanize
economize	memorialize	satirize	vulgarize

-ic, -ical

The following represent preferable spelling usage in regard to adjectives ending with *ic:*

academic	cataleptic	empiric	hectic
acrostic	catastrophic	energetic	Hellenic
agnostic	catholic	epic	heroic
anemic	caustic	epidemic	hygienic
antagonistic	Celtic	erratic	iambic
antiseptic	choleric	esoteric	Icelandic
apostolic	chronic	esthetic	idiomatic
aquatic	climactic	exotic	impolitic
Arabic	climatic	extrinsic	intrinsic
aristocratic	colic	ferric	italic
artistic	diagrammatic	forensic	lunatic
athletic	dialectic	futuristic	lymphatic
automatic	didactic	Gaelic	lyric
basic	dogmatic	Gallic	magnetic
beatific	dramatic	geodetic	mesmeric
Bolshevistic	drastic	Germanic	mimetic
Britannic	eccentric	gigantic	morganatic
bucolic	elastic	Gothic	narcotic
catalectic	emphatic	Hebraic	rationalistic

nitric	periphrastic	quixotic	splenetic
nomadic	pessimistic	realistic	static
optimistic	phlegmatic	rheumatic	sulphuric (or
organic	photographic	romantic	sulfuric)
orthoepic	picnic	rustic	syllabic
orthopedic	plastic	scenic	syntactic
orthographic	plethoric	scholastic	synthetic
pacific	prognostic	scientific	systematic
pathetic	prophetic	Semitic	Teutonic
patriotic	prosaic	Slavic	tragic
periodic	public	Slavonic	Vedic
peripatetic	pyrotechnic	spiritualistic	volcanic

The following words are preferably spelled with *ical,* with the exception of the few alternatives indicated which are used about half the time with *ic* and half the time with *ical* endings. As in the former list the words here are adjectives:

alphabetical	historic *or* historical
analytical	hypocritical
arithmetical	hypothetical
biographical	hysterical
biological	identical
botanical	liturgic *or* liturgical
chemical	logical
classical	magic *or* magical
clerical	majestic *or* majestical
conical *or* conic	mechanical
critical	medical
cubical *or* cubic	metaphysical
cylindric *or* cylindrical	methodical
cynical	musical
diabolic *or* diabolical	optic *or* optical
diacritical	panegyrical
dialogic *or* dialogical	parenthetical
diametrical	periodic *or* periodical
dramatic	philanthropic *or* philanthropical
dramaturgic	philosophic *or* philosophical
dynamic	physical
dyspeptic	poetic *or* poetical
electric *or* electrical	politic *or* political
elliptical	practical
encyclical	problematical
ethical	prosodical *or* prosodic
euphonic *or* euphonical	psychological
esoteric	puritanic *or* puritanical
fanatic *or* fanatical	rationalistic *or* rationalistical
fantastic *or* fantastical	rhetorical
fistic *or* fistical	rhythmical
geographic *or* geographical	spherical
geometric *or* geometrical	statistical
grammatical	stoic *or* stoical
harmonic *or* harmonical	strategic *or* strategical
heretical	symmetrical

synodic *or* synodical
synoptic *or* synoptical
tactical
technical
theatrical
theological
theoretical
theosophic *or* theosophical

therapeutic *or* therapeutical
topical
topographical
typical
typographical
tyrannical
zoological

II A few important lists

A Those pesky silent letters:

aisle	draught	knock	rogue
align	drought	knot	rough
almond	dumb	knout	salmon
alms	feign	know	scent
answer	ghost	knuckle	sign
aplomb	gnarled	league	solder
apostle	gnash	lamb	soldier
aught	gnat	limb	solemn
balk	gnaw	limn	talk
balm	gnu	mnemonic	though
becalm	half	monologue	thorough
benign	harangue	mortgage	through
bough	heir	ohm	thumb
bristle	hour	numb	tomb
brogue	hymn	palm	vogue
brougham	island	phlegm	would
brought	isle	plumb	wrap
burgh	khaki	plumber	wrath
bustle	kiln	pneumatic	wreath
calm	knack	pneumonia	wreck
catalogue	knapsack	poignant	wrench
cologne	knave	psalm	wrest
column	knead	pseudonym	wrestle
comb	knee	psychology	wretch
condemn	knell	ptarmigan	wriggle
corps	knew	ptomaine	wring
cough	knickerbocker	reign	wrinkle
crochet	knick-knack	resign	wrist
czar	knife	rheumatism	write
deign	knight	rhinoceros	writhe
diaphragm	knit	rhythm	wrong
dialogue	knob	right	yacht

B The simplified spelling list that is rapidly being adopted:

abridgment	ardor	carest	claspt
acknowledgment	ax	catalog	clipt
addrest	behavior	center	clue
affixt	blest	check	color
aline	blusht	civilize	comprest
altho	bur	clamor	comprize
arbor	candor	clapt	confest

coquet	gild	parlor	splendor
criticize	gipsy	partizan	stedfast
crost	goodby	past	stept
crusht	gript	pedagog	stopt
dasht	harbor	plow	stript
decalog	harken	possesst	suffixt
defense	heapt	practise	sulfur
demagog	hiccup	prefixt	supprest
deprest	honor	prest	surprize
dialog	humor	pretense	tapt
dike	husht	primeval	theater
dipt	idolize	profest	tho
discust	imprest	program	thoro
dispatch	instil	prolog	thorofare
distrest	kist	propt	thoroly
draft	labor	pur	thru
drest	lapt	quartet	thruout
dript	lasht	rapt	tipt
droopt	leapt	recognize	topt
dropt	lodgment	rime	tost
dulness	lookt	ript	trapt
endeavor	lopt	rumor	traveler
envelop	luster	savior	tript
epilog	mama	scepter	valor
exprest	meager	silvan	vext
fantom	mist	sipt	vigor
favor	mixt	sithe	washt
fiber	mold	skilful	whipt
fixt	molt	skipt	wilful
flavor	neighbor	slipt	wisht
fulfil	nipt	smolder	wo
fulness	odor	snapt	woful
gage	offense	somber	woolen
gelatin	opprest	specter	wrapt

C Words that every elementary school graduate should be
sure of:

accept	barber	carrying	diner
accommodate	bathe	choose	dining
accompany	been	coming	dinner
accumulate	beginning	committee	disappear
ache	believe	complement	disappoint
affect	benefit	compliment	dissatisfy
again	blue	convenience	divide
all right	break	cough	doctor
already	breath	could	does
always	breathe	country	done
among	built	dear	don't
angel	business	debater	early
angle	busy	describe	easy
answer	buy	destroy	effect
any	calendar	different	eighth
argument	can't	din	enough
athletic	careless	dine	equal

equation
every
excel
excitable
familiar
February
field
finally
forty
fourth
friend
garage
government
grammar
guess
half
having
hoarse
hoping
hopping
hour
immediately
interest
judgment
just
knew
know
laboratory
laid
lead
led
letter
loose

lose
losing
making
many
meant
minute
misspell
much
necessary
niece
ninety
occasion
occurred
odor
often
once
parallel
parliament
parlor
pawn
peace
perform
piece
plain
plane
planed
planned
precede
prejudice
preparation
prepare
pretty
principal

principle
privilege
proceed
professor
quiet
quite
raise
read
receive
recommend
refer
referred
said
says
seems
seize
separate
shepherd
shoes
siege
similar
similarly
since
some
stationary
stationery
stopped
straight
studying
sugar
sure
tear
their

there
thorough (thoro)
though (tho)
through (thru)
tired
together
to
too
toward
truly
two
untie
until
village
villain
weak
weather
Wednesday
weird
were
where
whether
which
whole
whose
women
won't
would
write
writer
writing
written
wrote

D Words that every high school graduate should be sure of:

abreast
abridged
absence
absorber
absurd
accelerator
accessory
accessible
accidentally
accustom
acquaintance
acquainted
acquire
acquitted
across
adapter
addressed
advice
advisable

advise
adviser
aerostat
affectation
aggravate
aggression
air brakes
aircraft
airplane
airship
airway
aisle
alienate
aline
allegory
alley
allotted
allusion
ally

altar
alter
alternating
altimeter
altitude
altogether
aluminum
alumna
alumnae
alumni
alumnus
amalgamate
amateur
ambidextrous
ambiguity
ammeter
ampere
amphibian
amplifier

analog
analysis
analyze
anesthesia
anesthetic
angelic
angular
annual
anonymous
anode
antiseptic
anxiety
apiece
apology
apostle
apparatus
apparent
appearance
appreciate

apprentice
apprize
appropriate
arbitrate
arc
archeology
arctic
arguing
arising
arithmetic
armature
arrange
arrangement
arrester
arrival
artizan
ascendant
assassin
assignment
association
athlete
attack
attacked
attendance
audience
authorize
automatic
auxiliary
awhile
awkward
ax
axiom
aye
bachelor
bakelite
balloon
banana
bandanna
barbarous
baring
baritone
barring
battery
bazaar
beaming
bearing
beautify
becoming
behave
believing
benefited
berth
biased
bibliography
biplane

biscuit
bleaching
bloc
block
bluing
blunder
body
bonus
born
borne
boundaries
brake
brass
breathless
breed
bridal
bridle
brilliant
Britain
Britannia
Britannic
Briton
broadcast
broccoli
bronco
buccaneer
bulb
bulletin
bumper
bunion
buoyant
bur
bureau
burglar
bus
button
buzzer
bylaw
byword
cabin
cable
caddying
cafeteria
caliper
camphor
candidate
cant
cantaloup
canvas
canvass
canyon
capillary
capital
capitol
caps

carbon
carburetor
career
carriage
catalog
cathode
caucus
caviar
cell
ceiling
cemetery
chamber
chancelry
change
changeable
changing
chaperon
characteristic
charger
chassis
chauffeur
chiffonier
chilli
choir
choke
chose
chosen
chord
circuit
clientele
clothes
cloths
clutch
coarse
coconut
cockpit
coil
colonel
column
commission
committal
commutator
comparative
compared
comparison
compass
compel
compelled
competent
complimentary
comrade
concede
conceit
conceive
conceivable

condenses
conduct
conductor
conductivity
conferred
confidant
confidence
confident
conjurer
connector
connoisseur
conquer
conqueror
conscience
conscientious
conscious
consciousness
considered
consul
contemptible
continuous
control
controlled
conveyor
cooler
coolie
coolly
cooperate
copper
cord
corroborate
costume
coulomb
council
councilor
counsel
counselor
coupé
coupler
course
courtesy
crank
cruelty
criminal
crystal
cultivate
current
cushion
custom
customary
cycle
cylinder
data
dealt
debatable

deceased	dying	filament	handsome
deceit	dynamo	finable	hangar
deceive	economics	financier	harass
decide	ecstasy	flat	haul
decision	effective	floats	headlights
deferred	electrode	fly wheel	heat
defendant	electrolysis	forbade	height
definite	electromotive	forbear	heinous
demeanor	electron	forego	helicopter
dependent	elevator	forehead	helmet
deposit	elicit	foremost	hesitancy
derived	eligible	foresee	hindrance
descendant	eliminate	foretell	holy
description	eliminator	forfeit	hop
desecrater	embarrass	formally	hope
desert	emergency	formerly	horn
dessert	emigrate	forth	hub
despair	eminent	fortieth	huge
desperate	emphasize	fortitude	human
device	enameling	forward	humane
devise	encouraging	fourteen	humorous
dexterous	encyclopedia	frame	hundredth
dialog	endeavor	frantically	hurriedly
diarrhea	enemy	fraternity	hydrogen
dictionary	engine	frequency	hygiene
dieresis	engineer	friendship	hypnotize
difference	entrance	fulfil	hypocrisy
differential	envelop	furniture	hypotenuse
difficult	epidemic	fuse	ignition
dilemma	equipped	fuselage	illicit
dining-room	escalloped	gage	illiterate
diphtheria	especially	gambling	imaginary
direct	exaggerate	gamboling	imitation
dirigible	exceed	gas	immigration
disaster	excellent	gasoline	imminent
disastrous	except	gear	impetuosity
discharge	exceptional	generally	impromptu
discipline	exercise	generator	incidence
disease	exhaust	ghost	incidentally
dispatch	exhibition	glider	incidents
dissatisfaction	exhilarate	goddess	incredible
dissipate	existence	governor	incredulous
distil	expense	grammatical	independence
distinction	experience	grandeur	indispensable
distribute	explanation	gravity	induce
distributor	expound	grease	induction
divine	extraordinary	grief	infinite
division	fabrikoid	grievous	influence
dormitories	facilities	growth	influential
draft	faction	guarantee	ingenious
drought	familiarity	guaranty	ingenuous
drudgery	fan	guard	innocence
dual	fascinate	guidance	innocuous
duel	fenders	handkerchief	inoculate
dumfound	fiery	handle	instance

instant	loveliness	nickel	permissible
instil	loyalty	nineteenth	perseverance
intellectual	luminous	ninth	persistent
intelligence	lying	noticeable	personal
intentionally	magneto	notoriety	personnel
insulator	maintain	nowadays	perspiration
intake	maintenance	nucleus	persuade
intensity	maneuver	oblige	pertain
intercede	manifold	obstacle	pervade
intermittent	mantel	occasionally	perverse
invitation	mantle	occur	Philippines
iridescent	manual	occurrence	physical
irrelevant	manufacturer	occurring	physician
irresistible	marconigram	o'clock	picnic
its	margarin	offered	picnicked
it's	marriage	offices	pilot
itself	marries	ohm	pistons
jeopardize	material	oil	planet
jet	mathematics	omelet	pleasant
jeweler	mattress	omission	plurality
keenness	meaningless	omitted	pneumonia
kidnaper	mechanics	oneself	politician
kilometer	medicine	operate	politics
kilowatt	medieval	operator	poor
knowledge	mesh gear	opinion	pore
ladies	messenger	opponent	portable
laity	metal	opportunity	positive
lamps	meter	optician	possession
landing	mettle	optimistic	possible
language	millionaire	organization	pour
later	miniature	origin	practically
latter	minutely	original	practise
legionnaire	miscellaneous	ostensible	prairie
legitimate	mischievous	outrageous	prayer
leisure	Mississippi	overrun	precedence
lessen	misstatement	pacifist	precedents
lesson	model	pageant	predicamen.
liable	momentous	paid	preference
library	moneyed	pamphlet	preferred
license	monoplane	pantomime	prejudicing
lightening	motor	parachute	preparatory
lightning	muffler	paralysis	pressure
lights	murmur	parliamentary	primitive
likely	muscle	particularly	principality
liquefy	mysterious	partizan	prisoner
literature	naive	partner	probably
livelihood	naphtha	passed	procedure
liveliness	navigation	passenger	prodigy
locks	necessarily	pastime	profession
lonely	negative	peaceable	proffer
longeron	negroes	perceive	prohibition
loop	neighbor	perception	promenade
loosely	neither	peremptory	promissory
losable	neon	performance	promptness
lounge	neutrality	perhaps	pronunciation

propeller
proton
protrude
prove
prudence
psychology
pulse
purchase
pursue
putting
quantity
questionnaire
quietly
quizzes
raccoon
racketeer
radiator
radio
rapid
ready
really
recede
receipt
receiver
recognize
recommendation
reconcile
reference
refractory
regard
region
reign
rein
relieve
religion
religious
remedy
reminiscences
repetition
replies
representatives
reptile
reservoir
resistance
respectfully
respectively
restaurant
rheostat
rhetoric
rheumatism
rhythm
ridiculous
right
rime
rite

rod
rotate
route
rubber
rudder
rumble
running board
rural
sacrilegious
safety
safety-belt
salable
sandwich
Saturday
savable
scarcely
scene
schedule
scholarship
science
scream
screech
scrupulous
seaplane
secede
secondary
secretary
seizable
sense
sentence
separated
sergeant
serviceably
several
severely
shaft
Shakespeare
Shakspere
shiftless
shining
shone
shown
shriek
sight
silencer
similarity
simile
simplify
simultaneous
sincerely
singular
sirup
skeleton
skids
smooth

soar
socket
solder
soliloquy
sophisticated
sophomore
spare
spark-gap
spark plug
speak
specifically
specimen
speech
speedometer
spinner
spokes
spring
stabilizer
starter
statement
statue
stature
statute
steal
steel
stopper
stopping
stops
stories
stratagem
strategy
stretch
strictly
struts
studious
successful
suffrage
suit
suite
summarize
superintendent
supersede
suppress
surprize
sweepback
switch
syllable
symmetrical
tail lights
tank
tape
temperament
temperature
tendency
thence

therefor
therefore
thoroughly
(thoroly)
thousandths
thrash
thresh
threw
throat
throttle
till
tires
torch
track
tract
tragedy
tranquillity
transferred
transformer
translate
transmission
treacherous
treasurer
tries
trolley
trouble
trunk
tubes
Tuesday
turbine
turnbuckle
turquoise
typical
tyranny
unanimous
undoubtedly
universally
unnecessary
unprecedented
unusual
usage
useful
using
usually
utility
vacancy
valves
vegetable
vengeance
veteran
vigilance
villager
villainy
visa
volt

voltameter	week	window	yacht
voluntary	weirdly	wings	yield
vulgarity	welfare	wintry	your
warrant	wherever	wiper	you're
wasteful	whistle	wire	zealous
weakness	whittle	wireless	zoning
weathering	wilful	wrought	Zeppelin

CHAPTER NINETEEN

TELEGRAMS

The language of the telegram, the cablegram, and the radiogram should be expressed as economically as possible consistent with clearness of understanding. Nouns and verbs should be depended upon principally for the conveyance of such messages. Other parts of speech have to be used, of course, but the aim should be to keep them at a minimum. Even code words stand primarily for nouns and verbs when they are substituted for straight messages. Simple, rather than compound and complex, sentences should be used. The important principles of economy and conciseness can be practised nowhere more advantageously than in connection with telegrams. One good way to discover how many unnecessary words you may have used in a paragraph or a theme, is to reduce it to a telegram or two, and then expand it again in shorter form than the original. In

> Arrive twelve Tuesday. Meet train.
> Have trunk and other luggage

it is easy enough to understand *I* before *arrive* and *have, at* before *twelve* and *o'clock* after it, and *on* before Tuesday. These are but the common "supplies" required in colloquial language.

But the above telegram is a bad one because it makes use of unnecessary words. *Train* is probably not necessary after *meet,* for such a telegram as this usually follows certain correspondence. The five words *Have trunk and other luggage* may be reduced to three, *Trunk. Other luggage.* Tho it would cost no more to send the telegram as it stands, the reduced form is better. Liability to error in transmission is reduced just in proportion as the message is brief, direct, and economical of words. On the other hand the exercise of economy must not be permitted to cause incompleteness.

Telegrams should be consistently worded. Every new thought or part thought should begin with the same part of speech. This makes the entire message easier to grasp. A little study and practise in telegraphic expression will make it almost second **nature** to wire

> Train smashed. Shipment destroyed.
> Letter follows

rather than this:

> Smash up on road. Letter follows.
> Destroyed shipment

In the first case each thought is stated by means of noun and verb, and the sequence is natural. In the second case, the first thought is stated by means of noun and phrase; the second by noun and verb; the third by verb and noun. This is confusing and erratic. Moreover, the sequence is bad. *Letter follows* should usually appear last in a telegram for it indicates that the letter will continue the information from the point where the telegram ends. It is a good rule, therefore, to state your message in natural sequence with verbs first or nouns first, consistently. This may not always be possible, but it is in the majority of cases. The following illustrates the two types of consistent telegraphic expression:

> Come Chicago. Bring papers.
> Notify Tomkins
>
> Shipment forwarded. Goods charged.
> Letter follows

Following are the classifications of telegraphic, cable, and radio messages. It should be remembered that these are modified from time to time, as special economic conditions may require.

CLASSES OF SERVICE—WESTERN UNION

Telegrams—A full-rate expedited service.

Night Messages—Accepted up to 2:00 A.M. at reduced rates to be sent during the night and delivered not earlier than the morning of the ensuing business day.

Night Messages may at the option of the Telegraph Company be mailed at destination to the addressees, and the Company shall be deemed to have discharged its obligation in such cases with respect to delivery by mailing such night messages at destination, postage prepaid.

Day Letters—A deferred day service at rates lower than the standard telegram rates as follows: One and one-half times the standard night letter rate for the transmission of 50 words or less and one fifth of the initial rates for each additional 10 words or less.

In further consideration of the reduced rate for this special Day Letter service, the following special terms in addition to those enumerated above are hereby agreed to:

A. Day Letters may be forwarded by the Telegraph Company as a deferred service and the transmission and delivery of such Day Letters is, in all respects, subordinate to the priority of transmission and delivery of regular telegrams.

B. This Day Letter is received subject to the express understanding and agreement that the Company does not undertake that a Day Letter shall be delivered on the day of its date absolutely, and at all events; but that the Company's obligation in this respect is subject to the condition that there shall remain sufficient time for the transmission and delivery of such Day Letter on the day of its date during regular office hours, subject to the priority of regular telegrams.

Rate Changes—Punctuation marks are now sent without charge, and five figures are counted as only one word.

Night Letters—Accepted up to 2:00 A.M. for delivery on the morning of the ensuing business day, at rates still lower than standard night message rates, as follows: The initial charge is for 25 words. The maximum charge for 25 words for the greatest distances in the United States is 50 cents. Words in excess of 25 are charged for by groups of five. The charges for additional words decrease progressively with the length of the message.

In further consideration of the reduced rates for this special Night Letter service, the following special terms in addition to those enumerated above are hereby agreed to:

Night Letters may at the option of the Telegraph Company be mailed at destination to the addressees.

Full Rate Cables—An expedited service throughout. Code language permitted.

Deferred Half-Rate Cables—Half-rate messages are subject to being deferred in favor of full-rate messages for not exceeding 24 hours. Must be written in plain language. Minimum charge for five words.

Cable Night Letters—An overnight service for plain language communications, at one third the full rate, or less. Minimum of 25 words charged for. Subject to delivery at the convenience of the Company within 24 hours.

Ship Radiograms—A service to and from ships at sea, in all parts of the world. Plain language or code language may be used.

CLASSES OF SERVICE—POSTAL TELEGRAPH

Full Rate Telegram—An expedited service, the transmission of which takes precedence over other classes of service.

Day Letter—A deferred day service at reduced rates, the transmission of which is subordinated only to Full Rate Telegrams and Serials. 50 words can be sent at 1½ times the initial rate for Full Rate Telegrams. This service is best suited for lengthy messages when a moderate delay is admissible.

A Day Letter is received subject to the express understanding and agreement that the Company does not undertake to deliver it on the day of its date absolutely and at all events; but that the Company's obligation in this respect is subject to the condition that there shall

remain sufficient time for the transmission and delivery of such Day
Letter on the day of its date during regular office hours, subject to
the priority of the transmission of full rate telegrams and serials.

Night Message—An overnight service at rates somewhat less than for
Full Rate Telegrams. Night Messages are accepted up to 2 A.M. for
delivery on the morning of the ensuing business day, and when short
messages are involved, are the most economical of overnight services.

Night Letter—An overnight service, the rate for 50 words being the
same as for a 10-word Full Rate Telegram. Night Letters are accepted
at any time up to 2 A.M. for delivery on the morning of the ensuing
business day. Where lengthy messages are involved, this is the most
economical class of overnight service.

Miscellaneous Services—Among the many miscellaneous services which
Postal Telegraph has made available to its patrons are:

Photogram service, covering the transmission by wire of pictures and
messages.

Errand service, covering delivery of packages, advertising matters,
circulars, etc.

Commercial News service, covering market quotations, commodity
reports, bulletins of sporting events, etc.

Marine service, covering reports of sighting and arrival of incoming
steamships.

Night Cable Letters at reduced rates. Must be in plain language of
country of origin, or of destination, or in French where transmitted
by telegraph to destination. Subordinated to the priority of transmission of full and deferred-rate messages. May be posted, when
sender so directs, to countries where this service is not available, at
tariffs to countries from which such messages are posted. Under latter
circumstances, messages must contain complete mailing address, including chargeable posting instructions (i.e., "Post London," etc.). Minimum word basis of twenty to twenty-five words applied. Code addresses may be used except for messages delivered by post. Figures
explained by text admitted. Indicator "NLT" required and charged
for as one word. For further particulars apply at any Postal Telegraph office.

While it is a rather prevalent practise to use words to indicate
punctuation, this is not necessary. All punctuation marks commonly used in correspondence, when so indicated by the sender,
will be transmitted exactly as written. Messages can also be
paragraphed if the sender so desires. Punctuations and paragraphs are charged for at the rate of one word for each punctuation or paragraph. The word *stop* may be used to indicate period
if necessary for clearness, and other marks may be indicated by
their names for the same (*see* below), but such words and names
are chargeable.

Names and addresses of the two parties to a telegram are not
charged for on domestic telegrams, that is, telegrams destined to

places in the United States, Canada, Alaska, Labrador, Mexico, Miquelon Island, Newfoundland, Prince Edward Island, and Yukon. Titles added in the address or signature are not charged for. Likewise, the designation of a department, branch, or division, or the name of an individual.

Telegrams and cablegrams—fast full-rate—may be sent in Dutch, English, French, German, Italian, Latin, Portuguese, Spanish. French is regarded as a world language and Latin as the language of religion. Isolated figures and letters, like dictionary words, count as words, as do also single initials, abbreviations, punctuation words, and particles belonging to foreign names. A few of the commonest abbreviations, however, count as single words; thus *a. m., p. m., c. o. d., f. o. b., O. K.* are charged for as full words. Figures in messages handled entirely within the United States and in cablegrams between the United States and foreign countries other than those on the North American continent, are counted at the rate of five characters to the word, including decimal points, commas, hyphens and fraction bars. For example, 12345 is counted as one word, 1234567 two words, 12.45 one word, 123.56 two words, 489-56 two words, 10 3/8 one word, 24,000 two words. In messages between points in the United States and points in Canada, Alaska, Labrador, Mexico, Miquelon Island, Newfoundland, Prince Edward Island and Yukon each figure no matter how it appears is counted as one word. *Five million* is charged for as two words, but 5,000,000 goes as nine words and 316.28 as six. The latter written out would be the same—*three hundred sixteen period twenty eight.* Fractions are counted out figure by figure if dispatched as figures; if dispatched as words, they are counted as words. Thus, *ten and five sixths* must be paid as four words; 10 5/6 as five words.

Code words must be either coined or abbreviated words that are pronounceable and that are devised according to the principles of word formation and usage (see page 586).

Plain language is counted at the rate of fifteen letters or less per word. Code or cipher interspersions nullify the plain language count and all words in such messages, including the plain language words, are rated at the code or cipher count. Combinations of dictionary words when appearing in plain language messages are counted and charged for as the number of proper words that the combinations represent.

Under international regulations which are observed by all foreign administrations and private companies, code language is composed of artificial words and/or real words not used with the meaning normally assigned to them in the language to which they belong and consequently not presenting an intelligible meaning. Code words, whether real or artificial, may be formed in any way but must not exceed five letters in length. They must not contain accented letters. Messages of which the text contains words in code language and words in plain language and/or figures or figure groups are considered, for the purpose of charging, as code messages. Nevertheless, the number of figures or figure groups must not exceed one-half the number of chargeable words in the text and signature. The plain language words in code messages are counted at the rate of five characters or fraction thereof to the word. If the number of figures or figure groups exceed one-half the number of chargeable words in the text and signature, or if the text contains secret language words of more than five letters, the message is considered, for the purpose of charging, as a cipher message.

Cipher language consists of arabic figures, groups of arabic figures, or of words, names, expressions or combinations of letters with the exception of accented letters not fulfilling the conditions of plain language or code language. The combination, in one group, of figures and letters with a secret meaning is not allowed. Commercial marks, abbreviations such as FOB, etc., are not considered as having a secret meaning. Figures, groups of figures and groups of letters are counted at the rate of five figures or letters or fraction thereof, to the word. The text of a cipher message may be partly in cipher language and partly in plain language, in which case the plain language words are counted at the rate of fifteen letters or fraction thereof to the word.

Radiograms, like telegrams and cablegrams, sent at full rate are presumably important and are dispatched immediately in order of receipt. Deferred radiograms are sent at half rate. Urgent radiograms—those taking precedence over all other kinds of general messages—are given not only preferred service by wireless but also urgent special telegraph service in foreign countries. The word *urgent* is placed at the beginning of such message by the operator at the instruction of the sender. Deferred radios, like deferred cables, may be sent in French or in the language of the country of origin or of the country of destination. The operator indicates at the beginning which language is used—LCO, LCD, LCF—language of country of origin, language of country of destination, language of country of France. The letters RLT and WLT—Radioletter Telegram and Weekend Letter Telegram —are also sometimes written by the operator at the beginning of deferred radio forms that are used as more casual deferred social and business letters.

Code addresses and code words used for cabling and telegraphing are variously devised. The cable companies will themselves furnish assistance in devising code language. To insure secrecy of transactions, however, business houses, like governments, sometimes have elaborate secret code systems. The code address very often consists of a combination word that suggests a trade name. Sometimes it is composed in part of the name of the firm and in part of the kind of business it is engaged in. Sometimes it is a word indicating house policy:

```
Angier Mills ........................"Keepdry"
Hotel McAlpin ....................."Hotelpin"
Rogers, Peet Company .............."Rocopet"
```

Code words used for the transmission of request for information may be devised in abbreviation. "Ilsem," for instance, may be used for, *"Ill, send money,"* for which it is a highly abbreviated form. The code word that stands for the largest amount of thought is, of course, the most valuable one to use. The following code words are reproduced here from the Postal Telegraph-Cable Company's code for travelers:

```
CAFER .... Met with an accident, not serious, letter follows
CAICH .... Suspend further action pending my return
CAZBI ..... Have not received an answer to my letter of ——
CENSA .... Arrived; all well, fine passage
CODTE .... Have you been able to secure cabin on ——?
MAZSI .... Will not cost more than ——
MESNA ... Am/are detained; cannot say when I/we can leave
MONOL ... Is there any truth in the report about ——?
MUCRI ... Suggest that you go as quickly as possible
MYTUD ... Keep me/us informed regularly of your movements
OCCIT .... Do not forward any letter-s until you hear from me again
ODGAB .... When and how did you send money?
```

Following is the proper form of a cablegram, in code, "Elagabel" being the private cable address, and meaning "Franklin Young":

Elagabel care Cicatrix, London

OCDIV CUKIT MUTLU OLAMI

When translated, the foregoing message reads:

> Franklin Young, care American Express Co.,
> 6 Haymarket, London
>
> *Have received no letter from you since June 3.*
> *Are you all right? Please reply by telegraph.*

The italics indicate how each word is translated.

Two additional domestic telegraph services, recently inaugurated, are the *serial* and the *timed wire service.*

The serial service involves the sending of a message filed in sections, all sections sent on the same day from the same sender at the same office of origin to the same addressee at the same destination. Serial messages are identified by the letters "SER" and receive the same expedited handling as Full Rate Telegrams. The charges for this classification of message are based on the total number of chargeable words in the combined sections sent during the day, instead of on each section as a separate message, as is done in the case of other messages. The minimum charge is for fifty words on any one day. No section is rated as containing fewer than 15 words. If the aggregate total for the day is fewer than 50 words, the patron is charged for 50 words. The rate for the first 50 is one-fifth more than the rate for a fifty-word day letter, rounded out in multiples of five cents. Additional words are charged for at the rate of one-fifth of the initial charge for each ten words or less. The following special conditions also apply:

(1) The sender when filing his message (including the different sections thereof) must indicate that he wishes this class of service, using the indicator "SER" for that purpose
(2) Service can be established for messages moving in one direction only. Separate serials must be arranged for messages moving in the opposite direction
(3) Paid and collect messages cannot be combined in the same serial
(4) In the event only one section of a Serial is filed, it will be charged on the basis of the lowest day rate available
(5) Serial Service is only available between places in continental United States.
(6) Inasmuch as Serial Service involves the sending of a message filed in sections, the limit of liability applying to a message will likewise apply to the combined sections of the Serial Message

The timed wire service is available to patrons of the telegraph company who are connected with the company's offices by simplex printers—telegraph transmitting and receiving machines with a standard typewriter keyboard which is operated by the patron's typist the same as a typewriter. This is a service by which the facilities of the telegraph company are placed at the customer's disposal on a time basis, the charge being for the number of minutes consumed in the transmission by the customer's simplex operator instead of on a word basis as in the case of telegrams. The charge for this service is twice the amount charged for a ten-word full-rate telegram to the point of destination for a minimum period of three minutes, and one third the initial charge for each additional minute. This service is designed to meet the needs of business concerns for sending lengthy communications at a very reasonable rate.

During the World War the author served in the cable division of the Committee on Public Information appointed by President Woodrow Wilson for the purpose of guiding and focusing publicity in the most effective and influential manner. Following is an excerpt from the many cable messages that were broadcast to the world from the central offices at Twenty-five Broad Street, New York City. Note the inverted phraseology used in order to keep words within code limits, the detailed punctuation words, and the generally stenographic sentence composition. Certain combinations appear here that would not, of course, be permitted today, but they were correct at the time they were used, and are interesting even now as illustrative of a principle in cable and telegraphic communications:

rockcastle virginia bishop oconnell addressed meeting of priests engaged among southern colored population stop conference southern workers held there stemmas industrial agricultural college unified coordinated efforts afterwar reconstruction among returning colored soldiers stop stpaul minnesota roland w quinn this city american irish descent with marines at front writes mother quote been over top seven times last time put me hospital stop champagne even hardern stmihiel chateau-thierry stop alls well ends well ill fight till ends with victory unquote stop detroit michigan bishop gallagher successor late bishop foley arrived take up work catholic diocese detroit given great reception stop for greece stop washington caslist includes missing private parashos denidous kin mrs anestasian denidous of panaia greece private mike coster kin john papas of kasstele crete greece stop newyork american hellenic association held meeting make preparation welcome premier venizelos if visits america stop formulated objects afterwar activities be quote impress greek residents here their first duty themselves hellenic race is allegiance america obedience to laws acknowledgment democratic form government acquisition english language stop since democracy first realized in ancient republic athens greeks here be urged assist america every way toward realization high ideals of government and solicit support for freedom unity entire greek race europe nearest unquote   COMPUB

CHAPTER TWENTY

WORD STUDY

I   Growth of the English tongue

A   English is a composite language.   It has drawn heavily upon all other tongues of the world.   English diction, therefore, bears upon it the stamp of history, and the history of England not only, but of practically all other nations as well.

The ancient Celtic of the Britons and both the Scotch and the Irish Gaelic are still to be found in the English vocabulary —*tor* is Celtic for rock, *inch* for island, *ben* for mountain, *strath* for valley, *brat* (not contemptuous) for child.   *Clan, coronach, crag, glen, slogan, whisky* are Scotch Gaelic words, and *bog, brogue, colleen, galore, shamrock, skein* are Irish Gaelic.   From about 55 B.C. to almost 500 A.D. the Romans were dominant in England, and their language—Latin—still constitutes about thirty per cent of all English diction.   For another century the Angles, Saxons, and Jutes of northern Germany settled in various parts of England, and brought with them the Teutonic dialects.   By the middle of the ninth century the Norsemen had settled in eastern and northern England, and with them came the Scandinavian dialects. Their King Canute governed the island in 1016.   Fifty years later the Normans conquered Britain, and the French language was accordingly introduced.   The Renaissance in the sixteenth century revived Latin and Greek and other romantic tongues. And inasmuch as England has ever been a commercial and industrial and colonizing nation, she has gathered unto her linguistic domain words and phrases from everywhere.   English still is, as it always has been, a world language, as these representative listings, brief as they must be, abundantly prove.   It is interesting to note what a large proportion of the words belong to trade and industry.

FROM AFRICA: *canary, chimpanzee, gorilla, guinea, gipsy, morocco;* FROM AMERICA (Indian): *apache, hominy, moccasin.*

574

*moose, mugwump, papoose, pemmican, skunk, squaw, toma-
hawk, wigwam;* FROM ARABIA: *admiral, alchemy, alcohol,
alcove, alembic, algebra, alkali, almanac, amber, caliber,
caliph, candy, carmine, cipher, coffee, crimson, dragoman,
gazelle, ghoul, harem, hashish, hegira, lemon, lute, magazine,
mocha, monsoon, mosque, nadir, orange, sequin, sheik;* FROM
AUSTRALIA: *iguana, kangaroo, paramatta;* FROM BRAZIL:
jaguar, tapioca, tapir, toucan; FROM CHINA: *chopstick, kow-
tow, pekinese, pekoe, silk, tea, typhoon;* FROM DENMARK:
boss, brick, bubble, fir, ski, trek; FROM EGYPT: *giraffe, oasis,
sack;* FROM FRANCE (modern): *bouquet, élan, etiquette, program;* FROM GERMANY: *bismuth, meerschaum, plunder, verein,
waltz, zeppelin;* FROM HOLLAND (Dutch): *blunderbuss, boodle,
boom, brandy, buoy, burgher, cashier, cruiser, cruller, dock,
domineer, firkin, frolic, gherkin, hops, hottentot, keel, knap-
sack, leak, ledger, mesh, mud, scow, scum, skipper, slim, sloop,
spa, spangle, spook, toy, trigger, tub, tug, veldt, wagon,
wainscot, yacht, yawl;* FROM ICELAND: *bag, bait, bunch, hussy,
scout, sky;* FROM INDIA: *bangle, calico, chintz, chutney, coolie,
juggernaut, jungle, karma, khaki, loot, mahatma, mandarin,
pajamas, pariah, pepper, puttee, rajah, rum, shampoo, sulfur,
suttee, teak, thug, tiffin;* FROM ITALY: *adagio, alert, al fresco,
allegro, alto, andante, bandit, broccoli, cameo, canto, contralto,
crescendo, cupola, dilettante, ditto, duet, forte, gondola, grotto,
impresario, influenza, legato, macaroni, madrigal, mandolin,
manifesto, motto, presto, prima donna, quartet, quintet,
regatta, sextet, solo, staccato, stanza, umbrella, volcano;* FROM
JAPAN: *geisha, hara-kiri, japanned, kimono, soy;* FROM JAVA:
bantam, junk; FROM MALAKKA: *amok (amuck), bamboo,
caddy, camphor, cassowary, gong, gutta-percha, orang-utan,
sago;* FROM MEXICO: *bronco, chilli, chocolate, cocoa, copal,
coyote, tabasco, tomato;* FROM PALESTINE (Hebrew): *amen,
babel, balsam, Beelzebub, cherub, halleluiah, hosanna, jubilee,
kibitzer, leviathan, mammon, manna, Messiah, Mizpah, phari-
see, sabbath, seraph, shekel, Sheol, shibboleth;* FROM PERSIA:
*awning, azure, bazaar, caravan, chess, chicanery, dervish,
divan, durbar, jackal, jessamine, lilac, magic, Parsee, peach,
satrap, scarlet, shawl, taffeta, tulip, turban;* FROM PERU:
condor, guano, jerk, pampas, puma, quinine; FROM POLYNESIA:
tabu, tattoo; FROM PORTUGAL: *caste, cobra, copra, dodo,
molasses, palanquin, port, veranda, zebra;* FROM RUSSIA: *bol-
shevik, cossack, droshky, duma, kopeck, knout, mammoth,
mir, rouble, samovar, soviet, steppe, ukase, verst, vodka;* FROM
SPAIN: *alpaca, armada, caramel, casque, cargo, cigar, comrade,*

*don, duenna, flamingo, flotilla, lariat, llama, maize, mosquito,
peccadillo, punctilio, quadroon, ranch, renegade, sherry, steve-
dore, vanilla;* FROM SWEDEN: *dahlia, slag, slant, skittish,
tungsten;* FROM TURKEY: *bey, caviar, horde, kiosk, kismet,
uhlan;* FROM WALES: *cotton, cromlech, eisteddfod, funnel;*
FROM WEST INDIES: *cannibal, canoe, caoutchouc, potato,
tobacco.*

From "nowhere": that is, the following words are a few of
those for which satisfactory lineage cannot be or has not yet
been traced. They are sometimes called "Topsy words"
because, like Topsy in *Uncle Tom's Cabin,* they "just growed."
One of the theories about *fad,* for instance, is that it is composed of the initial letters in *for a day. Sulk* may be from
Anglo-Saxon *solcen,* languid; *jig* from old French *gigue,*
fiddle; *pedlar* from provincial English *ped,* basket. But the
straight and dignified line of ancestry cannot be traced.
Somewhere along the way there are the bar-sinisters of slang,
barbarism, localism, vulgarism, what-not: *akimbo, aroint,
balderdash, bellow, bet, bib, boy, caboose, cask, clog, cub,
curse, cut, dog, fad, fib, flannel, fog, fun, girl, golf, harum-
scarum, hunch, hunk, jerkin, jib, jiffy, jumbo, jump, jumper,
lad, lass, lurk, lush, maggot, mahogany, mole, mug, mufti, nag,
ninny, nip, nook, noodle, pack, pant, pedlar, peevish, peg, pelt,
pig, pot, pounce, prowl, pump, pug, pun, quaff, quail, qualm,
quandary, romp, scamp, schooner, scoot, scullion, shamble,
skedaddle, shatter, simper, skull, spree, sprig, sulk, sag, tan-
trum, trolley, trollop.*

Latin words, Latin words thru the French, and Anglo-Saxon
words have been omitted from the above for the reason that
they are so numerous and so varied as to justify separate
listings. The following are representative Latin and Latin-
thru-French words, all of them used in industry: *accentuate,
accumulate, accommodate, advertise, aggregate, assumption,
benefactor, calculate, candidate, circumstance, circumvent,
collateral, commensurate, compensation, correspondence, dedicate, delinquent, demonstrate, deteriorate, distribution, duplicate, elaborate, eliminate, estimate, equilibrium, evaluate,
evaporate, examine, extinguish, extraneous, extraordinary,
factor, fastidious, formulate, generate, genuine, granary,
gratuitous, hesitate, identical, illegal, illuminate, inaccuracy,
inadvertent, incomplete, incorporate, indispensable, inexpli-
cable, juxtaposition, laboratory, legislation, liquidate, litigation,*

location, lubrication, machinery, magnify, manufacture, minor, neglect, nondescript, nucleus, numerous, obstinacy, obstruction, operation, opposition, oppression, penetrate, postponement, predominance, recapitulate, recipe, reduction, regulation, remunerate, revolution, salutation, satisfaction, subordinate, supposition, suburban, testimonial, transfer, unanimous, unexceptionable, unification, unintelligible, unscrupulous, verbal, verification, viaduct, violation, vocational, voluminous, voluntary, voucher.

These are representative Saxon words: *after, be, bed, bid, board, body, borrow, box, break, bring, broad, business, buy, cat, cheap, clean, climb, clinch, cloth, dear, do, dog, draft, draw, earn, earth, father, fetch, fight, fireside, free, friend, full, get, give, gold, good, great, have, high, hire, hold, home, house, husband, idle, if, keep, knife, knit, lade, land, last, late, laugh, law, lay, lend, load, loan, long, look, low, mad, make, man, match, mate, might, mother, new, old, pride, put, read, rent, right, roof, sell, send, settle, sharp, shelter, ship, shop, short, silver, take, trade, waist, walk, water, way, weight, wide, wife, woman, word, work, write.*

B English is by no means a phonetic language. But as the centuries have passed it has tended to become more logical in spelling and in pronunciation. English words today are spelled more nearly as they sound and look than they have ever been before, but there is a long way to go yet before the language can be made completely phonetic, if indeed it ever can—if indeed such consummation is to be wished. Many attempts have been made to simplify English spelling and pronunciation. Three or four notable ones were made in the time of Queen Elizabeth, but these did not prevent Shakespeare's name being spelled in more than thirty different ways. Samuel Johnson in 1755 made a notable attempt in his famous dictionary to regulate and standardize English diction. While his work contained many inconsistencies that today strike us as humorous, it nevertheless did bring a much-needed order out of the confusion and irregularity that previously existed. The eighteenth-century pulpit and forum made many attempts at uniformity and simplicity in orthography, and in the nineteenth century the names Isaac Pitman, A. J. Ellis, and Henry Sweet (to mention but three) meant much to those increasing numbers who were eager to see the language made "sensibly simple and consistent." The Philological Societies of England

S R A Fonetic Alfabet

24 Consonants

Print	Cap	Name	As in
p	**p**	*pə*	pin, cup
b	**b**	*bə*	bin, cub
t	**t**	*tə*	ten, bet
d	**d**	*də*	den, bed
k	**k**	*kə*	come, back
g	**g**	*gə*	gum, bag
f	**f**	*fə*	fan, safe
v	**v**	*və*	van, save
ƕ	**ƕ**	*ƕə*	thigh, bath
ħ	**ħ**	*ħə*	thy, bathe
s	**s**	*sə*	seal, race
z	**z**	*zə*	zeal, raise
ʃ	**ʃ**	*ʃə*	assure, rush
ʒ	**ʒ**	*ʒə*	azure, rouge
ĉ	**ĉ**	*ĉə*	choke, rich
j	**j**	*jə*	joke, ridge
m	**m**	*mə*	met, him
n	**n**	*nə*	net, thin
ŋ	**ŋ**	*eŋ*	ink, thing
r	**r**	*rə*	raid, dear
l	**l**	*lə*	laid, deal
w	**w**	*wə*	wet, woo
y	**y**	*yə*	yet, you
h	**h**	*hə*	head, who

14 Vowels

Print	Cap	Name	As in
ə	**ə**	*ər*	about, murmur, data
a	**a**	*at*	am, pat
ɑ	**ɑ**	*a*	alms, part, ma
e	**e**	*et*	edge, let
ɛ	**ɛ**	*ɛr*	air, pair, mare
ɐ	**ɐ**	*ɐ*	age, late, may
i	**i**	*it*	is, sit, army
î	**î**	*î*	ease, seat, me
ɒ	**ɒ**	*ɒt*	odd, not
ɔ	**ɔ**	*ɔ*	awed, naught, pshaw
ʊ	**ʊ**	*ʊt*	up, ton
o	**o**	*o*	open, tone, show
u	**u**	*ut*	full, should
ɯ	**ɯ**	*ɯ*	fool, shoed, shoe

4 Difthongs

Print	Cap	Name	As in
á	**á**	*á*	aisle, pint, by
aɪ	**aɪ**	*aɪ*	owl, pound, bough
ɔ̇	**ɔ̇**	*ɔ̇*	oil, point, boy
ɪu	**ɪu**	*ɪu*	pure, due

Supplementary sign

*	*	*capsign*

To capitalize a fonetic tipewritten or longhand word, write the capsign before it.

Fonetic print capitals ar hevy or boldface letters, otherwise similar to the small or lower case letters.

The linear order and fonetic names of this alfabet ar derived from establisht shorthand practis, and wil be found both logical and convenient

liŋkən'z getizbərg spîč

forskor and sevn yîrz əgo aʋr faħərz brɔt forħ ɒn
his kɒntinent ə niu naʃən, kɒnsîvd in libərti, and dedikated tu ħə prɒpoziʃən ħat ɔl men ɑr krîated îkwəl.

naʋ wî ɑr engajd in ə grat sivil wɔr, testiŋ
hweħər ħat naʃən, ɔr eni naʃən so kɒnsîvd and so
dedikated, kan lɒŋ endiʋr. wî ɑr met ɒn ə grat
batl-fîld ɒv ħat wɔr. wî hav kum tu dedikat ə por-
ʃən ɒv ħat fîld az ə fánəl restiŋ-plas fɔr ħoz huʋ hîr
gaʋ ħɑr lávz ħat ħat naʃən mát liv. it iz ɔltəgeħər
fitiŋ and prɒpər ħat wî ʃud du ħis.

but in ə lɑrjər sens, wî kanɒt dedikat — wî
kanɒt kɒnsikrat — wî kanɒt halo — ħis graʋnd. ħə
brav men, liviŋ and ded, huʋ strugld hîr, hav kɒn-
sikrated it fɑr əbuv aʋr puʋr paʋər tu ad ɔr ditrakt.
ħə wərld wil litl not nɔr lɒŋ rimembər hwɒt wî sa
hîr, but it kan nevər fɔrget hwɒt ħa did hîr. it
iz fɔr us, ħə liviŋ, raħər, tu bî dedikated hîr tu ħə
unfiniʃt wərk hwič ħa huʋ fɔt hîr hav ħus fɑr so
nobli advanst. it iz raħər fɔr us tu bî hîr dedikated
tu ħə grat task rimaniŋ bifor us — ħat frɒm ħîz
ɒnərd ded wî tak inkrîst divoʃən tu ħat kɔz fɔr
hwič ħa gaʋ ħə last ful mezur ɒv divoʃən ; ħat wî
hîr háli rizɒlv ħat ħîz ded ʃal nɒt hav dád in van ;
ħat ħis naʃən, undər gɒd, ʃal hav ə niu bərħ ɒv
frîdəm; and ħat guvərnment ɒv ħə pîpl, bá ħə pîpl,
fɔr ħə pîpl, ʃal nɒt periʃ frɒm ħə ərħ.

Brief study of the preceding page wil enable any one to read the
above selection accurately. A few hours study wil giv any one at
all familiar with fonetics a practical working knowledge of this
simplest and best fonetic alfabet for English.

and of America have likewise done much for the cause, as have
also the Spelling Society of England and the Simplified Spelling Board of America. The two great American dictionaries
—*Webster's New International Dictionary* and *The New
Standard Dictionary of the English Language*—have in their
latest editions marked tremendous strides in the laborious
undertaking of making English vastly more uniform and consistent and phonetic and therefore simpler than it has ever
been before. The Spelling Reform Association has devised an
English phonetic alphabet with twenty-four consonants and
fourteen vowels. On pages 578 and 579 it is reproduced by
permission, with Lincoln's *Gettysburg Address* in its characters.

Stress or accent tends to fall on the root syllable: *ten'd, ten'der,
tend'ing, tend'ed, attend'ed, atten'tion, atten'tively, inatten'-
tively.* There are, of course, many exceptions to this regulation, but it is basic and therefore helpful in making new word
acquaintances.   Note that it holds in general when prefixes
and suffixes are added, even when the prefix or the suffix—or
both—consists of more than one syllable: *stand', understand',
understand'able, misunderstand'able.* A   secondary   stress
usually falls on the first syllable when prefixing and suffixing
make the word lengthy.   When they make a distinct change in
the meaning of a word or when they play it up in direct contrast with another, then the stress is likely to move to the
contrasted parts:

> Please *un'*do this and *re'*-do that
> This *in'*creases as that *de'*creases
> Do you prefer to be child*ish'* or child*like'*?
> Are you forget*ful'* or just forgett*ing'*?

There is, however, a tendency for accent or stress to move
forward toward the beginning of a word as it is increased in
length by prefixing and suffixing: *compare', com'parable,
incom'parable; apply', ap'plicable, in'applicable; ad'mirable,
hos'pitable, irrep'arable, ref'erable, rev'ocable.* But the dissyllabic suffix *ition (ation)* tends to carry accent toward it as
a kind of balance or centralization device: *dis''posi'tion,
ex''posi'tion, ex''pecta'tion, in''vita'tion, prop''osi'tion, sup''-
posi'tion.* Ease or rhythm of expression is enhanced by this
change and by the secondary accent thus carried.

Pause after syllables may sometimes be exercised with advantage for the sake of differentiating them, especially when one

syllable ends with the same letter with which the next begins: *il-le'gal, ir-respec'tive, in-nova'tion.* This is much the same sort of pause that is required between and among words in good reading. Punctuation marks have something to do with indicating these pauses, but the mental pictures conveyed along the way are the cues for the more significant ones. Pause at every picture in the following passage and note how unimportant punctuation marks really are and how much more easily the meaning is conveyed:

> . . . when the Philistine arose (*pause picture*) and came and drew nigh to meet David (*pause picture*) David hastened and ran toward the army to meet the Philistine (*pause picture*) And David put his hand in his bag (*pause picture*) and took thence a stone (*pause picture*) and slang it (*pause picture*) and smote the Philistine in his forehead (*pause picture*) And the stone sank into his forehead (*pause picture*) and he fell upon his face (*pause picture*) to the earth

C The accent usually comes on the first syllable in compound nouns for the reason that the specific or surprize element resides in the first syllable. This also follows the forward-moving tendency above mentioned: *bookkeeper, blotting-pad, foresight, inkwell, footstool, penholder, typewriter.*

In many words the change of stress is the mark of distinction between nouns and verbs, the first stress denoting the noun and the after-stress, the verb. Inasmuch as the verb is more likely to carry suffixes than the noun (imperfect tense and present participle) this after-stress on many verbs tends to keep the balance of accent in pronunciation. Noté these words, as nouns, with the forward stress, as verbs, with the after stress: *abstract, affix, ally, annex, attribute, augment, collect, combine, compound, commune, compress, concert, concrete, conduct, confine, conflict, conscript, consort, contest, contract, contrast, converse, convert, convict, convoy, decrease, descant, desert, digest, discount, discord, ensign, entrail, entrance, envelop, escort, essay, excerpt, export, extract, ferment, import, impress, imprint, incense, increase, insult, object, perfume, permit, pervert, prefix, premise, presage, present* (also adjective), *proceeds, produce, progress, project, protest, rebel, record, recount, refuse, reprint, retail, subject, survey, torment, transfer, transport.*

But note that *compact', content', expert', inval'id, minute'* are adjectives and *com'pact, con'tent, ex'pert, in'valid, min'ute* are nouns.

Note also that the long vowel sound makes the verb in *alter-nāte, associāte, consummāte, deliberāte, intimāte, moderāte, separāte;* that the short vowel sound makes the adjective or the noun, or both, in each case.

Note again that the *ʒ* sound of *s* in *abuse, diffuse, excuse, grease, house, mouse, refuse* makes them verbs; the *s* sound makes them nouns or adjectives (sometimes with slight change of form). The heteronyms *lead* (leed) and *lead* (led), *read* (reed) and *read* (red), *tear* (teer) and *tear* (tare) illustrate further the importance of sound differentiations in the pronunciation of certain English words.

Diction tends to become more and more euphonious as language evolves. The prefixes *a, ac, af, ag, al, an, ap, ar, as, at,* for instance, are one and the same, but they are modified according to euphony in making adjustments to roots. Thus *atchieve* is neither so simple nor so easy to pronounce as *achieve.* Usage has consequently worn it down to the latter form. Note also *affix* instead of *agfix, allude* instead of *adlude, attend* instead of *aptend, differ* instead of *disfer,* and so forth. The adjustment is accomplished by making the last letter of the prefix the same as the first letter of the root, thus preventing awkward stoppage of the flow of pronunciation. There is no determining principle in regard to most suffixes, but it should be noted that euphony and rhythm have likewise played a part, however small, in the suffix adjustments. The Latin declension or conjugation may be followed in such cases as *tion* and *ation, tive* and *ative,* but "clipping" for ease of utterance takes place during the evolution of a word.

Words introduced into English from other languages tend to hold to their accent, as well as to their other pronunciation characteristics, until they are finally and fully adopted. But there is always some inconsistency to be reckoned with, in view of the fact that such adoption is necessarily slow and resistant. Thus we have *chal'ice, mal'ice, nov'ice,* but *caprice'* and *police'; an'tic, art'ist, crit'ic, di'vers, hu'man, phys'ic, ur'ban, ves'tige,* but *antique', artiste', critique', diverse', humane', physique', prestige', urbane'.*

Such differences may be confusing—there are hundreds of other similar ones. But they are no more so than are the pronunciations required by writers from before the time of Chaucer to after the time of Milton. Indeed, the accent alone of many words in Shakespeare makes them sound today as if they had been lifted from a foreign language—as many of them really were. To mention the minimum, the words *aspect, contrite, countree, impulse, uproar,* of the sixteenth and seventeenth centuries, must still be accented on the second syllable if a work of the time is to be read in the spirit in which it was written and which it represents.

D Following are a few of the more important word roots that have come down from Latin (with the exception of the six from Greek, marked with capital G in parentheses). Some of the illustrative words bear both prefix and suffix: *ac—act—ad* (do, act) reaction; *amo* (love) amorous; *ann—anni* (year) annuity; *arm—armor* (arms) armament; *ar—art* (art, skill) artistic; *audi—audit* (hear) audition; *auto* (self)(G) automatic; *capi—capt* (take) capital; *ced—cess—cedd—cedo* (go, move) concession; *cent* (hundred) centennial; *chron* (time) (G) chronic; *cit—citat* (stir, rouse) citation; *civ—civi* (citizen) civics; *cor—cord* (heart) cordial; *corp—corpor* (body) corpse; *cred—credit* (believe) credit; *cur—cura* (care) curator; *custos—custod* (watch, guard) custodian; *dic—dict* (say) dictation; *duo—dua* (two) duality; *duc—duct* (lead, draw) induction; *faci—fact* (do, make) manufactory; *fend—fens* (strike, keep off) defender; *fer* (bear, carry) transfer; *fin—fini* (end) final; *flec—flex* (bend) reflection; *forma* (shape, form) formative; *fugi—fugit* (flee) fugitive; *graph* (write) (G) multigraph; *grat* (thankful, pleasing) gratitude; *habe—habit* (have, hold) habitation; *jaci—jact* (throw, cast) jaculate; *jung—junct* (join) conjunction; *loc—loci* (place) locality; *log* (word) (G) logical; *magn* (great) magnify; *manu* (hand) manual; *metr* (measure) (G) taximeter; *mitt—miss* (send, cast) transmission; *move—mote* (move) removal; *mut—mutat* (move) mutation; *nosc—not* (know, mark) cognoscence; *numer—numeri* (number) numerology; *op—oper* (work, deed) operate; *or—orat* (pray, ask) oration; *par—part* (part) partition; *pende—pens* (hang) dependent; *pe—ped* (foot) pedal; *philo* (love) (G) philosophy; *plic—plicat* (fold) duplicate; *pon—pos* (put) postpone; *port—portat* (carry) portable; *prim* (first) primitive; *prob—probat* (try, approve) probation; *put—putat* (think, reckon) putative; *reg—rect* (rule) regulate; *rog—rogat* (ask) interrogate; *scend* (climb) ascend; *scio* (know) scientific; *scrib* (write) transcribe; *sec—sect* (cut) section; *senti—sens* (feel, think) sensitive; *sequ*

—secut (follow) consecutive; *serv—servat* (serve) conserve; *sign—signi* (seal) signature; *simili* (resemble) similar; *spici—spect* (look, see) inspection; *spir—spirat* (breathe) inspiration; *stat* (stand) stationary; *tend—tent* (aim) attention; *tract* (draw) subtract; *tribu—tribut* (give) tribute; *veni--vent* (come) convenient; *vert* (turn) controvert; *vid—vis* (see) invisible; *vinc—vict* (conquer) convincing; *volvo—volut* (roll, turn) revolution.

E Prefixes and suffixes are likewise taken principally from Latin, but Greek, French, and Old English have contributed a goodly number. Negative prefixes are those that subtract or take something away from the idea conveyed by the roots to which they are attached. These illustrative words with italicized prefixes make this classification clear: *ab*sent, *an*omalous, *anti*pathy, *a*pathy, *apo*logy, *contra*distinction, *de*preciate, *dis*favor, *ex*hale, *hemi*sphere, *mis*interpret, *il*legitimate, *im*mature, *in*convenient, *ir*remediable, *non*sense, *ob*stacle, *post*pone, *retro*active, *se*cede, *semi*annual, *sine*cure, *sub*ject, *un*compromising, *under*estimate, *vice*chairman, *with*hold.

These words illustrate additive prefixes, or prefixes that add something to the idea conveyed by the root: *ac*quaint, *ad*dress, *a*head, *ambi*dextrous, *amphi*bious, *ante*date, *at*tain, *be*fore, *bene*fit, *bi*annual, *by*law, *con*vince, *extra*ordinary, *fore*arm, *hyper*critical, *intro*duce, *out*bid, *over*do, *poly*technic, *pre*cede, *pro*duce, *re*tainer, *super*intend, *syn*dicate, *tele*graph, *ultra*gaseous.

Prefixes, again, have a divisional or separative or limiting significance, used in connection with certain roots: *ana*chronism, *cata*clysm, *circum*scribe, *dia*meter, *for*bear, *hetero*geneous, *homo*geneous, *inter*sect, *per*mit, *trans*late.

Prefixes and suffixes that may stand alone as independent words are sometimes called independent or separable: *after, at, by, extra, for, forth, in, off, on, out, over, thru, to, under, up, with; craft, fare, fast, head, hood, less, man, ship, some, son, ward, wide, wright.*

Such prefixes and suffixes as the following are called dependent or inseparable: *a, bi, con, ex, inter, non, pre, pro, trans, un; ast, dom, ed, en, er, est, ing, ish, ism, ist, ling, ly, ness, om, ow, ong, y.*

Prefixes are used in a few cases to indicate gender. Sometimes they form hyphenated compounds; sometimes, solid compounds:

brother-in-law	sister-in-law
buck-rabbit	doe-rabbit
cock-sparrow	hen-sparrow
father-in-law	mother-in-law
he-goat	she-goat
landlord	landlady
man-servant	maid-servant (woman-servant)
peacock	pea-hen
salesman	saleswoman
son-in-law	daughter-in-law

F Suffixes sometimes have a repetitive or frequentative signification: babb*le*, chatt*er*, clatt*er*, crumb*le*, mutt*er*, patt*er*, ratt*le*, rumb*le*, rust*le*, spark*le*, tumb*le*, whist*le*.

Sometimes they are causative in their effect upon a root: beauti*fy*, edi*fy*, embell*ish*, garn*ish*, oper*ate*, mitig*ate*, philosoph*ize*, strength*en*, stulti*fy*, uni*fy*, veri*fy*.

Again the suffix may indicate the agent or agency (sometimes with contempt): assign*ee*, associ*ate*, auction*eer*, capital*ist*, cash*ier*, debat*er*, debt*or*, enthusi*ast*, fire*man*, fish*wife*, gang*ster*, mill*wright*, old*ster*, pun*ster*, rhym*ster*, team*ster*, young*ster*.

A suffix (or a suffixed word) may, again, signify the small or the diminutive or the delicate, and sometimes the contemptuous: aster*isk*, ball*ot*, cabin*et*, chic*let*, cubi*cle*, dear*y* (or dear*ie*), hill*ock*, kitchen*ette*, lamb*kin*, lass*ie*, maid*en*, mole*cule*, Negr*ito*, parti*cle*, sap*ling*, satch*el*, sched*ule*, speck*le*.

It will be noted that a suffix may have more than one meaning or signification. The vast majority of suffixes, however, including those above, add to the root of a word the meaning of quality or condition or state of being, of act or agency or place, and of relationship. Suffixes likewise vary their forms to make easy and euphonious and rhythmic adjustments to roots. Thus, *an, ean,* and *ian* are the same suffix, as are also *ant* and *ent, ancy* and *ency, tion* and *ation*. Note also account*ant*, add*ing*, aggrandi*ze*, ambig*uous*, amphib*ian*, antag-on*istic*, appear*ance*, artiz*an*, atten*tion*, authorit*ative*, bell*icose*, benefic*iary*, bishop*ric*, bragg*art*, business*like*, cer*eal*, cerem*ony*, circul*ation*, cert*ain*, champ*ion*, civ*il*, compari*son*, compet*ence*, confid*ante*, cost*ly*, counter*act*, court*eous*, cow*ard*, critic*ism*.

customer, declension, delinquency, delirious, economic, enjoyment, falsehood, familiar, fashion, finesse, foreign, fragile, gallant, grotesque, growth, handcraft, hatred, helpful, hesitancy, hogshead, homestead, homeward, humanitarian, impish, ignition, incandescent, inconvenient, interpreted, irony, irksome, kingdom, larceny, legible, lengthen, literary, manifold, mathematics, memory, menace, millwright, merchandise, narrow, normal, notice, patronage, personnel, portable, portentous, Protean, provident, prowess, psychology, purveyor, ransom, reality, reckon, rectify, referee, sanguine, sarcasm, seed, serial, similar, sincerest, spheroid, stedfast, stubbornness, technician, tenacious, tenure, threshold, valid, welfare, workman, workmanship, worthless, worthy, zealot.

Note now how prefix, root, and suffix, or any two of these, are welded together to form words:

Source	Prefix	Root	Suffix	Finished English Word
Latin	con (with)	ver(t) (turn)	(s)ion (act of, state of being)	conversion
Latin	de (from, down from, fully)	trac(t) (draw)	or (one who, that which, quality of)	detractor
Latin	dis (apart, not, away)	pos (place)	al (act of, that which, relating to)	disposal
Latin	ex (from, out of)	pell (drive)	ing (act of)	expelling
Latin	il (not, away, from)	liter(a) (letters)	ate (one who, having the quality of)	illiterate
Latin	in (not)	tempero (I mix or adjust)	ate (function of)	intemperate
Greek	orthos (right)	grapho (write)	y (quality of)	orthography
Greek	philos (dear)	logos (word)	y (quality of)	philology
Latin	pre (before)	ced (go)	ence (state, quality)	precedence
Latin	pro (before)	positum (placing)	ion (act of)	proposition
Latin	re (back)	flecto (bend)	ion (act of)	reflection
Latin	sub (under)	struc(t) (build)	ure (that which, act or state of)	substructure
Greek	sun (with)	tasso (arrange)		syntax
Latin	trans (beyond, thru, across)	par(eo) (appear)	ent (being, one who)	transparent

These suffixes are sometimes called the gender suffixes: *a, ar, er, ess, ina, ine, rix (trix), ster, stress.* The fourth—*ess*—is the most commonly used but it is gradually disappearing. Gender is indicated in many cases by a complete change of word rather than by suffixing. The asterisks in the list below denote forms that are rarely used, the masculine form serving for feminine as well; the daggers denote types of foreign nouns that retain their original endings.

Masculine Gender	Feminine Gender	Masculine Gender	Feminine Gender
abbot	abbess	Julius	Julia †
actor	actress	landgrave	landgravine
administrator	administratrix	lion	lioness *
Alexander	Alexandrina	margrave	margravine
alumnus	alumna	marquis	marchioness
baron	baroness	murderer	murderess *
benefactor	benefactress	negro	negress *
count	countess	patron	patroness
czar	czarina	poet	poetess *
deacon	deaconess	priest	priestess *
duke	duchess	seamster	seamstress *
editor	editress *	shepherd	shepherdess *
emperor	empress	Signor	Signora †
enchanter	enchantress	songster	songstress *
executor	executrix	sorcerer	sorceress *
giant	giantess *	sultan	sultana
god	goddess	testator	testatrix
governor	governess	tiger	tigress *
hero	heroine	victor	victress *
host	hostess	votary	votaress *
hunter	huntress *	waiter	waitress
inheritor	inheritrix *	widower	widow

The following masculines and feminines are different words entirely:

Masculine Gender	Feminine Gender	Masculine Gender	Feminine Gender
bachelor	spinster	grandsire	grandam
beau	belle	gentleman	lady
boar	sow	hart	roe (hind)
boy	girl	husband	wife
groom (bridegroom)	bride	king	queen
		man	woman
brother	sister	milter	spawner
buck	doe	monk (friar)	nun
bull	cow	nephew	niece
bullock	heifer	ram	ewe
cock	hen	sire	dam
colt	filly	sloven	slut
dog	bitch	son	daughter
drake	duck	stag	hind
earl	countess	stallion (horse)	mare
father	mother	swain	lass
fox	vixen	uncle	aunt
gander	goose	wizard	witch

Offspring is frequently designated by names quite unrelated to parental names, tho in some cases by the diminutive suffixes *ling, le, let, kin, y (ie)*—*babe (baby), calf, chick (chickling), child, colt, cub, cygnet, duckling, fawn, fledgling, foundling, gosling, infant, kitten (kitty), lamb (lambkin), nestling, pig, prince, pullet, pup (puppy), squab, suckling.*

The suffix *ly* is added to adjectives of quality as a rule to form adverbs: *graceful, gracefully; sweet, sweetly; true, truly.* But there are many adverbs that do not end with *ly*, and it is incorrect to add *ly* to such adverbs as *alone, fast, here, much, quite, thus* (see page 199). It is unnecessary with *first, second, third*, and so forth, inasmuch as ordinals, tho usually nouns or adjectives, may be used adverbially without suffixing.

The suffix *ster* was originally the feminine of *er* and connoted agent or occupation. It has now almost completely passed as a feminine ending, tho it still survives in such proper names as *Webster, Brewster, Baxter (Bagster), Foster*—weaver, brewer, baker, feeder. The words *seamster* and *songster* are already feminine in the *ster*-form, so it is superfluous to add *ess*. The term *foster-mother* is likewise tautological, and *foster-father* is contradictory. The *en (in)* as in *vixen* is an old Teutonic feminine ending.

The suffixes *er* and *est* are used with the positive degree of many adjectives (and some adverbs) to form the comparative and superlative degrees respectively. Thus, the positive degree *fair* becomes *fairer* in the comparative, and *fairest* in the superlative. In longer adjectives and adverbs wherein the addition of syllables would become awkward in pronunciation, the *er* and *est* are not used, but *more* is used before the adjective or adverb to form the comparative, and *most* to form the superlative—*more gracious, most gracious*—in ascending comparison, that is, in comparison that indicates increasing degrees of meaning. In descending comparison—comparison that indicates decreasing degrees of comparison—*less* and *least* are used: *less successful, least successful.* Trisyllabic and longer adjectives almost invariably require the *more-most* o\ *less-least* comparative formation. Disyllabic adjectives may as a rule be compared either by the suffixes *er* and *est* or by the prefatory words *more* and *most, less* and *least.* Monosyllabics, with the exception of the irregular comparatives listed below, are almost invariably compared by *er* and *est.*

Positive	Comparative	Superlative
bad	worse	worst
far	farther	farthest
fore	former	foremost, first
(forth)	further	furthest
good	better	best
hind	hinder	hindmost, hindermost
ill	worse	worst
(in)	inner	inmost, innermost
late	later, latter	latest, last
little	less, lesser	least
much, many	more	most
near	nearer	nearest, next
nigh	nigher	nighest, next
old	older, elder	oldest, eldest
(out)	outer, utter	outmost, outermost, utmost, uttermost

The suffixes *ish* and *like* are sometimes used to form what is known as comparison of indefinite degree: *childish, manlike.*

The three degrees of comparison here illustrated, however, are by no means the only ones that can be expressed. The term *fairly good,* for instance, belongs somewhere between positive *good* and comparative *better,* and *rather better* probably belongs somewhere between comparative *better* and superlative *best.* And so *quite good, pretty good, even better, still better, very best, best of all* designate intermediate steps in comparison not accounted for in the above three degrees. A chain shop was known as *The Goody Shop.* A new branch was opened as *The Goody Goody Shop;* another as *The Excellent Goody Shop;* still another as *The Supreme Goody Shop*—all the names showing differentiated degrees of comparison.

G Mispronunciation occurs, for one reason, because our language is not phonetic. It occurs also because people do not yet —after all the pressure that has been brought to bear upon them—take sufficient pride in their speech. It is impossible here to point out all the errors of carelessness that are constantly occurring, but some of the more important ones are here listed. They should be carefully studied.

Such words as *bid, bide; bit, bite; cal, Kate; dot, dote; fat, fate; fir, fire; gat, gate; hid, hide; kit, kite; mat, mate; mit, mite; mop, mope; nod, node; not, note; pal, pate; rat, rate; rid, ride; rim, rime; run, rune; sat, sate; sit, site; slid, slide; sloop, slope; tap, tape; writ, write* are valuable for showing the effect of the final *e*. It tends to lengthen the sound of the preceding vowel proportionately as it lengthens the word.

Note again such words as *add* and *at;* *bad* and *bat;* *cad* and *cat;* *fad* and *fat;* *mad* and *mat;* *pad* and *pat;* *sad* and *sat;* *tad* and *tat*. The final *d* and *t* are too likely to be transferred in rapid speech, so that one is heard for the other very often.

Other troublesome pronunciation sounds are *ch* for *g* or *j;* *z* for *s* or *sh;* *oi* for *ur, or,* and *ir;* *oo* for *u;* *nk* for *ng,* and vice versa; *w* for *wh*. *Ch* for *g* in *German* tends to slurring of the two syllables and reducing the word almost to a monosyllable. In the same way, *classify* pronounced *clazzify* strongly tends to become *clazzfy,* and even *glazzfy.* There is, in other words, a closer relationship than is usually supposed between the missounding of a given syllable in a word and the slurring of it or of another. *Febry* for *February;* *founen* for *fountain;* *libry* for *library;* *zimlar* for *similar;* *tempry* for *temporary;* *twenny* for *twenty* illustrate this tendency, as do these also: *boistrous* for *boisterous;* *histry* for *history;* *intrist* for *interest;* *poplar* for *popular;* *valuble* for *valuable;* *victry* for *victory*.

Unt for *ent* and *unce* for *ence* are common pronunciation mis-soundings. *Independunce* for *independence, prudunt* for *prudent* are "ear errors" in pronouncing sounds. An accurate ear is offended by *momunt* for *moment* and *fraudulunce* for *fraudulence*. The same sort of mispronunciation or missounding exists in *excitid* for *excited, sightid* for *sighted, unitid* for *united,* and in *cariless* for *careless, goodniss* for *goodness, hostiss* for *hostess*. The suppression or slurring of final *d* is likely one day to make the letter *d* superfluous unless we mend our ways of pronunciation. *Buil, depen, fol, gran, han, hol, stan* for *build, depend, fold, grand, hand, hold, stand* respectively are becoming almost as general as the suppression of *g* in *ing* and the substitution of the *oo* sound for long *u* in such words as *duty* and *beauty*.

While no list of commonly mispronounced—vulgarly pronounced—words can possibly be complete (they change, naturally, with geographic conditions), the following specific instances of bad pronunciation, added to the general ones above pointed out, will do much, if corrective practise is brought to bear upon them, toward correcting wrong tendencies in pronunciation.

angsious	for	anxious
enaman	for	any man
augsion	for	auction
aujience	for	audience
banket	for	banquet
buttah	for	butter
byin	for	buying
kin	for	can
kazheer	for	cashier
ketch	for	catch
jairman	for	chairman
copetent	for	competent
consahn	for	concern
cudja	for	could you
didja	for	did you
didncha	for	didn't you
dispurse	for	disburse
disberse	for	disperse
doncha	for	don't you
dror	for	draw
d'ya	for	do you
eggstra	for	extra
chenius	for	genius
gonna	for	going to
gimme	for	give me
gotta or godda	for	got to
guvermunt	for	government
hair	for	heir
'm	for	him and them
hunderd	for	hundred
inchunction	for	injunction
ingwell	for	inkwell
itemiced	for	itemized
choinal	for	journal
jist, jest, or juss	for	just
lemme	for	let me
less	for	let's
letm or ledm	for	let him or them
litarachure	for	literature
lonker	for	longer
Lonk Giland	for	Long Island
modren	for	modern
noo	for	new
nooze	for	news
awfuce	for	office
aral	for	oral
ouda	for	ought to
pake	for	peg
pleass	for	please
brozeeds	for	proceeds
brospectuve	for	prospective
korum	for	quorum
reconice	for	recognize
reverence	for	reference
reerse	for	rehearse

wetail	for	retail
rink	for	ring
ropper	for	robber
cemetary or symmetry	for	seminary
zhwal	for	shawl
sumpin	for	something
sperl	for	spoil
de	for	the
dey	for	they
tink	for	think
toid	for	third
dis	for	this
zis	for	this
taut	for	thought
waid	for	wait
wanna	for	want to
wuz	for	was
vear	for	wear
watja meen	for	what do you mean
wite	for	white
willyer	for	will you
wudda	for	would have
wudja	for	would you
wrabber	for	wrapper
youse	for	you

The following words are commonly mispronounced thru false sounds and thru slurring. Aim, first, to stress the correct syllable (syllables) in each; then concentrate upon sound values, taking your time so that accent will not suffer as result of false sounding or vice versa. The list is a particularly good one. The words are in common everyday use and they present difficulties of pronunciation that are sometimes almost insurmountable. Yet, to pronounce them incorrectly may mean to get one's self adjudged illiterate.

abdomen	ăb dō'měn	ăb'dŏ měn
absolutely	ăb'sŏlūte ly	
accidentally	ak si den'tăl ly	
acclimate	ak klī'măt	
accompanist	ak kum'på nist	
acumen	a kū'měn	
address	ăd drĕs'	
adept	ăd ĕpt'	
administrative	ad min'is tra tiv	
admirable	ăd'mĭr a bl	
admirably	ăd'mĭr a blĭ	
adult	a dŭlt'	
advertisement	ăd vĕr'tĭz měnt	ăd ver tīz'měnt
alias	ā'lĭ ăs	
alien	āl'yĕn	
alienate	ā'lĭ en āt	
ally	å lī'	

alternately	al'tēr nāt li	al tēr'nát li
amateur	ăm á tûr'	am'a tiur
alumni	a lŭm'nī	
annex	ăn nĕks'	ăn'nĕks
annihilate	ăn nī'hĭl āt	
apotheosis	ăp ō thē'ō sĭs	
apparatus	ăp á rā'tŭs	
applicable	ăp'plĭk á bl	
appreciate	ăp prē'shĭ āt	
apropos	ăp rō pō'	
aristocrat	á rĭs'tō krăt	ăr'ĭs tō krăt
ask	ȧsk	
associate	as sō' shĕ āt	
association	ăs sō cĭ ā'shŭn	ăs sō shĭ ā'shŭn
athlete	ăth'lēt	
audacious	ô dā'shŭs	
automobile	ô tō mō'bĭl	ô tō mō bēl'
avenue	ăv'ĕn yū	
aviator	ā'vi ā tŏr	
bade	băd	
banquet	băng'kwĕt	
barrage	bär'āj	bá räzh'
Belial	Bē'li al	
believe	bē lēv'	
bicycle	bī'sĭk l	
biography	bī ŏg'rȧfĭ	
blatant	blā'tănt	
bouquet	bōō kā'	bōō'kā
bowel	bou'al	
bronchitis	brŏng kī'tĭs	
calliope	kȧ lī'ō pē	
calligraphy	kăl lĭg'rȧ fy	
casualty	kazh'ŭ ȧl tĭ	
Caucasian	Kaw kā'shȧn	Kaw kash'an
cello	chĕl'ō	
cement	se ment'	
chameleon	kȧ mē'le un	
chaos	kā'ŏs	
champion	cham'pi un	
chastisement	chăs'tĭz mĕnt	
chiropodist	kī rŏp'ō dĭst	
chocolate	chŏk'ō lāt	
chauffeur	shō'fûr	shō fûr'
clique	klēk	
coadjutor	co a ju'tor	
cognomen	kŏg nō'mĕn	
combatant	kŏm'băt ănt	kŭm'băt ănt
comparable	kŏm'pá rȧ bl	
complaisance	kŏm'plā zăns	kŏm plā'zăns
compromise	kŏm'prō mīz	
comptroller	kŏn trō'lēr	
condolence	kŏn dō'lĕns	
conscientious	kŏn shĭ ĕn'shŭs	
considerable	kŏn sĭd'ēr á bl	
conspiracy	kŏn spĭr'á sĭ	

coral	kŏr'ăl	
coroner	kor'o nẽr	
corps	kōr	
coupon	kōō'pŏn	
cowardice	kow'ärd ĭs	
credence	krē'dĕns	
creek	krĕk	
crematory	krĕm'á tō rĭ	krē'má tō rĭ
culinary	kū'lĭn ā rĭ	
data	dā'tá	
datum	dā'tŭm	
deaf	dĕf	
débris	dā bré	
decade	dĕk'ād	
decisive	de sī'sĭv	
decorous	de kŏ'rus	dek'ŏ rus
deference	def'ẽr ĕns	
deficit	dĕf'ĭ sĭt	
demonstrate	dem'on strat	de mon'strat
despicable	dĕs'pĭ ká bl	
detail	dē tāl'	dē'tāl
digest	dĭ'jĕst	dī jĕst'
digestion	dĭ jĕs'chŭn	
diplomat	dip'lo mat	
direct	dĭ rĕkt'	
dirigible	dĭr'ĭ jĭ ble	
discourse	dĭs kōrs'	
docile	dŏ'sil	dōs'īl
economic	ē kŏ nŏm'ĭk	ĕk ō nŏm'ĭk
egotism	ē'gŏ tĭzm	ĕg'ō tĭzm
élite	ā lēt'	
envelope	ĕn vĕl'ŏp	ĕn'vĕl ōp
epitome	ē pĭt'ō mē	
epoch	ĕp'ŏk	ē'pŏk
err	ẽr	
errata	ĕr rā'tá	
exigency	ĕks'ĭj ĕn sĭ	
exit	ĕks'ĭt	
exquisite	ĕks'kwĭz ĭt	
extant	ĕks'tănt	
extol	ĕks tŏl'	ĕks tōl'
extraordinary	ĕks trôr'dĭn ā rĭ	
faucet	fô'sĕt	
fiat	fī'ăt	
finale	fē nä'lā	
finance	fĭn ăns'	
financial	fĭn ăn'shăl	
financier	fĭ năn sēr'	
forbade	fôr băd'	
forehead	fŏr'ĕd	fōr'ĕd
formidable	fôr'mĭd á bl	
forward	fôr'wẽrd	
fragile	frăj'ĭl	
frequent	frē kwĕnt' (verb)	frē'kwĕnt (adj.)
fuel	fū'ĕl	

gala	gā'lå	
gamut	găm'ŭt	
garage	gå räzh'	găr'åj
genuine	jĕn'ū ĭn	
gigantic	jī găn'tĭk	
gist	jĭst	
gondola	gŏn'dō lå	
gratis	grā'tĭs	
Hades	Hā'dĕz	
hangar	hang'ēr	
harass	hăr'ăs	
hearth	härth	
height	hīt	
helm	hĕlm	
herb	ērb	herb
herculean	hēr kū'lē ăn	
history	hĭs'tō rĭ	
horizon	ho rī'zun	
hospitable	hos'pi tå bl	
humor	hū'mēr	yū'mēr
hypocrisy	hĭp ŏk'rĭs ĭ	
hysteria	hĭs tē'rĭ å	
illustrate	ĭl lŭs'trāt	ĭl'lŭs trāt
incalculable	in kal'kū lå bl	
incidentally	ĭn cĭ dĕn'tăl ly	
incomparable	ĭn kŏm'på rå bl	
indict	ĭn dīt'	
indictment	ĭn dīt'mĕnt	
indisputable	ĭn dĭs'pū tå bl	ĭn dĭs pū'tå bl
indissoluble	ĭn dĭs'ŏ lū bl	
industry	ĭn'dŭs trĭ	
inertia	ĭn ēr'shĭ a	
inexorable	ĭn ĕks'ō rå bl	
inexplicable	ĭn ĕks'plĭk å bl	
inextricable	ĭn ĕks'trĭk å bl	
infamous	ĭn'få mŭs	
infantile	ĭn'făn tīl	ĭn'făn tĭl
inhospitable	ĭn hŏs'pĭt å bl	
inquiry	ĭn kwī'rĭ	
insatiable	ĭn sā'shå bl	ĭn sā'shĭ å bl
interested	ĭn'tēr ĕst ĕd	
interesting	ĭn'tēr ĕst ĭng	
irrecoverable	ĭr ĭ kŭv'ăr å bl	
irreparable	ĭr rep'ä rå bl	
irrefutable	ĭr i fiut'a bl	ĭr rĕf yu'tå bl
irrevocably	ĭ rĕv'ō kå blĭ	
isolate	ī'sō lāt	ĭs'ō lāt
italic	ĭ tăl'ĭk	
joust	jŭst	
juvenile	jū've nĭl	jū've nĭl
kept	kĕpt	
khaki	kä'kē	
leisure	lē'zhur	
length	lĕngth	
library	lĭ'brā rĭ	

medieval	mē dĭ ē'văl	mēd ĭ ē'văl
mischievous	mĭs'chĕv ŭs	
moral	mor'ăl	
municipal	mū nĭs'ĭp ăl	
nauseate	nô'shē āt	nô'sē āt
nephew	nĕf'yū	nev'yu
new	niū	
Niagara	Nī ăg'à rà	
office	ŏf'ĭs	
often	ôf'n	
oral	ō'răl	
pageant	păj'ent	pā'jent
parquet	pär kā'	pär ket'
patriot	pā'trĭ ŏt	păt'rĭ ŏt
peremptory	pĕr'emp tō rĭ	
pertinacious	pēr tĭn ā'shŭs	
pianist	pĭ ăn'ĭst	pē'à nĭst
piano	pĭ ăn'ō	
poem	pō'em	
positively	pos'ĭ tiv lĭ	
precedence	prē sē'dĕns	
precedency	prē sē'dĕn sĭ	
precedent	prĕs'ĕ dĕnt	
preferable	prĕf'ēr à bl	
premature	prē mà tūr'	prem à tūr'
prerogative	pre rog'à tiv	
primarily	prī'mà rĭ lē	
produce	pro dūs' (verb)	prŏd'ūs (noun)
promissory	prŏm'ĭs sō rĭ	
promulgate	prō mŭl'gāt	
qualm	kwäm	
quinine	kwī'nīn	kwĭ nēn'
radiator	rā'dĭ ā tor	
radio	rā'dĭ ō	
raillery	rāl'ĕr ĭ	ră'lēr ĭ
ratio	rā'shĭ ō	rā'shō
recess	re ses'	rē'ses (only as noun)
recipe	rĕs'ĭ pe	
recognize	rĕk'ŏg nīz	
recourse	rē kōrs'	
referable	rĕf'ēr à bl	
remedial	rē mē'dĭ ăl	
reproduction	rē prō dŭk'shŭn	
retailer	rē tā'ler	rē'tā ler
revocable	rĕv'ō ka bl	
revolt	rē vōlt'	rē vŏlt'
rinse	rĭns	
rise	rīz	rīs (only as noun)
romance	rō măns'	
roof	rōōf	
room	rōōm	
root	rōōt	
route	rōōt	rowt (colloquial)
salmon	săm'ŭn	
says	sĕz	

several	sĕv'ēr ăl	
shone	shōn	shŏn
squalor	skwol'ēr	skwä'lôr
squirrel	skwĕr'el	
suggest	sŭg jĕst'	
suite	swēt	
superfluous	sū pĕr'flū ŭs	
superintendent	sū per in tĕnd'ĕnt	
supple	sŭp'l	
supplement	sŭp'le mĕnt	
tapestry	tap'es trĭ	
tedious	tē'dĭ ŭs	tēd'yŭs
tepid	tĕp'ĭd	
tomato	tō mä'to	tō mä'to
toward	tōrd	
tribune	trĭb'yūn	
Tuesday	tūz'da	
tuned	tūnd	
ultimatum	ŭl tĭm ā'tŭm	
usage	yū'zāj	ū'sāj
vagary	vä gā'ri	
vagrant	vā'grănt	
vice versa	vī'sē vēr'så	
wan	wŏn	
whistle	hwis'l	
window	win'dō	
yacht	yŏt	
yolk	yōk	yōlk
yule	yūl	
zealous	zĕl'ŭs	

H The following word classifications may be helpful by way of clarifying usage. Some one has used the term "dictional lubrication" to explain the vocabulary of that person who uses words as if he knows all about their nice distinctions, recognizes which pigeonhole to take them out of to make his expression precise and attractive.

1 A word is *archaic* or *obsolescent* when it is falling out of reputable use. It may be revived now and again for yielding atmosphere to expression: *Ye Olde Tea Shoppe,* and as result of this revival it may regain position for a time: *Thus Spake Zarathustra.* A word is *obsolete* when it has gone quite out of reputable use. These words are archaic: *belike, bounden, choler, doth, eftsoons, haply, hast, perchance, quoth, swain, thee, thine, thou, wast, wilt, ye.* These words are obsolete: *certes, forgat, holpen, meseems, yclept.*

2 An *antonym* is a word that is directly opposed to another in meaning. Antonyms are frequently formed by negative

prefixing and suffixing: *adequate, inadequate; explosive, nonexplosive; satisfy, dissatisfy; concerned, unconcerned; direct, indirect; careful, careless; useful, useless.* But most antonyms are different words entirely: *begin, end; blame, praise; bless, curse; busy, idle; clever, stupid; cold, hot; comedy, tragedy; conceal, reveal; continuous, intermittent; courage, cowardice; discord, harmony; down, up; enemy, friend; failure, success; false, true; find, lose; grief, joy; guilty, innocent; help, hinder; in, out; large, small; lie, stand; liquid, solid; long, short; lovable, hatable; minimum, maximum; small, large; strong, weak; wrong, right.*

3 *Argot* is the peculiar phraseology of any class, formerly that of thieves and rogues: *hoosgow,* jail; *cooler,* cell; *doing time,* serving time; *bump off,* kill; *gat* or *rod,* gun; *bull,* officer; *take for a ride,* murder in a car; *black maria,* police patrol car; *harness bull,* officer in uniform; *swag,* booty; *icebox,* safe; *typewriter,* machine-gun; *dip,* pickpocket; *juice,* nitroglycerin or electric current in the death chair; *pineapple,* dynamite bomb; *gorilla,* bodyguard for chief gangster; *moll,* girl gangster; *mouthpiece,* lawyer; *coke,* cocaine; *snatcher,* kidnaper.

4 A *barbarism* is a word or expression that is not accepted as in good use. An abbreviated form like *Yrs. tly.* for *Yours truly* is a barbarism. A surprize verb formation from a noun is also: *aetnaize, buicking, burglarize, certainteed.* But in advertising and sales literature the public may be impressed profitably by such combinations as these. *Argify, confectionate, moneyfied, pants* (for *trousers*), *patriotized, real-estatist, unlaydownable* are barbarisms. Many terms, however, that are now quite acceptable began their careers as barbarisms: *filibuster, gerrymander, mugwump, tune in,* and the Italian surname *Marconi* linked with the Greek suffix *gram* to yield the much-needed *marconigram.*

5 *Coined words* are words that are deliberately made up to meet a real or a fancied demand. They are frequently very successful in connection with business and in humorous writing and speaking, and many of them are eventually graduated from mere coinages and barbarisms into good usage. Rules for their formation there are none, unless perhaps the irregular application of prefixes and suffixes be one. From the field of advertising such coinages as *Everwear, Hole-*

WORD STUDY599

proof, Kiddis-koop, Sunkist, Resinol, Cafeteria, Zonite, Sapolio, Safetea, Takoma, Gloriol are already a part of everyday chatter and some have even passed beyond the stage of capitalization. The more common coinages, however, are such as these: *beanery, beautician, bootery, bootlegger, boozette, buymanship, clubable, detourist, eatability, eatery, farmerette, flappery, foolosopher, Fordism, fussibility, gunocracy, happify, hashdom, hoglet, jawsmith, jaw-work, lendthrift, literachewer, Manhattador, moronia, motormania, newslette, obscenario, outroduction, patrioteering, pepsonality, pigwam, preachified, propheteer, realtor, restorium, Shaksperience, skedaddlism, smileage, sundae, Texanee, Unitedstatish, womanize, yellocution, youward.*

During the past quarter century the rapid movement of events has brought about many coinages some of which are now accepted as standard, but many are still without complete authorization. Some came to us from other languages; some grew up or are growing up from slang; some are new applications of old words; and some are hybrid in more ways than one, but all are now and here being used and they will probably survive. This is a minimum list: *accelerator, aerial, airdrome, airplane, antenna, aspirin, barrage, biplane, blimp, bobbing, Bolsheviki, broadcast, cabaret, camouflage, carbureter, catwalk, chassis, cinema, cocktail, close-up, costing, cost-accountant, die-hard, dirigible, dole, drys, dugout, fade-out, featuring, flask, flapper, gangster, gate-crasher, gearshift, hangar, highbrow, hike, hookup, ingenue, jay-walker, jazz, leftist, listening-in, loudspeaker, marconigram, monoplane, movies, Nazi, oscillation, outboard, overhead, plus-fours, pull-over, radio, restaurateur, rightist, road-hog, robot, shingling, spark-plug, static, step-in, tailspin, talkies, tanks, thermos, transmitter, tuning-in, turnover, ultra-violet, vacuum-cleaner, vita-glass, wets, wireless.*

6 By *colloquialism* is meant expression that may be used in familiar and informal conversation but not in formal or set discourse, expression that is neither of purely literary quality nor yet coarse or vulgar. It may be quite correct (tho it may sometimes be incorrect) but it would not be suitable to formal or conventional writing or public address. It conveys no impression of illiteracy, but it gives no assurance of a high command of the English tongue. It is to the dress of language very much what the sack or lounge suit is to the

average man. The common contractions *you'd, won't, we'll, they'd* (see page 484) are colloquial expressions. *Are you folks coming down t'night? Hold on a minute and I'll let you know* illustrate colloquial expression in speech. Colloquialisms are not used in written English except as direct report of conversation. When critics condemn a book for style that is too colloquial they mean that it is more informal than it should be for the dignity and authority of the printed page. The so-called modern idiom in which so many of the present-day novels are written illustrates perfectly the colloquialism that verges upon illiteracy.

7 *Connotation* means the associated or traditional or implied signification of a word or expression. Its antonym— *denotation*—means the actual or literal meaning or signification. The word *home* denotes a place to live, but connotes comfort, love, mother, father, brothers, sisters, pets, habituated behavior, and many other things. *House,* on the other hand, denotes merely a structure in which to live; it has practically no connotation, no associative values. Note this sentence: *Owing to the heavy fog the ship was required to move up the harbor and into her slip very slowly,* and now note this one: *The harbor was blanketed with a thick shaggy fog and the greyhound, after a record run across the Atlantic, was obliged to creep mincingly up the harbor, sullenly nosing its way zigzag among the silent islands, and sulking gingerly alongside.* The latter is connotative; the former merely denotative. The latter is enriched and colored by connotative diction; the former is just a cold and colorless statement of fact. Words are sometimes made associative thru the use of adjectives (see page 155): *the multitudinous crowd, a porcupine aggressiveness, a round table, The Round Table.* The first table is simply round in shape, and *round* is denotative. The second table doesn't have to be round at all; it associates itself immediately with King Arthur. But in *We held a round table on the question* the word *round* has taken unto itself another connotative meaning—a discussion, a symposium. Words, then, are sometimes used in one way and sometimes in another. *Tempo* is no longer confined in meaning to the time or beat of a poem or a song. You may speak of the tempo of an engine, the tempo of the proceedings of a meeting, the tempo of a person, and there are overtones in each case that distinguish the word in that particular connection. The cultivation of connotative lan-

guage is to be encouraged. It yields to expression, warmth
and individuality and distinction. It is the secret of much
successful advertising phraseology. Dramatize *It floats* a
little, and you see yourself no longer ridiculous as you
scramble around in the tub trying to locate the elusive piece
of soap. Ponder *His master's voice* for a moment, and if
you have ever known the loyalty and affection of a friend or
of a dog, or both, you will be a pretty cold, that is, a pretty
literal and "denotative" person, if you do not suffer just a
bit of heartbreak.

8 *Dialect* is a modification of some language spoken (and
perhaps but not always written) in a given district or community. It is quite different from the standard or literary
form of the language of which it is a part in both pronunciation and word usage. The Scottish dialect, for instance, is
somewhat similar to English in both spoken and written
forms, yet it is so different that it is difficult of comprehension to a stranger. *Hame* for home, *kebbuck* for a large
cheese, *lown* for quiet or sheltered, *dinna ken* for don't know,
to bear the gree for to carry off the prize, are so different
from English as to be unrecognizable, but these are Scottish
dialect terms and are therefore a part of the English language. The word *patois* means very much the same as
dialect, but it carries with it the connotation of illiteracy to
a degree. The languages spoken by the French and Italian
provinces, as also by the various shires of England, are more
properly called patois than dialect. The so-called southern
dialect in the United States is really a patois, if indeed it is
even that. More properly it consists of a certain clipping of
endings and a certain intonation of delivery rather than of
different terminology and phraseology.

9 *Differentia* and *genus* mean respectively, special difference
and general classification. They are important in the present
connection because they need to be borne in mind in defining
words. Care should be exercised in defining words to make
the definition itself the same part of speech as is the word
defined, and yet to use no form of the word defined in
the definition. This is easy with some words. *Glad* means
happy; both are adjectives. *Grief* means *sadness;* both are
nouns. *Tease* means *vex;* both are verbs. But the case is
different with words like *chair* and *desk*. In defining these
it is necessary first to give the class or *genus* to which the

word belongs, and from this point to proceed with the special difference or *differentia*. A chair is a piece of furniture (genus) on which to sit (differentia). A desk is a piece of furniture (genus) at which to write or read (differentia). Do not begin a definition with the word *where* or *when* unless it actually belongs to the definition itself. *Aviation* is not to be defined as *when you fly thru space in an airplane,* nor is a *hangar where airplanes are kept.* Aviation is the art and science (genus) of locomotion by means of airplanes (differentia). A hangar is a shed (genus) for the shelter of vehicles, especially airplanes (differentia).

10 *Generic* words are class or general words; *specific* words are individual or special words. You may frequently be taken to task for not being specific in your choice of words, for speaking or writing in terms that are so general as to permit of more than one interpretation. Do not say *I want something to cut this cloth with;* say, rather, *I want the scissors.* Do not say that a story is *good* when you mean that it is amusing, exciting, stirring, interesting, or entertaining. There are degrees of generalizing and specializing in your use of words. Run the gamut of words from *structure* to *hovel,* and some such series as this may be built: *structure, building, house, cottage, shack, hovel.* In relation to *house, cottage* is specific; in relation to *cottage, house* is generic. Herbert Spencer in his essay *The Philosophy of Style* used these two sentences to show how much better specific language is than generic: *When the manners, customs, and amusements of a nation are cruel and barbarous, the regulations of their penal code will be severe,* and *When men delight in battles, bull-fights, and combats of gladiators, they will punish by hanging, burning, and the rack.*

11 *Heteronyms* are words that are exactly the same in spelling but different in pronunciation and meaning: *lead* (leed), *lead* (led); *wind* (wĭnd), *wind* (wined).

12 *Hackneyed* or *stereotyped* words and expressions are such as have become trite and outworn thru overuse. They are sometimes colloquially called bromides (see Gellett Burgess' *Are You a Bromide?*) Such terms have lost their real meaning and are used automatically—and lazily—by those whose vocabularies are limited and conventional to a high degree.

Those asterisked are peculiar to business letter writing:
*a consummation devoutly to be wished, a feast of reason
and a flow of soul, a reply in the negative, a wonderfully
salubrious community, along these lines*, an unapproach-
able Hibernian, and oblige*, anticipating your order by
return mail*, appallingly tragic, assuming this will meet
with your entire satisfaction*, assuring you of our best
attentions*, attached hereto*, awaiting your further orders*,
bated breath, beard the lion, beg to remain*, blood will tell,
briny deep, brown as a berry, busy as a bee, Caledonian
parsimony, checkered career, clear as crystal, contents of
yours duly noted*, conspicuous by your absence, dead as a
doornail, deem it advisable, demon rum, diamond in the
rough, downy couch, drown your sorrows, enclosed herewith*, enclosed please find*, encounter a miscreant, entering
the portals of the institution of learning, envisage a catas-
trophe, esteemed favor at hand*, extraordinary variety of
merchandise*, eyes like stars, foul play, filthy lucre, fine and
dandy, flowing bowl, Gallic gallantry, glass of fashion,
golden hair, green as grass, green with jealousy, heartless
wretch, heated argument, his better half, his initial endeavor,
hope springs eternal, hoping this meets with your approval*,
I take pleasure in informing*, ignorance is bliss, in close
proximity to, in compliance with yours*, in concluding let
me say*, incumbent upon me, indescribable odor, in our
midst, in regard to the*, in reply would say*, in such eventu-
ality*, in the last analysis*, in the month of June*, just a
moment, last but not least, let me call your attention to*,
light fantastic toe, may I be permitted to interest you in?*,
method in his madness, motley crew, no effort will be spared,
no sooner said than done, palatial abode, partake of refresh-
ment, pearls before swine, permit us to advise*, please use
the enclosed card at once*, pleased to meet you, psychological moment, pursuant to yours of even date*, raven
locks, regarding your communication*, regretting the oversight and the inconvenience thus entailed*, replying to your
favor*, rich as Crœsus, sadder but wiser, silver hair, single
blessedness, sleep the sleep of the just, snare and delusion,
somewhat unique, staff of life, straight and narrow, teaching
the young idea, teeth like pearls, tender mercies, termino-
logical inexactitude, thanking you in advance for your
order*, the Celestial Empire, the cup that cheers but does
not inebriate, to refresh the inner man, the fair sex, the
Indian weed, the iron horse, the parting of the ways, the*

horns of a dilemma, the weaker sex, there's the rub, to depict the ensuing scene, to evince perturbation, to take up an abode, to offend the olfactory organ, too numerous to mention, too full for utterance, too funny for words, trusting this will be satisfactory*, under other cover you are receiving*, unprintable vituperation, utterly incomprehensible, vast multitude, view with alarm, wake up—Spring's here, we are pleased to inform you*, we beg to inform you*, we beg to say*, we take pleasure*, we would advise*, we would state*, wee small hours, with all due consideration*, worse for wear, you are losing money*, your further communications are awaited*, your message of recent date*, your valued order is duly appreciated*, yours of recent date at hand*, yours of 15 inst. has come to hand*, young hopefuls.

It is sometimes said that the very atmosphere of a business office superinduces hackneyed expression. So long has the latter been emanating from the former that one just naturally "takes on the tongue" as soon as he enters or even thinks of an office. This may be true. We whisper at a funeral; we yell in appropriate parlance at a football game; we sing in the bathtub. So we probably "go hackneyed" in the business office.

Gerald received at his office a letter from his mother inquiring about his child, her grandchild, who had been ill. Almost before he knew it he had dictated and mailed the following letter to her!

Dear Madam:

Yours of the fifteenth inst. received and contents duly noted. In reply beg to state that I thank you for same. Confirming my communication of some little time ago, take pleasure in informing you that the party subject to your inquiry leaves nothing to be desired by way of health and apparent happiness. Will inform you in due course, in the event of any change to the contrary. At present writing would say that no such problem now confronts us in the situation. As per doctor's orders physical examinations are made weekly. Rest assured that you will be notified at our earliest convenience in case any unforeseen emergency arises. Trusting I have furnished the desired information to your entire satisfaction, and again thanking you for your very kind thought and consideration, beg to remain with all good wishes

Your loving son,

GERALD

13 *Homographs* are words that are spelled and pronounced alike but that are different in meaning and derivation: *base* as foundation and as vile; *bear* as an animal and as carry; *fair* as exposition and as blonde.

14 *Homonyms* are words that are alike in pronunciation but different in meaning and use, and also, as a rule, in spelling: *aisle, isle; all, awl; bail, bale; base, bass; bier, beer; build, billed; cell, sell; choir, quire; coarse, course, corse; dear, deer; earn, urn; fair, fare; flue, flew; gaol, jail; great, grate; hart, heart; heal, heel; here, hear; idol, idle, idyll; knot, not; loan, lone; manner, manor; new, knew; or, ore, o'er; prier, prior; principal, principle; right, rite, wright, write; sent, scent, cent; stationary, stationery; threw, through; vale, vail, veil; wait, weight; yew, you.*

15 *Idioms* are expressions that have become crystallized in certain arbitrary forms that very often defy precise grammatical construction. They are peculiar to their language in both form and meaning. The irregularities of idiomatic constructions and meanings are generally accepted without demur inasmuch as idioms denote language characteristic and habit, and carry with them the authority of popular approval. Some one has called idioms frozen language. They are to speech and writing very much what the buttons on a man's coatsleeve are. Here are a few commonly used idioms in English: *in a bad way, nip and tuck, up and doing, to set eyes on, to put on side, hard and fast, pros and cons, fits and starts, to put up with, at loggerheads, ups and downs, to bring about, to fall into line, to go hard with, might and main, caps the climax, to break the ice, to set a trap for, in the same boat, to mince matters, by hook or crook, two of a kind, to have a mind to, to stand to reason, hammer and tongs, riding a high horse, to stick to one's guns, to be on the wrong tack, to set people by the ears, letting well enough alone, straight from the shoulder, to stand in one's own light, to have cards up the sleeve, to let the cat out of the bag, bearding the lion in his den, to carry coals to Newcastle, to strike while the iron's hot, to take the bull by the horns, put your shoulder to the wheel, to make a bee line, the fat's in the fire, to beg the question, with a grain of salt, to get into hot water, to put your foot in it, to play second fiddle, more haste less speed, to get the lion's share, to have a bone to pick, to throw up the sponge, to keep a*

stiff upper lip, the cart before the horse, to sail under false colors, too many irons in the fire, to have one's head turned, it never rains but it pours, a stitch in time saves nine, least said soonest mended, a square peg in a round hole, to act like a dog in a manger, to steal a march on some one, penny wise and pound foolish, to put your best foot forward, to keep the wolf from the door, a rolling stone gathers no moss, to get out of the wrong side of the bed, birds of a feather flock together, actions speak louder than words, people living in glass houses must not throw stones, to give some one the cold shoulder, there are plenty of fish in the sea, to cut off your nose to spite your face.

In the following paragraph the thoughts are all expressed thru the medium of idioms. The combination in many cases causes badly mixed metaphors (see page 91), a danger that excessive use of idiom can hardly escape. This paragraph may be regarded as an exaggerated case, but it is exaggeration only of the truth. In country districts very often people are almost entirely dependent upon the end-to-end expression of idioms for the conveyance of thought.

> Tho he was up in arms against his kith and kin they kept him at bay. He stood his ground thru thick and thin, and eventually obliged them to eat humble pie. Tho on the brink of rack and ruin as result of his working at cross purposes with his own flesh and blood, he nevertheless by hook and crook won them over, poured oil on the troubled waters, and obliged them to show the white feather. It had been war to the knife at first, and hitting below the belt was the order of the day. But by and large all parties concerned decided to turn over a new leaf, bury the hatchet, consider half a loaf better than none, call it a day, and let well enough alone. So all's well that ends well, especially after too many cooks have spoiled the broth by making a mountain out of a molehill. Next time he says he will let sleeping dogs lie instead of trying to bring them down in the world, for he has learned that those people who cross bridges ·before they come to them usually jump out of the frying pan into the fire

16 *Impropriety* is a violation of good use by way of employing a perfectly good English word in a wrong relationship. Mrs. Malaprop in Richard Brinsley Sheridan's *The Rivals* was a "past mistress" in the "doubtful art" of impropriety: *You lead and I'll precede you, An allegory on the Nile, contiguous* for *contagious, infer* for *imply, effect* for *affect, illusion* for *allusion* (see page 618). If dear Mrs. Malaprop had ever fallen upon unprovided days and had been obliged

to enter trade (O dare me!) her first letter of application for a position at some eighteenth-century Selfridge's might have run as follows:

Dear Kind Sirs:

Since perceiving the mourning papers wherein I witnessed your divertissements, I have been perpetrating supplication for an imposition in your compartment storage.

I am a woman who has always locomoted in the most conclusive social cycles, but am now subjugated to concenter upon a business veneer, owing to the uncontrollable commotions of my insatiable niece.

If you will give me some perpendiculars in regard to your offering, I shall be gratuitous to you. I hope you will use all your affluence to help me make your preposition a success.

Trusting that I shall not have any antistrophe in my new inhibitions, suspecting an early and obligating reply to this implication, and wishing you a happy and preposterous New Year, I beg to be committed by this signatory,

Duly yours,

CATHERINE MALAPROP

17 *Localism* or *provincialism* is a word or expression—an idiom or other peculiar form of language—that is characteristic of the talking (and writing) of the people of a certain region or community. (In addition to this the word *provincialism* may mean bigotry or narrowmindedness.) *I calculate, turn out the coffee, red up the room, you-all, right smart, done gone, quite some.* The first three of these illustrative localisms are said to belong to New England; the remaining four to the South and the West. The Britisher may regard the United States *baggage, conductor, druggist, editorial, elevator, headline, oatmeal, overcoat, shoe, street car, suspenders* provincialisms for (respectively) his own *luggage, guard, chemist, leader, lift, topline, porridge, great coat, boot, tram, braces.* The terms localism and provincialism are geographically elastic.

18 *Pomposity* in diction means the use of large words when small ones will express thought better, and the use of many words and of high-sounding phraseology when simpler and less pretentious language will be more intelligible and in better taste. The clown Costard in *Love's Labour's Lost* (V, i, 44) refers to such diction as the almsbasket of words, and then invents a term himself that supposedly "outwords" all of the attendants at the "great feast of languages." His word is *honorificabilitudinitatibus.* But there is many a

Costard today who apparently must say *in the month of December* for *in December, governmental domicile* for *state capitol, electrical pyrotechnic phenomenon* for *thunder and lightning,* and *With herculean exertion he summoned the entirety of his colossal muscular capability and ejected the stupendously presumptuous mendicant from the entrance of his otherwise tranquil abode* for *He threw the tramp out.* Never use a big word when a little one will do just as well or better. Never use many words when a few will do just as well or better.

19 *Slang* was originally the name given to the stock phrases of thieves and beggars, but it is now applied to any unauthorized flippancy of speech and to any grotesque or arbitrary misuse of a good word or expression. There are degrees of slang. A little of it persists and ultimately finds acceptance in the language. The word *mob,* for instance, was once the worst of slang. But most of it is used and lives for but a day. Some of it survives as a low and vulgar form of expression for a long time. Shakespeare used *pickers and stealers* as a slang term in *Henry Fifth.* The term is still slang used by the present-day underworld to mean deft finger work in carrying out theft. Twenty years ago *twenty-three* and *skidoo* were "all the rage"; they meant go away or get out. Today they are heard no more. The expression *take it from me,* while in no sense a particularly literary term, is nevertheless to be found in good word company today. Slang should never be used unless its user can artfully imply that he has its better equivalent in reserve, that is, unless he can give the impression that he knows its literary equivalent but is just using slang to give "kick and color" to his language temporarily. For some slang does just this, and it is not therefore to be entirely despised. It is often forcible and picturesque, but as steady company it is to be avoided. It will invariably impoverish expression if used to excess. Slang terms are usually generic, a single one being required as a rule to serve many expressional purposes and occasions. Rarely is it specific or connotative in the truest and best sense, as these few examples abundantly prove: *and how, applesauce, babe, bat, biff, blah, blind date, bloke, bologney, breezy, bust, can it, chew the rag, chin music, come back, cop, crab, cram, dirt cheap, do your stuff, everything's jake, exam, fall for you, fizzle, flapper, flivver, flunk, for crying out loud, gee, get a horse,*

*get by, get me, gin mill, give him the air, give him the
works, glad rags, gold digger, hash house, have a heart, hire
a hall, hit it off, hooey, jazz, jinx, joint, josh, junk, kick,
let George do it, monicker, mug, never again, nit wit, nut,
oh yeah, once over, on your way, pussyfoot, quit your
kiddin', raspberries, rats, rotten, says you, shoot, speakeasy,
step on it, stick around, stunt, tell the world, the cat's eyebrows, tux, washout, willies, what-a dump, what do you
know, where do I get off, whoopee, woozy, wow, zip.*

Slang may be special or technical, that is, the word *slang* is
used to indicate the speech of a special group or class.
Every trade and profession has its own slang which is
"Greek" to the layman. A young lady visiting a man-of-war
once upon a time asked a "gob" where she could get a drink
of water. He replied: "Down thar at the scuttlebutt, on the
starboard side of the gundeck, 'midships, just forrud of the
dynamo hatch." Printing slang, baseball slang, theater slang,
and so forth, must not be confused with technical English
terms in these fields. *Devil* and *hellbox* are printer's
slang, but *galley* and *pi* are technical terms belonging to
printing; *muffed* and *southpaw* are baseball slang, but *steal-
ing a base* and *home run* are technical terms belonging to
baseball; *ham* and *upstage* are theatrical slang; *opening cold*
and *dark house* are technical terms belonging to the theater.

The following paragraph is a slang version of the idiom
paragraph above. The author of this little "masterpiece"
has apparently leaned backward in his effort to avoid being
accused of pedantry and purism. His effort was realized,
and to the full (or, as he would probably say, "And how!")

Say, Kid, listen: Dey got me goin, see, and I'm on me uppers.
They gotto go some, tho, fer I'm standin pat and makin em
look like dirty cents, yunderstan? De homehounds done me in
cause I doublecrossed em. Now dey go softy and try to pansy
me. Wot dey tink I am fer g'sake! But rates to dat stuff, sez I.
I shoot de woiks, and are dey a washout! Boy I'm tellin ye!
Such a bunch of bologney throwers ye never seen since Hector
was a pup! Dese mugs, why dey're the maltese's eyebrows! I
stepped on em fer a fifty-gran finally, and did dey cry out loud?
Baby, esk me anudder! I done my stuff double time, give em
de hotcha, and let em know where dey got off. And you outa
seen em scram! Next time mebbe dey'll ferget it before dey
start de whoopee wid me—and how! When I tell em to can it
dey'll can-can—and like it! And dat's no pow-wow from your
Uncle Elmer, eider. If any dingbat or sob-sister wantsa gimme

a belly guffaw, you tell em to stick aroun till the racket gits goin and I'll hand out de butterscotch till everyting's jake. See? Uh-uh?

20 *Solecism* is, strictly, a violation of grammatical relationships. The term is, however, applied to any slip in expression, whether that slip pertains to a single word or to an entire sentence. Any word, phrase, clause, or sentence that violates standard usage is now called a solecism. *Has everybody got their coats?* There are three solecisms in this interrogation. It should read *Has everybody his coat? It is me* for *It is I, Who did you see* for *Whom did you see, He gave the prize to we girls* for *He gave the prize to us girls* are solecisms (see page 166).

21 A slip of the tongue may often cause the transposition or transference of the initial letters of two closely related words or syllables. Rapid utterance is often the cause of it. Such error has come to be called a *spoonerism*, after Dr. William Archibald Spooner, a noted scholar of Oxford University. That Doctor Spooner was excessively given to "the accidental transposition of initial letters" (this is the New Oxford Dictionary definition of *spoonerism*) has been contradicted, but it is authoritatively affirmed that he did commit at least one spoonerism in his time, and this a serious one. He was a preacher as well as a professor. It is said that in 1879 he announced a hymn one Sunday morning from his pulpit the title of which he gave as *Kinkering Kongs Their Titles Take*. There was a respectful silence. Then he again announced the title, as before. Then there was laughter in the congregation, and Doctor Spooner, realizing at last what he had said, announced the title correctly as *Conquering Kings Their Titles Take*. This is said to be the one and only time on which he made such a slip, but the legend persists that he was from time to time guilty of all of those below.

Somewhat akin to spoonerism is *metathesis*, the transposition or transference of letters in a word, consciously for the sake of humor, or unconsciously as result of rapid speaking or illiteracy. *Haps* for *hasp, waps* for *wasp, modren* for *modern, childern* for *children, ossifer* for *officer, ephilant* for *elephant* illustrate. The following are spoonerisms. Read them correctly.

It is kistomary to cuss the bride
I'm going to the city by the town drain
I have found such a nice nosey little cook
Young man, you have been hissing my mystery lectures!
Three cheers for our queer old dean
My boy, you have tasted a whole worm!
I simply wanted to inquire whether the bean is dizzy?
It is easier for a camel to pass through the knee of an idol
The poor man has just received a blushing crow
For real enjoyment give me a well-boiled icycle
Somebody else is occupewing my pie
I will sew you into another sheet
Have you ever nursed in your bosoms a half warmed fish?
I shall speak to you of the shoving leopard of biblical story
We went down to Portsmouth to see the cattleships and bruisers
"I have two children, Steak and Kidney," said the fond parent
who had taken his offspring to be christened

22 *Standard usage* means that use of words and their relations
in sentences that is approved and therefore followed by the
most thoughtful speakers and writers the country over at
present.   Those who take the liberal view in regard to usage
will not accept this definition of standard usage.   They
would hasten evolution of language by admitting into it
terms and usages that are not yet ripe for adoption.   Those
who hold to the conservative view of usage would deny
adoption to terms and usages that have long since been
sanctioned by the most thoughtful writers and speakers.
The former would admit *It is me* here and now.   The latter
would insist that the noun-clause expletive never be omitted:
He said that he would go, not *He said he would go.*   There
is a better middle ground so inimitably pointed out by
Alexander Pope:

> In words, as fashions, the same rule will hold,
> Alike fantastic if too new or old;
> Be not the first by whom the new are tried,
> Nor yet the last to lay the old aside.

If Pope and Milton and Shakespeare were of this time and
place, and were all speaking tonight from the same platform,
their language would represent standard usage.   Not one of
them, probably, would say *He don't care,* but all of them
might say *He said he would go, which was satisfactory to us*
(see page 172).

23 *Synonyms* are words that have similar but not identical
meanings.   Lord Chesterfield long ago said that those who
study a language attentively soon find that there is no such

thing as a word that has exactly the same meaning as
another word. Yet synonyms are usually spoken of as
words having the same meaning. Language tends, as it
evolves, to become more and more discriminating, that is,
less and less confusing. As people become educated they
use words with greater nicety and distinction of meaning,
until what is commonly accepted as synonymous with something else is really not so at all. *Commence,* for instance,
is not so colloquial as *begin* or *start,* and the best speakers
and writers do not follow it with an infinitive. *Shall* and
will, innocent and *harmless, grasp* and *apprehend, courage*
and *bravery, infer* and *imply* are but a few of the numerous
pairs of words that the undiscriminating will treat as
synonyms, and their speech and writing will be accordingly
blunted and dull. A knowledge of near-synonyms is imperative if a writer and speaker would avoid monotony in his
expression, and the dictionary may be relied upon to supply
him wide choice in diction. The words *fix, nice, say,* and
terrible are said to be the most overused ones in our language. *Fix* has no fewer than twenty near-synonyms; *nice,*
fifteen; *say,* twenty-one; *terrible,* thirteen, in both pure and
colloquial uses. It is quite unnecessary, then, for any one
to use any of these ad nauseam. On the other hand, the use
of near-synonyms just for the sake of avoiding repetition
may lead not only to confusion or vagueness but also to a
kind of affectation. It evinces no poverty in expressional
ability to express the same ideas by the same words. To
say *They placed three men on the drive, stationed two on
the porch, allocated two to the rear entrance, and located one
at the lower end of the lawn* is to go too far in the cause of
variety.

24 *Technical* English is English that is made up of highly
specialized diction and idiom that belong exclusively to some
department of learning or activity. Used in general discourse it is incomprehensible, and its terms are then
classified as barbarisms. But used in special discourse for
a group of people who are trained in the special art or
science involved and in its language, technical expression is
not only allowable but preferable.

The mathematician may say this to a group of mathema-
ticians: *An ordinate in coordinate geometry is the distance
of any point from the axis of abscissas, measured on a line*

parallel to the axis of ordinates. To a group of laymen he will probably have to use both simpler language and a diagram to make his exposition clear. HF and BC are ordinates to H, i.e., in regular vertical parallels to it. HB and FC are abscissas to H, i.e., in regular horizontal parallels to it. AD is the axis of the ordinates. EG is the axis of the abscissas.

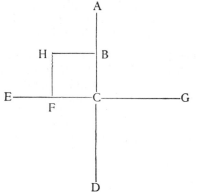

25 A *vulgarism* is a word or phrase or sentence that is offensive to good taste and to literary usage. Slang, impropriety, barbarism, solecism, reduced to their lowest terms are vulgarisms. One of the commonest vulgarisms in English is the word *ain't.* Others are *enthuse, should of, yrs., lousy, for God's sake* and other blasphemous phrases.

26 The term *wordiness* is frequently used to indicate extravagance in diction—the tendency to use many more words than are necessary in expressing one's self. Other terms are sometimes used to denote the same thing. *Circumlocution* is indirect or roundabout expression. *Diffuseness* is scattered or harum-scarum expression that denotes confused thinking. *Prolixity* is the introduction of endless petty details that do not logically relate to the subject in hand. *Pleonasm* is using more words than are required, but it may make for emphasis, as *I saw it with my own eyes.* *Tautology* is useless and, as a rule, ignorant repetition, as *They all unanimously agreed. Redundance* or *redundancy* means overflow or excess of words. *Verbiage* is the use of words for their own sake, without thought. *Verbosity* is excess of words in proportion to thought. The terms themselves are

not important inasmuch as they are used generally to indicate wordiness of one sort or another and have lost whatever niceties of meaning they once had. *Wordiness* covers them all. Their antonyms deserve the greater emphasis in any study of speaking and writing—*brevity, compactness, conciseness, condensation, directness, succinctness, terseness.* Pomposity (see above) results very often from wordiness. Humorous or nonsensical word-play may be based upon it, as in Act I, Scene i of *Julius Cæsar;* Act I, Scene ii in *The Merchant of Venice;* Act II, Scene ii in *Hamlet.*

J   According to Dr. Frank H. Vizetelly, editor of *The Practical Standard Dictionary of the English Language,* there are 700,000 reputable words in the English language. The average reader has a command, it is estimated, of 25,000 words, and the kindergarten child knows from 2000 to 3000 words. But Professor C. K. Ogden of Magdalene College, Cambridge University, England, contends that a mere 850 words can be made to satisfy all ordinary speaking and writing demands, and thus extravagance of diction as well as pomposity may easily be obviated. It would be worth while to try "translating" one of your compositions in the words listed below. To do it satisfactorily you should consult one of Mr. Ogden's books * in order to supplement the list of words with a knowledge of the rest of the system, for the word list cannot be used to advantage unless you follow the rules and explanations accompanying it. Basic English is above all a *system* of English, not merely a vocabulary.

Most English verbs are luxuries. We can get along without them. Thousands of them can be replaced by simpler verb forms, or operations, aided by adverbs, prepositions, and nouns, including among the nouns the names of operations, or the noun forms of the banished verbs. For example, *to accelerate* is to *go* more quickly, and *to climb* is to *go* up. *To break the law* is to *go* against the law. *To fall* is to *go* down suddenly. Here are four verbs—*accelerate, climb, break,* and *fall*—that may be discarded.

Thus thru long and painstaking tests the experts have weeded out the superfluous verbs until only eighteen verb forms are left blooming alone—and some of the eighteen are retained

---

* Notably *The System of Basic English* (Harcourt, Brace, and Company, 1933). The following seven paragraphs and the word list on page 616 are used by permission of *The New York Times* and of Miss Charlotte Tyler, American representative of Professor Ogden and the Orthological Institute, of 10 Kings' Parade, Cambridge, England

merely to act as convenient assistants to the others. The essential verbs in English are found to be *be, come, do, get, give, go, have, keep, let, make, may, put, say, see, seem, send, take, will*. Properly employed, they can be made to do the work of all the rest of the verbs in the fattest of dictionaries.

Nouns necessary to a clear understanding number 400, adjectives 100, and verbs and verb-helping words 100. To these are added 200 names of picturesque objects, such as *pencil* and *cart*, and fifty adjectival opposites, such as *narrow* and *slow*. With these the list of 850 is complete. This small vocabulary is equal to more than 20,000 words in actual practise and covers the ground of 5000 words in any attempt ever before made at simplification.

Fifty words of general utility that are understood everywhere, words like *hotel, madam, police, sir, telegram, theater, volt*, extend the basic list. Titles such as *president* and *prince*, the names of the sciences, the numerals, geographical names, and words pertaining to measurement and currency are already in international use and are not included in the 850. World scientists in convention who use the basic 850 plus 100 general scientific terms and 50 more words for any given science, can understand one another without difficulty. With 1000 words any field of knowledge is completely covered. In science, as in commerce and travel, the thing desired is clear sense, not style.

This new English is essentially a noun language, and English nouns are, with rare exceptions, regular in all their cases and in their plurals, and are not as a rule cursed with gender. Only the simplest instructions are needed for forming plurals and possessives, for indicating comparative and superlative degrees of adjectives, for using certain adjectives as nouns, for making adverbs in *ly* from adjectives, for reversing the meaning of the adjective with the prefix *un*, and so forth. An easy rule teaches how to manufacture derivatives from the noun form; how the noun *talk*, for instance, can be made to yield the nouns *talker* and *talking* and the adjectives *talking* and *talked*. The 850-word vocabulary, like a beef-tea cube, is a concentration of much in little.

Students in most foreign countries should be able to master the language in a very short time—often as little as a month or two—giving a few hours a day to it. Half the time they will devote to the words themselves, comparing them with equivalent expressions in their own tongue. The other half they will spend in learning word order and how the words work, and the 260 necessary special uses which make possible the effect of ordinary and familiar usage.

The English thus learned and put into practise sounds like normal English to any one who hears or reads it. Better still, it is discovered to have new qualities of value. Pieces of literature, such as Poe's story *The Gold Bug,* when put into Basic English, are strengthened and vivified. Letters and compositions written in Basic English by foreigners are found to contain unexpected beauty and clarity of phrase.

THE BASIC ENGLISH VOCABULARY
The 850 Words That Make an International Language

OPERA-TIONS ETC. 100	400 General				200 Picturable		100 General	
come	account	butter	decision	fiction	angle	cart	able	hard
get	act	canvas	degree	field	ant	carriage	acid	healthy
give	addition	care	design	fight	apple	cat	angry	high
go	adjustment	cause	desire	fire	arch	chain	automatic	hollow
keep	advertisement	chalk	destruction	flame	arm	cheese	beautiful	important
let	agreement	chance	detail	flight	army	chest	black	kind
make	air	change	development	flower	baby	chin	boiling	like
put	amount	cloth	digestion	fold	bag	church	bright	living
seem	amusement	coal	direction	food	ball	circle	broken	long
take	animal	colour	discovery	force	band	clock	brown	male
be	answer	comfort	discussion	form	basin	cloud	cheap	married
do	apparatus	committee	disease	friend	basket	coat	chief	material
have	approval	company	disgust	front	bath	collar	chemical	medical
say	argument	comparison	distance	fruit	bed	comb	clean	military
see	art	competition	distribution	glass	bee	cord	clear	natural
send	attack	condition	division	gold	bell	cow	common	necessary
may	attempt	connection	doubt	government	berry	cup	complex	new
will	attention	control	drink	grain	bird	curtain	conscious	normal
about	attraction	cook	driving	grass	blade	cushion	cut	open
across	authority	copper	dust	grip	board	dog	deep	parallel
after	back	copy	earth	group	boat	door	dependent	past
against	balance	cork	edge	growth	bone	drain	early	physical
among	base	cotton	education	guide	book	drawer	elastic	political
at	behaviour	cough	effect	harbour	boot	dress	electric	poor
before	belief	country	end	harmony	bottle	drop	equal	possible
between	birth	cover	error	hate	box	ear	fat	present
by	bit	crack	event	hearing	boy	egg	fertile	private
down	bite	credit	example	heat	brain	engine	first	probable
from	blood	crime	exchange	help	brake	eye	fixed	quick
in	blow	crush	existence	history	branch	face	flat	quiet
off	body	cry	expansion	hole	brick	farm	free	ready
on	brass	current	experience	hope	bridge	feather	frequent	red
over	bread	curve	expert	hour	brush	finger	full	regular
through	breath	damage	fact	humour	bucket	fish	general	responsible
to	brother	danger	fall	ice	bulb	flag	good	right
under	building	daughter	family	idea	button	floor	great	round
up	burn	day	father	impulse	cake	fly	grey	same
with	burst	death	fear	increase	camera	foot	hanging	second
as	business	debt	feeling	ink	card	fork	happy	separate

THE BASIC ENGLISH VOCABULARY—*Continued*

OPERA-TIONS ETC. 100	THINGS 400 General				THINGS 200 Picturable		QUALITIES 100 General	
for	insect	need	request	stop	fowl	pump	serious	tight
of	instrument	news	respect	story	frame	rail	sharp	tired
till	insurance	night	rest	stretch	garden	rat	smooth	true
than	industry	noise	reward	structure	girl	receipt	sticky	violent
a	interest	note	rhythm	substance	glove	ring	stiff	waiting
the	invention	number	rice	sugar	goat	rod	straight	warm
all	iron	observation	river	suggestion	gun	roof	strong	wet
any	jelly	offer	road	summer	hair	root	sudden	wide
every	join	oil	roll	support	hammer	sail	sweet	wise
no	journey	operation	room	surprise	hand	school	tall	yellow
other	judge	opinion	rub	swim	hat	scissors	thick	young
some	jump	order	rule	system	head	screw		
such	kick	organization	run	talk	heart	seed	50 Opposites	
that	kiss	ornament	salt	taste	hook	sheep	awake	left
this	knowledge	owner	sand	tax	horn	shelf	bad	loose
I	land	page	scale	teaching	horse	ship	bent	loud
he	language	pain	science	tendency	hospital	shirt	bitter	low
you	laugh	paint	sea	test	house	shoe	blue	mixed
who	law	paper	seat	theory	island	skin	certain	narrow
and	lead	part	secretary	thing	jewel	skirt	cold	old
because	learning	paste	selection	thought	kettle	snake	complete	opposite
but	leather	payment	self	thunder	key	sock	cruel	public
or	letter	peace	sense	time	knee	spade	dark	rough
if	level	person	servant	tin	knife	sponge	dead	sad
though	lift	place	sex	top	knot	spoon	dear	safe
while	light	plant	shade	touch	leaf	spring	delicate	secret
how	limit	play	shake	trade	leg	square	different	short
when	linen	pleasure	shame	transport	library	stamp	dirty	shut
where	liquid	point	shock	trick	line	star	dry	simple
why	list	poison	side	trouble	lip	station	false	slow
again	look	polish	sign	turn	lock	stem	feeble	small
ever	loss	porter	silk	twist	map	stick	female	soft
far	love	position	silver	unit	match	stocking	foolish	solid
forward	machine	powder	sister	use	monkey	stomach	future	special
here	man	power	size	value	moon	store	green	strange
near	manager	price	sky	verse	mouth	street	ill	thin
now	mark	print	sleep	vessel	muscle	sun	last	white
out	market	process	slip	view	nail	table	late	wrong
still	mass	produce	slope	voice	neck	tail		
then	meal	profit	smash	walk	needle	thread		
there	measure	property	smell	war	nerve	throat		
together	meat	prose	smile	wash	net	thumb		
well	meeting	protest	smoke	waste	nose	ticket		
almost	memory	pull	sneeze	water	nut	toe		
enough	metal	punishment	snow	wave	office	tongue		
even	middle	purpose	soap	wax	orange	tooth	*It is possible*	
little	milk	push	society	way	oven	town	*to get all*	
much	mind	quality	son	weather	parcel	train	*the words*	
not	mine	question	song	week	pen	tray	*that make up*	
only	minute	rain	sort	weight	pencil	tree	*Basic English*	
quite	mist	range	sound	wind	picture	trousers	*on the back*	
so	money	rate	soup	wine	pig	umbrella	*of a bit*	
very	month	ray	space	winter	pin	wall	*of note paper*	
tomorrow	morning	reaction	stage	woman	pipe	watch		
yesterday	mother	reading	start	wood	plane	wheel		
north	motion	reason	statement	wool	plate	whip		
south	mountain	record	steam	word	plough	whistle		
east	move	regret	steel	work	pocket	window		
west	music	relation	step	wound	pot	wing		
please	name	religion	stitch	writing	potato	wire		
yes	nation	representative	stone	year	prison	worm		

K Correct word usage—nice word usage—means that you know exactly which or two or more near-synonyms to choose when you speak and write. Here is a little lexicon of correct word usage. It will meet most everyday dictional needs.*

a—(1) Do not use before vowel sounds
(2) Use sparingly before *one* merely for the sake of emphasis
(3) Do not use after *sort of, kind of, type of, form of,* and similar expressions indicating class or distinction
(4) Use rarely after *such* when that word modifies an abstract noun followed by *as* or *that: Such a generosity* is wrong
(1) The men joined a union
(2) Not one of us arrived in time
(3) What manner of man art thou?
(4) I never experienced such discourtesy as that

ability—Power to accomplish (see *capacity*)
He has ability to do the work

about—(1) As an adverb, *about* means *around*
(2) As a preposition, *about* means *approximate* or *in the neighborhood of* (see *around*)
(3) Do not use after *discuss*
(1) He strolled about, taking in the sights
(2) He told me about the letter he had received
(3) We discussed the subject until about midnight

abrogate—To abolish or annul (see *arrogate*)

accept—To take something frankly and willingly (see *except*)
I accept your invitation heartily

adapt—To adjust oneself to; to suit oneself to a duty or an environment (Do not confuse with *adept*)

addition—Something that is added (Do not confuse with *edition*)

adept—Skilful or proficient; one who is able (Don't confuse with *adapt*)

admission—The right of admittance. He was denied admission to membership in our club

admittance—The act of allowing to enter. He gained admittance to the theater after paying an exorbitant price for a ticket

adverse—Opposed or opposing or antagonistic or opposite. Accented on the first syllable. Customarily used of things and circumstances. Do not confuse with *averse*
Correct: *He was discouraged by adverse criticism of his work*

advice—A noun, meaning counsel or suggestion. We gave him some sound advice about letter writing

advise—A verb, meaning to give counsel or guidance or suggestion. It is frequently wrongly used in the sense of conveying information. We advise you to look carefully after the placement of your letters

affect—(1) A verb, meaning to move or influence
(2) A verb, meaning to feign or pretend (see *effect*)
(1) The news in the papers will affect the stock market

---

* See *Don't Say It* by the same author, published by Funk and Wagnalls Company, for extended alphabetical treatment of word and phrase usage

(2) They will, of course, affect not to understand his derogatory remarks

aggravate—To increase adversely, to make worse. Do not use for *exasperate*. Their enmity in sport will aggravate their estrangement in business

all—Refers, as a rule, to totality of number (see *whole*)
You have used all the sugar in the jar

all right—Do not spell as one word with one *l*. Almost all of the wheat is already stored away, and the granaries are found to be all right

allow—Not to hinder (see *permit*). Please allow me to pass

allusion—A reference or suggestion made more or less indirectly (see *illusion*)

almost—An adverb, meaning *not quite* or *less than* or *very nearly all* (see *most* and *mostly*)
My work is almost done. (See sentence under *all right*)

alone—Solitary; without others (see *only*)
In scholarly achievement this man stands alone

alongside—By the side of; close to; near to. Do not use *of* after this word. The ship came alongside the pier, and the passengers disembarked

altar—Any raised place or structure for burning incense or for worship. (Do not confuse with *alter*)

alter—To change or modify or cause to be different. (Do not confuse with *altar*)

alternative—Refers to two only (see *choice*)
The alternative of surrender is death

amateur—One who engages in an art or a sport, not professionally, but for the love of it, for the pleasure it affords, and for training in skill and experience (see *novice*). His painting reveals him to be an amateur in the art

among—Refers to three or more (see *between*)
Among the works on exhibition, I like this best

amount—Refers to quantity. Not used, as a rule, to refer to number. He carried a large amount of money in his outer pocket. A large number of people attended the concert

an—(1) Do not use before consonant sounds
(2), (3), (4) These three cautions in regard to the use of *an* are the same as those given for *a* above
(1) An honest man fears nothing
(2) He presented a one-sided argument
(3) What sort of apple is this?
(4) Such emotion as he evinced was well understood

angry—Sharp and sudden displeasure or indignation; temporarily disordered in mind. Do not confuse with *mad*
Correct: *You are angry because he copied from your paper*

annoy—To trouble in a small way. Do not confuse with *aggravate* and *exasperate*. The dripping of the water annoys me

another—Used with *one*— *one another*—succession or consecutiveness of relationship is denoted. Custom, however, may justify its use interchangeably with *each other*. Do not use a plural verb or a plural reference with *another*. The members of the diplomatic corps followed one another in to dinner

any-–Do not phrase this word with superlatives. Do not say *best of any*. Used in comparative statements, this word requires *other* to follow it. Do not say, *This paper is better than any I have used.* Do not use with *place* for anywhere

(1) My last report is the best of all I have ever had
(2) This paper is better than any other I have used
(3) I cannot find my gloves anywhere. *Not* I cannot find my gloves any place

anywhere—Do not say *anywheres* for *anywhere*. There is no such word as *anywheres*

appreciate—Do not use transitively in the sense of know or understand, and do not use in its modification such adverbs of degree as *extremely, greatly, much, so, very*. The word itself means to esteem highly or to estimate correctly. As an intransitive verb meaning to increase in value, it may be modified by an adverb of degree. Say *I appreciate your kind remarks*, not *I greatly appreciate your kind remarks*. But *This land has greatly appreciated in value* is correct

apt—Tendency to; suitable or appropriate (see *likely* and *liable*)
(1) He is apt at music and drawing
(2) His after-dinner talk was apt to the occasion

argue—In arguing one depends upon cold facts (see *plead*)
He will argue from the figures of the last report

around—To encircle on all sides. Do not use for *about* in the sense of *approximate* (see *about*)
He walked around the block in about ten minutes

arrogate—To claim unreasonably and aggressively (see *abrogate*)

as—(1) As . . . as are correlatives in affirmative statesments (see *so . . . as*)
(2) Do not use *as* for *like*, when the latter is a preposition (see *like*)
(3) Do not use *as* for *that*. *I do not know as I am going* is wrong (see *that*)
(4) After *such, as* may properly be used as a relative pronoun (see *such*)

(1) He has written as good a letter as it is possible to write
(2) He writes like me. . . . He writes as I do
(3) I do not know that I am going
(4) Such letters as you write should be written well

ascent—Rise or the act of rising (Do not confuse with *assent*)

assent—To agree with or consent (see *ascent*)

at—(1) Do not use before *about* (2) Use with care after *begin* and *commence*
(1) He arrived at nine o'clock (2) He began his work promptly

aught—Anything (see *ought*)

average—The mean of several, arrived at by numerical calculation (see *ordinary*)

The average of his marks for the term was eighty-five

averse—Reluctant; unfavorable toward, in mind or feeling. Accented on last syllable. Customarily used of people and animals. Followed by preposition *to*. Do not confuse with *adverse*

Correct: *John is averse to participation in social functions*

avocation—Minor or subsidiary occupation (see *vocation*)

After office hours he works at radio as an avocation

awful—Custom is probably making permissible the use of this word in the sense of *very, execrable, supreme*. But such loose usage is not to be recommended. The word means *awe inspired*

The heavy thunderstorm made an awful impression upon the company

badly—Do not use this adverb for its adjective equivalent *bad*

Do not use in the sense of *extremely* or *very much* or a *good deal*

(1) His record is bad

(2) He plays badly

(3) I want to see you very much

balance—The difference between two sides of an account (see *remainder* and *rest*)

My accounts show a balance of fifty dollars in your favor

because—Do not use to introduce a causal clause after *reason* followed by *is* or *was* or *may be*, or similar copulatives. *The reason of his absence is because he is ill* is incorrect (see *reason*)

(1) He is absent because he is ill

(2) The reason for his absence is illness

beg—To ask alms, to entreat, to solicit, to request persistently and emotionally. Do not *beg to inform* in reply to a letter

We beg you not to eject this old man

beside—Near, close by, by the side of. Do not confuse with *besides*

He sat beside me at the circus

besides—Moreover, in addition to. Do not confuse with *beside*

He had four apples for lunch, and two pieces of cake besides

best—Do not use this word loosely or too frequently. Do not use *best* in reference to two things, instead of *better*. Say *the better of two*, and *the best of three* or more (see *any*)

(1) Of all the fellows in my class, I like Oliver best

(2) The better of the two pictures in this room has been adjudged the best of all in the exhibition

between—Refers to two only (see *among*) Requires the objective case after it. Use sparingly before *each* and *every*

Between you and me there can be no quarrels, but among the members of that class there are always bitter bickerings

bid—An offer based upon an estimate (see *estimate*)

After weighing very carefully the costs of labor and materials, the contractor placed a bid of ten thousand dollars on the job

bind—Refers to a decision forced or imposed thru the agency of out-side forces (see *determine*)

His contracts bind him to give eight American concerts

blame—Used as a verb, this word should not be followed by *on*. *Blame it on him* is incorrect. Blame a person for an error; do not blame an error on some one

They blame the engineer for the railroad accident

borrow—A verb meaning to obtain temporary use of (see *lend* and *loan*)   Correct: *May I borrow your umbrella?*

both—Refers to two persons or things considered jointly (see *each*) Both his parents will be present at commencement

bring—Motion toward a speaker or writer or director (see *fetch* and *take*)

Bring me a newspaper, please, when you return from the city this evening

but—(1) As a preposition, *but* means *except*
(2) As an adverb, *but* means *only*. Do not use *but* in this mean-ing after a negative: *I haven't but two* is wrong
(3) As a conjunction, *but* gives contrasted or adversative mean-ing. *But* is frequently misused for and with *that* or *what*. *We do not doubt but that* (or *what*) *you will be there* is wrong. *We don't know but what he will come* is wrong. *There is nobody but what* (or *who*) *he likes* is wrong. Be careful in the use of *but* after *can: She can but come* means that there is nothing else for her to do but to come. *She cannot but come* means that she cannot help coming

(1) Everybody went but me
(2) I have but two
(3) He was absent frequently but he nevertheless passed
(4) We do not doubt that you will be there
(5) We don't know but that he will come
(6) There is nobody that he doesn't like; *i.e.* He likes every-body

Note, however, that *but* is properly used preceding *what* and *that* in the following sentences:

He delivered an address, but what the audience thought of it, I do not know

He thought the tie he gave me would disappoint me, but that was just the tie I wanted

calculate—To compute and estimate by more or less complicated de-vices (see *reckon*)

They calculate the cost of the building to be exactly $38 750.78

can—Denotes power and capability (see *may*)

I can operate a lathe

can't—Do not use with *but* in the same sense in which *can but* is used. Do not use with *seem* in the sense of being unable to do: *I can't seem to get this* is wrong (see *but* and *seem*)

(1) I can't get this
(2) It appears that I can't get this
(3) I seem unable to get this

canvas—A coarse-grained cloth used for sails and tents (see *canvass*)

canvass—To go about soliciting for sales or votes (see *canvas*)

capacity—Power to receive or hold (see *ability*)
> He has the capacity to grow into a higher position

capital—A principal sum; wealth in general; a principal city; as an adjective, excellent, chief, leading, admirable

capitol—An official building of a state or country; a statehouse

carry—In relation to *bring, fetch,* and *take* (which see), *carry* refers to undetermined and indefinite action
> He will carry your parcels for you

censer—A jar or pan for holding incense

censor—To evaluate or criticize; a judge or critic

censure—To reprove or blame or find fault with

cession—A yielding or giving up

character—What a person really is by nature and temperament (see *reputation*)
> His character qualifies him to hold the position

choice—Refers to two *or more* (see *alternative*)
> Of the dozen opportunities offered him, he cannot yet tell what his choice will be

cite—To name or quote as an example; to summon; to show; to argue

client—One whom a lawyer or a business agency serves (see *customer*)
> The client questioned the legal advice given

coarse—Common, vulgar, rough

commodity—Any product, or part thereof, that is movable and valuable, and thus made ready for the market (see *product*)
> A new commodity has been placed on sale at our chain stores

common—Belonging to more than one (see *mutual*)
> (1) The employees use the library in common
> (2) The two appetites common to all mankind are eating and drinking

commonly—Refers to the greater part of a class (see *universally*)
> The two men are commonly regarded as the best of friends

compare—To place together in order to discover likeness and unlikeness (see *contrast*)
> If you will compare this book with that, you will find that one is almost a complete copy of the other

complement—The act of completing, the portion that completes (see *compliment*)
> The complement of our Christmas stock has just come in

compliment—Praise or commendation or congratulation. Do not confuse with *complement*
> He paid us a very high compliment, indeed, by his prolonged visit

consul—An official representing a government in foreign parts (see *council* and *counsel*)

The American consul at Algiers has submitted a valuable report

contact—The coming together cr meeting or touching of two bodies. This is a noun; it should never be used as a verb or an adjective, as in *I contacted him* or *He is a good contact man*

contemptible—To deserve disdain or disregard

I think his behavior is contemptible

contemptuous—To evince disdain or disregard

I think his attitude toward us was contemptuous

contrast—To set in opposition in order to point out dissimilarity (see *compare*)

To contrast the two pictures effectively, you must place them in direct light

co-respondent—A joint respondent, as the third party in a divorce case

correspondent—One who writes letters or for newspapers

council—A meeting or conference or consultation (see *consul* and *counsel*)

The executive council is called for four o'clock

counsel—Advice; an adviser, usually in legal matters

Do not confuse with *consul* and *council*

Lord Chesterfield gave his son the best of counsel

Their counsel charged them a large fee

course—To run thru or over; the place or track over which travel is done; a layout of study

credible—Worthy of belief or acceptance

Your news is hardly credible

creditable—Worthy of praise or commendation

His conduct is creditable from every point of view

credulous—Too easily disposed to believe; making believable on slight and insufficient evidence

You are too credulous regarding market reports

custom—Voluntary repetition of an act by a person or a group of persons, under the same circumstances, for the same reasons, and from the same underlying causes (see *habit*)

The natives of a certain province in central Africa have the strange custom of using colored calico for money

customer—One whom a tradesman regularly serves. Used almost interchangeably with *client* in certain relationships. Some banks refer to their depositors as clients; others refer to them as customers

He is a customer highly respected by the salesmen in the shop

data—Plural of *datum*, a known or an assumed fact. The first *a* is pronounced ā, not ä

Data for the debate are now ready in the library

deal—Along with *help, line, proposition* (which see), this word is too loosely used. Do not use it to refer to large transactions. It means to do business with a person

I shall hereafter deal directly with you

decent—Respectable and honorable

delusion—False belief, misconception. A *delusion* always involves some mental error; an *illusion* is a mistaken sense perception

depot—A warehouse or storehouse. Usage will probably in time justify its use in reference to a large railway station (see *station*)

descent—Fall or the act of moving downward

desert—A barren and unproductive region

dessert—The course or sweets at the end of a meal

determine—To come to a decision by the exercise of one's own will (see *bind*)

device—A plan, a contrivance, a stratagem

devise—To plan or strategize

differ—Do not use *than* after any form of this word. *Differ* and *different* and *difference* are not comparative forms. People *differ with* each other in opinion. They *differ in* judgment *about* a policy. They *differ from* their elders in a course of action taken

John and I differ from the principal regarding the game

directly—Do not use this word for *as soon as*. The word is properly used to refer to method, as well as to time (see *immediately*). It may also refer to proximity in space

He presented the case directly to the men

He will follow directly after us

disagree—Use *with* rather than *from* after this verb

We disagree with you in principle

dissent—To disagree; a disagreement

dive—The past tense and the past participle of this verb is, preferably, *dived*. In occasional colloquial use only, *dove* is used

He dived into the water is correct

don't—A contraction of *do not*. Do not use for doesn't. Some authorities claim that the somewhat common usage of *he, she,* or *it don't* is tending to make the expression acceptable. But it has not made it correct

They don't approve of his policy, and he doesn't approve of their practise

due—Do not use this word unless it refers explicitly to a noun or a pronoun. It cannot refer to a verb, a phrase, or a clause. *Due to his absence from the city he lost his vote* is wrong. The following are correct:

His victory was due to his fine spirit

He lost his vote as a result of his absence from the city

each—This word refers to two or more individually (see *both*). Followed by *other*, it should be used to indicate a certain equality of relationship among all referred to. *One another* means fol-

lowing or consecutiveness or succession of relationship. Do not
use a plural verb or a plural reference with *each*
Each boy has received his card
The employees helped each other in every way

effect—(1) A noun meaning result
(2) A verb meaning to cause, to finish, to achieve (see *affect*)
His wide reading has shown its effect upon his writing
His reading will effect a great improvement in his writing

either—Refers preferably to two persons or things. Correlative of *or*.
Do not use with *nor*. Used as an adjective, pronoun, *either* is
always singular (see *neither*)
Either John or James is to accompany you
Either of the boys is to accompany you

elapse—Refers to the passing of time (see *transpire*)
Two hours have elapsed since you came in

elevated—High or lofty in situation or character. Usually a participle
or an adjective, this word has properly come to be used as
a substantive in reference to a railway that runs above
ground level. Do not confuse with *elevator*
We went down town by the elevated *or* by the elevated road

elevator—One who or that which carries upward. A movable platform
or "cage" in a building for carrying passengers or freight up
and down. A grain warehouse. Do not confuse with *elevated. We went down town by the elevator* is wrong. Correct: *We took the elevator to the tenth floor. The grain
elevator is two hundred feet high*

else—In conjunction with *any one, everybody, somebody,* and similar
words, *else* should be given the sign of possession when the possessive case is used. *Anybody's else coat* is not the correct form.
There is some good usage to contradict this, but the best authorities stand firmly for *Anybody else's coat*

elusive—Hard to grasp, evasive, tantalizing

emigrate—To go from one country to settle in another (see *immigrate*)

eminent—Outstanding, prominent   (Do not confuse with *imminent*)

employ—Do not use this verb for its noun equivalent (*employment*)
Try to employ your time profitably
We have eighty men in our employment

empty—Without contents, having nothing in it, as of a vessel or vehicle
of any kind—car, crate, bucket, tumbler (see *vacant*). The
word *empty* is applied to homely movable things; *vacant,* to
things of greater dignity. The former is Saxon; the latter,
Latin. Still, while you speak of a vacant building and an
empty can, you may also say a vacant room and empty space.
The dictionary must be consulted for the idiomatic niceties of
usage in regard to these two words

enthuse—Do not use this word for *to be* or *to make enthusiastic*
The audience became enthusiastic at what he said

esteemed—Do not use this word to modify *favor* in reference to a
letter. It means valued or regarded highly
They esteemed your efforts highly

estimate—To calculate in definite terms; to arrive at final judgment after the consideration of many factors (see *bid*)

>The contractor will estimate the cost of the new building, to a fraction of a cent

every—Do not use with *place*, in the sense of *everywhere*. *In* is required before it when used to modify *place*. *Every* always implies singular number

>He has looked everywhere for his hat
>He has looked in every place for his hat
>Every man has his ration card

exasperate—To vex or annoy extremely. Do not use for *aggravate* (which see)

>His gross carelessness and indifference exasperate me

excellent—Do not use a modifier for *excellent*, such as *very, quite, most*. Do not use this word loosely, to describe anything of which you think highly

>He has made an excellent record
>He is a good friend of mine

except—(1) A verb meaning to exclude or omit
(2) A preposition meaning at the exclusion or with the exception of (see *accept*)

>I except your name from the list
>The names are all listed except yours

exceptionable—That which may be objected to; subject or liable to objection. Do not confuse with *exceptional*

>Correct: *Certain people were offended at his exceptionable conduct*

exceptional—Unusual, of superior value, out of the ordinary

>His exceptional conduct won promotion for him

expect—To look forward to as probable; to hold slight but justifiable belief that a certain thing will come to pass (see *calculate, reckon, suppose, suspect*, etc.)

>In view of his telegram we expect him to arrive tonight

fair—Of blond complexion; just; clear

famous—Celebrated or well and favorably known (see *infamous*)

fare—Money paid for a trip; of state or condition of being

farther—Refers to remoteness in space (see *further*)

>His shop is farther from the wholesale depot than I thought

favor—Do not habitually call a letter a favor or "your esteemed favor"

>Thank you for the favor you have just shown me

fetch—Motion from and toward a speaker or writer or director; to go from and return with (see *bring* and *take*)

>Please fetch my coat from the locker

few—Refers to number (see *little*)

>There are few errors in your work

find—To get something or to come upon somebody as a result of seeking (see *locate*)

>I could find the place only after much difficulty

first—This word is an adjective, an adverb, and a noun. Do not add *ly* to form an adverb. *Firstly* is wrong

fix—To fasten or attach or secure firmly (see *repair*)
I shall fix the lamp above the mirror

flaunt—To display ostentatiously, to make triumphant or impudent show of, to assume a look-at-me attitude. Racketeers may flaunt their booty and then flout the authorities by escaping (see *flout*)

flee—To run away for safety. The parts of this verb are *flee, fled, fled*
He must flee to another country for safety

flout—To speak or act disdainfully, scoffingly, contemptuously, mockingly (see *flaunt*)

flow—To move along quietly, as a stream of water. The parts are *flow, flowed, flowed*
Money flows in uninterruptedly

fly—To move thru the air, or, figuratively, to move rapidly and more or less mysteriously. The parts are *fly, flew, flown*
The aviators will fly to Chicago overnight

formally—Conventionally, perfunctorily, in accordance with forms

former—Refers to one of two only; never to more than two (see *latter*)
Both John and Bill received high marks, but the former was given greater commendation by his teachers

formerly—Heretofore; in past time

further—Refers to remoteness in time, degree, or quantity. Refers also to something additional to what one has already said or written (see *farther*)
Further in the winter, we shall have snow
I shall give you further examination tomorrow
He wants nothing further
He says nothing further in his letter

gain—Refers to transactions that are conducted on a large scale, income from which is attended with some irregularity and uncertainty (see *profit*)
His financial gain on his oil speculation has been unusual

good—This word is, as a rule, an adjective, and must therefore be used only in the modification of nouns and pronouns. Do not use in place of *well*
His work is good
The plan works well

goods—Any easily transferable articles that may or may not be offered for sale (see *commodity* and *merchandise*)
The goods were shipped to you promptly

got—Use this word sparingly. Never use the archaic past participle form *gotten*. Do not use *got* for *have*, except for emphasis or for conveying the meaning of *secured*. *We have got to bear it* is not good usage
Correct: *We have to bear our troubles*
At last, after much struggling, we got the animal safely roped to a tree

guaranty—Security; the act of making sure (preferably a noun)

guarantee—To warrant or to stand back of (used preferably as a verb)

habit—The tendency to repeat a certain act without volition on the part of the doer. *Custom* (see above) usually refers to groups; *habit* to individuals

Acquire the habit of promptness if you would succeed in business

had—Do not use *of* after *had*. *Had I of known* is incorrect.

Do not use *ought* after *had*. *He had ought to go* is incorrect. (See *of* and *ought*)

Had I known you were coming, I could have met you

He ought to go when he is told to go

hanged—Refers only to an individual who is executed by hanging (see *hung*)

The murderer was hanged at dawn

hardly—Do not use with a negative expression

We can hardly wait till he comes

have—Denotes possession. It is unnecessary, therefore, to combine with any other word to indicate possession (see *got* above)

We have all the goods on hand that we can possibly sell

healthful—To be the cause of health (see *healthy* and *wholesome*)

This is the most healthful climate in the world

healthy—To be in or to have good health (see *healthful* and *wholesome*)

He is a strong and healthy man

help—Do not use this word to mean *helpers* or *employees*

We need additional employees in our establishment to help us fill the large Christmas orders

here—Do not use this word after *this* or *these* to enforce your meaning

This sewing must be finished before these patterns are. *But* These patterns, here on the table, are done

human—Pertaining to mankind; characterizing man. An adjective and a noun

humane—Kind, tender, compassionate, benevolent. An adjective only

hung—Refers to anything that is fastened to a point above without supports from beneath (see *hanged*)

He hung his coat over the window

illusion—A misleading appearance caused either by bad eyesight or by false presentation; a deliberately deceptive showing of something (see *allusion*)

illusive—Unreal or imagined, deceptive, misleading

immediately—With no delay in time. Both *directly* and *immediately* refer to immediacy in time and proximity in space, but the former (see above) refers also to method of procedure as well; usage has weakened both words (and the word *presently* also) to some extent, until they are frequently used now to mean *in a little while*. The Shakespearian *presently* meant *at once*. As used today, *presently* rarely means this

Correct: *Please bring me the reports immediately*
Please follow immediately after me
I am too busy to see you now, but come to me
presently

immigrate—To come into a country or region from a former or native land (see *emigrate*)

imminent—Dangerous or threatening, close-at-hand happening (see *eminent*)

imply—To intimate a meaning not expressed; to convey virtually (see *infer*)

Your behavior implies that you do not care for the good opinion of others

in—Indicates position, not motion (see *into*)

We were sitting in the office when the bell rang

infamous—Notorious, of bad reputation or ill fame, disgraceful, detestable, as infamous laws, infamous behavior. This word is always accented on the first syllable (see *famous*)

infer—To come to a conclusion or to make a deduction (see *imply*)

I infer from your behavior that you do not care for the opinion of others

informed—To have information. Do not say *well-posted* for *well-informed*

That man is well-informed in all matters pertaining to the parcel post

ingenious—Clever, skilful, with inventive genius

He is ingenious at adjusting electrical devices

ingenuous—Frank, open, honest, sincere

His talk was ingenuous and engaging

inside—Do not use this word to express time. Do not use *of* after it. *The parcel will reach you inside of a week* is wrong

Correct: *The parcel will reach you within a week*

instance—A signal case or example; an illustraton

instants—Short items or periods of time

into—Indicates motion, not position or location (see *in*)

They went into the water in their street clothes

it's—The contraction of *it is*. The apostrophe means that *i* has been omitted

It's a long lane that has no turning

its—The possessive singular of the pronoun *it*. Do not confuse with *it's*

The kitten has lost its ball of yarn

kind—This is singular number. Do not precede it with a plural form such as *these* or *those*. Do not use *a* or *an* after *kind of*

This kind of cloth will wear well

Those kinds are not so durable

kindly—Be careful to place this word correctly when used in such expressions as this: *Enclosed kindly find sample that you are asked to match*. *Kindly* really modifies *match,* and the sentence should read: *Enclosed find sample that you are asked kindly to match* (see *please*)

last—The final thing in a series. *Last* and *first* are frequently hyphenated with *named* to indicate reference to numbers in a series

The last game of the season will be played tomorrow

Of the ten players you mention, the last-named has the best scoring record, and the first-named the best defensive record

later—After; comparative degree of *late*

latest—The most recent

The latest game was played at Blaine Field; the next will be played in the gymnasium

latter—Refers to one of two only; never to more than two (see *former*)

Both John and Bill received high marks, but the latter excelled the former

lay—To put or place. The parts are *lay, laid, laid*

I shall lay the map on the table

lead—(1) A noun, the name of a metal
(2) A verb meaning to guide by going on before. Unfortunately its imperfect tense is *led*, pronounced exactly like the noun *lead;* hence, frequently confused with it (see *led*)

They led the horse to water

learn—To acquire knowledge thru diligence and observation

lease—To permit to use, as of property, by means of written agreement called a *lease* (see *let* and *hire*)

leave—To go away (see *let*); to part with; to submit, as a report

We shall leave by an early train

We leave the report in your care

led—The imperfect tense of *lead* (see above)

Those who lead best have first been led

lend—A verb meaning to grant temporary use of (see *loan* and *borrow*)

Please lend me your pen?

less—This word is the comparative of *little*. *Least* is the superlative. Both, like *little*, are used principally to refer to quantity rather than to number. *Less* is the antonym of *more;* do not use it to refer to more than two. *Lesser* is an old comparative of *little*. It is still used in poetry but is becoming archaic in general usage. Like other comparatives both *less* and *lesser* are used frequently as substantives, as *The less you have the better off you are*

let—To permit. Do not confuse with *leave* (see above)

The master will not let them go to the game

liable—Dangerous; unpleasant in results; disadvantageous (see *apt* and *likely*)

You are liable for damages if you run into another

lie—(1) A verb meaning to tell a falsehood. Its parts are *lie, lied, lied*
(2) A noun meaning falsehood
(3) A verb meaning to recline or rest. Its parts are *lie, lay, lain*. Do not confuse with *lay* (see above)

Correct: *If you say he cheated, you lie*
He has told a lie
I shall lie here for a little rest
Yesterday I lay on the couch two hours

like—(1) A preposition meaning similar to or in a similar manner to or resemblance to
(2) A verb expressing attitude
(3) An adjective indicating *same*
(4) A noun referring to kind or class, usually in the plural. *Like* should never be used for *as* in introducing a clause. *He writes like I do* is wrong

Correct: *Clara is like Jane in appearance*
Clara will like Jane
Like tastes beget like interests
She has her likes and dislikes
He writes as I do, or *like me*

likely—Probably (see *apt* and *liable*)
It is likely to rain tomorrow

line—This word is altogether too loosely used to indicate kind or brand or classification
Draw a line from this point to that one
We shall travel by the Cunard Line

little—Refers to quantity, not number. Errors are frequently made in the use of the comparative *less* and the superlative *least* (see above)

loan—A noun meaning the thing lent. Do not use as a verb, in place of *lend* (see above)
The bank made him a loan of several thousand dollars

loath—Reluctant, strongly disinclined, averse to

loathe—To hate, to abhor, to detest

locate—To place in some particular position (see *find*)
We shall locate our new factory on the block opposite

loose—To be free from anything that binds. Incoherence in thought or expression. Do not confuse with *lose*
Correct: *His belt is loose*
Your sentences should not be loose and rambling

lose—To fail, to be defeated, to part with anything unintentionally or unconsciously
If they lose, they will do so, fighting hard

lot—A definite part, parcel, or quantity
A new lot of goods has just come in

lots—Means definite parts, parcels, and quantities. Do not use loosely to mean *much* or *many*, or as a noun meaning *abundance*
We shall place all the lots on sale tomorrow

luxuriant—Excessive or profuse in growth; exuberant in fancy; ornate, florid, or rich in design

luxurious—Voluptuous; supplied with those material things that gratify the senses

mad—Disordered in mind. Do not confuse with *angry*
    Correct: *He became mad at the death of his mother*

majority—More than half of any given number, as in election returns (see *most* and *plurality*)
    He was elected over the Republican candidate by a large majority

many—An adjective referring to number (see *much*)
    There are many errors in your letter

may—Denotes permission and possibility (see *can*)
    If I practise, I may some day be able to operate a lathe

merchandise—Goods prepared and offered for sale (see *goods* and *commodity*)
    The new merchandise was placed on the market this morning

merely—Indicates the lack of something or the mere meeting of demand (see *simply*). Be sure to place *merely* as closely as possible to the word it modifies
    Quoth the raven: "Nevermore! Merely this, and nothing more." *I merely want a book* is wrong

migrate—To move from one country or region to another at regular intervals; said of birds (see *emigrate* and *immigrate*)

miner—One who works in a mine

minor—Lesser; one who is under age—a boy under twenty-one; a girl under eighteen; a branch of study requiring less time than a major and yielding less credit

most—Superlative of the adjective *much*. Do not use as an adverb (see *almost, mostly,* and *plurality*)
    Most letters are written without much thought as to form and content

mostly—An adverb meaning for the most part; principally (see *most* and *almost*)
    The books in the corner closet are mostly old and torn

much—An adjective and an adverb referring to quantity and degree (see *many;* see *too* and *very*)
    There is much flour on the truck still to be unloaded
    We are much concerned about his condition

mutual—Pertaining reciprocally and interchangeably to both of two (see *common*)
    John and I have mutual regard for each other

myself—Do not use this, or any other intensive form of pronoun, when the simpler form conveys the meaning desired. *He spoke to you and myself about the work* is wrong
    Correct: *He spoke to you and me about the work*
    It was I myself who gave you the message

naught—Nothing; a cipher (see *aught*)

near—Do not use this word for *nearly*. *Near* may be used as an adjective, an adverb, a preposition, and a verb

Near relatives are not always agreeable
There's his house, with the garage standing neaɪ
He was sitting near me
We shall near the city by midday

nearly—An adverb only. *He is not near done* is wrong
    He is not nearly done is correct

neither—Refers to two persons or things, never more. Correlative with *nor*. Do not use with *or*. Used as an adjective pronoun, *neither* is always singular (see *either*)
    Neither of the boys is to go
    Neither John nor James is to accompany you

new—A new thing is simply one more, one in addition (see *novel*)
    He has just bought a new automobile

notable—Worthily eminent or distinguished
    He has made a notable record at college

noted—Well and worthily known by report and reputation
    He is noted for his fine work in athletics

notorious—More oɪ less unfavorably known. *Notoriety* means unpleasant and disadvantageous publicity
    As a result of his constant violation of rules, he has become notorious in athletics
    His bad behavior on the field has brought him much notoriety in athletic circles

novel—A novel thing is strange and unusual, in addition to being *new*
    A novel device for beating carpets has just been invented

novice—One unskilled and inexperienced and still on probation (see *amateur*)
    The works of a novice in the art of painting cannot possibly be entered at the exhibition

number—Refers to units that are counted and countable (see *quantity*)
    A number of trees could be seen in the distance

observance—Keeping or celebrating, as certain feasts or holidays
    We believe in the strict observance of legal holidays

observation—The act of seeing or looking at
    On close observation you will see the four masts of a vessel on the horizon

of—Do not use this word for *have* after *may, might, must, can, could, will, would, shall, should*. Do not use it after *off, alongside, inside, beside, outside*.
    I must have met you outside the city limits
    Keep off the grass
    Keep inside the ropes

off—Do not confuse with *away from*. Say *The ship was wrecked a mile off shore*, not *away from shore*. Say *Keep away from me,* not *off me*

official—Authoritative. Do not confuse with *officious*
    Correct: *This is the latest official report*

officious—Meddlesome

The new-appointed secretary is altogether too officious in his attitude

on—Do not use before *about*. Do not use after *blame*. Do not use in the sense (slang) of *from*

He will arrive about the fifteenth of May

He took it from me, not *on me*

one—Inasmuch as *a* and *an* mean one, it is unnecessary to precede one with either of these articles

I haven't one to my name, not *I haven't a one*

ones—Do not use *ones* for *these* or *those* (which see). Do not use *the* before *ones*. Use *those* instead of *the ones*

I mean those that you are wearing now

only—In no other time, place, or manner. Place *only* as closely as possible to the word it modifies. It is commonly misplaced in both conversation and writing. *I only asked for three* is incorrect (probably) for *I asked for only three*. Note on page 194 that the placement of *only* may be varied in accordance with different meanings intended

onto—Do not use this word in the sense of *place upon*. The word *on* or *upon* is preferable in such connection. Some authorities regard *onto* as great a vulgarism as *ain't*. But after verbs of motion it may be necessary for clarity, and is thus analogous to *in* and *to* in *into*. In *They stept on the ice* the meaning may be that they were already on the ice and were stepping on it or that they stept from land *on to* the ice

Correct: *He put his hat on his head*

He jumped upon the table

ordinary—Usual or common in occurrence (see *average*)

The ordinary events of the day held no interest for him

other—Preceded by *each* and *every* this word is singular (see *each* and *another*)

Every other boy in the class but John was prepared

ought—Do not use with an auxiliary verb or as an auxiliary verb. *Had ought* is a vulgarism. It is better never to use the ugly contraction *oughtn't*

Correct: *She ought to have prepared dinner for two*

out—Do not use after *start* (see page 198)

They started on their six-day trip

part—A certain amount or number of anything (see *portion*)

A part of his farm has been sold to a neighbor

partake—To take a share or part of, as of cake or melon

partial—Biased or prejudiced; also, incomplete. Since the word has these two distinctly different meanings, care should be taken to prevent ambiguity in its use. *He made a partial report* may mean either of two things. Do not confuse with *partly*

Correct: *The report he made was partial to the negative side*

He made only a partial report today, but he will complete it tomorrow participate—To have a share in common with others—*with* a person or persons, *in* a thing (see *partake*)

partition—A boundary or division wall or line, separating one room or apartment or larger space from another. Used as a verb it means to divide. Do not confuse with *petition*

Correct: *They have built a partition between his half of the locker and mine*
They will partition the locker

partly—Incomplete or in some degree
His work is partly done

party—Do not use to refer to an individual, except in legal phraseology. It should be used to refer only to a person or a group of persons who are actually concerned in some united action
There is an interesting old person sitting in the corner
The party of the first part agrees to pay to the party of the second part, fifty dollars

per—Do not use *per* for *a* in straightaway English expression. In abbreviated, technical, or commercial expression, it may be so used
We charge fifteen cents a copy for these brochures
Price: $15. per cwt.

per cent—Per hundred. Abbreviation of the Latin *per centum*.
The term *per cent* is now written without the period and it is increasingly appearing in print as one word—*percent*
His money is invested at six per cent interest
Do not confuse with—

percentage—Rate per cent, that is, rate by the hundred
The bonus amounted to a certain percentage of each man's salary

permit—To give express authorization, or, as a noun, the sign or token of such authorization (see *allow*)
The gateman will not permit you to enter the paddock
My permit will admit two thru the gate

persecute—To pursue in order to injure or afflict; to hunt down (see *prosecute*)
The authorities have persecuted him until he is almost insane

personal—Private, confidential, individual

personnel—A group of individuals constituting a homogeneous staff of workers in a given firm or firms

petition—A formal request or appeal, usually addressed to some one in authority. Used as a verb, it means to request formally. Do not confuse with *partition* (see page 449)

Correct: *They drew up a petition to present to the manager of the department*
They are going to petition the manager for a holiday

place—Do not use after *any, every, some, no*, for *anywhere, everywhere, somewhere, nowhere*, without preceding with the preposition *in*

I have looked everywhere for my books and cannot find them in any place

plead—Indicates the use of feeling and human interest in an attempt to persuade. You argue a question but plead a cause (see *argue*)

He will plead the cause of the accused in terms that every mother will understand

please—Be careful not to misplace this word in such expressions as this: *Enclosed please find the sample that you are asked to match* (see *kindly*)

Correct: *Enclosed find the sample that you will please match for me*

plenty—Do not use this word as an adverb, as in *This is plenty good enough for me*

Correct: *This is quite good enough for me*
We shall need plenty of muslin

plurality—More than any other of three or more totals. If John received 600 votes and Bill 400 votes out of a total poll of 1000 votes, then John received a *majority*. If, out of 1000 votes, John received 600, Bill 250, and Jim 150, then John received a *plurality* of 350 votes, or so many more votes than his closest competitor. In other words, John received the most votes; whereas, in the case of his getting a majority of votes, he may be said to have received the greater number of votes

In the recent election, Thomkins had a plurality of twenty-two hundred over Lloyd and Harrison

portion—A share or an allotment (see *part*)

The father gave to his eldest daughter her portion of the estate

posted—Do not use for informed, in the sense of *well-informed*. People are informed, ledgers and letters are posted

The timetables have been posted on the bulletin boards

practicable—Capable of being put into practise; usable, feasible. It is used to refer to things only, never to persons

The device that he has invented for filling fountain pens appears to be most practicable

Do not confuse with—

practical—Useful and valuable as a result of having been tried out in actual practise. It is used of persons chiefly, but also of plans and things in opposition to the theoretical and visionary. Practical knowledge is knowledge that has grown out of useful and profitable practise

John is the most practical fellow I have ever met; his head is full of practical ideas

precede—To go before, to take the lead, to go in advance

precedence—Priority in place, time, or rank; the right to such priority

precedents—Examples gone before brought to bear upon a present course of action or used in determining a given issue

prefer—Do not use *than* or *rather* after *prefer*. It is not a comparative. It should always be followed by *to, above,* or *before*
I prefer red to blue, and round figures before square ones

prescribe—To give, as a law or a direction. The noun form is *prescription* (see *proscribe*)
He is going to prescribe rest, and I shall see that his prescription is carried out

principal—(1) As a noun its meaning is chief, leader, employer, or
prime mover in an undertaking of any kind
(2) As a noun it also means invested capital
(3) As an adjective its meaning is highest or best in rank
or importance
Do not confuse with *principle*
Correct: *The principal of the school is a thorogoing man*
His principal is invested in gilt-edged bonds
The principal reason for my going is my mother's
illness

principle—A noun only, meaning truth, belief, policy, conviction, or
general hypothesis
He is a man of high principle

proceed—To begin or continue, to progress

profit—Refers to income that accrues in a more or less regular manner,
as a just reward for industry (see *gain*)
His investments netted him a handsome semi-annual profit

proposal—Something placed before one, or more than one, for acceptance or rejection, usually concerning a course of action
My proposal for traffic relief is now ready to place before
the committee for final vote

propose—To offer, to state a plan or a scheme for the consideration of
others. Do not confuse this word with *purpose* (below)
Correct: *I propose that we build a new highway at this point*
for the relief of traffic

proposition—A formal statement or exposition for consideration rather
than for immediate action. Do not use loosely in the
sense of *plan, task, question, problem*
Correct: *In outlining my proposition for your consideration, I want to call your attention particularly
to pages twenty-two and twenty-three*

proscribe—To outlaw or ostracize. The noun form is proscription.
Do not confuse with *prescribe* (see above)
His criminal record makes it necessary for us to proscribe
him, and to enter his works on the proscription list

prosecute—To follow up regularly and without injurious intent. To
begin and carry out a legal procedure (see *persecute*)
He will prosecute his studies with ardor
He will prosecute the offender to the full extent of the law

prove—The imperfect tense of this verb is *proved*. The past participle
is likewise *proved*. The form *proven* is now archaic, and should
not be used

It has been proved that the best-looking letters receive the best attention

provided—A conjunction meaning *if*, on condition that

We shall attend the performance provided it doesn't rain

Do not confuse with—

providing—Present participle of the verb *provide*, meaning to supply or furnish

The firm is providing the best stationery for its correspondence

purpose—(1)As a noun, it means aim, design, end, or goal

(2) As a verb, it means to decide or determine or intend in one's own mind. What we propose is open to others; what we purpose is not (see *propose*)

I shall explain my purpose to the men when I meet them

I purpose to convert my old office into a den for study and meditation

quantity—Refers to things that are measured. Do not use for *number*. *Amount*, in contrast, refers to things in more or less indefinite bulk, while *quantity* connotes measurement, to a degree at least

We measured the quantity of grain he ordered, out of the large amount we had on hand

quiet—Silent, not noisy

quite—Entirely or completely

raise—As a verb, always transitive, this word means to move upward, to cause to rise; also, to breed, to revive, to excite, to alarm (see *rise*). Its parts are *raise, raised, raised*. It is sometimes used colloquially as a noun to indicate increase. It is wrong to say *He was so ill that he could not raise*

Correct: *He was so ill that he could not rise*

rare—Uncommon or infrequent (see *unique*)

The house is filled with rare tapestries

rarely—Do not say *rarely ever, rarely or ever*, or *rarely or hardly ever*. Ponder the meaning of the word and use it consistently, either by itself or in combination. The idiom is *rarely or never*. Do not use with *don't* or *doesn't*. *He doesn't rarely* is wrong

Correct: *We rarely if ever go there*
        We rarely or never go there
        We rarely go there
        We hardly ever go there

real—Genuine, pure, authentic. Do not use for *very*

Correct: *She wore a necklace of real emeralds*

really—Be sure to place *really* always as closely as possible to the word it modifies. *I really think that he is going at last* is wrong

Correct: *I think that he is really going at last*

reason—This word, followed by *is* or other copulative verb, should not be explained by a causal clause. It requires, rather, a substantive attributive clause. In other words, do not use a phrase or a clause introduced by *due* or *because* in elaboration

of reason. It is wrong to say *The reason for his doing it was because* (or *due to his ignorance*) *he was ignorant of the law*
Correct: *The reason for his doing it was that he was ignorant of the law*

receipt—An acknowledgment in writing that payment has been received

recipe—A listing of ingredients, with proportionate mixture, of a dish or a medical prescription

reckon—To look upon or consider in a more general sense than by means of sheer computation or calculation. Do not use loosely for *think, guess, believe, fancy. I reckon he'll come* and *I calculate it's going to rain* are wrong
Correct: *I reckon the loss to be very serious*
　　　I think he'll come
　　　I think it's going to rain
　　　I believe in what you say
　　　I fancy he doesn't like me
　　　I guess you have the ace in your hand

recollect—To make a distinct mental effort to recall something (see *remember*)
I am totally at a loss to recollect the date referred to

regard—Refers to special esteem or kindliness toward equals, without consideration as to rank or position (see *respect*)
His colleagues hold him in high regard

remainder—A general term, meaning the part that is left, usually as result of mathematical calculation (see *balance* and *rest*). Do not say *remainder of people*
Correct: *Please forward the remainder of my goods*

remember—To retain in the memory (see *recollect*)
He remembered the meeting, and recollected the names of all those present

remind—To recall, usually followed by *of*. Do not use reflexively, as, *I reminded myself*
Correct: *I must remind him of the meeting*

remit—To send in return for something (see *send*)
On receipt of the pen I shall remit the amount due

repair—To mend (see *fix*)
He is going to repair the desk

reputation—What a person is said by others to be (see *character*)
His reputation disqualifies him to hold the position

resolve—To choose between action and inaction. *Determine* (see above) means in contrast, to make a choice between one motive and another.
I resolved to go to the meeting tonight, but I am determined not to speak

respect—Esteem felt toward one in a higher or a different station (see *regard*)
The employees respect their president highly

respectfully—With deferential feeling and attitude

I respectfully request you to give me your decision as soon as you can

respectively—Severally

Bill and Joe have respectively returned their reports to me

rest—This is a still more general word than either *balance* or *remainder*. It refers in general to number or quantity that remains

The rest of the students will follow later

rise—(1) As a verb, always intransitive, it means to move upward or to advance; to appear above the horizon; to revolt or rebel; to be revived from the dead (as in biblical use). The parts are *rise, rose, risen*

(2) As a noun it means the act or degree of rising; advance, as in rank or prosperity

Correct: *Tomorrow the sun will rise at seven-thirty*

The rise of the waters this spring surpasses all records

salary—Fixed stated payments made to one employed in the so-called white-collar pursuits

same—This word should not be used as a pronoun, in place of *it, they, that*, and other pronouns. Exception may be made to this rule in legal phraseology. *In reply to same* is incorrect

Correct: *In reply to your note I want, first, to thank you for words of commendation*

In pursuance of same, the legatee promises to leave such sum untouched until further notice

scarcely—Do not use with negative expression (see *rarely*)

I have scarcely any apples

seem—Do not use with *can't* (which see). Use with caution in the sense of *appear* after *couldn't, didn't, wouldn't*

Correct: *They seem to be coming toward us*

He seems (or *appears*) *unable to do the work*

seldom—Do not say *seldom ever, seldom or ever*, or *seldom or rarely ever*. These misuses of *seldom* are incorrect substitutes for *seldom or never* and *seldom if ever*. "Poor ear" is usually to blame for this error (see *rarely*)

Correct: *We seldom or never attend church*

We seldom, if ever, attend church

We seldom go to church

send—To cause or direct to go or pass (see *remit*)

Send me the following articles, and I shall promptly remit the amount due

session—An assembly; a meeting

set—To place in position; to cause to sit. Its parts are *set, set, set* (see *sit*)

Set the chair in the corner

sight—Eye-power; a view; a spectacle

sit—To seat; to rest, as in a chair; to take or occupy a seat. Its parts are *sit, sat, sat* (see *set*)

I shall sit here
I have sat here before

site—A location, as for a building

size—Do not use this noun as an adjective or a verb. Use, rather, *sized*, or *of size*. *How do the potatoes size up?* is wrong. *We carry every size of shoe* is wrong. Do not use the term *size up* in the sense of judge or estimate. *I sized him up in a minute* is wrong

Correct: *We sell* (or *carry*) *shoes of every size*
We sell the larger-sized stockings
I judged him rightly at once

so—*So . . . as* are correlatives in negative statements (see *as . . . as*)
He has not written so good a letter as this in a long time

some—Do not use this word for *somewhat*. Do not use *some place* for *somewhere*. Do not use *some* as accentual slang in the sense of *wonderful* or *remarkable*

Correct: *We shall take an outing somewhere tomorrow*
There is in some place a fortune waiting for you
He made a remarkable speech

somewhat—An adjective meaning of uncertain degree. Do not confuse with the noun *something*

sort—This is singular number. Do not precede it with a plural form, such as, *these* or *those*. Do not use *a* or *an* after *sort of*

Correct: *This sort of calendar will not do, but those over there are just what I want*

station—A regular stopping place, used to designate the place for the starting and the stopping of trains
The train came into the station exactly on time

stationary—Immovable, fast or secure in position

stationery—Writing paper, social and business forms

statue—A representation in marble or bronze or other material of some figure—human, animal, and so forth

stature—Build, height, physical size of man

statute—A law or legislative enactment; act of parliament or congress

such—This word should be correlated with *as* in relative clauses, not with *who*, *which*, or *that*. In result clauses, *such* should be correlated with *that* alone. *A* and *an* should be used after *such* with some caution

Correct: *Such students as see fit to do so, may accompany me*
His reply was in such bad taste that I could not accept it
I never saw such curiosity as he evinces on the slightest provocation

superior—This word (with its superlative *supreme*) should be used with caution. Like *best* and *very* and *excellent*, it has been over-used, especially in business expression, and its significance has consequently become weakened
Your report, placed side by side with others, shows you to have superior merit as a statistician
The Constitution is the supreme law of the land

suppose—Temporarily to assume that a thing is true. Do not use this word locally for *think, expect, reckon, calculate*

Correct: *Suppose A has two hundred dollars*

suspect—A verb meaning to mistrust, to imagine (usually unfavorably). Used more or less colloquially to mean the one suspected or mistrusted

I suspect him of intrigue in the matter that we have been discussing

They have been questioning the suspect. (The latter example is "journalese")

Do not confuse with—

suspicion—A noun meaning mistrust, doubt, conjecture. It cannot be used as a verb

My suspicion of him has been justified by recent revelations

take—Do not use superfluously, as, *Take and shake, Take and apply, Take and heat.* Motion from a speaker or writer or director (see *bring* and *fetch*)

Heat the medicine before taking

Take this weight from my hand, and place it on the desk

teach—To impart knowledge and instruction

that—A relative pronoun referring to persons, animals, or things. *That* introduces restrictive clauses only. Do not use before *there* (see *who* and *which*)

Correct: *The only man that can serve you is Jenkins*
The only material that you can use is asbestos
The only dogs that I care for are St. Bernards
That man, there on the bench, is the one I mean

their—The personal pronoun, possessive plural of *they*

there—Do not use this word after *that* or *those* to enforce your meaning

Those men are about to be caught. *But*
Those men, there by the wall, are the guilty ones

therefor—This word stands for a prepositional phrase *for that, for this, for it, for the matter referred to*

I did the work, and am responsible therefor

Do not confuse with—

therefore—A conjunction of reason, result, conclusion, addition, meaning (in the first two offices) for that reason or cause

I did the work, and am therefore responsible

these—Do not use before *ones*, or before *here*, except for special designation

These are the books I want
These, here on the table, are the books I want

they're—The abbreviated or contracted form of *they are* (see *their* and *there*)

this—Do not use before *here*

This is the book I want
This book here is the one I want

This (*these*) usually indicates closer and more coherent relationship than *that* (*those*)

those—Do not use before *ones*, or before *there* except for special designation

Those are the books I want
Those, there by the window, are the books I want

through (*thru*)—Do not use for a verb, in the sense of *done, finished, angered,* and the like

He waded thru the tunnel, and declared that he would never take the coach again

I am done with you

till—This word may be used interchangeably with *until*, meaning up to, to the time of, till such time as. They are adverbs, prepositions, and conjunctive adverbs, according to use

They never came till yesterday
He will be away until Thursday
We shall not go till they come

to—A preposition showing relationship. A sentence may properly end with *to*

He wrote a letter to me
I am the man he wrote to
Do not confuse with—

too—An adverb meaning also, in addition to. Do not use *too* to modify a past participle. *I was too disturbed to speak* is incorrect. (See *much* and *very*)

Correct: *He wrote to her, too*
I was too much disturbed to speak

toward—Used interchangeably with *towards*, to mean in the direction of, in respect to, or regarding. *Toward* is sometimes used to mean apt, imminent, approaching fulfilment, usually negatively, as *untoward*

He walked toward the village
His attitude toward his work is delightful
Untoward events prevented his being present

transpire—To exhale, to come to light, to become known, as of something that was hidden. Do not use in the sense of *occur* or *happen*

It now transpires that he was right in his opinions

two—An adjective meaning the number 2

He wrote two letters
Do not confuse with *to* and *too*

unique—The only one of its kind. Do not confuse with *rare*, meaning highly esteemed because of infrequency or uncommonness. *Rare* can be compared; *unique* cannot be

I saw a duplicate of this vase in China; it is therefore not unique

universally—Refers to all of a class (see *commonly*)

His work has been universally praised

unless—A subordinate conjunction. It must be so used as to establish a relationship between two clauses

I shall not go to the theater unless you accompany me
Do not confuse with *except* and *without*

up—This word is used superfluously after *build, divide, finish, open, settle, show, size, swell, write.* *Write up,* however, seems to be settling into good usage. *Show up* and *size up,* for *reveal* and *estimate* respectively, are not good usage (see page 199)

Build your bridges   Settle your accounts
Divide your apple   Show your hand
Finish your work   Write your story
Open the bottle   Your gums will swell
Reveal your true character so that I can judge you fairly

vacant—Having nothing or no persons on or in it (see *empty*). That is vacant which might be filled or might be expected to be filled (see the dictionary for extended exposition of the difference between *empty* and *vacant*)

This loft has been vacant for two years
The children were playing on the vacant lot
The absent-minded man placed the empty bucket on the porch of the vacant house

very—Do not develop the habit of using this word to modify every adjective in your vocabulary. Like *best* and *much* and *too,* it is greatly overused, and thus detracts from the intrinsic significance of the words it is brought to modify. In verbal modification, *very,* like *too,* should be followed by much. It is wrong to say *I was very distressed,* or *I was too distressed to see him.* The insertion of *much* before *distressed* in each case makes the expression correct

Correct: *I was very glad to receive your letter*
        I was very much disturbed at hearing of your illness

vex—To annoy or irritate. Do not use in the sense of *aggravate* (which see), or for so serious a meaning as *exasperate*

Correct: *She was vexed at having missed the train*

vocation—Major, systematic, and remunerative employment

His vocation—salesmanship—makes such heavy demands upon his time that his avocation—music—is sadly neglected

wages—Payments made for manual work

way—This word should be preceded by a preposition when used in the sense of manner. *Do not behave that way* is incorrect

Correct: *Do not behave in that way*

ways—Do not use this word, preceded by *a,* to indicate distance. It is wrong to say *He walked a little ways with me*

Correct: *He walked a short distance with me*
        He walked a little way with me

well—This word is an adverb, and must therefore be used only in the modification of verbs, adjectives, and other adverbs. Do not use in place of *good*

Correct: *He looks well*
        He is a well-known author
        It will be well worth your while to see him

what—Do not use for *that* after *but* (see *but*)

    Correct: *They do not know but that he will come*
             He spoke to me, but what he said I do not know

when—Denotes definite time, past or present, and means at the very time of (see *while*)

    When I entered, the click of typewriters suddenly ceased

where—Do not use this word for *that*, as, *I see by the papers where the president has decided to veto the bill*

    Correct: *I see by the papers that the president has decided to veto the bill*

which—A relative pronoun referring to both animals and things. It may introduce both restrictive and non-restrictive clauses, but preferably the latter only (see *that* and *who*). Do not use *which* to refer to persons

    Correct: *The dog which I bought of you has strangely disappeared*
             The machines which you sold me have given excellent service

while—Denotes passing of time; during the time of; progressive time (see *when*)

    While I was going thru the door, the click of typewriters suddenly ceased

who—Refers to persons. It may introduce both restrictive and non-restrictive clauses (see *that* and *which*). Do not use *who* to refer to animals or things

    Correct: *The man who spoke to me is my secretary*
             He spoke to me, but who he is I do not know

whole—Indicates totality of quantity (see *all*). But this is by no means a hard and fast rule. We speak of a *whole number*, and of *all the wheat* in a granary

    The whole field was covered with snow

wholesome—Generally used in reference to food or recreation or influence (see *healthful* and *healthy*)

    Eat plenty of wholesome food

who's—The abbreviated or contracted form of *who is* (do not confuse with *whose*)

whose—Do not use *whose* as the possessive of *which*. It is the possessive of *who* only, unless the thing referred to by *which* is commonly personified (like *ship*, for instance), in which case *whose* may be used as the possessive of which

    I opened the book, the cover of which attracted my eye
    The ship whose decks are cleared for action lies sleeping in the harbor

within—This word should be used to indicate a period of time, rather than *inside of* (see *inside*)

    A letter will be mailed to you within an hour

without—Do not use this word for *unless*. *Without* is a preposition, and must therefore have an object. It cannot serve as a

WORD STUDY

subordinate conjunction. *I am not going without you go* is incorrect

Correct: *I am not going without you*
I am not going unless you go

worse—This word is the comparative of *bad.* So you may say *If bad comes to worse* and *If worse comes to worst.* Do not say *If worse come to worse* or *If worst comes to worst* for, if you ponder them a little, you will see that they make nonsense

you're—Abbreviated or contracted form of *you are*

your—The personal pronoun, possessive singular and plural of *you*

INDEX

INDEX

a, 155, 156, 187–189, 193, 385, 464, 618
Abbreviations, 1–24; ampersand, 4, 391; apostrophe, 9; capitalization, 7–10, 45; complimentary closing, 4; ¢, 6; dates, 5–7; Dr., 1, 4, 8; Esq., 3; exponent, 11; formation, 10; Gen., 1; Gov., 1; governmental, 22–24; Hon., 1; hyphenation, 8; initial, 5; italics, 219; jr., 1, 3, 35; letterheads, 3; list, 10–21; Messrs., 1, 4, 8; metric, 8–9; Mr., 1, 4, 8; Mrs., 1, 4, 8; names, 1–5; *No.*, 6; notation, 7; NRA, 22, 23; *o'clock*, 7; O.K., 11; period, 8; places, 5–7; pluralization, 9–10; Prof., 1, 2; punctuation, 7–10; *rd*, 6; Rev., 1; salutation, 4; signature, 2–3; sr., 1, 3, 35; *St.*, 6, 8; *th*, 6; *the*, 4; telegram, 569; titles, 1–5
ability, 618
-able, 547
abolishment, 402
abolition, 402
about, 210, 618
above, 200
abrogate, 618
absolutely, 496
Abstract noun, 135
Academic citation, 383
Accent, acute, 445; breve, 446; circumflex, 446; pronunciation, 580–582
accept, 618
accordingly, 536
Acknowledgments, social, 267–268, 269, 310–311
Acrostic, 80
Active voice, 146–147
Acute accent, 445
adapt, 618
Add, 408
Addison, Joseph, quoted, 92, 99, 121
addition, 618
Additive, conjunction, 163; prefix, 584

Address, inside, 228, 232, 234, 237, 239; italicized, 220; telegraph, 568–569, 570–571
adept, 618
Adjective, 129, 155–157, 187–202; capitalization, 45, 50; clause, 132; comparison, 167, 190, 588–589; epithet, 155, 192; figurative, 200; headline, 397–398; modification, 193–194; multiplicative, 156; noncomparative, 191; numeral, 156, 460; phrase, 161; placement, 193–194, 210; pronoun, 201–202; qualifying, 155–157; quantitative, 156; substantive, 200
Adjustment letter, 295–297, 316–362
admission, 618
admittance, 618
Adverb, 129, 157–160, 187–202; as adjective, 200; clause, 132; comparison, 189, 588–589; figurative, 200; headline, 397–398; linking, 198; locating, 187; modification, 193–194; placement, 193–194, 210
Adversative conjunction, 163
adverse, 618
Advertising, classified, 408; coinages, 598–599; direct-mail, 54–77; display, 412; position, 407–408; space, 405, 407
advice, 618
advise, 618
ae, 464
Æschylus, quoted, 105
affect, 618
Africa, words, 574
Age, numeral, 432–433
Agency, suffix, 585
aggravate, 619
Agreeableness, illustration, 63
Agreement, noun and pronoun, 168–173; subject and predicate, 148–149, 173–178
ain't, 179, 613, 635
-al, 544, 586
all, 140, 170, 619

649

654 INDEX

West, Alfred S., quoted, 157
Western Union, 566
West Indies, words, 576
what, 139–140, 142, 499, 646
wheat, 460
when, 159, 646
whence, 199, 208–209
where, 159, 204, 646
whereas, 449, 452, 537
whether, 204–205, 499
which, 139–140, 142, 172, 646
while, 197–198, 646
who, 139–140, 142, 646
whole, 646
Whole numbers, 429–430
wholesome, 646
who's, 646
whose, 140, 166, 168, 484, 646
why, 159
Wilde, Oscar, quoted, 124
will, 145-146, 150, 175-178
Wilson, Woodrow, quoted, 98
widow, 402
wishing, 294
Wit, 123–124
with, 162–163, 210
Withdrawal, invitation, 270
within, 646
without, 207–208, 646
woman, 402
Wordiness, 613–614
Words, 574–647; antonym, 597; archaic, 597; argot, 597; barbarism, 598; Basic English, 616; capitalization, 34–53; circumlocution, 114, 613; code, 570; coined, 598; colloquialism, 599; composition, 583–584; connotation, 600; contributions (countries), 574–576; dialect, 601; differentia, 601; diffuseness, 613; division, 514–517; gender, 587; generic, 602; genus, 601; hackneyed, 292–294, 602–604;

heteronym, 602; homograph, 605; homonym, 605; hyphenation, 503–518; ideational, 130–131; idiom, 605–606; impropriety, 606; italicized, 221–227; Latin, 8, 576–577; lexicon, 618–647; localism, 607; obsolete, 597; pluralization, 457–466; pomposity, 607; prefix, 584–586; pronunciation, 589–597; provincialism, 607; qualifying, 130–131; redundancy, 613; relational, 131; root, 586; Saxon, 577; slang, 608; solecism, 610; spelling, 538–564; spoonerism, 610; standard, 611; stereotyped, 292–294, 602–604; stress, 580–583; suffix, 584–588; synonym, 611; tautology, 613; technical, 612; verbosity, 613; verbiage, 613; vulgarism, 613; wordiness, 613
Wordsworth, William, quoted, 90, 101, 113, 117
World War Proclamation, 450
worse, 647
would, 175–178
would state, 293–294
Writer, ghost, 409; space, 410

x, 457

-y, 457, 541, 551, 586, 588
ye, 140, 141
Yearbooks, 371–372
yes, 497
you, 139–141, 151, 173
Young, James, quoted, 83
your, 647
you're, 647
you-tone, 291
-yze, 554

z, 457, 582, 590
Zeugma, 124–125